A WICCAN BIBLE

Exploring the Mysteries of the Craft
from Birth to Summerland

A.J. DREW

New Page Books
A division of The Career Press, Inc.
Franklin Lakes, NJ

A WICCAN BIBLE
EDITED BY LAUREN MANOY
TYPESET BY STACEY A. FARKAS
Cover design by Cheryl Cohan Finbow
Printed in the U.S.A. by Book-mart Press

To order this title, please call toll-free 1-800-CAREER-1 (NJ and Canada: 201-848-0310) to order using VISA or MasterCard, or for further information on books from Career Press.

The Career Press, Inc., 3 Tice Road, PO Box 687,
Franklin Lakes, NJ 07417
www.careerpress.com
www.newpagebooks.com

Library of Congress Cataloging-in-Publication Data

Drew, A. J.
    A wiccan Bible : exploring the mysteries of the craft from birth to summerland / by A.J. Drew.
        p. cm.
        Includes index.
    ISBN 1-56414-666-9 (pbk.)
        1. Witchcraft. I. Title.

BF1571.D74 2003
299—dc21
                                                                            2003053998

Dedication

For Damien Echols, Jessie Misskelley, and Jason Baldwin;
you have not been forgotten.

For Steven Branch, Christopher Byers, and (James) Michael Moore;
you have not been forgotten.

For the seated Governor of the State of Arkansas, I beg
that the principles founding this great nation not be
forgotten by your state's legal system.

Acknowledgments

Normally, I would have a much longer list of acknowledgments. It took a great many people for this book to manifest, but two people stood out so much, that their names have to appear by themselves. Thank you, Mother, for your eternal love. Thank you, Paula 'Ravensfyre' Newman, for your eternal friendship. Thank you both for the months of time you dedicated to the creation of this book.

Contents

Section Three: In Apprehension, How Like a God, 227

Preface

(Otherwise Known as My Last Ritual)

 am a creature of habit. I find things in this world that I like, and I do those things again and again because they make me feel good. These regular rituals are usually simple things. I meditate with my iguana on my lap or let my ferret run around my bedroom, her little butt running faster than her front end until she trips over herself again and again. At night, I watch the *O'Reilly Factor* at 11 p.m. with my mother, and in the morning I buy a bottle of Mountain Dew on my way to work.

In the course of writing this book, almost all of this has changed. My iguana and ferret died within days of each other, despite every effort to save them. It felt as if my heart had been ripped from my chest. I had fed my iguana Fred some grapes from Chili, and the next morning she was horribly ill. Then I fed a grape to Thumper never thinking that grapes from a grocery store could be poison. Shortly thereafter, she took ill. In my attempts to save them, each of these friends took their final breath after days of being stuck with needles and IVs. So not only did I kill them, but in my great effort to save them I caused them to leave this world thinking I was a monster.

Right when I thought my heart couldn't feel any more pain, the war in Iraq began. At the time, I assured my mother that the people of this great nation would rise to support its brave men and women. I was confident that despite politics and party lines, despite opinions on the war itself, folks would realize combatants do not determine politics, and that in the United States military our soldiers follow the orders of the Commander In Chief without respect to political parties or leanings.

I was wrong. In trying to extend the lives of Fred and Thumper, I extended their suffering. In assuring my mother that Americans would all rally and show support for their soldiers, I set her up for a fall. Now there is no more Fred to meditate with, there is no more Thumper to run around and make me laugh, and there is no more O'Reilly at 11 p.m.; he has been pre-empted for reports on the war. We all make mistakes and those mistakes are part of the people that we are. We make mistakes, we learn from them, and we move forward. We manage this because we cling to the good things in life. Even when we might not see those good things in the moment, we know that they are just right around the corner. I can deal with this because I still have my morning Mountain Dew.

But it isn't just soda that starts my day; it is the smiling face of the young lady who sells me that soda. It is all part of the ritual. We never really talk much, but one can begin to see the nature of someone's soul, even from the smallest of exchanges. One day after I asked her how she was, she told me she was in pain because she thought her foot was broken. She laughed as she told me she called her father and he said if it was *still* broken when she got off work, that he would take her to the hospital. The next morning I asked her if her foot was still 'broken' and she said no. I told her that her father loves her a great deal. She said, "I know."

I think my morning breath of optimism is a high school student. If she is in college, I imagine she hasn't been there long. I hate to admit it, but I have become old and jaded. So this last ritual—my morning Mountain Dew—does my heart good. It reminds me of when I was young, before I became as jaded as I am. It is a good thing because if you believe in magick, then you know that this morning ritual marked me younger and less jaded. It reminds me that there is hope and that some children do continue to love their parents, even though it sometimes seems as if none do.

Recently, she asked me what I do for a living. I refused to say. So what was originally asked the way one might ask "How ya doing" has turned into a game. I am afraid that if I answer, I might not have that last daily ritual anymore, and right now I need it more than ever. I need the youthful optimism. I need something, anything, to tell me there is hope for this world. It doesn't take much, just a cheerful face now and then, just one person who still loves the world no matter how ugly it seems at the moment. If I were to answer her question and end the game, she might misunderstand my answer. It is so easy to misunderstand and so hard to find the words that appropriately express my job. Should I tell her what I do for a living?

In a broader sense of the question, should I tell you what I do for a living? If I tell her, she might think I am insane. Maybe she would rebuke me in the name of her god. It has happened so often that I have come to expect the occasional rebuking. If I tell you, you might also think I am a bit loopy. Pagan leaders might come out and say I am dangerous and ask the gods to protect the community from the likes of me. That, too, has happened.

You see, the status quo doesn't like people like me. The status quo wants you to just accept what you have been told and not question the world in which you live. Follow the standard operating procedure. Conduct business as usual. Oh, I am not always right, and sometimes it takes me far to long to admit when I am wrong. But that which drives my spirit, the *Ka* that motivates my *Ba*, the *Yang* that rocks my *Yin*, the *Yo* that completes my *In*, and the *mind* that guides my *soul*, leaves me with no choice but to put forth to this world the many things that it has seen and the many questions that it has formed.

So what do I do for a living? I am a professional Witch. "Professional" because such is my love of Witchcraft that I have worked it into not only my personal life, but into that which I do to fund that personal life, my work. "Witch" because I question the world in which I live. Oh, I know some folk have heard stories that Witchcraft involves the worship of Satan or other boogiemen. Others have been convinced that Witchcraft is the oldest religion the world has ever known. But the truth is where it is often found—someplace in the middle.

Witchcraft is not the world's oldest religion by any stretch of the imagination. Should one insist that words have specific meaning, then Witchcraft is much too diverse to be called a religion. While one might say that Witchcraft is a religion, one would be in error if they put a period at the end of that definition because it is so much more. It would be better to say Witchcraft *can* be a religion.

While definitions come and go, when I think of a Witch I think of someone whose spirit has a certain quality. Half of that spirit is a zest for life and all things living. The other half asks why there is this zest for life and why there are all things living. So when I think of one who is a Witch, I do not think of one who follows one religion or the next. Instead, I think of someone whose soul gives one no alternative but to love life as well as to identify why it is that we live. A Witch is one who, in determining what is what and who is who, allows his or her Spirit to decide, rather than simply believing what one is told.

Is Witchcraft the worship of Satan? Well, what is Satan? When we consider the word *satan*, we see that its original meaning was nothing more than 'to accuse' or to 'act as adversary.' With this understanding of the word *satan*, the next step in answering the question is obvious: *What is it that you are asking if Witches are averse to?* If you are asking if Witches are averse to being told what to think, then you probably think you know my answer. Chances are you are wrong. You see, while Witches are definitely averse to being told what to think without being allowed to think for themselves, they do not *worship* that aversion. Their Spirit *is* that aversion.

Witches are averse to the standard operating procedure that has caused this world to slip into the place where it now rests. Not only does the potential for World War III loom over our heads, but even if we survive man's inhumanity to man, the rate at which plants and animals are becoming extinct has now reached a point not even rivaled by the global extinction rate that destroyed the dinosaurs. Our world is dying, and the folk who refuse to accept the standard operating procedure that has brought this on are called extremists. Like Witches, they are taunted, laughed at, and vilified. Like Witches they are rebuked, and the gods are called upon to protect the world from their alarm. It should not come as a surprise, because although these so called alarmists might not all call themselves Witches, they are the very Spirit of Witchcraft.

You may have heard of a religion that has become popular that is often confused with Witchcraft. That religion is Wicca. It has been all the rage. You can find its name in movies and on TV. Recently, it has become rather fashionable to call oneself Wiccan—so fashionable that a great many people have come forth in an effort to squash this new religion. They have claimed it was invented by a man named Gerald Gardner, even though what Gardner called Wicca has very little resemblance to what it is today. It is said that the worship of the personification of evil, even though Wiccans do not so much as believe in the existence of that personification.

In response to these allegations, many of the folk who have flocked to Wicca because it is all the rage have fought back, defending their fashion statement with great amounts of energy. Recognizing an opportunity to profit, an industry has risen to meet the demand of these many people. Unfortunately, the majority of books that the industry offers to these folk who have rushed forth are lacking in many secrets, without which Wicca can be little more than a fashion statement. You see, if those secrets were told to the uninitiated, they might no longer seek Initiation. They fear that letting those secrets loose would result in a dramatic loss of book sales and the great ride that folk have had capitalizing on the popularity of Wicca would come to an end.

Fewer people would rush forth to sound that alarm if they knew that it came with horror and dread. Now to the initiated, to those who have received the secret names of our Lord and Lady along with their great lore, that knowledge is known. To the initiated, the name of that alarm is Pemphredo, who is accompanied by Enyo (Horror) and Deino (Dread), who are collectively known as the Graiae, three daughters born by Ceto whose husband is Phorcys.

Now, what do most people do when they see horror and dread? Do they turn away or do they sound the alarm? Although it is sad, the truth is that most people don't even see the horror and dread, much less sound the alarm. Most people look at that accident on the side of the road, but they do not see. They do not say to themselves, "My gods," and they do not cry.

So in writing a book for the few folk that do feel, for the few that do cry, one might think I am taking a great chance. But I have faith in humanity, and I believe Wicca is the religion that will prove that faith is well-placed. I believe there are enough people out there who will hear what I (and other so-called alarmists) say: We can still prevent our world from becoming that accident by the side of the road.

So for you sweet child, my goddess Caffeina, I answer your question thus:

I am a professional Witch. My profession is reminding people that their Mother and Father love them. If that scares you, I am sorry. But these are scary times.

Introduction

What a piece of work is a man!
how noble in reason!
how infinite in faculty!
in form and moving how express and admirable!
in action how like an angel!
in apprehension how like a god!
the beauty of the world!
the paragon of animals!

—William Shakespeare, Hamlet act 2 scene 2

f you have seen the ceiling of the Sistine Chapel, you are blessed. If you have not traveled that far, I am sure you can find an art print of Michelangelo Buonarroti's work. If you have never seen it, go take a look before you read any further. Make sure you find the portion of the immense work where God is depicted reaching his finger to Adam.

With that image fresh in your mind, tell me who the woman is. You know, the one who has God's arm is casually wrapped around like a lover. As a child, it never occurred to me that people do not think about it. It was my natural conclusion that it was God's wife. Then someone told me that God was a woman and I became terribly confused. If God is a woman, who is that big almost-naked guy with his arm around her? In answering that question, I found a beautiful religion called Wicca. But something there was also missing.

Within the Wiccan religion, I found many books that spoke about Goddess, but very few who listed her husband. Everywhere I looked, I could find information about Brigit but very little information about her husband Bres. Also within the Wiccan religion, I found many books that spoke about God, but very few that listed his wife. I could find reference to Wicca borrowing the Great Spirit from Native American traditions, but not with his wife Eschetewuarha.

This book is how I address that confusion.

You will note that the title of this book begins with the word *A*. This is because I in no way consider this *The* Bible. It belongs to me; I wrote it and gave it to someone to share it with you. They didn't think it would be a very popular book if we called it *A.J. Drew's Wiccan Bible*, so they shortened my name a bit and just called it *A Wiccan Bible*. Ok, actually that last part was just a bad joke, but I hope it made you smile.

You will also note that the title does not end with a period or with the word *complete*. This is because it's not finished yet. In fact, in trying to fit all that I would like to say under this title, I managed to write two different books. The first, this book, is dedicated to the discussion of the Wiccan religion. The second is dedicated to the discussion of Wiccan magick. This book is first because Wiccan magick is built on the religion, not the other way around. But even when these books are side by side, I will not be finished answering that question. You see, that answer is one's lifetime, and I am not ready for the grave quite yet. There are entirely too many things left to do.

In between the word *A* and the word *Bible*, there is a word that confuses a great many people. Exactly what it means is a bit confusing as it tends to mean something different to each person. Recently, a man by the name of Edred Thorsson published his research into the etymology of this word in a book called *Witchdom of the True*. There, he traces the word *wicca* past the Old English and into what may well be its true origin. This must have taken a great amount of research and work on his part, so instead of being one of the first to cite his book, I will be one of the first Wiccans to say that you should buy his book. That way his work is rewarded. I respect Edred a great deal. His research into the Old Norse traditions seems rivaled only by the soul of Freya Aswynn. However, I do not think the etymology of a word is a good way of addressing the meaning a word currently has. Yes, we are nothing without our past. But we are little more than a memory if we do not also have our present and our future. Please do read *Witchdom of the True* by Edred and also read *Leaves of Yggdrasil*.

If you have already read these books, you are probably wondering why a Wiccan author would recommend them. After all, they are both written by authors who are generally considered Asatrú rather than Wicca. Well, this Wiccan sees something very interesting in Norse lore. I see not only the Aesir (mind) but also the Vanir (soul), and

I see spirit in the unification of mind and soul. Now, I am not saying that Asatrú folk should all embrace Wicca, and I am not saying that Wicca folk should all embrace Asatrú. The word one uses to denote his or her spirituality is unimportant because it is what we have in common that is more important than what we do not. No matter what one calls this recent spiritual awakening, it cannot be experienced without both mind and soul because spirit is the very union of mind and soul.

I do not know what the future will hold, but I do know where the Wiccan religion is currently. In fact, while not uniquely qualified to report on the state of Wicca, I am certainly one of the few. You see, I live immersed in its diversity. Unlike many of the very founders of the modern Wiccan religion, I see firsthand what folk are doing and saying. Unlike the founders of specific organizations or traditions of Wicca, I have the blessing of witnessing a wide sampling of the Wiccan community. Yes, sometimes it feels more like a curse, but the good outweighs the bad. Some folk have taken great objection to my observations, and sometimes those objections have been voiced in very hurtful ways. I try not to get angry, knowing that their harsh words are brought on by the sense of love for Wicca that I share. So who am I? What gives me this relatively unique vantage point?

I am nobody. Sure, I have a few books in print and a few to come, but you wouldn't know it by looking at me. What gives me this vantage point has nothing to do with writing books. No, it has more to do with selling books. Although I own the place, my chief occupation is bookstore clerk, that being a rather unique position because the store in question is a Pagan book store specializing in the Wiccan religion, its books, and its supplies. I am also the host of *www.PaganNation.com*, an online community whose growth has been beyond my wildest expectations. Combining these occupations is where we see my unique position. Not only can I observe the Wiccan community, but because I am an author, I can report on it. I am not removed from my audience in any way, and I do listen. You see, the main reason I have these occupations is because I want to answer that same question I mentioned a few paragraphs back. Loosely, that question is: What is god? In a grander sense of the question: What does it all mean? This book is what I have found thus far in my quest to answer that question. It is how I answer five questions about myself and about humanity:

- ✦ What a piece of work am I?
- ✦ How noble am I in reason?
- ✦ How infinite am I in faculty?
- ✦ In form and moving how expressive and admirable am I?
- ✦ In action, am I like an angel?

It is in the questioning of these things that we find our place in the world, the natural order to our existence. It is the expression of doubt. A comment on how I question my own existence: While such questions might seem a bit pompous, anyone who has honestly asked them of oneself knows the answers are rather humbling.

Understanding This Book

Understanding this book requires that we suspend our instinct to interpret the written word literally. I have drawn on many world sources to structure my belief system. Although the stories on which I have built are themselves sacred, they should not be considered fundamentally true. This is especially true of time periods. Just because the oldest known story of the Great Flood can be found in Sumerian writings of about four thousand years ago does not mean the Great Flood took place four thousand years ago. Just because the story was told by the Sumerians with characters in the Sumerian pantheon does not mean that the story took place within the Sumerian culture. Indeed, that same story has been told by several cultures at several different points in history. So in reading of such matters, ignore entirely any reference to the time in which the culture telling the story existed because the time in which the story is told in that particular culture is not necessarily the time in which the event took place.

You see, this book is not the story of any one people or any one tradition of Wicca. Instead, it is the story of humanity and how the strivings of humanity have resulted in the evolution of this religion. It is a journey from the very beginning of humanity to what may seem like its end, all shown in the lifetime of a single Wiccan from birth until death. In this story, I hope the whole of what I intend to bring to your attention is seen because I believe the story given here in many parts is much greater than the sum total of its parts. Although Wicca was born in this past century, its birth took place only after its evolution and only when it was divinely needed. I hope here you will see that although there is widespread belief that Gardner or others created Wicca, belief in creation and evolution can coexist. For with this knowledge, although we may now be facing the end of one world, with Wicca we may welcome the birth of another.

The Recipes

In this book are included several recipes for natural incense and oils. To save space and connect the recipe to the rite or instance in which it is used, those recipes have been worked into the context of the book without an explanation of how to use them. In using those recipes, one should keep in mind that these are what have worked for me. You may need to modify these recipes to suite your needs.

Oil Recipes—On the market today there are several different types of oil, which range greatly in price. Unless otherwise noted, when I refer to oils herein, I am referring to pure, undiluted, natural essential oils of the plant listed. Wow, that was a mouthful. However, it had to be stressed. The market place is filled with synthetics and with blends of essentials in less expensive base oil. Generally speaking, true essential oils should not be placed on the skin. Although there are a few that do not seem to promote a reaction, such as patchouli, there are also some that will raise welts, such as cinnamon. However, oils should be purchased in their purest and most concentrated form because the recipe given includes the dilution.

That dilution and base oil can make or break the oil. In the recipes of this book, I have given the concentrations that have worked best for me. Your skin might be more sensitive than mine, so you may have to change the recipe to accommodate. The key to adjusting the concentration is to maintain the number of drops of oil that are in the recipe such that the ratio of the different essential oils remain consistent to one another. Either raise the amount of base oil used to further dilute the mixture, or lower the amount of base oil used to increase the concentration of the mixture.

When a specific base oil is not listed, it is best to pick one from the following list that will further the intent with which the oil will be used. Jojoba oil is the preference for any oil that is going to be stored for any length of time as it does not go rancid. Additionally, one can guard against rancidity by adding a few drops of wheat germ oil to each half-ounce of base oil. Potential base oils include almond, apricot kernel, avocado, coconut, grape seed, hazelnut, jojoba, olive, palm, sesame, and sunflower.

Incense Recipes—Generally speaking, natural incense is preferred to stick or cone for use in Wiccan ritual. Natural incense is usually ground in a mortar with a pestle, but if large amounts are to be made I will freely admit I am sometimes lazy and use my electric mortar—the coffee bean grinder. If you go that route, don't even think about putting whole roots in the thing unless you are prepared to purchase another one. Also, never use the coffee grinder for coffee or anything that you will eat or drink after it has been used for making incense. Some herbs that are perfectly safe in the censor are not all that safe in your digestive system. Likewise, if you are going to explore herbal teas or will be using your mortar and pestle for preparing food or drink, always have two sets, one for things you won't be eating and drinking and one for edible things.

Loose incense is burned over charcoal. But don't worry, you won't need a barbecue grill in your temple room. Instead, it is burned in a censor (burner) over a charcoal disk. These disks are sold in most New Age and Pagan shops in rolls of five and 10 at an affordable price. When you unwrap a roll of disks, you will notice there is a cup in one side of the disk; that is where the natural incense is sprinkled. To light the disk, hold it such that the cup is facing down, and light the cup side. It will spark a bit; this is normal. Turn the disk right side up, and place it in the censor on top of either gravel or sand. The gravel or sand is important, as the temperature the charcoal disk will reach is high enough to glow brass, shatter glass, and pop glazed ceramic burners. Once the edges turn white, the disk is ready to be sprinkled with natural incense.

How This Book Is Arranged

Because Wicca is a Nature-based religion, it recognizes that most things have a natural beginning, middle, and end. When applied to living things, these three states are seen as youth, adult, and senior. The three stages of life are more than literal ages that denote those years. Those phases are a way of addressing all things as having a beginning, middle, and end. In training covens, these stages of life are represented as degrees of initiation, which represent the initiate's life within the coven. First degree is the beginning, second degree is the middle, and third degree is the end. Although third degrees are not tossed out, they are generally welcome to leave their coven and start their own. In so doing, they bring the lore of the first coven, begin their own coven, and start the initiation process again. To maintain that natural order, I have arranged the whole of this book in three sections.

Section One: The Beauty of the World
Dedicated to our Lady and Lord as Maiden and Master

Here we discuss matters of birth, Wiccaning, and Self-Dedication. You will find not only ritual ideas, but why those ritual ideas exist. Here, too, are the basic ideas behind the Wiccan religion as applied to a worldview. The book of lore associated with this section is the Book of Plants.

Section Two: The Paragon of Animals
Dedicated to our Lady and Lord as Mother and Father

Here we discuss coven and household Initiation and mating customs. Building on the ritual ideas presented in Chapter 1, we see the development of the Wiccan soul. The book of lore associated with this section is the Book of Animals.

Section Three: In Apprehension How Like a God
Dedicated to our Lady and Lord as Crone and Sage

Here we see a further exploration of the Wiccan soul, building on that soul with mind, which yields Spirit. The book of lore associated with this section is Book of Humanity.

The Degree System

One might see a loose degree system begin to emerge in these three sections. If one were to see such a thing, one would be about half right. Although I am not a fan of the degree system, it is a convenient way of marking knowledge and the evolution of the soul. However, as stated earlier, I look on this book as the first half of a larger work. As you read this book, you will begin to understand why I have decided to separate these books and present them as I have.

Know first that the book Liber ab Planta (first degree study material) and Liber ab Familia (second degree study material) have been greatly condensed due to editorial space considerations. I hope at some time in the future to publish the missing material. So, please do not believe that in reading Section One, you are a first degree Wiccan. Not only is section one only half of the story that a first degree might possess, the truth is that each and every one of us is whole. If your soul is Wiccan, than you are already a first degree, a second degree, and a third degree. All I am doing here is reminding you of that fact. You see, I do not believe being Wiccan is a matter of birth or hereditary lineage, nor do I believe being Wiccan is a matter of being made or of coven initiation. Instead, I believe that when the world is in need, the souls who satisfy that need are reborn, and we have been. However, we must recognize that need and educate our minds to address it.

SECTION ONE

The Beauty of the World

Dedicated to our Lady and Lord as Maiden and Master

Section Introduction

This is the first of the Three-fold Path of Wicca.

Wicca is a personal religion. The exact format of the religion will change from one Wiccan to the next. The names used to call our Lord and Lady will change from group to group, coven to coven, and household to household.

Wicca is a mystery religion. Although a relatively clear structure has risen from about 150,000 years of human experience, the religion is more experiential than educational. The basics are provided, the references are pointed to, but what develops within you is what the religion is, not what you read in books.

Wicca is an initiatory religion. If you have heard anything about Wicca, you have probably heard about a degree system. I am not a fan of the way this degree system is used as a rank structure. But the degree system does serve to mark rites of passage, of which there are three. This section contains those first passages, the Rites of Name. It also contains the information on which that Rite of Passage is based. As all Wiccan rituals follow the same format, here too is the basic format for Wiccan ritual, the what (ritual) in the first chapter and the why (explanation) in the other chapters of this first section. Even if you are a long time member of Wicca, you would do very well to read on and learn the many things that have not been mentioned in other books. You see, Wicca is not a Path that has an end. It is a process of learning and relearning which continues throughout one's life.

Even if you are a second generation Wiccan, having received the Rite of Wiccaning when you were young, this section is most applicable as it examines Wiccan ritual from a view that I do not believe has ever made it to print. Even if you have already performed a Self-Dedication Rite, I think this section is important. Although you may have gone through the motions listed in previous books, you may not have given much thought to what was behind those rites. Why do we do these things? What are they based on?

Now, let me humble myself for just a moment. I do not say this because I think I have vastly more education than you. I say this because I was there. I was self-dedicated, coven initiated, and yet I did not understand the application of my own religion. I did not consider the message behind the rituals. I had not experienced that portion of the mystery that I now relate. Yes, you will discover it on your own but the Path of that discovery is dangerous. Although I am often called an alarmist for saying this, it has taken at least one life and years earlier it nearly took mine. Wicca is a very dangerous religion in many ways. Consider just one of those dangers to understand why I say this.

The Wiccan religion teaches that all acts of love and pleasure are our rituals. What about sexually transmitted disease? What about the carnage that infidelity can bring to a monogamous relationship? Other religions say, flatly, that sex prior to marriage is wrong and that sex outside of marriage is wrong. If both members of a marriage listen to these commandments, both members are safe from sexually transmitted disease as well as the results of infidelity. Wicca, on the other hand, has no set standard for the sexual conduct of consenting adults. Instead, Wicca insists that you decide what is right for you and what is not. You can see how a bad decision (cause) will lead to unpleasant effects.

So if Wicca is so dangerous, then why follow it? Those of us who are Wiccan do so because we have no choice. Our souls scream to us, so our minds create a structure in which that soul can be tempered with mind such that our Spirit does sing more than it does cry. The structure or Path of that tempering is the religion Wicca.

Liber ab Nomen

(Book of Name)

The Path to the
Inner Circle of Wicca

This is the Book of Name. Here we see two Rites of Passage in which a new name is given. In the first rite, the Wiccaning, a name is given to the, for lack of a better term, initiate. I say 'for lack of a better term' because although the Wiccaning is indeed a rite of initiation, it is not one in which the initiate is being initiated. It is a rite in which the community is initiated to the initiate. The second Rite of Passage discussed here is the Rite of Self-Dedication. This rite is just as the name implies; it is the rite of an individual's dedication not only to Wicca but also to the Wiccan community. As such, it is often conducted first in private and later in public. To understand why this is so, talk to someone who is gay or lesbian who has come out of the closet. Often there is first a step where one comes out of the closet only to oneself, followed by a time when one comes out to the community. So know right now that in my view of Wicca, there are no solitary practitioners and, at the very same time, everyone is a solitary practitioner.

Know also that these Rites of Wiccaning and Self-Dedication are not finite. They can be repeated when necessary. Such might be the case if a community feels it has strayed from one of its members. If that is the case, a second Wiccaning might be performed to apologize to the member and to reaffirm the community's commitment. Likewise, should a member of the community feel he or she has strayed, that person might want to perform another Self-Dedication rite to tell oneself that they have strayed but reaffirm their original commitment to the ways of Wicca.

There are other instances where the Rite of Wiccaning and Dedication can be conducted for the purpose of Rededication. Consider the effects of rape. I am sorry to say that in the greater community, the victim is sometimes blamed and treated as if dirty. A Wiccaning might be performed such that the immediate community can tell the victim that we do not accept the ways of the greater community. That our eyes are open to the horror and that we support that person in our community now more than ever, because that person probably needs the immediate community now more than ever.

On the Rite of Self-Dedication, consider the Wiccan who strays not only from his or her religion but from the nature of one's soul discovered in the mysteries that are found in the path of Wicca. Now and then, we all do incredibly mindless things, things we would rather forget. But in forgetting them, we cannot learn by them. So the Rite of Self-Dedication is sometimes performed again to reaffirm one's dedication to the principles of one's own heart.

The Rite of Wiccaning

Born with that beat
The trembling voice
Listen to that beat
You have no choice

Contrary to popular opinion, Wiccans are not made. Nor are they born. Born with potential and born with a Wiccan soul, yes, but neither made nor born Wiccan. Instead, Wiccans are discovered, and that discovery is the process by which the Wiccan discovers his- or herself, as well as the process by which the greater community discovers him or her and also that process by which he or she discovers the community. The Wiccan is born with that beat, that trembling voice, and no matter how one tries to deny it, one eventually has no choice but to listen to it.

It is the cycle, the power, and the energy (for lack of better words) of the very world in which we live. I say for lack of better words because if I told you it was a pattern you might not understand the depth of what I mean. It is the rhythm of all that lives, all that has lived and all that ever will live, a voice that beckons the Wiccan soul and while it pains me to say it, a voice that beckons none other. This does not mean that none other than Wiccans hear this voice, but none without the potential of becoming Wiccan can hear the voice, and those who do have that potential have no choice but to listen to it.

For this reason, the Wiccan community is charged with making itself available to the seeker. Not because I say this here, but those who are truly Wiccan will remember what it felt like when they heard that voice and did not know there were others who heard it, too. The Wiccan community is charged with making itself available to the seeker because we have compassion for the seeker, we know what that seeker must be feeling. We know that being lost in a dark place feeling utterly alone is horrific and we wish it on no living thing.

Naming a seeker is the first Rite of Initiation, better known as the Wiccaning. It was the first rite of Llew Llaw Gyffes who was initially denied a name by his mother but whose mother was later tricked into giving him one (see Book of Humanity). Having been separated from his mother for some time, raised instead by his mother's brother Gwydion, his mother did not recognize him when she saw him hunting one day. He fell a bird with a single stone and she proclaimed that he was a 'Bright lion with a sure hand,' and thus was he named Llew Llaw Gyffes. This naming is the acceptance of one's responsibility for all life that appears on this planet, a matter we will discuss in the following chapter. It is in so much as to say to our Mother Earth that we know we have been undeserving of a name, but here we demonstrate our worthiness.

The Rite of Wiccaning is both something a Wiccan couple might do for its child as well as something the community should perform for anyone of good report. As such, I believe that any *public* Wiccan organization that desires to be known of good report should offer such rites once in a month. After all, this rite is simply the affirmation that the community is present and available to the seeker. If an organization is not willing to do that much, just what does it do for the *public*?

The rite need not be formal. But performing it formally will better educate an adult seeker in the case of this rite being performed by a public group. In the case of parents Wiccaning their child, the formality of this rite goes a long way towards educating the participants, the friends and family, in the nature of the Wiccan religion. As the family and friends of the parents might not be Wiccan, the rite is an excellent way to further understandings.

Know first that should the seeker desire Wiccaning but not be of legal age, that not only should a parent's written and notarized permission be secured ahead of time, but that a consent-giving parent or legal guardian should be present just as if the seeker were an infant. While there is no hard rule that a body of Wicca not interact with someone under the legal age, Wicca insists that all rituals be conducted with the full consent of all who are involved. As we live in a society that chooses to protect its children by stipulating a legal age of adulthood, should one be below that legal age he or she cannot offer consent.

The Rite of Self-Dedication

Self-Dedication to Wicca does not make one Wiccan. If you already have a Wiccan soul, then you are already Wiccan. Although discovering that you are not alone might feel as if you are blessed, do not think for a moment that having such a soul is a blessing alone. It is also a curse. History has shown that those born with such a soul will be persecuted simply because they are different. Think about your life and the way you have felt about the world in which you live. Have you always felt different? Like no one understands you or like you think in a way that others do not?

When your friends talk about casual sex, do you dream about falling in love? Do you somehow know that racism is contrary to the nature of humanity? Have you always suspected that there is not much of a difference between the world's races, even though the greater community seems hell-bent on destroying the world over race? If you are white, have you noticed that you do not really fit the stereotype for being white? If you are black, have you noticed that you do not really fit the stereotype for being black? If you are one of the many shades between white and black, have you noticed that you do not really fit whatever the stereotype is for being whatever shade that is?

Have you always suspected that there is not much of a difference between the world's religions even though the greater community seems hell bent on destroying the world over religion? If you are already involved in the Wiccan community, have you noticed that you do not really fit in with the stereotype of being Wiccan? If this is you, then you have a Wiccan soul. I know, because so do I.

If this is not you, then you do not have a Wiccan soul. Although you might like the Wiccan community that you have met, there is no reason to dedicate yourself to something you do not honestly believe. Now this does not mean that your soul might not change or maybe that your understanding of that soul will grow, but embracing a religion that does not offer you the support you need would be like using an automobile repair manual to fix your VCR. It just won't work and it might cause you to harm your VCR. As that VCR is your soul, it would be a good idea to find the right repair manual before taking the lid off.

Basic Wiccan Ritual Formula

In discussing the aspects of Wiccan ritual, I have included examples of words that might be spoken at those points in ritual. Chances are there are many words you will not recognize. For this reason I say please know first that the words should come from your own heart. Given here are only examples. Know also that you should read Section One prior to conducting any ritual here. Without an understanding of the rite, it will serve no purpose to perform it. On some aspects of Wiccan ritual I will be very long winded, and on others I will be very brief. This is because the story that follows this explanation, the many chapters that follow this one, explain that which is briefly touched on here in greater detail. In my last book, *Wicca for Couples*, I explained that although Wiccans have no central bible, they do have a common ritual format and that ritual format is our bible. So in continuing through this bible, what you will see is basically the one Wiccan ritual format. That format starts with the lustral bath.

The Lustral Bath: All Life on Earth Came from One Initial Source

If you have ever worked with the general public, you might have noticed that perhaps personal hygiene should be better promoted. In my view of Wicca, every ritual and event in which one will interact with others requires first the lustral bath as a matter of personal hygiene and a whole lot more. In other cultures, group bathing does not have much of a stigma. But those cultures are in the minority. Not only does group bathing promote a sense of uneasiness among folk raised in the greater community, it can be down right painful if you happen to be the one who has to sit with your back to the faucet. So in addressing the lustral bath prior to public ritual, the best method I have found is to make a gift of bath salts to the guests you know will be attending.

Should a person arrive at the monthly meeting of a public organization and ask for the Rite of Wiccaning, by all means welcome the person, but ask them to return to the following month's meeting after having first followed certain instructions. Give to them those instructions along with the bath salts of Initiation, instruction as to their use, and a parental consent form should the person be under legal age. Those instructions should be clear in why the lustral bath is important so the seeker does not think he or she smells bad (even if he or she does indeed smell bad).

So why is the lustral bath so important? Because Wicca is a religion that embraces both creation and evolution. Although one might think the two are mutually exclusive, Wicca is a fertility religion, so it sees the creation of humanity as similar to the creation of a child. A child is not conceived in finished human form. Instead, a child begins his or her life as a cell, then two cells, then four, then eight, then 16...All of which took place in the womb of that child's mother.

Wiccans view the ocean as the womb of our Mother Earth, not just because it is nicely poetic, but because science tells us that the ocean is the womb in which all life on this planet started. Per common scientific convention, the primordial oceans of the Earth were once filled with the building blocks of life (the ovum) but it remained without life until gradually the conditions became such that the relationship between the Earth and the sky built potential between the two. With the Earth's rotation and the churning of the sky, that potential became greater and greater, the way rubbing a cat produces static electricity. When the potential became too great for the separate poles to contain, that electricity (sperm) was released. Like human conception, the first orgasms probably did not result in life, but as the ocean was joined with lightning over and over again, the chances increased until those building blocks of life (simple proteins/ovum) were eventually moved in such a way that they became amino acids. Eventually those amino acids joined in such a way to form the very first string of viable DNA for the first life. Those simple strings of DNA became the first single celled life—fertilized ovum—which in turn grew into the plethora that we now see, the beauty of all life. Thus, the lustral bath reminds us that plants, animals, and humans may have distinct differences, but they are all in the same order of Life itself. Thus, they are all sacred in a religion that praises Life.

Wicca is first and foremost a cult of science. Right about now you are probably flinching because I used the word *cult*. You shouldn't because of the word I used after that spooky term, *science*. The word cult means nothing more than 'a following,' and science is a way of explaining the truths of the world which can at this time be explained. So when I say Wicca is first and foremost a cult of science, all I am saying is that Wicca is first and foremost a following of the truth.

Now, I know other religions have used the word science in their titles. But I am not talking about other religions. No one has a trademark or copyright on the word. Think back on what you know about the Church State of Medieval England. Who did it persecute? Midwives and healers perhaps? Is not medicine a form of science? Maybe people who said the Earth was round? Or was it folk who dared to say that the Earth was not at the center of the universe? Oh no, that whole heliocentric thing isn't in the Bible, so we can't have that now, can we?

The fact that Wicca is a religion of science is almost completely overlooked if we do not include the lustral bath and its deeply founded connection to science in the start of each and every seeker's introduction to our religion. To do otherwise would be to perpetuate the myth that Wicca is something other than a Nature-based religion. After all, science is nothing more and nothing less than an attempt to explain Nature.

So then, what is this lustral bath? It is a time not only of the body, but of the mind and soul as well. It is a time to forget, a time to return to that moment when there was no mind, body, or soul, a time when there was no life on this Earth and thus not a care in the world. To that end and in accordance with the intent of the specific ritual, to that bath certain blends are sometimes added.

Unless one enters the ocean for the lustral bath, the recipe for the lustral bath always begins with sea salt. This is the symbol of our Lord, and the water is a symbol of our Lady. Adding sea salt to the lustral bath symbolizes the introduction of sperm into the womb, and your exit from that bath symbolizes your birth and the birth of all life within the womb of our beloved Earth. As you step from that bath, your footfalls are the very first creatures to leave the ocean as well as the very first steps a child takes when it learns how to walk. It is a common act that speaks volumes. Recognize it for what it is and you realize that the daily bath, even when not conducted for a specific religious purpose, is an affirmation that you will spend that day celebrating the life that you have.

In the case of an infant's Wiccaning, it is best to use nothing more than a very sparing amount of sea salt. Infant's skin, eyes, and mucus membranes are typically very sensitive to bath additives. If you decide to use something in addition to a tiny amount of sea salt, please ask your pediatrician first. This should also be the case for anyone under legal age unless their parent is directly involved in the selection of herbs and other additives. In the case of someone who is of legal age who can make educated decisions for themselves, I suggest the following in accordance with a ritual's intent:

Lustral Bath Recipes

Each recipe refers to the weight of dried herbs. With each recipe, mix equal amounts of the recipe (by weight not volume) with sea salt. It is okay to guess at the relationship between sea salt and the herb blend, but do not guess when it comes to the herb proportions to each other. Bundle into a cheesecloth or fabric with a weave no looser than burlap and then tie the end. This way your herbal bath will not turn into a cleaning nightmare. Because our eyes are linked our minds, it is a good idea to add an additional measure of sea salt such that you witness its entrance into the bath.

When drawing the lustral bath, do not use cold water. Instead, turn the hot water on such that it is absolutely scalding. Then add to the bath your herbal bundle, and let it soak until the water is comfortable enough to enter. During the time in which the water is cooling, try to think of nothing at all. Try to empty your thoughts. Then take a palm full of sea salt and slowly let it run from your hand into the water. As you do, see the union of sky and Earth in your bath. Making sure that your water is at a safe temperature, enter and relax. Feel the water pulling from you all the cares of your world. After you have soaked, unplug the drain but do not exit the tub. Instead, stand and watch the water travel down the drain, bringing with it anything that you do not want to take with you from your bath. Then step from the tub and remember the symbolism of those first few steps.

There are two additional ways to use these recipes. If you do not have a bathtub, use the herb pouch as a scrub in the shower. If you want to be extra sure not to mess the tub, you can use my preferred method.

First, boil the ingredients in water over the stove or ritual fire. Then allow to cool, strain, and set aside for when needed. The fancy word for this is *infusion*. The term basically means tea, but as the word tea implies that a mixture is to be consumed, the term *infusion* is used to insure that no one makes a potentially fatal mistake. Some things were just never intended to be on the inside of the human body.

Initiation Bath

2 parts Rosemary

1 part Sandalwood chips (powder will make a mess)

Used in the lustral bath prior to Self-Dedication and Rites of Initiation.

Divination Bath (Simple)

2 parts Rose

1 part Yarrow

This blend is intended for the lustral bath prior to Rites of Divination. However, even if a ritual is to be conducted for a purpose other than divination, if a Seer is used to divine the disposition of the gods at the end of the rite, this or the other given recipe for a divination should be used in the bath water of the Seer.

Divination Bath (Better)

3 parts Damiana

2 parts Thyme

2 parts Yarrow

1 part Rose

1 part Nutmeg

1 part Cinnamon (if you are brave)

I have had no problem with this recipe, and it seems to provide a much better result than the simple version. However, putting cinnamon in the bath is not generally a very good idea. I have heard that this can set mucus membranes on fire and act as a general skin irritant. Maybe I just have particularly tough mucus membranes. Everyone should be careful with this one, but women should be extra careful for obvious reasons.

General Lustral Bath

3 parts Rosemary

2 parts Galangal

1 part Ginger

1 part Cinnamon (if you are brave)

Also called a Sabbat lustral bath, this is a general mixture to use prior to any Wiccan ritual. It is intended to both cleanse the soul as well as put the mind in the proper mode for the general format of Wiccan ritual. Omit cinnamon if you have sensitive skin. See "Divination Bath" (page 27) for a further warning.

Habit Breaking Bath

3 parts Lemongrass

2 parts Sage Brush (common sage will do)

2 parts Rosemary

1 part Lavender

This blend is also called the Outsider Infusion. It is used as a bath every day while one tries to break a bad habit as well as a blend for asperging during the Outsider banishing.

Healing Bath

3 parts Rosemary

2 parts Peppermint

1 part Rose

1 part Lavender

This blend is not used for healing oneself. Instead, it is used when one will be working magick to heal another. The exception is that when one hopes to heal a relationship or mend one's own broken heart, this bath is most appropriate. For the actual physical healing of your body, please first see your doctor and ask if this bath may be used in conjunction with prescribed methods of healing.

Love Bath

3 parts Lovage

2 parts Rose

1 part Orris root

1 part Dill seeds

Inspires a sense of love within the heart of the bather, which might just be contagious.

Lust Inspiring Bath

2 parts Jasmine

1 part Rose

2 Vanilla beans

Bathe with this one if you wish to inspire lust in a man. It will only work if you have the opportunity to be close to that man after your bath. However, it will likely backfire if you break conversational distance before he responds with lust.

Lust Inspiring Bath

2 parts Patchouli
1 part Rose
1 part Myrtle

Bathe with this one if you wish to inspire lust in a woman. It will only work if you have the opportunity to be close to that woman after your bath. However, it will likely backfire if you break conversational distance before she responds with lust.

Prosperity Bath

3 parts Patchouli
2 parts Basil
1 part Cedar
1 part Clove

Bathe with this one prior to an interview for a new job, raise, or when conducting yourself in a situation which lends itself to prosperity.

Protection Bath

2 parts Pine needles
1 part Bay leaf
1 part Basil

This seems to cause a heightened awareness to negative influences encountered during the day and particularly effective against peer pressure.

Sleep Bath

3 parts Lavender
1 part Rose

Relaxing and sleep inspiring.

Dressed versus Skyclad Rites

I think that if the event is grand, the dress should be grand. If the event is relaxed, the dress should be relaxed. If everyone involved wants to be skyclad (naked) for the rite, then so be it. But be aware of the fact that you will probably be making some folk uncomfortable despite them saying they are not.

However, in the case of a personal Self-Dedication, I think one should go skyclad. It is how you entered this world, so it seems only right that it should be how you enter this religion. Besides, if you are uncomfortable being naked in front of no one but yourself, I still believe that you should seek professional help. Let's just face it, if you are not willing to take your clothes off for so much as a shower you are not going to fit in well with others because you will smell bad.

Preparing the Temple

At the very core of Wicca, the temple is the home. This is the base for the Wiccan view of community, that the largest of community is a collection of smaller communities and that the smallest community is the family. But rites do not always take place in the home; offering rites that are open to the public should not be conducted in the home, lest the home be identified to the potentially baneful actions of hateful people.

Instead, a place large enough for the rite is established. If indoors, part of preparing the temple might involve renting a facility or maybe getting a permit to use a local park. Should the rite be held outdoors, ensuring there is nothing for someone to trip over is a good idea. Make sure there are no holes even if you were certain there were none yesterday. Remember that our furry critter friends sometimes work long hours.

Just prior to the rite, with guests now in attendance, either host, hostess, or both stands in the center of the area where the ritual will take place with brooms called besoms in their hands. For added effect, small bells can be attached to the besoms. Starting from the center of the Circle and moving in the direction of banishing (counter-clockwise), the area is swept with the intent of cleansing. However, it is not necessary for the brooms to hit the ground or move any dirt at all. The idea here is to instill the intention of cleaning in your guest's mind, not to soil their feet with dirt or pelt them with bits of gravel. So if the area is in need of a good sweeping, do so prior to your guests' arrival and then again symbolically once they are present.

Asperging and Smudging

The acts of asperging (blessing with water) and smudging (blessing with smoke) are done with the intent of putting your guests in the right atmosphere for what will be taking place in the rite. As such, the smudging and asperging will change with intent.

As with the lustral bath, one can use water that has been salted with sea salt for asperging. Some folk use plain water, but using the given recipes for the lustral bath will work well so long as you use a very weak concentration. That way, the water of asperging can be used to influence your guests towards the matter at hand, but their clothing won't be stained in your attempt to do so.

I have seen some truly inventive tools used for the asperging, but my favorites remain the hand or a branch of wood selected in accordance with the intent of the rite. However, on a hot summer night using the besom for asperging is not only appropriate, it is welcome. Keep in mind that if you are going to dip your besom into a cauldron of water and shower that water down on your guests, you should probably get their consent ahead of time. Later on in the ritual, if dance is involved during a hot summer rite, keeping someone by the cauldron with that besom at hand is a great idea. Let your guests know that if they dance by the cauldron, they will be cooled down by a goodly amount of water cast by a besom holder.

Smudging is most often accomplished with sage bundles called smudge sticks, which are commonly available from New Age, Pagan, and other shops that cater to folk who practice Native American spirituality. However, when a rite is performed for a particular intent, there are specific recipes for incense that can be used to increase the effectiveness of that rite. Listed here are my two favorites for general smudging and initiation rites.

Incense Recipes

General Incense (1)

2 part Frankincense

2 part Sandalwood

1 part Myrrh

An incense of choice for initiations, add enough frankincense or sandalwood oil to bind.

General Incense (2)

2 parts Frankincense

2 parts Sandalwood

2 parts Copal

1 part Myrrh

Another good incense for initiations, add enough frankincense oil to bind.

Offering the Challenge and the Outsider Offering

The challenge has two parts. The first part of that challenge is to the folk who are in attendance. Although challenge sounds like an awfully scary term, it is simply that point in ritual prior to the casting of the Circle where it is explained that once the Circle is cast, it should not be broken. At a public rite, this might be the act of assuring folk that they can observe or they can participate, but that they should decide which it is they are going to do prior to the casting of the Circle. At a wedding, this might take the form similar to asking if everyone present consents to the marriage.

In a Wiccaning, this is the act of asking everyone in attendance if they welcome the new person to the community. The person being Wiccaned is also pledging that he is dedicated to that community and asking if folk accept his or her dedication. In a Self-Dedication, this is the act of pledging and affirming to oneself that Wicca is indeed the path on which one has chosen to walk.

The outsider offering, sometimes a banishing, centers around the idea that we each have things within us that we wish to place outside us. Greed, racism, bigotry, and bad habits come to mind. As Wicca is a path towards self improvement, many Wiccans have taken to the inclusion of an outside offering or banishment within their rites as an affirmation that those things, the outsiders, are still an influence in our lives even though we have time and time again rejected them. By recognizing these demons, it is hoped that we can then begin to remove them from our being.

Casting the Circle of Art

The term 'Circle of Art' has fallen from favor in the Wiccan community. It has been replaced with the shorter term 'Circle.' I believe this has come about not out of simplification but because the masses are looking for something dark and spooky, and the word art tends to bring about pleasant thoughts. As art is the act of creation, and creation is exactly what the Wiccan rites celebrate, I have chosen to again use this term.

The casting of the Circle has many symbolic meanings. In the largest symbolism, it represents the Earth. In its smallest symbolism, it represents the self. Somewhere in between its largest symbolism and its smallest symbolism, it represents one's country, one's state, one's city, and one's home. It is a boundary, a place where the rite ends and is separate from the outside world. It is often viewed as a place that is not of this world as if to say, this is where my concentration will be, here in this world that I have created by casting the Circle.

Generally speaking, the Circle is cast twice. If cast by a solitary, it is cast once for our Lord and once for our Lady. If cast by two people, presumably a male and a female, the male (host or priest) will go to the east most part of the ritual area and point the athame at the ground and visualize our Lord Father Sky reaching down to our Lady Mother Earth through his body. The female (hostess or priestess) then does the same, only she points the athame to the sky and visualizes our Lady rising to meet her Lord's embrace. Both begin in the East and walk clockwise around the ritual area to form a circle ending in the East. I do not believe the order in which this occurs is of great importance, but generally speaking Wicca conducts its rites with the belief that Darkness comes before Light, so for reasons we will explore later, it is a good idea that the first casting of the Circle be done to draw up Mother Earth.

Inviting the Four Quarters

Wiccan ritual includes an invitation to the Four Quarters because it is a world religion. Wiccans accept the fact that all life is sacred, including plant, animal, and human. But it also recognizes that we have been given a unique position in this world. The invitation at the Four Quarters is an affirmation that we draw on all of humanity to meet the demands of that position. Because humanity has spread to the four quarters of the world, seeming to take on different races and cultures, we call the Four Quarters to rally our troops. We call the Four Quarters to state firmly that the task of protecting that which is sacred is much larger than any one person, tribe, culture, or religion can accomplish. So we call them all into our effort and into our sacred duty.

Facing East

> 'Before me I see my breath. Thee who has been called in times of old the White King, Shu, Duamutef, Neith, Indra, Long, Chung, Jikoku, Raphael, Eurus, Vulturnus, Dragon, and Eagle.
>
> Before me do I see Jotunheimr and before me do I see Air. May that which fills my lungs with the breath of life breath life into this rite.'

Facing South

> 'Before me I see my spirit. Thee who has been called in times of old the Blue King, Nut, Imset, Isis, Yama, Feng-huang, Hung, Komoku, Michael, Notus, Auster, Phoenix, and Elk.'
>
> Before me do I see Muspellsheimr and before me do I see Fire. May that which fills my spirit with flames bring fire into the spirit of this rite.'

Facing West

> 'Before me I see my blood. Thee who has been called in times of old the Red King, Tefnut, Kebechsenef, Selkhet, Varuna, Ch'i-lin, Hai, Zocho, Gabriel, Zephyrus, Favonius, Unicorn, and Bear.
>
> Before me do I see Vanaheimr and before me do I see Water. May that which flows as the blood of the Earth flow in the heart of this rite.'

Facing North

> 'Before me I see my body. Thee who has been called in time of old the Green King, Geb, Hapi, Nephthys, Kubera, Gui Xian, Shou, Bishamon, Auriel, Boreas, Aquilo, Turtle, and Wolf.
>
> Before me do I see Niflheimr and before me do I see the firmament of Earth and ice. May that which is firm be to this rite as body that we may stand proud in our rite.'

Invitation to our Lord and Lady

The invitation to our Lord and Lady is a positive affirmation that Wiccans do not see male superior to female or female superior to male. As with all words given here, the following is just an example. Your words should come from your heart and be applicable to the rite itself.

> Here do I invoke to aid my goal
> My father above and Mother below
> Here do I invoke to bless this rite
> Our Lord and Lady upon this night

Here do I invoke that I may be whole
There love into
My mind, body and soul

For thou art the gods that were
Thou art the gods that will be
And thou art the gods that are

For thou art the gods of my father and mother
Thou art the gods of my sons and my daughters
And thou art the gods of my love and my self

For thou art my father and my mother
Thou art my sons and my daughters
And thou art my love and I

The Symbolic Great Rite

The symbolic Great Rite is an affirmation that Wicca views the Creator as both Lord and Lady. To be blunt, it is symbolic sex. The athame (masculine) is held over the chalice (feminine) and then slowly lowered into the chalice as a symbolic act of sexual union. This is a visual reminder that Wiccans view the creation of life as the union of man and woman because that is how we create life. If a host and hostess are conducting the rite together, an affirmation for their love of each other is made. Asking members of the Circle who are themselves couples to hold hands for this portion of the rite is most applicable.

As our beloved Lord is to our beloved Lady
So is the athame to the chalice
That union being the Creator
That union being all that has been created
That union being my love and I

The Body of the Ritual

The body of the ritual is that which is being celebrated. Should this be a Wiccaning, this might be a time when a child is given presents by the members of the Circle. Should it be the Wiccaning of an adult, it is a time when that adult is brought to each member of the Circle and introduced. In both cases, if the body of the ritual is a Wiccaning, it is a time when the host and hostess of that Circle give a new name to the child.

Should the reason for the rite be a holiday, this is where the celebration of that holiday goes. Should it be a handfasting, celebration also goes here. A handparting, the same. Whatever the intent of the ritual, whatever the purpose, it occurs after the symbolic Great Rite.

This is because although there is no insistence that a Wiccan couple have children, Wicca is a fertility religion. Its rituals are designed around the natural life cycles of beginning, middle, and end—birth, life, and death. Thus the body of the ritual, the magickal child that it produces, is marked after the symbolic Great Rite. The symbolic Great Rite is the conception, the body of the ritual is the growth of the magickal child within the womb of the Circle, and the end of the ritual is the birth of the magickal child. That magickal child is the product of the intent of the rite.

Stating Intent: The first half of the body of the ritual

Although every Wiccan ritual has clear intent, many fall short of letting the guests know what that intent is. Often, we become so concerned with using archetypes and hidden meaning that we forget hiding meaning from our guests is not only rude, it is counter productive to intent. Yes, it is possible to solicit the experience of a mystery from a person by exposing them to influences that bring on that experience. If that is the intent of the rite, by all means continue to practice in that manner. However, the dynamics of raising group energy for a specific intent demands that those involved understand exactly what that intent is. So telling them to chant in some dead language they do not understand will not be effective in causing the manifestation of the magickal child. If you doubt me, try this magickal chant taken from my Book of Shadows and see where it gets you: 'Ego similis nutrio asinius vomer.'

So instead of baffling guests, make the body of the ritual as clear as all other portions. If you choose to use symbolism that may be missed by your guests, explain as you go so everyone is on the same track. This is important because the power of group ritual is lost when the group is not focused on the intent of the rite. Methods for conveying clear intent include techniques seemingly as mundane as speech. I remember the first time my Roman Catholic mother saw a video tape of my leading of a Circle maybe 800 guests in number. She cried with pride as she mumbled forth that her son was a preacher. While acting in such a capacity might not seem overly Wiccan, speech is certainly one of the most direct ways to convey intent. Although modern Pagans might run away from this simple technique, it is clear that the ancients embraced such methods as sacred.

Bikeh Hozho—Male—North America
Found in many Native American tribes as the personification of speech, but most notably in the Navaho creation story where he has human form.

Tirawa—Male—North America
Pawnee creator and sky god who was said to have either gifted or taught speech to humanity.

Vach (Also known as Vac)—Female—Near East
Hindu goddess whose name literally means speech. Eventually, her lore was observed by Sarasvati where it was expanded to create a goddess of not only speech but of fertility and the wealth that often accompanies the ability to read, write, and speak elegantly.

Ve—Male—Northern Europe

After Odin created Ask and Embla (the first of humanity), it was Ve who gave them speech.

Waramurungundi—Female—Australia

The Creator Mother of the Gunwinggu people. She is said to have created the languages of Australia and given those languages to the many tribes.

Raising Energy and Releasing Intent:
The Second Half of the Body of the Ritual

Chances are you have heard the term 'Raising the Cone of Power.' While it might sound rather spooky, it is nothing more than creative visualization on a group level. The idea is that if one mind can focus on a specific thought and send that thought into the universe with the hopes that it will manifest, than a group mind will be able to accomplish such a task with even more effectiveness. The principle is the core of Wiccan spellcraft—not that all the candles, incense, oils, and chants are themselves magick, but that human consciousness is magick, that human consciousness has the ability to manifest change outside of itself. Generally speaking, the props of spellcraft are there to stimulate the mind into a thought. This is why specific colors, scents, words, and other props are used in ritual—not because those colors, scents, words, and other props are magick in and of themselves, but because they stimulate the human mind. They set the tone or mood in which the human mind is most likely to be focused on the intention.

If the intent of the rite is the exploration of mysteries, there might not be a need for raising energy. This might be the case in rituals such as the Rite of Persephone (discussed later). However, where a rite has an intent other than to expose one to the rite itself, it is often helpful to raise energy for that purpose and then to release that energy to the universe. In keeping with the principle that Wicca is a fertility religion, this practice is thought to be the conception, gestation, and birth, or release, of the magickal child. This is calling on that beat or rhythm of life to swell up in the participants and then be released into the universe.

In a structured Circle, participants should be well versed on the construction of the cone of power, and everyone must work in synchronicity. The idea is that the same thought, the same intent, will be focused upon by all who are in the Circle. Even with a clearly stated intent and the guest worked up by the stating of the intent, the chant used for the raising of the cone of power should be clear and bring about further concentration on the intent. The following would be appropriate in raising energy against the unethical treatment of animals, maybe against needlessly barbaric killing practices.

Earth, Air, Fire, Water
Give us strength
To end this slaughter

The safest but least effective method for accomplishing such a raising of energy is to have all participants sit in a circle around the host and hostess who guide the chant.

Start the chant slowly and quietly, and then build in speed and volume. As the chant grows, everyone in attendance visualizes the energy necessary to accomplish the goal swelling up within them and then joining the swirling mass of energy created by the other members of the Circle. That energy is seen as swirling around and up in the shape of a cone. A drumbeat is vital here, and best there be no less than three drummers in the center of the Circle. When the first person falls backwards, signaling they just cannot keep up with the chanting, the drummer who sees that person fall stops his or her beat immediately and indicates as much to the other drummers. When the drum beat stops, everyone falls backwards, ends the chant, and launches the cone of power.

A far less safe, but infinitely more effective method for raising a cone of power is to have three Circles, one within the other. The innermost circle is drummers facing outwards. The outermost circle is chanters facing inwards. Between the two Circles stand dancers. In this situation, should a dancer simply tire they move to the outside Circle to either join the chanters or take a break. Likewise, if a chanter decides to become a dancer, he or she simply moves into the area where the dance takes place.

The dancers serve two purposes, the first being that they are themselves raising energy. Their dance is the chant just as the drum beat is the chant, only without words. The reason this method is more dangerous is simple: It is more likely to stress the limits of a person's physical ability. Should the rite be for a specific purpose, there should be a sudden release of the energy. So the safety net here might protect the majority, but there is some level of risk to the first person who drops because they are in such a frenzied but controlled situation, the signal for everyone to release the energy at the same time is the first dancer that hits the ground instead of joining the chant circle and resting. When that person hits the ground, the drummers signal the stop and everyone hits the ground, dancer and chanter alike. There they visualize the raised energy shooting to the intended target. Again, I warn that this is not the safest practice. While it is the most effective, if you allow dancers to continue until someone drops out it is likely that you will encounter epileptic, diabetic, and more serious medical conditions if your guests are prone to those illnesses.

In a less structured or general rite, it is often unnecessary or impractical to raise the cone of power as a synchronous group. As an example, in a public Samhain Rite where each person is asked to remember and welcome their departed loved ones, one chant simply won't do; however, a group setting might. Here a dance can be led for the purpose of raising energy with the idea that the dancers are showing their departed loved ones that while they do miss them, they are happy to be alive and convey that message by demonstrating that they feel the beat, that rhythm of life so strongly that they have no choice but to dance to show them. In such situations, what will inevitably happen is a few folk who have worked with groups will gather up others who have not and form a Circle or Circles within Circles. As this is almost guaranteed, the drummers should be cued to the same set of circumstances for safety precautions. One person drops to the ground, the drumming stops. In this case, not for the benefit of simultaneous release of energy but for the purpose of safety.

Raising Energy and its Relationship to Sex

Here, too, is the reason for sex magick as a sacred rite in the Wiccan religion. Now, please do not understand me to say that public rituals should include sex as a method of raising energy. Although Wicca in no way forbids such choices when all involved are consenting adults, such activities are in the smallest of minorities within our community. Instead, please understand me to say that what is previously described as the raising of energy is, itself, another symbolic Great Rite. In this instance, the dance is foreplay when it is slow, coitus when it speeds, and simultaneous orgasm when the first dancer or chanter falls out. So then, the actual act of sex is, in and of itself, sacred ritual and thus can include the raising of energy.

Should a couple make love with intent of exploring mysteries, in this case of each other's soul, then like the raising of the cone of power in public ritual, there might not be a need for a deliberate attempt to raise energy. However, if that lovemaking should have an intent, then the intent should be clear. The act of sexual union, when done right, causes certain chemicals to be released into the blood stream. So do ecstatic dancing, chanting, and drumming. Those chemicals are similar in effect to the drugs used in brainwashing and behavioral modification techniques. Interestingly enough, similar drugs are sometimes used in conjunction with hypnosis for the reported purpose of recalling suppressed memories. However, those practices have been all but abandoned because rather than causing the recall of memories, the process tends to *implant* memories. You can see why this would be a very powerful tool. When those chemicals are present in our system, our minds become susceptible to the implantation of thoughts. So during both ecstatic ritual and sex, our minds become more willing to accept an intent. In the case of public ritual and ecstatic states being achieved by drum, chant, and dance, the intent is that which is stated. In the case of lovemaking, there is no difference other than it is more casually called pillow talk. Please understand I do not draw a large line between ritual and real life. Making love is sacred with or without candles and incense burning, and the most important altar in a marriage is the marital bed.

If lovers are open to the idea of using sex to raise energy for a purpose, there are many avenues that could be explored with the words spoken or chanted during sex. We can use these principles to not only further our relationships but to bring into manifestation the dreams and aspirations of those relationships.

Thanking our Lord and Lady

On the surface, the thanking of our Lord and Lady seems to be just common courtesy. However, it is a great deal more. It is an affirmation that we understand the principle that we are separated for the sake of union. Without separation, the creation of potential, there could not be union—creation itself.

Thanking the Four Quarters

Typically this thanks comes in the form of thanking each of the Quarters for their attendance, but not banishing them as some suggest. Instead, they are thanked and told that they may stay if they wish but go if they must. Your hospitality continues.

Opening the Circle

The Circle is either walked down in a counter-clockwise motion, or it is simply opened. I prefer it to be walked down with host and hostess holding hands and walking the Circle counterclockwise from East to East and then back to the center of the Circle. Then they return, they hold up their hands so that all can see they are united, and announce:

> Host and Hostess: *'The Circle is open but never broken.'*
> Host: *'Merry did we meet.'*
> Hostess: *'Merry do we part.'*
> All: *'And merry will we meet again.'*

Liber ab Genesis
(Book of Creation)

'Lo, I see here my father and mother';
'Lo, now I see all my deceased relatives sitting';
'Lo, there is my master, who is sitting in paradise.
Paradise is so beautiful, so green.
With him are his men and boys.
He calls me, so bring me to him.'

—*Norse Prayer recorded by Ahmed ibn Fadlan in 922 C.E.*[1]

Scribbled in my Book of Shadows is a quote that once saved my life. It reads "Our creator is evidenced by our creativity." There is no note next to it as to the statement's origin. I had assumed for many years that it was attributed to a very close friend, but even she did not remember its origin. In preparation for this book, I very much wanted to include that quote, so I did what I could to discover its origin. From what I can tell, it was the motto of someone who had written a computer screen saver back in the age of DOS.[2] Imagine that! It wasn't

Shakespeare or any of my other favorites. It was just some Joe trying to squeak out an existence by writing computer programs. The phrase that saved my life is just something someone made up. But isn't that what mythology is—bits and pieces of knowledge that folk created in their effort to understand the nature of life such that they can exist within its confines? Sure, some mythology is incredibly old and some was invented yesterday. But the test by which we determine if it is or is not sacred should not be its age or lack thereof. The test is if it is empowering. That simple quote from some Joe that I have never met saved my life, so it is sacred.

I was not there at the beginning of the world and will not pretend to know what I have not seen first hand. Neither was anyone else. I don't know how the world was created, and I don't know for a fact that its creator is evidenced by our creativity, but it works for me. Failing first-hand knowledge, we soothe our desire to understand with the explanations that we can muster; we create what I call 'constructs of understanding.' These are the stories that help us to understand things that we cannot know by science alone. In a way, they are magick because they give us the ability to understand the nature of something whose nature has not yet been explained. In reading the Book of Genesis, it is important to understand that this is a construct for understanding.

What follows is not sacred because it was written by a great prophet of any one god or goddess. It is sacred because I wrote it. Now before you think I am the most pompous author you have ever encountered, note that I did not say it was sacred to you. This is my sacred truth, just as I imagine the motto of that computer programmer is sacred to him. While I do hope you gather inspiration from this story, as did I from that motto, it should in no way be cited as a supreme truth.

It might sound a bit strange, but I hope that no one takes this book so seriously as to interpret much of it literally or any of it fundamentally. While I have pulled from ancient lore spanning thousands of years, the fact is I made it up. That's right, I took what I believe and made the story fit. Now, while that might not sound like the ideal way of addressing the issue of creation, the truth is none of us were there. So why would someone else's story be any better than that which someone creates for himself or herself? I just cannot judge a story based on the depth of the dust that has accumulated on it. New or old, if it works it works and if it does not work then it does not work.

I have created this story because the others just weren't working for me. I looked at the creation stories of major world religions and found the same great gaping hole. I look at my own religion and there I find the same gaping hole again. For a time, I thought I could live with that problem. I thought I could just believe what I believe and find other people who believe much the same. But then I turned on my television set and realized that not only can I not live with the problem, neither can anyone else. You see, that problem is that we have given a name to the Creator and called that Creator our own. Could a person become more pompous than to think they have a copyright on anything that grand?

A Creation Myth

"For if it were a simple fact that insanity is an evil, the saying would be true;
but in reality the greatest of blessings come to us through madness,
when it is sent as a gift of the gods."

From Socrates' second speech, as recorded by Plato in Phaedrus

In some versions of the Greek creation story, before there is Chaos (*'Void'*) there is Achlys (*'dark mist'*), who is the personification of misery. She is depicted as a pale woman with cheeks sunken from not eating. Her eyes are swollen and red from endless crying brought on by perpetual loneliness, those tears going unnoticed because she is alone in a way that none other could ever know. Think on that for a moment. That which existed prior to even the void from which existence sprang is misery.

Call it misery, pain, loneliness, or whatever word describes the feeling that comes when one feels utterly alone—that feeling is a universal concept. Not being able to touch, to feel, to connect with another being brings on a very special form of mania, the mania of creation and destruction. A baby who is not touched will certainly die. A person who feels truly alone will take his or her life. This too is mania. Creation and destruction, Life and Death—it is the very principle that caused the evolution of the French phrase for sexual orgasm, *le petit mort*, which means 'a little death.'

Who can argue that the world's greatest creators have not been touched with that mania? Who can argue that the world's greatest destroyer's have not been touched with that mania? So just what is this mania? The ancient Greeks used the word to personify madness, calling her the Goddess Mania. The ancient Romans also called her Mania but connected her to death. The Etruscans used the word mania as the name of the goddess of the Underworld. The Finnish used the root of the word in the name of their Underworld, Manana.

I have sat alone, cold and hungry but wanting neither companionship, nor warmth, nor food. Either would only prolong the suffering. It was in that moment that I understood the note from my Book of Shadows: "Our creator is evidenced by our creativity." In that instant of memory, I knew the gods had not forsaken me; I had forsaken them. They had not given me dreams that I had no hope of fulfilling. In that sacred moment, in choosing Life, I was reborn. In that rebirth, I truly understood the first mystery of my religion and the secret of genesis. But before I can tell you of that mystery and share its many secrets, you must first understand the nature of these words, mystery and secret.

A secret is, simply, something that is not told. Anything can be kept secret. The pin code for your ATM card is a secret. In a religious context, a secret is a bit more. It is a piece of information that either supports or leads one to understanding a mystery. As it is information it can be exchanged, sometimes even when it should not be. But unlike a secret, a mystery is experiential. It is something that can not be exchanged.

If you have been in that dark place, you will understand my creation story and will fondly receive the secrets that I share. Those secrets being the names and the expressions of countless others who have been in that dark place as recorded in the stories of the many gods and goddesses themselves. The secret is that we are not alone in our grief even when that grief is brought on by being truly alone.

The Nameless One: A Creation in Separation
Whose Holy Formula is (-1) + 1 = 0

"The nameless is the origin of heaven and earth"

—*From* Tao Te Ching

In a time before time, in a place before places, there was only the Nameless One, who was neither god nor man, neither male nor female. Because order had not yet emerged from the Nameless One, there was no disorder. Neither was there day and night, nor hot and cold, nor life and death. The dark was darker than the absence of light and the cold was colder than the absence of warmth.

The Nameless One was alone in a way that none before could have known because there were none before the Nameless One. The Nameless One was alone in a way that none since will ever know because there would never again be such loneliness. Nor would there be again anything darker than the absence of light, nor colder than the absence of warmth.

Overwhelmed with the sorrow of being alone in a way that none can begin to imagine, the Nameless One slipped into mania. The Nameless One found itself in that cold dark place where most of us have visited hoping never to return. But unlike us, the Nameless One had no other place to go. The Nameless One had no lore, no faith with which to ease the suffering. So the Nameless One chose death in a time when there was no death. It was the first act of love and the sacrifice from which we, this world, and all other worlds did come.

Darkness and Light: A Creation in Union
Whose Holy Formula is (-1) + 1 = 2

From the division of the Nameless One by the first act of love and sacrifice came forth a single son whose name is Light and a single daughter whose name is Darkness. With their creation, the Nameless One was no more. For a time, Light and Darkness were the sum total of the universe, but neither was content knowing each was not whole without the other. Just as the Nameless One felt alone for there was no other, both Light and Darkness felt alone because they were separated from one another. Neither whole, they were indeed alone. Desperately they tried to unite, but much to their surprise, they discovered the bliss of union to be so desirous that they would bear the pain of separation for the sake of reunion's splendor. Thus, in the first Great Rite did Light and Darkness discover the first mystery: We are separated for the sake of union.

With that separation we see the nature of the Nameless One as the union of that which is male and female. As a mystery, that observation is experiential. It manifests in all forms of love. It is, in essence, the Fifth Element. Known variously as Spirit, heart, and love, it is this force by which creation takes place in all orders. One of the manifestations of that Fifth Element is in the desire for sexual union. There we find the story of the Nameless One told in many lands by many cultures.

Africa—The Egyptian Atum, was driven to unite in the same way as his children would be: through sex. However, being all that existed, he had no one to experience union with. Egyptian lore thus records his creation of two children, Shu and Tefnut, as an act of masturbation.

Middle East—Before Eve, there was Adam's first wife Lilith. Although stripped from Christian lore, she is still found in older accounts. Lilith (Darkness) and Adam (Light) initially came into existence as conjoined twins. Lilith demanded autonomy, sometimes cited as sexual autonomy, thus leading to their separation and eventually to her replacement with the more passive Eve.

Mediterranean—The Roman Diana is a name used to describe both Diana (Darkness) and Lucifer (Light) before their separation and then to refer to Diana alone, after the separation. That separation came into play because Diana desperately wanted no longer to be alone and to have a mate of her own.

Sky and Earth: Children of Union

From the union of our Light and Darkness came many children, none of which are more beloved than the two we would come to know as Earth and Sky. It is here that we find the story of the Wiccan religion begins. You see, Wicca is an Earth-based religion. While Light and Darkness may have indeed caused life to start elsewhere, we have yet to meet those brothers and sisters. Instead, we see our creation story similar to the many Nature-based religions that have come before. As those many cultures evolved, they also looked back and attempted to explain the Nameless One.

Africa—The Egyptian Shu and Tefnut unite in the Great Rite. Later, Tefnut gives birth to Geb (Earth) and Nut (Sky).

China—The Chinese lore gives us the story of P'an Ku, who is also known as P'an-Gu. In the story of P'an Ku, the Nameless One is a cosmic egg that splits open to reveal a child or dwarf. As the child grows, the top half of the egg forms P'an Ku's head and upper body and becomes the Sky and its Heavens, the sacred Yang. The lower portions of P'an Ku become the Earth and its oceans, the sacred Yin. In the story of the Chinese Taoists, we see a similar separation of the male and female, which is Yang in the East and personified as Mu Gong and Yin in the West, personified as Hsi Wang-Mu.

Japan—The Shinto Izanami (female/darkness) is the Earth Goddess. Her husband Izanagi (male/light) is the God of the Sky. Also in Japan we see the principle of the Chinese Yin and Yang as In and Yo.

New Zealand—The tribal folk of New Zealand, the Maori, offer a story similar to P'an Ku. Here the Sky is Rangi or Raki (both male), depending on what part of the island you are on. The Earth is Papi (female). The creation of our world is a result of the two being separated by their children, who are a product of their great love for each other, the Fifth Element.

Summer and Winter: Creation in Union and Separation

		Winter
	Masculine	*Dark Half of the year*
Light Half of the year	*Feminine*	
Summer		

Summer and Winter

From the union of Earth and Sky came Winter and Summer who were named in honor of their grandparents. Winter, their son, was called the Dark half of the year in honor of his Grandmother Darkness. Summer, their daughter, was named the Light half of the year in honor of her Grandfather Light. It was their hope that by naming their son Winter after his grandmother Darkness, those generations to come would understand that although masculine, he would not exist without his feminine half. In like fashion, it was their hope that by naming their daughter Summer after her grandfather Light, those generations to come would understand that although feminine, she would not exist without her masculine half.

Here again we see culture after culture attempt to explain the mystery: We are separated for the sake of union.

Mediterranean—The Greek Persephone was kidnapped by Hades and brought to the Underworld. Her mother, the fertility goddess, Demeter, mourned her loss so much that she fell into depression and neglected her ability to provide fertility to the green of the Earth. The world fell barren, and the first Winter began. Realizing what had happened, Zeus sent Hermes to recover Persephone. But Persephone had already fallen in love with Hades. Although the story is sometimes told differently, the story of how Persephone took vengeance on a Nymph named Minth for having slept with Hades makes the story a bit clearer. Persephone agreed to spend part of the year with her mother Demeter because she loved her dearly and the other part of the year with the one who had won her heart, Hades. Thus, Summer returned to the Earth with Persephone's exit from the Underworld (separation), but leaves with the arrival of Winter and Persephone's love affair (union) continues. The story is virtually retold in the Etruscan story of Persipnei and the Roman story of Proserpina.

Near East—The Akkadian green man, Tammuz, presents the story of Persephone with a reversal of both gender and climate. At the time and location of his lore, the colder months were the ones to produce crops and the hot months were seen as barren due to the intense sun. Each year he is taken to the Underworld by demons. Without his fertility blessing the green of the Earth, the Summer begins. With his return, the Earth cools and the green returns to the land. This story is virtually retold in the Sumerian story of Damuzi.

Central and Northern Europe—When the Finnish Sampsa sleeps (separation) there is Winter. When he awakes he is reunited (union) with his bride in Holy Matrimony and Summer returns. In the Autumn he again sleeps, and Winter returns.

North America—Onatha, the Iroquois personification of Spring and Summer was kidnapped by a demon and brought to the Underworld. There she remained and her mother, Eithinoha, mourned her loss. As a result, fertility left the land until the Sun went looking for her, casting his rays and warming the soil as he did. Eventually she saw the light and snuck up from the Underworld as the new wheat crop. Every Autumn she is kidnapped again by that demon, and every Spring she returns. When she is in the Underworld, we see Winter. When she is not, we see Summer.

The Creation of the Sun

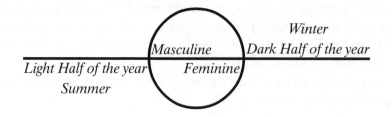

The Splitting of the Solar Year

As children who are themselves parents often turn to their parents for advice, so did Sky and Earth turn to their mother Darkness for advice. In response to and with permission from her Lord, Darkness took from her Lord enough Light to create the Sun. Then she set both Earth and Sky rotating about the Sun such that they would see the answer. Although the Sun was created by Darkness, it was created of Light.

From the Sun's interaction with Earth and Sky, we received the solar year as the amount of time it takes Earth and Sky to revolve around the Sun. And on that year does fall Winter and Summer, each being one half of the whole.

The First Order of Life—Plants:
Born of the Separation of Summer and Winter

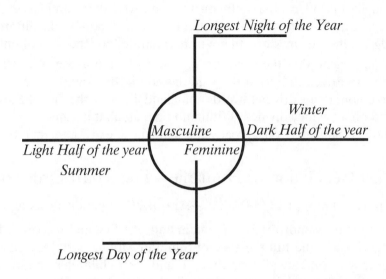

The Quartering of the Solar Year

From the union of Winter and Summer did come forth many splendid and sacred things, many of which sunk roots deep into the darkness of the Earth hoping to unite with the feminine half of their line, Mother and Grandmother, as well as branches high into the light and Sky hoping to unite with the masculine half of their line, Father and Grandfather. But neither remembered that sacred mystery discovered so long ago, for while they did see Winter and Summer neither were present at the same time. Try as they might, Winter and Summer gave birth to no children that could experience the first mystery. And so were born many lines in this order of life, but none which would become successful. Instead, the children of Winter and Summer quickly starved and almost faded entirely.

The longest night falls at the peak of the Dark half of the year, and the longest day falls at the peak of the Light half of the year. In the heart of Winter (masculine) we find the peak of Darkness (feminine); in the heart of Summer (feminine) we find the peak of Light (masculine). Thus, the solar year, again, is divided with the longest night at the mid of Winter and the longest day at the mid of Summer.

The Creation of the Moon

Again, as children who are themselves parents often turn to their parents for advice, so did Sky and Earth turn to their parents for advice. This time they spoke with Light. In response and with permission from his Lady, Light took from his Lady enough Darkness to create the Moon. He then set the Moon about both Earth and Sky, so they would see the answer. Although the Moon was created by Light, it was created of Darkness.

The Second Order of Life—Animals

With Earth and Sky set spinning around the Sun, so did the second Great Rite of Earth and Sky take place. In that union was conceived all the animals that we have ever known. Thus, the two lines became that of Plants and Animals, the difference being the knowledge of the first mystery, that we are separated for the sake of union.

And so it came that the order brought forth by the union of Earth and Sky, the animals, were driven to both union and division in the way that Earth and Sky were driven to union. Being driven towards union and division, the line of Earth and Sky did unite, and oh, how they divided. Within no time at all, it became clear that the line of Earth and Sky (animals) would greatly dominate the line of Summer and Winter (plants).

The First Generation of Humanity—The Third Order of Life

Between 169,000 to 148,000 B.C.E.—About 7000 generations ago

With so many wondrous lives found in both the first and second order of life who would never know the full message of Sun and Moon, Earth and Sky realized that although they indeed loved their children and their children's children, they needed assistance. So Earth and Sky created the third order of life—Humanity—as caretakers of all animals brought forth by the union of Sky and Earth and the plants of Winter and Summer.

Because these caretakers understood the value of the first order of life, it was decided that they would come from the first order of life, knowing those things that the body of a plant can know. Looking at the many children of Summer and Winter, they saw three that stood above the others, not looking down upon them but over them. These three were Ash, Elm, and Citron.

Taking the tallest of these children of Summer and Winter whose name was Ash, Sky formed it into his image, the first man, in the image of all animals male. As he did, so did Earth take the slightly shorter Elm and fashion it into her image, the first woman, in the image of all animals female. This creation of those who have already been born was not in the visual image, but in the image that is soul. For unto Humanity was given the soul that is distinctly male and unto woman the soul that is distinctly female, something found in the second order of life but not the first.

The Forbidden Fruit and the First Ascension of Humanity

This is the first ascension of humanity. To the first man and woman, Sky and Earth made a present the fruit of that third tree, telling them as they offered it that this was the Forbidden Fruit—forbidden because it is for humanity alone, but only should they take it of their own will. For, in the eating of this fruit, they would become more than plant or animal.

Upon eating that fruit, both man and woman did fall to the ground with much pain, for fruit of the citron brought with it both blessing and curse: empathy. This is the pain of birth, not one of union, but of separation. For, as surely as the child experiences the pain of being made separate from its mother, so does the mother feel the child's pain as if her own. And in this way, Ash and Elm knew the suffering of others. In that, so did Ash and Elm know the difference between right and wrong and so did they know sin. For there is no sin in the tormenting of a mouse by a cat because the cat does not know that it is wrong. Not knowing its pain, how could it? But humanity, the descendents of Ash and Elm, would never be able to so much as look at the cat tormenting the mouse without feeling the pain of the mouse.

So Ash and Elm knew they would not cause unneeded suffering because they would suffer as well. They would not toy with a mouse, as does the cat, simply for sport, unaware of the suffering incurred as the cat is unaware of the suffering inflicted. Where others may well say that the eating of that fruit may have been original sin, it certainly was not. The eating of the fruit was not sin; sin is the ongoing action and inaction that humanity commits having full knowledge that it is wrong. Some call this knowledge of right and wrong, good and evil, a conscience.

The First Praise of Our Lord and Lady

And when these new creatures spoke, they spoke the new names. To Sky, they spoke the word Father, and to Earth they spoke the word Mother. And so in respect for our line, so do we also call to these as Sky Father and Earth Mother. To their children, Mother Earth and Father Sky spoke, telling them that they were twice born. Plants were born of Summer and Winter. Animals were born of Earth and Sky. But humanity was born of Summer and Winter, as Ash and Elm, and then reborn of Earth and Sky, as Humanity. To them they also warned that while they would indeed fall and rise as do the plants of the Earth, they would one day die.

> *You were born of Summer and Winter*
> *Then reborn of Earth and Sky*
> *This is your blessing and your fate*
> *That one day you will surely die*

It was not long before their study of the first order of life found there was a cycle to things. Although it seemed at first on the surface that plants grew in the Light Half of the year and died during the Dark Half of the year, it was clear that after the darkest day of the year but before the first of Summer, there was a time in which the first sprouts had begun to break their shell. This they called the first Cross Quarter because it crossed the quarters set by the division of Winter and Summer, as well as the division made by the Earth's travel. And so it went that Ash and Elm would mark a second, third, and fourth Cross Quarter based on their study of the orders of life that had come before them. From this was observed the solar calendar.

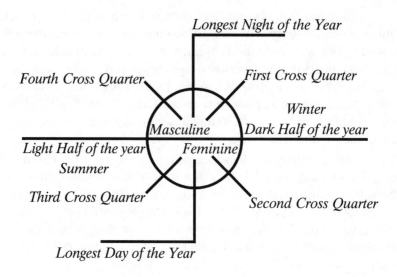

The Eight Spokes of the Solar Year

Being the first woman born under the Moon, Elm quickly discovered her cycles were different from that of the other orders of life. Where the females of other creatures moved to the rhythm of the Sun, her cycle moved to the rhythm of the Moon. Like the womb of her beloved Earth Mother, her tides rose and fell with the Moon. From this was observed the lunar calendar.

Commentary on the Book of Creation

In Wicca, neither is the Creator male nor female, neither Lord nor Lady. Instead, Wicca views the Creator as the union of Lord and Lady. Our Lord is the masculine principle of the soul (Yang) as well as the masculine principle of all things. Our Lady is the feminine principle of the soul (Yin) as well as the feminine principle of all things.

My view of Wicca strictly forbids the naming of the Creator. While I doubt this fact can be found plainly in any other book on Wicca, it is there for anyone to see. You see, part of the very fabric of the religion Wicca is the view of the Creator as Lord and Lady. Should one call the Creator by one name, whatever that name be, one is no longer practicing the religion that is Wicca. While the word 'forbid' is not generally used in our religion, it is used here for good reason, but only in the sense that being submerged naked in a pool of water forbids one from being dry. One may always leave the water to be dry and one may always leave Wicca to see the Creator in a way other than the Wiccan way. But in so doing, understand that there is a reason Wicca does not view the Creator as a single being by any name and there is a reason I have used the word 'forbidden.'

That name is forbidden because knowing the name of a thing grants one power over that thing and is blasphemous against that which Wiccans truly worship: Life itself. For when that Nameless One is given a name, the sum total of all that which is sacred, all life, is devalued. This is the nature of things, that when one gives name to the Creator, one looks at his neighbor's soul and sees diminished value. That act of naming the Creator is the very act that allows one to look at those who do not agree and say of them 'They are all godless,' or 'They are with a false god.' It also creates room for the idea that the Creator has an adversary or something apart from itself.

In giving the Creator the name Allah, one also names the adversary as all who are not followers of Allah, thus making it easy to take lives by saying they are all without Allah. In giving the Creator the name Yahweh, one also names the adversary as all who are not followers of Yahweh, thus making it easy to take lives by saying they are all without Yahweh. This principle was just as true on the eleventh day of September in the year 2001 as it was at the beginning of the Crusades. So know then plainly that the Creator is all these things—Allah, Yahweh, and all other names given unto the Creator. So many in fact, that that which is the sum of Creation can have no name.

Forbidden in the same sense in my view of Wicca is the use of the name God to refer to the Creator. Also forbidden is the word Goddess. For when we call the Creator God male, all who are female are devalued. Equally true is that in calling the creator Goddess female, all who are male are devalued.

So then in Wicca, the name God or Lord is the name of the masculine principle of all things; the name Goddess or Lady is the name of the feminine principle of all things. Additional names are given to each as Allah is given to our Lord, so is Allat given to our Lady. As Yahweh is given to our Lord, so is Aholibah given to our lady. For there is no masculine aspect of the Creator without a balancing feminine aspect, no God without Goddess, no Lord without Lady, and no father without mother.

So then what of the word Creator used as the name for the Creator? In my view of Wicca, the use of the word Creator is not a name for the Creator. It is a tool by which we can communicate belief with those who have chosen to give that Creator a name. Should the people of Allah ask what does a Wiccan worship, the Wiccan might answer, "The same holy Creator as you." Should the people of Yahweh ask what a Wiccan worships, the Wiccan might answer, "The same holy creator as you." For this is how the Wiccan views the many names given to the Creator by the many different religions, all the many faces of one Creator.

Liber ab Tres I
(Book of Three—Part I)
Book of Potential and Fate

"Mind the Three Fold Law ye should—three times bad and three times good"
Line 23 From Rede of the Wiccae
As submitted to Green Egg magazine by Lady Gwen Thompson

"Less in thy own defense it be, always mind the rule of three"
Line 23 From the Wiccan Rede
From my own Book of Shadows

 ne of the jokes about Wicca is that there are as many different traditions in Wicca as there are Wiccans. Although there is some truth to this statement, there are a few documents that practically every Wiccan counts as sacred. The first of these to be discussed is the Wiccan Rede. No one can be 100 percent sure where the Wiccan Rede came from so no one can be 100-percent sure exactly how it should be quoted. I received it with line 23 as quoted above from my Book of Shadows when I was a teen. It appeared in *Green Egg* magazine in 1975 with line 23 a bit differently and under a different title. Certainly the

52

term 'Rule of Three' is as popular an expression as 'the Three Fold Law.' The only real difference in the two quotes seems to be that in one we are told to always mind it and in the other we are told to always mind it unless it is in one's self defense. The second quote does not state that in self-defense the Rule of Three does not apply. It simply says that the exception to always minding it is in matters of self-defense.

I prefer the second quote, not because I received it before the first, but because without dismissing the Rule of Three, it tells us there are indeed times when one should not stop and think, times when you should act instinctively, from the soul rather than the mind or the Spirit (a combination of mind and soul). If one is clearly at risk, a gun is in one's face, one simply does not have time to consider the ethical ramifications of one's actions. I find the second quote much more empowering to any who might find themselves in a situation where such quick thinking is necessary. Yes, a Wiccan should consider the ethics of becoming a soldier, but having made that decision one does not stop on the field of battle to decide if it is right to return fire. Yes, a Wiccan should consider the ethics of becoming a police officer, but having made that decision a Wiccan police officer should not stop (as a fight begins) to decide if it is right to return fire. Yes, a Wiccan should consider the ethics behind actions in a life-threatening situation, but this should be conducted prior to the emergence of that life-threatening situation. So what is that rule of three?

The Wiccan Rede

(From my Book of Shadows)

1 Bide the Wiccan laws ye must, in perfect love and perfect trust.
2 Ye must live and let to live, fairly take and fairly give.
3 Throw the circle thrice about, to keep unwelcome spirits out.
4 To bind ye spell every time, let ye spell be spake in rhyme.
5 Soft of eye, light of touch, speak ye little, listen much.
6 Deosil go by the waxing moon, chanting out the Witches Rune.
7 Widdershins go by the waning moon, chanting out a baneful tune.
8 When the Lady's moon is new, kiss the hand to her, times two.
9 When the moon rides at her peak, then your heart's desire seek.
10 Heed the North wind's mighty gale, lock the door and trim the sail.
11 When the wind comes from the South, love will kiss thee on the mouth.
12 When the wind blows from the West, departed souls will have no rest.
13 When the wind blows from the East, expect the new and set the feast.
14 Nine woods in the cauldron go, burn them fast and burn them slow.
15 But elder be the Lady's tree, burn it not or cursed you'll be.
16 When the Wheel begins to turn, let the Beltane fires burn.
17 When the Wheel has turned to Yule, light the log, let the Horned One rule.

18 Heed ye Flower, Bush and Tree, by the Lady, blessed be.
19 Where the rippling waters go, cast a stone and truth you'll know.
20 When ye have a true need, hearken not to others' greed.
21 Never a season with a fool shall ye spend, lest be counted as his friend.
22 Merry meet and merry part, bright the cheeks and warm the heart.
23 Less in thy own defense it be, always mind the Rule of Three.
24 When misfortune is enow, wear the blue star on thy brow.
25 True in Love ever be, lest thy lover's false to thee.
26 These eight words the Wiccan Rede fulfill: An ye harm none, do as ye will.

In line 23 of the Wiccan Rede is the instruction, perhaps a warning, about the Rule of Three. Some have taken the Rule of Three to mean that anything one casts will return three-fold. If you believe this, I invite you to send me ten dollars, for surely someone will send you thirty. For that matter, send me a hundred dollars, a thousand, ten thousand. Send me $333,333.33 and I promise I will return to you a penny. With that penny and the $999,999.99 that the universe magickally returns to you in accordance with that interpretation of the Rule of Three, you will be a millionaire. Of course, that won't actually happen because the universe does not follow laws made up by folk who think they know better than Isaac Newton. Instead, the universe follows the laws set by Nature which are sometimes illuminated by men who know that they do not know better than Nature.

Called magicians in time of old and scientists today, these are the folk who create the expression of Nature's law after discovering it for themselves. The principle is represented again and again. In the science of thermal dynamics, the study of gravity, and any form of energy ever considered by a scientific method. No matter how much force you put into throwing an object into the air, that object will not return to the ground with an equal amount of energy, much less with three times that amount of force. In short, the previously mentioned interpretation of the Rule of Three is trumped by the scientific observation of the law of Nature governing all forms of matter and energy: The return is never greater than the investment. If it were, working perpetual motion machines would be common place and I would never have to pay an electric bill.

The number 3 is a magickal number—not because if we make a wish three times it will come true, and not because if we light three green candles we will win the lottery. It is a magick number because it unlocks the totality of that that which we are. It tells us that the whole of our being is mind, body, and soul. It uncovers our very essence and divines our fate. It is the key to understanding our past, present, and future.

Three is the Number of Humanity

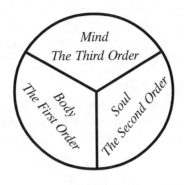

The Number of Humanity

In the Book of Genesis, we saw three orders of life. This is not a new concept. In Brazil we see the description of the three orders of life reflected in the gods Jacy, Guaracy, and Peruda. Jacy is said to have created all the plants of the Earth, giving them body as he did. Guaracy created all the animals of the Earth, giving them both body and soul as he did. Peruda created human consciousness and was particularly involved in human procreation and love. In fact, the three orders of life are a central concept in many Pagan cultures, most notably in the Norse. This is the Rule of Three:

> *All that one does will affect the mind, body, and soul; that these three aspects*
> *of humanity are inseparable; that causing harm to one will surely harm the*
> *other two and that causing benefit to one will surely cause benefit to the other*
> *two. In abstract we also see this in the Greek Three Graces and The Horae.*

Norse Creators of Humanity—Male—North Europe

After the great flood, Odin created the bodies of the first humans by carving them from two trees (plants). Embla, carved from the elm, became the first woman. Ask, carved from the ash, became the first man. But it took other gods to finish the task: Lodehur to give warmth and coloring (like that of animals) and then Hoeni to give them reason.

Name	Gift Given	Order of Life	Association
Odin	Gave breath	First order (plants)	Body
Lodehur	Gave warmth and coloring	Second order (animals)	Soul
Hoeni	Gave reason	Third order (humanity)	Mind

The Three Graces—Female—Mediterranean

Also known as the Three Charities. Three Greek goddesses who bestow beauty, charm, and merriment. With the rest of the Muses, they are the source of all inspiration.

Name	Her name means	Order of Life	Association
Thalia	'She who brings flowers'	First order (plants)	Body
Euphrosyne	'She who rejoices the heart'	Second order (animals)	Soul
Aglaia	'The brilliant'	Third order (humanity)	Mind

The Horae—Female—Mediterranean

Greek sisters who keep track of time and the seasons. The first brings the peace that is found in the elder forest. The second brings the natural order and justice under the law of the wild (survival of the fittest). The third brings deliberate order, those laws written by man.

Name	Gift Given	Order of Life	Association
Irene	Peace	First order (plants)	Body
Dike	Natural law and Justice	Second order (animals)	Soul
Eunomia	Deliberate Order	Third order (humanity)	Mind

Three times good...

Three is the number of the good things that come our way. It is the number of fortune as work product and the number that reminds us that there is creation in mania (inspiration). Not only did the Three Graces speak to our mind, body, and soul; as they themselves are muses, the message they spoke was of inspiration. Like the Nameless One, who can argue Odin had not given into mania when he hung from the tree called Yggdrasil, The Terrible One's Horse? The result of that mania was the inspiration for written language and the magick of the runes.

San-xing—Male—Central Asia

Chinese gods of fate, the San-xing are a likely source of the post modern expression 'Early to bed and early to rise make a man healthy, wealthy, and wise.'

Name	Fate/Association
Fu-xing	Luck and health
Lu-xing	Honor and prosperity
Shou-xing	Longevity and wisdom

Brigit—Female—Central Europe

A Celtic triple goddess of inspiration. Her three aspects are as follows.

- ✦ Fire of inspiration (patron of poetry and poets).
- ✦ Fire of the hearth/home (patron of fertility and healing).
- ✦ Fire of the forge (patron of metal smiths and craft folk).

Three times bad...

Ah, remember that forbidden fruit, the citron which gave Ash and Elm the ability to distinguish between right and wrong, good and evil? There is a tremendous argument in the Wiccan community: Most are very quick to say that Wicca does not believe in the existence of evil. If one were to redefine the word evil I might agree, but looking in my dictionary, I have to believe evil does indeed exist in this world. It exists in the hearts of men.

1. Morally bad or wrong; wicked: *an evil tyrant.*
2. Causing ruin, injury, or pain; harmful: *the evil effects of a poor diet.*
3. Characterized by or indicating future misfortune; ominous: *evil omens.*
4. Bad or blameworthy by report; infamous: *an evil reputation.*
5. Characterized by anger or spite; malicious: *an evil temper.* [1]

Now, I do with all my heart believe Wicca is a religion, but just for the sake of argument, let's see if Wicca can be a religion without a belief in the dictionary definition of evil.

1. If there is nothing that is 'morally bad or wrong,' then there is nothing that is morally good or right. That is to say, one could not identify something as being day if there exists nothing that can be identified as night. So, if Wicca is a religion which does not believe in evil, it can have no sense of morality.

2. If Wicca does not acknowledge that one can cause 'ruin, injury, or pain,' wouldn't it be just a little bit nonsensical to warn within the body and ending of the Wiccan Rede that one can indeed cause harm?

3. If Wicca does not believe that one might face future misfortune, why would we incorporate divination into the Wiccan Rede? I cite what is contained in most versions of the Wiccan Rede: 'Where the rippling waters go, cast a stone and truth you'll know.' If Wicca does not believe in evil, we are again nonsensical. Of course, we could believe that when we discover the truth of the future, all events that take place there are good. But in that case, we would be just a little bit overly optimistic for my taste.

4. If we do not think anything can be 'bad or blameworthy by report,' do we not say things such as child molestation are bad? Should we not report such matters?

5. Ah, maybe we are saying that anger and spite do not exist.

In my view of Wicca, we can say we strive not to promote evil. We can say that we do not worship evil. But what folk are trying to express in saying that evil does not exist is that Evil (note the capital E) does not exist. Wiccans do not acknowledge any one name for evil, any one personification because, like giving a name to the Nameless One, the moment you do you have devalued life. For certainly if there is a master of Evil, there are his or her servants.

On the existence of evil in the hearts of men, the ancients were rather clear. They believed it existed. Again, we see that three is the number of Humanity. Only here we see that it is a number applied to the other side of the Rule of Three. Here we see three times bad...

The Three Sons of Carman—Male—Central Europe
Three gods born to the Celtic Carman who are described as being an evil witch.

Name	Attribute
Dian	Violence
Dother	Evil
Dub	Darkness

The Graiae—Female—Mediterranean
In Greek lore, two sets of triplets were born to Phorcys and Ceto. The first three are called the Graiae. They were perhaps lesser known than the Gorgons were (the other set of triplets) but just as important. Each of the Graiae was born old, with gray hair and only one tooth and one eye to share between the three. As guardians of the Gorgons, they controlled the fate given out by those creatures.

The Sister	Attribute
Pemphredo	The Alarm
Deino	The Dread
Enyo	The Horror

The Erinyes—Female—Mediterranean
Three Greek goddesses born when Chronos killed Uranus and the blood of Uranus fell on to the belly of his wife Gaia (also Uranus's mother).

Name	Attribute
Alecto	Anger
Megaera	Jealousy
Tisiphone	Vengeance

The Gorgon—Female—Mediterranean
The second set of triplets born to Phorcys and Ceto.

Name	Attribute
Medusa	The Ruler
Euryale	Far Roaming
Sthenno	The Forceful

The Harpies—Female—Mediterranean

Here we see not only evidence that the ancient Greeks saw a clear difference between right and wrong, here we see the face of each. Initially, the Harpies were depicted as beautiful winged maidens, perhaps virgins. They were set about the world to insure that peace and lawfulness prevailed. But when it became necessary to carry off the evil of the world, they became hideous.

Name	Attribute
Aello or Podarge	Swift Storm/Fleet Foot
Celaeno	The Dark
Ocypete	Swift Wing

Three is the Number of Fate

Three is the number of fate. This is not a fate that is predetermined by a supernatural force. Three is the number the fate that we choose. We are each born, and we will each die. Three is the number of these two points and all that is in the middle. It is a number that speaks to the whole of that which we are without the limitation of time. It is the sum total, our beginning, middle, and end. It is the net result of that which we will be when we are no longer. In its essence, this is the expression 'by the power of three times three' which is the power of every moment in a person's life.

	Past	Present	Future
	Mind	Mind	Mind
	Body	Body	Body
	Soul	Soul	Soul
Total:	Three+	Three+	Three = Nine (three times three)

(Mind, Body, and Soul) x (Past, Present, and Future) = Fate

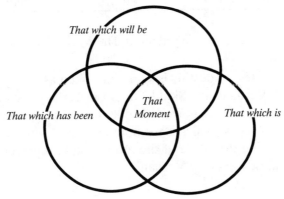

That which will be

That which has been

That Moment

That which is

The Moment

The idea that any one moment in a person's life is a dance between the past, present, and future is not a new concept. Nor is the idea that all things have a beginning, a middle, and an end. However, from the viewpoint of that moment we just spoke of, the future is seen as changing because it has not yet taken place.

The Three Fates (Also known as The Moirae)—Female—Mediterranean

Greek goddesses and daughters of Zeus and Themis who presided over the destiny of mortals. Calling them to bless a handfasting shows respect for natural law and can be seen as the more common Wiccan pledge 'A year and a day or for as long as love shall stay.'

Goddess	State	Tense	Condition	Description
Clotho	Potential	Past	Unchanging	Spins the thread of life
Lachesis	Opportunity	Present	Transitional	Presents opportunity
Atropos	Conclusion	Future	Changing	She who cuts the thread

The thought of having an outside force cut your thread does not, on the surface, sound very Wiccan, especially not when we make such an objection to a great record keeper in the sky. But when we recognize the potential with which we are born and the opportunities that are presented during our lifetimes, we see that we show Atropos exactly where to cut our threads.

Carmentis Sisters—Female—Mediterranean

Roman goddesses who expanded on the idea of the fates to apply to the totality of things that have come, are here, and will come. We see the development of the Triple goddess as associated with past, present, and future as well as an association to the unchanging and changing.

Goddess	State	Tense	Condition
Postvorta	Potential	Past	Unchanging
Carmenta	Opportunity	Present	Transitional
Porrima	Conclusion	Future	Changing

The Norns (Also called The Three Wyrds and The Weird Sisters) (Shakespeare)—Female—North Europe

The Teutonic Triple Goddess of destiny is sometimes seen as a single goddess, Wyrd, with three aspects: Urd, Verdani, and Skuld. Other times, the principle is seen as three entirely separate goddesses of which Wyrd is one, the other two being Verdani and Skuld. Urd represents one's past, which is the potential for destiny. Verdani represents the present, forever weaving the fabric of the future. Skuld represents the future and the ability to tear the fabric woven by Verdani.

Goddess	State	Tense	Condition
Urd	Potential	Past	Unchanging
Verdani	Opportunity	Present	Transitional
Skuld	Conclusion	Future	Changing

Three is the Number of Wiccan Self-Dedication

The Promise of Our Lady Ishtar

Here do I invoke that I may be whole
Their love into my mind, body, and soul

Three is the number of Wiccan Self-Dedication. It is the number of our Lord, our Lady, and their children, us. When one dedicates oneself to Wicca, one invites our Lord and Lady into the mind, body, and soul. This invitation replaces the adult baptisms and adult rites of other religions where the dedicant is said to be absolved of sin. When one dedicates oneself to Wicca, one's sins are not removed, they are acknowledged.

The act of dedicating oneself to Wicca is the act of declaring to oneself, 'I am responsible.' It is saying, 'I did these things.' It is accepting once and for all that there is no Satan or boogieman controlling one's actions. It is an acceptance of the fact that everything we have done, are doing, and will do affects our mind, body, and soul in the holy formula that is three times three. This is not to say that Wiccans do not feel remorse. Indeed, it is often remorse for unjust actions that brings one to Wicca. Upon seeing the carnage brought on humanity as a result of her words before the assembly of the gods, Ishtar fell to her knees and wept for what her words had brought about. In tears, she swore to the gods upon her lapis that she would never again act so mindlessly.

'Ye gods here, as surely as this lapis
Upon my neck I shall -not forget,
I shall be mindful of these days, forgetting never.'

Ishtar speaking of the Great Flood
From the Gilgamesh Epic [2]

Make no mistake; this is not a Path one should choose lightheartedly. There is great comfort in being led, in being able to blame someone else for one's own actions. This is the nature of Aleister Crowley's statement; 'The slaves shall serve.' Never can a Wiccan speak of such excuses and remain true to the Rule of Three:

'Satan made me do it.'—Wiccans do not believe Satan exists. Certainly evil exists, but that evil is in the hearts of men, so you did it yourself and should just admit it.

'It wasn't me. It was the [insert drug or alcohol of choice].'—Who put that
alcohol into your mouth? If it wasn't you, then where is the police report?

Wiccans refuse to be slaves to Satan, the boogieman, or any other excuse. We are not sheep. If you are a slave, sheep, or any other colloquialism denoting a follower, then Wicca is not the religion for you. You see, in Wicca, you must decide for yourself what is right and what is wrong. In this, I do not mean what is right and wrong just for yourself, but what is right and wrong in the totality of the terms. To be Wiccan, one must decide what is good, what is evil, and then look inside oneself, recognize both, and take action to remove that which is evil. Wicca is a religion in which one seeks to improve oneself.

In this I have seen the downfall of many that have come to Wicca for superficial reasons. If one becomes Wiccan and does not recognize the need to identify good and evil within ones self, there is no moral authority as guidance. No one to state firmly that one's actions are right or wrong. Consider the abortion issue, in Wicca, and the Catholic Church. Most Catholics will tell you that the Church finds abortion to be a sin so great, it is punishable by excommunication. Most Wiccans will tell you that the Wiccan religion is pro-choice. Note that the Catholic Church addresses the issue of abortion but Wiccans tend in conversation to address only the political stance on the legality of abortion. What benefit is Wicca to a person considering abortion if she were not willing to do that which Wicca insists? That is, to consult one's own soul and that which has been uncovered of that soul during the path of initiation into the mysteries of Wicca.

Now, I know I just pressed a few buttons by using the abortion issue. A great many people insist that the issue is not a matter of religion. Those folk like to tell us that abortion is a personal choice, not a religious edict. Those folk are exactly who I do not believe should be Wiccan. While such matters are not best decided by some group of priests in Rome, if one is not willing to accept a religion as personal, becoming ones own priest/ess, making decisions mindful of right and wrong, then having some moral authority other than one's self is in fact needed. Our actions do have consequences. As example, if abortion is wrong for you, then it is an immoral act. If you have searched your soul and found that it is not a wrong decision for you, then it is not an immoral act. However, do not think that it has no consequence, and do not think that the issue of having or not having an abortion is not a matter of morality. In Wicca, morality is of the highest order. That order is a morality in which the individual must decide for oneself what is right and what is wrong.

Take issue with this as you will. With or without your agreement, the fact remains that in our society, failing the ability to know the difference between right and wrong negates a person's ability to participate in the legal system. In our society identified sociopaths are generally institutionalized such that someone else makes decisions for them. This does not mean there is anything inherently wrong with the Catholic religion or other religions. Some religions say one thing on matters such as these, other religions say the opposite. The Wiccan religion, when it is truly asked, says something different to each person. This is because the Wiccan religion speaks from one's own heart. Do not make an honest attempt to listen to that source and you can be just as much a member of Wicca as an African-American Jewish lesbian can be a member of the Ku Klux Klan.

Three is the Number of the Outsiders

Three is the Number of Hope and of Afterthought

I draw you up
I bind your ways
I cast you out
I end your days

—A simple chant to banish the Outsiders

The Outsiders are those baneful things within each and every one of us that we wish we could rid ourselves of. Each year at the Real Witches Ball, I host a simply huge Samhain Rite in which everyone in attendance is asked to fork over their outsiders. Sometimes we come around the Circle with a box in which to place them, other times I have asked each person to pick up a pebble, see that pebble as the Outsiders and then toss it out of the Circle. Each year about half the folk look on as if they are utterly baffled. The idea that I might think there is something inside them that they don't want is confusing as if to say 'Who me? No, I am perfect thank you.' If one has already arrived at perfection, what purpose does a religious path serve?

If an offering is made, the idea is that an appeasement is made outside of the place in which the Circle is to be cast. The hope is that the Outsiders will leave the ritual space to receive the appeasement. If banishing the Outsiders, my preferred method, the Outsiders are collected from everyone in attendance and then either destroyed or removed from the circle. An excellent way to symbolically collect those outsiders is with a Pandora's Box. Per Greek lore, Zeus punished humanity for having received fire (symbolic of Mind) from Prometheus, who had stolen it from the gods. The form of that punishment was to unite Pandora, whose name means 'all gifted,' with Epimetheus, whose name means 'after thought.' With Pandora came a box that she was told not to open under any circumstance. She gave in to curiosity and opened the box. From within came all the evils of the world. She quickly slammed shut the lid, hoping to prevent further release, but by the time she got it shut there was only one thing remaining—hope. Three is the number of Pandora, Epimetheus, and their magickal child, the Outsiders.

Our recognition of the Outsiders in our rites is to say we still have hope. It is in this box. And with that hope, we are going to capture those Outsiders and return them to this box. In ritual, this is often done by asking guests to write down their own Outsiders and place them inside a box while telling them what doing so means. This is why my view of Wiccan ritual incorporates an offering to or banishing of the Outsiders prior to the casting or closing of the circle. Although this portion of the Wiccan ritual structure takes place with every Wiccan ritual, it is of even greater importance during a Self-Dedication rite.

Three is the Number of Who We Are

Three is the number of who we are. It is the number that says that while we embrace our Father above and Mother below, we are ourselves at center. Although we have branches reaching into the sky and roots stretching into the Earth, but bulk of who and what we are is found in the trunk, our own individual mind, body, and soul in the past, present and future. Although there is very little written material which can prove the ancient Druids saw the Principle of Three represented in the roots, trunk, and branches of the tree; there is certainly a lot of modern Druid literature that states this view was held by the ancient Druids. Finally, three is also the number of Wicca, a religion of not only old and new, but also of balancing the ancient and the modern in the needs of its followers.

Chapter Dedication

This chapter is dedicated in loving memory of my father, Robert, who in the way he both lived and died, demonstrated:

> The serenity to accept the things he could not change,
> The courage to change the things he could
> And the wisdom to know the difference.[3]

Liber ab Exodus
(Book of Departure)
Our Separation Began
Approximately 7,000 Generations Ago

We are the old people
We are the new people
We are the same people
Some will never die

We are the old ways
We are the new ways
We are the same ways
Some will never die

We are the old gods
We are the new gods
We are the same gods
Some will never die

—Author Unknown

n June 26 2002, a 73-year-old widow, grandmother, and Cherokee, by the name of Barbara Crandell, was arrested while praying, sitting on a sacred site of her ancestors in Newark, Ohio, a site where she had gone to pray for over 20 years. That sacred site is the worlds largest—note: I did not say one of, but *the* world's largest—earthworks. In reference to its world significance, it has been called the Stonehenge of America. Various attempts to date it have resulted in an age of between 2,000 and 5,000 years of age. Described as a *problem* when it comes to the history of North America, the Octagonal Earthworks of Newark, Ohio, were not originally built by the Cherokee. Certainly the Cherokee adopted it and used it as sacred ground long before those who currently use it, but the truth is that at this time we cannot be 100-percent sure who built it.

Although she had with her a copy of the lease that grants the current users permission to use the site only if they keep it 'open to the public at all times,' the folk currently using that land seem to think that 'all times' means the four days of the year on which the site is 'open to the public.' But that fact did not impede her taunting and arrest:

> *"They cuffed her hands behind her back and ordered her up. When she couldn't rise, she said, they dragged her to her feet. Snapshots show a ladder of fingerprints down her bruised arms." (From* The Columbus Dispatch, *July 19 2002, describing Barbara Crandell, written by Barbara Carmen)*

How did we get to the place in which our COPs, our *Champions of the People*, believe it is acceptable behavior to handcuff, drag, and bruise a 73-year-old grandmother because she decided to pray on the sacred ground of her ancestors? Was her crime really so horrible that the police could not wait until she was done praying before they inflicted her bruises? Despite the letter of the lease and the statements by the Ohio Historical Society found in literature and their Websites over and over again that the Octagon Earthworks are open year round, Barbara Crandell was found guilty of trespassing. The Ohio Historical Society declined comment on the verdict.[1]

So what is this Eighth Man-Made Wonder of the World currently used for? Realizing the site had great significant meaning, it was purchased with public money in 1893. Eventually it was leased to a country club, which did not sit very well with many folk, so the matter came before the courts of Ohio who ruled that because the property was of such significant historic value, that it be deeded to the Ohio Historic Society.

With what seems like very questionable wisdom, the Ohio Historic society then leased the land back to the country club until the year 2078. While one might think the Ohio Historic Society had the forethought of preserving the site and keeping it open to the public, great amounts of damage have now been done to the land in the Country Clubs efforts to maintain and expand their spacious golf course.

So why did someone handcuff, drag, and bruise a 73-year-old widowed grandmother? Because someone wanted to play golf. Why isn't the letter of the lease respected, allowing the public access to this sacred site on a more regular basis? Because someone wanted to play golf. How can historic sites be purchased with our tax money and then used for a country club? Because someone wanted to play golf.

According to Barbara, prior to her arrest she was taunted, 'Haven't you people got anything better to do?' My gods, our gods, who are these 'you people'?

Our Story Begins in Africa

If all of current humanity began with only one mother, how is it that we look so different? Do we each not have two feet, two hands, two eyes? And what of race? If we were all born of one mother, why is it there are different races of human beings?

In this matter, better questions are: Do we look all that different? Are there multiple races of humanity? The answer to both is a resounding no. In fact, any two members of humanity are about as closely related as two can be without being the same person. In the vastness of the human race, there are no two human beings that are further apart then two members of even the smallest community of other creatures. That is to say, if you take a tall black man with brown eyes and a short white woman with blue eyes, the amount of genetic diversity between the two is less than the amount of genetic diversity found within any one pack of wolves. There is only one race of humanity, that being the human race. As such, in my view of Wicca, there is seen only one Mother and only one Father.

Of the few differences seen within that race, few can be attributed to anything other than sexual selection. Skin color is an example. You may have noticed that in colder climates folk tend to have lighter skin. In warmer climates, folk tend to have darker skin. This is because skin pigment is humanity's way of protecting it from dangerous ultraviolet radiation. Dark skin inhibits the absorption of the ultraviolet spectrum of sunlight like a natural sun tan lotion. However, if we do not receive enough exposure to ultraviolet radiation, our skin cannot produce vitamin D. Without vitamin D, we develop rickets, which is characterized by defective bone growth. In Africa, where all life began, dark skin means a healthy body because it prevents one from being repeatedly burned by that ultraviolet radiation, resulting in horrible disfigurement due to cancerous growths. Because the amount of ultraviolet light striking the earth of Africa is great, there is little concern or worry about vitamin D deficiency or the development of rickets even if one has the darkest of skin. But as one moves away from the intense ultraviolet radiation, dark skin pigmentation causes one to suffer from vitamin D deficiencies and become horribly disfigured due to rickets. The fact of the matter is, folk who are horribly disfigured do not tend to breed as often as folk who are not horribly disfigured. This observation is called sexual selection. While it is not the only way in which we evolve, it is certainly a major contributor.

As we migrated away from the birthplace of Ash and Elm, we changed—not in a thought out or deliberate attempt to adapt to our environment, but in a constant ongoing attempt to select the best possible genes for our children. I hesitate to call this evolution because that would give the idea that a white person is more evolved than a black person is, and that simply is not the case. A light-skinned person is simply the product of a line of folk who preferred sex with lighter-skinned people because the darker-skinned people were either becoming disfigured or dying due to a vitamin D deficiency. The end result of that process was the appearance of white folk, black folk, and a variety of folk between black and white, all with the same mother.

In my view of Wicca, we state firmly that all humans are the children of the one Mother Earth and Father Sky for two reasons. One's mother, no matter what she might tell you, is still one's mother no matter who one chooses to have sex with. It is also now more or less scientific fact that all humanity has a genetic link to one woman who lived in Africa.

The great religions and sciences of the world have been wrong. You might recall mention of Eden where for a time lived Adam and Eve in your Christian Studies class. Maybe you were raised in Islam where you read about Adan where for a time lived Adam and Haiwa. Well, each of these world religions was wrong and dangerously so.

Science seems to have come to replace religion. You might have learned about Lucy and perhaps of the 'Scopes Monkey Trial' (*State v. John Scopes*) in public school. That information is wrong as well. In fact, although folk seem to think that John Scopes won his case, he in fact lost. Later it was overturned, but never won. They just decided the thing made a monkey out of the courts so they dropped it because there was little to be gained by punishing Mr. Scopes.

That was then and this is now. Today, recognizing the fact that the religion and even the science of past generations were wrong is critical. In the past, nuclear, biological, chemical, and other weapons had not been invented. Folk could go to war over which religion or science was right and which was wrong with little concern for devastation on a global scale. It was more or less globally safe to perpetuate the myth of the current concept of evolution. That myth is that Lucy (ape-like ancestor) lived in Africa and was the predecessor to the wandering Homo Erectus who moved into Europe and Asia and then evolved into modern humanity.

The great religions and science of the world have been right. What's that? Didn't I just say that both science and religion had been wrong? Why, yes I did, thank you for noticing. Religions have been right in stating that humanity emerged from the garden as just that, humanity, or modern man. Science is probably right in stating that humanity evolved, but it was wrong in the idea that we left Africa as anything other than modern humans. Oh, maybe some distant cousins did leave Africa, but without exception those cousins died.

My view of Wicca (and I hope yours) is that Wicca is a living religion. It evolves with the times, accepting new science and disregarding the mistakes we have made in the past. So where we once felt there were 'races' of humanity, today Wicca teaches that we are one race, one people —not because it is politically correct, but because our very survival demands it. Now that we have the ability to destroy our world many times over, we must grow in understanding such that we do manifest that potential eventuality. In other words, we must evolve or we will become extinct.

In essence, Africa is the womb of the family that we call humanity. While one can easily argue for evolution, does not a child evolve in the womb of his or her mother? Is a sperm cell or an ovum a human being? Do we hold funerals every time a man masturbates or a woman menstruates? Is the union of a sperm cell and an ovum a human being? Again, do we hold a funeral every time a woman menstruates? After all, the great majority of miscarriages occur without the woman's knowledge of ever being pregnant. Maybe we did evolve in the womb of Africa but we emerged from that womb just as human as any human child emerges from his or her mother. We are one people.

Today, science has a wonderful new tool called DNA by which to determine this. Within the makeup of each and every human being is something called mitochondrial DNA. It is found in virtually every cell in the human body but it is not a part of the normal chromosomal DNA. Of the more than three billion base pairs of human DNA, only about 16,500 are mitochondrial. The other more than 99.99 percent is found in the chromosomes. Unlike chromosomal DNA, only the mother passes mitochondrial DNA. Because it is separate from the typical chromosomal DNA, it can be used to trace genetic lineage all the way back to one woman who lived in Africa. Often called the Mitochondrial Eve, she is not the Elm spoke of in the first chapter. Nor is she the child or grandchild of Ash and Elm. Instead, Mitochondrial Eve, the Eve of most modern religions, lived approximately 2,200 generations after Ash and Elm in or about location one on the map on page 70, which is where our story begins.

In or around what we now call the Congo, Ash and Elm were born about 169,000 to 148,000 BCE, or about 7,000 generations ago. From Ash and Elm did come many children, who left to the four corners of their garden Africa. These were the first modern humans, not at all unlike you and I. They were hunter-gatherers, negotiating in nature with an intellect unrivaled by any other creature in their world.

But even with the same mind that just 7,000 generations later placed a man on the moon, their first exodus from the garden was ill-fated. In the north, they found their world ended in desert, in the west and south they found their world to end in ocean, but to the east they could and did pass. Their first attempts at exodus brought them to the east shore of the Red Sea where they followed the coast line north, passing the Valley of the Kings and crossing through Gaza into the Middle East as far as Galilee and maybe a bit further. But that is where this first exodus would end. The next attempt would not be for thousands of years.

The First Exodus: Map Location 2

Approximately 110,000 B.C.E.
Approximately 2,200 generations after Ash and Elm

Changes in the climate caused the polar ice caps to swell. With the growing ice at each pole, the amount of water at the equator decreased dramatically. The majority of the African continent north of the equator was engulfed by the Sahara dessert as it grew due to severe drought. The portions of humanity that remained in Africa could migrate south as the northern portions of the continent turned into dessert. But those who had left Africa through Gaza were trapped, unable to return to the garden that was Africa and unable to move much further into the Middle East. As the deserts approached from all sides, their entire line died.

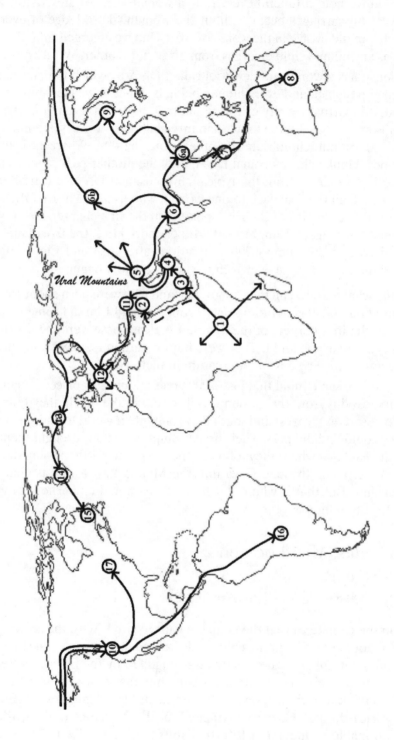

Migration from the Womb

In Africa, our ancestors huddled along the Southeast Coast. To survive, they changed from hunter-gatherers to beachcombers. Shellfish and other seafood became their primary diet. Forced into smaller areas, their increasing population grew to a point where the shores of Africa were no longer able to support them. A second attempt at exodus became a matter of survival. From the East Coast of Africa at the Gates of Grief, the sea level was 150 feet lower than it is today. From the African coast, one could look across the Red Sea to see the green of the Yemen Mountains.

The Second Exodus: Map Location 3
Approximately 78,000 B.C.E.
Approximately 3,500 Generations after Ash and Elm

The second exodus at about 78,000 BCE landed one community of people safely in Yemen, on the East Coast of the Red Sea. This is the beginning of all humanity outside of Africa. It was in essence the first New World. The community may have been as small as 250 people. Within its small number were two women of unique importance to this story. They were both descendants of our Elm as well as descendants of her offspring, Mitochondrial Eve. Their exodus from Africa is the single event that would eventually lead to the population of every corner of the globe.

This is not saying that everyone who migrated from this point were the children of these two women. However, before leaving the area of Yemen, about a thousand years later, all people outside of Africa would carry the unique mitochondrial DNA of one of these two women, if not passed on directly from one of the two, then from one of their descendants intermixing DNA with another line.

Migration Along the Coasts: Map Locations 4, 5, and 6
Approximately 77,000 B.C.E.
Approximately 3,550 Generations after Ash and Elm

Map Location 4—After about a thousand years, our family again separated. One group remained in the Middle East, spreading into Saudi Arabia. The other moved east into Iran, following the coastline.

Map Location 5—Some settled in Iran, moving inland to the east of the Ural Mountains. Others continued to move along the coastline into India.

Map Location 6—From India, our family splits again. One group continues its coastal migration into Malaysia (6a) and south towards Sumatra. The other group (6b) moved inland, heading towards the Himalayas.

The Toba Volcano Erupts: Map Location 7
Approximately 72,000 B.C.E.
Approximately 3,800 Generations after Ash and Elm

The Toba volcano in Sumatra erupted, sending plumes of ash 25 miles into the sky. The resulting cloud of ash reached as far as Northern Malaysia and India. The Middle East experienced a volcanic winter for 6 years. It was the most destructive event in the last two million years. Probably in an attempt to flee the affected areas, the group that had moved towards the Himalayas (6b) crossed the Himalayas, moved through the Mongolian steps, and into Siberia. The group that was north of the Toba eruption moved north along the east coast of Vietnam, and into China.

The Survivors of the Toba Eruption: Map Location 8

Approximately 68,000 B.C.E.
Approximately 4,000 Generations after Ash and Elm

The survivors of the Toba explosion that escaped by the southern route entered onto the landmass that is now the islands of South East Asia. But they didn't stop there. Within just a few thousand years, they faced the second successful exodus of the human race, crossing more than 100 miles of ocean to a world they could not have known existed prior to their arrival. Unlike the crossing of the Red Sea, there were no friendly shores visible before they left and to this day a reason for their journey has not been found. These members of our family found their home, remaining in Australia and becoming known today as the Australian Aborigines.

The Extinction of Megafauna: Map Location 8

Approximately 51,000 B.C.E.
Approximately 4,700 Generations after Ash and Elm

When our family arrived in Australia, just 700 generations earlier, they discovered a new world filled with wonder. They were met with 9-foot kangaroo, tortoises the size of cars, and an array of other megafauna. By 51,000 B.C.E. all megafauna had become extinct. There is no sign of over-hunting or any large-scale slaughter, just the first example of how the presence of humanity tends to have a dramatic influence on his environment whether or not that influence is intended.

The First Great Flood: Map Locations 4 and 11

Approximately 48,000 B.C.E.
Approximately 4,900 Generations after Ash and Elm

'The olden days are alas turned to clay,
Because I bespoke evil in the Assembly of the Gods,
How could I bespeak evil in the Assembly of the Gods,
Ordering battle for the destruction of my people,
When it is I myself who give birth to my people!
Like the spawn of the fishes they fill the sea'

—Ishtar speaking of the Great Flood
From the Gilgamesh Epic [2]

As humanity migrated along the coastline, we left behind settlements that later became the great cultures we see today. The community that formed in the Middle East, in the area of Saudi Arabia, might have migrated north prior to the Great Flood, but the Lebanon and North Saudi Arabian deserts prevented that migration. The first Great Flood changed that, opening up the Fertile Crescent and making the northern deserts passable.

Although this event took place about 50 thousand years ago (48,000 B.C.E.), the oldest surviving stories are only about four thousand years old. The oldest is probably the Sumerian story (2000 B.C.E.). This does not mean the story was not told much earlier, it just means that we have not yet found earlier record of the story. We have, however, found archeological and anthropological evidence that places the event about 50 thousand years ago (48,000 B.C.E.). With this evidence of Earth and man, we can speculate that the Earth event that allowed migration into Europe was also the event on which humanity based its many stories of the first Great Flood. Many European cultures attribute the entrance of humanity into Europe to this event.

The earliest known reference to the first Great Flood can be found in the Sumerian story of an elder citizen named Utnapishtim. Having received knowledge of the pending flood from Ea (Sumero-Babylonian god), Utnapishtim built a great ship and stocked it in preparation. After seven days of flood, he sent out a dove; it returned, indicating that it found no other place to land. He then sent out a swallow, and it too returned. Finally, he sent a raven, which did not return. Believing it must have found another place to land, he knew the flood was over

After finding dry land, he made sacrifice for his deliverance. So humbled were the gods by this mortal's act of sacrifice even after witnessing the utter destruction of his world, that they felt great remorse for having killed so many with the flood, and they granted Utnapishtim immortality, promising never again to cause such an event.

Babylonian—Ishtar, a Sumero-Babylonian evolution of the Babylonian Nuah, became concerned about the conduct of humanity and spoke her concerns to the Assembly of the Gods. In response, the gods brought forth the flood. After witnessing the destruction of humanity, Ishtar swears on her lapis that it will never again take place. In the Babylonian story, Utnapishtim's name is Ziusudra and he is warned by Anunna (the Assembly of Gods) rather than an individual, but other than those variances the story is essentially the same.

Hindu/Near East—Prior to the Great Flood, a man named Manu was fishing when he came upon a small fish with a talent unusual for most fish; this one could talk. And talk it did, telling Manu that its name was Matsya and pleading that Manu not kill him, but instead grant protection from the other fishermen until he could grow into an adult. Manu granted the small fish his desire and placed him in a pot of water just to make sure no one else would catch the poor little thing. When it grew, he put it into a bigger pot and then a bigger pot until he had to place it in a lake and then the ocean itself. Upon placing the huge fish in the ocean, it warned Manu of the impending flood and instructed him to build an ark. Manu, realizing the fish was an incarnation of Vishnu, did as the fish instructed. When the flood came, Matsya connected a rope to the ark and pulled the ark to safety.

Central Asian—The Chinese god Gun is cited as being responsible for not preventing the Great Flood.

The Story of the Flood Moves North

Greek account—Warned of the Great Flood by Prometheus, Deucalion built a great ship, an ark, which carried him, his wife Pyrrha, and stores necessary to repopulate the Earth. Deucalion's name means 'New-wine Sailor,' which might be a commentary on his replanting of the vineyards.

The survivors of the Great Flood moved into Europe. As they did, they, too, left behind communities and pockets of humanity that eventually became the great tribes of Europe. Many of those tribes later described their exodus from the Middle East and entrance into Europe in the mythology that followed.

Irish account—Warned of the impending flood by his father Noah (root of the Christian story), Bith and his wife Birren traveled to the west most point of the known world. With them, they brought their daughter Cesara, her husband Fintaan, and a tribe of maybe 200 people. When the flood receded, Bith and Birren became the first couple to enter Ireland, leading the way for their tribe.

Welsh account—Dwyvan and his wife Dwyvach built a ship named the Nefyed Nav Nevion, filled it with animals, survived the flood, and then seeded the Welsh tribes.

Scandinavian account—This event is marked in the Scandinavian tale of the first man and woman into Europe. In Norse lore, Odin created Ask and Embla from the Ash and Elm tree (some say Ash and Vine), but only after the Great Flood made the land livable. Some accounts state that, rather than from living trees, Odin selected two logs that were floating in the receding waters of the flood from which to carve humanity.

Neandertal Man: Map Location 12

Some cite Germany as the first place humanity meets Neandertal. If this meeting occurred, it is likely that Neandertal man was a migration out of Africa that occurred much prior to the migration of humanity. If that is the case, by 38,000 B.C.E. we see no further evidence of the existence of Neandertal. Like the extinction of megafauna in Australia, without any evidence of war or large-scale conflict, upon meeting humanity the Neandertal simply became extinct.

However, there are a growing number of researchers that believe Neandertal man simply did not exist. Instead, the evidence found might have been the remains of that portion of humanity that migrated too quickly for sexual selection to have lightened their skin. This school of thought says that the remains that were given the name Neandertal were actually shorter humans with sloped foreheads because they suffered from vitamin D deficiencies and the degenerative state of the bone structure known as rickets. If that is the case, those bones would not contain the DNA record of the migration out of Africa because they were most likely the ancestors of that first exodus from Africa, which are currently not thought to have made the migration as far north as Germany.

While both schools of science exist in conflict on this matter, there is absolutely no genetic evidence that would lead a person to believe Neandertal was an evolutionary step of humanity outside of Africa. Of that fact, both either agree or ignore.

The First East Coast Entrance into North America: Map location 6b

Approximately 22,000 B.C.E.
Approximately 6,000 generations after Ash and Elm

After crossing the Himalayas and moving through Siberia, this arm of our family moved east to cross into North America at the Bering Straits. When they entered North America, they continued to migrate along the coastline, this time in a southern direction because any migration west or north was blocked by the thick sheets of ice that covered the majority of North America.

The Second East Coast Entrance into North America: Map Location 9

Approximately 10,000 B.C.E.
Approximately 6,500 generations after Ash and Elm

Those members of our family that had moved up the coast of China entered into Siberia, continued north, and eventually went east into North America. These folk also headed south to escape the sheets of ice that covered North America. But the ice had started to melt as a result of similar climate changes mentioned earlier, thus allowing them to migrate not only south, but also southeast. Current thinking is that this sheet of ice, glaciers, were completely gone by about 8000 BCE. But where did they go?

While it has been speculated that there was one great world flood which is found in the lore of Eurasia as well as North, Central, and South America, I think such ideas rank right up there with the popular Fundamental Christian belief that biblical flood took place only 4,000 years ago and that our world is only 5,000 years old. Perhaps this is wild speculation on my part, but I think the result of great volumes of melting ice just might be great volumes of water. Again, perhaps this is wild speculation on my part, but I think that perhaps the Great Flood recorded in Eurasian lore was experienced by people who lived in Eurasia and that the Great Flood recorded in North, Central, and South America lore was experienced by people who lived in North, Central, and South America. After all, during the time of the first Great Flood (about 48,000 BCE), humanity had not yet entered North America.

North America—The Arapaho creator, Neshanu, is recorded as being responsible for the second Great Flood.

North America—The Pawnee creator Atius Tirawa/Tirawa, is recorded as being responsible for the second Great Flood.

Central America—The Mayan god Hurakan is recorded as having released the flood to punish the first of humanity who had dishonored and angered the gods.

South America—The Brazilian god Anatiwa is recorded in the lore of the Karaya as being responsible for the second Great Flood.

South America—The Columbian goddess Chia is recorded in the lore of the Chibcha as being responsible for the second Great Flood.

South America—The Peruvian God Paricia is recorded as causing the Great Flood.

The Third Entrance into North America: Map Locations 13, 14, and 15

Approximately 1000 C.E.
Approximately 6,950 generations after Ash and Elm

Here is where things get just a bit tricky. It is clear that Northern Europeans migrated to North America as early as 1,000 years ago. Evidence has been found and documented in Newfoundland and at each of the points indicated on the map as leading there, Iceland, and Greenland. So, we know for a fact that our family that separated when leaving Africa found union in North America. In fact, there is clear evidence that they traded with the folk who entered at the West Coast.

Humanity Again Finds Union

Approximately 2000 C.E.

Approximately 7,000 generations after Ash and Elm

I have heard a great many stories that link Stonehenge, the Pyramids, and even the North American Earthworks to unidentified flying objects and extraterrestrial beings. The underlying theme in those stories is that humanity would not have been capable of creating such works. I am not proposing such an easily believed theory on this. Just the opposite, I am proposing the seemingly hard to believe idea that maybe, just maybe humanity was able to create these wonders of the world—that maybe, just maybe, 'Our creator IS evidenced by our creativity.' That, my friends, is what I hold as the single most sacred message behind the Wiccan religion!

> *What a piece of work is a man!*
> *how noble in reason!*
> *how infinite in faculty!*
> *in form and moving how express and admirable!*
> *in action how like an angel!*
> *in apprehension how like a god!*
> *the beauty of the world!*
> *the paragon of animals!*
>
> —*William Shakespeare,* Hamlet *act 2 scene 2*

The measuring system developed in Africa is discovered in North America. It does not really matter if it was carried with the Eastern Migration, the Western Migration, or even if it was developed independently in all the many places it has appeared. The fact is, by either archeological, anthropological, or DNA evidence, the story remains relatively the same. We are one people, separated as we left Africa only to find union in North America. We are one people 'separated for the sake of union,' and that knowledge in and of itself can be our salvation.

We live in a time when humanity is divided by both religion and region. The people of Palestine (predominantly Muslim) and the people of Israel (predominantly Jewish) continue to kill each other. The people of India (predominantly Hindu) and the people of Pakistan (predominantly Muslim) have strutted the newest addition to their armament, nuclear weapons. The people of the United States (predominantly Christian) and the people of Iraq (predominantly Muslim) are at tremendous odds as I write this and may well be engaged in all out war before it is published. Even when religions are so seemingly similar, as with the Irish Catholics and Protestants, it does seem as if we are wildly divided.

I am not saying that any one side in these matters is to blame. The gods know and my service record attests to the fact that I am a patriot. However, I am also a member of the human race. So I pray this message reaches the leaders of both sides in these and all conflicts. That message is that we are all members of the same family, that we are One People. In saying this, I do not mean that this book should be on the desk of my President or in the hands of every world leader. What is important is that this message, which is not at all an original thought, is presented to the world leaders in the way that we and the other religions of the world conduct ourselves.

In closing this chapter, I should mention that I am neither archeologist nor anthropologist. I am just some Joe trying to make sense of my world and sharing what has made sense for me with you. But even if I held a degree in these fields, the dates given will change with time and new discovery.

Chapter Dedication

For the Einherjar Barbara Crandell.

Thank you for the liberty and freedom by which I am allowed to write this book.

Liber ab Quattuor

(Book of Four)

Our Reunion Begins Now

Our Mother Earth and Father Sky are threatened. With that threat, our children are in great peril. Somewhere along the way of our migration, we forgot that we are one people! The Nameless One has been given several names, and Fenris is scratching at the door! Everywhere I look, I see Ragnarok just a stone's throw distant, the doom of the gods, and we are just not ready to ascend to their position. Is it not the sacred duty of an Earth religion to protect our Earth? Is it not the sacred duty of a fertility religion to protect our children? Do you hear the scream of the Valkyries? Do you hear them call to the Four Corners of the world, hoping the Einherjar will reply?

Four is the number of reunion and family. It is Darkness and Light, and it is their children Earth and Sky. It is Tefnut and Shu, and it is their children Nut and Geb. It is

79

Mother and Father, and it is their Daughter and Son. It is the sacred marriage in which one Mother and Father are united with another Mother and Father. It is that which we find sacred and the path by which we find it. At its very core, it is the number of re-union. And with that reunion, we remember and truly become as we were before separation, one people.

We live in a three dimensional world. But until relatively recently, we mostly moved about it in only two dimensions. Prior to the use of airplanes and submarines, one could move forwards, backwards, to the left and to the right, but neither up nor down for any appreciable distance. At a very early time, humanity must have felt the need to offer directions to others to assist them. Maybe someone found a really good apple tree, took a few apples, and brought them home for his wife and him to enjoy.

A second man saw the first and his wife enjoying those mighty fine apples and wanted one for himself. The first man knew there were plenty of apples back at the apple tree, so he didn't see any reason to fight over those apples, and he gave the second man an apple. A third and fourth man saw the second man eating one of those mighty fine apples and asked him where he got it; he told them he received the apple from the first man. So the third and fourth man went to the first man and told him they each wanted an apple.

Something had to be done. He couldn't just point to the apple tree because there were obstacles in the way. So he told the second and third man to go to the first obstacle, turn to the left, walk to a landmark, turn to the right, walk forward and there is the apple tree. The men went off to fetch some apples but did not return for a long time. When they finally returned, they were mighty put off. They had found the apple tree just fine, but then he turned around and tried to follow the directions in reverse to return home. They went back to that final landmark and again turned right, leading them in the wrong direction. It became obvious that to describe directions, they needed a fixed reference. Fortunately, they had exactly what they needed already provided.

Morning after morning, one could face the East and witness sunrise. Evening after evening, one could face West and witness the sunset. Because the sun always rose and set in the same place, those first four principle directions could be situated to either the sunrise or sunset. Using the constant direction of either, one could easily refer to the four key directions with a reference that all could relate to a single point. Because most journeys would be taken during the day, the logical choice to reference was sunrise. Our simple concept of forward, backward, left, and right become universal references in direction.

Facing sunrise, those directions are:

Description	Direction
Before me	East
To my right	South
Behind me	West
To my left	North

The Four Quarters

With a standard set of directions in place, it became easy to describe not only places to which one could travel, but also places from which one came. It became easy to state that the winds that come from the West bring storms and bad weather or that from the East come raiders from rival tribes. So we see the development of guardians for each of those directions. Certainly in early cultures these guardians may have been the position of sentries who watched over the tribe as it slept. But as religion developed, it did so right along side the very real world need for protection. We see the development of this principle in the four sons of Horus.

Egyptian Creation Story—Africa

Name	Gender	Direction	Element
Tefnut	Female	West	Water
Shu	Male	East	Air
Geb	Male	North	Earth
Nut	Female	South	Fire

Four sons of Horus—Africa

Four sons of Horus the Younger were born by Isis. Each was seen as guardian of one of the four principle directions and associated with an Element, a human organ, and a protective goddess. During the process of mummification, the associated organs were removed and placed in canopic jars that were carved, etched, or shaped like the god they represent.

Direction	Element	Organ	God	Goddess
East	Fire	Stomach	Duamutef	Neith
South	Water	Liver	Imset	Isis
West	Air	Intestines	Kebechsenef	Selkhet
North	Earth	Lungs	Hapi	Nephthys

But this principle did not stop with humanity's migration from Africa. While the names may change with time and migration, the principles remain the same. Migrating east along the coastal areas of the Indian Ocean, we see this principle appear in the Near East.

The Lokapalas—Near East

The Lokapalas are Hindu directional guardians. They first began with four key directions with four associated deities, but soon grew into eight.

Lokapalas Four—Near East

Direction	God
East	Indra
South	Yama
West	Varuna
North	Kubera

Lokapalas Eight—Near East

Direction	God
East	Indra
South East	Agni
South	Yama
South West	Surya
West	Varuna
North West	Vayu
North	Kubera
North East	Soma

Moving east along the Indian Ocean and inland into Central Asia, we see the Ssu Ling and the Mo Li.

Ssu Ling (Also known as Ling)—Male/Female—Central Asia
The four creature guardians of Chinese mythology similar to the Wiccan Four Quarters. They are Ch'i-lin, Feng-huang, Gui Xian, and Long.

Direction	Name	Animal	Gender
East	Long	Dragon	Male
South	Feng-huang	Phoenix	Male
West	Ch'i-lin	Unicorn	Female
North	Gui Xian	Turtle	Female

The Mo Li—Central Asia
Buddhist Four Quarters.

Direction	God
East	Chung
South	Hung
West	Hai
North	Shou

Tian-wang (Also known as T'ien-wang)—Male—Far East/Central Asia
Four Kings who guarded the Four Quarters in both Chinese and Japanese lore. Their images are still found in the temples of that area. Each is shown fully armored with a different skin color and holding different items in accordance with the direction they preside over.

King (no name given)	Color
King of the East	White
King of the South	Blue
King of the West	Red
King of the North	Green

Still migrating east along the Indian Ocean, we find ourselves in the Far East, on the island of Japan and the surrounding area where we see the development of the Shi Tenno.

Shi Tenno—Far East

Direction	God
East	Jikoku
South	Komoku
West	Zocho
North	Bishamon

Thus we see the principle of the four directions and the four guardians of those directions as far east as Japan waiting to make the cross to North America with the final leg of the eastern migration. But back in the Middle East, the great flood had opened up northern migration. Back in the Middle East, we see the northern migration bring the Hebrew principles of the four directions and their evolution into the practices of Christian ceremonial magicians.

Direction	Arch Angel	Element
East	Raphael	Air
South	Michael	Fire
West	Gabriel	Water
North	Auriel/Uriel	Earth

Into Europe along the Mediterranean, we see the development of the Greek and Roman pantheons. With those pantheons, we see again the principles of the four cardinal directions and their guardians. These guardians were known as the four Winds in both the Greek and Roman pantheon.

Greek and Roman Gods of the Four Winds—Mediterranean

Direction	Greek God	Roman God
East	Eurus	Vulturnus
South	Notus	Auster
West	Zephyrus	Favonius
North	Boreas	Aquilo

Although the Greeks did use a system in which the four cardinal directions were of key interest, they also included the cross Quarters of those cardinal directions as follows.

Direction	Greek God
East	Eurus
South East	Apeliotus
South	Notus
South West	Lips/Livos
West	Zephyrus
North West	Kaikias
North	Boreua
North East	Skeiron

With the passage way open to Northern Europe, we see the Norse and other European principles of the four directions develop.

Norse Four Directions—North Europe

Direction	Realm/World	Element
East	Jotunheimr	Air
South	Muspellsheimr	Fire
West	Vanaheimr	Water
North	Niflheimr	Ice

Svetovit—Male—Central/North Europe

Slavic god of the four directions. He is depicted as having four separate heads, one facing each direction and each associated with the four Elements: Air, Fire, Earth, and Water.

Now we leap ahead in time to the modern Wiccan movement in North America. Although this is indeed a tremendous leap forward, we see that a standardized view of the four directions and their association with the Elements has occurred. Today, they are generally seen as:

Direction	Element
East	Air
South	Fire
West	Water
North	Earth

Note that while this is how I associate the Four Quarters with the four Elements, this chart does not reflect how *all* Wiccans draw the association. Yes, this set of associations is the most often cited, but there are exceptions, and those exceptions are not wrong by any stretch of the imagination. As Wicca developed, it looked desperately for evidence of surviving tribal tradition, practices that were not entirely stamped out by the destruction of written and oral traditions by the burning of libraries and lives. In that search, the Wiccans of North America looked to the indigenous people of North America. There, too, they found cultures that were virtually destroyed, but cultures and traditions whose last gasps were still audible. One of the many things they discovered was the principle of the four directions and guardians of those directions.

Native American Quarter Associations—North America

It is important to note that the directional associations change with the part of North America and individual tribe being cited. I believe the following list, which seems to be most prevalent in Wicca, is a combination of the similar attributes of the Sioux and Cheyenne with reported influence from Celtic sources. This list varies from tradition to tradition. The most often seen difference is that Raven is substituted for Elk.

Direction	Animal
East	Eagle
South	Elk
West	Bear
North	Wolf

The Four Tools

Who hasn't been moved to tears by a movie or play? Who has not left a theater house with a new perspective on the world in which we live? Theater often provides us with secrets, which stir the mysteries of our soul. Wiccan ritual is no different. While the living of life is what is most important, ritual often stirs that living into action. It reveals secrets that cause the exploration and thus understanding of the mysteries of the world in which we live. Although our rituals are themselves theater, they are more because they represent that which we call sacred. Thus, we use the term sacred theater.

As with any theater, props are often used. Those props are more often called the Wiccan tools. Of these, there are many. One might say that each variety of incense is itself a tool. However, there are four tools that are considered primary or most important. This is because these are the four that have direct association with the four Quarters, the gender of those Quarters, and the principle of those Quarters and their partners.

Direction	Element	Tool	Gender	Partner
East	Air	Censer	Masculine	Pentacle
South	Fire	Athame	Masculine	Chalice
West	Water	Chalice	Feminine	Athame
North	Earth	Pentacle	Feminine	Censor

While these tools are not at all necessary to be Wiccan, neither is the performance of ritual. Being Wiccan is a matter of heart and the way one conducts themselves in life more than a matter of formality and the way one conducts ones self in ritual. So then look on these tools as just that, things used in ritual, sacred theater, to represent what should be taking place in the hearts of each and every one who would call themselves Wiccan.

The First Union—Censer and Pentacle

The Censer—The Censer is the incense burner which represents Air. It is a masculine tool associated with the Element Air and the prayers sent to our Father Sky.

Prior to its first use of the censor and whenever cleansing and charging (rededication) is felt necessary, the following recipes are used. These recipes are also useful in the working of spells that draw on Air energy and it is the preferred incense for burning in the censor during its use.

Air Incense
2 parts Lavender flowers
1 part Benzoin
Enough Air or Lavender oil to bind

Air Oil
9 drops Benzoin
9 drops Lavender
3 drops Pine
1/2 ounce Almond or Palm oil

The Pentacle—The pentacle is a disk that represents Earth. It is a feminine tool associated with the Element Earth and the prayers sent to our Mother Earth. Sometimes a pentagram is carved on the pentacle to indicate the whole of that which is humanity.

Humanity on Earth

Prior to the first use of the pentacle and when ever cleansing and charging (rededication) is felt necessary, the following recipes are used. These recipes are also useful in the working of spells which draw on Earth energy and it is sometimes burned at the Earth Quarter.

Earth Incense
2 parts Patchouli
1 part Cypress
1 part Gum Arabic (optional)
Enough Earth or Bergamot oil to bind

Earth Oil

12 drops Patchouli

9 drops Bergamot

1/2 ounce base oil

The Union—The union of censer and pentacle is like the Druid tree that we discussed in the first half of Book of Three. It is the symbol of Mother Earth (pentacle/roots) who is below, Father Sky (the rising smoke/branches) who is above, and we their children (the union of pentacle and censer) at center. In this union, the direction is ascending above as the smoke rises to the heavens. It is seen as Mother Earth reaching for Father Sky and Father Sky accepting her embrace

The Second Union—Athame and Chalice

The Athame—The athame is a knife that represents the lightning of our Lord. It is in essence the symbol of his phallus. Different traditions of Wicca have unique specifications for the athame. Most agree that the handle should be dark and that the blade be double edged. The reason for the dark handle is because darker colors absorb light more readily. It is thus believed that with a dark handle the athame will conduct magickal energy better. While this might indeed help one visualize the conducting of energy, I should point out that the logic behind this concept is rather flawed. Sure, dark colors absorb one form of energy more readily, but those same folk often insist that the hilt of the athame be wood, which is not one of the better conductors of a different type of energy, that energy being electricity. If indeed we are speaking about conducting thought, it is necessary to point out that the best description of that magickal energy is bioelectric. So I do not feel a dark handle is absolutely necessary, especially not when that inner voice has selected a tool with a light handle.

Generally speaking, the athame has a double blade, that blade being symbolic of our Lord and Lady. They are themselves separate, but merging as we move forward towards the tip. The hilt should fit comfortably into the palm and be no more than half the total length of the athame. The blade should be no less than half the total length. For practicality, the overall length should never exceed elbow to the tip of ones middle finger. Anything longer should be considered a sword and used appropriately.

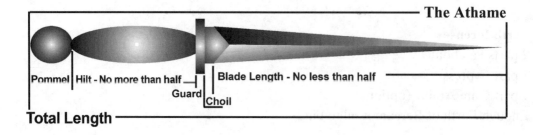

The Athame

Prior to the first use of the athame and whenever cleansing and charging (rededication) is felt necessary, the following recipes are used. These recipes are also useful in the working of spells that draw on Fire energy and are sometimes burned at that Quarter.

Fire Incense

2 parts Cinnamon

1 part Dragon's Blood

1 part Frankincense

Enough Fire or Allspice oil to bind

Fire Oil

6 drops Allspice

3 drops Bay

3 drops Ginger

1/2 ounce base oil

The Chalice—The chalice is a drinking vessel that represents the oceans of our Lady. It is in essence her womb. Although very few traditions have specific requirements for this drinking vessel, it is generally made from earth, glass, or metal, earth being my particular preference. Many folk give little thought to the selection of the chalice. Certainly it is not nearly as flashy as the athame, but keeping with the idea that it is the relationship that counts, I think it is a good idea to select chalice and athame such that they compliment each other. The depth of the chalice should then be no shallower than the blade of the athame is long.

Prior to the first use of the chalice and when ever cleansing and charging (rededication) is felt necessary, the following recipes are used. These recipes are also useful in the working of spells which draw on Water energy and are sometimes burned at the Water Quarter.

Water Incense

2 parts Jasmine Flowers

1 part Lemon Peel

1 part Camphor (natural)

Enough Water or Lemon oil to bind.

Water Oil

6 drops Camphor

3 drops Lemon

3 drops Eucalyptus

3 drops Cardamom

1/2 ounce base oil

The Union—The union of chalice and athame is a clear and obvious symbol of creation. It is the second union, often called the symbolic Great Rite. However, it is not simply a symbol of the sexual union by which humanity creates. It is also the marking of the initial creation of life on this planet. Science now believes that life began when the primordial ocean (chalice) was repeatedly struck with lightning (athame). In this union, the direction is descending below as the athame lowers into the chalice. Father Sky has already accepted Mother Earth's embrace with the union of censor and pentacle; here we see that embrace consummated.

The Fifth Element

So what should be going on in the hearts of each and every Wiccan? The answer to that is the influence of the Fifth Element, that force which causes both division and union, the mania by which we create. As our division has all so clearly taken place (see Book of Exodus) it seems rather clear that the time of union has come. While there does clearly remain times in which the Fifth Element will move us towards separation, when viewing Wicca as a religion dedicated to the preservation of the Earth and the betterment of that Earth for our children, we have now come to that point where the Fifth Element must be used to unite rather than separate.

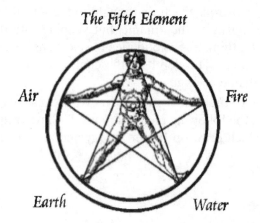

The Fifth Element

Air — Fire — Earth — Water

So important is the Fifth Element, sometimes called Spirit, that it has been incorporated into one of the predominant symbols of the Wiccan religion. It is the top point of the pentagram. This gives one the sense that creation is a matter of intellect. Indeed it is, but if we look at the format of Wiccan ritual and the use of the tools we see a different message coming through.

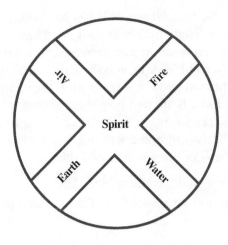

Spirit at Center

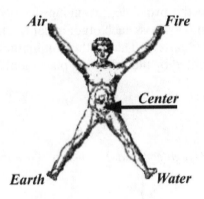

Ki and the Four Quarters

The diagram "Ki and the Four Quarters" places the four Elements in accordance with how the pentagram is most commonly depicted. Understanding the meaning behind this placement is a bit more difficult than can be drawn. Should you wear a pentagram around your neck, do the Elements apply to someone looking at you or you looking at the person? In respect to the Fifth Element, it is always the top point in the pentagram. However, when we address the principle of Spirit being center, we see a reason for the placement of the other Elements. Air and Fire are placed with the upper portion of the torso because the upper world (Sky) is considered masculine. Earth and Water are placed with the lower portion of the torso because the lower world (Earth) is considered feminine (see P'an Ku). What is important in the placement is not actually which Element goes where, but the relationship between the masculine Elements and the feminine Elements.

If you are involved in the martial arts or if you have taken even the most introductory course, right about now a light bulb over your head has just been switched on. Yes, this is the same principle discussed in just about every form of martial arts that has come out of the Near East, Central Asia, and the Far East. It is the source of all cosmic energy in relation to the human body. It is the center, the balance point, the part of the human body from which force is applied (separation) or drawn (union), the center of the Wiccan ritual, and the center of our body. It is not surprising that this point is also related to the center of our world, the Earth itself —not the center of the world, but the center of 'our world' and of our Earth-based religion.

Ki—Female—Middle East/Mediterranean/Near East
Sumerian personification and goddess of the Earth. Her Mesopotamian (Akkadian) counterpart is Aruru.

Aruru—Female—Middle East/Mediterranean
Mesopotamian personification of the Earth. Also known as Assyrian. Mesopotamian counterpart to the Sumerian Ki.

While it might seem at first glance that the position of Air and Fire should be reversed to better represent the principle, arranging the Elemental mates (Air/Earth) and (Fire/Water) such that they cross each other at center, this negates the principle of three as seen in the four Quarters. That is the commentary of union in the form of marriage, which is represented by the following placement.

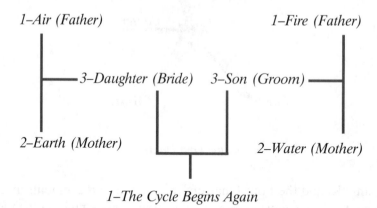

1–Air (Father)   *1–Fire (Father)*

3–Daughter (Bride) *3–Son (Groom)*

2–Earth (Mother)   *2–Water (Mother)*

1–The Cycle Begins Again

Marriage and the Four Quarters

To preserve this message in the four Quarters, Fire is placed above Water as opposed to being placed across from Water. Likewise, Air is placed above Earth, not across from it. Ah, but which combinations go where? I put Fire on the right because Fire represents sudden change, the type of thing one might expect from the right half of the brain. I put Air on the left because it seems more associated with intuition and the left half of the brain. However, I do not think this is set in stone. I have met several

folk who reverse the association based on the predominance of their hands. Sho
they be right handed, Fire is on the right. Should they be left handed, Fire is on the left.
I believe this is because the dominant hand is considered the one most likely to cause
sudden change (like the Element Fire).

When we acknowledge that the force that brings those Elements and tools together
in Wiccan ritual, we see that the four Elements, brought together by humanity, are
indeed the very Druid tree we spoke about in Book of Three Part I. Our arms (branches)
reach for the Sky (Air and Fire). Our legs (roots) are firmly planted in Mother Earth
(Earth and Water). Our body (trunk) is the Fifth Element (Spirit) that unites the two
worlds. We are that Spirit and thus, the four Quarter's union. For it is the power of
three that drives the principle of the four Elements to cause all life.

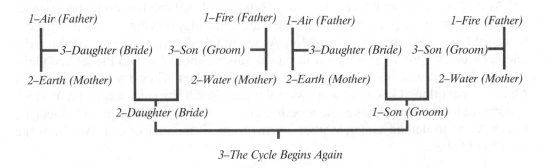

Generations and the Four Quarters

The Four Quarters as Union

I was first introduced to the principle of four long before my eyes were opened to
it. I had seen the four Quarters called time and time before, but the tremendous significance had escaped my young mind. As an adult, I had written a handfasting ritual
for two friends who were getting married. In that ritual, I suggested that the parents of
both groom and bride stood at the four Quarters of Wiccan ritual. That ritual appears
in *Wicca for Couples*. However, it was not until I saw that ritual performed that the
significance really sunk in.

Role in Handfasting	Apparent Ethnicity
Father of Bride	Central Asia
Father of Groom	North Europe
Mother of Bride	African American
Mother of Groom	French Canadian

four people of wildly different ethnicity who had come together
woman as husband and wife. The rule of three created the groom in
other and father. The rule of three had also created the bride in the
ther and father. But it was the love of groom for bride and bride for
ught these parents together. That love is the Fifth Element.

er, I learned about mitochondrial DNA, and my long-standing magickal
belief ᴄ we all started out as one people was confirmed by science. That confirmation caused me to think about those friends whose lineage is so wildly mixed and their
wedding. It struck me like a brick. This is the knowledge that would save our world. I
thought it was so profound, that I brought it up to my mentor. She was thrilled with my
'discovery' but also used the opportunity of our discussion to ask me to babysit the
following Saturday morning while her kids watched cartoons.

After arriving at her house, I was surprised to find that she had no plans. Instead,
she handed me some popcorn and had me watch Saturday morning cartoons with her
6-year-old son and 4-year-old daughter. As we watched cartoons, we talked further
and her kids each interrupted to say that I was talking about Captain Planet and Gaia.
I knew who Gaia was, but had to ask about Captain Planet. They described the Green
Man. The next thing I knew, we were watching a nationally broadcast cartoon in which
children of four distinct races come together in a single love to call Captain Planet (the
Green Man) to defend Gaia (Mother Earth) from all manner of evil. Ah, from the
mouths of babes...

> *I am a circle*
> *Within a circle*
> *With no beginning*
> *And never ending*
> *We are a circle*
> *Within a circle*
> *With no beginning*
> *And never ending*

—Popular chant, original author unknown

How Did Wicca Decide Which Quarter Is Which?

Warning: Rethinking Ahead!

If you are happy with the four Quarters presented most often in texts on the Wiccan
religion, you might want to move on to the next chapter. Indeed, most folk like them
just as they are. However, if you have thought about changing the associations used in
ritual, please consider the following as a reason why everyone is welcome to do so.
Keep in mind, if you are going to be leading public rituals, changing the Element associations with the Quarters will likely lead to confusion, and of course a few folk will tell

you that you are wrong. So be prepared for criticism if you vary from the accepted norm. But here is some fuel for your rebuttal.

You might have noticed that when I spoke about the blending of Native American spirituality with Wicca to form the four Quarters, I did not say the European influence was Celtic in nature but that it is reportedly Celtic in nature. You also may have noted that the system of assigning Elements to the Quarters most often used in Wicca corresponds best to the system that is perpetuated by Hebrew-based ceremonial magicians. Here we see something truly interesting about Wicca. While I firmly believe the modern movement began in the late eighteen hundreds along with many other Neo-Pagan movements, the idea that Wicca is an ancient Celtic religion seems to have come about with the introduction of the Gardnerian tradition and those who created similar 'traditions.'

In my opinion, Gardner was divinely guided to make a boob of himself as were the folk who later claimed to be following traditional Celtic Wicca. You see, like the eight Sabbats that we will discuss later, there is virtually no reference outside of Neo-Pagan books to a Celtic set of four Quarters with the modern Wiccan Elemental associations. You see, not only did the Celts not keep clear records of their traditions, those traditions were as diverse as the Celts themselves. Saying any one thing is Celtic is difficult because even if one does discover a set tradition in one of the Celtic tribes, the next Celtic tribe over probably did it completely differently.

Now, one might argue that as a result of the invading Norse, a quasi-Celtic tradition may have been formed in which the four Quarters and eight Sabbats were included, but stating that quasi-Celtic tradition was practiced by all Celts is just downright silly. Here we again see clear proof that Wicca is not a Celtic religion. Gardner simply borrowed the associations from the Ceremonial magicians when he and his friends invented his 'tradition.' From there, the so-called traditional Celtic Wiccans either lied or gullibly accepted and spread misinformation about the origin of their four Quarter mythos.

But in all that borrowing, misinformation, and lies, I believe there was divine intervention. When Gardner took the principle of the four Quarters specifically from Hebrew traditions of ceremonial magick, I doubt he or those who would later insist the principles were Celtic could have known just how universally important those principles were. In all the talk of how much research Gardner conducted, very little of it shows in any of his writings. If he or anyone else knew that these principles are found in as many Pagan cultures as are available to the seeker, they certainly did a good job of hiding that knowledge. So why did Gardner take the four Quarters from ceremonial magick and incorporate them into this modern religion? Why did so many people just blindly accept the idea that the tradition originated with the Celts? Because our Lord and Lady needed this concept to be present in our religion such that years later it would be explored and discovered to be an almost universal concept.

You see, the *what* of the matter is not nearly as important as the *why* of the matter. It is nice to be able to point at a specific historic cite (the what), but it is why those ancients conducted themselves in that manner and why our modern Pagan religion continues to do so. In modern Wicca, the four Quarters are drawn in as an act of union;

it is the gathering of our many tribes at center that they might find strength in both number and diversity for the many tasks ahead. I hate to cite a cartoon, but it is the calling of Captain Planet to defend Mother Earth and it is the affirmation that we accepted the role given to us by our Lord and Lady as guardians of this world.

In the glory of our Lord and Lady, so mote it be!

Chapter Dedication

This chapter is dedicated to the Einherjar, the men and women who live and died bravely, defending that which is good against the onslaught of that which is evil (the Outsiders). May your stay in Valhalla be long as we in Midgard stave off Ragnarok as long as we are able by uniting that which should be united, dividing that which should be divided, and by the wisdom to know the difference.

Liber ab Tres II
(Book of Three, Part II)
Confessions of an Idol Worshiper

Here do I invoke to aid my goal
My father above and Mother below
Here do I invoke to bless this rite
Our Lord and Lady upon this night

Here do I invoke that I may be whole
Their love into
My mind, body, and soul

Because three is the number of humanity, it is the number by which we see our Lord and Lady. Again, our Creator is evidenced by our creativity. This does not mean that we dictate the form of the Creator. One religion views the Creator one way, the next religion views that a different way. Wicca's very structure dictates that the Creator be viewed as Lord and Lady. Now, I realize a great deal of people do not like the idea that some central body dictates anything to the members of Wicca, but that is not the nature of the use of the word 'dictate' in this sense. Instead, it is the dictation that fire is hot. If you were touching something that feels cold, to describe it as 'hot' would defeat the purpose of language and communication. As I mentioned in Book of Genesis, this is not something that I am forcing on all Wiccans everywhere. It is simply part of what the word *Wicca* has come to mean.

By assigning name and form to our Lord and Lady, we allow ourselves to interact with them on a more intimate level. I am sure you can see how it is much easier to develop a close personal relationship with someone you can see, feel, and touch. This is why religions that are dominated by a central authority tend to forbid the use of idols. How much authority would the central authority have if they did not work as the middle-man between you and the Creator—in Wicca, that Creator being our Lord and Lady?

You can easily observe this in the bickering between Christian denominations. The Baptists tend to bash the Catholics because the Catholics tend to use a crucifix on their altars. Because there is a depiction of Jesus on the cross (an idol), the Baptists tend to think the Catholics worship idols. I can't begin to describe the look on my Catholic mother's face the first time someone explained that Catholics are all Pagan idol worshipers. There is one flavor of fundamental Christian who bashes the Baptists for allowing pictures of Jesus on their Christmas cards, another flavor of fundamental Christian bashes still other fundamental Christians because that flavor allows their teenagers to wear t-shirts with pictures of Jesus. They and many more do not want you to develop a close personal relationship with your view of the Creator, so the tools by which one can do so are forbidden. Around and around it goes. Where does it stop? Right here.

Catholics do not worship idols; they worship that which the idol represents. Baptists do not worship Christmas cards; they worship what those greeting cards represent. Fundamental Christian teenagers do not worship t-shirts, they worship... wait a minute, according to many parents, some teenagers do just about worship clothing. Those parents tell me it is one of the most expensive religions available to our youth. But guess what? Some Wiccans do worship idols.

In many respects, Wicca is not unlike other religions. Just like other religions of the world, it is possible to look at Wicca and see only that which is plainly visible while being blind to the significance, the hidden meaning behind that which is seen. With that knowledge, one might then repeat the observed actions and call oneself Wiccan. By that standard, one might then run down to their local Wiccan bookstore and purchase the largest, coolest statue of our Lord and Lady. Far be it for me, the owner of one of those local stores, to deter you in that purchase. But please do not think that such a purchase will make you the largest, coolest Wiccan.

The statues and even the images themselves are tools by which we further our understanding. Yes, they are idols but who does not see the gods through idols? An idol is not just a statue or even a picture on your coffee table. It is a concept, a mental image. An idol is a construct for understanding. Should one claim not to incorporate idols into their religion, ask them to describe the Creator. If they answer the question, then they have a mental image of that Creator. They are in fact using an idol in their worship and understanding.

In my view of Wicca, our religion witnesses our Lord and Lady in each and every thing, inanimate or animate, living, dead, or never having lived. While one can have a relationship with a rock or other inanimate object, it is much easier to establish relationships with living things. Again, one can have a relationship with a plant, but that plant does not respond to the relationship nearly as clearly as does an animal. I have yet to meet the fern that can purr. Finally, one can have a relationship with an animal, but that animal does not respond nearly as understandably as a human being. So then, we could choose to view our Lord and Lady as rocks. After all, rocks are indeed part of that which the Lord and Lady are — the sum total of all that is, was, and will be. There is in fact historical precedence for such a view. Mesenet is the name given to the Egyptian personification of a birthing stone. When a woman gave birth, it was believed this boulder provided the 'ka' or life force to the new child.

But how close of a relationship can one have with a rock? For that matter, how close would a relationship be with a plant? Yes, plants can be shown to respond to human touch and even to emotion and sound. But bring one home to mother and she is going to think you are the black sheep of the family. Speaking about sheep, this brings us to animals. There is definitely a significant amount of deity forms in Pagan lore that appear strictly as animals. There is a larger number whose image is a combination of animal and human form, and there are an even larger number of deities that switch or shape-shift between human and animal form. Indeed, many of these deity forms have been incorporated into Wiccan ritual. With respect to strictly animal forms, this is most notable at the four Quarters when folk incorporate Native American lore.

However, and speaking very generally, most deities that assume only animal form are cited as not having much to do with the creation of humanity. As such, while they are a clear part of our Lord and Lady, they do not make for good 'idols.' Yes, Norse creation lore involves a giant cosmic cow but it took Odin, a god of human form, to carve the image of man from the ash tree and the image of woman from the elm.

Do we create the gods? No. We are part of the gods, but we create only their image. Although some might take issue with this view, is it not the human mind that perceives information from the eye that creates the specific image of a tree for any individual? If a colorblind person were to look at that same tree, would not his or her image of the tree be different from that belonging to a color seeing individual's image of the same tree? Sure, we could say there is one true image of that tree and the colorblind person is incorrect, but in respect to viewing our Lord and Lady, that very act is the act of giving name to the Nameless One. It is to say my view is correct and your view is not.

Three Is the Number of Mother Earth

Three is the number of our Earth Mother because she is seen through the eyes of Humanity. Where we have youth, maturity, and senior, so does our beloved mother. Thus, we call our Lady with words that are our own, but always remember that three is her number. She is Maiden, Mother, and Crone, and so much more...

Canaanite Triple Goddess—Female—Middle East/Mediterranean

Name	Description
Arsai	Earth Maiden
Pidrai	Light Maiden
Tallai	Rain Maiden

The Three Mothers—Female—Middle East/Mediterranean

The Hebrew/Cabalistic trinity of the Three Mothers with Elemental association and a correspondence to the Hebrew alphabet.

Name	Element
Aleph	Air
Mem	Water
Shin	Fire

She has been called on many ways by the many different cultures of humanity, but none in the Wiccan religion more often than in what has become an almost universally accepted document called the Charge of the Goddess. Know that Gerald Gardner and Raymond Buckland referred to this Charge over and over simply as either The Charge or A Charge. Indeed, during the time of its creation there seems to be little reference to its current most commonly accepted title, so I prefer the title that accompanied it as I originally received it, A Charge of Our Mother. Please note that in using this title, I am not renaming either piece of work. I am simply addressing the many different variants as Charges of Our Mother, each individual Charge being called A Charge of Our Mother.

Our Lady is called, invited, or invoked in many ways—so many different ways that even though you will find half the books on Wicca state that the Charge of Our Mother (more often called the Charge or the Charge of the Goddess) has become beloved by Wiccans everywhere, you will find just as many different versions for that Charge. The following version is what I copied into my Book of Shadows when I was a teen. I have seen it attributed at least 20 different ways to Doreen Valiente, but few can be exactly sure who wrote it. Not only did Doreen Valiente not write the Charge of the Goddess, I do not believe she ever published it. Instead, she was rather clear that Aleister Crowley wrote the original Gardnerian Charge of the Goddess, and that she had only *rewritten* it with great inclusions from *Aradia: Gospel of Witches*. She did, however, state that it appears in works by the Farrars with very little difference from her version. It is also important to note that there are not only many wildly different variations attributed to Doreen Valiente, but there are also versions almost word for word that are not attributed to Doreen Valiente. The following version is not the same as the Charge of the Goddess cited in the Farrars' work. Therefore, I do not believe it is the work of Doreen Valiente, although perhaps similar.

What is reportedly the traditional way to call upon our Lady is not only different from book to book, but also different from version to version attributed to Doreen Valiente. So the "traditional" method of calling on our Lady can be one of many different versions incorrectly attributed to Doreen Valiente from an unknown piece of text written by Aleister Crowley, with inclusions from *Aradia: Gospel of Witches*, which Charles Leland claimed to have received from someone called Maddelena—who received it from an as yet unknown source. Ah, traditional Celtic Wicca at its finest.

I would have liked very much to have included Doreen Valiente's Charge of the Goddess to illustrate the differences between it and the many versions attributed to her, but I just could not bring myself to submit to the dictates of the current copyright owner. To do so would have been akin to a Catholic author having his work and audience approved by the Pope and then paying a fee to include the Lord's Prayer.

What matters is what you find in your own heart. While the Charge of the Goddess, in its many incarnations and with its many sources and several modifications, is beautiful each and every time, it is not yours. Sure, you can write to the current copyright holder and inquire about including it in your work, you can have that work and your audience approved and then pay X amount to use it, but you did not write it. So although it might indeed speak to your heart, it cannot speak from your heart.

A Charge of Our Mother
(Traditional)

—*Author Unknown*

Listen to the words of the Great Mother, who of old was called Artemis, Astarte, Dione, Aphrodite, Cerridwen, Diana, Arienrhod, Brigid, and by many other names: *

Whenever you have need of anything, once in the month, and better it be when the moon is full, you shall assemble in some secret place and adore the spirit of Me who is Queen of all Witches.

There shall you assemble, who have not yet won my deepest secrets and are fain to learn all sorceries.

To these shall I teach that which is yet unknown.

You shall be free from slavery, and as a sign that you be free you shall be naked in your rites.

Sing, feast, dance, make music and love, all in My presence, for Mine is the ecstasy of the spirit and Mine also is joy on earth.

For My law is love unto all beings.

Mine is the secret that opens upon the door of youth, and Mine is the cup of wine of life that is the Cauldron of Cerridwen that is the holy grail of immortality.

I am the Gracious Goddess who gives the gift of youth unto the heart of mankind.

I give the knowledge of the spirit eternal and beyond death I give peace and freedom and reunion with those that have gone before.

Nor do I demand aught of sacrifice, for behold, I am the mother of all things and My love is poured upon the earth.

Hear the words of the Star Goddess, the dust of whose feet are the hosts of heaven, whose body encircles the universe:

I who am the beauty of the green earth and the white moon among the stars and the mysteries of the waters.

I call upon your soul to arise and come unto Me.

For I am the soul of nature that gives life to the universe.

From Me all things proceed and unto Me they must return.

Let My worship be in the heart that rejoices, for behold—all acts of love and pleasure are My rituals.

Let there be beauty and strength, power and compassion, honor and humility, mirth and reverence within you.

And you who seek to know Me, know that your seeking and yearning will avail you not, unless you know the Mystery: for if that which you seek, you find not within yourself, you will never find it without.

For behold, I have been with you from the beginning, and I am that which is attained at the end of desire.

Three Is the Number of Father Sky

Three is the number of our Sky Father because he is seen through the eyes of humanity. Where we have youth, maturity, and senior, so does our beloved Father. It is the number of that which protects and provides, forever watching over his beloved wife and us, his beloved children. Three is Master, Father, and Sage. Three is the Hindu trinity of Brahma, Vishnu, and Shiva, as well as so much more...

The Syrian Triad—Male—Middle East

A pre-Islam triad as Sky God.

Name	Role	Name Means
Bel	Sky God	The Lord
Yarhibol	Sun God	Message/Messenger of the Lord
Aglibol	Moon God	Calm of the Lord

San-Ch'ing—Male—Central Asia

San-Ch'ing is the name of both the collective of the three Taoist Heavens and the gods that preside over each.

Heaven Level	Heaven Name	Lord of the Heaven
Lowest Heaven	Tai-qing	Tao-de tian-zong
Middle Heaven	Shang-qing	Ling-bao tian-zong
Highest Heaven	Yu-qing	Yuan-shi tian-zong

He has been called on many ways by the many different cultures of humanity, and although there is no generally accepted way of calling on him in the Wiccan religion, there is rumored to be a central document entitled the Charge of the God. While the Charge of the God has appeared in several books and been cited by many folk, the author of that text is almost always given as "unknown," and the words contained in that text are even more wildly different from version to version than are the words found in the many incarnations of the Charge of the Goddess.

A Charge of Our Father

Listen to the words of our Great Father, who of old was called Apollo, Adoni, Cronos, Hephaestus, Gwion, Lucifer, Llew, Bres, and by many other names:

Whenever you have need of anything, once in the month, and better it be when the moon is dark, you shall revel in My spirit and know that with that spirit you are Kings among men.

There shall you assemble, you who have not yet won My deepest strength but are who are brave enough to seek it.

To these shall I teach that which is yet unknown.

You shall be free from slavery, and as a sign that you be truly free you will free those still enslaved.

Only then shall you sing, feast, dance, make music and love, in My name.

For My law screams one is not free while others remain enslaved.

Mine is the secret that makes men of boys and mine is the sword in the stone.

I am the Strength of Righteousness who gives the gift of strength unto the heart of men who would be righteous.

I give the knowledge of the spirit eternal and beyond death I give peace and freedom and reunion with those that have gone before.

But know that I do demand sacrifice, for behold, the price of freedom is often high and yours was purchased by the sacrifices of those who came before.

Hear the words of our forgotten father, he who stands against injustice and beckons men to come forth into his service.

I who am the force of the blue sky, the thunder therein found, and the rain without which there would be no waters.

I call upon your soul to rise and come unto Me.

For I am the soul of nature that preserves and protects life in this universe.

From Me all things proceed and unto Me they must return.

Let My worship be in the heart of the just, for behold—all acts of justice are My rituals.

Let there be beauty and strength, power and compassion, honor and humility, mirth and reverence within you.

And you who seek to know Me, know that your seeking and yearning will avail you not, unless you know the Mystery: for if that which you seek, you find not within yourself, you will never find it without.

For behold, I have been with you from the beginning, and I am that which is attained at the end of desire.

Note on Charge of the God: This is an obvious attempt to echo the Charge of the Goddess. Please remember that the words that appear in your own heart are the ones that are important, not the words that appear here.

Using the Charges to Invite Our Lord and Lady

The key to understanding both a Charge of Our Mother and a Charge of Our Father is to know that the first line of each is generally not spoken by the person who speaks the rest of the charge. That is, if a host (priest) and hostess (priestess) are performing an invocation, the host invites the hostess (line one of a Charge of our Mother) to become the earthly representative of our Lady in this rite. The hostess then speaks the remainder of a Charge of Our Mother. The hostess invites the host (line one of a Charge of our Father) to become the earthly representative of our Lord in this rite. The host then speaks the remainder of a Charge of Our Father.

The reason neither Charge is simply read out of a book that someone else wrote is because it would be entirely too silly. Doing so would be like playing house rather than maintaining a household, it is playing Wicca rather than being Wiccan. While the practice might be fine and dandy for a training coven or for practice, in the real world it just does not cut it.

Consider the ritual structure of the first handfasting. When our Lord and Lady are invited into the rite, when the invitation of the Lord and Lady is given, that invitation is a public proposal and declaration, which might look like this: On one knee, host asks hostess to be his fiancée in accordance with his varar (a special form of a promise we will discuss later), then she speaks her acceptance. She then takes his hands and helps him to his feet. She, then on bent knee, does the same. He accepts and helps her to her feet. The festivities (body of the rite) then continue with the future bride and future groom as the earthly representatives of our Lord and Lady for the celebration. The same would be true of the exchanging of the varar at a wedding. Note that I used an example of a monogamous heterosexual couple only for ease of conversation.

And what of a child's Wiccaning? Who better to be host (priest) and hostess (priestess) than the father and mother of the child who is being Wiccaned? Why then would their words, their public declaration of their role in the child's life, come out of a book written by Doreen Valiente, Aleister Crowley, Charles Leland, or myself? Would a rite of adoption (also a Wiccaning) be any different? What about a rite of passage or of death? A celebration of the Holidays? A prayer over the meal? While the so-called traditional Charges might be pretty and fanciful, they are no equal to the words found in one's own heart.

Three Is the Connection Between Above and Below

As the trunk of that tree reaching for both Sky and Earth, we are the connection between our Lord and Lady. Because we see our Lord and Lady through human eyes, it is natural that in seeing these three states in ourselves, we would see the same states in them. This is where Wicca has found its concept of the Triple Goddess and her husband the Triple God to also have a beginning, middle, and end.

Three Daughters of the Dagda (and their husbands)—Female (male)—Central Europe
Irish lore gives us both a Triple Goddess and her husband in the three daughters of the Dagda. Here we see the principle of potential, opportunity, and conclusion shown on a more personal level. Here they are personified as youth, adult, and senior.

Relation	Name	Life State	Condition	Element
Husband	Mac Greine	Master	Changing	Fire
Wife	Eire	Maiden	Changing	Water
Husband	Mac Cecht	Father	Transitional	Earth
Wife	Fodhla	Mother	Transitional	Air
Husband	Mac Cuill	Sage	Unchanging	Ether
Wife	Banbha	Crone	Unchanging	Ether

Allat—Female—Middle East/Mediterranean
She is known in her totality as Allat, Wife of Allah who bore Al-Uzza and Menat (daughters and aspects of the whole). She is also known as one of the three daughters of Allah, probably the result of a patriarchal shift. Although she is not generally connected to the three phases of life in her appearance, her three aspects are connected to the lunar cycle, which is in turn connected to the three stages of life.

Name	Life State	Lunar Cycle	State
Allat	Maiden	New Moon	Changing
Al-Uzza	Mother	Full Moon	Transitional
Menat	Crone	Dark Moon	Unchanging

Haitian Voodoo Triple Goddess—Female—Africa/Caribbean

Name	Life State	Condition	Element
Erzulie Freda Dahomey	Maiden	Changing	Fire
Gran Erzulie	Mother	Transitional	Earth
La Sirene	Crone	Unchanging	Water

The Three Marys—Female—Middle East/Mediterranean

The Christian Trinity of the Three Marys is often overlooked. But before there was Father, Son, and the Holy Ghost there were the Three Marys and their reverence by many of the early Christians.

Goddess	Life State	Condition	Element
Virgin Mary	Maiden	Changing	Fire
Mary Magdalene*	Mother	Transitional	Earth
Mary Cleopas	Crone	Unchanging	Water

Note: Mary Magdalene is sometimes cited as one of the Virgin Mary's sisters. Additionally, that sister is sometimes cited as wife to Jesus.

Wicca and the Worship of Idols

I am an idol worshiper. I think that if everyone were to convert to worshipping idols this very instant, the world would be a much better place. Now before you think that I want everyone to get down on their hands and knees and worship some statue I carved out of wood, let me tell you about the words *idol* and *worship*. The very first definition for the word *idol* in my dictionary (1) includes 'An image used as an object of worship.' The definition found there for worship as a verb is:

1. To honor and love as a deity.
2. To regard with ardent or adoring esteem or devotion.

So then when I say that I am an idol worshiper, I am saying that I honor and love an image of deity. Were we not created in the *image* of our Lord and Lady? Now what would the world be like if all of humanity felt the same way? What would the world be like if we all honored and loved humanity? Now take that just one step further. Although Wiccans view the Creator as Lord and Lady, that which we worship is Life itself. So then, what would the world be like if we all honored and loved all living things? What would the world be like if we treated plants, animals, and humanity as sacred images of the divine?

> *For thou art the gods that were.*
> *Thou art the gods that will be.*
> *Thou art the gods that are.*
>
> *For thou art the gods of my father and mother.*
> *Thou art the gods of my sons and my daughters.*
> *Thou art the gods of my love and my self.*
>
> *For thou art my father and mother.*
> *Thou art my sons and my daughters.*
> *Thou art my love and I.*

Liber ab Planta

(Book of Plants—Condensed[1])

The First Order of Life

Study Material for the First Degree

"In Jamaica, if you want to purchase a candle wrapped with a piece of paper on which a prayer to lift sickness is written, you go to the 'drug store.' If instead you want to purchase the prescription that was given to you by one with a degree [in medicine] you go to a 'pharmacy.' Who be these doctors that would dare not prescribe prayer? Who be these priests that would dare not prescribe medicine? Being a civilized woman, I'll not call for their heads but instead for their shame, for a graduate of either school is ignorant having not at least respect for the other school."

—Tatia Kingslady, January 1982 [2]

y first book began with "Double, double toil and trouble" to paint the picture of three old hags stirring a cauldron as the classic Witch characters in Shakespeare's *Macbeth*. My second book cited the ingredients in that cauldron:

"Eye of newt and toe of frog,
Wool of bat and tongue of dog,
Adder's fork and blind worm's sting,
Lizard's leg and howlet's wing."

—*William Shakespeare,* Macbeth *act 4 scene 1*

Of course I wasn't the first to address the connection between Witchcraft and these seemingly disgusting ingredients. If you have read any recent examinations of Witchcraft, chances are you already know that the ingredients listed above are merely folk names for plants. Yes, there are exceptions to this. There are a few rather disgusting ingredients in a few of the classic recipes that are not innocent reference to herbs, but there are also a great many disgusting ingredients in modern day French cooking. Let's just face it, without our cultural bias, a blind worm's sting is no more or less disgusting than a plate full of snails.

In our rebirthing of the elder Pagan religions, we have included those elder religion's involvement with plants so much that today it is hard to find a book on Wicca that does not have a recipe or two for incense, oils, or other brew. One can look at this in two ways; they can look at the 'what' or the 'why' of the matter. Look at the 'what' and you will probably see recipes for magick potions to do just about everything from making money to winning back a departed love. I have even seen recipes for raising the dead. Now, one can look at all of this and say Wiccans are some truly zany people, or one can examine the 'why' of the matter.

The why of the relationship between Wiccans and plants is humanity's symbiotic relationship with the first order of life. This is reflected, in part, in the use of the phrase *first order of life* to describe plants. Although we weren't there at the moment of creation, it seems reasonable to believe plants came first because the animals that inhabit our world simply cannot live without the oxygen created by plants. Even fish need oxygen, although they acquire it in a different way.

So when you see the myriad of Wiccan books that provide incense recipes based on sandalwood, know also that at least one variety of sandalwood (*Santalum freycinetianum var. lanaiense*) was placed on the endangered species list in January of 1986. Here we see that the secrets of Wicca, the recipes, are built into our religion in the hope that they will guide the Wiccan's initiatory path in the direction where they discover the mystery that plants are sacred. Sure, someone might just build the statement into the Wiccan religion, but what will it mean to you if you just read it rather than discovering it for yourself? Would you better understand water as wet if someone tells you or if you put your foot into a puddle? Would you better understand fire is hot if someone tells you or if you put your foot into a bonfire? The answer is that you will better understand water and fire if you put your foot into them.

As reported by Alex Kirby of the BBC, the World Conservation Union estimates that in 1998, more than 12 percent of our world's plant species faced extinction. The WCU further estimates that if current rates continue, between one third and one half of the current plant life found on the Earth will become extinct by the latter half of this century. Think on that for just a moment and imagine half of the variety of flora gone without any sudden or Earth-wide event. No comet, no nuclear winter—we just wake up and they are gone. One of our duties as Wiccans is to see that folk get that wake up call early enough to prevent that prediction from becoming manifest.

One could take the stance that plants as a whole will survive, and there will be plenty of oxygen and food to go around. But in taking that stance, one demonstrates a complete ignorance for the nature of medicine. You see, although modern pharmaceuticals are often synthetics, virtually every medicine ever developed was observed first in its natural state in plants. So in our search for a cure for such diseases as cancer, that is exactly where we look. Yet every day there is less of a variety of plant life to examine. How many cures have already been lost? How many more will be lost before we discover this mystery? What are we going to do about it?

While you might not come to the same conclusion as I have on this matter, I very much believe we have been created to be dependent on plants for a reason. The reason is that we were created as caretakers and caregivers of this world. In case we forget that fact, our Lord and Lady have built in little reminders. Consider what lore tells us about the Yew.

Yew—Feminine, Saturn, Earth
Common Yew—*Taxus baccata*
Japanese Yew—*Taxus cuspidata*

Primary astrological association: Aquarius, Capricorn
Secondary astrological association: Capricorn, Taurus, Virgo
God association: Odin, Mimir
Goddess association: Athena, Banbha, Bestla, Hecate, Saturn
Celtic tree calendar: Idho, Winter Solstice

It does seem that Yew has been considered sacred for some time. By some accounts, it is from whence Odin received the inspiration for the runes. Other accounts state that Yew provides shamanic visions, extends life, and restores youth. Modern medicine has now shown that the drug paclitaxel may be tremendously effective in treating breast, ovarian, and lung cancer. Now take a look at the Latin names for the Yew and see if you can guess where one might find paclitaxel in nature.

In the words of one of my mentors, if you guessed it comes from a variety of Yew, you are 'smarter than the average bear.' Paclitaxel is extracted from the bark of the Pacific Yew tree. Unfortunately, the Yew is one of the slower growing trees. The current supply of paclitaxel is estimated to be able to treat only about 8,000 people annually because each patient's annual supply of the drug is made from about 60 pounds of the bark. To generate that much bark, one needs between three and six mature trees.

What would have happened if the Yew had become extinct prior to the discovery of paclitaxel? What would happen if it were to become extinct before there is a way to create a synthetic version? How many people would suffer and die simply because no one stopped and thought about the symbiotic relationship between humanity and the many plants which can prevent such suffering and premature death? Perhaps more importantly, how many will suffer and die because the plant that holds the secret to their health has already become extinct? Having witnessed the final hours of my father's life, I can tell you that I wouldn't wish death by cancer on my worst enemy.

Although we cannot state that the ancients knew the Yew would one day be used in the battle against cancer, it does seem as if there was at least a little bit of divine intervention in establishing the plant as sacred. Interestingly enough, plant lore works the other way as well. Not only does it tell us to preserve plants because they are sacred, it sometimes warns against their use because they are sacred.

"But Elder be the Lady's tree, burn it not or cursed you'll be."

From The Wiccan Rede

The Wiccan Rede does not say this because our Lady loves the Elder more than any other plant. It says this because if you regularly burn elder, you are likely to become very ill (cursed you'll be). Consider its lore in both the Wiccan religion and older sources:

Elder—Feminine, Venus, Water
English Elder—*Sambucus nigra*
American Elder—*Sambucus canadensis*

Primary astrological association: Libra, Taurus
Secondary astrological association: Cancer, Pisces, Scorpio
God association: Olocun
Goddess associations: Hel, Hulda, Ochun, Venus
Celtic tree calendar: Ruis, November 25 through December 21. The 13th month of the year.

Pendants and talismans made of Elder offer protection and encourage one to be faithful to his or her spouse. Elder berries and flowers are scattered to the four Quarters during the opening of Wiccan rites to call the blessings of the four Quarters upon the magick that is to be worked. Elder trees planted in the four corners of a property also lend protection, prosperity, and call forth blessings. But the wood is again and again forbidden from both ritual and utility fires.

Although the ripe berries are used to make wine and the flowers are used to make tea, the bark, leaves, roots, and unripe berries are poisonous. It is the one wood warned against inclusion in ritual fires as cited in both The Wiccan Rede and its most cited source, Rede of the Wiccae, because it is likely that the smoke from the burning of elder will cause a person to become sick and might bring on death. How's that for a curse?

The religions that currently dominate this world seem to feel as if all living things are here for our benefit. Now do not get me wrong, Wiccans have been just as guilty of objectification as any other world religion. We have scores and scores of books that tell us what plants can do for us and very few books that tell us what we can do for plants, but that is the mystery part of our religion, the part that only a handful of people seem to have understood thus far.

That mystery is very similar, albeit greatly expanded, to the teachings of another religion that also go mostly ignored. Although I cannot honestly say that I have observed it in the actions of many folk who call themselves Christian, I believe it was one of the teachings of Jesus that what ever a Christian does to the least of humanity, one does to him. In Wicca, that principle is a bit expanded. Rather than including just the third order of life, the teaching includes the first and second orders of life. The mystery that is arrived at by understanding the connection between humanity and plants is the view that whatever one does to the least of plants, one does to our Lord and Lady. While it is necessary for the perpetuation of life for one to cause death, it is most certainly not necessary to do so arbitrarily or without due cause.

> *Corn and grain, corn and grain*
> *All that falls shall rise again*

This is why even without having put it into words, Wiccans tend to either have a green thumb or (in my case) lust after a green thumb. We might not all be able to live off the land as did the ancients, but that does not mean we must forgo the connection that our soul insist we forge with the green world. Wiccans instinctively tend to welcome the green world into their home. They plant gardens where they can and share the produce from those gardens with their kith and kin. Even when full-blown gardens are out of the question, it is not uncommon to see a small herb garden in the window of a Wiccan kitchen. We do these things because they feel like the right thing to do, they feel good. But in so doing, we further our connection to the green world in such a way that when faced with the cold statistics of what is happening to that green world, we are motivated to action.

Note: This condensed version of Liber ab Planta has been shortened for space considerations. I hope to present the removed material separately such that this book can fulfill its intent as study material for the first degree.

Chapter Dedication

This chapter is dedicated to every editor I ever upset.
Except for that first one. That one really deserved it.

SECTION TWO

The Paragon of Animals

Dedicated to Our Lady and Lord as Mother and Father

Section Introduction

This is the second of the three-fold Path of Wicca.

This is approximately the place where most folk who become interested in Wicca stop. Either they become bored or they just do not find the information necessary to further their exploration. This is sad. Sad too is the idea that Wicca can be practiced as a solitary practitioner. Now, that does not mean that we must all practice with covens or households, but the idea that one would celebrate the holidays alone is not what is intended by the term 'Solitary Practitioner.'

If Wicca is the celebration of life, and if the celebration of life is more important than the rituals themselves, then we see that one is never a solitary when one has kith and kin, even when that kith and kin is not Wiccan. Of course, one will yearn for like minds, folk to do all the 'really, really Wiccan' things that we do in ritual. But that does not necessitate joining a coven. In fact, if you hear someone using the word coven but not putting the word *training* in front of that word, then you stand a very good chance of meeting up with folk who are playing Wicca rather than being Wiccan. While there are very sincere covens, the fact of the matter is that Wicca is a family religion and if that coven is not either family (meaning kith and kin) or training one in matters of family, then it is a farce which only fains belonging to the Wiccan community. It is my sincere hope that legitimate covens do not take offense to this statement but instead embrace it and recognize that the actions of the insincere are greatly damaging your good name.

By our very nature, we need community. The rituals of Wicca are created to promote that community. So while you might consider yourself a 'Solitary Wiccan', please do not think that term means 'Isolationist Wiccan.' In other words, get out of the house! Find a local Pagan bookstore and ask about groups in your area. If you still cannot find them, write one of the addresses in LIber ab Gens, or come visit the online community that I host at *www.PaganNation.com*. There you will find people from all walks of life that are not only willing to talk and chat with you, but who are also willing to put a wealth of information at your fingertips. You need only ask.

Section Two begins with the Rite of Handfasting and then moves on to a discussion of the eight Sabbats, Esbats, and the ancient Pagan holidays on which they were based. I have presented this information in this order because I see the natural progression of Initiation/ascension in three steps. The first is the Rite of Name, the second is the Rite of Handfasting, and the third...you will have to wait and see.

It is that natural order which I believe is the building of so called 'covens.' I know you have probably seen coven calls posted at Pagan stores or received one as a part of some Pagan spam effort. Today there is a coven on just about every city block. But in those covens is rarely seen the deep connections that Wicca promises. In an effort not to step on toes, I have been gradually using the term 'household' rather than coven. The first chapter of this section explains why I feel this way and the following chapters explore the many things these households or covens might celebrate together.

Liber ab Matrimonium
(Book of Marriage)
The Birth of the Magickal Child

ell me if this sounds familiar: 'I am Master of the Universe, a third degree exalted Grand Puba of the Order de Wicca Extraordinaire! I am heap powerful mojo man who knows the secrets of the universe. I can shoot lightning bolts from me fingertips and blow fireballs out of me arse. I sit in coffeehouses, probably don't have a job, and spout my supreme wisdom wherever I go. If I were a Super Hero, my name would be 'Super Wicca Man'! And I want you to join my Coven.'

Every day, folk walk into my store and ask: 'Are there any good covens in this town?' I suggest to them that they join one of the local public organizations and meet some folk, but they want the real thing and they want it now. Don't we all? After all, the real thing is a deeply committed relationship. It is a spouse, children, friends, family. The real thing is kith and kin. Unfortunately, that does not advertise on bulletin boards or via bulk email. Instead, the foundation of what is commonly called a coven is today the way it was in time of old, marriage.

Here is how I see the difference between finding a coven by looking and finding a coven/household in a sincere manner:

1. Walking into a Pagan bookstore or answering an advertisement for a coven.

This is similar to walking into a pet store and picking an animal on display. Maybe you want a cat and don't care that there are several available from Cat Welfare or other like organizations. Maybe you want a dog and don't care that there are several available from the Humane Society or other like organizations. How much is that coven in the window?

2. You realize that your family and friends are what a coven is.

This is similar to realizing that the relationship between an animal and a human is what is important. It does not matter where that animal came from, but that there are plenty of folk who will purchase an animal and few who will adopt.

Again, I stress that it is possible for someone to select their family and friends from an advertisement on the Internet or the wall of a bookstore. It is possible for that to be a very sincere union between the folk of a coven and yourself, but it is not likely because they are drawn together not by the things that bind finally and friends, but by a common religion. So what does this have to do with the Book of Marriage?

Marriage
Whose Holy Formula is (-1) + 1 = 2 = 3

The word *marriage* is most often used to note the marking of legal union between lovers. However, the idea of marriage is not based on romance in the least. In nautical terms, when one ties two ropes together, that person is said to 'marry' the ropes by interweaving their strands, effectively making the two ropes as one. Indeed one of the definitions of the word marry is 'to unite.'

While I have no issue with the modern use of the word, it is important to recognize its original meaning. Without that understanding, two people who enter into the sacrament of marriage might think they remain nothing but two separate entities. This is not the case in what I see as the Wiccan view of marriage. Instead, in my view of Wicca, the union of two people in the sacrament of marriage is magick. In mathematical notation, this is 1 + 1 = 3. Again, like in the first section of this book, we see a mathematical equation that does not seem to make sense. How is it that 0 can equal 1 and how is it that 1 + 1 can equal 3? The answer being that it is magick.

A whole person (masculine) unites with a whole person (feminine) in the sacrament of uniting as one, and the result is greater than the union of those two whole people. Now, I am not only speaking of physical flesh and blood children. As I have said, religion is a construct, so in Wicca as a fertility religion there is no mandate to have children. Instead, while children born to a Wiccan couple are most assuredly a blessing, anything that comes from such a union is the Magickal Child.

So too is the coven/household Initiation a rite of marriage. Now, let us get one thing absolutely clear right from the start. I am not stating that Wiccan covens/households are group marriages. While there are many fine Wiccans who are involved in group marriages and while several of those group marriages consider that marriage to be the base of their coven/household, they also have children and friends who are not a part of the group marriage.

Now that we have that clear, I tell you that the Rite of Coven or Household Initiation is a rite of marriage. It is the union of the initiate with the coven in the way the sailor marries two ropes, not just by tying them together, but by merging and intertwining their strands. It is the declaration that the initiate is not just joining some fancy group for name sake, but that the group will provide that person with the support and love that would be provided by a family. It is also the rite in which that member provides the same support for and love for every member of that coven/household.

Coven or Household Initiation Ritual Ideas

A Coven Initiation is a rebirth. It can be equated to an adoption, but to say that the adoption of a child is not as sacred as the birth of a child is rather insulting to folk who were adopted. Part of the format of a coven Initiation should involve a symbolic rebirth. While some have said this should take the form of blindfolding and binding the person, symbolic of the darkness and confines of the womb, I think the practice is rather insulting. When I think of my life in the womb of my natural mother, I think of a nurturing state. As I had not yet exited the womb, I did not know I was restricted or without light. Why then would a ritual that reminded me of something I did not know be appropriate? Instead, as the initiate makes the choice to enter the coven with his or her will unrestricted and with the full light of choice, I say let that rite be conducted unrestricted and with the full light of choice. In designing Initiation rites, let the initiate see fully where he or she is going and let them pass through that gate of his or her own accord.

The most beautiful way I have seen to symbolize both the rebirth and the freedom that an adult has to choose is to have all the women of the coven or household make two lines standing next to each other. Each stands in the pose found in the expression of center (See Chapter 4, Diagram 13), legs spread and arms reaching for the sky, but with one hand and foot joined to the person next to them such that the two rows of women form a symbolic birth canal. In larger groups and with large initiates, this becomes impractical. So we see an alternative, instead of putting the feet together and holding hands, the women can join by each holding a red piece of silk. If you object to using an animal product, use cotton. The color red is the symbol of blood and the association of blood made not only to birth, but also to marriage as seen in the rites of the Japanese god Gekka-o.

Whichever method is used, the men of the coven stand on the opposite side of birth symbolic birth canal and call the initiate forth, stating that 'Through woman you entered this world, through women you enter this family.' When the initiate reaches the men on the other side, the women say to him or her that 'But not without the union of men.' Each man of the coven/household then shakes the initiates hand. In large groups, the timing of the speaking of the words can become confused. If that is the case, the host can speak the men's words and the hostess the women's words.

The Three-Fold Name

Another matter that does sometimes occur during the coven or household Initiation is the giving of a new name, that being the name of the coven or the household. By this we see the principle of the last name being carried forward much the way it is done in marriage and thus respecting much of what was discussed previously as to the nature of three.

First name	Wiccaning	Given
Second name	Self-Dedication	Taken
Third name	Initiation	Given and Taken

So then, should one receive the name Golden at their Wiccaning, take the name Crow at their Self-Dedication, and then be initiated into a the household named Coyote, their three-fold name would be: Golden Crow Coyote.

Know that although this convention of a three-part Wiccan name is in play in the Wiccan community, it is neither mandated nor even very popular. Usually when you see a person with a three-part name, they just thought it sounded cute and has no reference to Wiccaning, Dedication, or Initiation. That is fine, too. However, it does not express the pride of family (Initiation), the Dedication of Self (Dedication), or commitment that one's community has for the individual (Wiccaning).

The Varar

Prior to the Rite of Initiation, the initiate should have reviewed the coven rules. These rules are sometimes called the *varar*. They are to a coven/household Initiation what a prenuptial agreement is to a marriage. While many might shriek at reading the word 'prenuptial,' no one should be initiated into a coven or household without first clearly understanding what is expected of him or her. While I have heard many times that such matters are not parts of the Pagan path, that a person's word is his or her bond, there is certainly historic documentation of such bonds being sacred to ancient Pagan folk. In fact, the word *varar* comes from the goddess Var of Norse mythology who listens to vows and agreements. She is also the one who punishes those who break such agreements.

If the coven/household should keep a group Book of Shadows, the varar should be placed there. If the household is founded by a couple that has formed a couple's Book of Shadows, the varar is placed there as well. Should each member of that coven or household keep a book of shadows of its own, they too should receive a copy of the varar for inclusion in their book of shadows. Remember that this is not just a coven's promise to the initiate, it is also that initiate's promise to the coven. Let the varar spell out as much of that bi-directional agreement as possible. Should coven/household members later find themselves at odds with each other, the first matter of that dispute should be addressed by examining the varar.

The exchange of that promise is the central focus of the rite. As such, making a present of an almost blank Book of Shadows to the initiate is most appropriate. If that is done, perhaps the very first page should be the initiate's varar itself, that page followed by each member's varar, symbolic of a new start and that new start being supported by the pledge of each member.

Earlier I mentioned that many folk would object to the varar as a sort of prenuptial agreement. It is true that we want to be taken at our word. However, spoken words are often forgotten—not for baneful cause, but because the way we remember things tends to change with time. Not long ago, there was a rash of folk on the TV talk shows who all reported to having participated in the most monstrous of rites. Reportedly, they had given birth to and sacrificed children for Satan. Sometimes they reported eating those children and the world wondered why the FBI or some other organization did not act on those reports. Some of the most paranoid viewers even went so far as to say the FBI was involved in the great satanic conspiracy along with the US government, the Royal Family of England, and anyone who did not go along with the paranoid delusion that satanic cults were taking over the world.

The FBI did investigate those allegations and found they were mostly fabrics of delusion. Not illusion or lie, but of delusion. Most of the claims were honestly believed by the folk who reported them. They had gone to a therapist for one reason or another, with hypnotism and a little help from the science of chemistry, presto-chango, a victim of a satanic conspiracy was created. Chances are even the therapist thought he or she was uncovering legitimate suppressed memory, but instead what was found was 'false memory syndrome.' If our memory is faulty (it is), then you can see the reason for agreements to be written down. So important is the written language that the development or reception of it has been recorded in the lore of our gods and goddesses.

Written Language as Sacred

Although there is nothing that states the varar must be written, we have a wealth of knowledge that shows the ancient Pagan folk on which our modern religion is based had a clear belief that written language is sacred.

Cherokee alphabet—Per North American lore, the inventor of the written language is Sequoya, also called Sint Holo.

Druid Runic alphabet—Remember, the term 'Celtic' is far sweeping. So when I tell you that Ogmios is the inventor of the runic language of the Druids, please do not get too upset. Certainly matters such as the written language were exchanged and built upon. One can easily see this by looking at the alphabets side by side. But what is important here is that those alphabets, whatever their historic origin, were all thought so sacred that it was said to have been invented by a god. The word *rune* denotes a poem or a piece of a poem, usually Finnish in origin. Incidentally, it might be the root for the word *tune* which is probably why The Wiccan Rede in its many incarnations alternates between the two words.

Greek alphabet—Per lore, the muse Clio, also called Kleio, was responsible for bringing the written language to the Greeks. She is almost always depicted with scrolls and quill in her capacity as muse of history and the heroic poetry found the telling of a historic tale. Although Clio brought the Greeks their alphabet, their lore says Cecrops initially taught the first people of Athens how to write. He is half snake and half man, born of the soil itself and thought to be the father or grandfather of the Greek people.

Irish Ogham alphabet—Oghma Grainaineach, also called Oghma and Ogma, reportedly either invented or received (depending on the story) the Ogham. This is the oldest form of the written language attributed to the Irish. Many believe this alphabet is also a calendar describing the Celtic view of the year.

Japanese written language—Per lore, it was Tenjin who taught the Japanese how to write their language. He is also god of learning and educational systems.

Roman alphabet—Per lore, it was Evander, also known as Euandros, who brought written language to the Roman people. He also resided over law and the arts.

Norse Rune alphabet—Odin is most often considered a god of war and death. However he is also cited as having received knowledge of the runes while hanging for nine days from the world tree, wounded by his own spear. Whether this form of written language was first a magickal tool and later an alphabet is a great debate; however, it is clear that at some point they were the written word.

So in writing the varar we make it sacred. We include it in our Books of Shadows because we want to remember that the union of initiate to coven or household is sacred. We want to keep a record of who has come and who has gone the same way one might keep the birth certificate or adoption papers of a child who is brought into a family.

There is another side to the varar, a more practical side. I do not think it is wise to initiate a person into a coven until they are of legal age. The Rite of Wiccaning is different from the Rite of Initiation in that Wiccaning is a dedication of the community to the child and not the child to any one religion. I do not believe one should be dedicated to a religion until that person can consent to such matters. Although we might bicker over what age a person can give that consent, our culture has established some rather clear ages for this purpose. If you decide it is acceptable to initiate someone under that legal age, let the varar be signed by that person' legal guardian and notarized. Even then, it is best that legal guardian stand at the Initiation.

Another practical reason for keeping a written varar is the matter of contact information. The initiate's contact information should be included in the varar and kept updated at regular coven or household meetings, sometimes termed Esbats. This way, the initiated and coven or household members are always able to contact each other.

Marriage as Matrimony

Like Coven or Household Initiation, marriage is a second rite of Initiation. It is the second rite of passage of Llew Llaw Gyffes, who was denied a mortal wife. That he would not be alone, he was given an immortal wife. That is the key to the Wiccan concept of marriage. When a Wiccan greets someone 'Thou art God' or 'Thou art Goddess,' that is exactly what he or she means. When a Wiccan makes love with a woman, that Wiccan makes love with our Lady Immortal. When a Wiccan makes love with a man, that Wiccan makes love with our Lord Immortal. Not only is this the building block of the family, it is the very foundation of the household or coven—not the act of making love, but the act of two people seeing our Lord and Lady incarnate in each.

From this foundation, children are born and adopted. From this foundation, friendships are forged. It is a foundation not only in the sense that the living space of that couple provides a place to meet (a household) but that their kith and kin are also in the order of the term household (coven). This is as it was among the pre-Christian fertility religions on which Wicca is based and it will likely be the way Wicca continues in the future. Why? Because the natural foundation of love and union is much more stable than covens built by Super Wicca Man.

Although handfastings are commonly entered whimsically by some Wiccans, it is fairly easy to see that such behavior is not unique to the Wiccan community. Interestingly enough, this conduct is probably more likely a recent phenomenon than anything else. If it were not, I doubt we would see as many gods and goddesses of matrimony as we do:

Gods and Goddesses of Matrimony

Atahensic (Also known as Ataensic)—Female—North America
Iroquois goddess who presides over marriage and childbirth.

Bhaga—Male—Near East
Hindu god and patron of marriage who is also associated with wealth and prosperity.

Chalchiuhtlicue—Female—North America
Aztec goddess of all the waters of the Earth who presides over the Rite of Marriage and the agreements made during those rites.

Cinxia—Female—Mediterranean
Roman goddess of marriage and particularly of the struggles of life being overcome by the joys of marriage.

Demeter—Female—Mediterranean

Not only is she one of the major goddesses of Greece, she is patron of marriages and married women. As Demeter Thesmophoros, her role as goddess of marriage is celebrated at the Thesmophoria. In times of old, folk traveled from great distances to be initiated to and participate in her mysteries.

Freyr—Male—North Europe

Norse god of rain and crop fertility who is called upon to bless marriages.

Frigg—Female—Northern Europe

Norse goddess of matrimony and pregnancy, she is wife to Odin and the highest of goddesses in her pantheon. This speaks volumes for how the Norse folk felt and feel about marriage.

Gekka-o—Male—Far East

Japanese god of marriage who binds the feet of lovers to one another with red silk, so they are forever attached.

Hera—Female—Mediterranean

Greek queen of the Olympians who was worshiped mainly as a goddess of matrimony who brought good fortune and favor to marriages and childbirth.

Hulda—Female—Central Europe/Northern Europe

Elder German goddess who presides over and blesses marriages.

Hymen (Also known as Hymenaeus)—Male—Mediterranean

Greek god of marriages and the celebration of marriage.

Janus (Also known as Bifrons)—Male—Mediterranean

Roman god who is primarily cited as god of doorways and gates. As he is also a god of matrimony, one sees a reference to the ancients recognizing marriage as a rite of passage.

Juno—Male/Female—Mediterranean

Sometimes cited as aspects of the goddess Juno, other times as unique deities, the Juno are a variety of ancestral spirits which protect and guide a woman through her life. On the issue of marriage these were Juno Pronuba (brides and brides-to-be), and Juno Iugalis (married women, mothers, and the Juno of marriage itself).

Mangar-kunjer-kunja—Male—Australia

Creator god of the Aranda who presides over the institution of marriage.

Musubi-no-Kami—Male—Far East

Japanese god of marriage and the courtship that leads to marriage, he is also a god of love, but such references rarely appear except when in courtship or the promise of courtship for marriage.

Nuwa (Also known as Nugua, Nu-kua, Nu Kwa)—Female—Central Asia

Chinese goddess of the institution of marriage and the agreements made between husband and wife.

Ot—Female—Central Asia

Mongolian Fire goddess who presides over and blesses marriage.

Pattini (Also known as Patni)—Female—Near East

One of the most praised goddesses on Sri Lanka (Ceylon), she is patron of marriage as well as a goddess of rice, grain fertility, and preventing plague.

Svarog—Male—Central Europe/Northern Europe

Slavic god of marriage, Fire, and the sun, he is said to have created marriage as a universally recognized rite of passage and an institute or convention that was respected as a matter of law between different people.

Var—Female—Northern Europe

Norse goddess of marriage agreements. She listens to the promises (varar) between married couples and brings punishment to folk who break those promises.

Vor—Female—Northern Europe

Norse goddess of marriage and contracts, whose name means 'faith.' She is also a goddess of monogamy and is said to guard against temptations of that matter.

The First Marriage

Although I do not feel the first marriage is any more or less sacred than the next, I should point out there are at least a couple of goddesses and festivals that were, in times of old, reserved for women in their first marriage. Two examples are Eos, the Greek goddess of the dawn who is the patron of first marriages, and Matuta, Roman goddess whose festival, Matralia, was attended only by women in their first marriage. I believe this supports two principles: that marriage is indeed sacred and that sometimes the first marriage needs just a little bit of extra help. After all, before you do something, can you really know how to do it?

The Second, the Third, and the...

Lore also tells us that choosing an appropriate partner is important. It does seem logical that if that choice is important the decision should be given time. So let me tell you about Kaik from the lore of the Salish the northwest tribes of North America. Kaik is a mink who first married a frog, but the frog hurt his paws, so he married an Eagle.

While riding on his wife Eagle, he saw a salmon and he leaped off Eagle and dove towards Salmon, hurting himself as he hit the water. So he then married Salmon and the story ends when he is swallowed by a whale.

Pagan lore is so clear that making the right decision about marriage is important that a test period is built into the Wiccan rite of marriage. Let's face it, if Zeus and Hera had spent any time together before their marriage, they never would have gotten married in the first place. They would have been much happier, their pantheon would have been much happier, and so would a great many others (Heracles being at the top of that list).

Marriage is so sacred and important a rite that it needs a test period to see if folk are right for each other and a way to conclude the marriage should they later discover either they were wrong about that test or that they have grown apart since that test.

The Rite of Handfasting

The Wiccan rite of marriage is called *handfasting*. Unlike what is all too often a lie, the Wiccan rite of marriage is not until death do us part. Instead it is said to be for a period which is the longest of 'A year and a day or for as long as love shall stay.' The meaning is that the couple will remain in accordance with their varar for a term no less than a year and a day but no longer than how long love shall stay. Thus, should a couple be handfasted for three years and they are still in love, they are still bound by that agreement, even if a year and a day has come to pass. If they should despise each other after six months, they are still bound by that varar for the remainder of the year and a day. The term 'year and a day' is actually a fancy way of saying a year. It is also a comment on matters of divorce. The term and the concept that a couple should always devote at least a year and a day to the marriage is Celtic in origin.

Many agreements other than marriage were made for a year and a day, but we see the most notable reference in the marriage of Rhiannon and Pywll. Rhiannon was married to Gwawl, but was not in love. When approached by Pywll, she told him to return in a year and a day. After that year and a day, they went to her father's court where Pywll did win her hand away from Gwawl. However, we see that one of the reasons Pywll won the hand of Rhiannon from Gwawl is, in part, due to another year and a day.

Earlier, Pywll once traded places with Arawn, Lord of the Underworld, for a year and a day. Along with position and duties, Pywll took on Arawn's appearance in all ways, so much so that Arawn's wife had not discovered the switch. However, Pywll had a noble and just heart, so he did not bed Arawn's wife. So Arawn and Pywll became the closest of friends. I am sure you can imagine that a friendship with Arawn would swing just a little bit of weight.

Pywll became Arwan's friend by the virtue he demonstrated in not taking advantage of Arawn's wife during that year and a day. Pywll won his lady's hand by the virtue he demonstrated by waiting a year and a day and then returning to Rhiannon after that year and a day. This is the basis for the Wiccan handfasting, virtue, and the demonstration thereof.

The First Rite of Handfasting

The first Rite of Handfasting is the engagement. It is what happens at the conclusion of courtship and not during. While it saddens me to say this, many of our younger folk tend to see this rite whimsically. I cannot tell you how many folk have asked me to perform the first Rite of Handfasting after a month-long courtship or after a few months trading emails on the Internet. Only if a couple can be judged to be serious in their dedication should anyone perform such a rite. Some argue that a couple should be allowed to court first. Of course they should be allowed to court, but courting comes before an engagement. Others argue they want a promise of monogamy now. Sometimes that is what is on their mind, but they won't admit it. Or maybe they want to make sure a person is bound to them. Well then, ask for a promise of monogamy or some binding now, but don't involve a Rite of Handfasting to establish monogamy or binding because handfastings do not automatically assume such a thing unless the couple builds that into the varar. And even once they are included in the varar, the first Rite of Handfasting does not magickly bind two people together. Instead, it celebrates and marks the magick that binds people together.

The commitment is always for a year and a day or for as long as love shall stay. Generally speaking, this commitment is also to live together under the conditions in which they will be legally joined at the second Rite of Handfasting. Thus, the first rite is a marriage itself under the Wiccan religion, but it is one that is much easier to dissolve. Yes, you still have to live by the varar for at least a year and a day to complete your promise; however, should you complete that promise you do not have the matters of a divorce by law. Instead, a simple Handparting will do.

Now, the proposal is a very interesting question. If the first Rite of Handfasting is the engagement, doesn't that absolutely destroy the surprise of a proposal? No, it does not. When I say the first Rite of Handfasting is the engagement, I mean that it is what is done to mark the engagement. Remember, Wiccan rituals are sacred theater that celebrate life by imitating life. The rite itself is no more the act of proposing than is the symbolic Great Rite the consummation of that union.

Should one want to propose to another, let that person go to his or her love. Should he or she desire to exchange a ring at that time, then he should bring it along. But do so with your varar, your promise. Let the person know what you are asking, and be specific. Trust me, it is more romantic to extend the moment on bent knee reciting the poetry of your varar to the person you love than to ask if he or she wants to get hitched. Should the other person accept the varar, they write theirs and offer you their promise as well. Together, the couple then discusses the varar until they arrive at a realistic plan for their first handfasting. They then pick a date, perform the rite, and at that point the varars are officially marked and exchanged. So, instead of the first Rite of Handfasting preventing romance, it furthers romance while also insisting that those who would be wed take some time to think about that union long enough to write it down and discuss it.

The Second Rite of Handfasting

The second Rite of Handfasting is a legal marriage. If conducted under barbaric marriage laws (laws which restrict consensual sexuality), then instead of the permission of those barbaric communities to be wed, a varar of equally legal binding nature should be devised. I am told that in many areas such barbarism is combated with something called a *domestic partner agreement*. In short, if you are a couple of different sex you should combine the second Rite of Handfasting with the legalities of marriage. If you are a same-sex couple or if the marriage involves more than two people and you live in a barbaric community (one that will not let you be legally wed), you should enter into a legally binding agreement similar to the binds of a legal marriage.

In an ideal world, the legal portion of this Rite might not be necessary. Frankly, I am disturbed by governments that regulate religious rites. However, if a Wiccan marriage is to command the same respect as any other marriage in the greater community, it should be just as subject to government authority as any other. In fusing matters of law and religion, the legally binding part of the union can be conducted as a part of the rite itself or it can be performed beforehand. In my view, it should not be performed after the second rite of hand fasting because I have seen too many people show disrespect for this rite by not following threw with that step. If the legal union is performed before the Rite of Handfasting, it can be a simple matter or grand. Thus, there is no encouragement in Wicca to deny family even when they refuse to attend the hand fasting out of religious intolerance. Remember, Wicca was never intended as a tool to break up families. If you should find yourself at odds, then be bigger than their bigotry and have it both ways. After all, if you are truly Wiccan then their Creator is your Creator as well.

The Third Rite of Handfasting and the Rite of Handparting

Because Wicca sees all things with a beginning, a middle, and an end, the third Rite of Handfasting is either a Rite of Handparting or a deathbed promise to continue loving the partner who is leaving this world. The intent is the same in both, that the marriage is coming to an end and that the two should part as friends, welcoming reunion if it should come again.

Handparting is a divorce. The spirit here is to acknowledge that it has indeed been more than a year and a day from the second handfasting, but that love did not stay. The spirit of the Rite is that although the union has parted, they do so as friends and should they desire union once again, it is welcome. This is also a rite in which the community is told that although the couple tried, their union is dissolved.

As Handfasting, this is a deathbed promise, something entered into only if death seems near. The spirit of the rite is that although a very real parting is in the near future, the couple does not want the end of their marriage to be the end of their union. That they will continue on into the next life and welcome reunion should it occur in accordance with free will. But it is also a handparting, one that tells the other that once death has caused an end to the marriage, the varar is released.

Why Three Handfastings?

There are three Rites of Handfasting in the Wiccan religion because there are three states in all things, a beginning, a middle, and end, as we discussed in Book of Three. There are three because the first one proves virtue (the first year and a day of Pywll), then one proves virtue again (Pywll waiting for Rhiannon), and then one proves virtue again (the marriage of Pywll to Rhiannon). First an agreement is made, then the agreement is tested, and then the marriage is made. However, making the marriage is not a promise for this world, it is a promise for the next.

Why Public Rituals for Engagement, Marriage, and Partings?

One of the failings of many views of Wicca is that the non-Wiccan community is not involved. If Wicca is truly built on the pre-Christian fertility religions, our celebrations should include much more than just Wiccans. Until very recently, survival depended on the entire family pulling together for common goals. Is not the blessing of a marriage one of those common goals? Historically and today, such matters are the very roles of religion. While you might have a knee jerk reaction to this statement, thinking religion should not be involved in such matters as social law and conduct, if it is not providing those services then what is it doing?

One can be spiritual without being religious. So why then would we need a religion if not to establish social standards within our community? Not to force those standards on folk who accept it, but to provide a community of like-minded folk. When one says he or she is Wiccan, the only value that word can have is if that word has meaning beyond whatever a person wants it to mean. Let's face it; if the word has no meaning, one might as well call one's religion Crack and it would mean just as much.

So how can Wicca be a religion when it says that one must decide these matters for oneself? It does so by the Wiccan's estimation of what those things are and then by marking those matters with public ritual to tell their community what those things are. Wicca does not decide if your marriage will be monogamous or not. Wicca does not decide if you will have two members to that marriage, three, or whatever number. Wicca does not decide if you marry a same-sex partner or a member of the opposite sex. In all these things and more, you decide. But then you let the rest of us know what that decision is by your varar which is read during ritual. So should your engagement state that you will be monogamous, your community knows that it would be wrong to intrude upon it. Should your marriage be open, your community knows that potential inclusion is welcome. It is in making these things known that your Wicca can interact with other people's Wicca. It is in making these things known that Wicca can be a community religion.

Ritual Ideas for the Rite of Handfasting

Lustral bath—Taste and smell are of prime concern as smelling and licking might follow. Myrtle is said to bless unions of marriage.

Dress—Personally, I will be married in a tux because the greater community says it is the finest way a man can dress, and I want only the finest for my love. Medieval weddings are fun and they do tend to be popular in the Wiccan community. However, if it is a medieval wedding, please do let your guests know that Wicca is not a medieval religion.

Asperging—Consider using branches of Myrtle as they seem to pop up over and over again in lore surrounding weddings.

Smudging—Experiment with incense by blending herbs and resins in accordance with the bride's and groom's astrological signs. There are many books that provide this information. A quick reference can be found in *Wicca Spellcraft for Men* (New Page Books).

Challenge/Outsiders—Here one might want to ask if anyone opposes the union to speak now. If one does, that person can choose to stand for the wedding, but only if he or she will ignore that objection after the Rite is concluded. If he or she does not agree, they should be asked to leave the Circle. Including a final opportunity for the bride or groom to reconsider is also a good idea.

Casting the Circle—Consider using petals from flowers that correspond to the bride's and groom's astrological signs. Perhaps the Circle could be cast the first time by a flower maiden or maidens scattering the bride's flowers and then by a flower master or masters scattering the groom's flowers. Those flowers mingling and falling to the ground together as a symbol of the union being marked.

Inviting the Four Quarters—Ah, what better job for the in-laws?

Invitation to Lord and Lady—It is rather beautiful to incorporate the invitation to our Lord and Lady in the exchange of varar. After that invitation, the couple could perform the symbolic Great Rite, only while the athame and chalice are joined, someone joins their hand with a red silk cloth and then takes the athame and chalice away, so they can kiss safely.

Chapter Comments

Further information on the Rites of Handfasting can be found in *Wicca for Couples*. I know I have already said at least a dozen times that this is only my view of Wicca. I know that I began this book by saying that as well. But please, please, please remember that more in this chapter than any other place. What is in my heart might not be what is in your heart. In all matters, but especially in matters such as these, listen to your own heart first. This is not everyone's view of Wicca. Even if it were everyone's view, there is nothing that says you have to listen to them.

Liber ab Sol

(Book of Sun)

A Discussion of the Sabbats

ere you will not find specific instructions for conducting rituals for each of the Sabbats, the eight solar Holidays. You will find no drawings to tell you where to put your feet or sequence of events. This is because there is no set place for you to put your feet or sequence of events that you must follow. Surely if you wish to incorporate a waltz or tango into the celebration of these rites, you will likely seek a book or instruction for doing so. Therein you will find such instruction, but that is not the order in which I address these celebrations. I am not a dance instructor.

Instead, here you will find the heart of what I find important about each of the Wiccan Holidays, the heart behind the rituals. Typically, they are the activities and rites that are conducted between the opening and closing of Wiccan ritual as discussed earlier. However, there need not be the formal opening or closing of a rite for that rite to be sacred. Certainly it is more important that the rite be experienced than the formalities be conducted. While it is ideal that both formality and experience occur, the world in which we live does not always afford this option. Wicca should never drive apart kith and kin because someone is uncomfortable with formalities, so if it is not appropriate that a formal Circle be cast then so be it, for the celebration is much more important.

You will notice I have not spelled out specific rituals for each of these Holidays. Generally speaking, Wiccan rituals open and close as discussed in Section I. That ritual format is one of the things noted by the word Wicca. Although rituals vary from group to group, the theme remains the same. That which we find in the middle, the celebrations themselves, will vary greatly from person to person and group to group. Although the central theme is the same, the marking of the Wheel of the Year, the format should be interpreted by the individual heart and how that heart interacts with all who attend the rite.

The Eight Solar Holidays

Known variously as the Sabbats, High Days, and Holy Days, these are the eight days of the year that are defined by the sun's travel. They are the four days defined by the two equinoxes and the two solstices as well as the four days that fall between those events. Although calling these *Sabbats* is most common within the Wiccan community, the word that would better express meaning to non-Wiccans is *holiday*. When we consider the purpose of words is communication, we see that if our intent is to communicate what we mean when we talk about these days, we could use the word holiday to refer to them. Using the word Sabbat just seems to further the rift between Wicca and other mainstream religions. Of course, if your intention is more in the order of being spooky and mysterious, then by all means use the word Sabbat among cowan friends. I am sure it will impress them greatly.

Truth be known, there is almost nothing of the pre-Christian fertility religions in the word Sabbat. It was mostly likely invented for the purpose of connecting Witches to yet another group of folk who were persecuted for their religious beliefs. I am, of course, speaking about the Jewish faith. It is interesting to note how many people with distinctly Jewish sounding names were put to death on the charge of witchcraft in or around Germany. This causes me to wonder if the atrocities committed by Nazi Germany against the Jews were not a continuation of the assault on pre-Christian religions. The earliest use of the word that I have discovered is in the medieval demonologists and witch hunters. So, much like wearing all black, there is probably more of Hollywood than religion associated with the word.

Sometimes the Sabbats between solar events are called the Greater Sabbats and the ones marked by the solar events are called Lesser Sabbats. This is an old reference from when folk still clung to the lie that Wicca is an ancient Celtic fertility religion. You see, the Celts did indeed celebrate the days between the solar events, but it was not until they were invaded by Norse tribes and others that the solar days became times of celebration. I choose to ignore these distinctions because I accept the fact that Wicca is a post-modern religion that draws on the ancient practices and beliefs of many cultures. To readily consider a Celtic Holiday as Greater to the Lesser Germanic Holiday is an insult to the Celtic and Germanic blood that dwells harmoniously with each other in my veins and the veins of a great many Wiccans. Instead, I use the terms Quarter Days and Cross Quarter Days to mark the difference but even in marking the difference, I don't see a great deal more significance in one or the other.

Quarter Days:

Winter Solstice: the shortest day of the year. The Sun is Dark/New.

Spring Equinox: the day and night are equal length. The Sun is waxing.

Summer Solstice: the longest day of the year. The Sun is full.

Fall Equinox: the day and night are equal length. The Sun is waning.

Cross Quarter Days:

Imbolg: the day that falls between Winter Solstice and Spring Equinox.

Bealtaine: the day that falls between Spring Equinox and Summer Solstice.

Lughnasadh: the day that falls between Summer Solstice and Fall Equinox.

Samhain: the day that falls between Fall Equinox and Winter Solstice.

Note: In naming the Cross Quarter days, I have used the Celtic names not to show preference or dominance, but to ease understanding and reference. With the exception of spelling variations, these are the names most often cited.

Collectively, these eight days form the Wheel of the Year, the solar calendar discussed briefly in Book of Genesis. It is important to note that the dates given here are only generally accepted dates that are cited in many books. The actual dates will change with each year. Your best source for the specific dates marked by the sun is your local newspaper. For the Cross Quarter days, just do the math.

Winter Solstice	Solar Quarter	December 21 or 22
Imbolg	Solar Cross Quarter	February 2
Spring Equinox	Solar Quarter	March 21 or 22
Bealtaine	Solar Cross Quarter	April 30 or May 1
Summer Solstice	Solar Quarter	June 21 or 22
Lughnasadh	Solar Cross Quarter	July 31 or August 1 or 2
Fall Equinox	Solar Quarter	September 21 or 22
Samhain	Solar Cross Quarter	October 31

Now to make things just a little bit more confusing, everything that has been said above this sentence is for the Northern Hemisphere. South of the equator we see a different story:

Summer Solstice	Solar Quarter	December 21 or 22
Lughnasadh	Solar Cross Quarter	February 2
Fall Equinox	Solar Quarter	March 21 or 22
Samhain	Solar Cross Quarter	April 30 or May 1
Winter Solstice	Solar Quarter	June 21 or 22
Imbolg	Solar Cross Quarter	July 31 or August 1 or 2
Spring Equinox	Solar Quarter	September 21 or 22
Bealtaine	Solar Cross Quarter	April 30 or May 1

Because Wicca was born/reborn in the Northern Hemisphere and due to the influences of larger religions, these Holidays are not typically respected in this way. Now, do not take this to mean that Wiccans south of the equator do not make an effort to celebrate the Sabbats in accordance with this concept. However, consider the south of the equator Wiccan who celebrates Yule at Summer Solstice when the rest of the non-Wiccan community is celebrating Yule at or around Winter Solstice. Because the cultural Holiday of Christmas is celebrated on December 25th by most Christian cultures, the sense of a larger community is lacking at Summer Solstice. The sense that all of humanity is rejoicing, without regard to specific religion, is missing.

This state is sad, as it is a further distraction from the concept of Lord and Lady. The Christian religion with its concept of god being set only in the masculine does not allow for the balance of masculine and feminine principles, so of course it is not built into their Holidays. Those masculine and feminine principles are at the very foundation of the Wiccan religion, and thus built into our Holidays. The confusion only comes in with the idea of static dates. If we are in the Northern Hemisphere we see that the Holidays are:

Holiday	Counterpart	Approximate Date
Samhain (masculine)	Bealtaine (feminine)	October 31
Winter Solstice (masculine)	Summer Solstice (feminine)	December 21 or 22
Imbolg (masculine)	Lughnasadh (feminine)	February 2
*Spring Equinox (m & f)	Fall Equinox (f & m)	March 21 or 22
Bealtaine (feminine)	Samhain (masculine)	April 30 or May 1
Summer Solstice (feminine)	Winter Solstice (masculine)	June 21 or 22
Lughnasadh (feminine)	Imbolg (masculine)	July 31 or August 1 or 2
*Fall Equinox (f & m)	Spring Equinox (m & f)	September 21 or 22

However, in the Southern Hemisphere we see that the Holidays are:

Holiday	Counterpart	Approximate Date
Samhain (masculine)	Bealtaine (feminine)	April 30 or May 1
Winter Solstice (masculine)	Summer Solstice (feminine)	June 21 or 22
Imbolg (masculine)	Lughnasadh (feminine)	July 31 or August 1 or 2
*Spring Equinox (m & f)	Fall Equinox (f & m)	September 21 or 22
Bealtaine (feminine)	Samhain (masculine)	April 30 or May 1
Summer Solstice (feminine)	Winter Solstice (masculine)	December 21 or 22
Lughnasadh (feminine)	Imbolg (masculine)	February 2
*Fall Equinox (f & m)	Spring Equinox (m & f)	March 21 or 22

* Note that the equinoxes are both masculine and feminine. The Spring Equinox is masculine in transition into feminine. Fall Equinox is feminine in transition into masculine.

One can easily argue that the names of these Holidays are important, and that being of Celtic origin, we should preserve the dates that have been traditionally associated with them. But that argument pales when we accept the simple fact that it is the associations made by our connection to the natural rhythms that are important. Remember that I only choose to use the Celtic names because they are most used. What is important is not the name, but the relationship represented.

Our language is such that it is difficult to express the idea of the sacred dance that requires both advance and retreat. Imagine a couple waltzing; one person leads the dance, and the other is lead in symmetry. In this example, the important issue is that the couple is dancing, not who is leading the dance. It is the relationships between the Holidays and their mates that are important. It is also not important that the couple is male and female; the principles of the dance are the same. There is advance (masculine) and retreat (feminine) in all things that are not stagnant. Summer causes a seed to grow into a plant, but it is the Winter that cracked the seed such that it could grow into that plant. This is the Wheel of the Year as discussed in the Book of Genesis.

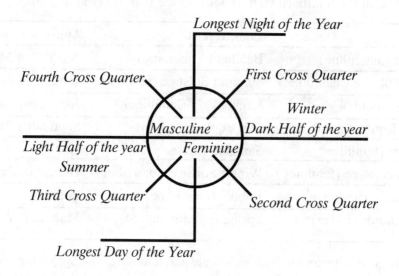

The Eight Spokes of the Solar Year (reprinted from page 50)

The Wheel of the Year

Darkness Before Light

When considering the traditional date of a Holiday it is important to remember that in ancient times the day began and ended at sundown; thus the light of each day is preceded by the darkness of that same day. This principle is represented in such lore as Diana (Darkness) and Lucifer (Light). Prior to their separation into two beings, that which came before was simply called Diana.

In ordering the Wiccan Holidays, many folk are inclined to begin with the Winter Solstice, stating that the Winter Solstice is the beginning of the solar year and then counting each by degree around the Wheel of the Year. This method counts Winter Solstice first, or at 0 degrees on the Wheel. These opinions no doubt come from a stressing of the importance that the Germanic tribes associated with the solstice. To a much lesser degree, some choose to begin with Fall Equinox, commenting that the Fall Equinox marks the division between Summer and Winter, so that day would be both the end of the old year as well as the beginning of the new. Those folk would mark the Fall Equinox as at 0 degrees, Samhain at 45 degrees, and Winter Solstice at 90 degrees.

In considering these two ideas of where to start the new year, I find myself in the middle. Yes, the new solar year is marked at the Winter Solstice, but that is the day on which our Lord Winter is at his strongest. Certainly we are not at either our strongest at the moment of our birth. Instead, I find Winter Solstice to align with our Lord's attribute of maturity, his Father stage. Keeping in tune with the threefold path of masculinity (Master, Father, Sage) this means that He would have been at the youth/Master stage during Samhain and at the Holiday prior (Fall Equinox) His state would be newborn/infant. Consider the following from the Wiccan Rede:

> *When the Wheel has turned to Yule*
> *light the log,*
> *let the Horned One rule*

—*From the Wiccan Rede, Author Unknown* [1]

I begin my list of Wiccan Holidays with Samhain, not because it is the Holiday that marks the end of Summer, but because it is the first Holiday of Winter, said to be the first in the Dark half of the year. As we are all born (beginning) in darkness, it just seems like the natural way to do things.

In our larger world culture, the calendar day is considered the 24 hours between midnight and midnight. In some Eastern and Native American cultures it has been considered sunrise to sunrise. Finally, in many Western cultures it has been seen as the amount of time between sunset and sunset. Here again we see the principle of Darkness coming before Light.

Making matters even more confusing, the actual dates of the Solar Cross Quarters were far more flexible prior to the invasion of Germanic customs. As an example, Bealtaine hopped around so much that some folk cite it as being a month and a half either prior to or after its current position on the Wheel of the Year. By introducing the idea that these things are marked by the Earth's travel around the sun, things become much easier to place.

So, when is the best actual date to celebrate these events? Well, that is what all Wiccans have to decide for themselves. After many years of thought, I have decided it is more Wiccan that I celebrate Winter Solstice on December 24th because that is the day my family has chosen, and I cannot imagine belonging to a religion that would not promote family relationships.

Seasons of the Sun

The final consideration before discussing the Holidays themselves is to state that the Holidays are not simply days. Yes, those days are often marked on a calendar, but those days are simply the peak of the season by the same name. We celebrate the Holidays on a more or less specific date, but that date should be thought of as the culmination of the season. Samhain, for example, is most often celebrated on October 31st; however, the season of Samhain runs from Fall Equinox through Samhain. Likewise, we typically see Winter Solstice marked and celebrated on or around December 21st; however, the season of Winter Solstice runs from Samhain (the end of the Samhain season) through Winter Solstice, the day on which the season is marked. Although this has not been the typical Wiccan view, it does seem rather naive to think that a harvest or planting would last only a single day.

While this might sound a bit confusing at first, this way of viewing the year denotes that each day is sacred. It is also in keeping with the cultural norm of marking a thing at its conclusion. A child is said to be one year old at the conclusion of his or her first year. When an adult marks his or her 21st birthday, he or she marks the completion of the 21st year and the entrance into the next year of life, the 22nd.

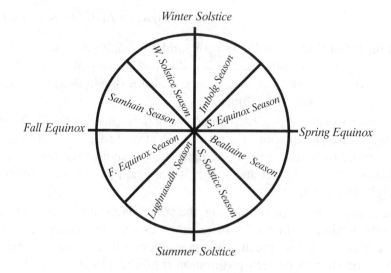

Seasons of the Sun

Here we begin to see four seasons instead of just two, each season having a beginning, middle, and an end, as do all things. With this explanation, we see that at Samhain we can be truthful in saying that we are celebrating the peak of Fall. After all, as a nature based religion that is exactly what we are celebrating, even if a small portion of our community wants to continue to confuse and scare the general public.

Season	Beginning	Middle	End
Fall	Fall Equinox	Samhain	Winter Solstice
Winter	Winter Solstice	Imbolg	Spring Equinox
Spring	Spring Equinox	Bealtaine	Summer Solstice
Summer	Summer Solstice	Lughnasadh	Fall Equinox

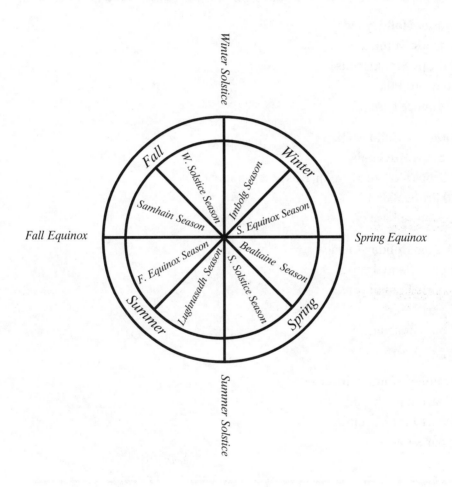

The Four Seasons

General Recipes

If possible, it is best to use recipes intended for specific Holidays. If that is too much work for the occasion, a general use recipe is the next best bet.

Winter Holiday Oil
4 drops Nutmeg
4 drops Frankincense
10 drops Pine
1/2 ounce base oil

Summer Holiday Oil
4 drops Patchouli
4 drops Otto of Rose or Rose Geranium
10 drops Pine
1/2 ounce base oil

Winter Holiday Incense
4 parts Sandalwood
4 parts Frankincense
2 part Myrrh
2 part Benzoin
1 part Clove

Summer Holiday Incense
4 part Sandalwood
4 part Frankincense
2 parts Lavender

Samhain

Winter is at the youth/Master stage. Summer is entering the first trimester.

Also known as All Hallows Eve, All Saint's Eve, Blood Feast, Blood Harvest, Calan Gaef, Celtic New Year, Day of the Dead, Feast of Spirits, Hallowmas, Last Harvest, Martinmas, Samonios, Samhuinn, Santos, Third Harvest, Winter's Eve.

Date: Approximately October 31st, this Holiday is actually found on the day that rests in the middle of Fall Equinox and Winter Solstice.

God association: Oengus Mac Oc.

Goddess association: Bhavani, Carlin, Cerridwen, Hecate, Moingfhion, Nicneven.

Gemstone associations: Obsidian, Onyx, and Carnelian.

Plant associations: Allspice, Apples, Catnip, Chrysanthemum, Corn, Gourd, Grains (all), Hazel, Pears, Pomegranates, Sage, Squash (especially pumpkin), Thistle, Wormwood.

Color associations: Black, Orange.

Samhain Incense

1 part Allspice

1 part Sage

1 part Frankincense

1 part Gum Arabic

Samhain Oil

8 drops Allspice

6 drops Sage

6 drops Frankincense

1/2 ounce base oil

Solitary/General—When first considering where to divide the Wheel of the Year, many look to Samhain because it is the Celtic New Year. If that were the case, the line dividing the year into Summer and Winter would be drawn from Samhain to Bealtaine. That is just as valid a way of looking at the Wheel of the Year as any. However, when we consider the names of the two halves of the year, we see a reason not to split the year that way. Winter, called the Dark half of the year, implies that it would be the half of the year in which there is the least amount of light or sun. That half of the year is better marked at the Fall and Spring Equinox because the length of days is the shortest on one side of that line and longest on the other side of the line, thus making an even division of the darkest half of the year and the lightest half of the year. So I choose to separate Winter (the Dark half of the year) and Summer (the Light half of the year) at the Equinoxes, making Samhain the first Holiday of the year rather than the last. This means that while Samhain can most definitely be considered New Year's day, because that day is part of the New Year, it most certainly is not akin to New Year's Eve as New Year's Eve would be connected to the former year.

It is a time of reflection on the past year and a time to plan the new year. The association between Samhain and fresh meat comes from this reflection and from how the ancients viewed this time of the year. Known variously as the Blood Feast or Blood Harvest, it was the time when the ancients assessed the harvest of the previous year and determined how much food was available to keep cattle and other livestock through the winter. If it was determined that there was not enough food to keep the animals fed throughout the winter, it was necessary to cull the herd.

This Holiday speaks to us of insuring that last year's matters are complete and are put to rest. It's when you make sure the storm windows are all closed and you have extra stores (money) to pay the utility bills that rise as the temperature lowers. Generally speaking, my store does not accept new business contacts or expand our merchandise offering during this time of the year, going instead with the tried and true. Many covens do not take on initiates during this time, for the same reason.

But this is so much more the case after Samhain. If we have not done business with you before, we will not start a relationship during this time of the year, asking instead that you contact us again after Bealtaine. Why? Because the Pooka will surely destroy all attempts to harvest between Samhain and Bealtaine. While it may sound incredibly superstitious, ancient lore warns that the Pooka will curse all crops not taken in on the night of Samhain. While I do not believe some dark force roams the countryside looking for that last pumpkin to curse, the story of the Pooka does well to remind us that this is a time for new beginnings and as such, we are best to move on.

In its aspect as being the day on which the veil between worlds at its thinnest, we can compare this day to Mardi Gras. No, it is not so much the day that is between the last and the new year, but it is the last day of that transition. This is much the way Fat Tuesday is not the whole of Mardi Gras, but it is the last and most celebrated day. Which brings us to our ancestors and why they are celebrated on this day.

Like no other Holiday, Samhain speaks to us about death, thus reminding us of the value of life. On this day, it is considered common courtesy to invite our passed relatives back into our lives by preparing their favorite meals, telling their stories, and calling their names to the night. Candles are placed in bowls of milk and honey to invite wayward spirits. And what do we tell them when they arrive? That while we miss them, we know that we will be with them again, and for now we celebrate the days we have left.

Couples—When a couple addresses the grief of loss together, there is a symbiotic bond made. Yes, the member experiencing grief is most comforted, but the relationship between the two is strengthened, thus bringing benefit to both members. It is sometimes easier for a person to share grief and honestly address the issue with someone to whom that person is intimate.

In keeping with the theme of reflection, this is an excellent time for a couple to enter into their Book of Shadows their hopes for the new year, as well as to look back at what they wrote last year and discuss both successes and failures. It is also a time to reflect on matters that didn't make it into the book of shadows over the past year. Grievances and problems can be discussed, settled, and then written on a piece of paper for use in an outsider offering. This can be done simply by placing them into a burning fireplace.

Coven/Household—Where some would celebrate this Holiday solemnly, as one would a funeral, I say this more than any other Holiday is a time to dance and sing, showing those in our line that we enjoy and appreciate the gift of life that they bestowed upon us. What better way to do that than with kith and kin?

Standing in a circle, the host and hostess begin the Dance of the Dead by calling forth to the night the names of those who have come before, especially their mothers and fathers should they have passed. The prayer found in the introduction to this book is most appropriate. If you want to be dramatic, the host can hold the hostess to the sky as she reads the prayer. Yes, it was done in a movie, but as you will see when we come to our discussion about Winter Solstice, just because someone else does, it does not mean that you cannot.

The host and hostess are then charged with inviting others to call to their loved ones. If you have guests who are not members of your household, use your household members to guide them in these invitations. They can be loud, soft, spoken, or unspoken, but the spoken ones will cause others to come out of their shell and share the grief of loss. If host and hostess have achieved the right frame of mind ahead of time, their invitation will be sincere, and tears may flow. Those tears will lubricate the emotions of coven/household members and guests.

While the calls are going on, the host and hostess then invite folk to dance for their departed loved ones, to show those who have joined us from other realms that while we do miss them, we celebrate the life that they have given us. The dance can be of any theme. For the young and healthy, a slow drumbeat working into a frenzy can bring with it revelations from beyond. If this is the nature of your celebration, make sure everyone knows that they should identify their own limits and make allowances for the limits of others. There is no shame in retiring to the outside of the circle when exhaustion sets in. If the crowd is older or if you have chosen a more formal setting for the rite, something as slow as a waltz is most appropriate. Believe it or not, combining the two works well as demonstrated at The Real Witches Ball 2002.

Winter Solstice

Winter is at the mature/Master stage. Summer is entering the second trimester.

Also known as: Alban Arthan, Day of Children, Midwinter, Mother's Night, Return of the Sun, Saturnalia, Yule.

Date: Approximately December 21st or 22nd, this Holiday is actually found on the longest day of the year.

God associations: Cernunnos, Herne, Odin, Pan.

Goddess associations: Angerona, Colleda, Frigg, Koliada.

Gemstone associations: Bloodstone, Garnet, Ruby.

Plant associations: Apple, Bay, Cedar, Cinnamon, Clove, Ginger, Frankincense, Holly, Ivy, Juniper, Lemon, Mace, Mistletoe, Myrrh, Nutmeg, Orange, Sage, Pine, Rosemary.

Color associations: Gold, Green, Red, White, Yellow.

Winter Solstice Incense
4 Part Frankincense
1 Part Juniper Berry
1 Part Cedar

Winter Solstice Oil
10 drops Pine
4 drops Clove
2 drops Cinnamon
2 drops Juniper
1/2 ounce base oil

Solitary/General—If you have never read another book on Wicca, you can ignore this paragraph. If you have read other books on Wicca, this paragraph is vitally important in understanding my take on this Holiday. From my creation story, you understand that I consider the sun to be created of the masculine, but created by the feminine. This is important because although I do not personify the sun, I most certainly give it gender (not sex), that gender being feminine. Now if we were to personify the Sun, being created of masculine energy we would state that He is male. Note the use of the word male and not the word masculine.

Winter Solstice is one of the strongest reasons for associating the sun with the feminine half of divinity. We don't have to look beyond the Wiccan Rede to see that our Lord rules this Holiday, so why then would our Lord be associated with the Sun as the Sun is riding at its lowest point (the shortest day of the year). The answer is that the Sun is associated with the feminine half of divinity, so when it is at its lowest the masculine is at its highest. Of course the shortest day of the year is the one associated with the peak of our Lord's influence.

While all night drum circles are traditionally held to greet our Lord as the sun returns, I find those same drum circles are held to welcome the return of our Lady into his arms. What man can argue that he is not at his strongest when his love is returned to his arms? This season is, after all, also the Roman celebration of Mother's Night (Dec. 24th) and is followed by the Day of Children (Dec. 25th). If not in the arms of our Lord, just how would our Lady become Mother?

With this view we see that Winter Solstice is a Holiday of reunion and of returns. No wonder one of the most popular songs on the radio this time of the year is "I'll be home for Christmas." It has achieved such popularity because the old Pagan ways simply will not die, even when they are hidden in new religions. It is a time when we remind ourselves of what is important in life, our kith and kin.

Even though most of us no longer live directly from the harvest of previous Holidays, life has become harder since Samhain. Remember that this is the season where the suicide rate skyrockets, violent crime increases, and drunk drivers are at their worst. Your household might escape these things, but does it escape cabin fever? Remaining mostly indoors and in close contact with members of our household can often elevate minor annoyances into seemingly serious issues. Friends without a place to go often sit alone in tears, wondering if someday they will have a family of their own. Seasonal affective disorder nips at our soul even more than Jack Frost does at our toes. The driveway has to be shoveled; the heating bills rise, gas prices soar, slips and falls abound. All this and more brought out by the Dark half of the year. What better time for a party?

Couples—While it might seem difficult to separate couple from children on this Holiday, few can argue that in popular culture December 24th belongs more to the couple than the children. Sure, chances are they are only pretending to be asleep, but still there they are in the other room providing quiet time for Mom and Dad. Is there a better time for celebrating the joy of one's relationship? Even without having children, there is the celebration of the joy of other pleasures that have come from the couple's union. Taking time for just the two of you is most appropriate. Perhaps a romantic dinner or maybe something as simple as stealing some of Santa's cookies and sharing them under the mistletoe.

Take turns writing in your couple's Book of Shadows what has come from the relationship that you are thankful for. Exchange personal gifts. If it has been a particularly hard year, gifts of massage are most appropriate.

Coven/Household—I had a conversation with a friend who felt that her children were left out of the fun of Christmas because she was raising them in a traditional Pagan manner. "What do you mean?" I asked. She told me that she wanted to celebrate Yule on the right day, but her children are surrounded by the cultural celebration on December 25th. I was shocked. Has Wicca really come so far in our rebellion that we would reject traditional Pagan ways just because Christianity has capitalized on them?

Few disagree that the Pagan Yule was not a specific day; it was a range of 12 days, as evidenced by the popular Christmas carol "The Twelve Days of Christmas." Although there is some argument as to when the first day begins, I think the great amount of argument can be found in the same issues discussed in context of when any Holiday begins. For the 12 Days of Yule, I choose to think of the first day as beginning at the evening prior to the day of Solstice.

Counting 12 days forward, this yields the last day of Yule on approximately January 1st. An alternative way of looking at the Holiday is to blend it into popular culture and count backward from January 1st to find the first day on December 20th. Either way will only find a variance of a day or so. Now then, what does this say of the 25th? It says that the 25th falls almost perfectly at the center of the 12-day season of Yule. This is rather important when a study of the celebration of Yule finds that this mid-point was called Mother's Night. The day after was the Pagan celebration of children, Day of Children. When we take into consideration the ancient way of looking at the new day as starting at sundown, we see that a traditional Pagan celebration of Yule might indeed fall on December 25th. But why stop there? From both a modern cultural and ancient traditional viewpoint, this Holiday can be seen as beginning at Winter Solstice and ending on January 1st, so why not make use of each of those days?

Imbolg

Winter is at the senior/Sage stage. Summer is entering the third trimester.

Also known as: Anagantios, Blessing of the Plow, Candlemas, Disting, Disting-tid, Feast of Brigid, Feast of the Virgin, Festival of Milk, Ground Hog's Day, Imbolc, Oimelc.

Date: Approximately February 2nd, this Holiday is actually found on the day that rests in the middle of Winter Solstice and Spring Equinox.

Goddess associations: Brigid.

Gemstone associations: Amethyst, Turquoise.

Plant associations: Cinnamon, Dill, Dragon's Blood, Frankincense, Red Sandalwood, Snow Drop, Rosemary, Rowan and the wildflowers that have already started to flower.

Colors associations: Pink, White, Yellow.

Imbolg Incense

6 parts Frankincense

4 parts Dragon's Blood

2 part Red Sandalwood

1 part Cinnamon

Imbolg Oil

8 drops Frankincense

6 drops Rosemary

2 drops Cinnamon

Solitary/General—Imbolg is a fertility celebration of the first order of life. In popular culture, this is Groundhog's Day. While that might seem too pop culture for inclusion in a Wiccan bible, it is yet another Holiday that illustrates just how Pagan contemporary culture is. When German settlers arrived in Pennsylvania in the 1700s, they brought with them a Holiday they called Candlemas. The Holiday itself has deep Pagan roots, but the name Candlemas comes from the Christian service in which a priest blesses candles which are later placed in the windows of every home, welcoming the birth of Spring in the Pagan tradition.

At the time, the two seasons had already been replaced by four, so the point between Winter Solstice and Spring Equinox was seen as the middle of the Winter. German lore stated that if the day brings with it good weather, the second half of Winter (Candlemas till Spring Equinox) would be kind. There the tradition would have remained if not for the fact that the German settlers were not alone. At about the same time, the Delaware Indians established a campsite about half way between the Allegheny and Susquehanna rivers. That campsite would later be called Punxsutawney Pennsylvania, established in 1723. Today, the town is found 92 miles northeast of Pittsburgh at the crossroad of route 36 and route 119.

Those Native Americans believed humanity evolved from animals. In their lineage, they counted Wojak who was himself a groundhog and from whose name the common name woodchuck evolved. By February 4, 1841, we see the German tradition of Candlemas and the Native American tradition honoring the groundhog to have merged so well that Groundhog's Day was recorded as if it were a German Holiday:

"Last Tuesday, the 2nd, was Candlemas day, the day on which, according to the Germans, the Groundhog peeps out of his winter quarters and if he sees his shadow he pops back for another six weeks nap, but if the day be cloudy he remains out, as the weather is to be moderate."

—From the diary of James Morris' (shopkeeper from Morgantown, PA) [2]

So what is commonly called Groundhog's Day was a traditional Pagan rite of spring, adopted by Christianity, brought to the United States, mingled with Pagan traditions, and then introduced to a modern culture as folklore. It does seem like it would be an ideal choice for inclusion in our post-modern religion. After all, the Wiccan community has embraced the term Candlemas to refer to this Holiday, and that word is much more of the Catholic Church than is Groundhog's day.

Although this Holiday falls in the Dark half of the year, its name connects it to our Lady rather than our Lord. Imbolg literally means 'in belly.' In essence, the child that is Summer has entered the third trimester. Although not yet born, this is the point where parents and doctors can relax, knowing the as yet unborn child has reached a point where many developmental concerns are no longer issues. So pronounced is this stage in development that even the strongest proponent of the pro-life movement shudders at the idea of abortion in this stage of development. Indeed, this is the point where a child has a chance of living outside of his or her mother's womb.

This thought applied to the Wheel of the Year tells us that although Winter was certainly hard that we can relax just a bit because we know that Summer will surely be born at the next Holiday. Although they are not all visible, the signs of life are everywhere, just under the soil. The changing temperatures and melting snow have helped seeds to crack their outer shell, and sprouts have begun exiting their shell, slowly but consistently.

Couples—This is an excellent time to plant seeds indoors for later transfer to your garden. Done in Circle or in the kitchen, a couple that plants seeds together can watch their relationship grow with the season, then harvest the fresh seeds for the next, symbolically replanting the seeds of there love each year and harvesting the fruits of that love on later Holidays.

Coven/Household—In most parts of the world, it doesn't really matter if that groundhog sees his shadow or not. Either way it is still entirely too cold for outdoor rituals. But there is always the chance that the sun will be out and with a little bit of work, a group can stay warm. Why not honor the old ways brought from Germany and plan the coven/household celebration in two parts, one indoor and the other outdoors.

When everyone has gathered, break out a couple shovels and see if you can turn the earth in your garden. If so, the celebration is outdoors and involves getting the garden ready for planting. If not, then the celebration moves indoors where you can ready seeds into peat pots to give them a head start indoors.

Spring Equinox

Winter is at the death stage and begins the cycle of rebirth. Summer is at the birth stage and ends the cycle of rebirth.

Also known as: Alban Eilir, Bacchanalia, Bealtaine, Beltane, Children's Bealtaine, Easter, Eostre's Day, Lady Day, Ostara, Waxing Equinox

Date: Approximately March 21st or 22nd, this Holiday is actually found in the Spring on the day when the length of night and day is equal.

Goddess association: Aurora, Black Annis, Eos, Eostre, Ostara

Gemstone associations: Aquamarine, Moonstone, Rose Quartz

Animal associations: Chicken, Duck, Bee

Plant associations: Daffodil, Dragon's Blood, Benzoin, Ginger, Frankincense, Gorse, Iris, Jasmine, Narcissus, Nutmeg, Olive, Orange, Peony, Rose, Sandalwood, Violet, Woodruff, and all flowers that have already started to bloom.

Color associations: Blue, Pink, Red, *Yellow or White & Black (together equally)

* Yellow or White to represent the day with equal amounts of Black to represent the night. Each is appropriate only with an equal amount of the other.

Spring Equinox Incense

4 parts Frankincense

2 parts Benzoin

1 parts Dragons blood

1 part Rose petals

1 part Orange peel

Spring Equinox Oil

8 drops Frankincense

6 drops Nutmeg

6 drops Rose or 3 drops Orange and 3 drops Ginger

Solitary/General—Spring Equinox is a fertility celebration of the second order of life. From culture to culture, Bealtaine moves either direction on the wheel of the year by 45 degrees. Most often, when it was not celebrated between Spring Equinox and Summer Solstice, it was celebrated here on Spring Equinox. As such, the associations between Bealtaine and Spring Equinox sometimes cross. Generally speaking, both Spring Equinox and Bealtaine celebrate fertility in all orders. However, Bealtaine stresses human fertility and Spring Equinox celebrates the fertility of other animals (let's say rabbits and egg laying critters). Surprise, surprise…one of the folk names for Spring Equinox is Easter.

Around this time of the year, customers often walk into my shop chuckling about the fertility images they saw on Christian gravesites. I have to chuckle a bit myself, but not with them. No, I find myself chuckling at those customers. Yes, the eggs and bunny rabbit imagery is associated with fertility and with birth, but this Holiday does not just mark the rebirth of Summer and of our Lady. It also marks the death of Winter and the cycle of rebirth beginning for our Lord. Here, we see again the connection between life and death, neither existing without the other. It seems only natural that we would decorate those gravesites with the symbols of life.

Sometimes called Children's Bealtaine (or Beltane), this Holiday is not only a celebration of animal fertility, it is a celebration of the common result of human fertility: children. Donations to charities that serve children are most appropriate at this time as are presents given to children of all relations. Chocolate and other candy shaped in the symbols of the season are most appropriate. For older children, nuts and eggs make great gifts. Remember that children are not only a blessing to the mother and father. They are a blessing to the Coven/Household. Share them with your kith and kin. Your kids will love it, as it will provide them with multiple streams of candy.

Couples—Because we live in a predominantly Christian culture, there is a great chance the extended family will be Christian. As such, there may well be a rift between the couple and extended family. In some cases, one family might be accepting of the couple's Wiccan ways, and the other might not be to keen on the idea. This is an excellent opportunity to bridge that gap. Couples focussing on making Equinox (Easter) eggs and baskets in their own private rites might go a long way towards furthering communication by sharing those creations with the extended family.

Coven/Household—Culturally speaking, we see public Easter egg hunts and games designed to promote community. Why not? After all, not only are those eggs a symbol of the animal fertility associated with this Holiday, but the very practice of hunting those eggs comes from the ancient practice of hunting for eggs and nuts to be given as gifts of fertility. Today, some of the largest of these community egg hunts are often held at local zoos. What better way of sharing the true Pagan meaning of this celebration with our children?

Ah, but what about those of us without children? Well now, we are all still children somewhere inside.

Bealtaine

Summer is at the youth/Maiden stage. Winter is entering the first trimester.

Also known as: Beltane, Cyntefyn, May Day, May Eve, Lover's Beltane, Lover's Bealtaine, Roodmass, Cetsamhain, Walpurgis.

Date: Approximately April 30th or May 1st, this Holiday is actually found on the day that rests in the middle of Spring Equinox and Summer Solstice.

God associations: Bile, Cernunnos, Herne, Pan.

Goddess associations: Green Lady.

Gemstone associations: Bloodstone, Sapphire.

Plant associations: Frankincense, Hawthorne, Honeysuckle, Jasmine, Sandalwood, St. John's Wort, Rose, Rosemary, Woodruff, and all flowers in bloom.

Color associations: Green, Yellow, Red.

Bealtaine Incense

4 parts Frankincense

2 parts Gum Arabic

2 parts Sandalwood

1 part Jasmine

1 part Rosemary

Bealtaine Oil

8 drops Frankincense

6 drops Rosemary

4 drops Rose

1/2 cup base oil

Solitary/General—Bealtaine is a fertility celebration of the third order of life and the first Holiday of Summer in the same way Samhain is the first Holiday of Winter. As a result, Bealtaine is sometimes cited as the point where the Light and Dark Halves of the year are split. The line is drawn on the Wheel of the Year between Bealtaine and Samhain. However, keeping with the theme that the Holidays are marked at the end of their season and observing the fact that we see rather clear lore that Bealtaine was celebrated at different points on the Wheel, most notably at Spring Equinox, I choose to recognize Bealtaine as the season that begins at Spring Equinox and is celebrated on this day. Thus, rather than drawing a line from the day of Bealtaine to the day of Samhain to separate Summer and Winter, I draw the line 45 degrees earlier, separating the two seasons at the beginning of the Bealtaine season.

More than any other association, this is a celebration of human fertility, but do not confuse that fertility with sex. Certainly, sex is an aspect of this Holiday that is rarely ignored, but when we say Wicca is a fertility religion we mean only that we use sex or symbolic sex (ritual) to illustrate what is really going on. No more is the actual Great Rite a reference to sex than it is a reference to the union of athame and chalice. The real Great Rite in Wicca is the mingling of souls, and the real fertility of Wicca is that which comes from the mingling of those souls. It is in that order of fertility that we receive the hidden knowledge of the magickal child, that which is conceived in union— not a physical manifestation of fertility (a baby), but that which is fertility itself, Love. That, my friend, is what Bealtaine is all about. Love in the order of romance.

Couples—Far be it for me to dictate love sport or the way that couples express their mind and soul with their body, but I will make suggestions in the hopes that you understand the nature of this Holiday. Yes, it is associated with sex but it is more so associated with the chase and game of courtship. It is a playful Holiday and with that in mind, I suggest the following sport. However, feeling very much that the first time a couple makes love should be unrehearsed, I suggest these activities only to lovers already initiated to each other.

Sometimes called Lover's Bealtaine (Beltane), this is a day of love sport. Yes, I did say sport. It is a time to make a game of the art and act of physical love. If you want to be bold, visit your local adult bookstore and bring home a few games designed for you and your partner. If you want something a bit more modest, find a public park and play a game of tag. Set a time limit and then stand facing each other, one partner the chased and the other the pursuer. The chased is given a head start and the game begins. If the pursuer can catch the chased within the designated amount of time, the pursuer wins. If not, the chased wins.

Ah, but what does a person win? Be inventive with love sport. Perhaps, after moving to a more private and preferably legal location, the looser lays completely motionless as his or her lover provides pleasure. It has been my observation that in symbiotic relationships with any degree of shared empathy, this prize causes both partners to be winners. If the lover's sport leading to this suggestion of reward does not suite your taste, consider making sport of the reward I suggested.

Ask your partner to lie completely still and completely sky clad on your bed. Using light touch and kiss, see if you can't get your partner to move. If s/he does move of his/her own accord, switch so you are the one attempting to remain motionless. This game has no point system or designated method of conclusion. You will know it is over when you both toss out the rules.

Another simple love sport is for two lovers to stand clad only by the sky at about conversational distance from each other. Looking directly into each other's eyes, caress each other's bodies without actually touching each other. Imagine there is an infinitely thin force field around each other and try to skirt the boundaries of that force field while not entering it. If you touch skin, your partner receives a point. After a predetermined amount of time, maybe the time it takes for a stick of patchouli incense to burn from top to bottom, the one with the most points wins and receives whatever prize was predetermined. Alternatively, you can do away with the idea of a prize or point system and simply allow this game to end as did the one I listed prior.

Coven/Household—Of course, Bealtaine is not just about having sex. It is the connections, romantic in nature, which we have made, as well as the connections others have made. If your brother or sister has children but you do not, consider offering to baby-sit for this Holiday such that s/he can enjoy love sport with his or her spouse. Make it clear in your offering that you want them to have a romantic evening and then celebrate a second Children's Bealtaine with their children. If you have children of your own, take turns with another responsible couple.

Summer Solstice

Summer is at her mature/Mother stage. Winter is entering the second trimester.

Also known as: Alban Hefin, *Beltane, Litha, *Midsummer, Vestalia, Whitsuntide.
Date: Approximately June 21st or 22nd, this Holiday is actually found on the longest day of the year.
God associations: Jahnis, Mannan, Puck.
Goddess associations: Vesta, Xilonen.

Gemstone associations: Emerald, Jade, Lapis, Tigers Eye.

Plant associations: Apple, Benzoin, Carnation, Chamomile, Daisy, Dragon's Blood, Elder, Fern, Frankincense, Gardenia, Ivy, Lavender, Lemon, Lemon Balm, Lilly, Mugwort, Oak, Orange, Rose, Rosemary, Saffron, Sandalwood, Thyme, Vervain, Yarrow.

Color associations: Gold, Green, Yellow, White.

* Summer Solstice is an example of how the traditional Holidays sometimes jumped around. There is clear indication that Bealtaine was celebrated by some at this point on the Wheel as is Midsummer, whose name is sometimes seen to denote the middle of the two seasons, Winter and Summer, or to Lughnasadh, which is found at the middle of Summer with the view of the year as having four seasons. Additional confusion comes into play when we consider the fact that Lughnasadh is often cited as a month-long festival. Again we see the reason each Sabbat should be considered a season between spokes, ending on the day typically marked by the spoke of the Wheel of the Year.

Summer Solstice Incense

4 parts Sandalwood

1 part Benzoin

1 part Dragon's blood

Summer Solstice Oil

8 drops Lavender

4 drops Lemon

4 drops Sandalwood

2 drops Orange

     Solitary/General—Summer Solstice is the longest day of the year. As such, we revel in the Sun but also celebrate its dwindling. This day is a day to say thank you for all the things that the Sun brings (growth) but also what it does not (draught). Remember that as seen in Babylonian and Sumerian lore, in some parts of the world this is the peak of the barren summer months when sweltering heat destroys crops and vegetation. While we do not generally experience such solar destruction on a regular basis, there are definitely seasons in which draught and excess heat is abundant. In such circumstances, this is a celebration to mark the end of the heat and draught as the sun travels past its peak. Much like Winter Solstice celebrates the waxing of the Sun because lack of Sun is a hardship, this Holiday celebrates the waning of the Sun because too much sun is also a hardship. At the moment of imbalance we celebrate the return to balance.

     Couples—Couples wishing to conceive should make love in a fertile field. Should a woman's partner not be able to join her in this rite, simply walking in a fertile field is said to improve her chances of conception later that night.

     Coven/Household—Cakes and cookies shaped like the sun are often baked as a part of the household activities. These are served during the feast as a reminder of what is being celebrated. This Holiday is associated with both Fire and Water. As you can well imagine, the season itself has probably provided the fire, so why not take it upon yourself to provide the water? Gatherings around swimming pools and other spots where a person might cool off and restore balance are very appropriate. Vanilla and mint ice cream make wonderful deserts for this celebration, as does lemon Italian ice.

If the summer heat is not enough or if you want the visuals of a fire, the evening will be greatly complimented with a roaring bonfire, drumming, and dancing. However, hosts and hostesses should pay close attention to their guests' hydration and signs of hot weather injuries. Remember that ritual is sacred theater that celebrates real life, and as the heat is very real it will be an influence on your ritual. Should the Summer be particularly hot, rites based on the story of Persephone are appropriate without respect to which side of the equator one finds oneself. This is a wonderful way to educate children as to the importance of balance.

Lughnasadh

Summer is at the senior/Crone stage. Winter is entering the third trimester.

Also known as: Ceresalia, Elembius, First Harvest, Lad Day, *Midsummer, Lammas, Thing's Tide.

Date: Approximately July 31st, August 1st or 2nd, this Holiday is actually found on the day that rests in the middle of Summer Solstice and Fall Equinox.

God associations: Lugh.

Gemstone associations: Citrine, Peridot.

Plant associations: All Grains that Harvest Early (especially Rye), Blackberry, Crab Apple, Frankincense, Ginseng, Grapes and Grapevine, Heather, Lavender, Pear, Potato, Sloe Berries.

Color associations: Green, Orange, Red, Yellow.

* See Summer Solstice

Lughnasadh Incense
4 parts Frankincense
2 parts Lavender
1 part Heather

Lughnasadh Oil
10 drops Frankincense
10 drops Lavender

Solitary/General—It is likely the name Lughnasadh comes from the god Lugh. In their book *Eight Sabbats for Witches*, the Farrars tell us the translation is 'the commemoration of Lugh.' I like to call it 'Lugh's Night'. Now remember, I do very much believe Wicca is a world religion, but as this is the name so many use to note this Holiday we should wonder: Just who is Lugh?

Lugh is sometimes called Lugh Samhioldanach, which means 'Lugh of the many arts.' Other times he is called Lugh Lamhfhada, which means 'Lugh of the long hand.' Although Winter Solstice and the cultural gift giving season is still several months off, this is an excellent time to incorporate crafts into one's Holiday activities. The weather is good enough that spending long hours looking for pinecones, acorns, and other natural materials to make Yule ornaments and gifts will be pleasant and fruitful.

Couple—Love sport is most appropriate to this Holiday, especially games involving a chase theme. This Holiday often marks the first harvest, the first capture (harvest) after a season of tending to the crops (chase). Even if finances are a bit stretched, spending a bit of extra money on a nice dinner or entertainment with the theme of ushering future harvests is an excellent way to include sympathetic spellcraft into this rite. Remember, like attracts like. Lughnasadh celebrates much more than the fertility of the field. It is also tied to the marriage and fertility rites of Lugh and his bride. This is the day on which the first Wiccan rite of Handfasting is based, the day of the Brehon marriages, which are trial marriages that could be undone by returning to the same spot after a year and a day.

Coven/Household—This is a time of introspect for Covens and Households. The first harvest has been taken in and from it one can begin to judge what the next harvests will be like. With that information, one can begin to judge what the Winter food supply will look like. Although most of us do not live directly off the land, there are some equally pressing issues facing covens and households.

In general, many covens do not take on new members in the Winter because traditionally that which a coven or household requires to survive that winter (food and supplies) has already been calculated and set aside. An interesting correlation to this principle is that when one faces reality, a modern household or coven has certain monetary requirements. As heating bills rise, household income decreases. Soon the cultural Holidays will be upon us, and our income will be taxed. This is a good time to discuss pooling resources, maybe setting aside coven monies should one member find themselves short when trying to pay their heating bills or buying gifts for their children. Hosting public festivals in order to raise capital for such eventualities is not overly capitalistic.

Fall Equinox

Summer is at the death stage and begins the cycle of rebirth. Winter is reborn.

Also known as: Alban Elfer, Harvest, Mabon, Festival of Dionysus, Second Harvest, Waning Equinox, Wine Harvest.

Date: Approximately September 21st or 22nd this Holiday is actually found in the Fall on the day when the length of day and night is equal.

God associations: Dionysus, Damuzi.

Gemstone associations: Amethyst, Topaz.

Plant associations: Acorns, Apple, Aspen, Corn, Cypress (especially cones), Frankincense, Grape, Hazelnuts (and to some extent all nuts), Hops, Juniper, Oak, Oak Moss, Pine (especially cones), Sandalwood, Wheat (especially stalks).

Color associations: Brown, Orange, *Purple, **Yellow or White and Black (together equally).

* Purple is an association if observing this Holiday with its associations to Dionysus.

** Yellow or white to represent the day with equal amounts of black to represent the night. Each is appropriate only with an equal amount of the other.

Fall Equinox Incense

4 parts Frankincense

2 parts Sandalwood

1 part Cypress

1 part Juniper berries

Fall Equinox Oil

6 parts Frankincense

6 parts Sandalwood

4 parts Cypress

2 parts Juniper

Solitary/General—We find ourselves again at a seasonal balance. The days and nights are equal, and the second harvest is in. Feasting is welcome, but excess is ill advised, as this is a day of balance. Remember that there is only one more harvest before Winter. It is a time of meditation and thought. How has the year gone? What will be needed for the pending Winter?

It is also a good time for the Solitary to find community. The nights will get longer and longer for each of the next six months. With those long nights comes depression as our bodies give into seasonal affective disorder. The cultural holiday season is right around the corner, and minds tend to turn inward if they have no place to turn outward. That is to say, get out of the house because in just a short time it will be difficult to do so. It is also a time for the general community to find solitaries for the same reasons.

Couples—When someone thinks of Wiccan holidays, they typically think of a full moon and bonfire late at night. Now I am sure everyone loves a good bonfire and moonlit evening, but there is something very special about this holiday for parents of school aged children. It is the first one after their children's Summer vacation. While that might not seem like much for those without children, I am told it is a great blessing to parents. As such, this is an excellent day for both parents to take off from work and enjoy the day rekindling their love for one another. After all, the stress of being cooped up in the home is right around the corner with Winter's approach.

Coven/Household—This is a grain harvest. Although corn has not been a traditional part of European lore, today it is a staple. As such, if you should live in a region where corn is ready to come in, kettles and grills can be used to create a veritable corn feast. If you can, find a farmer willing to sell whole stalks. Soak the ears in seawater without shucking them and place them on the grill. If you do not have access to seawater, mix sea salt with fresh water and soak away. Then make it a feast of shucking as you eat.

Ah, but what of the stalks? Although we are still a month and a half away from Samhain, we are only a day until the season of Samhain begins. Why not put those stalks to good use, making dolls and stands of corn stalks for decorations, protection, and blessings? Remember, in just a month and a half the Pooka will begin cursing whatever crops have not been harvested, so he is probably starting to have a look see right now.

Liber ab Luna
(The Book of the Moon)

An Exploration of the Esbats
or The Book of Twelve, Part I

 started the research for this chapter what seems like decades ago. Someone asked me why it is that Witches' covens have 13 members. I explained the idea that a Coven must have 13 members is a myth. Sure, it was perpetuated in the early days when Wicca was first being introduced, but the word coven is simply a spooky term for a collection of kith and kin, and any specific number is just a misconception. The research started when my friend asked why there is a perception that Witches' covens have a leader and 12 Witches, and I had no answer to give. This chapter is my answer.

In addition to the eight solar Holidays, many Wiccans mark the cycles of the Moon. As you recall, I mentioned the belief that the word *Sabbat* is probably just another one of those spooky words invented by demonologists for the purpose of slandering the religious practices of folk who were not Christian. Perhaps you have heard another scary term, *Esbat*. Chances are, this is yet another made up term. The difference between the words *Sabbat* and *Esbat* is that one was made up a lot later than the other was.

Prior to the 20th century, the word *Esbat* seems to have appeared only once. In the writings of Pierre de Lancre, the author claims one French Witch used the word *Esbat* to refer to a Witches' gathering. The use of the word was likely either a misprint, misunderstood, or slang version of the French term *s'esbattre*, which means 'to frolic.' Although Pierre de Lancre was clear in the use of that word being a general reference to the gatherings of Witches, by the time Dr. Murray encountered the reference she had already decided that all Witches everywhere used the word *Sabbat* to describe those gatherings. This is an important point because a great deal of what Gerald Gardner claimed was an ancient religion when he introduced his tradition to the public was in fact based largely on Dr. Murray's books. Rather than recognizing the fact that different cultures use different words to describe the same thing, she took it upon herself to decide the word *Esbat* was another of the universal Witch words. As such, she had to invent a meaning other than the one she assigned to *Sabbat*. As she had decided the word *Sabbat* was a reference to a holiday, then *Esbat* must be a workday despite its origin in a word denoting frolic. Eventually, maybe via Gardner, the note that the *Sabbats* were marked by the sun probably lent itself well to the evolution of the *Esbats* as being marked by the moon. Today, many folk use the word Esbat to refer to the full moon.

In the Book of Sun, I said the Sabbats are better termed holidays. Here I tell you the Esbats are better termed meetings. Although not nearly as spooky as the other words, they do convey meaning much better. It's not really a hard concept to grasp; a household/coven celebrates Holidays together and it has household/coven meetings separate from those celebrations. Although the word *Esbat* was not used by pre-Christian fertility religions, if a group were to schedule monthly meetings they would have likely based those meetings on the lunar cycles because those cycles were their calendar. Setting a date like the full moon is not unlike a modern group stating that it will meet on the second Tuesday of each month.

This is not to say that Wiccans do not mark the cycles of the Moon with holidays and celebrations. In fact, a large amount of lunar lore has come to be connected with the eight solar holidays. Although it might seem shocking, although we celebrate the eight solar holidays on dates determined by the Earth's travel around the Sun, that concept is not exactly universal. This is most notably with Samhain and Bealtaine. Before the modern Pagan movement decided to place Samhain between the Fall Equinox and Winter Solstice, its day of celebration was marked by lunar cycles. Likewise, prior to Bealtaine being marked half way between Spring Equinox and Summer Solstice, it was marked by lunar cycles as well.

As mentioned in Book of Three Part II, the cycles of the moon have been connected to our Lady in popular lore. As Maiden she is connected to the new and waxing moon, as Mother to the full moon, and as Crone to the dark and waning moon.

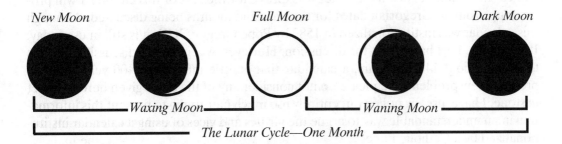

New Moon   Full Moon   Dark Moon

Waxing Moon   Waning Moon

The Lunar Cycle—One Month

'The Waxing and Waning Moon'

Chances are you will not often find a similar association to our Lord. Instead, you are more likely to see a solar cycle assigned to our Lord. Looking at popular books on Wicca, one might think that all goddesses are Moon Goddesses and all gods are Sun Gods. Historically speaking this simply has not been the case. There have in fact been many masculine personifications of the moon and moon gods.

Some of the Many Moon Gods

Moon God	Origin	Moon God	Origin
Aglibol	Middle East	Menu	Middle East/
Amm	Middle East		Mediterranean
Aningan	Greenland	Meness	Central Europe
Apocatequil	South America	Menulis	Central Europe
Arebati	Africa	Metztli	North America
Arma	Middle East	Nannar	Middle East
Avatea	Polynesian Islands	Napir	Near East
Chandra	Near East	Si	South America
Fati	Polynesian	Sin	Middle East
Gou	Africa	Soma	Near East
Ilmaqah	Middle East	Ta'lab	Middle East
Igaluk	Arctic North America	Taukiyomi	Far East
Itzamna	Central America	Tecciztecatl	North America
Jarih	Middle East	Terah	Middle East
Jayce	South America	Toruguenket	South America
Khons	Africa	Varuna	Near East
Kusuh	Middle East	Wadd	Middle East
Mah	Middle East	Yerah	Middle East
Mao	Near East		

To make matters just a bit easier to express, for the rest of this chapter I will provide approximate Gregorian dates for the days and months being discussed. Although this calendar was institutionalized in 1582 by Pope Gregory XIII, it is still in use today. It makes the best base point for discussion. However, when we are discussing matters that span about 140,000 years, a calendar that is little more than 400 years old will present a few problems. So please do not consider any of the dates given here to be set in stone. I have already pulled out entirely too much hair trying to present this information in an understandable way to argue the virtues and vices of using a calendar institutionalized by a Catholic Pope.

The Hindu Calendar

In the Middle East, a god was associated with each of the year's moons (each month). The following are those gods presented with the name of the moon they are associated with and the modern approximation. Collectively known as the Adityas, the Hindu moon gods sometimes appear with a few alternative names. The most common are: Ansa, Aryman, Bhaga, Daksha, Dhatri, Indra, Mitra, Ravi, Savitri, Surya, Varuna, and Yama. Historically, the names have changed, sometimes seemingly to exchange with the name of the month itself. Please note that the Hindu calendar begins with Chaitra on March 22nd; however, I have arranged the months starting with the first month, which has days in January, to relate more easily to our modern Gregorian calendar.

The Hindu Wheel of the Year

Month	Gregorian Start	Gregorian End	God
Pausa	December 22	January 20	Pusha
Magha	January 21	February 19	Bhaga
Chaitra	March 22	April 20	Vishnu
Vaisakha	April 21	May 21	Aryman
Jyaistha	May 22	June 21	Vivasvana
Asadha	June 22	July 22	Amshumana
Shravana	July 23	August 22	Parjanya
Bhardra	August 23	September 22	Varuna
Asvini	September 23	October 22	Indra
Kartika	October 23	November 21	Dhatri
Agrahayana	November 22	December 21	Mitra
Phalguna	February 20	March 21*	Tvashta

* 21 on leap year.

So just why is the moon found in so many different religions? The most obvious answer is because it is there. That might sound like a very short answer, but the existence of a thing is all it takes for religion to address its existence because that's one of the primary functions of religion. Religion, science, and magick were for a time inseparable subjects. They were separated by power structures that didn't have much faith in the religion they used to assert their authority. Fearing science might some day prove the earth was not the center of the universe, they made the heliocentric (sun at center) view of the universe illegal and imprisoned its teachers. It is not an unfamiliar story. Remember the Scopes Monkey trial discussed earlier?

Like science, one of the roles of religion is to explain why things exist and what their nature is. At the dawn of humanity, someone looked up and asked, "Hey, what's that?" Not long after that, someone came along and explained it: That is god. Sometime before Newton, someone observed that the ocean's tide rose and fell with the cycle of the moon and someone said "That is goddess," because they observed that the tides of menstruation seemed to come and go with various stages of the moon, both on a monthly cycle.

From observing those cycles, a pattern emerged to compliment the pattern of Summer and Winter. That pattern, the lunar cycles, served as a primitive calendar. I say primitive because as we will soon see, the calendar was not all that accurate in keeping track of seasonal changes. In short, the seasons are a function of the Earth's relationship to the sun. The cycle in which the Earth travels around the sun is called the solar year. The lunar cycle (month) is a function of the relationship between the sun, moon, and the Earth. The solar cycle (year) is approximately 365 days. The lunar cycle is 29 days long, but let's use modern science to be a bit more exact: One day is 24 hours, or the amount of time it takes the Earth to rotate once; one month is 29.531 days, or 708.744 hours, or the amount of time it takes for any one phase of the moon to be repeated, dark to dark, full to full, new to new or any portion thereof.

One year is 12 months, so to find the length of a year we can take 29.531 and multiply that by 12, and we should come up with that familiar figure 365 days. And that is exactly what we would come up with if there were indeed 12 months in the year, but there are not. If there were, the year would be 354.372 days long. What about those other 10.62 days? Wouldn't they accumulate and wind up adding an extra month every 2.78 or so years? They would, which is why the lunar calendar is not the best choice for tracking annual events. It is, however, an excellent tool in tracking monthly events when a modern calendar is not available. One needs only look into the sky to get a general idea what time of the month it is.

But instead of adopting a strictly solar calendar, attempt after attempt was made to justify the Moon and solar cycles. Now, many of them were rather ingenious, but none were ideal for the masses that did not possess a level of education that permitted their understanding. So chances are Murray, in inventing the modern use of the words *Sabbat* and *Esbat,* was on to something after all. Not because either word was used by the ancient Pagans, but because once a year events (celebrations) were best marked by a solar calendar, and routine things, matters of kith and kin, were best marked as by a lunar calendar.

This is about how most Wiccans find their practice today. Larger festivals are marked on the solar calendar and private or small group celebrations sometimes occur on the full moon. But in saying that, please do not confuse the idea of a lunar month with the current 12 months of the year. Although those months were definitely fashioned on the many attempts to synchronize the lunar months with the solar year, our modern calendar is a strictly solar calendar with nothing more than the names of the months borrowed from the older attempts at fusing the two. It could just as easily have 11 or 12 months. For evidence of this fact, just look at your calendar and notice how the full moon wanders about it from month to month.

The Celtic Moon Calendar

This is why the so-called 'Celtic Moon Calendar' of popular-Pagan culture seems to change from book to book. Even if we set aside the fact that the Celts were a vastly diverse group, having different words, cultures, and names not only for the lunar cycles but for the gods and goddesses themselves and also set aside the difficulty in determining the number of months in a year, we are left with the question: When does the year start? Although it might seem like a no-brainer that the solar year starts at Winter Solstice, we have to remember that the Winter Solstice was not marked by the ancient Celts.

To make matters even more maddening, I am sure you have heard Samhain called the Celtic New Year. Well, Samhain's counterpart is Bealtaine, which has historically been referenced as Cetsamhain, which means 'opposite Samhain.' Now, we know that Bealtaine moved about on the calendar by about a month and a half in either direction, so it stands to reason that Samhain—which is 'opposite' Bealtaine on the Wheel of the Year—also moved around a bit. Does anyone really believe that the moon accommodated the placements of these celebrations? So then, if the names given to the lunar cycles are valid and are in the right order, where on Earth would we start counting them? Let's say the Wolf Moon is the first moon of the year. Is that the first moon after the Winter Solstice that the ancient Celts did not mark? Or is it the first moon after Samhain, which could occur more than a month prior to October 31st or a month after? Is there an answer?

I think the answer is that it does not matter. A far superior calendar has been invented, and that calendar is so ingrained into our culture that it will be around for a long time. However, for the sake of discussion I will share how I count the lunar cycles by name should I ever want to do that. Please note that in the past, I have counted these by the full moon. Today I have a greater understanding of the Greek and Roman calendars that led to our modern calendar, so I count them by the new moon. I begin with the first new moon after the Winter Solstice.

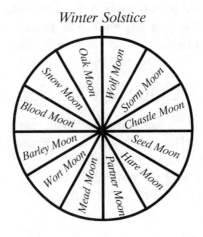

The Celtic Moon Calendar

Moon Count	Name of Moon	Pop Pagan Month
First New Moon	Wolf Moon	January
Second New Moon	Storm Moon	February
Third New Moon	Chaste Moon	March
Fourth New Moon	Seed Moon	April
Fifth New Moon	Hare Moon	May
Sixth New Moon	Partner Moon	June
Seventh New Moon	Mead Moon	July
Eighth New Moon	Wort Moon	August
Ninth New Moon	Barley Moon	September
Tenth New Moon	Blood Moon	October
Eleventh New Moon	Snow Moon	November
Twelfth New Moon	Oak Moon	December

Ah, but what about the Blue Moon? Well, that is a tough one. Most folk like to say that the Blue Moon is a full moon that occurs as the second full moon of any given month. As a lunar cycle is a month, I do not entertain such nonsense. Instead, I just set aside those 10.62 days and don't give them a name. Or I say they are part of the Blue Moon that occurs every 2.78 or so years and I am saving them up until it comes around again. The Blue Moon is thus the full lunar cycle of the solar year that begins with the thirteenth new moon of a solar year and ends in that same solar year. It is not an exact system, but as you are about to discover it is as good as any.

The Celtic Tree Calendar

Another interesting calendar found in pop-Pagan culture is the Celtic Tree Calendar. It is sometimes called the Druid Tree Calendar or the Ogham Tree Calendar. Like many things adopted by the Pagan community as fact, this is also speculation. Now, do not misunderstand my position. I am not convinced the tree calendar is bunk at all. I just don't believe there is significant historic fact to believe it is entirely as it is often presented.

The premise of this calendar was supported in one of the books most often cited on the subject within the Pagan community, *The White Goddess* by Robert Graves. The author supports the theory of the Tree calendar with a historic poem, which has come to be known as "The Stag of Seven Tines." Despite the fact that Graves' support of the Tree Calendar has been widely challenged by current academic authors who have the benefit of the years of discovery that were not available to Graves at the time his theory was put forth to support the Tree Calendar, the poem itself has been embraced by the Wiccan community. Most notably, it has been included in the rituals presented by our beloved Janet and Stewart Farrar. Despite the difference in opinion between the Pagan and academic communities, I feel the Tree Calendar deserves a place in our community and believe the information presented here will help to further its inclusion by addressing not only its supporters but also its detractors. With that goal, I present three theories about the ancient Celtic year.

The Ancient Celtic Tree Calendar (Theory 1—The least accurate)

Presented as the first theory is how I received it as a teen. Since that time, I have noted that this system is also the most often cited in the Pagan community. It is a 13-part division of the year with an extra day or two at the end of the year to adjust the lunar cycle to the solar cycle. The last day of the year is seen as a day outside of the year, and while this may be confusing, calling that day a day is not very accurate. It might be a couple of days depending on how the solar year and lunar months line up. This is the source of the Wiccan term 'A year and a day.' Most claim it means one year (365 days) and a day (1 day) for a total of 366 days. It is actually a Celtic year (approximately 364 days) and a day (approximately 1 day) for a total of 365 days or modern year.

To add just a bit more confusion to the matter, Samhain (Gregorian approximation October 31) is often cited as the Celtic New Year's Eve with November 1 cited as the first day of the Celtic Winter. Thus, because the Celts followed the principle of counting in the order of Darkness before Light, the new year began on November 1st— the first day of Winter and the Dark half of the year. I believe this is not true if we consider Samhain to be a single day. Instead, if we consider it to be a season that is marked at conclusion, we see a different story unfolding. If that is how we address the months, we see that a more accurate way of approaching the months of the Celtic Year would be to start at the first new moon after Fall Equinox. That being the case, the first month in the Celtic Tree Calendar would be Gort. If, on the other hand, we say that the first day of the new year is the day after Samhain, then we would say that the first month is Ruis.

Whichever you choose, I have arranged the chart to depict the Celtic Tree Calendar starting with Beth for two reasons. First, Beth is most representative of January, and January is where we start the new solar year. The second, and perhaps more entertaining reason, is that if we choose to believe what all those Pagan books say about Samhain being the Celtic New Year and we choose to believe that the Celtic Tree Calendar is valid, then we are left with a major paradox. You see, if we use the Celtic Tree Calendar, we are forced to accept that which Robert Graves used to support its premise, "The Stag of Seven Tines." In doing that, the first month of the year is Beth, which is as I have ordered the months. To be most accurate, the chances of a solar-marked day (Solstice or Equinox) and a lunar-marked day (new moon) lining up perfectly are slim. Therefore, in considering the approximate Gregorian dates, know that I have set these dates as the most commonly cited but rectify them against the first new

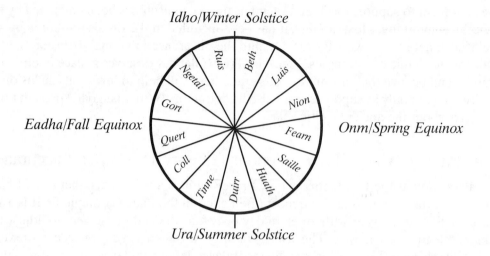

Idho/Winter Solstice

Eadha/Fall Equinox

Onm/Spring Equinox

Ura/Summer Solstice

The Celtic Tree Calendar

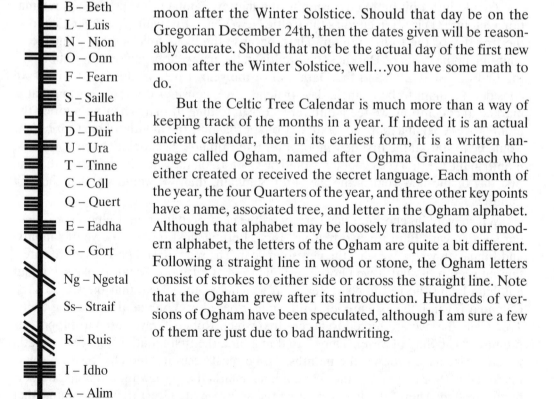

B – Beth
L – Luis
N – Nion
O – Onn
F – Fearn
S – Saille
H – Huath
D – Duir
U – Ura
T – Tinne
C – Coll
Q – Quert
E – Eadha
G – Gort
Ng – Ngetal
Ss– Straif
R – Ruis
I – Idho
A – Alim
Ph – Phagos

The Ogham

moon after the Winter Solstice. Should that day be on the Gregorian December 24th, then the dates given will be reasonably accurate. Should that not be the actual day of the first new moon after the Winter Solstice, well…you have some math to do.

But the Celtic Tree Calendar is much more than a way of keeping track of the months in a year. If indeed it is an actual ancient calendar, then in its earliest form, it is a written language called Ogham, named after Oghma Grainaineach who either created or received the secret language. Each month of the year, the four Quarters of the year, and three other key points have a name, associated tree, and letter in the Ogham alphabet. Although that alphabet may be loosely translated to our modern alphabet, the letters of the Ogham are quite a bit different. Following a straight line in wood or stone, the Ogham letters consist of strokes to either side or across the straight line. Note that the Ogham grew after its introduction. Hundreds of versions of Ogham have been speculated, although I am sure a few of them are just due to bad handwriting.

The Celtic Tree Calendar at a Glance (Theory 1—Least Accurate)

Month	Tree	Gregorian Start	Gregorian End	Ogham Letter
Beth/Beith	Birch	December 24	January 20	B
Luis	Rowan (Mtn. Ash)	January 21	February 17	L
Nion/Nuin	Ash	February 18	March 17	N
Fearn	Alder	March 18	April 14	F
Saille	Willow	April 15	May 12	S
Huath	Hawthorn	May 13	June 9	H
Duir	Oak	June 10	July 17	D
Tinne	Holly	July 18	August 4	T
Coll	Hazel	August 5	September 1	C
Quert/Muin	Apple/ Vine (grape)	September 2	September 29	Q
Gort	Ivy	September 30	October 27	G
Ngeatal	Broom/Reed	October 28	November 24	Ng
Ruis	Elder	November 25	December 21	R

Quarter Days:

Day	Tree	Quarter Day	App. Gregorian	Ogham Letter
Onn	Gorse	Spring Equinox	March 21	O
Ura	Heather	Summer Solstice	June 21	U
Eadha	Aspen	Autumn Equinox	September 21	E
Idho	Yew	Winter Solstice	December 21	I

Additional days of note:

Day	Tree	Quarter Day	App. Gregorian	Ogham Letter
Straif	Blackthorn (Sloe)	Samhain	October 31	Ss
Alim	Pine	Last day of year	December 23	A
Phagos	Beech	All except December 23		Ph

The Celtic Calendar (Theory 2—Most Accurate)

This theory is most commonly accepted among scholars but is almost entirely missing from the Pagan community. Here we see a calendar reconstructed from large bronze plate called the Coligny Calendar. Measuring 5 feet by 3 1/2 feet, the Coligny calendar was discovered in France. Its language is clearly Gaulish, but its letters and numbers have obvious Roman influences. The lunar cycles were counted in 19-year increments for a total of 235 lunar cycles with two extra months inserted for every 62 standard cycles. It was precise enough to yield only a 12-hour error after the full cycle of 19 years.

The problem with this calendar is that it is anything but user friendly. Maybe the term would be 'user surly.' A 5-foot bronze plate is not exactly a Palm Pilot. For this reason, I do not believe it was the calendar of the common (pagan) folk. Instead, I believe although the Coligny Calendar is a valid representation of the way the ancient Celts measured time, it was probably only the very well educated that used it or a similar system.

The Celtic Tree Calendar (Theory 3—The Middle Ground)

The third and least accepted idea is that theory one and theory two were more or less both right. This theory is that the older of the two calendars was the Tree Calendar and that the Coligny Calendar represents a Romanized view of the Celtic year. Those folk educated enough to use the Coligny Calendar or those like it would do so to determine the application of the Tree Calendar while using those days Ruis (December 21) and Beth (December 24) to make it fit. I believe this hybrid theory is the best way for Wiccans to view the Celtic year, as our modern Gregorian Calendar most represents the ancient Roman Calendar.

The Astrological Calendar

Interestingly enough, we see yet another attempt to connect the solar year and lunar months in modern pop astrology. I say 'pop astrology' because as any trained astrologer will tell you, there is a great deal more to astrology than looking up your sun sign on a chart. However it is very interesting to note that there is no real reason to have created a system with 12 signs unless one began with a connection to the lunar cycles. Why 12 signs when just about anyone can look at the stars and a number of constellations limited only by one's imagination?

The Astrological Wheel of the Year

Month Name	Begins	Ends	Planet(s)	Element
Capricorn	December 22	January 19	Saturn	Earth
Aquarius	January 20	February 18	Saturn/Uranus	Air
Pisces	February 19	March 20	Jupiter/Neptune	Water
Aries	March 21	April 19	Mars	Fire
Taurus	April 20	May 20	Venus	Earth
Gemini	May 21	June 20	Mercury	Air
Cancer	June 21	July 22	Moon	Water
Leo	July 23	August 22	Sun	Fire
Virgo	August 23	September 22	Mercury	Air
Libra	September 23	October 22	Venus	Air
Scorpio	October 23	November 21	Mars	Water
Sagittarius	November 22	December 21	Jupiter	Fire

Why so many Twelves?

I believe the number 12 became sacred because it is the number of full lunar cycles in the solar year—not the number of Full Moons (single days), but of the full cycles. Thus, a further example that the relationship, not the thing, is important. You see, that's how Wicca sees the world in which we live—not in a collection of things (objectification), but in our relationship with those many things (sometimes by personification). Therefore, the Moon was personified as opposed to objectified. Many further examples can be found in ancient Pagan lore, which tells us the number 12 is of great religious significance. Moses led the 12 tribes of Jewish people out of Egypt. Jesus selected 12 apostles. Odysseus had twelve crew members. Arthur initially selected 12 Knights of the Round Table. Modern juries typically contain twelve jurors and, of course, Witches Covens are often thought to have a leader and 12 members. All because someone looked up and saw something larger than the stars in the night sky. All because there is one Sun and 12 lunar cycles. All because it was there.

The 12 Labors of Heracles—Roman—Mediterranean

Although it might be wild speculation on my part, 12 Labors of Heracles could be a reference to a year of servitude.

Kill the Lion of Nemea

Kill the Hydra

Kill the horrific birds of Stymphalis

Kill the Boar of Erymanthus

Capture the Ceryneian Hind

Capture the Bull of Crete

Capture man-eating mares of Diomedes.

Capture the oxen of Geryon

Clean the Augean Stables

Retrieve the girdle of Hippolyta

Retrieve the golden apples from the garden of the Hesperides

Retrieve Cerberus from the underworld (bring it to the surface)

The Statue of Crom Cruach—Irish—Central Europe

The Statue of Crom Cruach that once stood in Ulster was made of gold. Surrounding this huge statue were 12 lesser statues made of stone. This is probably a recognition of Crom as a solar deity (one solar year) with lesser deities (each lunar cycle) surrounding him.

Gladsheim—Scandinavian—North Europe

Meaning 'place of great joy,' Gladsheim is the hall of the Asgard, which contains 12 high chairs, one for each of the major gods of the pantheon.

Consentes Dii—Rome—Mediterranean

The equivalent of the Greek Olympians, there are 12 major gods in the Roman pantheon, six male and six female.

God	Goddess
Apollo	Diana
Jupiter	Juno
Mars	Venus
Mercury	Ceres
Neptune	Minerva
Vulcan	Vesta

The Olympians—Greek—Mediterranean

God	Goddess
Hephaestus	Aphrodite
Apollo	Athena
Ares	Artemis
Zeus	Hera
Hermes	Demeter
Dionysus	
Poseidon	

The Titans—Greek—Mediterranean

The Greek personification and gods of Nature. They are the 12 children of Gaia (Mother Earth) and Uranus (Father Sky). They are presented here as couples as each can be found that way in lore.

God	Goddess
Cronos	Rhea
Iapetus	Themis
Oceanus	Tethys
Hyperion	Theia
Crius	Mnemosyne
Coeus	Phoebe

The 13 Moon Myth

And yet, with all of these cultures incorporating the lunar cycles into their 12 month years, when my first book came out a fellow author took me aside and told me that I did a good job on everything except the Moons. Per that friend's observation, there are not 12 lunar cycles in the year, but 13. Could I have been that poorly informed?

In a desperate attempt to discover if I had just made a fool of myself, I must have read every Pagan book on Moon lore. In so doing, I'd almost thought I was misled. It seems the majority of our books do state that there are 13 moons in a year, not 12.

I wondered how that could be so when just about every book outside of the Pagan community said there were 12 and some change. And then it struck me: It is objectification.

Instead of being predominantly concerned with the relationship of the lunar cycle, folk were concerned with the event of the Full Moon. You see, that extra change often produces a 13th full moon in the year, but it is incapable of producing an additional lunar cycle, even if one does use new math. This is perhaps a result of the advice giving in the traditional version of "The Charge of the Goddess."

> *"Whenever you have need of anything, once in the month,*
> *and better it be when the moon is full,*
> *you shall assemble in some secret place and*
> *adore the spirit of Me who is Queen of all Witches."*

—Author Unknown (see Book of Three Part II)

Whatever the reason, the Full Moon is only part of the story. The rest of the story in Moon lore is that like all things, the lunar cycle has a beginning, middle, and an end. It is New, Full, and Dark, and it is an expression not only of our Lord as Master, Father, and Sage, our Lady as Maiden, Mother, and Crone, but of ourselves as youth, mature, and senior.

Iao Abrasax, thou art the Lord

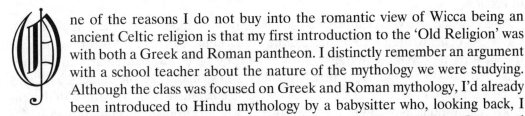

Liber ab Solemnitas

(The Book of Holidays)

A Further Exploration of the Sabbats and Esbats
Or the Book of Twelve Part II

One of the reasons I do not buy into the romantic view of Wicca being an ancient Celtic religion is that my first introduction to the 'Old Religion' was with both a Greek and Roman pantheon. I distinctly remember an argument with a school teacher about the nature of the mythology we were studying. Although the class was focused on Greek and Roman mythology, I'd already been introduced to Hindu mythology by a babysitter who, looking back, I believe may have been involved in the Krishna Consciousness movement. It seemed reasonable to believe that if the mythology of one people was in fact their religion, then the mythology of another people would be their religion. I claimed the material at hand was an ancient religion; he claimed it was just stories and not religion. I asked, "What then is the difference between the Christian Bible and any particular version of mythology?" His answer was that what is in the Christian Bible really happened. "According to who?" I asked, offering "You perhaps?" Well, the teacher sent me to the principal's office. There, I later explained that I was just curious about the subject, the teacher explained his side of the story, and the principal explained that I was not allowed to discuss the matter in class because we were not allowed to discuss religion in class. Needless to say I was very, very, very confused.

Shortly thereafter, I found a Pagan group who indeed followed the Roman pantheon with a hint of the Greek names. The word Wicca was not used much, and when it was, it typically noted a leader or elder. Most of the printed material there was to read was academic, although there was a bit of Dr. Leo Martello, Sybil Leek, and the now infamous newsletters from New York. I think I remember reading material by Herman Slater, but to be honest I can not be sure. Published books were hard to come by and frankly, the majority of what I read was illegally photocopied.

While in the U.S. Military, I received dog tags that said 'No Preference' for my religion. I think it might have been abbreviated. I mentioned this to my Drill Sergeant and explained that I indeed had a preference. He sent me to the chaplain who asked me what I believed. I explained my belief system; he looked it up in a military manual, and then explained that I was Wiccan. Though I argued the point, thinking the word was just a bit too pompous for this simple Pagan, he insisted that it was the best thing the military had for my dog tags, so I reluctantly accepted.

When I returned to the United States, I found a group of folk in my home town called the Pagan Community Council of Central Ohio. I attended their meetings and talked with them. Although there were a few folk following Native American and a couple following Northern European Pagan paths, the great majority claimed to be Celtic Wiccans. It seemed everywhere I went the only thing that outnumbered the percent of Pagans reportedly following a Celtic path was the percentage of shopping mall goers who wore Don Johnson-style baggy pants. The Celts were indeed the peak of fashion.

So I looked into what Celtic lore I could find and found a great difference between the books being written for Pagans and the books being written for historic value. For the most part, everything in the books written for Pagans was written as if the author was there to witness the event first hand. The straw that broke the camel's back was when I read that the ancient Celts used to make corn husk dolls as part of their religious celebrations. Now, I know the word corn was a European term used to describe many different grains and not the New World discovery of maze (the ancestor of modern corn), but the author was rather specific that these dolls were made from corn *husks*. There were even a few diagrams and I've got to tell you, if it was wheat husks that author was talking about, it was some mighty large wheat those ancient Celts were a growing.

In 1993, I opened a Pagan shop in Ohio and set about the task of stocking the shelves with books that I thought were applicable. Unfortunately, those books were hard to find and did not sell well. The Celtic craze had yet to die out, and being Celtic Wiccan was becoming more and more fashionable. To stay in business, I begun offering my customers what they wanted, and I bit my lip to fight back comments on the whole idea that Wicca is an ancient Celtic religion.

Then someone asked me the question that led to Chapter 9. The research that I conducted for that chapter led to the following information, and I discovered the so-called Eight Sabbats of the Wiccan religion are actually modern constructs. The ancient Celts did not celebrate four quarter days and four cross quarter days, they celebrated what can best be described as this, that, and the other thing. You see, those folk whom we typically call the Celts were so incredibly diverse, the only thing they had in common is that among their many tribes, each wrote down just about nothing.

The Holidays

Wicca is a world religion. It embraces universal ideas such as the Creator being Lord and Lady and it embraces specific incarnations of those universal ideas, such as individual names for our Lord and Lady. As such, its eight major holidays are an amalgam of the holidays celebrated by the many cultures that have led to the union of religious observances that we today call the Wheel of the Year.

Unfortunately, even if the ancient cultures on which Wicca is based had kept clear written records of their traditions and holidays, the past five or six hundred years have seen a level of religious intolerance previously unknown during the many tens of thousands of years that humanity has walked this Earth. Some traditions are being pieced together. Many more have been lost forever. But records of one Pagan civilization have survived much better than others. It language is in use in modern medicine, botany, animal husbandry, and a variety of other sciences. From that Pagan civilization, we have received the basis for modern government. From that culture we received the Edict of Milan as the basis for the First Amendment to the Constitution of the United States of America. I am of course speaking of the culture formed by the fusing of the Roman and Greek cultures.

In understanding the modern Wiccan Holidays, we do well to examine the ancient Pagan holidays. In examining the ancient Pagan holidays, we do well to look at the Greek and Roman—not because they are ultimately better than the holidays of any other group of people, but because their culture most resembles ours and because their holidays were recorded well enough that they survived the test of time and the onslaught of intolerance.

The Ancient Greek 'Hellenic' Calendar and Holidays

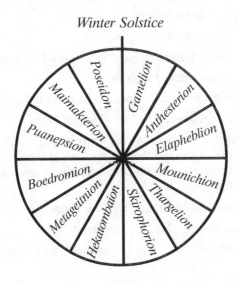

The Greek Wheel of the Year

Approximated Gregorian dates are provided; however, these dates would only be valid if the first New moon after the Summer Solstice were to fall on the Gregorian date of June 22nd and then if each following new moon fell alternating 28 and 29 days after each other. Of course the lunar cycle does not alternate neatly to fit into the solar year, so the given dates are not to be considered accurate. They are provided only such that the reader can receive a sense of where in the year these celebrations fall.

It is also important to note that as of about the 6th century before common era, the Greek year began on the first new moon after the Summer Solstice. Then each month that followed keyed its start on the next new moon. Because 12 lunar cycles do not fit neatly into a solar year, the month of Poseideon was repeated. To present this in better relation to the modern concept of the year, instead of presenting it here beginning with the traditional first month Hekatombaion (which begins shortly after Summer Solstice), I have started with Gamelion, which is closest to being the modern January.

Greek Holidays

Gamelion—*January*—Approximation December 27—January 25

Gamelion actually begins on the seventh new moon after Summer Solstice
This is the preferred month of handfasting in Greek traditions

Gamelion 1	**Noumenia**—Celebration of the new moon.
Gamelion 2	Sacred to Agathos Daimon.
Gamelion 3	Sacred to the Three Graces and Athena.
Gamelion 4	Sacred to Aphrodite, Hermes, Hercules, Eros.
Gamelion 6	Sacred to Artemis.
Gamelion 7	Sacred to Apollo.
Gamelion 8	Sacred to Poseidon. Sacrifices offered to Apollo and the Nymphs.
Gamelion 9	Sacrifices offered to Athena.
Gamelion 14	**Lenaia**—Festival to honor Dionysus on the day of the Full Moon.
Gamelion 27	Sacrifices offered to Poseidon and Demeter.
	Gamelia/Theogamia—Festival to honor Zeus and Hera as a loving couple. Although there are numerous cites to this couple having wild arguments (especially over infidelity), their marriage was honored at this festival.
Gamelion 28	Sacred to all Chthonian (Underworld) deities
Gamelion 29	Sacred to all Chthonian deities.
Gamelion 30	**Dark Moon**—Sacred to Hecate and all Chthonian deities.

Anthesterion—*February*—Approximation January 26—February 23

Anthesterion actually begins on the eighth new moon after Summer Solstice.

Anthesterion 1 **Noumenia**—Celebration of the new moon.

Anthesterion 2 Sacred to Agathos Daimon. Sacrifices made to Dionysus.

Anthesterion 3 Sacred to the Three Graces and Athena.

Anthesterion 4 Sacred to Aphrodite, Hermes, Hercules, Eros.

Anthesterion 5 **Soteria**—Festival honoring Zeus.

Anthesterion 6 Sacred to Artemis.

Anthesterion 7 Sacred to Apollo.

Anthesterion 8 Sacred to Poseidon.

Anthesterion 11–13 **Anethesteria**—Three-day festival Honoring Dionysus and Hermes. Reflects greatly on the three stages of life, which Wiccans know in the feminine as Maiden, Mother, and Crone and in the masculine as Master, Father, and Sage.

Day one is called Pithoigia, which means 'from the jar' or 'jar opening.' On this day, the bottles of new wine are opened and shared, however intoxication is generally frowned upon. This day is more of tasting of the wine to decide which will be best for the following day. Crowns of flowers are given to the children who were born during the previous year, welcoming their soul into the community. Day two is called Khoes, which means 'from the cup.' On this day the wine selected the day previous is shared in great revelry and accompanied with feasting, games, and rituals honoring marriages. Day three is called Khytroi, which means 'from the cauldron' or 'from the kettles.' On this day, cauldrons were filled with flowers and kettles were used to cook great vegetable feasts for the dead. With the assistance of Hermes, the dead are called to visit the living.

Anthesterion 14 **Full Moon**—Also gatherings in preparation of the Eleusinian Mysteries.

Anthesterion 23 **Diasia**—Festival honoring Zeus, which is held away from the city in some relatively secluded area. Great feasting took place with the sacrifice of breads to the wild (scattered into the woods). In the evening, bonfires, dancing, and chants to call on Zeus to help welcome and return Spring.

Anthesterion 27 Sacred to all Chthonian deities.

Anthesterion 28 Sacred to all Chthonian deities.

Anthesterion 29 **Dark Moon**—Sacred to Hecate and all Chthonian deities.

Elaphebolion—*March*—Approximation February 24—March 25

Elaphebolion actually begins on the ninth new moon after Summer Solstice

Elaphebolion 1	**Noumenia**—Celebration of the new moon.
Elaphebolion 2	Sacred to Agathos Daimon.
Elaphebolion 3	Sacred to the Three Graces and Athena.
Elaphebolion 4	Sacred to Aphrodite, Hermes, Hercules, Eros.
Elaphebolion 6	**Elaphebolia**—Festival to honor Artemis. Sweet breads made with honey and sesame seeds are made in the shape of Deer (stag) and scattered in wooded areas. Although this day celebrates Artemis as hunter, it was celebrated with the abstinence from meat. Instead, competitions of archery were conducted using deer poppets.
Elaphebolion 7	Sacred to Apollo.
Elaphebolion 8	Sacred to Poseidon.
	Asklepia—Festival in honor of Asklepios.
Elaphebolion 9–14	**Greater Dionysia**—Festival to honor Dionysus. Revelry, both modest and sexual, with public celebration, sacred theatre, and a procession leading to the crowing of a phallic symbol, symbolic of sexual union.
Elaphebolion 14	**Full Moon**—Marks the last night of the Greater Dionysia.
Elaphebolion 15	**Galaxia**—Festival to honor Rhea. The festival takes its name from the food Galaxia. Similar to hot oatmeal, galaxia is barley flour boiled in milk and sweetened with honey. Candy was made in the same way by decreasing the amount of milk and increasing the amount of honey. Those sweets were given to children in celebration of their relationship to Rhea, an Earth Mother, and the community itself.
Elaphebolion 28	Sacred to all Chthonian deities.
Elaphebolion 29	Sacred to all Chthonian deities.
Elaphebolion 30	**Dark Moon**—Sacred to Hecate and all Chthonian deities.
	Pandia—Festival to honor Zeus. Sometimes cited as being on the 17th day.

Mounichion—*April*—March 26—April 23

Mounichion actually begins on the 10th new moon after Summer Solstice

Mounichion 1	**Noumenia**—Celebration of the new moon.
Mounichion 2	Sacred to Agathos Daimon.
Mounichion 3	Sacred to the Three Graces and Athena.

Mounichion 4	Sacred to Aphrodite, Hermes, Hercules, Eros.
	Eroteia—Festival in honor of Eros. This day celebrates love, especially new love.
Mounichion 6	Sacred to Artemis.
	Delphinia—Festival to honor Apollo. Virgin girls brought offerings of sweet breads and cakes to his shrine. Offerings and praise is given to call on safe travel throughout the pending Summer.
Mounichion 7	Sacred to Apollo.
Mounichion 8	Sacred to Poseidon.
Mounichion 13–14	**Demetreia**—Festival honoring Demeter.
Mounichion 14	**Full Moon**—Marks the end of Demetreia.
Mounichion 16	**Mounykhia**—Festival honoring Artemis. The festival begins with the rising of the moon and ends with the setting of the moon. In part, this was a celebration of female youth and beauty (teenagers). Traditionally, skyclad girls would dance and play games through the night. Today such practices are tainted with the sexual undertone of nudity, so such practices are not conducted with our youth. Even if one is pure of heart, such practices are best not conducted unless participating teenagers are in the order of 18 and 19 years of age for obvious legal reasons and because while you may be pure at heart you cannot speak for the hearts of any but yourself.
Mounichion 17	**Brabroneia**—A continuation of the festival honoring Artemis held the previous day. This day celebrates younger girls (pre-teen). It is not an initiation rite, but an introduction of young girls to our Lady by her name Artemis.
Mounichion 19	**Olumpeia**—Festival in honor of Zeus.
Mounichion 20	Sacrifices offered to Leucippe.
Mounichion 27	Sacred to all Chthonian (Underworld) Deities.
Mounichion 28	Sacred to all Chthonian (Underworld) Deities.
Mounichion 29	**Dark Moon**—Sacred to Hecate and all Chthonian deities.

Thargelion—*May*—April 24—May 23

Thargelion actually begins on the eleventh new moon after Summer Solstice

Thargelion	**Noumenia**—Celebration of the new moon.
Thargelion 2	Sacred to Agathos Daimon.
Thargelion 3	Sacred to the Three Graces and Athena.
Thargelion 4	Sacred to Aphrodite, Hermes, Hercules, and Eros. Also, sacrifices made to Apollo, Hermes, Leto, and Zeus.

Thargelion 6–7	**Thargelia**—Festival to celebrate the birthday of Artemis (day 6) and Apollo (day 7). On the first day, breads were made and baked communally for use on the second day. This practice illustrates how the preparations for a festival were thought a part of the festival itself, as opposed to the more modern approach to celebration where one or two people prepare everything for guests. On the second day, the breads made the previous day were sacrificed (scattered to the woods) in the hopes that the offering will bring fertility to the land. In ancient times, two criminals who had been sentenced to death were sacrificed on this day. Later, they were excommunicated. Today we can see this day mark a time when those who have wronged us are banished from our hearts. The festival winds down with a procession to honor Helios (Sun), Selene (Moon), and the Horae (Seasons).
Thargelion 7	On this day, children who had been adopted were registered with the presiding government such that they were respected under Greek law as if they were born to the parents who registered them.
Thargelion 8	Sacred to Poseidon.
Thargelion 15	Full Moon celebrations.
Thargelion 15—19	**Bendideia**—Festival honoring the Thracian goddess Bendis. Could be one of the festivals of which are referred to in *Aradia Gospel of Witches* as 'the game of Benevento.'
Thargelion 16	Sacrifices are offered to Zeus.
Thargelion 22	**Kallynteria**—The cleaning of the temple of Athena, which is sometimes celebrated as Spring cleaning of the home and especially the altar room in modern Wicca.
Thargelion 25	**Plynteria**—Festival that includes the cleansing of the temple of Artemis, which is sometimes celebrated as Spring cleaning of the home and especially the altar room in modern Wicca.
Thargelion 28	Sacred to all Chthonian deities.
Thargelion 29	Sacred to all Chthonian deities.
Thargelion 30	**Dark Moon**—Sacred to Hecate and all Chthonian deities.

Skirophorion—*June*—May 24—June 21

Skirophorion actually begins on the 12th new moon after Summer Solstice
The entire month is sacred to Athena.

Skirophorion 1	**Noumenia**—Celebration of the new moon.
Skirophorion 2	Sacred to Agathos Daimon.
Skirophorion 3	Sacred to the Three Graces and Athena. Sacrifices offered to Athena, Aglaurus, Poseidon, and Zeus.

Arrephoria—An alternative day often cited. See Skirophorion 22 for details.

Skirophorion 4   Sacred to Aphrodite, Hermes, Hercules, Eros.

Skirophorion 6   Sacred to Artemis.

Skirophorion 7   Sacred to Apollo.

Skirophorion 8   Sacred to Poseidon.

Skirophorion 12   **Skirophoria**—Festival in honor of Athena, Demeter, Persephone, and Poseidon. Although there is no hard rule, speaking in general historic terms Skirophoria was celebrated only by women. Today its celebration is participated in by both men and women. Great offerings are made of cakes and baked goods shaped like snakes and the male phallus. Those offerings are placed in hidden places where animals can not eat them. They are later retrieved at Thesmophoria for use as fertilizer.

Skirophorion 14   **Full Moon.**

Skirophorion 22   **Arrephoria**—Festival honoring Athena. In day of old, four virgin girls (ages 7 to 11) were elected on this day and then placed into the a cave on Pyanepsion (Gregorian approximation October 17th). And the four virgins placed in the cave the previous Pyanepsion also released from the cave. Modern Wiccans do not hide their children in a cave for four months. Or do we? Certainly in Northern climates the majority of the time between October 17th (their entrance to the cave) and June 14th (their release) we do spend cooped up in our homes due to the cold weather. Perhaps this holiday can be honored by electing four young girls from our community each year who will promise to spend their Winter planning and preparing for the Arrephoria where they lead a celebration of Winter's release of Summer.

Arrephoria is sometimes cited on the third day of Skirophorion instead of the 22nd.

Skirophorion 27   Sacred to all Chthonian deities.

Skirophorion 28   Sacred to all Chthonian deities.

Skirophorion 29   **Dark Moon**—Sacred to Hecate and all Chthonian deities.

Hekatombaion—*July*—June 22—July 21

Hekatombaion actually begins on the first new moon after Summer Solstice

Sacred to Apollo

Hekatombaion 1   **Noumenia**—Celebration of the new moon.

Eiseteria—Festival which honors Athena and Zeus.

Hekatombaion 2   Sacred to Agathos Daimon.

Hekatombaion 3   Sacred to the Three Graces and Athena.

Hekatombaion 4	**Aphrodisia**—Bathing festival of Aphrodite and her daughter Peitho. Celebrated with the ritualistic bathing of statuary as well as feasting, dancing, and athletic games. This was also a celebration of love, romance, and sex. The fourth day of Hekatombaion is also sacred to Hermes, Hercules, and Eros.
Hekatombaion 6	Sacred to Artemis.
Hekatombaion 7	Sacred to Apollo.
Hekatombaion 8	Sacred to Poseidon.
Hekatombaion 12	Sacrifices are made to Artemis. **Kronia**—Harvest celebration in honor of Cronos.
Hekatombaion 14	**Full Moon** celebration.
Hekatombaion 15–16	**Synoikia**—Festival to celebrate community in memory of the merging of villages by Thesus, to form the city of Athens.
Hekatombaion 27	Sacred to all Chthonian deities. **Ponnykhis**—All night festival fire and dancing. Associated with youth, boys and girls would dance and compete in torch lit foot races. Honors Adonis. Also sacred to the Chthonian deities.
Hekatombaion 29	Sacred to all Chthonian deities. **Lesser Panathenaia**—Celebration of Athena's birthday. The Panathenaia was celebrated annually as a one day holiday (Lesser/Minor Panathenaia). Sacrifices were made to Athena, Hygeia, and Nike. **Major Panathenaia**—Every fourth year, the Panathenaia is expanded to a 12-day holiday (Greater Panathenaia).
Hekatombaion 30	**Dark Moon**—Celebration sacred to Hecate and all Chthonian (Underworld) Deities.

Metageitnion—*August*—July 22—August 19

Metageitnion actually begins on the second new moon after Summer Solstice

Metageitnion 1	**Noumenia**—Celebration of the new moon.
Metageitnion 2	Sacred to Agathos Daimon.
Metageitnion 3	Sacred to the Three Graces and Athena.
Metageitnion 4	Sacred to Aphrodite, Hermes, Hercules, Eros.
Metageitnion 6	Sacred to Artemis.
Metageitnion 7	**Metageitnia**—Festival honoring Apollo which celebrates community.
Metageitnion 8	Sacred to Poseidon.
Metageitnion 10	Sacred to Hercules. **Heracleia Kynosargous**—Festival celebrating the lives of illegitimate children.

Metageitnion 15	**Full Moon**—Celebration marks the beginning of the Eleusinia.
Metageitnion 15–18	**Eleusinia**—A day of games and sport within the community. Not associated with the school of mysteries, but instead shares its name because this festival started in the city Eleusis (as did the mystery school). See the Eleusinian Mysteries on the 14th day of Boedromion.
Metageitnion 16	Sacrifices made to Hecate and Artemis.
Metageitnion 20	Sacrifices made to Hera.
Metageitnion 25	Sacrifices made to Zeus.
Metageitnion 27	Sacred to all Chthonian (Underworld) Deities.
Metageitnion 28	Sacred to all Chthonian (Underworld) Deities.
Metageitnion 29	**Dark Moon**—Sacred to Hecate and all Chthonian (Underworld) Deities.

Boedromion—*September*—August 20—September 18

Boedromion actually begins on the third new moon after Summer Solstice

Boedromion 1	**Noumenia**—Celebration of the new moon.
Boedromion 2	Sacred to Agathos Daimon.
	Niketeria—Festival to honor Nike.
Boedromion 3	Sacred to the Three Graces and Athena.
Boedromion 4	Sacred to Aphrodite, Hermes, Hercules, Eros.
Boedromion 5	**Genesia**—Festival honoring dead ancestors at which offerings are made to Agathos Daimon. Offerings of flowers, rice pudding, honey, and butter are made to Agathos Daimon. Offerings of ancestral favorite dishes are made to the dead. Gifts are exchanged between the living.
Boedromion 6	**Artemis Agrotera/Kharisteria**—Festival honoring Artemis in her capacity as huntress. Competitions of archery are often followed with a feast including much meat.
Boedromion 7	**Boedromia**—Festival honoring Apollo in his capacity as protector and savior from war. On this day we honor police officers, doctors, and others who protect our community.
Boedromion 8	Sacred to Poseidon.
Boedromion 12	**Democratia**—Festival in honor of democracy. Although the United States of America was built on the very principles put forth by the Greeks and later improved upon by the Romans, it seems a great many modern Pagans want to adopt socialism as a national policy. Yes, socialism existed well on a very small scale just as it does now, in families and marriages. But on a scale the size of a modern nation, here is clear proof that democracy trumps socialism in the view of at least one ancient Pagan culture.

Boedromion 14	**Eleusian Mysteries**—The Full Moon of this month marked the festival of the Eleusinian Mysteries. Held as a one day festival annually but expanded to nine days every fifth year. The Eleusinian Mysteries honor Demeter and Persephone and were the most sacred of all the Greek festivals.
Boedromion 16	**Epidauria**—Festival in honor of Asklepios.
Boedromion 27	Sacrifices are made to the Achelous, Athena, Gaia, Hermes, and the Nymphs.
Boedromion 28	Sacred to all Chthonian deities.
Boedromion 29	Sacred to all Chthonian deities.
Boedromion 30	**Dark Moon**—Sacred to Hecate and all Chthonian deities.

Pyanepsion—*October*—September 19—October 17

Pyanepsion actual begins on the fourth new moon after Summer Solstice

Pyanepsion 1	**Noumenia**—Celebration of the new moon.
Pyanepsion 2	Sacred to Agathos Daimon.
Pyanepsion 3	Sacred to the Three Graces and Athena.
Pyanepsion 4	Sacred to Aphrodite, Hermes, Hercules, Eros.
Pyanepsion 5	**Proerosiea**—Festival honoring Demeter and Persephone connected with the tending of farmland.
Pyanepsion 6	Sacred to Artemis.
Pyanepsion 7	**Pyanepsia/Puanepsia**—Festival honoring Apollo, Artemis and the Horae. Offerings of fruit were made in hope that blessings would be granted.
Pyanepsion 8	**Oskhophoria**—Festival in honor of Dionysus and Ariadne. Men dressed as women symbolizing the feminine side of masculinity present in all men. Women, carrying a sacrifice of a grand dinner, followed the cross-dressed men to the ocean where the food was thrown as sacrifice to Poseidon. Athletic games and general revelry followed, as did great lovemaking by couples in their homes and groups in public temples. This day is sacred to romantically involved couples as it celebrates the union of Dionysus with Ariadne.
	Theseia—A festival apart from Oskhophoria, which is far less frenzied. At Theseia, a procession of children would participate in military/formal games to honor Theseus (King of Athens). A feast of bread and meat was prepared and shared with or given to the poor.
Pyanepsion 9	**Stenia**—The first day of Thesmophoria. Stenia was participated in by married women and mothers. Men and single women did not attend. It was the marking of Demeter's mourning over the loss of her daughter

Persephone. Participation was only allowed after eight days of abstinence from sex with men prior to the holiday. The Stenia was the opening celebration of the Thesmophoria in which women jokingly taunted each other and symbolically whipped each other with branches, working themselves into frenzied ecstatic dances.

Pyanepsion 9–14   **Thesmophoria**—Festival in honor of Demeter which was participated in by women only. Although one did not need to be married to attend anything except the opening rites (Stenia), men were still not welcome. To participate, women had to be abstain from sex with men for nine days prior to the festival. On the second day of Thesmophoria, the women shared communal baths in the sea. A modern interpretation might be swimming in local ponds or even sharing a hot tub. Offerings of fruit and pork are made feasts of bread and baked goods are exchanged. The rotting food that remains in the temple from the previous offerings at the Skirophoria are collected and ground into fertilizer for future grain crops, especially barley. During the Thesmophoria, women remained barefoot and did not brush their hair or adorn themselves to share Demeter's loss. On the final day, they return home and bless their children.

Pyanepsion 14   **Full Moon** celebration.

Pyanepsion 27   Sacred to all Chthonian deities.

Pyanepsion 28   Sacred to all Chthonian deities.

Pyanepsion 29   **Khalkeia**—Festival to honor Hephaestus and Athena.

                        Dark Moon—Sacred to Hecate and all Chthonian deities.

Maimakterion—*November*—October 18—November 16

Maimakterion actually begins on the fifth new moon after Summer Solstice

Maimakterion 1   **Noumenia**—Celebration of the new moon.

Maimakterion 2   Sacred to Agathos Daimon.

Maimakterion 3   Sacred to the Three Graces and Athena.

Maimakterion 4   Sacred to Aphrodite, Hermes, Hercules, Eros.

Maimakterion 6   Sacred to Artemis.

Maimakterion 7   Sacred to Apollo.

Maimakterion 8   Sacred to Poseidon.

Maimakterion 14   **Pompaia**—Festival to honor Zeus takes place on the day of the full moon.

Maimakterion 20   **Maimakteria**—Festival honoring Zeus and asking him for a fair Winter. Men wore women's clothing and pretended to be the Horae. Both men and women covered their faces with see-through fabric as a sign that the veil between Winter and Summer is thin. Probably the origin of the expression used at Samhain that the veil between worlds is at the thinnest.

Maimakterion 28 Sacred to all Chthonian deities.

Maimakterion 29 Sacred to all Chthonian deities.

Maimakterion 30 **Dark Moon**—Sacred to Hecate and all Chthonian deities.

Poseideon (greater)—*December*—November 17—December 15

Poseideon actually begins on the sixth new moon after Summer Solstice

Poseideon 1 **Noumenia**—Celebration of the new moon.

Poseideon 2 Sacred to Agathos Daimon.

Poseideon 3 Sacred to the Three Graces and Athena.

Poseideon 4 Sacred to Aphrodite, Hermes, Hercules, Eros.

Poseideon 5 **Plerosia**—Festival in honor of Zeus.

Poseideon 6 Sacred to Artemis.

Poseideon 7 Sacred to Apollo.

Poseideon 8 **Poseidea**—Festival honoring Poseidon.

Poseideon 14 **Lesser Dionysia**—Festival honoring Dionysus. A procession is led by men with large wood phallus images symbolic of masculine fertility. They are followed by women carrying baskets (symbolic of the womb) filled with the feast preparations. After the feast was a masquerade dance. Full moon celebration.

Poseideon 16 Sacred to Zeus.

Poseideon 26 **Haloa**—Festival honoring Demeter, Dionysus, Poseidon, and Persephone. A procession with food and offerings followed by a feast. It is customary for the feast to contain breads and cakes shaped like reproductive organs. At the traditional Greek celebration, the evenings entertainment is in the order of sky clad women taunting each other with sexual innuendo and insults designed to stir the lust in their male audience.

Poseideon 27 Sacred to all Chthonian deities.

Poseideon 28 Sacred to all Chthonian deities.

Poseideon 29 **Dark Moon**—Sacred to Hecate and all Chthonian deities.

Poseideon (lesser)—*December Continues*—December 16–26

The lesser month of Poseideon is a short month, perhaps not a month at all, with approximately 10 days. It was used for the purpose of rectifying the discrepancy between the solar year and lunar months.

Poseideon 6   **Lesser Asclepieia**—Festival honoring Asklepios, Apollo and Hygeia.

Poseideon 10   **Heracleia**—Festival honoring Hercules. Could last three nights.

The Ancient Roman Calendar

Please note that the ancient Roman year started with March; however, I have arranged the year here starting in January for easier reference. In fact, depending on how one wants to use the word ancient we can also state that the ancient Roman calendar started in January, the change being made by Gaius Julius Caesar to align better with the solar year. The Roman calendar does not use the simple numbering system that we use today. Instead, it addressed the problem of lunar months not aligning to the solar year by ordering the months of each day to the Calends, Nones, or Ides of each month.

Calends: The new moon marks the first day of the month.

Ides: The 15th day of March, May, July, or October and the 13th day of all other months. Sacred to Jupiter.

Nones: The seventh day of March, May, July and October, but the fifth day of all other months.

Roman Holidays

Januarius—*January*—Sacred to the god Janus

Januarius 1   **Anno Novo**—Sacred to Janus and Asklepios.

This day is sacred to Janus, who is often depicted as having two faces, one looking forward to the future and one looking backwards to the past. It is a day of both reflection and planning. Ovidius asked of Janus, "Why do we now celebrate the New Year in the middle of Winter rather than as it was celebrated in the past during the spring?" Janus answered: "Midwinter is the beginning of the new Sun and the end of the old one. Phoebus and the year take their start from the same point." (Ovidius Fasti, classic tale). Phoebus is the Sun.

Januarius 3, 4, or 5	**The Campitalia**—Celebration of extended community. The celebration of Lares (of the crossroads) is a celebration of the countryside that takes place at the merging of roads between villages. This is a festival of community unity, a chance to reach out, greet, and exchange goods with your neighboring villages. Traditionally it has taken place between December 17th and January 5th but is most often recorded on January 3, 4, or 5.
Januarius 5	Sacred to Vica Pota.
Januarius 8	Sacred to the goddess Justitia.
Januarius 9	**Agonalia of Januarius**—Honoring Janus.
	The name of this holiday finds its root in the word *agonium*, meaning 'sacrificial rites.' This is one of four festivals by the same name December 11th honors Sol, March 17th honors Mars, and May 21th honors Veiovis.
Januarius 11	**Juturnalia**—A day to honor the goddess Juturna.
Januarius 11–15	**Carmentalia**—A festival honoring Carmenta.
	The focus of this festival is on divination and reflection on the past. This holiday is similar to the modern cultural New Year's eve in that we reflect on the past and seek to find closure on issues with kith and kin, but we also look to the future and consider resolutions hoping that those resolutions will change the future we are currently headed for.
Januarius 13	**The Ides**—Full Moon—Sacred to Jupiter.
Januarius 16	A day to honor the goddess Concordia.
Januarius 17	A day to honor the goddess Felicitas.
Januarius 24	**The Sementivae**—A festival of sowing or planting of seeds honoring Tellus Mater and Ceres. With the invention of modern machine farming and the difference between climate in Rome and where you might live, sowing seeds isn't always at the top of the list of things to do. However, the concept behind sowing seeds early is still valid. This is a time to consider potential business decisions one may make this Spring. Perhaps a time to research that book you have been thinking about writing. It is also a time of sacrifice. Traditionally, cakes and pork were offered to Tellus on this day. Today, sacrificing the value of a day's meal to your charity or maybe non-perishable pork products to your local food shelter. As you do, remember the relationship of Tellus and Ceres. Ceres provides the grain and Tellus gives it a place to grow. In sacrifice, you assume the role of Ceres giving your grain (work product) to Tellus (charity) that the grain (work product) will grow.
Januarius 27	A day to honor the twin brothers Castor and Pollux.
Januarius 30	Sacred to the goddess Pax (peace).

Februarius—*February*—Sacred to the god Mars and goddess Juno

Februarius 1 and 2	Festival day of the Juno.
Februarius 2	Sacred to Ceres.
Februarius 5	Festival day marking the beginning of Spring.
Februarius 5–7	**The Fornacalia**—The Feast of Ovens. Honoring the local community. The feast moved about on the calendar from about the fifth of the month till the seventh of the month depending on ones community needs. If one forgot or missed his or her communities feast, there was the Quirinalia to make up for it.
Februarius 9	Sacred to Apollo.
Februarius 12	Sacred to Diana.
Februarius 13–21	**The Parentalia**—Honoring dead kin, especially dead parents.

This holiday is the first of three in Februarius that seeks to honor and sometimes appease the dead. In the case of this holiday, the focus was on giving honors, praise, and sacrifice to departed parents and family members. That ceremony was traditionally led by a Vestal Virgin. Celebrated with the family, traditions include visiting grave sites and making personal sacrifice to the departed, perhaps preparing their favorite dish and leaving it on the grave site on which animals would dine. The first day being a private personal reflection with the rest of the week conducted in service to the relationships with surviving family members, knowing that they too will one day part.

Februarius 14	**Festival of Juno**—This day is sacred to Juno and her son Vali. With Juno's connection to love and her son Vali's description as an excellent archer, it is not hard to see where the idea of Valentine's day finds its Pagan roots.
Februarius 14 and 15	**The Lupercalia**—Honoring Lupercus (see Faunus).

On this day, animals are said to befriend humanity and offer their assistance in resolving problems. I can think of no better day on which to celebrate both kith and kin familiars.

Februarius 17	**The Quirinalia**—The Feast of Fools honoring Quirinus.

This holiday celebrated the larger community. Should anyone forget or miss their local Fornacalia, they would make sacrifice at the Quirinalia. This demonstrates the principle of community being a circle within a circle, a large community built upon many smaller communities.

Februarius 18	Sacred to Dea Tacita (a day of silence).
Februarius 21	**The Feralia**—Honoring the dead. This holiday is the second of three in Februarius that seeks to honor and sometimes appease the dead. In the case of this holiday, the focus was on giving honors, praise, and sacrifice to the dead. Unlike Parentalia which honors kin and Carista which honors kith, this holiday was held more to appease wayward spirits that were often thought not all that fond of strangers (us). On this day

we recognize that those who do not have kith or kin often do not for a reason. These forces are linked to the outsiders of Wiccan ritual, those who are not befriended as either kith or kin.

Februarius 22   **The Charistia/Carista**—Honoring the goddess Concordia.

This is the Feast of Favor or the Feast of Good Will. It is celebrated with a grand feast, at which differences between kith and kin are settled in a manner of compromise such that all participating are satisfied with the outcome. This holiday is also the third of three in Februarius that seek to honor and sometimes appease the dead. In the case of this holiday, the focus was on giving honors, praise, and sacrifice to departed friends. Note: Some cites place this holiday earlier in the month, making it the second of three.

Februarius 23   **The Terminalia**—Honoring Terminus. This is a Feast of Neighbors celebrating the old saying "Good fences make good neighbors." It is a day to celebrate the marking of boundaries both physical and emotional. It is a day one might want to spend with a lifetime friend, one who might have become a lover if circumstances had been different, but with whom your friendship has flourished because of the clear boundaries.

Februarius 24   **The Regifugium**—Honoring the principles of freedom. This is the celebration of the founding of the republic of Rome and the removal of the last King of Rome. This is a day of national pride, not only to the ancient Romans but also to the citizens of all current countries that embrace a democratic system. Its celebration as a religious holiday demonstrates the principle that religion and real life concerns such as government have not always been separate and reflecting the joy of living in a democratic republic.

Februarius 27   **The Equirria**—In honor of Mars. A day of horse racing dedicated to Mars. The modern equivalent is obvious, a day at the track. If you choose to gamble, perhaps some of the proceeds could be donated to the innocent victims of war or maybe the ongoing effort to identify and remove landmines left from previous wars. Also celebrated on March 14th.

Martius—March—Sacred to the god Mars

Martius 1   **The Matronalia**—Honoring the goddess Juno and god Mars (her son). This holiday began as a day in which mothers were honored by their partners. However, it grew to include wives who had or had not bore children, and now to a day in which any female lover (wife, girlfriend, or not) is honored. Gifts were given to wives and girlfriends in thanks for their feminine influence and companionship. It is tradition that husbands pray and make sacrifice for the well being of their wives, but it was in no way a somber event and celebrated with song, dance, gambling, and other revelry.

Martius 1	Sacred to Vesta. Her fires are rekindled by the Vestal Virgins on this day.
Martius 6	Festival day of household gods and goddesses.
Martius 7	Festival day of Juno.
Martius 14	**The Equirria**—In honor of Mars. Also celebrated on February 27.
Martius 15*	**Festival of Anna Perenna**—On this day there was singing, dancing and revelry in an order which many might view as excessive. One of the challenges was to drink as many glasses of wine as one hoped to live. Public sacrifice and prayer were incorporated in what many consider the most festive night of the Roman year.

* The Festival of Anna Perenna is actually held on the full moon of Martius but it is listed here on the 15th for simplicity.

Martius 15–29	Festival celebrating the union and mysteries of Attis and Cybele
Martius 16 and 17	**The Bacchanalia** —This holiday celebrating Bacchus became so decadent with its intoxicated orgies, that the Roman Senate made it illegal in 186 B.C.E. They went underground and some say such practices have survived into this day, hidden from the general public.
Martius 17	**The Liberalia**—Honoring Libertas (Liberty) and Liber Pater. This was a day to celebrate liberation, and liberation from youth in particular. It was to the young men of Rome the liberation of their youth and celebration of their ascension into manhood. It is when boys began wearing the *toga virilis* or in modern terms, began dressing as adults. In its association with Liber Pater, a sacrifice of sweet cakes made with honey were baked. These cakes were given to strangers as they passed by, celebrating the fertility of the land and the liberty that such fertility brings— enough liberty that food could be given to strangers. The fusing of Liber Pater and Liberalia into this one day of celebration brought about an interesting development. When first celebrated in honor of Liber Pater, a large penis shaped statue was carted around the villages and fields in an effort to bring fertility to the land. As they passed a farmer's field, the farmer would give them wine in thanks for the blessing. I am sure you can imagine that by modern standards a bunch of drunken men running around the countryside with a giant penis in tow might seem a bit funny. Eventually, it must have seemed so to them (although a similar practice continues in Japan to this day).

With the addition of Libertas, the size of that phallus became smaller and eventually the cart was replaced by a woman running marathon style around the village holding up the phallus for all to see. Wine was replaced with water as the association with Liber Pater (a god of wine) faded. Later, the phallus was set on fire and the symbol of masculinity was hidden in the shape of a torch. Now we know that the Olympic games were started by the ancient Greeks. But the next time you see that torch bearer taking a drink from an onlooker, please remember those drunks and their giant penis in a cart. It might bring a smile to your face. Better yet, call up a friend on March 17th and wish him or her a "Happy giant penis day."

Martius 17	**The Agonalia Martius**—Honors Mars and Liber Pater. The name of this holiday finds its root in the word *agonium*, meaning 'sacrificial rites.' This is one of four festivals by the same name December 11th honors Sol, January 9th honors Janus, and May 21st honors Veiovis.
Martius 19–23	**The Greater Quinquatrus**—Honoring Mars. This was a working festival at which the tools and weapons of war were made ready in preparation of the combat that would come in the pending year. Remember, March is the first month in the Roman calendar. The Lesser Quinquatrus is Junius 13–15.
Martius 19	**Festival day of Minerva**—A day to celebrate crafts, artistry, doctors, and other skilled trades.
Martius 23	**The Tubilustrium**—Honoring Mars and his wife Bellona. On this holiday, readiness was made for war. Weapons were cleaned as were the trumpets used in public ritual. A modern interpretation of this day might be that one should clean their ritual tools. After all, it is our ritual tools with which we combat negative influences in our life by ritual. Also celebrated on the 23rd of Maius.
Martius 25	Observation of Spring Equinox, the actual day changes with the year.
Martius 30	Festival day of Janus and Concordia.
Martius 31	Festival day of Luna.

Aprilis—April—Sacred to the goddess Venus

Aprilis	**The Veneralia**—Honoring Venus. In the ancient traditions, this was the day when women were allowed into the men's bathhouse. Held in honor of Venus in her aspect as Verticordia, 'the changer of hearts,' today this day is seen as a time to challenge gender roles in a Sadie Hawkins capacity.
Aprilis 1	**Sacred to Fortuna**—This day is also sacred to Fortuna. To some degree, on this day the upper class participated in the honoring of Venus at the Veneralia, but the working class honored Fortuna.
Aprilis 4–10	**The Megalensia**—Honoring Cybele (Magna Mater). This week is a festival of games and theater, but before you rush forward to join in on the procession leading to the festival, know that the cult of Cybele often castrated themselves and beat themselves bloody during her procession on this day. While this is not an absolute rule of all of her followers, it certainly was for her priests, all of which were eunuchs. Others, the Archigalii, sacrificed the genitals of bulls instead and did participate in the procession. The remainder of the festival was open to the non-castrated public as the priests of the cult of Cybele were performers, and the tithes given to her temple often came from non-initiates in exchange for performance and entertainment.

Aprilis 5	**Fortuna Publica**—'Luck of the People' Sacred to Fortuna.
Aprilis 10	Last day of the **Megalensia**—On the last day of Megalensia a closing procession is conducted in honor of Apollo, Castor, Ceres, Bacchus, Mars, Minerva, Neptune, Pollux, Venus and Victoria.
Aprilis 11–19	**Festival of Ceres** (ends on the Cerialia).
Aprilis 13	**Ides of Aprilis**—Sacred to Jupiter.
Aprilis 13	Festival day of Libertas.
Aprilis 15	**The Fordicalia**—Honoring Tellus Mater. Sacrifices were made to Tellus Matter in the hopes that she would bless the growing season with fertility. Historically, these sacrifices involved the slaughter of dozens of pregnant cows, hoping their fertility would transfer directly to the land. Perhaps this can be used as a day to build and tend a compost pile.
Aprilis 19	**The Cerialia**—Honoring Ceres. The Cerialia is the last and most grand day of the Festival of Ceres. The entire eight-day festival was conducted with games with the participants wearing finest white clothing. It culminated at the Cerialia with chariot races and sacrifices made to bring blessings of peace and a good grain harvest. Ceres is particularly fond of milk, honey, and wine. Her offerings were walked about the circumference of the festival three times in an effort to keep out spirits that would disrupt the peace associated with Ceres. This custom may be the origin of the casting of the Circle in the Wiccan religion. Consider the Wiccan Rede: "Cast the Circle thrice about to keep all evil spirits out." (Commonly cited as line three of the Wiccan Rede.)
Aprilis 21	**The Parilia/Palilia**—Honoring Pales. Historically, this was a day in which Pales was honored in the hopes that he would continue to smile on the shepherd. At first light, the shepherd's sheep were cleaned and tended and purified in sulfur smoke. Olive and pine woods were used to build a ritual fire stoked with bay branches and leaves. The shepherd, sometimes accompanied with one sheep at a time then leapt the fire hoping that its sacred flame would purify both. In a modern context, this is a day to honor our sacred kin familiar. While leaping a bonfire might be beyond the expectations of many of the animals we keep, especially the smart ones, sharing a ritual bath containing an infusion of bay leaf is certainly a good way to commune with our furry friends. Okay, maybe fitting them into a bathtub with yourself is not a bright idea, but a kiddy pool will do just fine. Traditionally wine and milk (both warm) were shared by sheep and shepherd. I am not sure giving a pet wine will be appreciated, but for those who don't appreciate baths (cats come to mind) sharing warm milk might be in order. No, its not the best thing to give a cat but once a year certainly is not excessive.
Aprilis 23	**The Vinalia Priora**—Honoring Venus and Jupiter. Festival of the first wine. On this day the first wine of the year was opened and offered to Jupiter. Only after this offering could it be consumed by humanity in the further celebration of the goddess Venus. Note that wine was generally available year round. The first wine refers to the wine that was set aside the previous year for fermentation. See also Vinalia Rustica on August 19th.

Aprilis 25	**The Robigalia**—Honoring Robigus and Robigo. One of the most unique holidays of the Roman year. Robigus or maybe Robigo (one being male and the other female) or perhaps both are the god/dess of wheat-rust, mildew, blight and other attackers of the grain crop, but also of rust on weapons and tools of war. On this day, the prayers were conducted asking that they bring rust onto weapons rather than on the crops. This is perhaps a reflection on the idea that when the crops do well there is little need for war as a source of income. Thus, the idea that plenty for all brings peace to all. In modern context, those who oppose war might see this as an encouragement to devote their protest efforts towards helping to promote prosperity rather than defeat a nation's intent on war because with prosperity wars are often avoided.
Aprilis 28–Maius 2	**The Floralia**—Honoring Flora. The festival of flowers. Flora is honored on this day with sacred theater, after which the performers were blessed with a shower of flowers (the offerings of Flora). Originally a festival of mild performances and games, the Floralia gradually became associated with prostitutes who brought a sense of sexuality into both performance and sport. Still the shower of flowers continued. Remember that many of those prostitutes were temple virgins who had sacrificed their virginity to their patrons very recently. Without the negative associations between sex and evil that are prevalent in today's society, the Floralia could be seen as these women's coming out. A statement that while they entered service to their temple as a virgin, they are now sexually educated (and thus empowered) women.

Maius—*May*—Sacred to the god Apollo and goddess Maia

Maius 1	Sacred to Maia.
Maius 1	**Festival of Bona Dea**—A festival celebration attended by only women. In time of old, wine was brought to her temple hidden in honey pots and referred to as milk in conversation, perhaps a deliberate misdirection or maybe a connection to the nurturing properties of celebrations involving wine.
Maius 1	**The Laribius**—In honor of the Lares—A celebration of the ancestral spirits of the community.
Maius 2	The last day of the Floralia.
Maius 9	**The Lemuria**—First annual feast of the lemures. There are three annual feasts of the lemures. The three days are the ninth, 11th, and 13th of Maius. The 10th and 12th are skipped because even numbers are considered unlucky. These are days to either appease the lemures or to drive them away in fear. The Lemures are baneful spirits that pester the household.
Maius 11	Second annual feast of the Lemures honoring Larvae.
Maius 11	Sacred to Mania.

Maius 13   Third annual feast of the Lemures honoring Larvae.

Maius 15   **The birthday of Mercury**—This is the festival day on which we celebrate the birth of Mercurius, one of the names of Mercury. Most often celebrated as a merchants' festival in Mercury's capacity as patron of merchants. Celebrated as a feast day.

Maius 15   Sacred to Maia and Vesta.

Maius 21   **The Agonalia of Maius**—In honor of Vediovis. A festival day in honor of Vediovis. On this day, the community celebrated the ascension of young boys into manhood. In ancient Rome, this was the day boys were given adult togas. The name of this holiday finds its root in the word *agonium*, meaning 'sacrificial rites'. This is one of four festivals by the same name: December 11th honors Sol, January 9th honors Janus, and March 17th honors Mars.

Maius 23   **The Tubilustrium**—A day of purification. On this holiday, readiness was made for war. Weapons were cleaned as were the trumpets used in public ritual. A modern interpretation of this day might be that one should clean their ritual tools. After all, it is our ritual tools with which we combat negative influences in our life by ritual. Also celebrated on the 23rd of Martius.

Maius 23   **The Rosalia**—Honoring Flora. A celebration of Flora as goddess and as the personification of greenery.

Maius 29   **The Ambarvalia**—Honoring Bacchus, Ceres, Janus and Mars. A ritual purification of the fields in honor of Bacchus, Ceres, and Mars.

Junius—*June*—Sacred to the god Mercury and goddess Juno

Junius 1   Sacred to Juno. A day of divination and honor of the warning aspect of Juno. It was her sacred geese who warned Rome of the pending invasion by the Gauls in 389 B.C.E. Offerings made to geese followed by hydromancy.

Junius 1   Sacred to Carna. On this day, offerings of pork fat and beans were made to Carna believing she would in turn grant health. This is interesting, as modern medicine has told us that doing without large amounts of cholesterol greatly improve the health.

Junius 1   Sacred to Mars and Tempestes.

Junius 2   Sacred to Vesta.

Junius 3   Sacred to Bellona.

Junius 4   Sacred to Hercules.

Junius 5   Sacred to Sancus.

Junius 7   Sacred to Tiberinus. A day of fishing and games played by those who fish in celebration of Tiberinus, the patron of fishermen.

Junius 7–8	Preparation for the Vestalia.
Junius 9	**The Vestalia**—Honoring Vesta. If you have ever seen those quaint bottles with pointed or rounded bottoms at a local import specialty shop, you will find this interesting. In preparation for the Vestalia, the Vestal Virgins retrieved water from a sacred Spring. Because the water was not allowed to touch the ground, they transported that water in bottles that had pointed or rounded bottoms such that no one could set them down. That water was used in the preparation of cakes for the celebration. On this day, only women who went barefoot to bring simple foods into the temple as offerings made sacrifices. Men were not allowed in the Temple of Vesta as it was home to the Vestal Virgins.
Junius 9–15	Cleaning the temple after Vestalia—Honoring Vesta.
Junius 17	Ludi Piscatori (Festival of Fishermen)—Honoring Tiberinus.
Junius 11	**The Matralia**—Honoring Matuta. Attended only by women who were still in their first marriage. On this day, household slaves (females) were sent from the homes and temples, save one who was beaten ritually as both a warning and clear statement that one should not tempt a husband to the bed of another woman.
Junius 11	Sacred to Fortuna.
Junius 13–15	**Lesser Quinquatria**—Honoring Minerva and Jupiter. Three days of celebration with wandering minstrels. Often these minstrels are hired by shopkeepers as a show of thanks to the shop's customers and to encourage patronage. This festival honors Minerva, as she is the patron of commerce, entertainers, and minstrels. The festival ends with a feast in honor of Jupiter. The Greater Quinquatria is from Martius 19–23.
Junius 19	Sacred to Minerva.
Junius 20	Sacred to Summanus (cakes offered in sacrifice).
Junius 24*	**Summer Solstice Observation**—Sacred to Fortuna. A day of festivals honoring Fortuna and the craft folk that she smiles upon. Celebrated with a festival resembling a festive farmers market, when the products of cottage industry and home gardens are brought to market. *Note that this date is an approximation.
Junius 25–26	**Ludi Taurei Quinquennales**. Two days of games, horse racing, and offerings to the gods and goddesses of the Underworld. Although each year is marked with sport, every fifth year the greater games are celebrated with fierce competition.
Junius 27	Sacred to Juno and Jupiter.
Junius 29	Sacred to Hercules and the Muses.

Quinctilis—*July*—Sacred to the god Jupiter

Quinctilis 1	Sacred to Felicitas.
Quinctilis 4	Sacred to Pax.
Quinctilis 6	Sacred to Fortuna. On this day the goddess Fortuna was honored by women who were in their first marriage.
Quinctilis 7	Sacred to Pales, Juno and Consus.
Quinctilis 7	**Ancillarum Feriae**—Festival of Working Women. After Rome had been sacked by the Gauls, the Romans were ordered to send out their women for the amusement and entertainment of the standing army. A servant girl named Philotis offered to the Citizens that she and the other serving girls go in place of the men's wives. They did, going to their captors dressed as Roman's finest women. Once their rapists fell asleep, they disarmed them and signaled the Roman men to attack. The battle was won and this day was set aside to forever honor the serving/common woman. A modern interpretation of this can be had in honoring Rosy the Riveter and other figures that represent women's non-combative role at time of war as one of the strengths of a fighting force or the liberty of a nation.
Quinctilis 17	Sacred to Victoria and Honos.
Quinctilis 22	Sacred to Concordia.
Quinctilis 23	**Neptunalia**—Honoring Neptune. A festival in honor of Neptune in his capacity as a Water god. His feast involved the quick construction of temporary shields from the sun (huts) under which light feasts were had, sacrifice was made, and much prayer for water was given in the hope that he would see fit to bring water to the land to protect the crops from the Summer sun.
Quinctilis 25	**The Furrinalia**—Honoring Furrina. A celebration similar to the Neptunalia in its connection to water but celebrated at home. On this day, the goddess Furrina, wife of Neptune, was honored in her capacity of Earth Mother and protector of the natural springs that come from the Earth.
Quinctilis 30	Sacred to Fortuna.

Sextilis—*August*—Sacred to the goddess Ceres

Originally called Sextilis (sixth month) in keeping with the original view of the year starting on the first day of March. It was renamed in honor of Augustus Caesar.

Sextilis 1	Festival day of Ceres.
Sextilis 1	Sacred to Victoria.

Sextilis 9	Sacred to Sol.
Sextilis 12	Sacred to Hercules and Venus.
Sextilis 13	Sacred to Castor, Flora, Fortuna, Hercules, Pollux.
Sextilis 13	Festival day of Diana.
Sextilis 13	**The Vertumnalias**—Honoring Vertumnus. A celebration of harvest and the ripening of both crop and wild crafted food (wild vegetables and fruits).
Sextilis 17	**The Portunalia**—Honoring Portunes. A celebration in honor of Portunes. Homes and places one hopes to keep secure are blessed on this day by throwing their keys into a ritual fire. If Portunes hears your prayers, he will assure that any ill intent placed on those keys is burned away.
Sextilis 17	**Tiberinalia**—Honoring Tiberinus.
Sextilis 19	**Vinalia Rustica**—Honoring Venus.
	A wine festival celebrating romantic love, the goddess Venus, and the fruits of harvest, especially wine. See also Vinalia Priora, Aprilis 23.
Sextilis 21	**The Consualia**—Honoring Consus.
	A festival to celebrate Consus, who protects stores of food. This holiday was celebrated on or about August 21 as grain is being stored and then again on or about December 15 when those stores were needed.
Sextilis 23	Sacred to Maia
Sextilis 23	**The Volcanalia**—Honoring Volcanus. Festival day honoring the Roman Fire god Volcanus. Celebrated with huge bonfires, feasting, and revelry. This day is a time of Fire divination.
Sextilis 23	Festival day of Ceres (day her world opens).
Sextilis 25	**The Opiconsivia**—Honoring Ops. Harvest festival celebrating Ops.
Sextilis 28	**Sacred to Sol and Luna**. This day is sacred to both Sol (Sun) and Luna (Moon). It speaks to us of balance between the masculine and feminine principles of our soul as well as how those principles interact and balance with our partners.

September—*September*—Sacred to the god Volcanus

September 1	Sacred to Juno (Regina).
September 5–19	**Ludi Romani**—Honoring Jupiter. Meaning 'Roman Games' or 'Games of the Rome,' the Ludi Romani were originally held on the 13th of September but gradually expanded to become two weeks of celebration and games.
September 13	Sacred to Juno and Minerva.
September 13	Sacred to Jupiter.

September 23   Sacred to Apollo, Ceres and Latona.

September 26   Sacred to Venus.

September 30   Sacred to Meditrina.

October—*October*—Sacred to the god Mars

October 1   Sacred to Ceres and Fides.

October 4 and 5   **The Mundus Cereris**—Honoring Ceres. Meaning 'Opening of the Earth Gate,' the Mundus Cereris was celebrated with games of endurance and the marking of trials of endurance that have been survived. Honors were given to the victims of rape and similar crimes for having endured and overcome. The order in this is to state firmly that survival is good.

October 7   Sacred to Jupiter and Juno.

October 9   Sacred to Felicitas and Venus.

October 10   Sacred to Juno.

October 11   **The Meditrinalia**—Honoring Meditrina. A holiday celebrating the last harvest of grapes or the wine harvest. This is a healing festival which draws its name from the same source as the deity Meditrina, the word *meden*, which means 'to heal.' This holiday is celebrated with toasts to one's health.

October 12–13   **The Fortunalia**—Honoring Fortuna. This day celebrates reunions. Unlike some of her other festivals, this festival welcomes both men and women to celebrate safe returns from travel and to pray for future safe returns.

October 14   **Feast of the Penates**—At each meal of other days, a portion of each meal was made sacrifice to the Penates so they would continue to protect the home. On October 14th, an evening feast was held and an entire portion of each item in the feast was made sacrifice by tossing it into the home's fireplace.

October 19   **The Armilustrium**—Honoring Mars. On this day the weapons of war were cleaned, purified, and made ready for storage over the winter months. In a modern context, this reflects the Wiccan principle that new ground is not taken during the dark half of the year. In business terms, this means new acquisitions are not made during this time. Instead it is a time to be sure that inventory has been acquired and made ready for the holiday season, which can make or break a business.

October 26–   **The Ludi Victoriae Sullanae**—Honoring Victoria.

November 1   These games honored Victoria and served as competition to replace war but also commemorating victory at war.

November—*November*—Sacred to the goddess Diana

November 1   Last day of Ludi Victoriae Sullanae (See October 26).

November 4—17   **Ludi Plebeii**—In honor of Jupiter. One of the most important games of the year, the Ludi Plebeii were celebrated with not only athletic games but with games of skill and strategy. On November 13th, at the peak of the celebration, a grand feast was held.

November 8   **Mundus Patet**—The Roman Samhain. A day on which the Earth is said to be open or the veils between worlds are thinnest. As the Roman months were not the set things that they are in the modern world, the dates of all events changed. The actual date of this one could easily fall on the current day of October 31st.

November 13   Sacred to Jupiter, Fortuna, Pietas.

November 13   **The Festival of Feronia**—On this day was celebrated freedom from servitude. In a modern context, here we celebrate sobriety if we happen to be dry addicts, or maybe being debt free if we once had debts. This is also a day to contemplate the role of slavery in our lives.

November 18   Sacred to Ceres.

November 29   Sacred to Jupiter, Neptune, and Pluto.

December—*December*—Sacred to the goddess Vesta

December 1   Sacred to Neptune and Pietas.

December 3   Sacred to Bona Dea and Ceres.

December 5   Sacred to Faunus.

December 8   Sacred to Gaia and Tiberinus.

December 11   **The Agonalia of December**—Honors Sol. The name of this holiday finds its root in the word *agonium*, meaning 'sacrificial rites.' This is one of four festivals by the same name: December 11th honors Sol, January 9 honors Janus, March 17th honors Mars, and May 21st honors Veiovis.

December 12   Sacred to Consus.

December 13   Sacred to Tellus Mater.

December 15   **The Consualia**—Honoring Consus. A festival to celebrate Consus, who protects stores of food. This holiday is celebrated on or about December 15th as grain is being consumed from storage and on or about August 21st as grain is being stored for winter.

December 17–23   **The Saturnalia**—Honoring Saturn and his wife Ops. The holiday on which many Christian traditions were based, the Saturnalia involved giving presents (especially to family members), making sacrifice (especially to the poor), and making a distinct effort at removing the barriers of class. Masters served the serving class and merriment for all was the rule. The underlying message was that thanks be given to god (in this case Saturn and his wife Ops), so considering the fact that the date given changes from year to year (depending on the date beginning the year) we see that December 25th (Christmas) often falls smack dab in the middle of the Roman Pagan celebration of Saturnalia. This I feel makes the rebellion against so called Christian traditions—which are actually Pagan traditions—rather silly.

December 19	**The Opalia**—Honoring Ops. This holiday was held in the middle of the Saturnalia. Where Saturnalia is a celebration of the marriage of Saturn and Ops, this day was a celebration that focused on Ops, especially in her role as wife.
December 19	**Day of Children**—Honoring Juventas. This day is known as the Day of Children or Festival of Youth. Although it honored Juventas, goddess who presides over boy's ascension into manhood, this holiday keys on the maiden and master stages of life and not the transition into adulthood. This is a day to give our children presents and enjoy their youth, realizing it dwindles day by day. The cultural celebrations this time of year fit right into the Wiccan religion and Pagan way of life.
December 21	Sacred to Ceres, Divalia, and Hercules.
December 22	Sacred to Lares.
December 23	**The Larentalia**—Honoring Acca Larentia. The last day of the Saturnalia honoring Acca Larentia in her uninhibited aspect.
December 25	**Observation of Winter Solstice**—The actual date changed year to year.
Winter Solstice	**The Angeronalia**—Honoring Angerona.
	This holiday celebrates the goddess of secrets. Celebration centered around games in which no one speaks.

Modern Wiccan Holidays

When considering the ancient Pagan holidays, we see something really interesting starting to emerge. When we consider the eight Sabbats in conjunction with these many ancient Pagan holidays, we see that although the standard eight holidays have become almost universal in the modern Wiccan movement, there is very little about their rigid structure that is from the practices of the pre-Christian Pagans. Instead, we see that what we consider the eight Sabbats is more of an amalgam of ancient ways combined with the new. Consider how many books have told us that Winter Solstice, which is a specific and measurable day, is the same as Alban Arthan, Day of Children, Mother's Night, and Saturnalia? And yet, Alban Arthan, Day of Children, Mother's Night, and Saturnalia were celebrated in time of old as distinctly separate events on distinctly separate days. What gives?

So how many book on Wicca have you read that talk about a person's birthday? How about a wedding anniversary? The anniversary of the first time a couple had sex? How often do you hear about Wiccan Rites conducted to celebrate a child's graduation from high school? One might think these matters would be marked as sacred days to the members of a fertility religion, especially considering the frequency in which we call our religion a 'family religion.'

The answer is that the folk who decided there would be eight major Holidays in Wicca did just that, they decided. Read that. They made it up. They did not receive it from any ancient source, and they could have just as easily chosen the number 4 (one for each of the modern seasons) or 12 (one for each of the modern months). So while we continue to mark those eight holidays because they have become the traditional way for modern Wiccans to mark the Wheel of the Year, what is important to the Wiccan soul is not so much the marking of those days, but the many days that come in between those days.

In looking at those eight Sabbats alongside these examples of ancient Pagan holidays, what we see eight seasons of celebration, not eight single days or evenings. We see that the ancients found reason to celebrate on just about a daily basis, and so should we. You see, if every day is sacred, then we see that every day we live is sacred, and we are reminded that Life itself is, indeed, sacred.

A Morning Prayer

Hail the hoof and hail the horn
Hail the day and praise the dawn
Bless this day with holy light
Bless this time, my holy rite

There is a great deal more to the ancient Pagan cultures than modern Pagan books let on. There is soulful insight to the nature of humanity and the cycles of the world. But chances are you will not find much of that information in fanciful books. I invite you to rediscover the ancient Pagans in modern academic references rather than popular Pagan pulp fiction. There is a whole world out there to discover.

Recommended reading list for this chapter

On the Greek Calendar and Holidays:

Chronology of the Ancient World, by E. Bickerman. (Ithaca, N.Y.: Cornell University Press).

Encyclopedia of Greece and the Hellenic Tradition, by Graham Speake. London: Fitzroy Dearborn Publishers, 2000.

Festivals of the Athenians, by H. Parke. (Ithaca, N.Y.: Cornell University Press, 1986).

Greek Religion, by W. Burkert. (Cambridge, Mass.: Harvard University Press, 1987).

Lost Goddesses of Early Greece: A Collection of Pre-Hellenic Myths, by Charlene Spretnak. (Boston: Beacon Press, 1992). Please note that this title includes a great deal of speculation. I found this tremendously useful, but if you want to stick with main stream thinking on the Hellenic and pre-Hellenic traditions, this one won't make you very happy. This book is greatly speculative, which is why I loved it.

Handbook to Life in Ancient Greece, by Lesley and Roy Adkins. Oxford: Oxford University Press, 1997.

Religion in the Ancient Greek City, by Louis Zaidman and Pauline Schmitt Pantel. Cambridge, Mass.: Cambridge University Press, 1995.

On the Roman Calendar and Holidays:

Festivals and Ceremonies of the Roman Republic, by H.H. Scullard. Ithaca, N.Y.: Cornell University Press, 1981.

Dictionary of Roman Religion, by Lesley and Roy Adkins. Oxford: Oxford University Press, 2001.

The Pagan Book of Days, by Nigel Pennick. Rochester, Vt.: Inner Traditions, 2001.

A Dictionary of the Roman Empire, by Matthew Bunson. Oxford: Oxford University Press, 1995.

Liber ab Anima

(The Book of Soul)

Also Known as Book of Mind and Soul Part I or the Book of Twelve Part III

In previous books I have said that plants have body, animals have body and soul, and humans have mind, body, and soul. Here I discuss the nature of soul. In so doing, I must first point out something very interesting. One of the several Latin names for soul is *anima*. Of the different Latin words I could have chosen I picked *anima* because it is not only the Latin name for soul, it is also the Latin root of the word Animal. While other religions continue to claim that animals have no soul, and can thus be treated any way a soul bearing human desires, Wiccans believe animals have soul because our religion is based on the ancient Pagan religions. Those ancient Pagans, in this case the Romans, did believe so strongly that animals have soul that it was built into not only their language, but has continued into our modern language.

In the introduction to this book, I said that no part of this book should be taken out of context. This is especially true of this chapter, for here we discuss the fire of the soul. Fire without water is dangerous. When it comes to soul, that water is mind. So please consider this not only The Book of Soul but also the first half of the Book of Mind and Soul.

The first observation of the nature of the soul is that it generally accompanies the body of living creatures but becomes separated at death. This principle is evidenced by the Roman god Viduus who is said to be responsible for that separation after the body dies. His name means 'divider'. As it is clear that the body remains present in this world upon death, it seems reasonable to believe the soul is not a function of the body.

In ancient Egypt, the soul was called *ba*. It was depicted as a bird or sometimes as a human with the head of a bird. Upon death, the *ba* left the body. Often times great leaders were said to have the *ba* of some of the most sacred animals. The gods were sometimes said to also have the *ba* of specific animals; however, the Pharaoh was also said to be the *ba* of the gods. The ancient Egyptians were rather clear that when discussing the soul, they were not speaking of a force that animates the body but instead a *pattern of consciousness*. The life force had a different name, *ka*. Again we see 'Our creator is evidenced by our creativity,' expressed here by saying the soul of the creator is found in both animals and humanity.

In the many Voodoo traditions, the word *zombie* is used to describe a human who has had his soul removed from his body. According to Caribbean Voodoo traditions (as opposed to Hollywood Voodoo traditions), the victim did not have to die before becoming a zombie. Instead, the soul of a living person could be removed either with or without tricking the soul into thinking it was time to leave. Even though there is a wealth of knowledge that tells us the death was faked and the soulless conduct of the victim is a result of chemicals used to fake death, the lore remains. So we have another insight into what the Voodoo traditions consider the soul to be—not something that animates the body because the body can be animate without the soul.

On the Polynesian islands, the soul is called *Mauri*. In Batak (Sumatra, Indonesia) it is called *Tondi*. It is the very nature of that which we are. Collectively, it is the very nature of that which the collective is. As the collective of a small group, it has been called the *Yamato*, or the soul of the Japanese. On a much larger scale, it has been described as the soul of humanity. The Hindu religion calls that great collective the *Atman*, the Greeks called it the *Aether*. In my view of the Wiccan religion, this collective is not the Creator itself, but the force by which the Creator acts in creation. It is the very soul of our Lord and Lady.

In Teutonic lore, there are creatures known as the Undine. They are female Water Sprites who are said not to have a soul until they marry a mortal man and have a child. The birth of that child causes the Undine to receive a soul. But where did it come from? For that matter where did the soul of the child come from?

In Roman lore, the goddess Psyche is the personification of the soul, her name meaning either 'breath' or 'soul.' She was so beautiful that Aphrodite became jealous and sent Eros to punish her by causing Psyche to fall in love with an ugly man. Upon looking just once at Psyche, he fell hopelessly in love with her. For that love, he had no choice but to visit her every night. Being in the service of Aphrodite, he had no choice but to insist that Psyche not know his true identity. One night, Psyche cheated and held a light to his face to determine his identity. When he discovered her attempt, he left her. Psyche (soul) then wandered the world desperately hoping to find Eros (love) again.

It seems rather clear that the ancients connected the soul with what Wicca calls the Fifth Element. It is the force that brings a man and a woman together to create a child, the force that brings lovers together in such a way that, once knowing each other, they might wander the world searching for reunion. Here we see that the soul is the center that we talked about in the Book of Four.

Of course, I cannot speak to the nature of your soul. That is a job that each individual must do for oneself. But I can use historic reference to the ancient Pagans, as seen in the Book of Holidays, and put forth speculation as to the nature of the soul most applicable to a modern interpretation of those ancient Pagan religions. You see, the nature of our soul can be seen in those things that give us joy and those things that give us grief. The ones that give us joy, we celebrate. So in understanding the nature of the Wiccan soul, we can look at those things that were celebrated by the ancients to determine what those ancients valued and if, indeed, the values we hold are Pagan.

The Wiccan Soul Screams for Beauty

The third day of every Greek month is sacred to the Three Graces. Also known as the Three Charities, they are the Greek personification of natural beauty. They are Aglaea (Splendor), Euphrosyne (Mirth), and Thalia (Cheer). In modern Wicca, this does seem clear in our many arts, in the celebration of human form by using it to view our Lord and Lady, by the inclusion of skyclad rites, and by reverence for the beauty of the Earth and all its creatures.

The Wiccan Soul Screams for Both Love and Lust

The fourth day of each of the Greek months is sacred to Aphrodite, goddess of love. While the three Graces are honored the day before Aphrodite, they are themselves the attendants of Aphrodite, thus marked plainly on the third day of every Greek month were the attendants of Love. While there are many things one might do to tend their love, one of the most sacred in the Wiccan religion is the act of romantic love itself. The Greeks also remind us of this with the Aphrodisia on Hekatombaion 5.

The fourth day of each of the Greek months is also sacred to Eros, the god so connected to sexual desire that his name is the root word for *erotic*. While the souls of all creatures scream with lust, the Wiccan religion embraces lust when this aspect of our soul is tempered with mind (as discussed in Book of Mind). But in identifying the lust in the Wiccan soul, we see the Bendideia celebrated in honor of Bendis for the days of Thargelion 15 through 19. While it is not clear if this reference in *Aradia* found its way into the Charge of the Goddess, it is clear that the Charge of the Goddess instructs that "all acts of love and pleasure are my rituals."

How could one say the Romans argue this point when we see the a clear origin of Valentine's Day in their Festival of Juno on Februarius 14 and the Lupercalia on Februarius 14 and 15? Then there is the Vinalia Rustica on Sextilis 19, which is presided upon by Venus and which celebrates not only romantic love, but also the passion that a bit of wine often inspires.

In modern day Wicca, this is manifested in our liberal views on human sexuality. Sex is pleasure and pleasure is good. Remember, it is that drive for sex that has preserved the human race during its exodus from Africa, making it possible for originally dark-skinned people to move north into parts of the world with less ultraviolet radiation. It was sexual selection, the lust that causes folk to select their mates, that changed the dark skin that protects from ultraviolet radiation into light skin that in northern areas protects from the degenerative results of rickets.

The Wiccan Soul Screams for Family and Community

The second day of every Greek month is sacred to Agathos Daimon (Agathadaimon in Egypt), or 'Good Spirit.' Monthly offerings included flowers, rice pudding, honey, butter, and the sweet things in life in conjunction with the more personal celebration of individual ancestry. On Boedromion 5, the Genesia was celebrated much the same way, but in grander annual style. The practice of honoring these ancestors and Agathos Daimon are said to bring good luck and fortune, indicating the ancient Greeks saw a clear connection between personal prosperity and the family structure, and that a great portion of one's wealth can be found in one's ancestors. Additional Greek celebrations of community are found in the Synoikia on Hekatombaion 15 and 16, and the Metageitnia on Metageitnion 7. On this the Romans were in great agreement, celebrating community at the Campitalia, one of the first festivals of Januarius and the Fornacalia from Februarius 5 to 7, which honors local community.

The last day of the Greek month, the dark moon, is sacred to Hecate. The last three days are sacred to the deities of the Underworld, where our departed ancestors are. When we consider the connection between the prosperity of humanity and the riches found in the Earth, we see clearly why the ancient Greeks marked the beginning and ending of each of their months with celebrations of our departed loved ones. Their soul screamed for family so loudly that their actions insured that even departed members of the family are heard.

On this, too, the Romans were in great agreement as demonstrated with the Parentalia from Februarius 13 to 21 and the Quirinalia on Februarius 17. If not for community, could we have migrated all this way?

The Wiccan Soul Screams for Life, Mirth, and Revelry

Even if we set aside the fact that each and every Wiccan ritual incorporated numerous symbolic Great Rites to mark the very nature of our religion as one which praises life, we see the Festival of Anna Perenna on Martius 15 at which one is challenged to drink a glass of wine equal to the number of years one hopes to live.

Although revelry for the sake of family, beauty, and love was clearly an indication that the ancient Pagan soul screamed for family, beauty, and love; they also demonstrated revelry for the sake of revelry. In so doing their actions tell us that their souls scream for celebration, dance, and merriment. From the Anethesteria which is held from Anthesterion 11 to 13, we see a celebration of our beloved Dionysus. We see also the Dionysia celebrated not once, but twice every year. First for a full week beginning on Elaphebolion 9 and ending on 14 and then for a day on Poseideon 14. We see the Bacchanalia on Martius 16 and 17.

And let's not forget the many Roman celebrations of wine; The Vinalia Priora on Aprilis 23, The Vinalia Rustica on Sextilis 19.

The Wiccan Soul Screams for Liberty and for Freedom

The Roman Festival of Feronia on November 13 tells us ancient Rome cared greatly for freedom.

When we remember the fact that all of humanity left Africa, spread to the four corners of the world, and then rejoined each other in North America, we see something truly amazing start to unfold. Right in the center of North America is the United States, where freedom of religion is considered so important that it was written into the nations very founding documents:

> "Congress shall make no law respecting an establishment of religion, or prohibiting the free exercise thereof; or abridging the freedom of speech, or of the press; or the right of the people peaceably to assemble, and to petition the government for a redress of grievances."

The First Amendment to the Constitution of the United States of America

Indeed liberty and self-determination was screamed by the ancient Pagan soul so loudly that modern nations were constructed with those very themes. Who can argue that the structure of the government of the United States of America is not founded on the principles set forth by the ancient Greeks and then developed further by the Romans? Who can argue that the very principles that caused the founders of the United States to scream the very same message as did the ancient Greek and Roman Pagans?

If the Pagan soul does not value and scream for liberty, why then did the Greeks celebrate the Liberalia? Why does their pantheon include Libertas, the goddess and personification of liberty. Why were the French, so moved by the thirst for liberty that they gave to the United States the giant idol of Lady Liberty to smile down on our nation?

Indeed the Pagan soul does scream for liberty and freedom. In the Roman Festival of Feronia, we see a celebration of freedom not only from that which is commonly thought of as enslavement, but from those things which bind our soul. That principle being summed up by the Devil card in a standard tarot deck.

It is this desire for liberation that has brought most folk to Wicca and yet it is mostly ignored. Again we see the two distinctly different paths of Wicca. The faddist who performs a self-dedication or a coven/household initiation being one branch of Wicca and the sincere path in which one recognizes the insatiable need to understand, to know, to liberate the mind and who, with that recognition, realizes Wicca is not a place to go, it is a journey to take. That journey being the initiation into the mysteries upon mysteries found within not only our own soul but the collective that is life itself.

The Wiccan Soul Screams for Victory

Finally, the Wiccan soul screams for victory in all things as demonstrated by the Ludi Victoriae Sullanae from October 26 to November 1. That very celebration being created because the ancient Romans knew that their souls screamed for victory, but that victory could not be achieved without a conflict to be overcome. So instead of allowing the desire for victory to become the motive for war, the celebration of sport was created.

Is Your Soul Wiccan?

In these questions, I am not asking if you have acted on your soul's desire. I am asking only if your soul has spoken these things to you.

Does your soul scream for beauty in a world that is sometimes very ugly? When you see an animal needlessly tortured and killed in the ugliest ways do you want to scream STOP! That is life that you are destroying! Do you cry for that creature because you feel its pain? Because you have the empathy given to Ash and Elm. Do you know the suffering of other creatures? Does it hurt so bad that when you think about it, when you lower the years of protective walls and shields intended to protect you from the pain, do you have trouble curling up into a little ball and cry in the dark?

Does your soul scream for love in a world that is sometimes filled with hate? When someone acts hatefully towards you, does it hurt? Does your soul scream out that you want to be loved? That you need to be loved? Does your soul tell you that unless you are loved, you will wither and die? Have you ever sat alone in the dark and given into the tears of a relationship gone bad? Has your soul ever brought you to the edge of insanity because someone you loved did not act with reciprocity?

Does your soul scream with lust so strongly that you can't imagine laws against satisfying those desires? If you are heterosexual, is your soul so clear that sex is sacred that you can not imagine laws against homosexuals. If you are homosexual, is your soul so clear that sex is sacred that you can not imagine laws against heterosexuals? Has your soul ever demanded that you say to your lover, take me and take me now! Have you been without a love and heard your soul demand that you have someone, anyone, in your bed? Have you ever been awakened to realize that while your mind was asleep, your soul was reviling?

Does your soul scream; "I cannot do this alone"? Does it demand that you find your tribe, your people, your Kith and your Kin? Do you feel your life is better when it is shared, not only with a lover, but with a good friend. Does it tell you that kith and kin are necessary for your very survival, that without friends you might well die? Does it tell you that you must build community and participate in that community? Does it cause you to participate in message forums and chat rooms? Does it cause you to seek out like minds and draw close those with whom you want to spend your life? Does your soul cause you pain when these people leave your life, when you loose community?

Does your soul scream for mirth? Does it tell you that you must rejoice and celebrate life, finding merriment where you may? When you sit in a club without dancing because you don't think you know how or maybe because you don't think you look good enough to get out on the dance floor, does your soul torment you? Does it say; 'Come on lets dance?" When you drink too much and your mind take a nap for a while, do you do things that you wouldn't do should your mind be alert? Do you ever wonder if your soul is telling you to lighten up? Do you sit and cry because you don't know how?

Does your soul scream for liberation from whatever force it is that restrains it? Does it demand freedom from that which is ugly and that which is unloving? Does it demand liberation from laws which oppressive sexuality? Does it scream for liberation from those forces which supress your mirth and destroy community? Does your soul scream to be set free from the Outsider's that we spoke of earlier? Does your soul demand liberation and victory over those forces?

Does your soul insist that the earth be liberated from the poisons that are being dumped into her ocean? Does your soul insist that the sky be liberated from the poisons that are being dumped into his air?

Does your soul insist that animals should be free from unnecessary suffering?

Does your soul insist that humans should conduct themselves humanly?

If it does, then STOP, relax, and calm down. In my view of Wicca, if that sudden stop felt very awkward, then chances are you have a Wiccan soul. Yes, I am shifting gears rather suddenly and might seem to be flying off on a tangent. But I am doing so to illustrate a very important point which we will discuss in the second half of The Book of Mind and Spirit, which is otherwise known as the Book of Mind. But before entering in to the Book of Mind, we should do what might seem like back-tracking.

Liber ab Familia

(Book of Familiars—Condensed[1])

The Second Order of Life

Study Material for the Second Degree

A s stated in the Book of Soul, that which drives human nature is shared by animals. Because animals possess soul but not mind as human consciousness, we can look to them to understand the nature of our soul without the mind obstructing that view. Human consciousness is not a bad thing, but it does tend to cloud the view of the soul. Consider the first impression, the animal impression, one might have of a potential mate—not just the look or body of that potential mate, but the impression one has of the nature of that soul.

History is filled with stories of the Witch and her cat familiar. Many feel those stories are just as silly a stereotype as the image of the almost classic Halloween Witch with the big wart on her nose. Others have recognized that a great many Wiccans are cat-lovers. Others are dog-lovers. And let's not forget the birds, lizards, snakes, rodents, rabbits, and all order of critters found to be loved by the modern-day Witch. Hopefully, most of us have done so mindfully.

Yes, modern day Wiccans do commune with their familiars. But the familiar is not nearly what most folk seem to think it is. As a noun, the first definition given by *The American Heritage Dictionary* is "A close friend or associate." It says nothing about that close friend or associate mandatory being a cat. Certainly one could have a cat as his or her familiar, but it is not necessarily.

209

Neither is having a familiar mandatory to being a Wiccan. If we were to insist that every Wiccan have a familiar, that again would be objectification. Instead, the Wiccan religion insists nothing but quietly observes that the very nature of the Wiccan soul causes the Wiccan to love animals. Hence, being mindful of those critters needs, should a Wiccan not be able to provide for those needs, that Wiccan does not take a familiar into his or her home.

The word familiar comes from the Latin *familiris*, which refers to family. This is why Wicca has involved familiars from its very beginning, not because doing so satisfies the need to approximate the historical (and sometimes hysterical) stereotype of a Witch, but because it hopes to guide Wiccans into experiencing the mystery of our relationship with animals.

Again we see that water is wet and fire is hot are matters better learned by discovery than by a book education. Yes, one could tell you that animals are sacred, but if one guides the student in the direction of involvement with animals, should they have a Wiccan soul they will arrive at that conclusion on their own. That having taken place, the connection already forged will be infinitely more valuable than anything one could read in a book. With that and the relationships discussed in Book of Plants, we see that all living things are part of one large family.

If you are not convinced, spend some time in study of our cousin, the rat. If you do not have one in your care, visit your local zoo or pet store and carefully watch how rats eat. Study their hands and how they use them. Study your own and compare them to Rat. Then leave and have lunch at the first fast-food restaurant you encounter. Carefully watch how humans eat. I think you will discover tremendous similarities, although rats do tend to have much better table manners and social skills.

The second definition given for the use of familiar as a noun is "An attendant spirit, often taking animal form." Again, the dictionary hit the nail square on the head. The familiar is an attending spirit or soul that has taken on animal form. Are not we all? Certainly no one can argue that humanity is not itself an animal. Yes, humanity possesses distinct traits such as mind that are not found in other creatures, but we are animals none the less.

So what of that stereotype of the old wart-nosed Witch and her familiar the cat? Science now tells us that healthy relationships with animals can greatly improve a person's health, thus extending that person's life. Programs have been established to bring animals into the hospital to visit the ill and to nursing homes and retirement villages to visit the elderly, bringing with them cheer and a sense of well being. Generally speaking, of all the animals domesticated by humanity, the cat remains the most independent, thus requiring the least amount of care. Such a creature would seem the animal of choice for one who is elderly and perhaps unable to tend to the needs of a more demanding critter. Now, if science is right about life extension being facilitated by a healthy relationship with a loving creature, one can easily see how it would not be uncommon to see the elderly with the creature that helped extend that person's life.

Of course science has not always been the acceptable thing that it is today. If the Witch-hunters of old had any logic behind their madness, their belief that the familiar communicated messages between the Witch and Satan can be found here, in the familiar's communication between anyone who would listen and the natural world of which we are part but which the Church desperately sought to separate from. Remember, the Church State of the Burning Times taught that their God was supernatural and widely opposed the concepts of gods and goddesses that had developed naturally alongside humanity. That Church opposed nature and the explanation of natural law (science) and attempted to snuff it out at every turn. The discovery of natural laws, like the Earth is round and in orbit around the sun, was met with execution. Science was then lumped in with the Church State's boogieman because their word *satan* comes from the Semitic word for adversary (sometimes incorrectly cited as Ha-Satan). Certainly any creature that spoke to us of all things natural would be viewed as adversarial (satanic) to their *supernatural* ("Of or relating to existence outside the natural world")[2] God and the heavens in which he ruled.

In embracing animals and the natural world in which we belong, we become the adversaries of any power structure that would think otherwise. When we stand and say no, you may not pit dogs against each other for amusement and betting, we become the adversaries. When we say yes, we will punish you for organizing cockfights, we become the adversaries of any power structure that would think otherwise. We are winning, and times they are a-changing. Promoting such events is now illegal in most of the civilized world. Yes, when the fight organizers are brought to court they quote the Christian Bible in defense of their actions. Yes, the punishments are far too low in the opinion of many, including myself. But these things will also change with the changing of our society's group consciousness. This is where Wicca and religions with similar ethics comes in. By conducting ourselves in accordance with the ethics that we arrive at by exploring the mystery of our religion, we find that those ethics manifest in our actions and in our words.

Think about those folk who organize dog fights and cock fights. More and more, their rants cause folk to become sickened. More and more, people turn away from the old Church State style of Christianity in disgust and perhaps more importantly, more and more Christians are accepting the idea that the translation of the word 'dominion' would have better been 'stewardship.' I say more importantly because no matter what one claims their religion to be, no matter what word they use or what they do in church or ritual, what matters is what their soul tells them that religion is and what they do in between church or ritual. Let's face it, most of us live in a Christian society and hope to do so peacefully. But it is impossible to do so with a Wiccan soul if that society continues to subscribe to medieval ideas that the animals exist for the amusement of men. So as that predominantly Christian society transforms its view on animal rights, we fall from the position of adversary, we become less 'satanic,' and in that transition we are instrumental in bettering the lives not only of humanity, but of all who share this world.

You see, the agents of the power structure are now on our side. Where once they sought those who would dare befriend our connections to the natural world, today law enforcement seeks those who would harm these critters without cause such that they can be brought before the courts—the power structures—and punished for their crimes against our Lord and Lady. No, the battle for animal rights has not been won, but with continued inroads being made in a sensible manner, we are certainly winning the war.

Before I begin a discussion of the Wiccan familiar, I must warn you that I am not talking about the fanciful stylish familiars or spirit animals that many folk lay claim to for fashion sake. If you want to claim a critter is your familiar just to have something neat to talk about with your friends, please do just that. Claim, and claim only! Adopting an animal is a serious responsibility that should only be taken by the most committed animal-lover.

Being involved with a familiar is a give and take relationship. When one truly welcomes a critter into one's heart, he or she welcomes that critter as family. So if you are not willing to give, please don't take because without that willingness to sacrifice for your familiar, neither you nor your familiar will receive the benefits of the relationship. You might think that without a pet your life is miserable, but that is no reason to make another critter's life miserable.

The familiar is much more than simple companionship. It is a connection to the world that we sometimes think lost when we moved into the cities. Prior to the Neolithic revolution some 8,500 to 9000 years ago,[3] humanity lived mostly as a migratory creature. We fueled our migration up the coastal areas and tributaries, living off seafood as well as the hunt for both flesh and fruit. The Neolithic revolution marks that point when we turned our attention inland and began building permanent communities. Many of those communities later became vast cities, and a difference could eventually be seen in the habitat of humanity and of all other creatures. Today, those differences are often defined as *natural* and *artificial* (man made) as if humanity were not a part of the natural world.

Our familiars remind us that we did not leave the natural world at all, that although our modern ways might seem artificial or removed from nature, there remains zero degrees of separation between humanity and the natural world. If we were not still connected to that natural world, we would not see extinction after extinction in direct relationship to the actions of humanity. If we did not have the arrogance to deceive ourselves into thinking we are not connected, we would not be shocked when we realize the scope of the destruction.

Bison, American—Feminine, Earth

Also known as: American Buffalo, Buffalo, Bison

God associations: Great Spirit, Tatanka

Goddess associations: Durga

While there are many animals that illustrate the need for Wiccans to embrace the children of Earth and Sky, few remain alive to tell their story. The American Bison is one of those few. Where their numbers once exceeded an estimated 75 million, humanity saw to it that by the beginning of the 20th century their herd had been reduced to a handful of about 1,000. To put that figure into perspective, that means that for every buffalo alive at the turn of the nineteenth century, at least 75,000 buffalo were slaughtered (most for neither meat nor hide). Today, they number approximately 30,000.

Elephant—Feminine, Earth

Also known as: African Elephant and Asian Elephant

God associations: Aeacus, Apedemak, Bacchus, Dionysus, Ganesha, Indra (white elephant), Krishna, Kurma, Minos, Rhadamanthus, Shiva, Vishnu, Vulcan

Goddess associations: Artemis, Diana

Most people do not realize that there are two species commonly known as the Elephant. These are the African and Asian elephant. The Indian, Sri Lankan, and Sumatran elephants are all sub-species of the Asian elephant. The Bush, Savannah, and Desert elephants are all sub-species of the African elephant. The African elephant entered the twentieth century with a speculative population of 5 to 10 million. By the time the twenty-first century rolled around, there were less than 600,000. More accurately, there were less than 600,000 when they were added to the endangered species list in 1989. The Asian elephant is in worse condition, having started the last century with even fewer numbers. At the turn of the twentieth century, approximately 200,000 Asian Elephants existed. At the turn of the twenty-first, there are no more than about 35,000, a decline in population of about 82.5 percent.

The Two Types of Familiars: Animal Kin and Animal Kith

Before you remodel your home to allow an elephant into the living room, know that familiars come in two varieties: kith and kin. Just as the process of adoption can change a human from kith to kin, so does the adoption of an animal other than human cause that creature to go from kith to kin. Those creatures brought into both heart and home are said to be kin creatures or kin familiars. In Wicca, these critters are typically known simply as familiars. However, one need not have an animal in the home to welcome it into the heart. Indeed, those creatures often reside in our hearts long before we recognize their residence. These creatures that are welcome in our heart but for whatever reason not in our home are said to be kith animals or kith familiars. In Wicca, these critters are most often known as power or totem animals.

Kith and kin familiars can be equally in our hearts, but just as with our human relations of kith and kin there are distinctly different ways in which we further our relationships. One might commune with the children of our friends (kith) by attending their birthday and graduation parties. Be it by adoption or birth, a person might commune with their own children (kin) by bathing them, taking them for their first hair cut, or tucking them in at night. Confusing the two can bring about misunderstandings. There is little difference in our relations with animals. Some relationships are appropriate and some are not appropriate. Determining which is which is relatively easy should one have a lick of common sense and an ounce of respect for our critter friends.

Common sense: It is not appropriate to take a human child from a shopping center and raise it as your own.

Respect for critters: It is not appropriate to take a baby bird from its mother's nest and bring it home to be your pet.

Kin Familiars

Most Wiccans have knowledge of the kin familiar and simply call it a familiar. Those who have shed the spooky names that seem to come with the Wiccan religion substitute the word *friend* for familiar. Although they might use the word *pet* to talk about the critter in mixed company, many know exactly what that critter is and commune with him or her every day. Others argue that the critter is not a familiar, demonstrating the belief that the word familiar is only used to describe animals that have a formal role in religious rituals. To those folk who believe the word familiar only belongs to animals used in formal rituals, I have to point out that real life is vastly more important than ritual. Not wanting to be redundant, but wanting to address those who are not already convinced of this, I ask that you please read Chapter 6 of my book *Wicca for Couples* (New Page Books, 2001) to understand where I am coming from on this issue.

If you have bonded with a specific animal, that creature is your familiar. It doesn't actually matter if you have welcomed it into your home or given it a name. Those actions are more a result of the bonding process. It is the joining of hearts that denotes the union and that union, rather than its formal marking is what is important. Except for the practicality of limiting factors, it also matters not if you have one or one hundred and one. Like relationships with humans, there is plenty of love to go around. But also like relationships with humans, there is only so much time in a day. I have observed that my closest friendships are shared with people who, like I, do not have a tremendous number of close friends.

One need not place his dog on his altar and bless him for that dog to be his familiar. Neither does one need to take one's cat everywhere one goes or buy it special jewelry to mark its rank as familiar. Oh, these things might seem fun, but often they are more for the amusement of the owner than the bond between one and his or her critters. It's not a hard concept to understand, and yet people sometimes seem completely blind in this regard.

If you were to ask a bare footed friend if they want to walk on hot pavement all afternoon, they would probably say no. Yet every year at our local Community Festival[3], I see dozens of dog owners walking their dogs on the blacktop, at a complete loss to understand why their beloved pets are practically goose-stepping. Finally, I figured it out. It wasn't that they did not care about their animals, it was because they did not communicate with them. Upon this realization I started attending with a sign on my canopy that reads: "Your dogs are walking funny because their feet are being burned." Amazingly, people read the sign and instantly brought their animals onto the grass of the park. One woman even dropped to her knees in tears and covered her dog's feet with water from one of those stylish bottles. More often than not, when we abuse our familiar it is because we are not treating them as a familiar. We are not listening to what they have to say because they do not use words. It wasn't until some kind organization funded a huge public service campaign that many people realized leaving a dog in a car during the summer might be a bad thing.

Thus, shattering the more popular conception that a familiar is defined as a critter that is involved in Wiccan ritual, the point at which our pet becomes our familiars is that point where we begin listening to them. After all, that is the classic definition of a familiar now isn't it? Our familiars communicate on a level that is far easier to understand than words. But one need not pry these messages from them with a ouija board, tarot cards, or psychic reading. Their messages can be found in their actions. Let me tell you about my ferret friend Thumper, whose name she received from the sound she makes when she has crawled into that space between the inner and outer wall of an electric oven. You know, the space between the outer and inner wall of your oven that is *supposed* to be filled with insulation to keep the heat in the oven that you find in the bottom of the oven should you take your eyes off your ferret for a few moments.

Always trying to get me into a foot race or a game of attack the toes, she tells me that when your needs are met, being playful is important to maintaining a healthy soul. Just watching her tells me that when playfulness gets you into a tight spot, flexibility can get you out of it. Of course, she also warns that playfulness can be misunderstood, especially when she tries to play with Fred, my 4-foot iguana. She also advises that sometimes things that seem fun for you will result in harm to someone you love even when it doesn't seem so at the time. Have you priced a new oven recently?

Now I am not about to try and crawl between the walls of an oven and displace the insulation, but I am involved in a monogamous but long distance relationship that benefits greatly from what Thumper has told me. You see, I am not without temptation, and it does sometimes seem as if I can have my cake and eat it, too. But there's Thumper's warning that what might seem like nothing more than playful fun might hurt someone that I love. Sure, it does seem that a roll in the hay with a local lass wouldn't hurt the woman to whom I am sworn. I might even be able to rationalize the action, tricking myself into believing it is just sex and doesn't mean all that much. But there is that insulation from my oven. It's just insulation and doesn't actually mean much. This being the first serious relationship I have been involved in since having that conversation with Thumper, the word is still out on how things will pan out. But it does seem like sound advice.

This brings up something very important about the advice given by our critter friends. Even more so than our human friends, critters do not listen to their own advice. When taking it, one must always do so from the stance of listening to what they do. You see, critters do not share a common language, so in essence that which they do is what they say. To tell me that playfulness might be misinterpreted, Thumper had no choice but to try to play with Fred. To tell me that one should keep potential harm from oneself until one is sure of its intent, Fred had no choice but to whap her with his tail and send her rolling across the floor. To tell me that sometimes my loved ones won't see eye to eye, they had to stage the entire incident. Make no mistake, when the message is important enough, critters will team up to deliver it.

Finding Kin Familiars

Generally speaking, it is not fair to take an animal from the wild and bring it into your home. There are exceptions, but with each comes tremendous responsibility. Remember that the Wiccan Rede specifically tells us that we should "fairly take and fairly give." I hope you will agree that deliberately kidnapping a critter and forcing it to live by your side is far from fair. But what about injured wildlife? Certainly a warm and loving home is superior to death in the wild.

Far be it for me to tell you that it is bad to assist an injured animal. One could not count the number of animals I have brought into my home this way. If you don't believe me, ask my mother who probably cannot count the ones I brought into her home when I was a child. But in making such a decision for a young critter, remember that if that creature should imprint upon you or not learn that which its parents would teach it about survival, there may be no way to return it to the wild.

Another way kin familiars come from the wild is by the actions of a just hunter. Should you take a critter's guardian before its young are able to fend for themselves, the just hunter is charged with the life of those children. Rather than turning a blind eye to the suffering and starvation that taking a guardian will cause to its young, a just hunter will, at a very minimum, swiftly end the life of those children, find an appropriate home for them, or adopt those children as one's own and raise them in stay of the life that one took. Incidentally, this has also been general policy of many tribal cultures when dealing with matters of war. But the injured and parentless animals are the least common source for familiars. The most common source is the pet store. While this might seem like the kindest way to bring an animal into your life, it is only kind in the way purchasing flesh from the grocery store is kind, that kindness being only the illusion of kindness.

As with hunting, here is a place where I believe I feel very differently than many folk. Where many folk see hunting as an unfair contest between man and beast, I see it as vastly more fair than the meat industry that supplies most grocery stores. The difference is that when one takes the life of an animal, the hunter witnesses the action from a viewpoint where one can decide if the action of taking that life was just. When one purchases flesh from most grocery stores, one can never be sure if the taking of that life was fair. At the risk of alienating the great majority of my readers, I urge you to at least allow yourself to make an educated decision. Before again eating flesh, just watch a video of the methods used to raise and kill the animals that feed the average grocery store. Realize that in purchasing that product you are supporting those methods and then ask yourself if doing so is living in accordance with the Wiccan Rede's advice to "fairly take and fairly give." I am not telling you to boycott grocery stores, I am just asking that your actions be taken mindfully.

When finding critters to become your familiar, I ask that you do the same. Discover where the pet stores are acquiring those animals. Investigate the methods by which those animals are bred and presented for sale. Are they conducting themselves as did the slave merchants of old? There are exceptions, but chances are great that you will discover treatment that is far beyond your definition of fair. Certainly, one can make the argument that the animals that are already in the pet stores need homes, but the counter to that argument is obvious. If they are in a pet store, it is because they sell well and will find a home without your assistance. I am not telling you to boycott pet stores, I am just asking that your actions be taken mindfully.

Although there is clearly a difference between kin familiars and kith familiars, in choosing one's kin familiars, one should remain loyal to the whole of its line to insure a proper match. This is much in the same order as human adoption. Hopefully, you can see how a card-carrying member of the Ku Klux Klan might not be the best person to adopt an African American child even if s/he honestly loves that child. One need only look at the history of slavery to know that when souls are sold mainly for profit, those sales are indiscriminant. While there is a difference between the way our society feels about the sale of human life and the sale of critters, the principle remains the same. The result is that generally speaking, pet stores buy and sell their product as did the slave trade, indiscriminately.

So what does happen to the critters that pet stores do not manage to sell? Many of them wind up further burdening one of the best kept secrets in the pet industry, the critter rescue services. With so many Wiccans demanding secrets be revealed by authors, I am surprised this one has not yet been printed. If you can think of an animal, you can probably find that animal at little or no cost in the care of many rescue services. As an example, a recent visit to a pet store to purchase some canned Iguana food showed me that the going rate of a Ferret is about $150.00 in the Central Ohio area. One search on the web using the words "ferret rescue Columbus Ohio" turns up the link to Mid Ohio Samoyed and Ferret Adoption and Information Services.

> *"MOSAFARI is a not for profit organization which takes in unwanted, abused, and neglected pets, rehabilitates them, and finds them new forever homes. We take in strays, owner surrenders, and some with health problems. We rehabilitate when necessary, vaccinate, and put them up for adoption after recovery from illnesses."*
>
> —*From the MOSAFARI Website*
> http://www.petfinder.org/shelters/OH48.html *January 17, 2003*
> *Note: This URL will soon change to www.morafari.org*

Of course, some folk might want to adopt only healthy baby critters. But even when that is the case, finding critters via the many rescue services is a good way to go. You see, most rescue services realize that demand and network with reputable breeders to help battle the hordes of unscrupulous breeders. By dealing with a reputable breeder, you will generally pay only slightly less than pet store prices, but you will have the advantage of knowing you have remained true to the line of your new critter by not promoting its exploitation. Why? Well, it is simple economics. The price of an animal in the pet store is set by the consumer. It is roughly that which the market will bear, as much as the store can get without lowering total income by reducing sales beyond that magickal point of maximum profit. To meet that price with a large staff, pay the electric, buy the store fixtures, and let's not forget the rent, they simply cannot afford to pay breeders top dollar. As a result, remaining in business requires breeders to do one of two things.

1. **'For profit' breeders**—If their primary intent is profit, they cut corners to lower their selling price. In so doing, they overpopulate living areas, decrease the genetic distance between mother and father (inbreeding), allow children to leave their parents too early, and decrease the amount of human attention each critter receives. The result, like almost any attempt at economizing a product, is a product that is inferior to other methods of production.

2. **'For love' breeders**—If their primary intent is focused more on their love for the animal they raise, they will refuse to cut corners to decrease the selling price. In so doing, they allow critters to have appropriate living areas, increase the genetic distance between mother and father (preventing inbreeding), insure that children are fully weaned before sale, and increase the amount of human attention each critter receives. The result, like most cottage industry, is that a superior product is produced and with it a higher price, although that price remains comparable because when one deals with a breeder they eliminate the many expenses involved in operating a pet store.

But there is still a source of critters that is superior to even the breeder or rescue service. Rescue the critters yourself, allowing destiny, karma, Wyrd, or whatever you want to call it to bring them into your life. Although they do not possess human consciousness, critters are in no way stupid. The absolute best dog I have ever had still lives with me this day. He is mostly blind, partly deaf, and a little lame, but he is the most loving and joyful animal I have ever had the fortune of encountering. Why? Because I rescued him from a miserable state and after a year of loving care, he came to realize his life is all the better for it.

Puppy (named after a roommate by the same name) and I first met during the night of a cold rainstorm. I was driving back from machinating at a festival an hour south when I found him in the middle of the road. At first I thought he was dead because honking solicited no response. I parked my truck blocking the road and put on the hazards to warn off other traffic. Upon approaching him, I discovered that he was indeed alive but trembling in fear as would be any blind, deaf, and partly lame human should he find himself in the middle of traffic. I took him to the vet, figuring I would get him fixed up and then give him over to an adoption agency. The vet told me that there was almost no chance of restoring his eyesight, nothing to do about his hearing, and that his hips would soon need an operation. She also told me that if I gave this animal to the humane society for adoption, they would certainly put him down because he was un-adoptable. Well, someone missed out because although he is not too good at playing catch, fetch, or anything that involves eyesight, he is a killer at playing tug of war with socks. Sure, it's usually the socks that I haven't donated to that cause, but that's just his way of telling me to pick up after myself.

Cat (named after my lawyer at the time) came into my life much as did Puppy. I was returning from visiting my lawyer Catherine when I stopped in Lancaster, Ohio to visit with friends. After my visit, I was on my way to my car when I spotted her in an over-grown grass field next to my car. She was dehydrated and seemed a bit lame, but I didn't think she was really in need of rescue. She insisted. Now I don't mean she opened up her mouth and talked to me, but she looked at me with those big loving eyes and I told her, "No, you might belong to someone, so I am not going to fall for that. If you really want to come home with me, you jump in that car yourself." Although it sounds boastful, she did just that. Yes, I did hold the car door open when I told her but she took it upon herself to jump into my car and my life. Ten years later, she is still in my life by her own choice. How do I know? The store door is propped open whenever it is hot and she remains inside because she knows who loves her.

Neither Puppy nor Cat participates in formal ritual with me, but they are most certainly part of my religion. They each speak to me of loyalty and of honoring the folk that choose to love me. During the time I have had them in my life, I have had many occasions to be down and out, doubting very much that I will ever find love with the end of each tormented relationship. Each time Cat would sit in my lap and Puppy made his cute little howling noise, both reminding me that I am loved in love's purest form. I don't know about you, but that message has surely extended my life.

Kith Familiars

Folk who identify with the term New Age (and a few Pagans) tend to call them power animals. Folk following the rediscovery of Native American ways sometimes call them spirit animals or totem animals. Those who have discovered the Dream Time traditions of South America and Australia sometimes call them dream animals. Folk who follow specific pantheons of gods and goddesses with specific animal forms often call them by the name of that god or goddess. Such is the case with gods like Horus (Hawk) and Bast (Cat), each having their god or goddess name even when depicted in purely animal form.

In formal conversation, I call them kith familiars, but mostly I just call them out-door critters. These are the animals that we do not know on a personal basis. We see their entire line as if it were one. When we talk about these critters, we call them by their collective name to honor their collective spirit. With this relationship, all wolves are called Wolf; all hawks are called Hawk. The order in which we relate to these critters is much the same way we relate to groups of people. Although much less accu-rate than the description of a specific person, this practice allows us the luxury of gen-eralized expression of common observations—a fancy way of saying stereotypes.

Now, before you experience a knee jerk reaction to the use of stereotypes, let me tell you how they are sometimes a good thing. You see, stereotypes let us discuss those traits belonging to a group that seem to represent the whole of that group. When we say Hawk has good eyesight, we do not mean that all hawks everywhere have good eyesight. When we say that humanity now knows that the Earth is round, we do not mean that all humans believe the Earth is round. When we acknowledge the existence of stereotypes, we can discuss a matter in that order.

This is one of the many reasons that when we are speaking about kith familiars, power animals, totems, or whatever we choose to call them, we are talking of the order of their entire line and not any one individually. This normal process of language is why I can make observations about the human race, such as males have greater upper body strength than females, without the expectation that I will widely be seen as sexist. Note that I did not say males *generally* has greater upper body strength than females because I was speaking of the entire line of humanity, a group in which the collective that is male does, indeed, have more upper body strength than the collective that is female.

Even if one develops a personal relationship with kith familiars, that relationship is with the whole of the line if it is in the order of kith familiars or it is termed kin familiar. This is important because the guide that follows speaks more the whole than to any one critter. For example, Bear being listed as having feminine attributes means simply that the attributes of most bears seem to be feminine. It does not mean that all bears every-where are females or even that all bears in every situation will be fiercely protective of their children. Instead, considering bears to be feminine in nature means that if you were to take the sum total of all bears everywhere it would be a safe bet that if Mama and Papa Bear are in the area, you don't want to mess with Baby Bear.

This principle can provide great comfort when considering the fact that for Life there must be Death. When we see a fox kill a rabbit, considering both fox and rabbit to be parts of their greater line, we see death as a necessary part of life. This allows us to recognize that although Fox does indeed kill Rabbit, it does not make Fox evil. It also allows us to recognize that although Fox must eat Rabbit to live, Rabbit is not evil for trying to escape. Instead we see Rabbit continuing to feed on greens, Fox continuing to feed on Rabbit, and the death of neither even though individual creatures do die. We see the Cycle of Birth, Life, and Death repeated again and again in the constant and yet sometimes seemingly mysterious ways of nature. But the moment we identify these critters as individuals, we move to protect rabbit from fox, thus causing the suffering of fox by starvation and the suffering of rabbit from over population.

Although it has been popular to link spiritual relationships with animal archetypes to Native Americans, virtually all religions have shared a deep connection with ani-mals. Cave paintings and primitive carvings that celebrated animal spirit have been found to be of an origin thousands of years before humanity ever thought to migrate to North America. Remember, there isn't really any such thing as a Native American. We are all Africans, so we all brought not only the genes but also the customs that those genes tend to promote when placed in similar environments.

Prehistoric Shaman from across the world dressed, acted, and danced as animals do to call on their spirits, hoping to bring that which they observed in nature into them-selves and perhaps to call on those attributes for their tribe. When they observed the sudden and silent swiftness of hawks as they snatched mice from the brush, they called on Hawk to lend his swiftness and keen eyesight to matters of hunting. When they saw bears bringing trees to the ground, they called on Bear for strength against all order of foe. When they saw the well-functioning communities created by Beaver, they called on Beaver for the order and wisdom to create and maintain well-functioning communities. Although the practice may seem either overly mystical or even a bit silly to some urban folk, it can easily be seen as nothing more than asking your neighbor to help you with a skill that you are lacking. If it feels a bit silly to you, think about this:

Overnight one of the tires on your car goes flat. You have never changed a tire in your life, so you go next door and ask your neighbor, the mechanic, if s/he can show you how. Of course if its a hot day and you know your neighbor likes Beck's Dark, you might want to mention that you have some when you ask. For larger favors, you might want to find out what type of pizza he likes and offer to have one ready. So is it really all that strange that I make a short journey several times each Spring and Summer to ask a favor of Duck? Or that I often bring him treats? After all, it wasn't until very recently that our critter friends were not our next-door neighbor.

You might have noticed I just personified Duck in the masculine. Later, you might notice the attributes for Duck are feminine. This is because although their are general guidelines for the gender associations made with animals, those gender associations change with our involvement with the critters. Gender is a very personal thing, and that is exactly the order of relationship we experience when we allow our hearts to be touched by kith familiars. So let me tell you the story of Duck in the hopes that you will understand my experience with kith familiar and use such critters to greatly advance not only your own life and relationship with critters, but the relationship between our immediate human and extended animal family.

I first met Duck a few years ago after coming out of an emotionally draining relationship. There is a waterfall not far from where I live, and I wanted desperately to get away from humanity, if only for a few hours. After hiking down to the stream fed by the waterfall, I spied Mama Duck and her five chicks walking towards the creek. I became completely still, hoping she would not notice me. I think she did but decided to take a chance. Her and her chicks entered the stream and started swimming towards the falls. I entered the stream and followed after them.

The shallow water was flowing strongly enough that I figured it would cover the sound of my footsteps, and it was a hot day, so cooling my feet seemed in order. What I hadn't counted on was that when I stepped into the stream, I placed myself in the one spot that was not shielded by the canopy of green. Mama Duck didn't have to hear my footsteps; she needed only to hear Papa Duck's warnings to know that I or some other threat was present. She and her chicks sped up and then disappeared somewhere far ahead of my position, although I tried to find them again it was as if they had become completely invisible.

The next day I returned with a camera and telephoto lens. That day, I kept my distance but knew that Papa Duck was again watching from above. When I came too close, he yelled his warning. I started to wonder if he was warning his family about my approach or warning me about his. It occurred that there was little difference. Each time I visited, he was always there, watching me more intently than I watched his family. Eventually I found myself watching him more than his family. That was about the time he relaxed and went about his normal routine of escorting his family to the water-fall and then back down the stream into the river that it feeds.

I hadn't dressed like a duck, walked like a duck, or quacked like a duck, but I had heard Duck speak even more clearly than some of the married men that I know. He said, "This is my wife and family. There is nothing else that is as important."

Note the period at the end of what Duck said. One of the reasons animals can so easily communicate their message is because their message is simple—not simple in the way one might call a person of low intellect, but simple in an uncluttered way. They say what they mean and mean what they say, period. Humans seem overly fond of saying that no sometimes means yes and wet sometimes means dry. Ask people about the movie *Gone with the Wind* and they will probably tell you how romantic it was when Ret whisked Scarlet off her feet, up the stairs, and into their bed. Ask an animal and you are likely to be told it was rape. You see without the clutter that fills our minds, no means no.

Animals also speak to us of purity in duty. Many Wiccans reject Aleister Crowley's law of Thelema, which reads "Do as thou wilt shall be the whole of the law," because they do not understand the nature of what Aleister Crowley called "will." In the Middle to Far East, this principle is called "duty" or "dharma." It is that which is your true will. Animals remind us of this purity. When Fox kills Rabbit, the action is not sinful. There are no karmic reactions in the order of punishment because the action was of duty. This reflects on the Pagan principle that for Life there must be Death and explains how one's kith familiar can even be the creatures that we hunt or harvest. This is the very nature of the Pagan god of the hunt being that which is hunted, the sacrificial god. As a result of this way of thinking, we see that although death is necessary for life, that which we kill is also sacred, thus should a Wiccan find it necessary to kill, he or she insists that the death be as painless as possible.

Although I am a vegetarian, I know that many of my readers are not. So I tell you that these kith familiars are also the animals raised or hunted for food. Considering any source of food to be anything short of sacred is a great mistake. Not only does it lead to the abuse of the food source, it leads to a spirituality that is deprived in many other aspects as well. But in taking animals for food, they must remain kith familiar and never kin. There is a custom among many who raise livestock that one does not kill an animal if that animal has been given a name. That same custom is alive and well in families that hunt. Should they befriend a deer and give it a name, the hunting of that deer is off limits. When a just hunter takes deer for food, that hunter takes Deer, not Bambi. When a just farmer takes a pig for food, that farmer takes Pig, not Wilbur. Keeping that distance clear is what allows humanity to conduct itself as just predator. Like Fox who takes Rabbit, when we perform a just killing for a just reason such as food, that death is just.

I have even seen this principle shared among some of the old-timers with whom I used to fish. Our local fishing hole had a legendary white catfish named Walt. Reportedly, Walt was 6 feet long if he was an inch. One night, one of the old-timers told us that Walt wasn't a legend, that he knew because he caught him just a couple years earlier. The other old timers believed his fish story but the young pups challenged him:

"So where's the proof if you caught him?"

"Out there in the pond. I put him back," the old timer told us.

"Why?" asked the younger fishermen.

"Because the pond just wouldn't be the same without him."

Well, old Walt was finally caught in a net. The property the pond was on was purchased at auction. The new owner decided to harvest the pond and sell the catfish stock off as farm raised, then restart the process by stocking the pond. Because he was caught in a net and not on a line, the find didn't draw much attention, no pictures or documentation in the local fishing journals, but there was a picture up on the bulletin board at the local gun and rod shop—up for about a week, that is. Then the owner of that gun and rod shop took the picture down, leaving pictures of other fish that had been up for years. Why? Because the owner knew Walt too, so leaving his picture up just didn't seem right.

I loved those old hicks because they had instinctively tapped into the use of the kith familiar and even gone so far as to fall into the same trap that has caused much grief for many Wiccans. They allowed a kith familiar to become kin familiar. Although the land owner was proud of his catch, no one would display it. Although he allows people to fish his pond with rod and reel, none of the old timers fish it. Although he desperately wants to be a part of the culture that had sprung up in that area, he never will be. You see, he just doesn't understand the sacred connection between humanity and the divine that is all of Nature.

Finding Kith Familiars

I have been Pagan for the great majority of my life. I was introduced to the movement years before I could so much as drive a car. But the last ten years of that life has been spent completely and totally emerged in the culture in a way that very few people experience. I own and work in a Pagan shop, live in a Pagan household, and as a result of my career as an author, my attendance of Pagan functions has risen greatly over the last ten years. So please do not be offended when I tell you that in observing the Pagan communities use of kith familiars/Spirit animals I have had many occasions to laugh hysterically. It seems these sacred critters are found mostly in books and movies. I have had many a conversation with folk who have only seen their totem in a dream.

While I have nothing against folk who are blessed with such a vision, I simply do not believe the vision was valid if they have made no real effort at meeting that creature in the flesh. Unless your kith familiar is an exotic, meeting that critter might mean something as simple as paying attention to your surroundings. While helping a friend to move, I once found Hawk to live on the balcony of a second floor apartment across from a self-service storage facility. Over the week that we made trips to and from her storage area, I must have seen Hawk sitting there three times.

Of course, going outside of the city will help greatly. Deer hunting with a camera is a great way to meet Deer and the many other animals that reside in your area. To my surprise, I have even met Fox, Lynx, and several other seemingly uncommon critters simply by finding a mostly human free area and walking around. The larger state and national parks are great for this introduction. Even if you do not meet your kith familiar on the first visit, if you do your research well enough to identify his or her habitat, just spending time in that habitat will greatly increase your connection. Often times on your first visit, you might not spot your familiar but you will feel as if you have. This is because that visit commonly involves a meeting, but your kith familiar didn't let you know that s/he saw you.

But your kith familiar is an exotic, you say. Where do you go to meet Tiger? Almost every major city has a zoo and while it is not the ideal place to meet one's kith familiar, it is certainly more affordable and safer than traveling to the natural habitat of some critters. There was a time in which I would never advise patronizing a Zoo. Back in those days, the zoo was similar to the "for profit breeders" I spoke of in reference to kin familiars. But those days are mostly behind us. Most modern zoos are staffed by some of the kindest loving people you will ever meet. Ok, some of them are a bit snippy after years of dealing with that portion of the public that still shops at pet stores, but when they get to know you for the animal loving soul that you are, they will lighten up.

Communing with Kith and Kin Familiars

There is little difference between communing with kith and kin familiars other than the level at which that communion can take place. We commune with both types of familiar with mind, body, and soul. The connection is in the order of our entire being or it is not termed familiar.

Mind—Reading about an animal does not make it a familiar, but it does greatly further the connection. Volumes of books are often written on each. Because most of these are academic, you can find them at your public or school library. Read as much as you can. Be able to talk about your familiar on an educated level. If one of your kith familiars is an exotic like Tiger, know how many different types of tigers there are. If one of your kin familiars is a domestic like a dog, know what kind of dog that familiar is. In both cases, know what their ideal food is, how fast they can run, how high they can jump, where their genes came from. Your dog might live in Ohio, but who created his breed and for what purpose? If he is a mutt, know what mixture he is, who bred the dogs that led to each portion of the mix and why. Tiger might live at the zoo, but where did tigers live before they were kept in zoos? Do they still live in their native habitat? Most importantly, do they need your help this moment? How many are still alive in the wild? How many are in zoos? Is there a crisis situation that demands your immediate assistance? Remember, if your familiar, kith or kin, has called to you, it is possible it felt you needed it, but it is equally as possible it did so because it needs you.

Body—In terms of kin familiar, we can make body connections by playing with our critters. Dogs love to play tug and ferrets love to play attack the toes. In the case of kith familiars, visit them. If they are an exotic, go to the zoo. If they are wild, go to the woods. If your kith familiar is Dog, go to the pound. Know that whenever your kin familiar is of a line, that line tends to become kith familiar as well. That is to say, if your kin familiar is a dog, then Dog is probably one of your kith familiars.

But don't fall into the trap of thinking that connections of the body are always a pleasant thing. If you have chosen Dog (or if Dog has chosen you) as kith, then donate your time to your local pound. If you have been adopted by Ferret, then donate your time to a ferret rescue service. This might mean shoveling manure, but in so doing you will receive the rewards of communion. While there might be blisters on your hand, there will also be love in your heart.

Spirit—In this world where we connect money to material things, we can see how releasing money is in the order of spirit. Support your kith and kin familiar. This can also be a viable way of bringing an exotic from the status of kith familiar into the realm of kin familiar without actually bringing an exotic into your home. Most zoos have adoption programs where you can pay either the total or even a portion of a critter's upkeep. Use the connections you made with your mind, your discovery of the critter's state, to fuel the spirit of protest and public outreach.

I have said that neither reading about, meeting, nor dreaming about a critter makes it your familiar. This is because the order in which we use the word familiar denotes a connection of mind, body, and soul. While two out of three is not a bad thing, or even one out of three, such connections do not denote the personal level at which the word familiar is used. It is kind of like being in love. Surely we have all used that term long before we knew what it meant, but when we really find ourselves in love, we know what it is with our mind, body, and soul. Unfortunately, that connection does not communicate well in words. When you meet one of your familiars, be it kith or kin, you will know it with your mind, body, and soul. Chances are that connection won't be easily communicated to other people, but what the hell? At least you will understand that crazy cat woman at the end of the block. That, and for whatever value it has, I will love you all the more for it. After all, us animal lovers have to stick together.

Note: This condensed version of Liber ab Familiars has been shortened for space considerations. I hope to present the removed material separately such that this book can fulfill its intent as study material for the second degree.

Chapter Dedication

This chapter is dedicated to my loving mother,
who was worried about how horrible I would feel after
a failed rescue effort, but who never discouraged me from
making the attempt. And to Thumper and Fred, my close friends,
who passed during the creation of this book.

SECTION THREE

In Apprehension How Like a God

Dedicated to Our Lady and Lord as Crone and Sage

Section Introduction

This is the third of the three-fold path of Wicca.

One of the things I am blessed with is my Website. In the years that it has been operating, it has become a living, growing thing with thousands of members who interact and participate in open debates frequently. I say I am blessed with this because it gives me an opportunity to bounce ideas off people long before a book goes to press. A lot of my ideas promote a knee jerk reaction, so by finding out what peope object to about an idea, I either find out I was having an off day or I find the many points of an idea that I have not addressed. Now that we have polls running, there is no telling where it will end.

One of those many ideas I posted was that maybe Wicca should adopt a standard set of ethics. The idea met a great amount of argument. Dogma, I was told, is the first step in totalitarianism and we know what happens when we go that route. My next question was that if Wicca does not have a set of ethics or any dogma, how can it be a religion if words have meaning? That is, if Wicca can be anything a person wants it to be, how does calling it Wicca (or anything in particular) make any sense? Overwhelmingly similar answers flooded in: Each Wiccan decides for his or her self what Wicca is, and we do not need a standard of ethics or a dictate of dogma.

So who decides what is moral or ethical in Wicca? Again, you do. Again, Wicca does not dictate what you are to think. Instead, Wicca presents a Path of initiation. As you walk on that path, you encounter the many mysteries. As you address those mysteries, you determine what Wicca is and is not. These are the many things that make Wicca what it is. For some reason, the folk drawn into these mysteries tend to come up with the same general beliefs. In this case I do not think it is a stretch to say Wiccans firmly stand against the molestation and rape of children. If in saying that, I have become the latest Wiccan Dictator, so be it.

Liber ab Gens
(Book of Tribe)

I wanted to include information on the Wiccan community, but I should tell you that this has been the hardest chapter to write. On one hand, I wanted to praise the many tremendously beautiful folk I have met on my Path. I wanted to share with my reader how beautiful what I found has been. On the other hand, I wanted to just scream that there is no Wiccan community.

If I am to fail in accurately presenting my view of the Wiccan religion, this chapter is going to be where I do just that. You see, more than anything else in the Wiccan religion, it is our community that simply must be experienced to be understood. Unfortunately, that community is not something one can define. Fortunately, it is one of those things that a person is absolutely sure of once one has found it. Your folk are your folk. In a way, finding one's tribe is akin to falling in love.

I believe that, like falling in love, community is one of the things that has allowed the human race to continue for as long as it has. We do not run very fast, we don't jump very high, we have no natural camouflage, and when pitted against many of the other creatures of this world, we don't fair well. Our only real strength is that we are driven to build community, to connect with like-minded folk for the betterment of both tribe and individual.

This importance of building community is a part of each and every Wiccan ritual. Yes, this step in ritual is often the symbolic sex of the Great Rite that marks union of two people along with the union of their families; however, the message is union of all kinds. And yet, with each and every Wiccan ritual pointing out the importance of building community, there is no central mailing list, no way to fully identify our tribe. You see, in all of our drive to unite in our commonalties, the very structure of Wicca demands that each person be an individual. As a result, there are great numbers of folk that have missed the point entirely. Even if a central community or mailing list existed, it would not accurately reflect the community to whom I write because as we have learned oh so many times, anyone can join a mailing list. In other words, if you have not heard it yet, you will surely hear someone call himself or herself Wiccan, and yet they have absolutely nothing in common with yourself. Now what kind of community would that be?

They might even perform the rituals perfectly, having memorized them from one book or the other. But if those rituals are performed without meaning, they do not make one Wiccan in anything except name's sake. What we do in ritual does not a community make. Instead, it is those things done outside of the formalities of ritual that makes for a community of like-minded folk. This is true of all religious communities.

During Catholic ceremonies, there is often a time to turn to your neighbor shake his or her hand and say 'Peace be with you.' But the action that makes community is not shaking your neighbor's hand in church, it is mowing his lawn when his leg is broken, watching his house when he is away, and being concerned about his or her children as if they were members of one's own family. One can define the Jewish community better by what takes place between visits to synagogue than what takes place in synagogue. One can define Christian community better by what takes place between visits to church than what takes place in church; one can define Krishna community better by what takes place between visits to the ashram than what takes place in the ashram; one can define Muslim community better by what takes place between visits to the mosque than what takes place in the mosque. So naturally one can define Wiccan community better by what takes place between our rituals than what takes place within rituals. In this manner, we see that what takes place outside synagogue, church, ashram, mosque, and ritual are infinitely more important than what takes place within those houses of worship.

The reality of Wicca is that there are two distinctly different types of people who call themselves Wiccan; thus, there are two distinctly different tribes. First, there are the folk who think Wicca is a soulful Path of duty in service to and kinship with our Lord and Lady. Then there are the folk who think Wicca is a reason to be all dark and spooky. Indeed, this split in Wicca has caused many to stop using the name Wicca to describe their religion in an attempt not to be identified with the faddists using the same word. Let's face it, tell people that you are Wiccan and the TV show *Buffy the Vampire Slayer* will come to some folk's minds. Others, like myself, have clung desperately to the word because we see the many noble battles fought to bring our religion into the position where it enjoys the same legally protected freedoms that other world religions do. We know that brave folk like Dr. Leo Martello and Herman Slater fought for these rights and we simply will not ignore their great effort on our behalf. We also know that while Pop-Wicca, McWicca, or WWR (Wicca Without Rules) continues to be a growing trend, the word that describes our religious Path has received meaning. While that meaning might not be set in stone word for word, it is certainly enough to define enough commonalties to call us a tribe.

On Dogma and Doctrine

The dogmas of the quiet past are inadequate to the stormy present.

—Abraham Lincoln

Before we can even begin to talk about finding community, we have to establish what that community is based on, what we have in common, because that is what community is. You might have noticed the words are even very similar in appearance. Indeed, they share the same linguistic root. So what do we have in common?

One Sunday I visited a Catholic and a Protestant church in an effort to discover the differences between the two. Of those differences, I observed that the greatest were that Catholics hold mass and Protestants hold services. A priest leads Catholic mass and a minister leads Protestant services. Catholic mass centers on an altar where a crucifix is displayed and Protestant services center on a table where a cross is displayed. So then, this must be why so many have lost their lives in the wars between Catholic and Protestant.

Catholic priests conduct Mass centered on an altar with a crucifix on it.

Protestant ministers conduct services centered on a table with a cross on it.

Is it really something worth fighting over? Most Pagans would say no. However, in their desperate attempt to avoid repeating the mistakes of other religions, they are very quick to fight over that of which we discuss here, dogma and doctrine.

The Dogma of No Dogma

The American Heritage Dictionary of the English Language offers three definitions for the word *dogma*. The first two definitions seem responsible for the bad reputation this very friendly word has received over the years.

1. A doctrine or corpus of doctrines relating to matters such as morality and faith, set forth in an authoritative manner by a church.

2. An authoritative principle, belief, or statement of ideas or opinion, especially one considered to be absolutely true. See Synonyms as doctrine.

3. A principle of belief or a group of them: "The dogmas of the quiet past are inadequate to the stormy present" (Abraham Lincoln).

But in running away from the "authoritative manner" of the church in definition one and the idea that anything can be "considered to be absolutely true" in definition two, shall we throw away the principles and beliefs spoken in definition three? What would our religion be without principles and beliefs? Would it be a religion at all if we had no principles and beliefs?

This does not mean that a person who does not subscribe to Wiccan dogma is of less value than one who does subscribe to Wiccan dogma. Of my love, no less worthy is my mother for being Catholic than would she if she were Wiccan. It just means that Wicca does in fact have principles and beliefs, but don't say that too loudly if you don't want an argument. You see, there are scores of Wiccans who insist that the Wiccan religions have no dogma.

The Doctrine of No Doctrine

Equally offensive to the ears of many kind Pagan folk is the word *doctrine*. Perhaps more so, the word indoctrination. Oh, we don't seem to mind the words teaching or student, but indoctrination seems to reek of the notion that one is being brainwashed. Indeed this battle of words continues in the Pagan community, yet it is exactly the same argument as the Catholics and their altar and the Protestants and their table. You see, these are simply words that mostly describe the same thing. While they most certainly have meaning, that meaning expresses the ideas of what a thing is, not what is right or wrong.

One of the definitions available for *doctrine* is "A rule or principle of law, especially when established by precedent." With all our talk of Wicca being a nature-based religion, one might think we would be more comfortable with accepting the law of nature. With all of our talk of Wicca being based on ancient fertility religions, that we might be especially comfortable with that law when established by the precedent of those ancient fertility religions. Wow, we do have doctrine. Is it so baneful that we would want to teach that doctrine to those who seek it? To *indoctrinate* them to the ways of Wiccan dogma? What would our religion be without this principle of law? Would it be a religion at all if we had no law?

Of course, this does not mean that a person who does not accept Wiccan doctrine is of less value than one who does accept Wiccan doctrine. Of my love, no less worthy is my mother not having formally accepted the law that Wicca insist be accepted.

The Religion of No Religion

Congress shall make no law respecting an establishment of religion...

—*The first 10 words of the First Amendment to the Constitution of the United States of America*

How could it be that a person who believes in neither dogma nor doctrine call that which they believe (or don't believe as the case may be) a religion? Because most of them are rebelling against the established religions of the world and using the principle set forth by the First Amendment to the Constitution of the United States of America. They don't want to ignore the word "establishment" in that sacred document, so a new establishment of dogma and doctrine has risen to serve their needs, that being the dogma of no dogma and the doctrine of no doctrine. Resembling more the spiritual choice of the agnostic, such views are neither Wiccan nor "an establishment of religion." If one chooses to dispute this, they may of course do so at their will. But they will look rather silly as they are disputing not me, but just about every dictionary. That religion which has neither dogma nor doctrine is not a religion.

This is not to say that someone making up his or her own religion is a bad thing. It doesn't mean that someone without any set custom, tradition, or teaching cannot live a religious life. However, it does mean that folk who use the word Wicca to describe a Path so alien from the laws of Nature and the observations of those laws as a fertility religion are simply causing confusion. You see, the word Wicca has come to mean something, so using it to mean something totally different will just cause confusion. This is not a matter of totalitarianism; it is a matter of language. If you disagree, please try using the word anchovies to mean pepperoni and then order a pizza.

The Ethics and Dogma of Wicca

So then what are the ethics and dogma of the Wiccan religion? What can we all agree upon in our effort to establish community and tribe? Despite the fact that getting Wiccans to agree on anything is akin to herding cats, there have been some rather widely accepted attempts to create a definition. In 1974, a newly founded organization called the Council of American Witches decided to define what it means to practice modern Witchcraft. In so doing, they created the 13 Principles of Wiccan Belief and released it to the world to be freely shared.

The 13 Principles of Wiccan Belief

1. We practice rites to attune ourselves with the natural rhythm of life forces marked by the phases of the Moon and the seasonal quarters and cross quarters.

2. We recognize that our intelligence gives us a unique responsibility toward our environment. We seek to live in harmony with Nature, in ecological balance, offering fulfillment to life and consciousness within an evolutionary concept.

3. We acknowledge a depth of power far greater than is apparent to the average person. Because it is far greater than ordinary, it is sometimes called "supernatural," but we see it as lying within that which is naturally potential to all.

4. We conceive of the Creative Power in the Universe as manifesting through polarity— as masculine and feminine—and that this same creative Power lives in all people, and functions through the interaction of the masculine and feminine. We value neither above the other knowing each to be supportive of the other. We value

sexuality as pleasure, as the symbol and embodiment of Life and as one of the sources of energies used in magickal practice and religious worship.

5. We recognize both outer worlds and inner, or psychological worlds—sometimes known as the Spiritual World, the Collective Unconscious, the Inner Planes, etc.— and we see in the interaction of these two dimensions the basis for paranormal phenomena and magickal exercises. We neglect neither dimension for the other, seeing both as necessary for our fulfillment.

6. We do not recognize any authoritarian hierarchy, but do honor those who teach, respect those who share their greater knowledge and wisdom, and acknowledge those who have courageously given to themselves in leadership.

7. We see religion, magick, and wisdom-in-living as being united in the way one views the world and lives within it—a world view and philosophy of life, which we identify as Witchcraft or the Wiccan Way.

8. Calling oneself *Witch* does not make a Witch—but neither does heredity itself, or the collecting of titles, degrees and initiations. A Witch seeks to control the forces within him/herself that make life possible in order to live wisely and well, without harm to others, and in harmony with Nature.

9. We acknowledge that it is the affirmation and fulfillment of life, in a continuation of evolution and development of consciousness, that gives meaning to the Universe we know and to our personal role within it.

10. Our only animosity toward Christianity, or toward any other religion or philosophy-of-life, is to the extent that its institutions have claimed to be "the one true right and only way" and have sought to deny freedom to others and to suppress other ways of religious practices and belief.

11. As American Witches, we are not threatened by debates on the history of the Craft, the origins of various terms, the legitimacy of various aspects of different traditions. We are concerned with our present and our future.

12. We do not accept the concept of "absolute evil," nor do we worship any entity known as "Satan" or "the Devil" as defined by Christian Tradition. We do not seek power through the suffering of others, nor do we accept the concept that personal benefits can only be derived by denial to another.

13. We work within Nature for that which is contributory to our health and well-being.

Unfortunately, shortly after creating the above document, the organization became defunct. Similar ethics can be found in the 13 Goals of a Witch. However, the exact wording in the 13 goals of a Witch is similar to the exact wording of The Charge of the Goddess that is often reported to belong to Doreen Valiente. The words change from reference to reference. The many incarnations of the 13 goals have been just as varied in their wording even though their likely origin was Scott Cunningham's book *Wicca: A Guide for the Solitary Practitioner*, from where I now quote:

The 13 Goals of the Witch

1	Know yourself
2	Know your Craft (Wicca)
3	Learn
4	Apply knowledge with wisdom
5	Achieve balance
6	Keep your words in good order
7	Keep your thoughts in good order
8	Celebrate life
9	Attune with the cycles of the Earth
10	Breathe and eat correctly
11	Exercise the body
12	Meditate
13	Honor the Goddess and God

—From *Wicca: A Guide for the Solitary Practitioner*
By Scott Cunningham

Did Scott Cunningham write this? Maybe and maybe not. Although it is often cited to Scott Cunningham, he presented it as if it were part of the Wiccan religion as already established. Now I do think Scott created *The 13 Goals of the Witch*, but I do not think that in so doing his writing becomes a sacred Wiccan text any more than the 13 Principles of Wiccan Belief, or the Charge of the Goddess or any other text unless it comes from one's own heart. In fact, I may only include it here because it is less than 250 words in length and used for academic purposes and to present critical commentary (exceptions to copyright law).

So then, like a Charge of our Mother or Father, the 13 (or whatever number) Goals of the Wiccan should come from the Wiccan heart, not a Wiccan book. This is not for legal concerns but because there is absolutely no point in creating a set of ethics or goals if you are not going to follow them and because you are not going to follow them unless they came from your heart rather than a book. In that matter, I feel the one primary Wiccan goal is the first of the 13 listed in Scott Cunningham's book: "Know yourself." No, those two words are not the sum total of Wiccan belief, but only with those two words can one listen to established Wiccan dogma and doctrine and determine if it sings to the soul or if maybe there is a better religious choice for you. You see, the rituals and teachings of Wicca are not the religion. Instead, your perception of those rituals and teachings are.

What Is Wiccan Community?

I called this chapter 'Liber ab Gens' because the Latin word *gens* translates well as both 'tribe' and as 'nation.' Here, hidden in the very nature of an ancient Pagan language we find the wisdom of that which is Wiccan community. We are not a group of folk who all think identically about any one subject because the very nature of our religion forces one to decide for oneself. Contained here in this book is my personal dogma and doctrine. You do not have to agree to be Wiccan.

For this reason, using the term *Wiccan community* does not accurately reflect the nature of our religion. Wicca is based on knowing oneself rather than knowing the words in a book. As a result, it is a very personal religion, and while any one Wiccan is likely to share many things in common with the next, our religion is based far too greatly on the individual to envision a large community without tremendous amounts of infighting on the subject of just what Wicca is. For that reason, here I use the term *Pagan community* rather than *Wiccan community* to discuss relations larger than those of kith and kin. While not every Pagan is Wiccan, in general terms there is no greater distance between the beliefs of any one Pagan and the other than between any one Wiccan and another.

Finding Pagan Community

Currently, the main problem with finding Pagan community is found in the same reason I choose to use the term *Pagan community* rather than *Wiccan community*. For the most part, each effort to establish Pagan community has found it necessary to become a tradition or denomination unto itself. Now this in and of itself is not a bad thing, so when I discuss the following Pagan organizations, please do not think I am attacking them in anyway. But the current structure does create an obvious problem: How does one find out what traditions or groups are available to the seeker? Not a reference or a listing, but how does someone meet folk from the many different groups and traditions? How does one find the community options?

Listed here are what I have found to be top of the list of Pagan organizations, these are the finest of the finest. However, only one of the three listed has not become a tradition unto itself.

A Druid Fellowship

In my opinion, this is one of three of the finest Pagan organizations available to the seeker. Founded by Isaac Bonewits, one of the better-educated authors in the Pagan community, the central idea behind its liturgy is that although local chapters (called *groves*) may change the pantheons used in ritual, the basic ritual construct are the same from group to group. This way, a member familiar with ritual structure in one grove can travel the world and still attend public religious services the same way members of most mainstream religions can.

Church of All Worlds

In my opinion, this is another of the three finest Pagan organizations available to the seeker. Founded by Oberon Zell-Ravenheart, incorporated 1968 and legally recognized as a church by the IRS 1970, this is the oldest Neo-Pagan Church in the United States. The Church of All World's local organizations are called nests and branches. A nest is usually a private organization similar to what I call a household in Wicca; others might call it a coven. Sometimes nests are public, but that is left entirely up to the discretion of the nest and not dictated by CAW. A regional collection of these nests as well as members unaffiliated with these nests is called a branch.

Comparing and Contrasting ADF and CAW

The structure of Church of All Worlds differs greatly from the ADF in that the ADF addresses its structure from the top down while CAW does just the opposite. The principle behind the structure of ADF is that if general community is made available by their local Groves, then deep personal friendships and loving relationships will form between members. Additionally, groups within each grove will mix with members of other groves in what is termed special interest groups or SIGs. Thus each Grove exists as a whole, but contains interpersonal relationships that develop naturally. The principle behind the structure of CAW is that if interpersonal relationships form into nests, then those nests will bundle together the way families do with neighbors and form branches (the public face of CAW). Both organizations attempt to achieve the same goal, approaching it from different direction, and both groups provide essentially the same form of community in doing so—circles within circles.

Spiral Scouts

This is the exception to the observation that Pagan organizations are traditions unto themselves. I would not normally list an organization that is only a few years old as one of the three finest; however, in the few years that Spiral Scouts has existed, it has far surpassed any other Pagan organization that I am aware of in approximating my view of the way the ancient Pagans must have formed community. And yet—surprise, surprise—they are of no specific religious affiliation whatsoever. Instead, they leave specific religious affiliations up to the individuals and families that unite with them. The only drawback is that Spiral Scouts was created in service to Earth-based families with children. While this is very much needed, it leaves those of us who do not have children feeling a bit left out, but we address that in just a moment.

The organizational structure of Spiral Scouts is exactly the way I envision the pre-Christian fertility religions must have been. While I detailed the structure of how I believe those communities must have been in my book *Wicca for Couples*, I did not have knowledge of the organizational structure of Spiral Scouts at the time. Their organization is the absolute best approximation of how ancient Pagan communities must have formed. Their organizational structure begins with the hearth (what I call a household). This structure is led by one or two parents (what I call the host and hostess). Should a Hearth grow to include three unrelated children, it becomes a Circle.

A circle is led by two people called 'circle leaders'; again, these are what I have called here a host and hostess. This is the core or basic Spiral Scout group. For practical reasons, these two must be members of the opposite sex, the reason being that there are matters a girl member would be best to turn to a female adult that is a woman and a boy member would be best to turn to a leader that is a man. However, these 'circle leaders' do not rule the circle, they simply provide structure and hospitality. All parents are not only welcome to participate, they are strongly encouraged. A clan is the next largest organizational structure. Generally speaking, a clan is made up of circles that are united by a geographical area such as a city. Those clans form the next largest organizational structure, a tribe. The tribe is made up of individual clans who are united by a geographical area, such as a county.

Spiral Scouts officially started in 1999. Although my book *Wicca for Couples* had absolutely nothing to do with the founding of Spiral Scouts formation, after reading their literature and meeting many of its members, both adult and child, I take immense gratitude in knowing that the concepts presented in that book are shared in part by an organization as fine as this, especially that a couple is the core of community, be that community Wiccan or other. Bless you Spiral Scouts! You are the salvation of the Tempest Smiths of this world!

In the glory of our Lord and Lady, so mote it be!

Circle Guide to Pagan Groups

The problem still remains: How does one find Pagan community? You see, each of these groups is part of the Pagan Community, but with the exception of Spiral Scouts (which is child-oriented) each is also an individual tradition or denomination unto itself. Despite my tremendous favor of the above listed organizations, they might not be the one you want to join. Where then does one turn?

Some folk might tell you that Web indexes are a good option. I think they are the worst way to find like-minded folk for two reasons. Web indexes are inevitably inaccurate because they are too easy to join. Click here, fill in this form there, and presto: You are now the head of an international Pagan organization. Most important, web indexes tend to be all-inclusive without respect to the organization's qualifications or if that organization is of good report. So what is a person to do?

Fortunately, there is a partial solution that has helped thousands of folk. That solution is *Circle Guide to Pagan Groups*, available from Circle Sanctuary. Circle Sanctuary is in and of itself a Pagan organization, but I have little experience with them other than to know that they are of good report. Their annual publication of which I speak is a collection of public Pagan groups and resources across the world. While Circle does not make an attempt to determine who is of good report and who is not, they do keep their list current, list national affiliations, and check their references annually by more than simply sending an email out and seeing if it bounces back. Yes, all this takes a bit of money, so there is a cost involved in acquiring their publication; that cost is well worth it. If you can not find it at your local Pagan shop, please write to the address given for Circle Sanctuary.

Organizations of Good Report Quick Reference

What follows is a list of public organizations I have found to be of good report. I neither belong to nor promote one over the other. I have mentioned having tremendously good experiences with two of these groups, ADF and CAW. However, this is not to say that these two organizations are any better than any others on this list. I have had close involvement with those two organizations, their members, and/or leadership, so I can form personal opinions on them. The other organizations on this list are those large organizations that I have been given good report of or those I have been involved with on a casual level and found of good report, but not so intimately involved that I can praise them:

A Druid Fellowship (ADF)
PO Box 17874
Tucson, AZ 85731-7874
Web address: *www.adf.org*

Church of All Worlds (CAW)
960 Berry Street
Toledo, OH 43605-3044
Web address: *www.caw.org*

Circle Sanctuary
PO Box 219
Mt. Horeb, WI 53572
Web address: *www.circlesanctuary.org*

Covenant of the Goddess (COG)
C/O Correspondence Officer
PO Box 1226
Berkeley, CA 19701
Web address: *www.cog.org*

Covenant of Unitarian Universalist Pagans (CUUPS)
PMB 335
8190 a Beechmont Avenue
Cincinnati, Ohio 45255-3154
Web address: *www.cuups.org*

Pagan Nation
1209 North High Street
Columbus, OH 43201
Web address: *www.pagannation.com*

Spiral Scouts International
48631 River Park Drive
PO Box 409
Index, WA 98256-0409
Web address: *www.spiralscouts.org*

Note: When contacting any of these organizations by mail, it is common courtesy to include a self addressed stamped envelope. I would also add one, two, or even three dollars and inform the organization that you have done so to defer the cost of printing literature and staffing a mailing list. Chances are these organizations either have a chapter in your area or have a program of offering support to folk who would like to form one, so if it is real life community you are looking for, please let them know when you inquire of them.

What about the Solitary Practitioner?

The question then becomes: What about solitary practitioners? This question is moot for two reasons. First, being a solitary practitioner does not mean one is an isolationist. If you are uncomfortable with group or public ritual, then do not attend group or public ritual. The only thing the phrase solitary practitioner means is that one performs ritual by oneself. It does not mean that one conducts the important part of the Wiccan religion by oneself because doing so is impossible unless you feel a religion is something that only takes place in Circle. While this might be true of other religions, the very nature of Wicca insists that it be included in our everyday life. The second, perhaps more comical of the two is that if you are a solitary practitioner but do not want community, why would you complain about the necessity to be involved in a group to find that community? Simply put, you can sit alone at home by your self night after night or you can be involved with other people (a group). You cannot do both.

Enter Pagan Nation: Stage Left

We are a Circle
Within a Circle
With no beginning
And never-ending

It is for these and like reasons that I have spent the last few years of my life creating a structure by which Pagan community can flourish, a Pagan organization that is not an organization in the traditional sense of the word. Instead of offering specific liturgy or being an organization unto itself, the organization has no rank structure, no politics, and no doctrine. Instead, the organization focuses on the idea of facilitating community simply by making it possible for folk to meet. Currently, the organization is predominantly Internet based, with an annual homecoming in Columbus, Ohio called The Real Witches Ball. We offer instant messaging and chat with a project underway to offer voice and video conferencing by the end of this year. Shortly thereafter, we will be establishing groups similar in structure to Spiral Scouts, but with the focus on providing similar contact and resources without the limitation of being focused on children or the Internet.

The idea of this organization, called Pagan Nation, is that the Pagan community is perfectly capable of establishing its own traditions and groups, but that it has fallen a bit short of providing an accessible community that is not limited by specific tradition. Our primary goal is to facilitate exchange, not dictate that exchange. As such, Pagan Nation's first and primary goal is to establish chapters which offer the chance to meet folk socially and then let those folk decide what feels right for themselves. To that end, each chapter is charged with providing social gatherings once a month (and better it be on the same Saturday each month). It is our hope that in so doing we will promote the formation of interpersonal relationships (households) as well as membership in and the creation of local chapters of nationally and internationally recognized organizations. A friend of mine likes to compare the principle to rush day in college, but I shy away from comparing Pagan Organizations to fraternities and sororities. Although facilitating social exchange between its members is the ultimate purpose of those monthly get-togethers, just putting people in a room and telling them to interact would be a bit silly. So we incorporate a three-fold path in providing those social gatherings.

Need—The First Path

Need is the first of the three-fold path of Pagan Nation. It can be equated to the first order of life, plants, and the first degree in the Wiccan religion. In addressing this path, chapters in Pagan Nation are charged with hosting a monthly potluck dinner. To that dinner, prosperous members are encouraged not only to bring a covered dish, but whatever non-perishable food they can offer in sacrifice to the community. This is conducted in accordance with the Wiccan Rede where we are instructed to 'fairly take and fairly give.' Although found in the Wiccan Rede, this principle is not unique to Wicca, thus I do not feel it is overly dictator like of me to say it should be included in Pagan Nation or any other such organization. The sacrifices are blessed in whatever way folk feel is appropriate and added to a pantry reserved first for the chapter. However, if that need is met, it should be shared with other food pantries without regard to their religious affiliations. Need is need, no matter what religion a person belongs to.

Service—The Second Path

Service is the second of the three-fold path of Pagan Nation. It can be equated to the second order of life, animals, and the second degree in the Wiccan religion. In addressing this Path, chapters in Pagan Nation are not only charged with the sacrifice discussed in the first Path, but in recognizing the duty that we as human beings are uniquely qualified to perform. Although this principle is presented here in the Book of Genesis as our duty to protect, tend, and serve our world, it is not a uniquely Wiccan idea. For this reason, every local chapter is charged with organizing the sacrifice of time and labor in service to our world. This can be in the order of adopting a waterway, park, or even a stretch of highway. It can be in serving meals to the elderly, reading to children in a hospital, or any other activity where one's time is spent each month for the betterment of our world.

Now, one might feel donating cash or gifts to a community service organization fulfills this obligation. While they are certainly encouraged, they are no substitute. Remember that the primary purpose to this organization is facilitating social exchange between its members. Sending a check to your favorite charity is encouraged, but it does not facilitate that social exchange.

Celebration—The Third Path

Celebration is the third of the three-fold Path of Pagan Nation. It can be equated to the third order of life, humanity, and the third degree in the Wiccan religion. In addressing this Path, chapters of Pagan Nation are not only charged with enabling celebrations. In this matter, chapters make available places for celebrations as well as instruct in general methods of Pagan celebration; the teaching of chants, drumming, dance, and other activities come to mind.

Need, Service, and Celebration

Now, I have spoken greatly about my aspirations for Pagan Nation the way a proud father might speak highly of his newborn child. However, the principles that I have discussed for Pagan Nation are not unique to my vision of a single organization. Instead they are found in virtually every Pagan culture one can document. Why? Because they are necessary to promote community, and community is necessary for the survival of the human race.

In short, if these three Paths were not addressed, then humanity would not have made it as far as it has. If these three Paths are not addressed by humanity, we will shortly fade from existence. You see, although I speak rather concernedly about the current state of our world, comparing the current extinction rate to that of the dinosaur's exodus from our world, the fact is it will be a great time until our sun supernovas and until then, the Earth simply will not die. Life will always find a way, even if we fail to insure it. However, if we fail to continue then we fail in our duty to our Lord and Lady. So to the survival of humanity Wiccans are also committed, and for that survival our needs must be met by the service to and from our community such that we can rejoice and celebrate. Remove any one of these three vital Paths and we crumble. This observance on a large scale, I call the Pagan community. This observance on a small (family and friends) scale, I call a Wiccan community. Within each of those communities we find both support and obligation.

Liber ab Arma
(Book of Arms)

Making a Difference in Your Community

We live in very scary times. As I send this manuscript to my publisher, there is a war unfolding in Iraq that may affect the stability of the Middle East or even the world. What follows should not be taken as commentary on that war or any specific war. I do have opinions on that war, and those opinions are easy to find at *PaganNation.com*. I do not try to conceal my convictions one bit. In fact, I seem to be at odds with the great majority of Pagan authors in respect to that war.

But this chapter is not about any one conflict. It is about the nature of conflict and how that nature determines that which is Wicca. So in this chapter, please do not read that I either support or do not support any one war. Instead, read into this chapter only what is there. See only what I have said for what it is, and do not impose upon it any prejudices based on one conflict. The ancient Pagans did experience conflict, they did make war, and they did take a firm stand on matters of right and wrong. If Wiccans do not recognize that there is a time and a place for standing on conviction, then they have very little right to call themselves Pagan as Pagan lore is absolutely filled with just that.

Consider this: You have probably heard that Wicca is a Celtic religion, which insists that conflict never solves anything. Why then did the British Celtic folk hero Cartimandua lead the descendants of the goddess Brigantia against the Roman Empire? If you answer is that Wicca is more Goddess focussed than the ancient Pagan religions, I won't even argue that Wicca is a balance between the feminine and masculine, I will just point out that Cartimandua was female.

Taking up arms is the third rite of passage of Llew Llaw Gyffes, who was initially forbidden the rite by his mother who demanded that he not be allowed to take up arms until she armed him. Arming him later became exactly what she did when she was in fear for the safety of her community, and that is exactly what we do when we take up arms. We defend our community.

Now this does not mean that Wiccans have an initiation rite where guns and ammunition are distributed. Instead, it is the point on the path of Wicca when one realizes that no matter how much one detests conflict, it is sometimes not only the best choice, but also the only choice. If we learn anything from the burning times, it is what happens when one does not stand against oppression. If we learn anything from the persecution of the Jews at the hands of Nazi Germany, it is what happens when one does not stand against oppression. Have we learned anything?

The mystery of how Wicca can be a religion and yet mandate absolutely no specific morality or ethics is conflict. This is the natural order of our world, survival of the fittest. At its core, it is the science of Darwin. This is not to say that the Wiccan religion promotes war or bloodshed, but it does promote conflict in encouraging individual thought and the expression of that thought. Someone says Wiccan rites should include child molestation, I say child molestation is an abomination to a fertility religion, and *you* decide who is right and who is wrong. This is the taking up of arms. So interwoven is this to Wicca that, long before we became an industry standard religion given into the mass media's desire to market books, we did not use the word *tools* to denote the props of our sacred theater (ritual). Instead, the athame, chalice, censer, pentacle, and other props in sacred theater were called *weapons*. That term fell out of favor because it was feared someone might misunderstand the word and think our religion presented a danger to the larger community—and that fluff bunny stuff seems to sell a great deal more books (read that it makes more money for Wicca's 'secret chiefs'). But it is in not recognizing those props as weapons that there is a danger, for it is in doing nothing, allowing the world to slip into disaster that we are all in danger.

Should we do nothing as the rate of extinction exceeds that of the dinosaur? Should we do nothing as entire lines of plants are destroyed? Should we do nothing as animals are needlessly made to suffer? Do we actually have a choice? We do. Having a Wiccan soul, we do not have a choice but to feel the pain of these things, but we have a choice in what we do about it. We could recognize these things and allow them to cause us to sit and cry, or we can turn that pain into rage and bring about the manifestation of a just world by taking up arms by the expression of thought, putting that rage forth into the world, thus seeking conflict with the forces that oppose such expression, and praying that our convictions prevail.

Yes, it is tempting to scream 'Make love not war.' But in that scream, still there is conflict, or there would be no reason to scream it. In that scream there is war, there is the demand that ones perception of that which is right be put forth to challenge that which is wrong. This is why Pagan lore is filled with gods of war—not because Pagans are desirous of war, but because they recognize that conflict is the nature of things, and because we need someone to receive the prayers that our convictions meet with victory.

Gods and Goddesses of War

Faces of our Lord and Lady

It is important to mention that these gods and goddesses have many other attributes, some of which are presented in the final chapter of this book. They are presented here in their attribute as warriors and gods of war to illustrate how important such attributes were to the ancient Pagans. Just like today's soldiers, the willingness to make war, to take a stand on conviction, is not the whole of the being.

Agasaya—Female—Middle East
Early Semitic goddess of war.

Ah Cun Can—Male—Central America
Mayan god of war.

Ah Chuy Kak—Male—Central America
Mayan fire god and god of war.

Ahulane—Male—Central America
Mayan god of war who is called the Great Archer.

Anath—Female—Middle East
Semitic goddess of not only war, but of motherhood. Perhaps a comment on the maternal instinct to protect one's children.

Andraste (Also known as Adraste, Andrasta) —Female—Central Europe
British Celtic goddess of war. She was prayed and made sacrifice to by Queen Boudicca in the Queen's charge against the Roman Empire.

Ankt—Female—Africa
Egyptian goddess of war.

Ara (Also known as Aray) —Male—Central Europe/Northern Europe
Armenian god of war whose name means 'the beautiful.' He can probably be linked to the Greek Ares.

Ares—Male—Mediterranean
Greek god of war whose constant companion is his sister Eris, the goddess of strife equated with the Roman Discordia.

Badb—Female—Central Europe

Irish Celtic goddess of war. She not only participates in wars, but also uses magick against the enemy to cause confusion and defeat. Interestingly enough, her lore is probably responsible for the term 'Bad Lands' as the traditional name her followers gave to the battle field is 'Land of Badb.'

Beg-tse—Male—Central Asia

Tibetan god of war who is often depicted with a sword by his side and wearing a full suit of armor. In some traditions, he is the keeper of the divine teachings of the Buddha.

Belatucadros (Also known as Belatu Cadros)—Male—Central Europe

Welsh Celtic god of war whose name means 'Fair Shinning One.' Obviously not a reference to war being viewed as a negative, even when it is required.

Bellona—Female—Mediterranean

Roman goddess of war. She accompanied Mars and has been cited variously as his sister, daughter, or wife.

Burijas (Also known as Burigas)—Male—Middle East

Early Iranian god of war.

Bugid Y Aiba—Male—Caribbean

Haitian god of war.

Buluc Chabtan—Male—Central America

Mayan god of war.

Camulus (Also known as Camulos)—Male—Central Europe/Mediterranean

Celtic god of war, particularly among the Gauls. He was identified with Mars by the Romans.

Cariocienus—Male—Central Europe

Spanish god of war. The Romans linked him to Mars.

Cartimandua—Female—Central Europe

British Celtic folk hero and queen who may be historic figure. Per lore, she led the descendants of the goddess Brigantia against the Roman Empire.

Caswallawn—Male—Central Europe

Celtic god of war, particularly on the British Isles.

Chemosh—Male—Middle East

Moabian god of war and the chief god of their pantheon. He is the giver of laws and the event that takes place when those laws are broken. He is equated to the Babylonian Shamash.

Ek Chuah (Also known as Ekchuah)—Male—Central America

Mayan god of war and patron of the merchant.

Enyo—Female—Mediterranean
Greek goddess of war. She is variously cited as mother, daughter, and sister of Ares. She is one of the Graiae, whose very name means 'horror.' As such, she is often depicted covered in blood.

Eshara—Female—Middle East
Chaldean goddess of war.

Futsu-Nushi-no-Kami—Male—Far East
Japanese god of war, as well as lightning and fire.

Guan-di (Also known as Emperor Guan, Kuan-ti, Kuan Yu)—Male—Central Asia
Taoist god of war in opposition to the disruption of peace. (Yes, I did say Taoist. Contrary to popular modern belief, most cultures, religions, and philosophies have recognized the need for war. Perhaps I should say most surviving cultures, religions, and philosophies.)

Gun—Male—Africa
African god of iron and war. His name and the attribute of iron affords some very interesting speculation.

Huitzilopochtli (Also known as Uitzilopochtli)—Male—North America
Aztec sun god and god of war. Interestingly enough, he is associated with the hummingbird. This could be a comment on the swiftness of war.

Ictinike—Male—North America
Sioux god of war, as well as the teacher of the Sioux tribes in the art of war.

Indra—Male—Near East
Hindu god of war from the time of the Vedics.

Inanna—Female—Mediterranean
Sumerian goddess of war.

Kartikeya (Also known as Karttikeya, Muruhan, Skanda, and Subramana)—Male—Near East
Hindu god of war and leader of the divine armies of heaven.

Korrawi (Also known as Katukilal)—Female—Near East
Dravidian goddess of war and victory.

Ku—Male—Polynesian Islands
Hawaiian creator and god of war.

Laran—Male—Mediterranean/Central Europe
Etruscan god of war who is depicted as a boy who is sky clad except for a helm and carrying only a spear.

Mars—Male—Mediterranean

Generally referenced as the Roman god of war; however, there is a great deal more to his story. He was first seen as a god of nature, fertility, and of the Earth. Gradually he changed into a god of war, as war became necessary for the survival of his people.

Maru—Male—Polynesian Islands

Maori god of war who instigates conflict for the purpose of being witness to the result of that conflict. He taught the use of weapons and the use of magick against the enemy.

Mentu (Also known as Menthu, Mont, Month, Monto)—Male—Africa

Egyptian god of war and patron of warriors.

Mexitl—Male—North America

The god of war from whose name the nation of Mexico comes.

Neith—Female—Africa

An Egyptian goddess of war. She is depicted with bow, shield, and quill. Although she is sometimes cited as a huntress, the shield indicates that she had other attributes as well.

Oro—Male—Polynesian Islands

Tahitian god of both war and peace. Another example of the need of one to enjoy the other.

Reshep—Male—Middle East

Syrian god of war, disease, and the Underworld.

Rugiviet—Male—Central Europe/Northern Europe

Slavic god of war.

Sakhmet—Female—Africa

Egyptian goddess associated not only with war, but also with revenge.

Samulayo—Male—Polynesian Islands

Fijian god of war who welcomes the slain in battle.

Segomo—Male—Central Europe

Celtic god of war and victory in all matters of conflict, particularly among the Gauls.

Septu (Also known as Sopd, Sopdu)—Male—Africa

Egyptian god of war and victory.

Set (Also known as Setekh, Setesh, Seth, Seti)—Male—Egyptian

Egyptian god of chaos, disorder, and the wars that bring those things.

Shamash—Male—Middle East

Babylonian god and giver of law. He becomes god of war when those laws are broken.

Si—Male—South America

The Mochica (pre-Inca) personification and god of the Moon. He is also a god of war depicted in full armor.

Svantetit (Also called Svetovit)—Male—Central Europe/North Europe

Slavic god of both field and war, that relationship being in the capacity of protector of the fields.

Triglawus (Also known as Trigelavus, Triglav)—Male—Central Europe/ Northern Europe

Slavic god of war with three heads representing heaven, earth, and the underworld. This is likely commentary on the fate of warriors. They might survive the battle (Earth), they might fall in a just cause (Heaven), or they might fall in a cause that is not just (Underworld).

Tu Matauenga (Also known as Tu)—Male—Polynesian Islands

Polynesian god of war. He is equated to Maru (Maori) and Ku (Hawaii)

Tyr—Male—Central Europe

German god of war and justice, which seems to predate the lore of Odin. There is some evidence that suggests Tyr was the predecessor to Odin, but that by the time of the Vikings, lore had grown in such a way as to record him as Odin's son.

Wepwawet (Also known as Ophois, Upuaut, Wep-wawet)—Male—Africa

Early Egyptian God of war who is depicted with a jackal head.

Wurukatte—Male—Middle East

Early Hattic god of war.

Zababa—Male—Middle East

Akkadian god of war.

Zi-yu—Male—Central Asia

Chinese god who invented both war and the weapons with which wars are fought.

The Need for Victory

Indeed, the ancients recognized the need for victory. They knew that without the sense of challenge and conquest, humanity becomes complacent. Realizing the great harm that war brings, they devised methods by which such challenges and conquests could be accomplished without the act of war. Not all of their ideas were the most humane. In fact, some were degenerative forms of entertainment in which men were pitted against each other not for their longing of victory, but because spectators wanted to feel what it was like to be pitted in life versus death combat while remaining in the relative safety of their Colosseum seats. The ancients were not perfect. But they did try. In fact, our modern Olympic games testify to the fact that the ancient Pagan Greeks sought appeasement to this lust for victory in the creation of great sport. Elsewhere we see limitations placed on war, such that single combatants meet on the field rather than entire armies.

Anguish, a king of Ireland, sent his brother-in-law Morholt to face single combat with the Cornish Tristan. In that combat, Tristan felled Morholt so it was not a death-less battle, but it was a battle that involved only one death. As such competition can be found in a great deal of Celtic lore, we can safely say that the Celts may have been dedicated to war when war was necessary, but when it was not they refrain from combat, and when combat was inevitable they did what they could to limit the loss of life.

Additional indications as to how the ancient Pagans felt about war can be found in the many connections between war and crop fertility, the central message being that should a nation be prosperous, war is not likely. Should a nation starve, war was inevitable. You might recall I mentioned the barbarism of one of Rome's most notorious forms of entertainment. History has shown that the Roman people should not be judged by one event alone and neither should their attitude towards war. Why? Well, there is very clear evidence that they were not the bloodthirsty monsters that the coliseum battles between Gladiators portrays. Indeed, one of their holidays even involves praying that the weapons of war rust. While that principle is represented widely in lore, it is found no more clearly than in the Robigalia celebrated on Aprilis 25. The Robigalia honors Robigus and Robigo, god and goddess of rust in one form or another. At their festival, prayers were conducted asking them to rust the weapons and tools of war rather than to rust (blight) their crops. Please let our crops do well, so our armies will not have to make war to feed us.

When to Fight

How do we decide what we should and should not take up arms against? Where is this great book of wisdom that tells us right from wrong? If it is so clear that the ancient Pagans were willing to stand against what they saw as wrong, why can we not just have a book to tell us what those wrong things are? The reason Wicca does not have a list of things one should or should not do is the creation of such a list would destroy the very nature of our religion. Doing so is why we see those most annoying sidewalk preachers who can tell right from wrong simply by reading the pages where those rights and wrongs were written.

At a march conducted in Columbus, Ohio for the National Organization for Women, there was one such preacher whose wife had a sign that read "Feminism is Satanism." She looked none too thrilled to be standing there with that sign. Normally, I tend to taunt such protesters, but I couldn't. The punishment for her ignorance was already standing right beside her, her husband. Now maybe, just maybe, there was a time in which men needed to be in charge. I have noted that patriarchal communities tend to develop where life is hard. Maybe, just maybe, the time in which that book of theirs was written was when such matters were life preserving. Even so, that time is not now. Yet, there it is in that book of theirs, that god is the head of every man and that man is the head of every woman.

I saw that same preacher protesting with a gas mask on the sidelines of the gay pride parade. His sign read "Homosexuality is Satanism." Again, I thought about taunting him, but I couldn't. It was about a hundred degrees and he was wearing a rubber suit and gas mask so he wouldn't contract AIDS from the gay and lesbian folk in the parade. To be perfectly honest, I can't say for sure that it was the same person. But I have seen that same person with a similar sign so often that I have come to expect to see him at Red Lobster with a sign that reads "Seafood is Satanism." You see, that book of his forbids that as well.

That is why we do not write down a set of 10 (or any other number) of commandments. Although Wicca is modeled on some truly ancient religions, we have the benefit of observing how other religions have failed. Should we write these things down, we become just like those failed religions that now threaten global peace.

On Crone and Sage

You will note that I equate the taking up of arms to the Crone and Sage state of our Lady and Lord. As such, I believe this to be the core knowledge of the third degree of Wicca: Now that you have knowledge of the first and second degree, it is time you do something with it. In the degree system more akin to Gardner's system, the third degree is the point where one can hive off of his or her original coven and form one's own. Remove that artificial coven system from the equation and we realize the third degree is the point where Wiccans are able to make their own stand (hive off). It is the point where they have received the secrets, explored the mysteries, and have awakened that Wiccan soul that I have spoken about so much thus far. It is the point when we welcome others whose hearts have awakened, but we no longer depend on their example. It is the point when we no longer mix our potions and play with our familiars because it is the Wiccan thing to do, but when we realize that although those practices are valuable in and of themselves, their main purpose was as a stepping stone from which to launch our understanding of our relationship to the world we live in. We have been there, done that, and are now moving out into the world to provide the same service to others who would listen.

In this, we see that the role of taking up arms is not only the act of speaking out and attempting to manifest our world for the better, but it is also the act of handing down our traditions to the folk who follow—not by writing books, forming covens, or any of the ways one might think, but in leading by example. Thus, the very act of assuming a posture in which one makes their feelings known is the act of handing down traditions and guiding our younger folk into the mysteries of our religion. Sure, there will be opposition to those opinions, but that is what the law of Nature is all about.

Liber ab Mentis
(The Book of Mind)

The reason I placed the Book of Familiars in between the Book of Soul and the Book of Mind is because that is exactly where we see them, somewhere between the soul that they possess and the mind that we use to understand that soul. That is how we decide the difference between right and wrong, somewhere between what our soul and mind tells us. That is where we find truth—right where truth is so often found, right smack in the middle.

This is also the conflict that I spoke of in the last chapter. It is the adversarial system by which we judge our own actions and inaction. It is similar in concept to the taking up of arms, but in the conflict between our nature (soul) and our nurture (mind), the assumption that emerges from this conflict is truth. Our soul (subconscious/ego) throws out a primal emotion and our mind (conscious/super ego) either puts it down or brings it into manifestation. In a court of law, this is the difference between premeditation and a crime of passion. This is a very important part of that which I term Spirit because without that mind causing intentional manifestation, the soul unchecked will produce unintentional manifestations.

In a previous book, *Wicca for Men*, I put forth the idea that there is a clear difference between animals and humanity. This is why I prefer the athame to the wand for use in ritual. You see, although animals have been proven to do just about all of the things we used to claim made them different, they have not as of yet developed the ability to work metal. Some animals do indeed build homes, have language, teach language to others, make love facing each other, practice monogamy, live in extended communities, and so on. Practically every thing we have used to separate humanity from animals has been disproved, except one. In reflecting on the Elements, other religions claim the one Element that animals do not demonstrate is Spirit.

It might surprise you to know that I agree, but only in the semantics of how I use the term. I do very much believe animals have soul, but when I use the term Spirit I mean much more than soul. I mean soul tempered with mind. Because that tempering process can be equated to Fire, I note Fire as the one Element of the four that animals do not possess a mastery of. I do not believe humanity has mastered Fire. But we are the only critter that has made an attempt thus far.

While presenting this concept in workshop forum, one person in attendance insisted that by acknowledging the difference between humanity and animals that I was claiming humanity is better than animals. I explained that I believe all Life is sacred, but could not resist the opportunity to do just a little bit of vegetarian proselytizing. "Do you eat meat?" I asked. The truth of the matter is that I have chosen to be a vegetarian, but do not generally think that eating meat is wrong. I think it is wrong for me but do not condemn others for doing exactly what I have done, which is to make an educated personal choice. The thing is, the person in that workshop had clearly not made an educated personal choice. He was telling me it is wrong to consider animals different than human beings, yet he doesn't eat human beings.

There is a clear difference between animals and humanity. That difference is represented in our lore, in our language, and in the way we conduct ourselves every day. I have shown that the ancients were rather clear in their belief that animals have soul. I have shown that so strong was their belief that it is built into our modern language. Now let's look at what animals and humanity do not share: mind. Again I turn to my dictionary where I find the very first definition for *mind* is:

> *"The human consciousness that originates in the brain and is manifested especially in thought, perception, emotion, will, memory, and imagination"*[1]

Human consciousness is the tempering fire that I speak of. Those same folk who argue that I should not point out the difference between humanity and animals are usually the first to point out that only humans have developed the nuclear bomb (fire). Of course I agree, yet even though they argue my very point, they still will not concede that there is a difference between humanity and animals. If there is no difference, then does it not stand to reason that humanity is just as responsible for this Earth as is my cat? Therefore, does it not stand to reason that we should do just as much to save the Earth as my cat, that being nothing at all?

The ancient Pagans saw the clear division between animals and humanity by the attribute of mind being given to only humanity, and they demonstrated that belief in their lore.

Alaghom Naom—Female—Central America
Mayan goddess whose name means 'mother of mind.' In the Mayan, pantheon she is chiefly responsible for the creation of human consciousness.

Mens—Female—Mediterranean
Roman goddess of human consciousness.

Naum—Male—Central America
Mayan god who is attributed as the father of mind. In the Mayan pantheon, he is chiefly responsible for the creation of human consciousness. He is either husband to or a male version of Alaghom Naom.

Sia—Female—Africa
Egyptian personification and goddess of human consciousness.

It is by recognizing that humanity has this unique attribute that we understand our unique responsibility. Can an animal be blamed for over-populating and causing environmental disaster as the foliage, their food, recedes, allowing the topsoil to be eroded and the land to become barren? When those animals do this, should they be blamed for their own starvation and the suffering of other animals in their area? If one does not acknowledge that animals are incapable of being mindful, then one must blame them for following their soul to the point of extinction.

If, however, we acknowledge that animals cannot make mindful decisions, then we begin to understand why the Earth is in the condition it now is. We, humanity, have not stepped up to bat in our capacity as caretakers of this planet. As a whole, we have not committed to the very duty to which we were created. As a result, we have become guilty not only of neglecting the world which our Lord and Lady have given us to shape, but we have become gluttons and allowed ourselves to harvest entirely more than we need. In that acknowledgement, we see that we have not only neglected our duty to maintain a healthy balance, but we have far tilted the scales. If something does not change, it will not be just the animals of this world that become extinct. It may well be the Earth herself.

Fire and the Mind

Fudo—Male—Far East
Japanese god of both fire and wisdom. An additional Japanese reference can be found in the trident named Kongo, which was originally owned by Koya-no-Myoin. Reportedly that trident provides men with wisdom from its flames.

Kali—Female—Near East
Hindu goddess described as the 'Black Flame' who blesses the seekers of knowledge, wisdom, and the secrets of the gods. She is referred to as she who destroys ignorance.

Svarog—Male—Central/North Europe

Slavic fire god is responsible for formalizing marriage with mindful contracts and obligations.

Perkons—Male—Central/Northern Europe

Russian and Lithuanian fire god by whom oral contracts were thought out and sworn to mindfully.

Accepting the Fire

Ancient Pagan lore is rather clear that fire sets humanity apart from animals. Although I would like to say that *mastery* of fire is what sets us apart, the ancient wisdom is rather clear that there was always speculation as to whether humanity was ready for that knowledge or if that knowledge might not be so great as to cause humanity to use it for great harm.

Prometheus—Male—Mediterranean

Prometheus stole fire from Zeus. Per Greek lore, the fire of which they spoke was not only sacred, but it was in the possession of the gods alone. It seems clear the lore is not talking about the fire that comes from rubbing two sticks together.

Yehl—Male—North America

Tlingit god who stole fire and gave it to humanity. As he is also the inventor of human culture, we see again the connection to mind, culture being a product of mind.

Ilmarinen—Male—North Europe

Finnish god who gave fire to man and instructed in the mindful art of the metalsmiths.

Wekwek—Male—North America

Tuleyone falcon who stole fire and in so doing set the Earth on fire, illustrating the instant repercussion for stealing fire. With what the world is experiencing right now in the Middle East, can there be no doubt this was a warning?

Is Not Fire More Akin to the Soul?

One might argue that if we are to assign the Elements Water and Fire to that which is soul and that which is mind, that it might be better to assign Water to mind and Fire to soul. But it is the very nature of Fire to consume its fuel and burn out, as does the mind. It is the nature of Water to remain eternal, as does the soul. Can we argue that a heated argument is not found more in the mind than in the soul? If we did, how would we explain the way lovers make up? The Fire, the thought of mind, burns itself out leaving the lover's souls like Water to mingle. If we were to take that stand that mind is best equated to Water, what would our view of humanity be? An eternal war maker?

I say nay, the soul of humanity is pure, but our thoughts sometimes muddy that purity. Our mind sometimes gets in the way. After all, Fire is the Element of war, and that Fire is exactly why Zeus and others were very guarded when it came to matters of Fire's possession by humanity.

Consider the Haitian Voodoo Ogoun, who is god of not only Fire and war, but also of politics. If that isn't a clear message about the nature of fire, mind, and war I do not know what is. Over and over we see the connection between fire and war: Futsu-Nushi-no-Kami (Japanese), Maru (Polynesian), Ah Chuy Kak (Mayan), Mixcoatl (Aztec), Camaxtli (Aztec), Resef (Egyptian & Phoenician), Bishamon (Japanese). These are all gods associated with both Fire and with war.

And of course let us not forget the Christian lore that actually predates Christianity. In mix of ancient Mediterranean lore on which the Christian story was based, we see that Yahweh told the other deities that he wanted to create Adam and give unto Adam the intelligence of the gods, the ability to think for himself. All of the other deities, including the Earth herself, opposed this creation because they agreed that the line of Adam would result in the fires of war.

Fire as Creative

This is not to say Fire is in and of itself a destructive force. Although it is the Element that promotes the fastest change and that fast change is sometimes described as being violent, Fire is also the tool of the craftsman. In the same Element that drives us to war, we find the soul driven to create. In this, we see that Fire by its nature might well be destructive, but when mastered it is creative. Who can argue that this is not the very nature of human intellect? That genius brings us such things as both our greatest artisans and our greatest villains.

Hephaestus—Male—Mediterranean
Greek patron of all forms of the arts, but particularly of the metalsmith.

Svarog—Male—Central/North Europe
Slavic fire god, mentioned earlier, who is also patron of the metalsmith.

Goibniu—Male—Central Europe
Irish god of the smith's fire who is said to create swords that remain so true, they were thought to possess great magick.

Fire and Water/Soul and Mind

Separating Fire and Water to explain the two has been difficult because they are so strongly fused. Once a blade is forged, can one separate the fire and the water used to temper it? Who can say where the fountain and the fountainhead separate? Just as that which a person is after being born of a mother and father cannot be separated back into mother and father without the destruction of self, that which is the nature of a person's being cannot be separated into masculine and feminine. Where Wiccan rituals mark life by noting the union of the feminine and the masculine, that speaks only to the union itself. The product of that union, the magickal child, is neither wholly male nor wholly female. Instead, it is a union of the masculine and feminine that can not be undone without destroying that which is created.

This is the Egyptian 'ba' (soul) and 'ka' (human life force). The 'ba' is present in both humans and animals, but the 'ka' is unique to humanity and the gods themselves. Seen in many facets of the Hindu traditions, it is the Water (soul/feminine) which is controlled by the fountainhead (mind/masculine). Neither male nor female should feel insulted by this, as we are not discussing that which is male or that which is female. Every man and every woman is a composite of that that which is soul (feminine) and that which is mind (masculine). Every man and woman is equal in that they are a composite of what the Chinese called the Yin (feminine, Earth, soul) and the Yang (masculine, sky, mind).

Culture	Feminine	Masculine
Egyptian	Ba	Ka
Chinese	Yin	Yang
Japanese	In	Yo
Hindu	Fountain	Fountainhead
Wicca	Chalice	Athame

The Conception of Spirit

This is one of the many reasons the Wiccan religion is applicable not only to heterosexual couples, but also to solitaries and the many gay and lesbian members of our community, as well. Some see the Great Rite as a symbolic act of heterosexual union, but it is not. Even the physical act of sex is nothing more than a symbolic Great Rite. While this is not to say that sexual unions are not sacred in and of themselves, that which is termed the Great Rite is greater than any physical act. It is the mingling not only of the soul, not only of two separate beings, but the mingling of the ba and ka within the individual. At its essence, the Great Rite is the symbolic conception of Spirit as the place in which soul and mind meet.

The symbolic Great Rite, as the athame of Fire into the chalice of Water or as penis into vagina is not only an affirmation of Life, the union of masculine and feminine. It is a promise. It is the acceptance of the responsibility given to humanity upon its first ascension. It is the affirmation that we have indeed accepted that fruit, and now we will revel in the rewards of empathy as seen in the great joys of one of the symbolic Great Rites, and we will also live up to our promise to temper that soul—joy, sex, revelry—with mind. The Great Rite is therefore the affirmation that our Spirit has been born, the sum total of soul and mind.

On Will, Dharma, Duty, and Soul

In Thelema, it is called *will*. In the many forms of Hinduism it is called *dharma* which translates loosely as duty. In Wicca, I say that it is best termed Spirit. It is what we mean when we say 'so mote it be,' an affirmation that both mind and soul agree. You see, the *will* spoken of in Thelema keys on duty to oneself, and the *dharma* spoken of in the Hindu paths speaks more to the duty to ones line. The Wiccan concept of Spirit recognizes both of these things in the Rule of Three times three.

Will	Father	Duty to oneself
Dharma	Mother	Duty to one's community
Spirit	The Magickal Child	Duty to oneself and one's community

Spirit is the sacred center, the place one cannot see by looking either outside of oneself or inside oneself, the place only seen by recognizing both. That recognition is the marriage of self with community, the knowledge that those things that benefit the self also benefit the community, and the knowledge that those things that benefit the community also benefit the self.

Wicca and Sex

Right about now a few folk are wondering why I have equated these matters to sex. My answer is rather simple: Wicca is a fertility religion. Now, this does not mean that Wiccan rituals involve sex; nor does it mean that all Wiccans must become parents. Indeed, there are many Wiccans who should not become parents just as there are members of every religion that should not become parents. Let's face it, the world is getting pretty crowded.

Instead, Wicca is a fertility religion because Wicca explains the world in which we live very much as did the ancient Pagans on which our religion is based. But it is also a modern religion, embracing science as well as lore. This is why we term these principles masculine and feminine—not because we think one is better than the other, but because natural observation has told us that the way we create life is by male flowing into female. If you think this view is sexist, please consider: That which is light (masculine) is said to flow into that which is dark (feminine). So is it the light (masculine) acting on the dark (feminine), or the other way around? That which is hot (masculine) is said to flow into that which is cold (feminine). So is it the warmth (masculine) acting on the coldness (feminine), or the other way around?

Thus, we see Spirit as the manifestation of the magickal child that is formed when mind (masculine) flows into soul (feminine). We see the active (mind) flowing into the potential (soul) as conception. Thus, the nature of the magickal child is revealed, and the core of Wiccan ritual is known. Although the symbolism of Wiccan ritual is most certainly sexual, it is not a celebration of the conception of a child as manifested in flesh and blood, but in the conception of one's Spirit as manifested in the people that we are and the people that we hope to become.

Liber ab Mortuus
(Book of the Dead)

There have been many cultural 'Books of the Dead,' none of which are titled the 'Necronomicon.' Instead, that title is what a fantasy novelist named Lovecraft invented for use in his stories of fiction. Although he reported being asked numerous times about a copy of the *Necronomicon,* he said over and over again that it did not exist. Then, seemingly out of the blue, a book by that title appeared on the pulp paperback market with that very title which alluded to a connection with Aleister Crowley. The book was not written by Crowley and probably not even by Lovecraft. You see, you cannot copyright a title, so it was probably written by someone hoping to capitalize on Lovecraft's fiction. That book has probably made the author more money than the *Satanic Bible* made for Anton LeVey. You see, books are judged by not only their cover, but also their title. Frankly, spooky titles sell books.

I have not titled this chapter to be dark and spooky. I have titled it because it fits. Although religion is a matter of how we live, it is also a matter of how we die. The word means to "re legion," to have union again. In this word, we see the nature of things. It is the path by which we find reunion, the Path we started at our birth, our separation, which leads us to our death, the reunion. But what then?

While assembling a video chat server for the online community at *www.Pagannation.com*, a friend of mine named Duane and I were descended upon by modern day missionaries. For some reason, they seem attracted to Pagan shops such as mine. After they dispensed with the formalities of determining that we are not saved, they moved on to what they must have thought would be our breaking point:

"A.J., what happens after you die?"

I answered by simply stating that because I am not dead, I don't know. They were happy to inform me, so I assume they were dead. After all, unless you are dead how would you know for sure? I couldn't provide them with an answer, and I cannot provide you with an answer. I cannot tell you what Wiccans think about death because it is far too personal a matter to dare attempt to speak for Wiccans in even the most general of terms. Nor can I provide you with rituals that will ease the heart's ache at such a loss. But I can tell you that the pain of loss is normal, and I can tell you how I feel about the subject.

I do not believe *ashes to ashes and dust to dust* is appropriate terminology to sum up the life and accomplishments of anyone with even the tiniest life. So rather than recognizing my death when it comes, I beg of my kith and kin that they recognize my life and the lives that I have touched rather than mourn my loss.

Do with my body what you will. Bury or burn it. Set it afloat, or feed it to the fish. I do not care because whatever my fate is, that fate is no longer attached to the flesh that I once inhabited. If you think it would raise a smile, prop it up at my wake with Guinness in one hand, and don't forget the Guinness for the folk who come to celebrate my life rather than wallow in my death.

That's it. No funeral, ritual, or large production, just a party so I can look down (or up, as the case may be) and see that the folk that I love will continue in love after I have died. Should you want to comfort the folk who were particularly close to my heart, then tell them my tales. Instead of rambling on about what a loss my death was to the world, ramble on about how different the world would have been should I have not lived and be grateful that I did. If that is too much to ask, then don't drink my damn beer.

You see, in all of our talk about there being no judgment day, when that thread is finally cut, I believe very much that a person's life can be judged by the stories one can tell of his or her life. After all, what else would our earthly legacy have to know us by if not our stories?

On Facing Death

"My name is Damien Echols and I am on death row in Arkansas."[1]

After receiving that letter, I spent weeks searching for help on how to reply. I have decided there is not one book on the subject of giving spiritual advice to someone on death row, much less for someone who is on death row with virtually no evidence brought against him except for his involvement in a minority religion. With the complete and total failure of Pagan books to address the issue, I turned to the more established clergy of other religions. Maybe it should not have surprised me that everyone I spoke to advised me that being right with God was in order. Maybe I should not have been surprised because I have always felt that living as a Wiccan is a harder path than that of other religions. Why would facing Death as a Wiccan be any different? "Thou are god," thought I. What about being right with yourself? How does a Wiccan face Death?

I thought long and hard on the subject, and then I remembered the circumstances that once caused me to be in that dark place with a twelve gauge in my mouth. I was sick and had given up on life. I had come to the conclusion that there was nothing I could to do to change the eventuality of my death. But I am only able to recount this story to you now because something happened to me that would forever change the way I live, thus changing the way I hope to face Death when it finally finds me. In that moment I received a simple message. If I wanted to live, then I should not support death. Of course, with the illness that ravaged my lungs and the belief that inaction is an action unto itself, that message meant one thing: Fight!

That is how I now hope to meet my death—not in peace, but in combat. Not in a battle against Death itself—no, Death is the natural conclusion to Life—but in a battle against the same forces that I combated during my lifetime. I hope to die combating those forces that stand in opposition to what my Spirit dictates. While I have been told that when death is seemingly imminent, one should comfort folk and convince the dying to accept that eventuality, I cannot in good conscience do so because I am living proof that some times death is only *seemingly* imminent, and the very thing that may cause Death to turn and look the other way is how we accept Life, not how we accept Death.

So what does someone say to someone that is on death row for a crime that he says he did not commit? One says the same thing one would say to anyone that is facing Death for whatever reason: One should face Death in the way one faces Life, by recognizing that which one's Spirit demands and fighting anything that would oppose those demands. One tells him that if Spirit demands that he scream his innocence, then he should do just that until the very last moment. For it is the very act of living at the moment one thinks he might die that may well be what is necessary to postpone that moment of death for many, many years to come. One tells him to never, ever give up or give in!

The Afterlife

Thus far, Wicca has not developed much of a detailed afterlife concept. As none of us have been there and returned to tell the tale, no one really knows. If the belief in reincarnation is a fact, then folk don't tell that tale much because they do not remember it to tell. In truth, I do believe firmly in reincarnation. The thing is, I do not generally believe folk when they tell me their wild tales. I have lost count of the number of folk who claim to be Hitler and Napoleon reincarnated. Okay, maybe Napoleon had some good points, but Hitler? I am reminded of the song Industrial Disease by Dire Straits: "Two men say they're Jesus. One of them must be wrong."

Ask a hundred Wiccans about almost any other subject and you will receive almost a hundred answers. Ask a hundred Wiccans about the afterlife, and you will probably receive only two answers: Reincarnation and Summerland.

Common Wiccan Reincarnation—The common Wiccan belief in reincarnation centers around the idea of learning and life on Earth being an educational Path. We live, we learn, we die, and then we start over, with no ending in sight or much of a speculation as to why it is that we are living over and over again. It is as if we are professional students, destined never to have a job, never needing to demonstrate that acquired knowledge or put it to work.

Common Wiccan Summerland—The common Wiccan belief in Summerland is similar to the Greek Elysian Fields, only everyone gets to go there, and everyone can leave whenever they like. It is to reincarnation what spring break or summer vacation is to college or the public school system.

What strikes me as odd is that if Wicca is a Nature-based religion, these common views of the afterlife do not seem to fit. From where I sit, life involves work and while education can be incredibly valuable, without putting that education to work it becomes rather useless. Even after working hard one's whole life, there is further work after retirement. So why then would the afterlife be any different?

Reincarnation?

Reincarnation has been a central belief in many religions, but not as the superficial thing that it often becomes in the superficial portion of the Wiccan community. In other religions, reincarnation could be used as a teaching tool, but it was also a punishment. In Hindu lore, one such punishment is to return as a *Preta*. This punishment was given to gluttons, folk who consumed far more than they need. The Preta are disembodied spirits sent to walk the Earth forever, always able to see those things they had been gluttonous for but never able to consume them, always thirsty but never able to quench that thirst. Additional tales of such punishment can be found in the many stories of the dead being chained just outside the reach of water for an eternity.

Generally speaking, the common Wiccan belief in reincarnation is unique to Wicca. While Pagan religions did demonstrate a belief in reincarnation, where one would reincarnate and what that person's next life would be was in direct relation to the way one lived his or her current lifetime. In other words, graduating from one grade level might have meant moving on to the next, but failing did not necessarily mean you would repeat the class. Instead, depending on how badly you failed, you might be expelled, as the Preta, or you might have to start again at the beginning.

Summerland?

Generally speaking, like the common Wiccan version of reincarnation, the common Wiccan version of Summerland is unique to Wicca. Nowhere in all of Pagan lore can we find a system in which everyone who dies goes to a pleasant place. Nowhere in all of Pagan lore is everything forgiven. Yes, the Wiccan version of Summerland resembles the Greek Elysian fields, but not all were welcome there. In all the modern Pagan community's declarations that they do not believe in the existence of Heaven and Hell, what they have effectively done is to rewrite Pagan lore. Yes, the ancient Pagans believed in Heaven (Summerland) but they also believed in Hell (Winterland). In fact, the very name *hell* comes from Pagan lore.

Traditional Pagan Winterlands

Norse Winterland

The Norse Underworld is called Helheim. It is ruled by the goddess Hell and also called by that name. The entrance to Helheim is guarded by a horrific flesh-eating hound called Garm, who stands aside to let all in but prevents anyone from leaving.

Greek Winterland

The Greek Underworld is ruled by Hades and his wife Persephone. Hades is judge and ruler of the dead. His name is also the name of the Underworld itself. The entrance to Hades is guarded by Cerberus, a monstrous three-headed dog who allows all to enter but none to leave.

Roman Winterland

The Roman Underworld is ruled by Pluto and his wife Proserpina, described as a place from where none return. Of course, there have been a few exceptions. Pluto's wife Proserpina comes to mind. The name of the Roman Winterland is Avernus, but they also called it by the Greek name Hades after the cultures merged. Avernus is also the name of a large opening in the Earth in Campania, which was thought to be the entrance to the Underworld. The entrance to Avernus is guarded by the goddess Mania, a goddess of horrific insanity. In the Roman Underworld is found the personification of hunger as Fames, poverty as Egestes, death as Letum, and many other similarly gods and personifications, the collective of which are called the Inferi Dii

Similarities in German, Roman, and Greek Winterlands

Culture	Name	Guard	Lord	Lady
Norse	Hell or Helheim	Garm	Ganglati*	Hel/Hell
Roman	Avernus	Mania	Pluto	Proserpina
Greek	Hades	Cerberus	Hades	Persephone

* Ganglati is Hel's servant.

Mayan Winterland

Mayan lore speaks of an Underworld with nine levels. Exactly which level a person would be sent to upon his or her death was determined by the actions of one's life. The lowest, most horrific, level is Mitnal. It is the place from which none ever return, the Mayan Winterland.

Aztec Winterland

Like the Mayan, the Aztec Winterland is the lowest level of the Underworld. It is ruled by Lord Mictlantecuhtli. After great challenges and dangers, the souls of all who travel here find rest in oblivion.

Traditional Pagan Summerlands

The ancient Pagans also saw a Summerland, a place where life was easy. I presented some of the many Winterlands first to illustrate the point that there are indeed places that are not too pleasant. Those things should be just as part of our lore as the following eventualities.

Aztec Summerland

In Aztec lore, everyone who dies goes to Winterland unless they died bravely or in the act of giving birth. For these souls is reserved a splendor which is not possible to imagine or describe.

Celtic Summerland

Called the Mag Mell ('plain of joy') or the Tir na n-Og ('land of youth'), this is what you have heard of the Wiccan Summerland. It is a perfect island or sometimes a realm hidden deep beneath the ocean.

Greek Summerland

This is the Elysian Fields, no doubt one of the sources for the neo-Pagan Summerland. What the neo-Pagan movement left out is that although this is a place of Nature's splendor where Summer never sets, only those chosen by the gods are allowed to reside here. Also called Elysium and Elysion.

The Judgement of Souls

So we see a Summerland and a Winterland, a nice place and a not so nice place. How is it that souls are sent to one or the other? The answer is that although we have a knee jerk reaction to the idea of a judgement day, this principle can be found in many ancient Pagan religions. You see, it is this judgement that sets Wicca apart from most mainstream religions. But it is not in denying the principle of judgement; it is in embracing it. It is in the idea that we are responsible for the things that we do and our sin (for lack of a better word) cannot be washed away by speaking a few words, changing our religious choice, or saying a few Hail Marys. Yes, we do decide what our afterlife will be. But we make that decision in the actions of our lifetime and our lifetimes.

Egyptian Judgement

Anubis takes the deceased to the house of Osiris and into the Hall of Two Truths. There, a court is held to determine what one's final disposition will be. Unlike the courts of men, here there are no lies because the prosecutor is Thoth, the personification and god of Truth itself. Sitting as judge is Osiris with the assistance of Isis and Nephthys who are at his sides. The soul, or sometimes the heart, is then placed on a balancing scale along with its sin, the actions of the mind. On the other side of that scale is placed a feather from the crown of Maat, goddess of truth. Should the weight of the soul with its sin be greater than the feather, it sinks and is devoured by Ammit such that there is no chance of afterlife or reincarnation. Instead, the soul becomes nothing.

Babylonian Judgement

Similar to the Islamic Katib, the Babylonian record keeper is Belit-Sheri. She records the actions and inaction of a lifetime and presents that record to the Queen of the Dead to determine final judgement.

Native American Judgement

The lore of several of the tribes of the great planes shows a bridge between this life and the next, The Bridge of Souls. Below that bridge is an abyss of darkness that consumes souls into its nothingness. Upon that bridge is a guardian, sometimes an Owl Woman, who looks at the spirit of those who would pass. If she recognizes that spirit as being kith or kin, deserving of the afterlife, she allows them to pass. If she should not, they are thrown from the bridge into the abyss.

Islamic Judgement

At birth, every person receives a Katib (writer) who throughout a person's lifetime keeps tracks of all actions and inaction and writes those deeds in the *kitab*, the book of deeds. On the day of one's death, the kitab is read to the recently released soul, and his or her final disposition is determined by its contents.

Why This is important to Wicca

Wicca is a modern religion, so one might say we can pick and choose what Pagan lore we desire and what we do not. While this is true, in asking what Wicca is we see guidance in what to choose and what not to. In looking at what Wicca is, we see a clear reason to recognize both a Summerland and a Winterland. You see, this book began with the separation of Light and Darkness, with the separation of Winter and Summer and that is how it will end, with Light and Darkness as well as Winter and Summer, in their reunion, in that which is the very end of the world.

You see, all things have a beginning, middle, and an end. We are all born, we all live, and we will all die. Our world was born, it is living, and it will die. We can extend our lives by living right and taking care of ourselves. We can extend our world's life by taking care of it. But in the end, we will die. In the end, our beloved world will die as well. In the end of our life, our birth (Light) and our death (Darkness) will meet and cancel each other out. In the end of the world, Summerland will meet Winterland and cancel each other out. In the end of Divinity, the Gods will meet the Outsiders and cancel each other out. So one is left with two potential ways of looking at things:

1. How one lives does not matter because one will surely die.
2. How one lives is the only thing that matters because one will surely die.

You were born of Summer and Winter
Then reborn of Earth and Sky
This is your blessing and your fate
That one day you will surely die

The Death of the World

1 – 1 = 0

Thinking about the end of days is so distasteful that, to date, I do not recall ever reading of such matters in a book about Wicca. As Pagan lore is filled with such matters and as Wicca sees a beginning, middle and end to all things, one would think mention of the end of the world might be included. After all, if we do not recognize that as a potential, why would we fight against it? If one does not believe we may one day cause the extinction of all living things on this earth, why bother to fight against that eventuality? So then, incorporated into our lore we do see and end of all days just as surely as we see an end of our days.

Ragnarok (Also known as Gotterdammerung or 'Doom of Gods')—Northern European

From the time of Ash and Elm, the Valkyries, Choosers of the Slain, have circled the world for the Einherjar, those who in life battled the Outsiders and in death have gone bravely. The Valkyries find these brave souls and bring them to the hall of Odin. Called Valhalla, the Hall of the Slain, it is not a place where the brave will live forever as the movie adaptation of the Norse Prayer suggests. It is a place where the Einherjar train for Ragnarok, the doom of the gods. It is a place where the brave are brave, not because they are promised immortality but because that is what they do and that is what they will do until the very end.

The Winter Fimbulvetr will mark the beginning of that ending. It is the Winter of all Winters, lasting three years with no summer between. All the earth will be blanketed with ice and snow. Battles will break out between nations as well as between kith and kin. Everywhere there will be war. A wolf named Skoll will consume the sun. His brother Hati will devour the moon. The stars will dwindle away, fading to sky that is nothing but black. Day will become as night, and night will become darker than any man can remember. The morning will be known only by the crow of three cocks. The cock named Fjalar will wake the Outsiders, those who have challenged the gods and lost. The cock named Gullinkambi will wake the Gods and a third cock will wake the dead.

The Outsider Jormungand, the great serpent, will rise from the sea and move towards land. In his wake, the oceans will swell, letting slip the ship Naglfar. In his wake will the land quake, letting slip the bonds of Fenrir. The Earth and sky will turn to poison in Jormungand's wake. Hymir will sail the Naglfar, the ship of the Outsiders, to

Vigrond. So too will come the slain of Hell in a ship sailed by Loki. And from Muspel in the south will come the Outsiders led by Surt, the fire giant. With him, Surt will bring a sword of flames that will scorch the Earth. Heimdall will sound the alarm, calling forth the sons of Odin and the Einherjar. They will come from the four corners of the world. Those who would stand with the Gods and those who would stand with the Outsiders, all meeting at the place of this, the final battle.

Odin and Fenrir will first meet, then Thor and Jormungand, then Heimdall and Loki. Though Freyr is unarmed, Surt will kill him without hesitation because that is what the Outsiders do. Though Tyr has but one arm, he will join the battle and attack Garm because that is what the Gods do. Thor will defeat Jormungand, but then himself die from its poison. Surt will kill the unarmed Freyr. Loki and Heimdall will kill each other, as will Tyr and Garm. Fenrir will swallow Odin and at the moment of Odin's death, when it seems clear to both sides that all is lost, Vidar and Surt will show one last time the difference between the Gods (good) and the Outsiders (evil).

With his father and friends dead and nothing to be gained but his own death, Vidar will leap at his fathers killer and ripe the jaw of Fenrir from its skull, killing Fenrir to avenge his fathers death, knowing very well that not retreating from the battlefield meant his own death. Why will he do this? Because that is what the Gods do. But that is not what the Outsiders do. When Surt, who kills the unarmed, realizes he will not win, he swings his flaming sword to the four Quarters, setting the world on fire such that all will lose—the armed, the unarmed, the combatants, the non-combatants. Why will he do this? Because that is what the Outsiders do.

Shortly after the fires have consumed all that is left of the Earth after the great battle, the land will sink into the ocean and there will be nothing left of that which we have loved so dearly. The Gods will seem dead, Humanity will seem dead, and the Earth itself will seem dead.

So tell me? Who are you? Are you one of the Gods or are you one of the Outsiders? This too is the meaning behind the Wiccan greeting 'Thou art god' and 'Thou art goddess.' No, Ragnarok has not fallen. But the Valkyries are circling overhead and the Fenrir is scratching at the door. Some might argue that it is too late, but it is never too late to decide who you are. That and not what you have read here or in any other book on Wicca is the mystery of Wicca. That single question and the things that we do to try and answer it: Who are you?

But with the passing of time, a new world will rise from the ocean and the floods will recede. The Gods will be reborn and two of Humanity's finest will have survived. Lif ('life') and Lifthrasir ('eager for life') will become as Ash and Elm, or maybe they are Ash and Elm. Maybe Ragnarok has already come and gone. Maybe it has come and gone many times over. Maybe it is a distant tale of our future, or maybe Fenrir scratches at the door even now. Do you see the Valkyries overhead? Are we at the beginning or the end?

In the glory of our Lord and Lady, the end becomes the beginning and the beginning becomes the end. So mote it be.

Chapter Dedication

This chapter is dedicated to Damien Echols and for anyone with a heart:

Damien, if you are innocent and there is nothing I, or those I rally,
can do to prevent the unjust taking of your life, then I urge you to spend
each moment between now and the moment of your death living as you have for
the last 10 years. I urge you to meet your death in the way I feel a Wiccan
would—in the unyielding battle to see that thy will be done. Thou art God!
Now manifest thy destiny in accordance with thy will!

To anyone with a heart. There is a distinct chance this man will be put to death
for little more than his involvement in the Wiccan religion. I am not going to tell you
that he is innocent, but I do think it is our responsibility as Wiccans to investigate the
matter. If he is guilty, then you have wasted a few minutes of your time. But if he is
innocent, the Burning Times have returned and the fires are being lit in Arkansas.
The difference being this time you might be able to do something about it.
Please visit *www.damienechols.org*.

Liber ab Clementia
(Book of Humanity)

The Third Order of Life

Study Material for the Third Degree

O f all the material presented herein, the title of this chapter is bound to be the most controversial. If we are discussing God and Goddess forms, why would I call this the Book of Humanity? Because it reflects the secret found in the three orders of life. You see, whatever you call our Lord and Lady, they are the sum total of all that lives. They are in essence, Life itself. Thus this book, the Book of Humanity, is the book of viewing our Lord and Lady alive in all humanity.

Ultimately, though we might be seen as worshipping our Lord and Lady by outsiders, the educated Wiccan knows that what is really being celebrated is Life and its splendor of diversity. This is why the Wiccan respects all order of plants, all order of animals, and all order of humanity. Black, red, white, yellow, or any variation between, in their many forms our Lord and Lady are us in our many forms. Like us, they started in Africa and circled the world to return and once again be united in the love in which they started, separated for the sake of union.

Here we find the Wiccan greetings: Thou art Goddess and Thou art God. Where we look to plants and animals as the creation of our Lord and Lady, here we have become God and Goddess in giving form to our Lord and Lady. No, we did not create them. But we have surely assigned them the many names and many forms by which we now recognize them.

Like any discussion of lore, this book is not complete in any sense of the word. Were it possible to create a complete reference, such a manuscript would fill the shelves of many libraries. Whenever possible, I have used the most current and credible reference material to expand and make corrections on the lore that has made its way into my Book of Shadows. However, with ongoing studies into these matters, reference material becomes outdated quickly. Making matters even more confusing, the same story told several times becomes different. In preparing this material, there were many instances where mythology provided two, three, or even more sets of parents/lines for a particular god or goddess. In those cases, I choose the lineage that not only seemed most current in academic reference but also the one that fits the underlying story presented by the whole of the line. That is, I have set my focus more on the relationships of the gods and goddesses rather than on individual deity forms.

We have traveled so many miles since our exodus from Africa. Along the way, we left behind pockets of humanity who developed unique cultures. But our journey has not been only along the coastlines and up through the Fertile Crescent. Our journey has not been only across land and over sea. It has also been a journey of time. As we migrated, those pockets of humanity grew into elder communities. Some of those communities prospered and grew. Others reached a peak and then fell from sight to be replaced by a different community in the same corner of the world. Other communities merged and mingled, sometimes as the result of war. Other unique cultures have been referred to as if they were one and the same for so long that folk have started to believe they are one and the same.

What is important in these matters is to remember that although we have been separated by both distance and time, we are one people. We are the children of Ash and Elm, who were themselves the children of Summer and Winter as well as Sky and Earth. This is why we can look to the many deities, separated by great distances of both land and time and see the same archetypes over and over again. To illustrate that point, I have diverged from the typical method of identifying the names of our Lord and Lady. Where most books list only the community who praised the deity, I have listed the general part of the world where that community is found. In so doing, I preserve the common reference to community in the context of the discussion of each particular deity, but I add the additional generalized geography of each as well. When I say generalized, I mean just that. Because I know that Ireland is not part of Central Europe, when listing the names of our Lord and Lady of Ireland, I include that reference in the context of those deities. However, I also note that when it comes to cultural migration, Ireland is part of Central Europe. After all, it is Irish lore itself that states the Irish people moved into Central Europe after the Great Flood and only later into Ireland.

Where cultures have moved about and intermixed enough that I can not be comfortable placing them with one migration or the other, I have listed the ones that seem most likely with respect to lore, elder science, and the newer science of mitochondria DNA. It is my hope that by doing so, I have illustrated that the many archetypes of our Lord and Lady are a matter of human migration (the general references) more than they are a matter of individual cultures (the contextual references) because I feel very strongly that these archetypes belong first to the world but that understanding their contextual basis helps us in their understanding. To that end, I identify the world as in the following diagram:

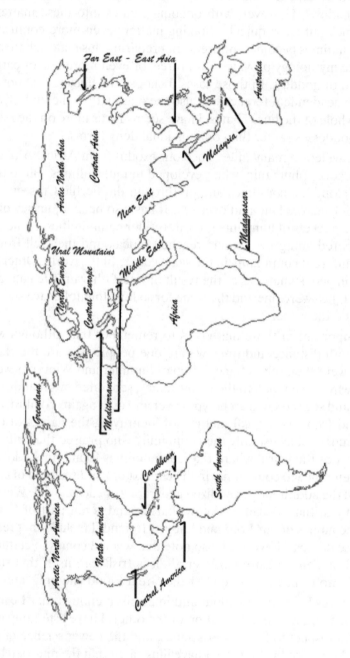

Homes of Our Lord and Lady

The Cultural and Geographical Names of Our Lord and Lady

Abraxas—Male—Middle East/Mediterranean
Animal association: Chicken, Horse (white)

Potentially an ancient Gnostic name used in place of the unspeakable name of the Supreme Being and to identify that being with solar energy. His name sometimes appears in reference by the medieval demonologists, but their opinion was obviously biased. His name is the most likely origin for the expression *abracadabra*, perhaps indicating the idea that with the Creator all things are possible. I say potentially because there is a distinct possibility this is a very modern myth.

Acat—Male—Central America

Mayan and Yucatan people prayed to Acat for healthy children. Acat was seen as a god of human development, shaping our children in the womb. He has been adopted by tattoo artists as patron deity.

Acca Larentia—Female—Mediterranean
(Also known as Lupa)
Husband: Faustulus
Lover: Hercules
Animal association: Wolf

In one version, an Etruscan goddess who adopted Romulus and Remus. Another version states that she is one of Hercules' lovers who is particularly promiscuous. In that aspect, she is sometimes either called or associated with the name Lupa. There she is seen as a charitable goddess, having married rich and upon her husband's death gave her inherited wealth to the citizens of Rome when they were in need.

Achelous—Male—Mediterranean
(Also known as Acheloos)
Father: Oceanus
Mother: Tehys
Lover: Melpomene

Animal association: Cattle (bull), Snake (serpent)

'He who washes away cares' —Greek god of the river by his name as well as other flowing bodies of fresh water. So much did he love Deianeira, that he wrestled with Hercules for her hand in marriage. He lost not only the competition but his arm. Sometimes cited as son of Helios and Gaia

Achilles—Male—Mediterranean
(Also known as Achilleus)
Father: Peleus
Mother: Thetis

'Lipless'—Greek god who warns that we are all vulnerable. From his story, we have the expression "Achilles Heel." His mother, Thetis, did her best to protect him from harm, dipping him in the River Styx so that all parts of his body which contacted the water would be invulnerable. To his downfall, Thetis had held him by his heel when dipping him into the water, leaving a vulnerable spot. Achilles fell when his heel was struck by an arrow shot by Paris at the Trojan War. Although he fell during that war, he was one of its greatest heroes.

Achlys—Female—Mediterranean

'Darkness' or *'Dark mist'*—Greek creator who gave birth to the creator Chaos. Her name shows a clear link to the story of Diana (Darkness) giving birth to Lucifer (Light) and the story given in the Book of Genesis.

Anchises—Male—Mediterranean
Father: Capys
Lover: Aphrodite

Roman mortal who did so love the goddess Aphrodite that she welcomed him to her bed and bore him a son, Aeneas. He was the owner of six incredible horses which he created by mating his own mares with six divinely bred stallions.

Adam—Male—Middle East

Father: Yahweh

Mother: Earth

Wife: Lilith, Eve

Although often cited as the Christian first man, even Christian scripture is rather clear that he was not. First Yahweh created life with Mother Earth: "Let the Earth bring forth the living creature after his kind.." (Genesis 1:24). Later, the line of humanity is created (presumably with the help of Mother Earth): "Let *us* make man in *our* image, after our likeness" (Genesis 1:26). After the week long process of creating not only Earth and sky but all the creatures of land, sea, and sky, after his rest on the seventh day, then God created Adam: "And the Lord God formed man..." (Genesis 2:7). But the creation of Adam was not without argument. After Yahweh told the angels that he had intended on creating Adam, he ordered them to bring to him clay from which he would sculpt Adam such that another line of humanity would follow. They strongly advised against the action, stating; "Humanity in the line of Adam will hatch hatred, jealousy and sin, he will light the brush-fire of war." So too did Mother Earth disagree at first, stating that 'No part of mine will be used to form a disobedient sinner." Although Mother Earth objected to the creation, Yahweh sent Azrael, the Angel of Death, to rob her of the clay necessary to create Adam, in effect bringing Adam into this world through an act of rape. That rape is the 'original sin' for which Yahweh would later suffer as Jesus Christ to wash away. See Jesus.

Adamah—Female—Middle East

Hebrew personification of the Earth, perhaps the victim of rape at the order of Yahweh. See Yahweh.

Adapa—Male—Mediterranean/Middle East

Father: Ea

Mother: Kishar

Babylonian god sent by his father to protect and watch over humanity. Paris (God) offered Adapa immortality for humanity, but Adapa refused. He reminds us that it is not always in our children's best interest to give them what they desire. In another story, he did not receive immortality because he did not conduct himself as would a god.

Addad—Male—Mediterranean/Middle East

(Also known as Iskur [Sumerian])

Animal association: Bull, Dragon (lion)

Babylonian god of rain and storms.

Adibuddha—Male—Near East

The Buddhist embodiment of the masculine principle of the Buddhist soul.

Adereosa—Female—Africa/Middle East

(Also known as Adra Nedega [Babylonian])

Egyptian and Arabian virgin who is seen nursing her child in the night sky as the constellation Virgo.

Adra Nedega—See Adereosa

Aditi—Female—Near East

Lovers: Brahma, Kashyapa

Animal association: Cow

'Limitless,' 'Free from bonds,' or *'The unbound'*—Hindu All Mother and sky goddess. Mother of the Sun (Mitra) and Moon (Varuna), which together define the solar year and the months of that year. She gave birth to the twelve Adityas, each associated with one of the Hindu 12 months of the year. See Adityas.

Adityas, The—Male—Near East

Father: Kashyapa

Mother: Aditi

Twelve Hindu sun gods associated with the 12 months of the year. They are: Vishnu, Aryman, Vivasvana, Amshumana, Parjanya, Varuna, Indra, Dhatri, Mitra, Pusha, Bhaga, and Tvashta. Alternatively, the Adityas are sometimes cited as: Ansa, Aryman, Bhaga, Daksha, Dhatri, Indra, Mitra, Ravini, Savitri, Surya, Varuna, and Yama.

Adoni—Male—Mediterranean/Middle East

Phoenician/Babylonian consort (lover) of Astarte, Adoni is associated with the waxing and waning of the solar year. A god of the green, Adoni was seen as dying at the onset of Winter and being reborn with the new Summer.

Adonis—Male—Mediterranean

Lover: Aphrodite, Dionysus

Animal association: Dove, Boar, Lion,

Plant association: Acacia, Adder's Tongue, Anemone, Bay, Corn, Daffodil, Fennel, Heather (especially white), Jojoba, Lettuce, Vine (grape), Lily, Myrrh, Olive, Rose

'Lord'—Greek patron of children, virgins, and anyone that feels alone or lost in the world. As one of Dionysus' male lovers, he has become one of the patrons of the gay, lesbian, and bisexual community. His holiday on July 19th is associated with his relationship with Aphrodite. So much did Aphrodite love Adonis that she begged him to give up hunting, but it was his favorite sport, so he refused and continued. Again she begged him, but he would not give up the pleasure of the sport of hunting. Eventually, just as she had worried, he was killed while hunting. A wild boar, who was Aphrodite herself, attacked and killed Adonis. From this I have taken the principle that when one has love in one's heart one cannot make sport of death. Although hunting may be necessary for survival, there can be no love in the act. This reflects strongly on the principle put forth in the Book of Animals in respect to not naming kith familiars.

Incense Recipe

2 parts Myrrh (sweet myrrh is best)

1 part Bay Leaf

1 part Gum Arabic

1 part Rose petals (red) or 9 pomegranate seeds*

Enough Adonis or Myrrh oil to bind

*If being used during Winter (Samhain through Beltane), use pomegranate seeds. If you will be using during the Summer, use the rose petals.

Oil Recipe

9 drops Bay essential oil

6 drops Myrrh essential oil

6 drops Otto of Rose (or 3 drops Rose Geranium and 3 drops Cypress)

1/2 ounce Olive oil

Adraste—Female—Central Europe

(Also known as Andrasta, Adraste)

Animal association: Hare

Celtic goddess of war during the Celtic British rise against Rome.

Aeacus—Male—Mediterranean

(Also known as Aiakos and Aeacos)

Father: Zeus

Mother: Aegina

Animal association: Ant, Elephant

Plant association: Allspice, Aloe, Cinnamon, Frankincense

'Earth born'—The Greek Aeacus tells us that appealing to higher powers is sometimes necessary to overcome obstacles. He tells us that our word is our bond and reminds us that judgement is most certainly part of the Pagan mindset. By many accounts, he was conceived after Zeus raped his mother Aegina, he went on to rule Attica (the island Zeus had kidnapped his mother to). Aeacus was one of the three judges of the Underworld, determining one's death based on how one lived.

Incense Recipe

3 parts Frankincense

3 parts Allspice berries

1 part Cinnamon

Enough Aeacus or Frankincense oil to bind

Oil Recipe

9 drops Frankincense essential oil

9 drops Allspice essential oil

3 drops Cinnamon essential oil

1/2 ounce base oil

Aeetes—Male—Mediterranean

(Also known as Aietes)

Father: Helios

Mother: Perse

Greek king of Colchia, son of Helios, and father of the sorceress Medea.

Aegina—Female—Mediterranean

Mother: Merope

Lover: Zeus

Greek woman who was kidnapped by Zeus as a girl, brought to the island Attica, and some say raped. As a result, she bore Aeacus who later ruled the island.

Aegir—Male—North Europe

Wife: Ran

Animal association: Fish and to some degree all creatures of the sea.

Norse god of the sea. Aegir speaks to us of human adoption, telling us that blood is not nearly as important as heart.

Aello—Female—Mediterranean

(Also known as Podarge ['fleet foot'])

'Swift Storm' —Greek Harpy charged with creating peace. In that capacity, she and the others are beautiful winged maidens (sometimes virgins). But to keep that peace, she and the others were also the punishers of crime. In that capacity, they are horrid winged beasts. One of the three Harpies. The other two are Celaeno and Ocypete.

Aeneas—Male—Mediterranean

(Also known as Aineias)

Mother: Venus

Father: Anchises

Roman mortal born of the goddess Venus. Aeneas is the founder of the Roman nation and patron of interracial/cultural couples. Sometimes cited as son of the Greek goddess Aphrodite.

Aengus Mac Og—Male—Central Europe

(Also known as Angus, Anghus, Aonghus, Angus Og, Angus Mac Og, Oengus Mac Og)

Father: Dagda

Mother: Boann

Plant association: Hazelnut, Heather, Witchhazel

'Angus the Young'—Irish god who speaks to us of trickery and the ability to outsmart an opponent.

Incense Recipe

2 part Heather Flowers

2 part Gum Arabic

1 part Witchhazel

Oil Recipe

Simmer Witchhazel and Heather flowers in Hazelnut oil, strain, and cool. This is not a strongly scented oil; if you want to scent it add a few drops of Heather scented oil after it cools.

Aeolus—Male—Mediterranean

(Also known as Aeolos and Aiolos)

Father: Poseidon

Mother: Arne

Wife: Gyane

'Earth destroyer'—Greek and Roman god associated with the winds. He invented sails and is thus associated with sea travel.

Aestas—Female—Mediterranean

Roman goddess of Summer.

Aesir, The—Male/Female—North Europe

Scandinavian tribe of Norse gods and goddesses who live in Asgard and initially battled the Vanir. The conflict was eventually settled, and the Aesir and Vanir allied. The allegiance of these two tribes may be found in the marriage of Odin (Aesir) and Frigg (Vanir).

Aganippe—Female—Mediterranean

'Mare who kills with mercy'—Greek nymph who is associated with fresh-water springs and the wells that they fed.

Aganyu—Male—Africa/Caribbean/South America

(Also known as Aganju)

In Santeria, he is called Aganyu-Sola.

In Voodoo, he is called Aganyu.

Wife: Yemaya

Holiday and Saint associations: Feast of Saint Christopher on July 25th, Feast of Saint Michael of Assisi on October 4th

Yoruba god of all Earth forces, especially volcanoes. In blending with the Catholic tradition, he became associated with Saint Christopher and to a smaller degree with the Archangel Saint Michael. He is called on to aid in control over baneful influences but only with Shango's intercession in much the way Christians look to the Father God for help through their Christ.

Agarou Tonerre—Male—Africa/Caribbean

Haitian Voodoo sky and thunder god.

Agassou—Male—Africa/Caribbean

(Also known as Ati-A-Sou)

Father: Agwe

Animal association: Panther

Originating as an African panther god, Agassou became the Haitian Voodoo loa of family/cultural traditions, as well as natural springs. He is the keeper of secret traditions and the guardian of ancient ways.

Agathos Daimon—Male—Africa/Mediterranean

(Also known as Agathadaimon [Egyptian])

Animal association: Snake (serpent)

Plant association: Rice

'*Good spirit*'—The personification of luck and of all things pleasant. Often cited to the Greeks as Agathos Daimon. He is sometimes cited as Egyptian Agathadaimon, probably migrating with cultural exchange. He is honored in connection with ancestral sprits. Offerings commonly made to Agathos Daimon commonly include flowers, rice pudding, honey, and butter.

Agayu—Male—Africa/Caribbean

Catholic Saint association: Saint Christopher

Holiday: Feast of St. Christopher on July 25th

Santeria patron of travelers. He protects all forms of travel, including air and water.

Agdistis—Male/Female—Mediterranean

(Also known as Agdos)

Father: Zeus

Mother: Cybele

When Zeus discovered Cybele hiding from his pursuit, he raped her. In so doing he brought about the conception of Agdistis, a hermaphrodite.

Aglaurus—Female—Mediterranean

(Also known as Aglaulus)

Greek woman who was told by an oracle that if she sacrificed herself, she would end the siege on her city, Athens. Upon being witness to her sacrifice, the siege was ended by the invading forces. Today, her name is what many Wiccans think of when swearing the oath upon joining the military. In time of old, young men joining the military to protect Athens did so in her name.

Agenor—Male—Mediterranean

Father: Poseidon

Lover: Telephassa

'*Very Manly*'—The King of Troy who, when his daughter Europa was kidnapped by Zeus, sent his sons to recover her. His story speaks to us of fathers passing family duty (dharma) to their sons.

Aglaia—Female—Mediterranean

Father: Zeus

Mother: Euronyme

Husband: Hephaestus

'*The brilliant and shining one*'—The youngest of the Three Graces found in Greek lore. Her parents are sometimes cited as Dionysus and Aphrodite. See also Euphrosyne and Thalia.

Aglibol—Male—Middle East/Mediterranean

'*Messenger of the Lord*'—Ancient Syrian (pre-Islam) sun god who forms a sacred triad with Bel and Yarhibol.

Agloolik—Male—Arctic North America

Animal association: Seal

Agloolik is prayed to for good fortune while hunting in cold weather. He is believed to live under the ice and lend assistance to hunting only when needed. Calling on him to assist in sport hunting provokes a baneful response, such as hunting accidents.

Agnayi—Female—Near East

Husband: Agni

Hindu fire goddess. She is prayed to by women when seeking sudden and irreparable change, often for revenge, especially of rape and abuse. Note that the reference to her husband is often disputed. Sometimes her name is said to be a female aspect (not wife) of Agni. See Agni.

Agni—Male—Near East

Father: Dyaus

Mother: Prithvi

Wife: Agnayi

Lover: Shiva, Svaha

Animal associations: Cattle (bull), Eagle, Goat, Horse, Ram

Plant associations: Dragon's Blood, Red Poppy, Hibiscus, Nettle (greater), White Poppy

Hindu fire god. His wife is most often listed as Agnayi, sometimes as Ushas (his sister), and sometimes his wife is cited as being his lover Svaha. I believe the name 'Svaha' could be a deliberate attempt to rename Shiva and thus cover the homosexual exchange between Agni and Shiva. Although most often considered heterosexual, a story survives that states Agni once swallowed Shiva's semen. But even with that story, there is not reference to it being a lustful act. He is also god of lightning, storms and rain. He is one of humanity's benefactors in fertility, bringing rain to crops and the lightning that caused all life to propagate (see the Book of Genesis). One of the eight Hindu guardians of the principle directions. Agni is the guardian of the South East. The other seven are Indra, Yama, Surya, Varuna, Vayu, Kubera, Soma.

Incense Recipe

2 parts Hibiscus flower

1 part Nettle

1 part Gum Arabic

1 pinch poppy seeds

Enough Agni or Dragon's Blood perfume oil to bind

Oil Recipe

9 drops Allspice essential oil

6 drops Frankincense essential oil

3 drops Cinnamon essential oil

1/2 ounce base oil

Agunua—Male—Polynesian Islands

Animal association: Snake (serpent)

Solomon Islands serpent god. Sometimes seen as a supreme god with the other gods and goddesses of the islands just aspects or personalities of Agunua. The first seasonal fruit of each tree is made sacrifice to him.

Agwe—Male—Africa/Caribbean

Wife: Erzulie (La Sirene)

Haitian Voodoo god of fish, sea plants, and to a lesser degree of the ocean itself. Sacrifice is made to him to insure a good harvest of fish and sea plants. Those offerings are cast into the ocean with the hopes that they will be returned in the harvest.

Ah—See Aha

Aholibah—Female—Middle East

Husband: Yahweh

Originally a Hebrew All Mother, wife to Yahweh. After creating all of humanity except Adam and Eve, she and Yahweh had a falling out. Humanity took her side in the matter, so Yahweh went on to create his own group of humanity in the Garden of Eden, who would follow him blindly. See Yahweh. She was later called the 'voluptuous whore' and still later the 'menstruating whore' by the line of Adam and Eve and virtually removed from their lore. Now is that any way to treat a lady?

Ahriman—Male—Middle East/Mediterranean (Also known as Angra Mainyu (*'fiendish spirit'*), Ako Mainyu)

Father: Zervan Akarana

Animal associations: Cat, Jackal, Wolf, Frog, Iguana, Lizard, Salamander, Snake (serpent), Toad

Note: Listed with masculine association due to modern convention. The original early Persian use of the word was feminine.

Perhaps the origin of the contemporary Christian concept of Satan. Although the name Satan most certainly comes from the earlier word for antagonist, the concept of an all evil antagonist to the Christian God did not come into play until the Persians were invaded by the Indo-Europeans. It is likely that the invasion resulted in mingling of the lore behind the antagonist and this entity, which was seen by the early Persians as being the leader of evil who is in opposition with Ormazd (good). It was Ahriman who led Mashia and Mashiane away from Ormazd, which is probably at least a contributor to the better known story of Adam and Eve.

Ahsonnutli—Male/Female—North America (Also known as the Turquoise Hermaphrodite)

Ahsonnutli is the Navajo creator of both Heaven and Earth. One can easily see the connection that can be made to the Nameless One in the creation story given here. But there is another important message given by Ahsonnutli. Seen variously as hermaphrodite and as bisexual, Ahsonnutli demonstrates yet again that any modern Pagan religion should welcome folk of all sexual preferences, as the ancient Pagans certainly did.

Ahti—See Ahto

Ahto—Male—Central Europe/North Europe (Also known as Ahti)

Wife: Vellamo

Finnish god of the sea, the shore, and all creatures which reside therein. He is also god of physical strength who is prayed to for assistance in overcoming attack, threat, or for ac-complishing a task which tests the limits of both strength or endurance.

Ahura Mazda—Male—Middle East (Also known as Ormazd, Ohrmazd, Ormuzd)

Father: Zervan Akarana

Son: Atar

Animal association: Hawk

'Lord Wisdom'—Persian personification of good. He created the first man, Gayomart, who died and from whose body came the first Couple. Ahura Mazda was then God of the first human couple; Mashia and Mashiane. In opposition to Ahriman (evil).

Aine—Female—Central Europe (Also known as Aine of Knockaine)

Father: Eogabail

Animal association: Cattle, Horse

Irish moon goddess who watched over crops and cattle as their caregivers slept. She is often cited as a goddess of love and fertility, sometimes as a fairy queen. Patron of farmers and domesticated animals, especially cattle.

Airmid—Female—Central Europe (Also known as Airmeith)

Father: Dianchecht

Irish goddess of healing and health. Patron of herbalists.

Aizen Myoo—Male—Far East (Also known as Aizen Myo'o)

Japanese Buddhist lion-headed god of love who watches over humanity, offering help when needed. Patron of all of humanity, but particularly of prostitutes and musicians.

Aji-Suki-Takahikone—Male—Far East

Father: O-Kuni-Nushi

Japanese god of storms, particularly thunder.

Aker—Male—Africa

Animal association: Lion

An Egyptian personification of the Earth and thus, god of the dead. Aker opens the gates to the Underworld.

Akaru Mime—Female—Far East

Japanese patron and protector of sailors.

Akibimi—Female—Far East

Japanese goddess presiding over Autumn (days between Fall Equinox and Winter Solstice).

Akka—Female—North Europe

(Also known as Yambe-akka)

Husband: Ukko

Holiday: Honored on July 15

Finnish goddess of the Underworld. Sometimes cited as Earth Mother.

Akna—Female—Arctic North America

Husband: Akanchob

'The Mother'—Eskimo goddess of childbirth and patron of both mother and child.

Akupera—Male—Near East

Animal association: Tortoise

Hindu tortoise god who supports the Earth on his back.

Alaghom Naum—Female—Central America

(Also known as Alaghom Naom Tzentel)

Husband: Patol

'Mother of Mind'—Mayan goddess and creator of human consciousness.

Albina—Female—Mediterranean

Plant association: Barley

Tuscan goddess of the dawn, of particular note in the lore of Tuscan Witches. Sometimes cited as a barley goddess.

Alcippe—Female—Mediterranean

Father: Ares

Greek goddess who was raped by Halirrhothius. See Ares.

Alcmena—Female—Mediterranean

Husband: Amphitryon

Lover: Zeus

Greek goddess who was condemned by her husband Amphitryon to burn to death as punishment for her infidelity with Zeus. Zeus saved her from that end.

Alecto—Female—Mediterranean

'Unceasing Anger'—Greek goddess of justice and vengeance. One of the three Erinyes. The others are Megaera and Tisiphone.

Aleion Baal—Male—Middle East

(Also known as Aleyin, Aleyn)

Father: Baal

Animal association: Boar and to some degree all creatures of the wild.

Phoenician god of Spring and of the weather necessary for abundant crop growth.

Alektraon—Male—Mediterranean

Animal association: Chicken

Greek deity hired by Ares to watch over Aphrodite as she slept and when Ares was parted from his love.

Aleyin—See Aleion Baal

Aleyn—See Aleion Baal

Alignak—Male—Arctic North America/North America

(Also known as Aningan)

Inuit/Eskimo deity who was banished on a charge of incest. After being banished, he became the Moon and his sister became the Sun, forever circling their home but never being allowed to return or again to be with each other. Their chase is responsible for earthquakes and weather changes. Their rare reunion is the solar eclipse. While some might joke that the moral of this story is sleeping with your sister will make you a god, the more practical observation is that where the earlier gods and goddesses were often seen as incestuous, the later developing deity forms stood clearly against such matters. I believe this shift was due to medical observations made on the dangers of incest. Like Jewish dietary law, religious taboo against incest came about due to entirely pragmatic concerns.

Allah—Male—Middle East

Wife: Allat (also daughter)

'The God' (derived from 'al-ilah')—Persian and Arabian All Father. Allah is to Islam what Yahweh is to Christianity. What is commonly called Islam today would better be termed Mohammedism because today's Islam reflects mainly on the teachings of Mohammed. It is interesting to note that of the worship of Allah, Mohammed saw both Jews and Christians as all worshipping Allah by different names, calling both Jews, Christians, and Moslems "Children of the Scripture." The primary difference is that neither Jesus nor his mother were viewed as being themselves part of divinity. Prior to Mohammedism, Allah was an Arabic Creator but not the one and only god as promoted by Mohammed's declaration. When we consider the recent and ongoing actions of fundamental Islam, we see the effects humanity receives for giving name to the Nameless One. Allah is said to have three daughters: Allat (also his wife), Menat, and Al-Uzza. Together, they make the Triple Goddess who is often known by the name of his wife and one of the daughters, Allat.

Allat—Female—Middle East

(Also known as Allatu and Al-lat)

Father: Allah

Husband: Allah

Holiday: New Moon

'The Goddess' (derived from 'al-ilat')—Persian and Arabian All Mother who was condemned by the followers of Mohammed the same way the wife of Yahweh was condemned by the line of Adam and Eve. However, she later appears as one of Islam's three daughters of Allah. This was perhaps a Mohammedan attempt at hiding her significance as Allah's equal. Her holiday is the New Moon, but the cycle of the waxing moon is also sacred to her. She is one of the many Triple Goddesses, her other names being Al-Uzza and Menat.

All Father—Male—Universal

Most often used as a name for Odin, the term has been used so universally prior to the modern Pagan movement that it is used almost interchangeably with the Neo-Pagan term Sky Father.

All Mother—Female—Universal

Most often used as a name for Gaia, the term has been used so universally prior to the modern Pagan movement that it is used almost interchangeably with the Neo-Pagan term Earth Mother.

Alphaeus—Male—Mediterranean

Lover: Arethus

Greek river god who fell in love with the nymph Arethus.

Aleitheia—Female - Middle East/Mediterranean

'Truth'—Gnostic Aeon of experienced truth and the hidden meaning behind the mystery. She is that which cannot be expressed in language either written or spoken, but that which must be experienced to be understood. She is often expressed with a sexual undertone, as if to say the reception of the truth behind a mystery is the act of experiencing orgasm within her embrace.

Althaea—Female—Mediterranean

Husband: Oeneus

Lover: Dionysus

Greek goddess of birth and, to some degree, of plant growth. A couple can call on her favors by sharing wine with the Earth as sacrifice. To do so, become skyclad with your partner outdoors on a slightly chilly night and share a bottle of grape wine, giving one drink to the potential father, one to the potential mother, and then one to the Earth (spill it to the ground). Repeat until you have consumed that which you intended and then make love outdoors where you made the offering. View your lovemaking to be an offering itself. Be aware that although filled with maternal instinct, she is not without limits. When her son Meleager was born, it was prophesized by the Three Fates that he would live only as long as a particular ember in the fireplace remained unconsumed. She immediately grabbed that ember from the fire, extinguished it and hid it to insure it never be burned. As an adult, Meleager killed his mother's brothers. In response, Althaea returned that ember to the fireplace, thus bringing about her own son's death.

Al-Uzza—Female—Middle East
Father: Allah
Holiday: Full Moon

An aspect of the Triple Goddess Allat. She is goddess of the morning star. See also Allat.

Amalivaca—Male—South America

Venezuelan god who taught man the arts of farming and negotiating with Nature.

Ama-No-Minakanushi-No-Kami—Male—Far East

Japanese supreme god and ruler of all other deities in his pantheon.

Amaterasu—Female—Far East
(Also known as Ama Terasu)
Father: Izanagi
Husband: Takami-Musubi
Animal association: Chicken (Cock), Crow

'She who shines in heaven'—Japanese Shinto sun goddess who rules the world with her husband Takami-Musubi. She banished her brother Susanoo, the moon god, from Heaven. Known to have a familiar named Yatagarasu who is a Crow.

Amathaon—Male—Central Europe
Plant association: Spikenard (ploughman's)
Father: Beli
Mother: Don

Welsh god responsible for causing the conflict between his brother Gwydion and Arawn, Battle of the Trees. Amathaon is a working man's god. His name comes from the Welsh word *amaeth,* which literally translates to "ploughman."

Amatsu-Mikaboshi—Male—Far East
(Also known as Ama No Kagaseo ['*Brilliant Male*'])

'August star of heaven'—Japanese personification and god of Evil. Similar to the Christian Satan.

Ambika—Female—Near East
Husband: Shiva

Hindu avatar/incarnation of Parvati as the creator and protector who transforms into the destroyer Kali. Her lust-inspiring beauty is her weapon. She first flirts with her enemy, telling them that she has sworn an oath never to allow anyone who has not bested her in combat into her bed or embrace. When fools take her up on her challenge, she uses words to defeat the challenger's friends, leaving the challenger to battle her on her own. She then transforms into Kali and makes short work of the challenge. Her story is classically told as the destroyer of demons who first releases a hum that kills the attendants of the demons who challenge her and then transforms into Kali to finish off the demons themselves. Other citations state that she uncurls her tongue and tricks the demons onto it. After their slaughter, she consumes them and their demonic blood causes her to become Kali, full of rage. Her rage and/or transformation into Kali is calmed when her husband Shiva throws himself at her feet. Unable to kill him, she then transforms back into Ambika/Parvati.

Ambisagrus—Male—Central Europe
Celtic sky god and All Father figure, sometimes associated with the Roman Jupiter.

Ame-No-Oshido-Mimi—Male—Far East
Mother: Amaterasu

Japanese god who was offered rulership of the Earth by his mother. He took one look and refused the offer.

Ame-No-Wakahiko—Male—Far East
Wife: Shitateru-Hime

Japanese ruler of the Earth until he was killed by Takami-Musubi

Amergin—Male—Central Europe

Irish mythical bard and perhaps historic character reportedly responsible for the creation of the poem 'I am a stag of seven tines,' which years later has been used to support the theory of the Celtic Tree calendar. (Per *The Witches God*, by Janet and Stewart Farrar, page 154.)

Am-Heh—Male—Africa
Animal association: Dog

Egyptian Underworld god with a human body but dog head.

Amphitryon—Male—Mediterranean
(Also known as Amphitryo)
Wife: Alcmena

'Harassed on all sides'—Greek general who found struggles at every step of his life. He fell in love with Alcmena and was wed, but his wife refused to (or could not) have sex with him until the death of her brother was avenged. While avenging that death, Zeus visited his wife's bed, making her pregnant with the child that would grow up to be Hercules. On discovering her infidelity, he condemned his wife to burn to death. Fortunately, Zeus saved her at the last moment.

Amshumana—Male—Near East
Father: Kashyapa
Mother: Aditi

Amshumana is one of the Adityas. The Hindu month Asadha (June 22–July 22) is sacred to Amshumana. See Adityas.

Amun Ra—Male—African
(Also known as Amun Re, Amon Ra)
Wife: Mut
Animal associations: Bee, Donkey, Duck, Frog, Goose, Ram, Sheep
Plant associations: Acacia, Amaranth, Aloe, Cedar, Frankincense, Myrrh, Olive, Palm (date), Saffron (Spanish), Water Lily

Egyptian unification of the Theban god Amun and the later Egyptian god Ra.

Incense Recipe
2 part Sandalwood (yellow)*
1 part Frankincense
1 part Myrrh
* Alternatively, 1 part Yellow Sandalwood and 1 part Cedar

Oil Recipe
10 drops Sandalwood
5 drops Frankincense
5 drops Myrrh
1/2 Ounce Safflower Oil or Sunflower Oil

Amenti—Female—Africa
(Also known as Amentet)
Animal associations: Dog, Hawk, Hippopotamus, Ostrich

Egyptian goddess who welcomes the dead to the Underworld at its west gate where the sun sets. Her name is synonymous with that entrance, where Osiris judges the hearts of those who have died.

Amor—See Cupid

An—Male—Mediterranean/Middle East
Wife: Ki

Sumerian sky god, sometimes associated with the Babylonian Anu as if they were the same; however, the lineage does not add up well for that association.

Anagke—Male—Mediterranean

Greek goddess whose name means 'necessity' but who is most often cited as a goddess of destiny. This speaks volumes about the ideas of dharma, will, true will, and free will.

Anahita—Female—Middle East
(Also known as Anaitis, Ardvi Sur, Aredvi Sura)
Animal association: Horse
Holiday : Ten days prior to each New Moon.

Persian Water goddess whose holiday may be associated with menstruation and the moon. After the Persians and Babylonian cultures mixed, she took on many of the attributes of Ishtar. Women's virginity was sacrificed to her. To support her temples, virgins would serve as sacred prostitutes until such time as their virginity was accepted, at a price, by visiting men. Although this practice may well seem disgusting by today's standards, the majority of those offering their virginity as sacrifice were from wealthy homes, went willingly, and received much training in the ways of physical love in exchange for their sacrifice.

Anait—Female—Middle East
Animal associations: Dog, Lion

Middle Eastern goddess who is sometimes identified with or described as being similar to the Hindu Annapurna. Other citations state that she was adopted by the Persian Ahahati.

Ananse—See Anansi

Anansi—Male—Africa
(Also known as Ananse)
Father-in-law: Nyame
Animal association: Spider

An Ashanti god who provided the material by which Nyame created the first human. He convinced his father-in-law, Nyame, to provide humanity with sun, moon, rain, and the other things necessary to farm, and later taught humanity the art of farming and negotiating with Nature.

Anatha Baetyl—Female—Africa/Middle East
Husband: Yahweh
Animal association: Owl

One of two Hebrew wives of Yahweh from the fifth century B.C.E. following at Elephantine, Egypt. The other was Ashima Baetyl. See Yahweh.

Anatina—Male—South America
(Also known as Anatiwa)

Brazilian god who was responsible for the Great Flood.

Anatiwa—See Anatina

Andromeda—Female—Mediterranean
Father: Cepheus
Mother: Cassiopeia
Husband: Perseus

'Ruler of Men'—Greek woman who was made sacrifice to a sea monster sent by Poseidon. She was rescued by Perseus and became his wife.

Angana—Female—Near East
Lover: Kasari

'Handsome Woman'—Hindu goddess of beauty and self-worth. Mother of Hanuman.

Angra Mainyu—See Ahriman

Angurboda—Female—Northern Europe
Lover: Loki
Animal association: Wolf

'Herald of sorrow'—Scandinavian giant who is sometimes seen by the Pagan community as a Crone Goddess. Called the 'Herald of Sorrow,' she can be seen as a goddess of ill-fate. With her three monstrous children Fenrir, Jormungand, and Hel we see again that three is the number of not only good fate but of ill-fate.

Aningan—See Alignak

Anna Perenna—Female—Mediterranean
Plant association: Barley

'Eternal Steam'(from *amnis perennis*)—Roman goddess of the solar year with a slightly heightened focus on the Light half. She has often been called the 'Grandmother of Time' as a reflection on her role in the Roman year, as well as her Crone position in the three stages of life. She is often cited as being associated with food or the harvest; however, this may be an association that came from confusing her with the Hindu Annapurna. On the full moon of Martius in particular, but also at all full moons, she is celebrated with the sacrifice of barley cakes. Preparing these cakes for kith and kin on the full moon of Martius is said to bring good bounty during the remainder of the solar year.

Annapurna—Female—Near East

Hindu avatar/incarnation of Durga who presided over mountains and provides needed food to humanity. Sometimes confused with the Roman Anna Perenna.

Anpu—See Anubis

Ansar—Male—Mediterranean/Middle East
(Also known as Anshar, Assorus)
Father: Lakhamu
Mother: Lakhmu
Wife: Kishar

Babylonian god. Father of many children, but most notably Anu and Ea.

Antaeus—Male—Mediterranean
Father: Poseidon
Mother: Gaia

Greek giant who was invincible in every way as long as he remained in contact with the Earth (Gaia, his mother). He was defeated by Hercules when Hercules picked him up off the ground, thus severing his ties with his mother and bringing his loss. This story speaks volumes to the connection between sons and their mothers.

Anteros—Male—Mediterranean

'Return'—Greek god of mutual love and the punisher of those who do not return love. Before his birth, his brother Eros was horribly lonely and depressed. So deep was Eros' depression that Aphrodite took notice and gave him Anteros as brother and companion. Anteros speaks to us of not only brotherly love, but love that is returned in the manner in which it is given. He tells us that mutual love and admiration is far superior to one-sided desire, for even Eros (god of desire) was humbled before the feeling that he was alone.

Anat—Female—Mediterranean
Husband: Anu

Babylonian goddess and mother of Ishtar.

Angerona—Female—Mediterranean

Roman goddess of secrets who is always shown with a finger to her lips in the way a librarian might to hush you.

Anu—Male—Mediterranean
(Also known as Anum)
Father: Ansar
Mother: Kishar

Lover: Ki
Wife: Anat
Plant association: Tamarisk

'Great above'—In the Mesopotamian pantheon, he is king of the gods. An All Father figure and sky god. Not to be confused by the Irish goddess of the same name. He was called on by the Mesopotamian pantheon to mediate disputes between the other deities, who called him Father. Sometimes associated with the Sumerian An.

Anu—Female—Central Europe
Animal association: Cat

Irish goddess of war and one of the Irish Triple Goddesses of Fate. The other two are Badb and Macha. See also Morrigan. Not to be confused by the Mesopotamian/Sumerian/Babylonian god of the same name.

Anubis—Male—Africa
(Also known as Anpu, Anup, Ienpw, Wip, Yinepu)
Father: Osiris
Mother: Nephthys
Animal associations: Cock, Jackal
Plant associations: Benzoin, Poppy (especially white), Sandalwood (yellow)

Sometimes cited as son of Set. Egyptian jackal-headed god who was born by Nephthys but later adopted by Isis. When Horus' body was scattered by Set, it was Anubis who helped his adoptive mother Isis reassemble his body, thus resurrecting him.

Incense Recipe

1 Part Benzoin
1 Part Poppy Flowers*
1 Part Sandalwood
Ok to use Blue, Red, or Purple as White is hard to come bye.

Oil Recipe

10 drops Benzoin oil

5 drops Sandalwood

½ ounce base oil*

If you simmer Poppy flowers in your base oil, strain, and then allow to cool before mixing the essential oils, the end result will be far more potent.

Anum—See Anu as Mesopotamia/Sumerian God, not Anu as Irish Goddess.

Anumati—Female—Near East

'Divine Favor' or *'Conclusion'*—Hindu goddess who is cited in distinctly different ways. According to some cites, her name means 'conclusion.' In that aspect she is associated with the waning and dark moon, as well as endings of all kind. Alternatively, her name is cited as meaning 'Divine Favor,' and she is thought to be a moon goddess who grants prosperity and children. Perhaps the confusion rests in the Western mind's attempt to grasp Eastern philosophy. Is not a birth the end of a previous cycle?

Anup—See Anubis

Apedemak—Male—Middle East

Animal association: Lion, Elephant

Sudanese lion-headed god of war.

Apeliotus—Male—Mediterranean

Greek personification of the South East Wind.

Apep—Male—Egypt

(Also known as Aapep, Apepi, Aepepi, Apophis [Greek])

Animal association: Scorpion, Snake, Wolf

Plant association: Cactus, Benzoin

Egyptian snake god (monster) who lives in darkness as the opposition to Ra (Sun/Light). Each night, he fights against Ra to prevent the new day. On the few occasions that he wins, the Earth experiences a solar eclipse. The Greeks associated him with Apophis.

Apesh—Male—Africa

Animal association: Tortoise

Obscure Egyptian god form.

Amphitrite—Female—Mediterranean

Husband: Poseidon

Greek goddess and ruler, with her husband, of the oceans.

Apisiharts—Male—North America

The name given to the god associated with the planet Venus by the Blackfoot Tribe.

Aphrodite—Female—Mediterranean

(Also known as Aphrodite Pandemos, Cerigo)

Husband: Hephaestus

Lover: Anchises, Adonis

Animal associations: Boar, Bee, Chicken, Deer, Dove, Fish, Frog, Hare, Heron, Sheep, Sparrow, Swallow, Swan, Turtle, Tortoise, Vulture

Plant associations: Apple, Cinnamon, Cypress, Daisy, Myrtle, Olive, Orris, Quince

'Foam Born' —Greek goddess of passion and sex. Unlike many other goddesses of passion, Aphrodite is just that; passion without a connotation of long term relationship Yes, she was called on by Melanion in his pursuit of his wife to be Atalanta, and she is often called on by Wiccans who desire the fire of passion. However, although she gave golden apples to Melanion to win the hand of Atalanta, she was also partly responsible for the Trojan war by demanding another golden apple be hers at the wedding of Peleus and Thetis. From these two stories we see how magick can stir what we commonly think of as love (Aphrodite) and sometimes provide events that are entirely unexpected. You see, although she is commonly called on in love spells, love is a spell unto itself. It needs no help and the help it receives tends to muddle things up. Remember, Aphrodite is also the woman who tired of the husband that adored her, took his gifts, and ran around with every bad boy she could get her hands on. She is the goddess of love who dumps you for the drummer in a bar band.

Incense Recipe

2 parts Orris root

1 part Cinnamon

1 part Cedar

Enough Aphrodite or Cypress essential oil to bind

Oil Recipe

10 drops Cypress essential oil

6 drops Cinnamon essential oil

6 drops tincture of Orris root

1/2 ounce base oil

Apollo—Male—Mediterranean

(Also known as Apollon)

Father: Zeus

Mother: Leto

Wife: Coronis

Lover: Cyrene, Calliope

Animal associations: Bee, Cock, Crane, Crow, Deer, Dolphin, Dragon, Goose, Hawk, Horse, Lion, Mouse, Quail, Raven, snake, Stag, Swan, Vulture, Wolf

Plant associations: Acacia, Alder, Apple, Bay, Cornel, Cypress, Fenugreek, Frankincense, Heliotrope, Hyacinth, Heliotrope, Leek, Lily of the Valley, Lotus, Mistletoe (European), Olive, Palm (date), Sunflower, Thistle, Wormwood

'Destroyer,' 'Excite,' or *'Exciting Destroyer'*—Initially Greek but adopted by the Romans when the two cultures merged. Brother to Artemis, Apollo is seen as a sun and fertility god. However, he is most often cited as a god of both scientific and cultural education, law, medicine, and fine arts. He was educated, as was his son Aristaeus, by Chiron. Apollo is an ideal deity to work with for assistance during academic pursuit.

Incense Recipe

1 part Acacia flowers

1 part Bay leaf

1 part Gum Arabic

Enough Apollo or Cypress oil to bind

(Add a date or two if using to make a tincture)

Oil Recipe

12 drops Bay essential oil

6 drops Cypress essential oil

3 drops Juniper essential oil

1/2 ounce olive, sunflower, or palm oil

Apsaras, The—Female—Near East

(Also known as the Vrikshakas)

Animal association: Swan

The female nature spirits of India, similar in nature to water and woodland nymphs. Each is a beautiful woman whose mate is one of the Gandharvas. As the Gandharvas play their drums and other instruments, the Apsaras dance to the natural rhythm of Nature's gentle cycles. The relationship is similar to the relationship shared between drummer and dancer at Wiccan drum circles. Their dance (both Apsaras and Wiccan) is said to inspire both love and lust. Here we see a rather interesting parallel between modern Wiccan and Neo-Pagan drum circles and ancient Hindu lore. Far be it from me to either condemn or condone (it is not my place to do either) the revelry at modern drum circles. I have certainly observed the use of not only alcohol, but also other mind and mood altering drugs. It seems that although the story of the Gandharvas and the Apsaras are not generally known in the modern Pagan community, we have certainly found their story in our lives. See Gandharvas for more.

Apsu—Male—Middle East

(Also known as Abzu, Absu)

Lover: Tiamat

Babylonian (maybe Sumerian) fresh water god from whose clay humanity was formed. He was himself formed when his lover, Tiamat (salt water), separated him from her much as Diana did Lucifer.

Aqas-xena-xenas—Male—North America

Wife: The Moon

Chinook hero who married the Moon. He later took his wife's side with his mother-in-law against his sister-in-law the Sun. This story again illustrates the feminine association of the Sun.

Aquilo—Male—Mediterranean

Roman personification and god of the North Wind associated with the North Quarter (Earth) in Wiccan ritual. The other three are Auster, Favonius, and Vulturnus.

Arachne—Female—Mediterranean
Animal association: Spider

'*Spider*'—Greek mortal who dared challenge Athena to see who was the best weaver. When they were finished, we see that what was being constructed was more than a craft, it was a story. Athena was outraged that Arachne had portrayed the gods as they had been and without embellishment. Athena punished her by turning her into a spider such that no matter how true she spun her web (history), humanity would run in fear (arachnophobia). Patron of the truly told tales.

Aradia—Female—Mediterranean
Father: Lucifer
Mother: Diana
Plant association: Rue, Vervain

Italian goddess who was sent by her mother Diana to instruct Witches in not only the use of magick, but also to rise against their tyrants and enslavers. Her instructions were recorded in *Vangelo,* published as *Aradia: Gospel of the Witches.* Published in the late eighteen hundreds, Vangelo was probably the single largest source of inspiration for the founders of the Wiccan religion.

Aramati—Female—Near East

Hindu goddess of devotion, especially to one's religion.

Arani—Female—Near East

Hindu fire goddess of female sexual desire. Her worship has involved lesbian and self-pleasuring acts, both without the involvement of men.

Arawn—Male—Central Europe
Animal associations: Boar, Horse (pale), Dog (hound)

Welsh King of the magickal kingdom of Annwn who became the god of the Underworld with a little help from his friend Pywll. Although Arawn and Pywll switched places for a year and a day, during which they took on all outward appearances of each other, Pywll never took advantage of Arawn's bed and the beautiful wife that waited there night after night unaware of the switch. Together with Pywll, their story speaks volumes about friendships and the value of monogamy.

Arcas—Male—Mediterranean
Father: Zeus
Mother: Callisto

To protect his lover and the son she bore him from Hera, Zeus raised both into the heavens where she became the Great Bear constellation and he the star Arcturus. Their story reminds us of the fact that indiscretions and jealousy can often affect those outside of a marriage.

Ardhanarisvara—Male—Near East

Hindu form of Shiva that demonstrates the historical acknowledgement of transgender and perhaps homosexual aspects of deity. In this form, Shiva is both definitively masculine God and woman at the same time.

Ariadne—Female—Mediterranean
Husband: Dionysus
Plant associations: Ivy (common), Pine

'*Very pure*' or '*Very pleasing*' —When Theseus volunteered to kill the Minotaur who demanded human sacrifice, it was Ariadne who gave him the magick sword to do so. As such, Wiccans often call on her during the consecration of both athame and sword. To Theseus, she also gave a bolt of thread that he might use it to find his way back out of the Minotaur's caverns once he had killed it.

Arianrhod—Female—Central Europe
Father: Beli
Mother: Don
Lover: Gwydion
Plant associations: Alder, Birch, Ivy (common)
Holiday: Full Moon

'*Silver Wheel*' (often translated as The Moon)—Celtic moon goddess whose story gives us the three rights of initiation seen in many Wiccan traditions. Arianrhod brought into this world two sons. One healthy, the other premature. Upon seeing the child born immature, Gwydion took the child as his own, hiding and tending it until it became healthy. Arianrhod allowed Gwydion to raise the child, but only under three conditions: The child would have no name unless she named him; the child would bear no arms unless she armed him; and the child would never come to know a human wife. Years later, Arianrhod saw a beautiful young man fall a wren with a single stone's throw. Not knowing he was her son and being greatly impressed, she called out that he was a bright lion with a sure hand. So he was named, Llew Llaw Gyffes. Gwydion then tricked Arianrhod into believing she and her people were under attack, so she armed him. And finally, his wife was created of flowers that his mother's demands would be circumnavigated.

Ares—Male—Mediterranean

Animal associations: Boar, Horse, Goose, Scorpion, Vulture, Wolf, Woodpecker

Plant associations: Benzoin, Buttercup, Cactus, Dragons Blood, Nettle (greater), Rue, Wormwood

'*Man*' (loose interpretation)—Greek god of war who speaks to us of doing battle when necessary. Upon discovering that his daughter had been raped by Halirrhothius, son of Poseidon, Ares immediately killed Halirrhothius for the crime. He was brought before the Olympians by Poseidon and freely admitted his taking of a life. He was acquitted. For that story, he is patron of the rape victims, especially children. His sister, Eris, is his constant companion. As she is the goddess of discord and strife, we see a clear message about the nature of war.

Incense Recipe

2 parts Dragon's Blood resin
1 part Benzoin
1 part Nettle

1 pinch Wormwood
1 pinch Rue
Enough Ares or Benzoin oil to bind.

Oil Recipe

12 drops Dragon's Blood perfume oil
9 drops Benzoin essential oil
1/2 ounce olive oil

Aristaeus—Male—Mediterranean

Father: Apollo
Mother: Cyrene
Animal associations: Bee, Cattle
Plant associations: Olive, Vine (grape)

'*The best*' or '*Very good*'—Greek god, patron of the hunt, bee-keepers, cattle, and negotiating with Nature. Made immortal by Gaia, he was educated in medicine and the science of divination by Chiron.

Oil Recipe

Simmer a mixture of Olive Oil, Raisins, and honey. Strain mixture still warm and then place aside to cool.

Arjuna—Male—Near East

Father: Indra

Hindu god whose conversation with Krishna forms the sacred manuscript known as the Bhagavad Gita. In that discussion, Arjuna contemplated the correctness of a war between two households who were kin. To take up arms was to raise those arms against his kinsmen. To not take up arms was to not raise arms in defense of his kinsmen. He wondered which was the correct course of action. Krishna explained that the course of action is that which is his duty, his dharma or will.

Arsai—Female—Middle East/Mediterranean

Canaanite Earth goddess of Nature. One of the aspects of the Canaanite's Triple Goddess whose name means 'Maiden of Earth.' See also Pidrai and Tallai.

Artemis—Female—Mediterranean

(Also known as Amarynthia, Cynthia)

Father: Zeus

Mother: Leto

Animal associations: Antelope, Bear, Bee, Boar, Deer (stag), Dog, Cat, Cattle (bull), Elephant, Goat, Hawk, Horse, Quail, Wolf

Plant associations: Almond, Aloe, Amaranth, Banyan, Camphor, Cedar, Cypress, Daisy, Damiana, Fir (especially silver), Frankincense, Ginseng, Hazelnut, Ivy (common), Jasmine, Ox-eyed Daisy, Mandrake, Mugwort, Myrtle, Palm (date), Pine, Tarragon, Willow, Wormwood

'Fashion'—Greek goddess of the wild. Within the city, she becomes a goddess of child birth. With associations to Selene, she is seen as a moon goddess, often depicted with a crescent moon. As with many moon goddesses, she is associated with both the tides and menstruation. Artemis speaks to us of our duty as caretakers to the animals of the world. She was huntress, most often depicted with bow and arrows, and chiefly concerned with matters of animal care with special attention to their breeding practices. She reminds us of the Wiccan principle that for Life there must be Death.

Incense Recipe (1)

2 parts Jasmine flowers

1 part Mugwort

1 part Camphor

Note: I think this Recipe smells horrible

Incense Recipe (2)

2 parts Frankincense

1 part Cedar

1 part Jasmine flowers

1 part Cypress

1 part powdered honey

Note: This one smells much better.

Oil Recipe

10 drops Cypress oil

5 drops Cedar oil

5 drops Jasmine absolute or Camphor oil

1/2 ounce base oil made by simmering a mixture of Palm or Almond Oil and Honey, strain, and allow to cool.

Artio—Female—Central Europe

(Also known as Artio of Muri)

Lover: Essus

Animal association: Bear

Celtic goddess of strength on whom the Celtic bear cults were based.

Arwen—Female—Central Europe

Lover: Aragorn

Plant association: Apple

There is a great deal of difficulty discussing Arwen because, due to her inclusion in the Lord of the Rings, great amounts of misinformation have been generated—so much so that even reputable sources seem to include great amounts of fantasy mythology. She is perhaps goddess of inspiration, maybe the elf of procrastination. Arwen is an immortal Elf/Goddess with whom the mortal Aragorn fell hopelessly in love. Her father advised against her returning his love because he did not want her to suffer as she watched him grow old. Upon her father's advice, she left his side but not his heart. In another version, her love wanted her to take her father's advice for her own safety.

Aryman—Male—Near East

Father: Kashyapa

Mother: Aditi

Aryman is one of the Adityas. He is associated with the Hindu month Vaisakha (April 21–May 21) See Adityas.

Asclepius—Male—Mediterranean

(Also known as Asklepios, Aesculapius)

Father: Apollo

Mother: Coronis

Animal association: Raven, Snake

Plant associations: Bay, Mustard (especially black), Juniper, Lily of the Valley, Mustard, Olive, Vine (grape)

'Cut up'—Greek god who was taught medicine and the science of divination by Chiron, who had also instructed his father Apollo. He became such a good doctor that the Underworld was becoming underpopulated. To maintain balance, Zeus struck him dead. His names means 'Cut up' and refers to his skill as a great surgeon. For this reason his favor is prayed for when facing surgical procedures. 'Here do I evoke Asclepius and bid him lend his hand unto my surgeon.'

Incense Recipe

2 parts Juniper berries
1 part Bay leaf
1 part Gum Arabic
Enough Asclepius or Juniper oil to bind

Oil Recipe

9 drops Bay essential oil
9 drops Juniper essential oil
1/2 ounce Olive oil

Asgaya-Gigagei—Male/Female—North America

(Also known as Asagaya Gigaei, Red Man, Blood Colored Man)

A bisexual or transgender Cherokee god of thunder and lightning.

Ash (1)—Male—Africa

Animal associations: Hawk, Lion, Snake, Vulture

Egyptian god of the desert before that job was taken over by Set. Sometimes seen as having the head of a hawk, other times completely human in appearance, and on rare occasion as human with three heads: lion, snake, and vulture.

Ash (2)—Male—Post Modern
Father: Summer then Light
Mother: Winter then Darkness
Wife: Elm

Like his wife Elm, Ash is said to be thrice born. First of body as are plants, then of soul as are animals, and finally of Spirit. Sometimes associated with Ask.

Ashera—Female—Middle East
(Also known as Asherah)
Husband: Ball, Yahweh
Animal associations: Dog, Cattle

'She who walks in the sea'—Canaanite/Phoenician who was worshiped as the wife and sometimes sister of Yahweh. She tends to overlap and merge with Anat and Astarte. A clear struggle is seen between her and Yahweh in the insistence of the Israelite clergy to remain devoted to Yahweh. Later condemned in Christian text under the name Ashtoreth.

Ashima Baetyl—Female—Africa/Middle East
Animal association: Owl
Husband: Yahweh

One of two Hebrew wives of Yahweh from the fifth century B.C.E. following at Elephantine, Egypt. The other was Anatha Baetyl. See Yahweh.

Ashi-Nadzuchi—Male—Far East
Wife: Tenazuchi-no- Kami

Japanese god of the Earth.

Ashtoreth—See Astarte

Ask—Male—Northern Europe
(Also known as Askr)
Wife: Embla

Scandinavian first man much like the Christian Adam. Created by Odin from the ash tree after the Great Flood, his story is most likely the story of humanity's migration into Scandinavia after the flood that opened up the Fertile Crescent and northern portions of the Middle East to migration.

Asopus—Male—Mediterranean
(Also known as Asopos)

'Never silent'—Greek river god who dutifully attempted to pursue Zeus after he kidnapped his daughter Aegina. Zeus prevented his pursuit, but could never silence his objection.

Asshur—Male–Middle East/Mediterranean
(Also known as Ashur)
Lover: Ishtar
Animal associations: Cattle (bull), Dragon (snake), Horse (white), Eagle, Goat (female)

Assyrian god who remains the patron of soldiers, although he did evolve into a fertility god. Asshur is one of the many moon gods of the area.

Astarte—Female—Middle East/Mediterranean
(Also known as Athtarat, Ashtoreth)
Animal associations: Antelope, Bull, Cattle (bull), Dog, Dolphin, Dove, Fish, Horse, Pigeon, Shark
Plant associations: Acacia, Apple, Cypress, Juniper, Myrtle, Pine, Saffron (Spanish), Sandalwood (yellow)
Holiday: Honored on the 23rd day of April

Phoenician and Canaanite fertility goddess who was sometimes described as a hermaphrodite but was more often shown strictly female. She has been adopted by the modern gay, lesbian, and bisexual community as patron.

Incense Recipe

2 parts Sandalwood (yellow)
1 part Juniper berries
1 pinch Saffron (Spanish) or Cypress
A few apple seeds
Enough Astarte or Pine oil to bind

Oil Recipe

8 drops Pine Oil
6 drops Cypress Oil
6 drops Juniper Oil
1/2 ounce base oil

Astraea—Female—Mediterranean
Animal association: Quail (common)

'Star maiden'—Greek goddess of justice who continues to watch over humanity from the heavens. She is associated with the constellation Virgo.

Astraeus—Male—Mediterranean
Father: Crius
Mother: Eurybia
Wife: Eos

'Starry'—Greek Titan, father of the four Winds; Boreas (North), Eurus (East), Notus (South), and Zephyrus (West).

Asteria—Female—Mediterranean
Husband: Perses
Animal association: Quail

Greek goddess with conflicting stories. One is that she changed into a Quail to escape the pursuit of Zeus (who wanted to rape her). Another version says that to escape, she flung herself into the ocean and became the island by her name.

Asvins, The—Male—Indian
Animal association: Horse

Hindu divine physicians. Sons of Saranyu and Surya.

Ataksak—Male—Arctic North America

Eskimo god of all things joyous.

Atalanta—Female—Mediterranean
Husband: Melanion

'Balanced'—Greek personification and goddess of the female athlete. Patron of women who play hard to get and especially of tomboys. See Melanion, her husband, for their story. She speaks to us of the difference between that which is female and that which is feminine, showing us that one can be a woman despite the possession of attributes commonly thought to be masculine.

Ataokoloinona—See Norianahary

Atar—Male—Middle East
(Also known as Atesh)
Father: Ahura Mazda

Persian god of purity who gave humanity fire and other gifts.

Atargatis—Female—Middle East

Animal associations: Dove, Fish, Pigeon, Snake, Spider, Shark

Mesopotamian/Aramaic mermaid like fertility goddess. She is depicted as half woman and half fish.

Athar—Male—Middle East

Arabian masculine form of Ishtar.

Athena—Female—Mediterranean

(Also known as Athene, Pallas Athena)

Father: Zeus

Animal associations: Chicken (cock), Cattle (Ox), Crocodile, Crow, Deer, Dog, Dove, Eagle, Goat, Heron, Horse, Owl, Peacock, Raven, Sheep (ram), Spider, Vulture

Plant associations: Amaranth, Apple, Asafoetida, Ash, Belladonna, Cypress, Coconut, Dragon's Blood, Geranium, Hellebore (black), Henbane, Lily (tiger), Olive, Poke Weed, Woody Nightshade, Willow, Yew

'Protector' or *'Protectress'*—Greek goddess who is most often associated with the art of war. She is also associated with the art of industry and skill. She is a goddess of divine justice and a woman with an open heart. Although her adopted son Erichthonius was born of Gaia and Hephaestus, he did so love his adopted mother Athena that when he rose to King he spread the praise of Athena, thus bringing forth much of her worship. Athena is a warrior goddess. Often called on to protect the home or other sacred space.

Athene—See Athena

Athtarat—See Astarte

Atlas—Male—Mediterranean

Father: Uranus

Mother: Gaia

Lover: Aethra, Pleione

Note: Sometimes cited as the son of Iapetus (father) by either Clymene or Asia.

'Endurer'—Greek god who conspired against Zeus in the war of Titans. His daughter

Maia was on of Zeus' many lovers. Rather than kill Atlas for his traitorous actions, Zeus forced him to endure the burden of the world upon his shoulders.

Atri—Male—Near East

Father: Brahma

Hindu bard who was deified for the great wisdom he expressed in the stories and songs. Prayed to for wisdom.

Attis—Male—Middle East/Mediterranean

(Also known as Atys)

Lover: Cybele

Animal associations: Lion, Ram

Plant associations: Adder's Tongue, Almond, Daffodil, Lily, Pine

A vegetation god. The story of Attis and his lover Cybele is listed under Cybele.

Atum—Male/Female—Africa

(Also known as Tum, Temu)

Animal association: Goose

Plant association: Water Lily

An early Egyptian creator who later became identified as god of the setting sun. He is the first land to emerge on the primeval waters. He created Shu and Tefnut in an act of masturbation.

Auahi-Turoa—Male—Polynesian Islands

Polynesian god who brought fire to humanity. Interestingly enough, the same attribute is sometimes cited under the same name as a god of Australia.

Aunt Piety—Female—Central Asia

Chinese goddess of magick and spellcraft.

Auriel—Male—Middle East/Mediterranean

Animal association: Finch (gold)

Semitic god of Earth. Gnostic Arch Angel who is associated with the North Quarter in Wiccan, Gnostic, and Ceremonial rituals. The other quarters are presided upon by Raphael, Michael, and Gabriel.

Aurora—Female—Mediterranean

Plant association: Rose

'The Dawn'—Roman personification and goddess of dawn. Similar to the Greek Eos. Mother of the four Winds who was mentioned in the story of Romeo and Juliet by William Shakespeare.

Avfruvva—Female—North Europe

Animal associations: Shark, Fish

Finnish goddess of the sea who is described much as a mermaid would be.

Audhumla—Female—North Europe

Animal association: Cow

In the Scandinavian creation story, she is the cow who nurtured Ymir.

Auf—Male—Africa

(Also known as Auf Ra, Efu Ra)

Animal association: Sheep (ram)

Egyptian avatar/incarnation of Ra, which describes Ra in his dark aspect. This is the name of the Sun God during the nighttime.

Aulanerk—Male—Arctic North America

Animal association: Fish and to an extent all sea creatures.

Eskimo Nature spirit who lives in the waves of the ocean and brings great joy to men with each of his waves.

Aumanil—Male—Arctic North America

Animal association: Whale

American Eskimo Nature spirit who guides the movement of whales.

Austeja—Female—Central Europe/North Europe

Animal association: Bee, Boar

Holiday: Festival celebrated in mid-August.

'Weaver'—Lithuanian goddess. Patron of bee-keepers who accepted honey and beeswax in sacrifice, granting unto bee-keepers who made sacrifice the continued prosperity of their profession.

Auster—Male—Mediterranean

Roman god of the South Wind. The other three are Aquilo, Favonius, and Vulturnus.

Avagdu—Male—Central Europe

Father: Tegid

Mother: Cerridwen

Welsh deity credited as the ugliest boy ever born.

Avalokitesvara—Male—Near East

Indian Buddhist who achieved enlightenment, but rejected ascension to remain on Earth for the betterment of the relationship between animals and humanity.

Aya—Female—Mediterranean/Middle East

Husband: Shamash

Babylonian goddess of the dawn.

Ayizan—Female—Caribbean

(Also known as Grande Ai-Zan, Aizan)

Plant Association: Palm

Haitian Voodoo first priestess of Voodoo. Patron of the market place and of initiation rituals.

Azazil—Male—Middle East

Islam adversary to Allah who refused to grovel after Allah created the first man (Adam). Sometimes associated with the Christian Satan.

Azrael—Male—Middle East

Plant associations: Cedar, Juniper, Sandalwood (yellow)

Islamic god/angel/messenger of death and divination.

Incense Recipe

2 parts Sandalwood (yellow)

1 part Cedar

1 part Juniper berries

Enough Azrael or Cedar oil to bind

Oil Recipe

8 drops Sandalwood oil

6 drops Cedar oil

6 drops Juniper oil

1/2 cup base oil

Baal—Male—Middle East

(Also known as Baal-Zebul)

Animal associations: Bull, Quail

Plant association: Frankincense

Sons: Aleion Baal

'Master,' 'Lord,' or similar translations—Canaanite/Phoenician fertility and storm god. The name 'Baal' is also a general term for god. This has led to a great amount of confusion in lore, most notably the Christian association with Beelzebub, who is in league with their Satan. In the Christian Bible, Baal is directly referred to as Beelzebub, a deliberate slur and attack on Baal-Zebul, one of the names of Baal. Interestingly enough, his wife is often listed as Ashera, who is also found sometimes as the wife of Yahweh.

Ba'alat—Female—Middle East/Mediterranean

(Also known as Baalat, Baalath)

Animal association: Snake (cobra)

'The Lady' or *'Divine Lady'*—Goddess of the written language and knowledge. She is the patron of authors and librarians. It is likely that the modern Wiccan use of the term 'The Lady' came from similar uses such as found here. The roots of the story of Adam's first wife Lilith might be found here with Ba'alat. There is a great deal of debate over the names I have listed here as belonging to Ba'alat. If they are linked as I believe they are, we see the connection through the Canaanites who called Lilith either 'Baalath' or maybe 'Baalat,' depending on how one wants to translate wildly different alphabets, vowel use, and spelling. Knowing Ba'alat is a goddess of knowledge and the written language, we see an interesting story unfold in the story of Lilith's transformation into the serpent who convinced Adam's second wife, Eve, into eating the forbidden fruit from what is sometimes called the 'Tree of Knowledge.'

Ba'al Gad—Male/Female—Middle East

Animal association: Goat

'Lord of Good Luck'—An amazingly complex amount of lore exists for this relatively simple deity of good luck. His name can be translated easily from the Hebrew. Ba'al (Baal) can be used as both a masculine noun or verb. As the title of a deity, it is a noun which means 'Lord', 'Master', or other similar translations. The word Gad is a feminine Hebrew noun meaning 'good luck'. Sounds simple right? Well, the problem is with the repeated translation of the word Gad into the word God simply because it the two words look and sound similar. Combine that with the word Ba'al (again meaning Lord or Master) and sprinkle in a major translation error in virtually every version of the Christian Bible, which associated the word Ba'al with the term 'false', and we see the emergence of the translation of Ba'al Gad as 'The False God.' As a result, I have found fundamental Christians (who worship the Lord) to be rather fond of claiming I worship Ba'al (which means Lord), which is entirely too funny.

Ba'al-Hammon—Male—Middle East/Mediterranean

Wife: Tanit

Animal association: Ram

'Lord of the Incense Altar'—Phoenician fertility god with lesser associations to the Underworld than to fertility. The Greeks associated him with Cronos, the Romans with Saturn

Babalu Aye—Male—African/Caribbean/South America

In Santeria his name is Babalu Aye/Chankpanna

In Africa his name is Obaluaye/Omolu/Sonponno/Soponno

Saint and Catholic association: St. Lazarus

Holiday: Feast of Saint Lazarus on December 17

Plant associations: Angelica, Allspice, Acacia, Almond, Anise, Asafoetida, Basil, Bay, Balm of Gilead, Bergamot (orange), Copal, Clove, Cumin, Cedar, Calamas, Carnation, Citron, Cinnamon, Coriander, Clover (red), Cypress,

Camphor, Eucalyptus, Fern, Frankincense, Fennel, Gardenia, Ginger, Garlic, Heliotrope, Honeysuckle, Hyssop, Hyacinth (wild), Juniper, Lime, Lotus, Lavender, Myrrh, Mistletoe (American), Mugwort, Orris, Palmarosa, Red Poppy (seed), Peppermint, Rosemary, Rue, Sandalwood (white), Sage (diviner's), Thyme, Yarrow

Yoruba god (king who owns the Earth) who migrated into Santeria to become an Orisha of healing. In the mixing of Yoruba and Christian tradition he became associated with Saint Lazarus.

Baba, The—Female—Central Europe

'Old woman'—Hungarian term used to denote a good Witch or a good fairy. Although they stood in opposition to the Baba Yaga (bad Witches), the Baba were eventually lumped in with the Baba Yaga as nasty creatures.

Note: Not to be confused with the Sumerian Bau who is sometimes called Mother Baba or Baba.

Baba Yaga, The—Female—Central Europe (Also known as Baba Jaga, Baba Yaga Kostianaya Noga, Jezi-Baba)

Animal association: Snake

'Bad Old Woman'—Hungarian and East European term to denote a bad Witch. Stood in opposition to the early view of Baba (good Witch).

Babelah—Female—Middle East/Mediterranean

Babylonian and Hebrew goddess of Babylon whose name is also connected by Islam to magick.

Babi—Male—Africa

Animal association: Monkey (baboon)

Egyptian baboon god associated with war and male virility. The modern Pagan community celebrates his lore in the common pendant depicting a phallus with a baboon/monkey riding on it. The charm is said to bring on male sexual virility and strength in conflict. In his role in the judgement of souls, he dines on the souls of those whose judgment was not favorable.

In the Underworld, his phallus is sometimes seen as the mast of a sail boat/ferry that bring new souls across the river to the Land of the Dead.

Bacabs, The—Male—Central America

The Mayan personification of the four principle directions. They are Cauac, Ix, Kan, and Mulac.

Baiame—Male—Australia

Wife: Birrahgnooloo, Birra Nulu

Lover: Yhi

Australian Aborigine moon god and All Father who was the personification of good who stood in opposition with Dardawigal.

Bacchus—Male—Mediterranean

Animal associations: Boar, Dove, Elephant, Panther

Plant associations: Beech, Broom, Fennel, Fig, Ivy (common), Patchouli, Pine, Tamarisk, Thistle, Vine (grape)

Roman god of wine. Greek equivalent Dionysus. His major holiday, the Bacchanalia, was celebrated with wild, intoxicated orgies until the Roman Senate forbade the practice. His cult then went underground, giving rise to the secret societies of Bacchus reportedly alive today.

Incense Recipe

2 parts Patchouli

1 part Thistle

1 part Gum Arabic

Enough Bacchus or a combination of red wine and field honey to bind

Oil Recipe*

1/2 ounce Patchouli essential oil

1/2 ounce Grape seed oil

3 drops Wheat Germ

2 drops Pine essential oil

2 drops sweet wine

2 raisins

* See *Wicca Spellcraft for Men* for an alternative Recipe.

Badb—Female—Central Europe

(Also known as Badhbh, Badb Catha)

Father: Delbaeth

Mother: Ernmas

Husband: Net

Animal associations: Cow, Raven

'Battle'—Irish goddess of war and one of the Irish Triple Goddesses of Fate. She is a shape-shifter, her favorite form being the Raven. In that form, she is called Badb Catha, which means 'Battle Raven.' The other two goddesses of fate are Anu and Macha. See also Morrigan.

Bahloo—Male—Australia

Mother: Yhi

Lover: Yhi

Overlaps with Baiame as Australian All Father. Australian Aborigine All Father who, with his creator (mother) Yhi, created all the animals of the Earth, including humanity. This was most likely not an incestuous relationship. See Yhi for details.

Balor—Male—Central Europe

Wife: Dana or Ceithlenn

Daughter: Eithne

Irish leader of the Fomorians, a tribe of Giants. Balor became god of the Irish Underworld.

Balarama—Male—Near East

Lover: Revati

Hindu god and dark skinned twin brother of Krishna. He is sometimes cited with his twin brother as the eighth avatar of Vishnu.

Baldur—Male—Northern Europe

(Also known as Balder)

Father: Odin

Mother: Frigga

Wife: Nanna

Plant associations: Daisy, St. John's Wort

Scandinavian god who was so loved by both gods and men that the jealous trickster Loki arranged a joke that caused his death. After all attempts to save his life, his wife Nanna died of a broken heart. Sometimes cited as the son of Freya, he is more properly listed as the son of Frigga.

Banbha—Female—Central Europe

Plant association: Yew

Irish warrior goddess and protector of Ireland. With Fodhla and Eire, she is an Irish Triple Goddess.

Banebdjedet—Male—Africa

(Also known as Ba-Neb-Tetet, Banebdjetet, Banaded, Binded, Baneb Djedet)

Lover: Hatmehyt

Animal association: Ram

Egyptian god who helped secure the throne of Horus.

Baron Cimetiere—See Ghede

Baron La Croix—See Ghede

Baron Piquante—See Ghede

Baron Samedi—See Ghede

Bast—Female—Africa

(Also known as Bastet)

Father: Ra

Animal associations: Cat, Lion, Lynx

Plant associations: Catnip, Vervain, Valerian

Egyptian sun goddess who is a prime example of how the genders assigned to the sun and moon changed quite a bit with time. Initially she was a solar deity, but with the introduction of the Greek association to Artemis, she became a lunar deity. She is often depicted with the head of a lion or desert cat and the body of a human. Other times, she is seen as having both head and body of a cat.

Bau—Female—Mediterranean

Also called Baba and Mother Baba

Animal association: Goose

Sumerian Mother goddess of healing. Sometimes associated with Gaia, thus becoming an Earth Mother goddess.

Note: Do not confuse with the East European Baba. They share similar names but are separate figures.

Befana, La—Female—Mediterranean
(Also known as La Strega, La Vecchia, Saint Befana)

'Unexpected' (see note)—Italian Witch who flies down chimneys and brings presents to children on Twelfth Night. The Italian story is that when the three wise men were on their way to welcome the Christian savior to this world, they passed La Befana and invited her along. She declined because she wasn't much for new fad religions and because she had better things to do, like cleaning her house. But then she had second thoughts. Although she didn't much agree with the Three Wise Men's opinion that the child was supremely sacred, he was none the less a child and thus sacred. She tried to catch up with them, but got lost. Feeling so sorry she missed the child's birthday, she spends the year getting ready for First Night when she flies down the chimney and gives presents to the deserving children whose birthday she missed. If she discovered that the children were undeserving and thus had wasted her valuable time, she instead places a rock or unburned lump of coal. In her story we see a wonderful cite supporting my belief that there is no reason to rob the cultural holiday typically known as Christmas from our Wiccan children. After all, here we see that Santa was once a Witch. Note on her name: The etymology of her name is often cited as 'Epiphany,' which is a Christian term for the January 6th feast celebrating the divinity of Jesus. However, the word far predates its Christian use and originally meant something more in order of a sudden and unexpected manifestation of divinity without reference to pantheon.

Begochiddy—Male—North America
Native American supreme god of the Navajo.

Behanzin—Male—African
Animal association: Fish
West African patron god of fishermen.

Bel—Male—Middle East/Mediterranean
(Also known as Bol)
Wife: Beltis
Animal associations: Cattle (especially Bull), Snake

Ancient Syrian (pre-Islam) sky and Supreme God. Forms a sacred triad with Aglibol and Yarhibol.

Beli—Male—Central Europe
(Also known as Bile, Belenus, Belanos)
Wife: Don
Holiday: Bealtaine

Celtic patron of metalworkers, especially creators of magickal tools. Also patron of sheep, cattle, and the folk who tend them. He is the father of the beloved Dagda and one of the male fertility gods that has managed to work his way into Wicca despite the goddess predomination. Of course he came in a rather hidden way. You see, although very few people realize it, the fertility Sabbat of Bealtaine is named after him. His name has had several changes as it moved from tribe to tribe. Some of those names have been based on a root word meaning 'Shining one,' others have meant 'Sacred tree.' Beli was chiefly a god of Summer. The beginning of his reign was marked at Bealtaine and ended at Samhain. When this principle was followed, Bealtaine was sometimes called *Cetsamhain,* which literally means 'opposite Samhain.' While this might sound strange considering the modern Pagan way of splitting the Light and Dark half of the year at the Fall and Spring Equinox, one should remember that the Celts were not overly interested in the Solar Days. As such, that which we now consider fixed Sabbats actually moved around on the Wheel of the Year quite a bit.

Belit-ili—Female—Middle East
(Also known as Baalat, Belili)
Animal association: Dog
Plant association: Willow

Babylonian patron and protector of newborn children who is probably the origin of the story of Lilith. More accurately, her Canaanite name was Baalat or Ballet, which later became

Lilith. This is interesting, as with Lilith's demonification came the stories of how she eats children.

Belitis—See Ninlil

Bellona—Female—Mediterranean
Husband: Mars
Plant association: Belladonna

'War'—Roman goddess of war and combat. She is depicted with spear and shield and accompanies her husband Mars into battle.

Beltis—Female—Mediterranean
Husband: Bel

Babylonian moon and love goddess. She is sometimes seen as wife to Bel and other times as his female equivalent.

Bendis—Female—Mediterranean
(Also known as Bendidi)
Husband: Sabazius

Thracian/Greek moon goddess. She was known to the Greeks as both Bendis and to some degree as Artemis, depending on the time in history. Her worship often involved wild orgies. Although this may be a wild theory, we see the Thracian Bendis/Bendidi with wild orgies over and over in mythology. We then see her adopted as Artemis by the Greek, and then we see the Roman Diana with her association to the Greek Artemis. Years later, we receive *Aradia: Gospel of the Witches* from Charles Leland, which in part reads: "And ye shall make the game of Benevento." Those words are the advice of Diana as presented by her daughter Aradia. Could the celebrations of Bendis/Bendidi be the origin of the seaport named Benevento? And if so, could the term 'game of Benevento' be a reference to the historically documented orgies associated with the worship of Bendis/Bendidi?

Benten—Female—Far East
(Also known as Benzai-ten, Benzai-tennyo)
Animal associations: Dragon, Snake (white)

Japanese love goddess of music and wealth. She is called on for luck, especially by gamblers.

Bertha—See Hulda

Berus—Female—Mediterranean
Husband: Elium

Phoenician All Mother.

Bes—Male—Africa
(Also known as Bisu)
Wife: Ta-Urt

Egyptian dwarf who protects women during childbirth. Prayed to by parents and couples for the betterment not only of children, but also the relationships that support them. He is often depicted skyclad with exaggerated genitals. The key to understanding Bes as a protective god is found in his tremendously ugly outer appearance. Evil cannot see his inner beauty, so it is driven off. The message here seems to be clear: Those with a pure heart are not intimidated or scared by external appearances.

Bestla—Female—North Europe
Lover: Bor
Plant association: Yew

Mother of Odin and goddess of the yew tree.

Bhaga—Male—Near East
Father: Kashyapa
Mother: Aditi

Hindu patron of marriage and god of prosperity. Bhaga is one of the Adityas. The Hindu month Magha (January 21–February 19) is sacred to Bhaga. See Adityas.

Bhairavi—Female—Near East
Husband: Shiva

Hindu avatar/incarnation of Parvati.

Bharti—Female—Near East

Hindu goddess of human speech and language.

Bhatta—Female—Near East

Hindu goddess of magick and spellcraft.

Bhavani—Female—Near East
Plant associations: Cypress, Myrrh, Poppy (especially white)
Holiday: Feast of Lamps on the new moon closest to Samhain.

Hindu goddess whose breasts are the sun and moon. Sometimes seen as a horrific form of Parvati, akin to Kali and Durga.

Incense Recipe
1 part Sandalwood
1 part Myrrh (best to use sweet myrrh if it is available)
1 part Cypress
Enough Bhavani or Cypress oil to bind

Oil Recipe
10 drops Myrrh oil
10 drops Cypress oil
1/2 ounce base oil (best base oil is made by simmering poppy flowers in sesame oil, straining, and then cooling before adding the essential oils)

Bhumi—Female—Near East
Hindu Earth goddess and mother of all living things.

Biliku—Female—Australia (Malaysia)
Husband: Buluga
Animal association: Spider
Spider goddess of the aboriginal Australians and on several of the Malaysian islands.

Birrahgnooloo—Female—Australia
Husband: Baiame
Australian Aborigine All Mother.

Birra Nula—Female—Australia
Husband: Baiame
Australian Aborigine goddess who was one of the wives of Baiame, but not chiefly involved in his role as All Father. She is most often cited for giving him grief.

Birren—Female—Central Europe
Husband: Bith
Irish first woman into Ireland. See Bith for her story.

Bishamon—Male—Far East
(Also known as Bishamon-ten, Bishamon-tenno, Tamomtennu)

Japanese god subordinate to Taishaku-ten who guarded the North. The other three were Jikoku, Kimoku, and Zocho. In Wiccan ritual he is sometimes connected with the South Quarter.

Bith—Male—Central Europe
Father: Noah
Wife: Birren
Irish God who was sent to the west most point of the known world by his father Noah. There they waited 40 days to escape the Great Flood. With him, he brought his wife Birren, daughter Cesara, her husband Fintaan and a small tribe. After the Great Flood receded, Bith and Birren became the first couple to enter into Ireland. This is no doubt a reference to the Great Flood presented in the Book of Exodus.

Black Annis—Female—North Europe
Animal association: Hare
Holiday—April 30th/May 1st
Scandinavian nymph who was associated with the hare and hunting of the hare. Later became associated with the Easter egg hunts of Christianity.

Blodeuwedd—Female—Central Europe
(Also known as Blodeuwydd)
Husband: Llew Llaw Gyffes
Lover: Gronw
Animal association: Owl
Plant associations: Birch, Broom, Hawthorn, Meadowsweet, Oak
Welsh goddess who was created specifically to be Llew Llaw Gyffes' wife. Not only was she unfaithful to Llew, but she plotted his death with her lover Gronw. Llew survived their attack and killed Gronw. Blodeuwedd was turned into an owl to forever mourn her lover's death during the night hours.

Incense Recipe
Burn the branches of birch, hawthorn, and oak

Boann—Female—Central Europe

Father: Delbaeth

Mother: Ernmas

Lover: Dagda

Animal association: Cow (white)

'She of white cattle'—Irish goddess of the River Boyne. Boann was known as a virgin, not in the sense that she had not yet had intercourse, but rather in the sense that she was an independent women and not subservient to her lover, the Dagda.

Bochica—Male—South America

Wife: Chia

Colombian champion who created/channeled the solar calendar and provided it, as well as knowledge of morality, ethics, farming, and the art of negotiating Nature to his people. He is considered the inventor of law, that which allows community to build.

Bolthorn—Male—North Europe

Scandinavian giant and grandfather to Odin.

Bona Dea—Female—Mediterranean

'Good Goddess'—Roman goddess of fertility and interestingly enough, virginity. She is a personification of the Earth who, in antiquity, was celebrated predominantly by women. During those times, men were forbidden to look on so much as her statuary. Today, she is praised by both men and women.

Bor—Male—North Europe

(Also known as Borr)

Father: Bur

Lover: Bestla

Commonly cited as a Scandinavian god, Bor is more of a pre or proto-god who, with his wife Bestla, had three children who are seen as the first gods. Those three are Odin, Vile, and Ve.

Boreas—Male—Mediterranean

Father: Astraeus

Mother: Eos

Greek god of the North Wind associated with the North Quarter (Earth) in Wiccan ritual. Associated with the Roman Aquilo.

Bragi—Male—North Europe

(Also known as Brage)

Father: Odin

Mother: Frigga

Wife: Iduna

Norse patron of poets and poetry who inspired men and gods with his magickal mead.

Brahma—Male—Near East

(Also known as Brahman)

Wife: Sarasvati

Animal associations: Eagle, Swan, Peacock, Raven

Plant associations: American Aspen (poplar), Ash, Common Aspen, Cedar, Cypress, Fig, Hyssop, Ivy (common), Oak, Olive, Saffron (Spanish)

Hindu god who formed the sacred triad with Vishnu and Shiva. Said to have split himself in half, much as the creation story presented in the book of Genesis. His male half is called Purusha and his female half, Satarupa. The two halves then combined to conceive and birth Sarasvati, who later became his wife.

Incense Recipe

2 parts Cedar powder

1 part Hyssop

1 part Cypress

Enough Brahma or Cedar Wood essential oil to bind)

(Add a fig or two if using to make a tincture)

Oil Recipe

12 drops Cypress essential oil

9 drops Cedar Wood essential oil

1/2 ounce Olive oil

Bran the Blessed—Male—Central Europe

Father: Llyr

Mother: Iweridd

Animal associations: Raven, Wren

Plant associations: Alder and all old world grains

Welsh god, brother of Branwen. So did Bran love his sister that when he realized she was abused by her husband Matholwch, the

King of Ireland, he and his kith and kin took arms against the King and his army.

Branwen—Female—Central Europe
Father: Llyr
Mother: Iweridd
Husband: Matholwch (King of Ireland)
Animal associations: Crow, Raven

'*White raven*'—Welsh goddess, sister of Bran the Blessed, who tells us that when a marriage has become abusive, it is acceptable to rely on kith and kin for help because it might be their will to do so. See Bran the Blessed.

Bres—Male—Central Europe
Wife: Brigid

Irish god of fertility. He was a horrible leader who at one point raised taxes so high that his people starved. After being dethroned, he raised an army to regain his kingdom. His attempt failed and he was taken prisoner. In exchange for his life, he offered to instruct the people of Ireland in the art of farming and negotiating with Nature. They accepted, and we receive an interesting observation on the quality of leadership or any specific job. Although Bres made a horrible leader, he was a splendid teacher. Ireland quickly became a fertile land under his guidance.

Bridhid—See Brigid

Brigantia—Female—Central Europe
Animal association: Cattle
Plant association: Mountain Ash (Rowan)

Celtic fresh water goddess from whom the Braint and Brent rivers were named. She became the patron of cattle and the folk who tend them by a combination of factors, first by the practice of raising cattle close to large supplies of fresh water, and second by Roman occupation. The Romans associated her with Caelestis thus creating 'Caelestis Brigantia.'

Brigid—Female—Central Europe
(Also known as Brighid, Brigindo, Brigit)
Father: Dagda
Mother: Boann
Husband: Bres
Animal associations: Boar, Cat, Cock, Sheep (ewe),Snake
Plant associations: Blackberry, Mountain Ash (Rowan)
Holiday: Imbolg

Celtic Triple Goddess of inspiration: fire of inspiration (patron of poetry and poets), fire of the hearth/home (patron of fertility and healing), and fire of the forge (patron of metalsmiths and craft folk). Although a separate name may have been used for each aspect at one time, those associations have been lost.

Brihaspati—Male—Near East
(Also known as Brahmanaspati)
Wife: Tara

Hindu personification and priest of prayer, chant, and mantra. His words are said to have brought about the creation of the world.

Britannia—Female—Central Europe
British personification of Britain.

Bubatis—Female—Africa (?)/Mediterranean (?)
Animal association: Cat

A goddess that seems to appear only in Neo-Pagan lore where she is said to be a Greek cat goddess. I am unable to locate historic cites other than those to the popularity of cat statuary and the goddess Bast/Bastet in the ruins of Tell-Basta (formerly the town/city of Bubatis).

Buddha, The—Male—Near East/Central Asia
(Also known as Gautama, Siddhartha)
Father: Immaculate Conception
Mother: Queen Maya
Wife: Yasodhara
Plant associations: Acacia, Amaranth, Bay, Bodhi, Frangipani, Vine (grape)

The word Buddha is more of a title than a name, meaning the 'Enlightened One.' This particular Enlightened One was an Indian man named Siddhartha. Born about 550 B.C.E., Siddhartha founded modern Buddhism after abandoning his son Rahula (on the day Rahula was born) and wife Maya, taking the alias Gautama, and wandering the country side pretending to be a poor monk although he was born a prince. After his following became large enough to present a clear threat to the Hindu religion, he was declared the ninth avatar (incarnation) of Vishnu to appease his followers. Note: Not to be confused with Budha or "Buddha, Dankinis."

Incense Recipe
2 part Gum Arabic
1 part Acacia flowers
1 part Bay leaf
A few raisins

Budha—Male—Near East
Father: Soma
Mother: Tara

Beloved Hindu god whose birth was the result of rape. See Tara for an account. Note: Not to be confused with "Buddha, The" or "Buddha, Dankinis."

Buddha, Dankinis—Female—Central Asia

Dankinis Buddha is the Tibetan goddess associated with Center, enlightenment, and understanding. See also Vajra, Ratna, Padma, and Karma.

Note: See separate listings for "Buddha, The" and Buddha

Bur—Male—Northern Europe
Son: Bor

Scandinavian grandfather of Odin

Buto—Female—Africa
(Also known as Edjo, Udjo, Wadjet, Wadjit)
Animal Association: Mouse, Snake (cobra), Vulture

'Papyrus colored'—Egyptian snake goddess. Her symbol, the cobra, is found on the crown of many Egyptian kings as a talisman of protection. Her name refers to the color of natural papyrus as the color of the female cobra.

Cadmus—Male—Mediterranean
Father: Agenor
Mother: Telephassa

'From the East'—Greek god responsible for inventing/channeling the Greek alphabet. Founder of the city of Thebes.

Cailleach—Female—Central Europe
(Also known as Cailleach Beara, Scotia)
Animal associations: Adder, Crane, Owl
Plant association: Wheat

Scottish All Mother who by some account was also the creator of the world. Her story gives us the custom of the corn doll. Originally made from local grains crops (called corn) to represent the goddess herself, with the introduction of the New World discovery of maize (also called corn) the tradition expanded to include dolls made from cornhusks. This was a doll made by the community farmer who finished the last harvest first. He then passed the doll on to the next farmer to complete harvest as he showed up with his kith and kin to assist in that farmer's harvest. The practice was repeated until all of the kith and kin of all of the farmers arrived at the last to finish. His was given the doll, his work was the easiest because everyone else helped, and thus in fair exchange for their help he was responsible for taking care of the doll (and the poor/elderly that needed food) over the Winter. If he should be unable or his resources depleted early, he would return the doll and responsibility to the previous farmer who had given him the doll; if that farmer's stores failed, it would again pass to the farmer before him. This was a form of work equity socialism where he who works the hardest (the ones who finished first and helped all others) is the last to bear the burden of social support because he was the one to offer the most at the harvest. This lore is key to understanding the modern Wiccan approach to the subject of socialism. Yes, we are a community based religion. Yes, we feel that members of our tribe/community should be supported by the whole. However, safeguards must be in place to insure that the lazy do not leech off of those who bear the brunt of the work necessary to keep the tribe/community going because they are already taxed by their own heart and work ethic. They have already given, and asking more of them might well cause them not to offer that which they already do.

Cain—Male—Central Europe

A name sometimes cited as the father of Lugh by Eithne. In those references his father is Dianchecht. However, the name is more commonly cited as the first son of Adam and Eve. In that story, Cain made an offering of grain to the Christian God. God rejected Cain's offering because he demanded the blood of death in exchange for blessings. This is the most likely reference found in *Aradia: Gospel of Witches* as the section in which his name is used is discussing a feast of grain.

Calliope—Female—Mediterranean

'Beautiful voice'—Greek muse of epic poetry. See also Muses, The.

Callisto—Female—Mediterranean

Lover: Zeus

Animal association: Bear

Plant association: Willow

'Fairest'—Greek nymph sometimes said to be a moon goddess. The title of moon goddess came about through a connection made to Artemis, whom Callisto very much adored. Knowing that Callisto had taken a vow of chastity and knowing how much she adored Artemis, one day Zeus took on the form of Artemis and found the young Callisto in the woods where she, thinking he was Artemis, let down her guard for just a moment. In that moment Zeus attacked and raped her.

Calypso—Female—Mediterranean

(Also known as Kalypso)

Father: Atlas

Mother: Aethra or Pleione

'Hidden'—Greek nymph who so loved Odysseus that even though he wanted to leave her island and return home, she refused and kept him prisoner, by some accounts for seven years.

Camazotz—Male—Central America

(Also known as Camazotx)

Animal association: Bat

Mayan bat god who was defeated in the struggles between the gods.

Carmenta—Female—Mediterranean

(Also known as Carmentis)

Lover: Hermes

Roman goddess of childbirth and divination.

Capys—Male—Mediterranean

The Trojan founder of Capua and father of Anchises.

Cardea—Female—Mediterranean

Plant associations: Arbutus, Hawthorn, and Beans (especially black beans)

Roman goddess and protector of the home and patron of children. She is said to protect children from baneful magick.

Carlin—Female—Central Europe

Celtic spirit who leads baneful spirits in Samhain mischief.

Carman—Female—Central Europe

(Also known as Carme)

Holiday : August 1st

Irish Witch/sorceress who bore the Irish Triple God of evil as her three sons: Dian, Dub, and Dother. She and her sons fought against the people of Danu. Carman lost and is now identified as an evil Witch who used all manner of negative magick and curses. However, it is important to remember that while the story might be true, history is told from the viewpoint of the winner.

Carmenta—Female—Mediterranean

(Also known as Carmentis)

Roman goddess of childbirth, writing, and the present. She invented the Roman alphabet and instructed (with her sister Porrima) on its use in divination and (with her sister Postvorta) the recording of the past. With her sisters Porrima and Postvorta, she is seen as a

Triple Goddess. She is one of the Camenae, a collection of beings similar to and later associated with the Roman Muses.

Carna—Female—Mediterranean

Roman goddess of health. She is strongly associated with the liver and heart, but is generally associated with all internal organs. This is extremely interesting as the number one food offered to her in sacrifice is pork and pork fat, showing us another side of sacrifice. If we want our hearts and other internal organs to remain healthy, maybe we should give up pork.

Castor—Male—Mediterranean
Father: Tyndareus
Mother: Leda
Animal associations: Magpie, Beaver
Plant associations: Lucky Hand, Morning Glory, Wormwood

'Beaver'—Greek and Roman god who was the son of Tyndareus, but who is sometimes cited as the son of Zeus. See Leda for the account. With his twin brother Pollux, he was called the Disocuri.

Cassiopeia—Female—Mediterranean
(Also known as Casseipeia)
Husband: Cepheus

Greek woman who tried to sacrifice her daughter Andromeda to a sea monster sent by Poseidon. Perseus saved Andromeda from that fate.

Cauac—Male—Central America
Father: Itzamna
Mother: Ixchel

One of the Bacabs, the four Mayan gods of the principle directions. Associated with the color red. In Wiccan ritual he is associated with the South Quarter. See also Ix, Kan, and Mulac.

Ceithlenn —Female—Central Europe
Husband: Balor
Daughter: Eithrene

Irish goddess sometimes associated with Dana.

Celaeno—Female—Mediterranean

'The Dark'—Greek Harpy who was charged with creating peace. In that capacity, she and the others are beautiful winged maidens (sometimes virgins). But to keep that peace, she and the others were also the punisher of crime. In that capacity, they are horrid winged beasts. One of the three Harpies. The other two are Aello and Ocypete.

Centon Totochtin—Male/Female—Aztec
(Also known as Centzon Totochtin)
Animal association: Rabbit

'Four Hundred Rabbits'—A group of Aztec deities who met frequently for great volumes of alcohol, revelry, and sex.

Ceres—Female—Mediterranean
Father: Saturn
Animal association: Ant, Boar
Plant association: Adder's Tongue, Bay, Daffodil, Leek, Lily, Narcissus, Pomegranate, Poppy (all), Wheat, Willow

Italian/Roman personification of the love that a mother has for her children. Also goddess of grain and crops. As she evolved, she has been associated with Tellus Mater and Demeter. The month Sextilis is sacred to Ceres.

Cernunnos—Male—Central Europe
(Also known as Hu'Gadarn, Herne, Kernunnos)
Animal associations: Antelope, Bear, Crane, Deer (stag), Wolf, Bull, Otter, Sheep (ram), Snake, Goat
Plant associations: Bay, Heliotrope, Oak, Orange, Patchouli, Sandalwood, Sunflower
Holiday: Bealtaine

'Horned One'—Celtic Horned God who tends to be associated in the Neo-Pagan community predominantly with the hunt. Historically speaking, he is more of a prosperity and fertility god, oftentimes being depicted (as was Pan) with an erect penis and sometimes with a bag of coins. When not shown with an erect penis, he is shown with a large snake that has the head of a ram. His most famous depiction in this capacity is on the Gundestrup cauldron, which was found in Denmark. He is god of Nature and especially of the woods. Said to marry the Earth Goddess at Bealtaine, but also associated with the Underworld and the Dark half of the year.

Incense Recipe

2 parts Gum Arabic
1 part Bay leaf
1 part Orange peel
1 part Sandalwood (yellow)
Enough Cernunnos Oil to bind*

Oil Recipe

10 drops Bay oil*
8 drops Orange oil
2 drops Sandalwood oil
1/2 ounce Sunflower oil
* Note: Some folk use either musk or patchouli oil.

Cerridwen—Female—Central Europe
(Also known as Ceridwen, Grandmother Moon, Kerridwen)
Lover: Tegid
Animal associations: Boar (sow), Chicken (hen), Dog (greyhound), Otter
Plant associations: Acorns, Apple, Vervain, Willow
Holidays: Samhain, all dark moons
    Welsh Witch and moon goddess most often associated with the dark moon. Mother of the ugliest boy (Avagdu/Afagddu) and most beautiful girl (Creirwy) in the history of the world. She is a goddess of shape-shifting and of being able to adapt to one's environment. She is prayed to for easing the suffering of childbirth, like the mother who comforts her daughter as she gives birth. She is the owner of a cauldron named 'Amen,' within which she stirs a magick potion named 'greal.' That potion is said to grant all inspiration and knowledge, which she created for her son Avagdu/Afagddu that he might compensate for his repulsive looks with great wisdom. See Gwion for more information.

Cesara—Female—Central Europe
Father: Bith
Mother: Birren
Husband: Fintaan
    Irish woman who led the journey west described under her father's name. Became the first woman into Ireland after the Great Flood. See Bith.

Chac—Male—Central America
(Also known as Chac Mol)
Animal associations: Jaguar, Panther, Snake (serpent)
    Mayan god of thunder and rain who is associated with crop fertility. May have been an early form of Cauac.

Chandra—Male—Near East
Lover: Tara
Animal associations: Antelope, Hare
Plant associations: Aloe, Almond, Camphor, Celandine (lesser), Hazelnut, Mugwort, Sandalwood (yellow)
    Hindu seventh avatar of Vishnu. He was originally also a moon god, but that association became absorbed by Soma. He is patron of couples who seek to have children and is prayed to for granting that aspiration.

Incense Recipe

2 parts Sandalwood
1 part Mugwort
1 part Gum Arabic
Enough Chandra or Sandalwood oil to bind.

Oil Recipe

10 drops Sandalwood oil
10 drops Camphor oil
1/2 ounce base oil (try a 50/50 mix of Hazelnut and Almond oil)

Ch'ang-O—Female—Central Asia
Husband: Excellent Archer
Animal association: Hare
    Chinese moon goddess who fled her husband in fear of his anger. When she did, she

stole from him the drink of immortality. She speaks to women of the strength necessary to leave an abusive relationship. Note: Do not confuse with the African/Caribbean Chango.

Chantico—Female Goddess—Central America
Animal associations: Dog, Snake (red serpent)
Plant association: Paprika

'She who lives in the home'—Aztec god of home, hearth, and volcanoes. Her story comments on the principle of the kin familiar. She was originally found in human form but violated a law that stated paprika would not be eaten on fast days. In punishment, she was turned into a dog, the most popular kith familiar in Arctic North, and North, South, and Central America. Interestingly enough, this is not so much the case in Europe and not at all in Asia, where her lore is geographically separated.

Charon—Male—Mediterranean
Father: Erebus
Mother: Nyx

'Fierce Brightness' or *'Fierce Brilliance'*—Greek god who conducted souls across the River Acheron into the Underworld. Later cites would say the river was Styx, but those cites seem far less accurate.

Chaos—Male—Mediterranean
Mother: Achlys
Daughter: Nyx
Animal association: Alligator

'Great Void' or *'Gaping Void'*—Greek origin/ Creator god similar to the Nameless One in the creation story given in the Book of Genesis. Nyx is sometimes listed as his wife and other times as his sister, with Erebus brother to both. I believe this came into play with the old question: Where did the first god come from if s/he did not have a mother and father? Note that the story of Diana and her brother Lucifer is told here as well. Chaos was born from his mother Achlys, whose name loosely means 'dark mist.'

Chasca—Female—South America

Inca goddess of flowers who protects young women.

Chia—Female—South America
Husband: Bochica

Colombian moon goddess who was patron of women and men who dressed like them. In other references, men dressed like women to escape her wrath after they had offended her. With her association to the moon, and thus the tide, she is sometimes cited as the one responsible for the Great Flood. Patron of cross-dressing men.

Ch'i-lin—Female—Central Asia

Chinese creature guardian of the West. She is similar to the unicorn in having a single horn, but is described as having the tail of an ox, the body of a deer, and the scales of a fish. She presides over that which is good and pure. The other guardians are Ch'i-lin, Gui Xian, Feng-huang, and Long. They are collectively known as the Ssu Ling.

Chiminigagua—Male—South America
Animal association—Blackbird

Chibcha Creator god who set order to the universe by causing light to come from eternal darkness. He spread that light across the world with the assistance of Blackbird.

Chiron—Male—Mediterranean
Father: Cronos
Mother: Philyra
Animal association: Horse

'Hand'—Greek educator who taught Apollo and the sons of Apollo: Aristaeus, Asclepius and Orpheus. In some references he was one of the Centaurs (half man and half horse).

Chung, Mo Li—Male—Central Asia

Mo Li Chung is the Chinese Buddhist guardian of the East. His statue is often included at the east point of Buddhist temples. In the modern practice of Feng Shui, his statue is placed in the East-most part of a home to protect from negative influences coming from that direction. In Wiccan ritual, he is one of the names for the Four Quarters, the other three being Hung, Shou, and Hai.

Chu Pa-chieh—Male—Central Asia

Animal association: Boar

Chinese student and guardian of the Tang Monk Tripitaka who journeyed to the western heavens to secure the knowledge of the Buddha.

Cinteotl—Male—Central America

Mother: Tlazolteotl

Plant association: Corn

Aztec and Toltec corn (maize) god. His suffering brought forth the corn that fed his people. Not that it made much difference to the brutal Spanish invaders, he was associated with the Christian Jesus such that his worship could continue in hiding. The attempt was similar to the African slaves' development of Santeria, only this one mostly failed.

Circe—Female—Mediterranean

Father: Helios

Mother: Perse

Animal association: Falcon, Hawk, Boar (sow), Wolf

Plant association: Belladonna

'Falcon' —Beautiful Greek Witch/sorceress who with her magick could and did turn men into boars, lions, and wolves.

Clio—Female—Mediterranean

(Also known as Kleio)

'Announcer' or 'Proclaimer'—Greek Muse of history. See also Muses, The. She is sometimes cited as the Muse who brought the Phoenician alphabet into Greece.

Cliona—Female—Central Europe

Father: Gebann

Irish goddess who possessed legendary beauty.

Clymene—Female—Mediterranean

Husband: Helios

'Famous might'—Greek nymph or maybe goddess who is cited as having several different potential genealogies.

Coatlicue—Female—Central America

Animal association: Snake

'Skirt of Serpents'—Aztec Earth and Fire goddess who wears a skirt of snakes. She was betrayed by her children and decapitated. In vengeance, she bore Huitzilopochtli in full armor, who later killed many of her children who had plotted against her. The theme behind her story is a similar one connecting birth and death in the never-ending cycle.

Cocidius—Male—Central Europe

Animal association: Deer (stag)

Celtic god of the hunt.

Concordia—Female—Mediterranean

(Also known as Charistia)

Roman goddess of order, peace, and harmony in opposition to Discordia. Her temple served as a meeting place. In her depictions, she demonstrates the principle of sacrifice. In one hand she holds a sacrificial bowl, and in the other hand, a cornucopia (horn of plenty). Sacrifice made to one yields benefits from the other is the order of the universe.

Consus—Male—Mediterranean

Animal association: Donkey

Roman god of harvest, especially grain harvests. His major holiday is the Consualia, celebrated twice a year, first after the planting season and then again after the harvest of those crops.

Corn Goddess—Female—North America/ Central America/South America

(Also known as Corn Mother)

Animal association: Grouse

Plant association: Corn

The principal grain goddess of North, Central, and South America found in many different cultures as simply Corn Mother, Corn Goddess, or by her many different names including Chicomecoatl (Aztec), Iyatiku (Keresan Pueblos), Xilonen (Aztec), Zaramama (Peruvian), and many others. Sometimes listed in other cultures as a reference to a grain goddess/

mother because the word corn is also a general reference to grain.

Corn Mother—See Corn Goddess

Coronis—Female—Mediterranean

Lover: Apollo

'Raven'—Wife to Apollo who, while pregnant with Asclepius, informed her husband that she was unfaithful. He killed her for her infidelity and set her on a funeral pyre. Before her body was completely consumed, he removed his son Asclepius and restored him to life. By some accounts, he also restored her to life, but not before the fire turned her white feathers black, thus explaining why the raven has black feathers. Although Asclepius is cited as son of Apollo, it is not clear if this story is an act of adoption or if it was Apollo's natural son. In another story, she was the hostage of Neptune who was changed into either a raven or a crow by Athena in order to escape.

Cotys—Female—Mediterranean

(Also known as Cottyto)

Greek and Sicilian fertility goddess who was celebrated with orgies. Her name is one potential source of the word *coitus,* which denotes sexual union. Her followers' orgies became so debauched that even she became disgusted with them.

Cronos—Male—Mediterranean

(Also known as Cronus, Kronos)

Father: Uranus

Mother: Gaia

Wife: Ashtart, Dione

Lover: Philya, Rhea

Animal associations: Crow, Donkey, Raven

Plant association: Beech

'Crow'—Greek god who is sometimes seen as the father of the Greek pantheon. One glance at associations and it is easy to see why one would make that observation. Not only did he father three of the major male figures in the Greek pantheon by his lover Rhea, he married both Ashtart and Dione (each one of his sisters).

Cihuatcoatl—Female—Central America

Animal association: Snake (serpent)

Aztec goddess of childbirth who was known as 'Serpent Woman'. Mother of Mixcoatl. Patron of pregnant women, especially at birth.

Coyote—Male—North America

Animal association: Coyote

Native American god form shared by many tribes. Like Loki, Coyote is the trickster.

Crom Cruaich—Male—Central Europe

Holiday: Lughnasadh

Irish god associated with Lughnasadh and the last Sunday in July, known as Domhnach Chrom Dudh (loosely, 'Chrom's Sunday').

Cuchulain—Male—Central Europe

(Also known as Cuchulainn, Cu Chulainn, Setanta)

Father: Sualtam, Lugh (adopted)

Wife: Emer

Irish culture hero, whose most often cited father, Lugh, speaks to us of kith turning into kin. His natural father is the mortal by the name of Sualtam, but Lugh adopted him.

Culhwch—Male—Central Europe

Father: Kilydd

Mother: Goleuddydd

Wife: Olwyn

Welsh culture hero who can be seen to have connections to the Wiccan reenactment of the Oak and Holy King story. Culhwch desired the hand of Olwyn in marriage. Her father, Ysbadadden, knew that should Culhwch take his daughter in marriage, he would himself die.

Cupid—Male—Mediterranean

Father: Mercury

Mother: Venus

Plant associations: Bay, Cypress, Juniper, Olive, Rose (especially red), Sugar, Violet (especially white)

Note: Some state Cupid was the son of Venus and Mars.

'Desire'—Roman god who is most often cited as god of love, but his stories better show him as god of lustful desire. Greek equivalent is Eros.

Incense Recipe

2 parts red rose petals and buds
1 part Cypress
1 part Juniper berries
1 part Gum Arabic
Best if you use enough Otto of Rose to bind. Ok to use Cupid oil or Juniper essential oil.

Oil Recipe

6 drops Cypress essential oil
6 drops Rose essential oil
3 drops Juniper essential oil
1/2 ounce Olive oil

Cybele—Female—Middle East/Mediterranean
(Also known as Magna Mater, Kybele)
Lover: Attis
Animal associations: Bee, Lion, Dog, and of all creatures of the wild.
Plant associations: Cypress, Heather, Oak, Poppy (especially white), Myrrh, Pine

'She of the hair'—Greek goddess of the Earth and of all creatures in the wild. She took rather serious action when she discovered her lover's intent to marry another woman. Upon discovering Attis' plans, she caused him to go insane. As a result, he castrated himself and presented her with his genitals. Her following started in the Middle East and then spread north into the Mediterranean, bringing along with it the practice of castrating oneself in her honor.

Incense Recipe

2 part Myrrh
1 part Cypress
1 part Heather
1 part Gum Arabic

Oil Recipe

8 drops Cypress
6 drops Pine
6 drops Myrrh
1/2 ounce base oil

Cyrene—Female—Mediterranean
(Also known as Kyrene)
Father: Hypseus
Mother: Creusa
Lover: Apollo

'Sovereign queen'—When she was seen wrestling with a lion by Apollo, it was love at first sight. He immediately carried her off and built a city in her honor and by her name.

Da-Bog—Male—Central Europe
Father: Svarog

Slavonic fire and sun god. Associated with a healthy home through his connection to fire and the hearth.

Dada—Male—African/Caribbean/South America
Saint association: St. Raymond Nonnatus
Holiday: Feast of Saint Raymond Nonnatus on August 31

Patron of newborns and protector of children.

Dagan—Male—Mediterranean
See also Dagon and Ben Dagon.

'Grain'—Babylonian god of agriculture and to some extent negotiating with nature.

Dagda, The—Male—Central Europe
(Also known as Daghda, Dagde, Dagodevas, Cian)
Wife: The Morrigan
Lover: Boann
Plant association: Heather, Hops, Oak

'The Good God'—Irish Celtic All Father and god of the Earth. Kind ruler of Life and Death, master of magick, warrior, and highly skilled at many crafts.

Dagon—Male—Mediterranean
See also Dagan and Ben Dagon as their names are often interchanged.
Father: Uranus
Mother: Gaia
Animal association: Fish and to an extent all creatures of the sea.

'Grain' or *'Corn'*—Mesopotamian god of crop fertility who invented the plough and instructed humanity on how to negotiate with nature. He is often depicted as a merman.

Daksha—Male—Near East

Father: Brahma

Hindu god whose 20 daughters were the days of each month (phases of the moon) who each married Soma, the 28th day and the moon itself.

Damballah—Male—Caribbean

(Also known as Damballah, Dambala, Bon Dieu)

Animal association: Snake (serpent)

Haitian Voodoo fertility god and All Father figure. He is the father or master of each of the loa and the most important deity in the Haitian Voodoo tradition.

Danae—Female—Mediterranean

An oracle told Acrisius that the son of Danae would one day kill him. To escape this fate, Acrisius locked Danae away. Because Zeus held great lust for her, he came to her as a shower of gold (one of his preferred tricks) and together they became the parents of Perseus who later killed Acrisius just as fate had said he would. The message here seems to be two-fold, the first being that lust tends to triumph over precaution. The second is that the ancient Greeks clearly believed in the concept of Fate founded in the nature of a person, as opposed to the will of the gods.

Dakini—Female—Near East

Hindu goddess associated with the Muladhara chakra (base of the spine). Sometimes described as an aspect of Shakti. See also Rakini, Lakini, Kakini, Sakini, and Hakini. Do not confuse with the Tibetan Dankinis.

Dankinis, The—Female—Central Asia

(Also known as The Kadomas)

Five Tibetan goddesses that represent the Tibetan model of five principle directions (North, South, East, West, and Center). They were often shown skyclad as a symbol that they

bring the naked truth. See Vajra, Ratna, Padma, Karma, and Buddha, Dankinis. Note: Do not confuse with the Hindu goddess Daikin.

Daramulum—Male—Australia

'One leg'—Australian Aborigine god to whom one prays and makes tribute to bring power in medicine and spellcraft. He is associated with initiation rites, especially of the ascension into manhood.

Dardawigal—Male—Australia

Australian Aborigine god who was the personification of Evil and antagonist to Baiame.

Dragon—Male—Middle East

Animal associations: Fish, Snake (serpent)

Most often cited as a mystical creature, some Neo-Pagan literature states that Dragon is also the name of a god in the early Middle Eastern religion of Philistia. I have not found this to be the case in mainstream scholarly works.

Daikoku—Male—Far East

(Also known as Daikoko-tenn)

Animal association: Rat (white)

Japanese god of prosperity, especially the prosperity of agricultural harvest.

Damkina—Females—Mediterranean

Husband: Ea

Animal association: Lion

Babylonian/Sumerian goddess and chief lover of Ea/Enki. Despite his seduction of many other goddesses, she remained by his side and worked with him as partner in most matters.

Damgalnuna—See Damkina

Dana—Female—Central Europe

(Also known as Danu, Dan, Dann)

Father: Delbaeth

Mother: Ernmas

Husband: Balor

Irish Mother and Earth goddess. Principle leader of the Tuatha Dé Danann, an Irish race of gods.

Danh—Male—Africa

(Also known as Dan Petro [Haitian Voodoo])

Animal association: Snake

African god of negotiating with Nature who migrated to the Caribbean to become Dan Petro, the Haitian Voodoo loa of farming.

Dardanus—Male—Mediterranean

(Also known as Dardanos)

Father: Zeus

Mother: Electra

Wife: Batea

Greek God and founder of Dardania (later called Troy).

Dea Artio—Female—Central Europe

Animal association—Bear

Celtic goddess of the Bear cults.

Dea Tacita—Female—Mediterranean

(Also known as Dea Tacti)

Roman goddess of silence, of keeping secrets, and of death. Associated strongly with Larentia.

Dechtire—Female—Central Europe

(Also known as Dectera)

Father: Cathbad

Lover: Lugh

Irish mother of Setanta by Lugh. Her son went on to kill the hound of Culann the Smith, after which he was known as Cuchulainn.

Delbaeth—Male—Central Europe

Father: Oghma Grainaineach

Lover: Ernmas

Irish god and father, by Ernmas, of the Morrigan.

Demeter—Female—Mediterranean

Father: Cronus

Mother: Rhea

Lover: Zeus, Iasion

Daughter: Persephone by Zeus

Animal associations: Cock, Crane, Dove, Lion, Pig, Fish, Ant

Plant associations: Barley, Bay, Beans (all), Cypress, Frankincense, Myrrh, Pennyroyal, Pomegranate, Rose, Sunflower, Wheat, Poppy (white), and all cultivated plants that bear food.

'Barley Mother'—Greek goddess associated with Spring Equinox and Bealtaine fertility rites. She is often cited as a 'corn goddess,' but with the modern use of the term corn to mean a specific plant, she is better termed a grain goddess, especially barley. She taught humanity how to plow and negotiate with Nature.

Oil Recipe

8 drops Frankincense essential oil

6 drops Otto of Rose

5 drops Cypress essential oil

1/2 ounce base oil

Deucalion—Male—Mediterranean

Father: Prometheus

Wife: Pyrrha

'New-wine Sailor'—Greek story of the Great Flood centered on Prometheus warning his son Deucalion, who built an ark capable of surviving the flood. Deucalion and his wife, Pyrrha, then repopulated the Earth.

Devaki—Female—Near East

Husband: Vaseduva

Hindu mother of Krishna. Sometimes cited as an avatar/incarnation of Aditi.

Devi—Female—Near East

Animal association: Swan

'Goddess'—Hindu All Mother. Goddess of both motherly and romantic love. She is the mother of the Hindu culture.

Dharma—Male—Near East

Wife: Sradda, Samnati, Medha

Hindu personification of duty (dharma) to community, self, family, and to the gods themselves. Husband to either one, two, or three of the listed wives, depending on specific cite. Similar to Pietas (Roman Goddess) and representative of the principle presented in the Wiccan Rede as *will*.

Dhatri—Male—Near East
Father: Kashyapa
Mother: Aditi

Dhatri is one of the Adityas. The Hindu month Kartika (October 23–November 21) is sacred to Dhatri. See Adityas.

Dianchecht—Male—Central Europe
Son: Cain, Miach
Daughter: Airmid

Irish god of healing and of medicine. He is often cited as the father of modern medicine. Patron of doctors, healers, pharmacists, and herbalists.

Dian—Male—Central Europe
Mother: Carman

'*Violence*'—One of the aspects of the Irish Triple God of Evil. The other two aspects are Dub and Dother. It is interesting to note the name similarity to the Roman Diana, who is said in *Aradia: Gospel of Witches* to have sent her daughter Aradia to show the Witches the ways of magick such that they can violently overthrow their oppressors. Dian's mother is said to be Carman, a Witch herself who taught her children the ways of Witchcraft that they might combat the people of the goddess Danu.

Diana—Female—Mediterranean
(Also known as Tana [Etruscan])
Lover: Lucifer, Endymion
Animal associations: Alligator, Bear, Cat, Dear (especially stag), Dog, Elephant, Antelope, Bee, Owl
Plant associations: Acacia, Almond, Apple, Banyan, Beech, Birch, Damiana, Dittany of Crete, Fir, Ginseng, Hazelnut, Jasmine, Mandrake, Mugwort, Mulberry, Oak, Rue, Willow, Wormwood

Roman moon goddess of Nature, childbirth, fertility, and hunting. Her sacred month is October. She has been associated with the fertility of the Earth, with mountains, and the deep forest. She was patron of the working and lower economic class, a goddess of slaves and wage slaves of past and present. Her following likely persisted well into the rule of Christian Europe when it was said she was the Goddess of Pagans. Her worship may have continued uninterrupted to the present day. See also Lucifer, Aradia, and Dian. Dian might be a male Irish counterpart, although this is wild speculation on my part.

Incense Recipe

2 part Gum Arabic
1 part Acacia Flowers
1 part Jasmine Flowers
1 pinch Wormwood
1 pinch Mugwort
A few apple seeds
Enough Diana oil or Jasmine absolute to bind

Oil Recipe

10 drops Jasmine absolute
10 drops Birch oil
1/2 ounce base oil (try a 50/50 mixture of Almond and Hazelnut oil)

Dianus—Male—Mediterranean
Plant association: Fig, Oak

Roman oak god who evolved into Janus.

Diiwica—Female—Central Europe
(Also known as Devana, Dziewona)
Animal associations: Horse, Dog

Slavic goddess of the hunt. Associated with Diana. There could be a root word connection between her name and the word Wicca/Wica, especially considering the late 1800s use of the word *Wicca* by Leland in reference to the worship of Diana and other remnants of the Mediterranean and European Pagans.

Dike—Female—Mediterranean

'*Justice*' or '*Natural law*'—Greek goddess of justice for humanity, but a justice connected with natural law rather than the law of man. When Zeus saw that her job of keeping humanity in tune with the laws of Nature was impossible, he recalled her to Olympus where she now resides. She is most often cited as a being virgin. However, sometimes citations indicate she never had sex with men, implying that her affections are lesbian in nature. She is one of the Horae with her sisters Irene and Eunomia.

Dionysus—Male—Mediterranean

(Also known as Dionysos)

Father: Zeus

Mother: Semele

Wife: Ariadne

Lover: Adonis, Althea, Hermaphrodite

Animal associations: Bull, Cheetah, Lion, Panther, Tiger, Fox, Donkey, Elephant, Goat, Ram, Bee, Deer (fawn)

Plant associations: Agaric Mushroom (also all toadstools and mushrooms to a lesser degree), Apple, Fennel, Fig, Ivy (common), Juniper, Patchouli, Pine, Pomegranate, Vine (grape)

Greek god of fertility in each order of life. He is most often cited as the god of wine. While that is certainly a valid association, he is called on more for the intoxication of love and of merriment than simple drunkenness. Dionysus is an educated god for an educated devotee. Having been the lover of Adonis and Hermaphrodite, he is an excellent example of bisexual deity forms and has thus been adopted by many in the gay, lesbian, and bisexual community as a patron. Although he is associated strongly with Bacchus, there is a clear difference. To understand that difference, consider James Morrison in his early years (Dionysus) and then in his later years just prior to his leaving the United States (Bacchus).

Incense Recipe

8 parts pine needles (or 2 part pitch and 6 part sandalwood)

5 part Sandalwood (white/yellow)

4 part Juniper berries

1 part raisins

Enough Dionysus or Patchouli essential oil to bind (better to use Patchouli)

Oil Recipe

9 drops Patchouli essential oil

6 drops Juniper essential oil

3 drops Fennel essential oil

3 drops Pine essential oil

1/2 ounce grape seed oil

3 drops red wine

2 raisins

Discordia—Female—Mediterranean

Roman goddess of disorder, discord, and chaos in opposition to Concordia. She was said to precede Mars, sometimes the chariot of Mars, thus noting that discord and chaos often lead to war. See also Eris (Greek equivalent).

Oil Recipe

Cover your skyclad body with baby oil and try to play Twister while balancing your checkbook.

Disocuri—Male—Mediterranean

(Also known as Dios kouroi)

'Sons of Zeus'—Greek title of the twin brothers Pollux and Castor born of Leda and Zeus who are associated with the astrological sign Gemini.

Diti—Female—Near East

Father: Daksha

Husband: Kashyapa

Hindu mother goddess of both Earth and the endless sky.

Dolma—Female—Central Asia

(Also known as White Tara)

Animal association: Lion

Plant association: Lotus

National goddess of Tibet before Tibet was illegally taken by communist China. An erotic goddess of passion and compassion. She tells us that wisdom can go hand in hand with sexuality, and that the faithful mother can also be a sensual wife.

Don—Female—Central Europe

Husband: Beli

Sons: Amathaon Caswallawn, Govannon, and Gwydion by Beli

Daughter: Arianrhod by Beli

Animal association: Gull

Welsh All Mother goddess similar to the Irish Danu.

Dother—Male—Central Europe

Mother: Carman

'Evil'—One of the aspects of the Irish Triple God of Evil. The other two aspects are Dub and Dian.

Duamutef—Male—Africa

(Also known as Tuamutef)

Father: Horus

Mother: Isis

Animal association: Jackal

Egyptian god associated with the element Fire and with the East. Associated with the Goddess Neith. Wiccans who have adopted an Egyptian pantheon often associate their Quarters to align with Egyptian associations made with the Four Sons of Horus. The other three are Hapi, Imset, and Kebechsenef.

Dub—Male—Central Europe

Mother: Carman

'Darkness'—One of the aspects of the Irish Triple God of Evil. The other two aspects are Dother and Dian.

Dumuzi—Male—Middle East/Mediterranean

Animal association: Bull

Holiday: Fall Equinox

Sumerian mortal who married Inanna to bring fertility to his land. So offended was his wife at his lack of sensitivity and concern for her needs, that she ordered him to leave the world of the living for six months out of the year, thus bringing the barren months of Summer. He was allowed to return to the land of the living at Fall Equinox (the beginning of the Sumerian new year) but then had to leave again at Spring Equinox. Upon his return to his wife's bed, all was well, as absence makes the heart grow fonder. Here we see clearly the principle of separation for the sake of union, but we see something else that is of key note in understanding Wicca as a world religion. The story of Dumuzi leaving every Fall Equinox is incredibly similar to the story of Persephone. The main difference is the gender of the two subjects and the time in which their story was told. During the time of Persephone's story, the area surrounding her story was overly cold and barren in the winter (while she was gone). During the time of Dumuzi's story, the area surrounding his story was overly hot and thus barren (while he was gone).

Durga—Female—Near East

Animal associations: Lion, Tiger, Bison

Husband: Shiva

Hindu avatar/incarnation of Parvati.

Dwyvach—Female—Central Europe

Husband: Dwyvan

See Dwyvan for her story.

Dwyvan—Male—Central Europe

Wife: Dwyvach

Welsh man who survived the Great Flood with his wife Dwyvach. Together, they built an ark called Nefyed Nav Nevion, filled it with animals, and survived the flood. Their story, combined with the Irish, seems the most likely origin for the Christian story of Noah and his ark.

Dyaus—Male—Near East

(Also known as Dyaush, Dyaush-Pitir)

Wife: Prithvi

'Sky father'—Hindu lord of the sky and of the clouds that float there. As such, a fertility god granting rain that fertilizes crops.

Dylan—Male—Central Europe

Animal association: Fish (silver)

Father: Gwydion

Mother: Arianrhod

Wife: Lady of the Lake

'Sea'—Welsh god who was born by Arianrhod before she relinquished her virginity.

Ea—God—Mediterranean
(Also known as Ea-Oannes, Ea-Onne, Enki [Sumerian])
Father: Ansar
Mother: Kishar
Wife: Damkina
Son: Adapa, Marduk
Daughter: Gasmu, Inanna, Nanshe, and Nina
Note: His mother is sometimes cited as Bau.
Animal associations: Dolphin, Goat, Fish, Turtle, Tortoise, Frog, Antelope, Ram
Plant association: Cedar

Babylonian/Sumerian god of magick, especially Water magick, and wisdom. He taught man about culture, community, and civilization building. Patron of community builders.

Incense Recipe
1 part Cedar
1 part Gum Arabic

Ea-Oanne—See Ea

Ea-Oannes—See Ea

Ebisu—Male—Far East
Father: Daikoku

Japanese god of labor, especially labor related to fishing and prosperity brought about by the sea.

Ehecatl—Male—South America
'Wind'—Aztec god of the Wind who fell so deeply in love with a mortal woman named Mayahuel that all of humanity learned love from his example.

Eingana—Female—Australia
Animal association: Snake

Aboriginal Australian All Mother and Creator goddess who resides in the dream time. Prior to her birthing of all creatures, she had no vagina but could not stop dreaming the wondrous creatures into existence inside her womb. Realizing she was in great pain as her womb swelled, Barraiya (a fellow god) sliced her open with a spear. From that womb sprang all the animals of the world. That they would not suffer the same pain, each female creature was born with the wound already in place. The link between dream time and creation speaks volumes to the Wiccan belief in, for lack of a better word, the Etheric World.

Eire—Female—Central Europe
(Also known as Eriu, Eyre, Eiriu)

With Banbha and Fodhla, she is an Irish Triple Goddess. Her name is the origin of the word *Ireland* in the former form Eire Land.

Eite—Male—Central Europe
Lover: Persipnei
Etruscan god of the Underworld.

Ek Chuah—Male—South America
(Also known as Ekchuah)
Animal association: Scorpion

'Black war lord'—Mayan god of war who was fierce in battle. Also a kind patron of merchants and travelers, but not both at the same time. His story, like so many others, tells us that prosperity and war are often opposite points on the same scale. Greater prosperity leads to less war. More war leads to less prosperity.

El—Male—Mediterranean
(Also known as El Elyon ['God Most Holy'])
Father: Uranus
Wife: Elat
Lover: Damkina
Animal association: Bull

'God'—Supreme Canaanite God who is the most likely source from which the story of Yahweh/Jehovah is most likely derived.

Elat—Female—Mediterranean
(Also known as Asherat of the Sea [Asheratian])
Husband: El

'*Goddess*'—Canaanite goddess and wife to El. She is associated with the ocean, especially the shores where she enjoys long walks, sometimes hand in hand with her husband, El, when not tending to her children.

Electra—Female—Mediterranean
Father: Agamemnon
Mother: Clytemnestra

Greek goddess of revenge. After her father was killed by his adulteress wife and her lover Aegisthos, Electra plotted revenge with her brother Orestes. There is some dispute to whether or not Electra helped execute the plot. At a minimum, she planned the murders and Orestes carried them out. Later, she stood loyally by her brother's side, defending him at every step. See Orestes for the rest of the story.

Eleggua—Male—African/Caribbean/South America

In Santeria, his name is Eleggua

In Voodoo, his name is Legba/Liba

In Africa, his name is Elegba

Also variously known as Esu/Eshu (West Africa) and Exu (Brazil)

Saint associations: St. Anthony (most often), others include St. Michael, St. Peter, St. Martin de Porres, St. Benito

Holidays: Feast of Saint Anthony of Paudua on June 13, Feast of the Holy Infant of Atocha on January 1

Plant associations: Allspice, Anise, Angelica, Asafoetida, Balm of Gilead, Basil, Calamus, Calendula, Camphor, Cayenne, Clove, Coffee, Copal, Cumin, Dill, Dragon's Blood, Eucalyptus, Garlic, Ginger, Grains of Paradise, Geranium, Heather, Heliotrope, Hibiscus, Honeysuckle, Horehound, Hyacinth (wild), Hyssop, Juniper, Lavender, Lemon Balm, Lilac, Lime, Lotus, Mallow (blue), Mandrake, Meadowsweet, Mimosa, Mint, Mistletoe (American), Mugwort, Myrrh, Orange (sweet and bitter), Orris, Orange Bergamot, Peppermint, Pine, Rosemary, Rue, Sage, Sandalwood (white/yellow), Snapdragon, Thistle (greater), Vetivert, Violet, Valerian, Vervain, Wormwood

In Africa, he is god of the crossroads. In migration into Santeria, he becomes Orisha and trickster similar to the North Europe Loki or the North America Coyote. He can be a powerful ally in both magick and the mundane. But in all matters he must be given great respect and accepted as he is rather than as one might want to see him. He treats his devotees with what can best be summed up as tough love.

Incense Recipe

2 part Dragon's Blood
1 part Copal
1 part Orris Root
1 part Juniper Berries
1 pinch ground coffee bean
Enough Eleggua or Lavender oil to bind

Oil Recipe

8 drops Clove oil
8 drops Lavender oil
4 drops Eucalyptus or Sandalwood oil
1/2 ounce base oil

Elihino—Female—North America
Cherokee Earth Mother Goddess.

Elium—Male—Mediterranean
Wife: Berus
Phoenician All Father.

Elli—Female—North Europe
(Also known as Elle)

Teutonic personification of old age. She was the only one to ever beat Thor at a wrestling match, the observation being that one cannot beat old age.

Embla Female Northern Europe
Husband: Ask

Scandinavian goddess much like the Christian Lilith prior to her replacement by Eve. Created by Odin from either the elm tree or, by a few references, grapevine after the Great Flood. Her story is most likely the story of humanity's migration into Scandinavia after the flood that opened up the Fertile Crescent and northern portions of the Middle East to migration.

Emer—Female—Central Europe
Husband: Cuchulain

Irish goddess who demonstrates an enormous amount of self-worth. Before she would allow Cuchulain into her bed, she insisted that he accomplish several great tasks—not that she needed them done, she just needed him to show her that he felt she was worth the great effort. With full knowledge that the tasks were given for this purpose, he accommodated her requests because he knew there was no other way to prove his devotion.

Endymion—Male—Mediterranean
(Also known as Endamone)
Lover: Selene

Greek mortal who was so loved by Selene that she begged Zeus to make him immortal. He did, but at the cost of Endymion's eternal sleep. Perhaps a god form that symbolizes humanity, visited nightly by the Moon (Selene) as we sleep. See Selene for more of the story. In the book *Aradia: Gospel of Witches*, this story is identified with Endymion and Tana (an Etruscan name of Diana) rather than Selene.

Enlil—Male—Mediterranean/Middle East
Father: Anu
Mother: Anat
Wife: Ninlil
Note: Mother sometimes listed as 'Ki' because she is wife to 'An' and in some views, An is a form of Anu (father to Enlil).
Animal association: Dragon (snake)

'Lord wind'—Babylonian/Sumerian storm god who holds the tablets of destiny and fate and who causes hardship when it is necessary. In Babylonian and Sumerian lore he is responsible, in part, for the Great Flood. Also seen as a god of the mountains.

Enki—Male—Mediterranean
Mother: Bau
Wife: Ninhursag
Lover: Ninsar, Ninkurra, Uttu
Animal associations: Antelope, Lion, Fox, Cattle (bull), Frog

Sometimes cited as the father of Ishtar. Enki is a Sumerian water god who had sexual relations with his daughter Ninsar, with his granddaughter Ninkurra, and with his great-granddaughter Uttu. As a result, his wife Ninhursag cursed him. Believing it was in Enki's nature to have conducted himself as he did, the gods convinced Ninhursag to change her curse to better address his nature. This speaks to us of our duty to negotiate nature. While the nature of a thing like water can be to kill (flood), it can be harnessed to provide clean energy. While the nature of a creature might be to love, we negotiate with that nature. That negotiation is the process by which we understand will and that negotiator is the will itself. Again we see: Love is the law, but love ONLY under will. Some cite Enki as another name for Ea. Those cites are probably the result of Bau (Mother of Enki) being listed as mother of Ea. Due to this link, Inanna is sometimes cited as daughter of Enki.

Enmesarra—Male—Mesopotamia
Wife: Ninmesarra
Animal association: Pigeon

'Lord of Law'—Sumerian god of the Underworld. In noting the meaning of his name, it is important that we do not interpret the word law to mean the law of humanity. The translation might better be to 'Lord of Mes,' mes being the power of the law (love) as expressed in 'Love is the law.' Not a written law. Enmesarra is Lord of that force by which communities and entire civilizations are built. That force is the unification principle of the Fifth Element.

Ennoia—Female—Mediterranean/Middle East

Gnostic Aeon of thought and clear intent.

Enodia—Female—Mediterranean
Animal association: Dog

Greek goddess of the crossroads and transition. Called on at the moment of decision to help bring that decision but not necessarily the right or most correct. Often there is not one choice more right or correct.

Enurta—Male—Mediterranean

Father: Enlil

Wife: Gula

Babylonian god of war and triumph over physical confrontations.

Eos—Female—Mediterranean

(Also known as Aurora)

Father: Hyperion

Mother: Theia

Husband: Astraeus (first)

Animal association: Horse (Pegasus)

'*Dawn*'—Greek mother of the four Winds and personification of Dawn. See also her sons Boreas, Zephyrus, Eurus, and Notus. She was much loved by Ares. That love brought the jealousy of Aphrodite, who also loved Ares greatly. As revenge, Aphrodite caused Eos to fall in love with several others, including Orion. Orion was later killed and Eos felt much grief. The story changed as did her men, but at the end of each relationship Eos was miserable, and Aphrodite was usually the cause. The story here seems to be a warning about the pains that love can bring one who does not have clear intent or who desires another woman's man.

Eostra—Female—Central Europe/North Europe

(Also known as Ostara, Eostre, Eastre)

Animal association: Hare

Plant association: Birch

Holiday: Easter

Germanic personification of sunrise who is associated with the Spring, and thus a fertility goddess in her own right. She is often cited as having a kin familiar of a hare whom she changes into a bird as a magic trick to amuse and entertain children, which she loves. As a result of the transformation, the hare laid wondrously colored eggs that she gave to the children. She is one of the many wonderful examples of why Wiccans have no reason to reject cultural holidays. After all, in her story we see that Easter (typically rejected by many Wiccans) is the celebration of the Goddess Eostra (or Eastre). It is interesting to note that the Christian celebration of Easter marks the celebration of the rising of the son of their god, and the Pagan celebration of Easter celebrates the rising of the Sun, Eostra (or Eastre).

Epona—Female—Central Europe/Mediterranean

Animal association: Horse, Goose, Dog

Celtic horse goddess who was involved in the judging of souls after human death. So popular did she become in the Roman army that a temple was erected to her in the Roman capital. From the spread of her worship from the Celts to the Romans, we see that conflict tends to generate a two-way flow of cultural traditions.

Epunamun—Male—South America

Araucanian god of war who was so vicious in battle that even his own people had occasion to fear him.

Erato—Female—Mediterranean

'*Lovely*'—Greek muse of love poetry. See also Muses, The.

Erh-lang—Male—China

(Also known as Er-lang)

Animal association: Dog

Master of the dogs of Heaven who destroys evil by sending his dogs to devour it in any form.

Erigone—Female—Mediterranean

Father: Icarius

Animal association: Dog

Plant association: Pine

Greek daughter of Icarius. When she found that her father had been put to death unjustly by her own people due to a misunderstanding, she committed suicide by hanging herself from a pine tree. Her kin familiar is a dog named Marea. When Dionysus found what had happened, he caused all the maidens of the land to become insane and to take their own lives as did Erigone.

Erinyes, The—Female—Mediterranean

(Also known as The Eumenides)

Animal association: Snake (serpent)

Three Greek goddesses of both justice and vengeance, reminding us that the lines between the two are often blurred. See also Alecto, Megaera, and Tisiphone.

Eris—Female—Mediterranean

'Strife'—Greek goddess similar to the Roman Discordia. She demonstrates how small actions of discord can turn into huge amounts of strife. Her constant companion is her brother Ares. As he is god of war, we see a clear message telling us that discord and strife are often accompanied by war. See Peleus for an excellent example of this principle.

Eros—Male—Mediterranean

Father: Erebus

Mother: Nyx

Lover: Psyche

Animal associations: Goose, Hare

Plant associations: Bay, Olive, Rose (especially red), Saffron (Spanish), Yarrow

'Desire'—Greek god who is most often seen as a god of love. He is also the god who calls attention to the value of a person's lineage and the importance of relationships over individuality. Historically and today, he is called on to bless both heterosexual as well as homosexual relationships. He was called on by gay soldiers to give them blessings before battle. When we consider the meaning of his name, we see an interesting commentary on the nature of soul (his lover Psyche). Soul is not without desire. This is the principle on which I base the principle of animals having soul, as they certainly have desire. See Psyche for more information.

Incense Recipe

4 part Rose petals (match color to intent)

2 part Bay leaf

1 part Gum Arabic

Enough Eros or Otto of Rose to bind (Otto of Rose is best)

Oil Recipe

9 drops Bay essential oil

6 drops Yarrow essential oil

6 drops Otto of Rose

1/2 ounce Olive oil

Erebus—Male—Mediterranean

Father: Chaos

Lover: Nyx

Greek god whose name is also a reference to a region in which souls must pass before entering the afterlife/Underworld. Nyx is sometimes cited as his sister, other times his mother. See Chaos for an explanation.

Ereshkigal—Female—Middle East/Mediterranean

Lover: Nergal

Sumero-Babylonian goddess of the Underworld. She is considered dark and violent, lashing at the souls of those who have not lived a good life. With her lover Nergal, we see a clear personification of many of the attributes Christianity has given to Satan. See Nergal for the rest of the story.

Erichthonius—Male—Mediterranean

(Also known as Erechtheus)

Father: Hephaestus

Mother: Athena by adoption, Gaia by birth

Greek god who was adopted and raised by Athena, who became King of Athens, where he sung the praises of his mother that the worship of Athena spread to all of Athens and beyond.

Erzulie—Female—Africa/Caribbean/South America

(Also known as La Siren)

Plant associations: Basil, Cardamom, Frankincense

May be a unique deity or may be another name for Oshun. There is evidence to support either. See Oshun.

Incense Recipe

2 parts Frankincense
1 part Cardamom
1 part Basil

Oil Recipe

10 drops Basil oil
10 drops Cardamom oil
1/2 ounce base oil

Esaugetuh Emissee—Male—North America
'Master of breath'—Muskogean (Creek) All Father and Creator god who repopulated the world after the Great Flood.

Eschetewuarha—Female—South America
Husband: Great Spirit
Chamacoco Mother Goddess who insures that humanity receives rain from the cloud bird Osasero. Her husband is the Great Spirit.

Essus—Male—Central Europe
(Also known as Esus)
Lover: Artio
Plant associations: Oak
Celtic god of agriculture and negotiations with Nature.

Eunomia—Female—Mediterranean
'Good order'—Greek goddess of order and the laws of man (legislature) who lives with humanity, assisting us to create legislature that will cause the laws of man to be in harmony with the laws of Nature. She is one of the Horae with her sisters Dike and Irene.

Euphrosyne—Female—Mediterranean
Father: Zeus
Mother: Euronyme
'Rejoices the heart' or *'Happiness'*—One of the Three Graces found in Greek lore. Her parents are sometimes cited as Dionysus and Aphrodite. See also Thalia and Aglaia.

Europa—Female—Mediterranean
Husband: Asterius
Lover: Zeus
Animal associations: Cow, Dog
One of the many loves of Zeus. To Europa, he gave a dog named Laelaps who became her kin familiar. After her relationship with Zeus, she married Asterius.

Eurus—Male—Mediterranean
Father: Astraeus
Mother: Eos
Greek god of the East Wind associated with the East Quarter (Air) in Wiccan ritual.

Euterpe—Female—Mediterranean
'Delight,' 'Source of Rejoice,' or *'Rejoicing Well'*—Greek muse of wind instruments. See also Muses, The.

Evander—Male—Mediterranean
(Also known as Euandros)
Father: Hermes
Mother: Carmenta
Roman deity who brought the Greek culture to Rome, thus mingling the pantheons and traditions in such a way that the citizens of Rome could see that although at odds with each other for some time, the two could coexist and even compliment each other.

Eve—Female—Middle East
(Also known as Haiwa [Arabic])
Second wife of Adam. See Adam and Lilith.

Evenor—Male—Mediterranean
Wife: Leucippe
Greek Earth-born/primeval man and husband to the nymph Leucippe. His wife accompanied Persephone when she was kidnapped by Hades.

Excellent Archer—Male—Chinese
Wife: Ch'ang-o
Chinese god whose anger was feared by all, including his wife. To escape his anger, she fled to the moon after stealing the drink of immortality from him. His story warns folk of the damage unchained anger can do to a marriage.

Fama—Female—Mediterranean

'Fame'—Roman personification of fame and goddess of rumor. Everything that she said was first said softly to the few to whom she spoke and then repeated over and over until it was almost deafening. Sometimes described as a terrifying creature with a great number of ears, eyes, and tongues. If she has a motto, it is 'No publicity is bad publicity.'

Fand—Female—Central Europe

Husband: Manannan Mac Lir

Irish fairy queen who married Manannan Mac Lir but whose marriage ended in divorce. Her story shows support for the Wiccan principle of handfasting being dissolvable.

Farbauti—Male—North Europe

Wife: Laufey

'Cruel striker'—Scandinavian god of fire whose story is partially responsible for the creation of Merlin. Seen sometimes as the Scandinavian Merlin, his more important story can be found in the relationship between he and his wife. She provided the wood for his fire, not for the fire created by him, but for his existence itself, his soul. This speaks of action being masculine, but the force behind that action being feminine. It is very similar to the Hindu principle that states the masculine is the fountainhead, but the feminine is the fountain or water.

Fates, The—Female—Mediterranean

(Also known as The Moirae)

Father: Zeus

Mother: Themis

Animal associations: Dove, Spider

Greek three daughters of Zeus and Themis who presided on the destiny of mortals. Their blessings are called at handfasting in so much to say that we respect the will of the gods even in the matters of human union. See Clotho, Lachesis, and Atropos.

Clotho—Spins the thread of life.

Lachesis—Presents the element of chance.

Atropos—She who cuts the thread.

Fati—Male—Polynesian

Father: Roua

Mother: Taonoui

Polynesian personification of the moon and moon god.

Fauna—Female—Mediterranean

(Also known as Marica)

Husband: Faunus

Plant association: Pine

Roman Earth and fertility goddess. She is sometimes said to be another name for Bona Dea. See also Faunus.

Faunus—Male—Mediterranean

(Also known as Lupercus)

Father: Picus

Wife: Fauna

Animal associations: Goat, Bee

Plant associations: Bay, Olive, Patchouli, Pine

Roman god of fertility and Nature. Provides visions as we sleep, especially when sleeping outdoors. With his wife, he shares the holiday Lupercalia. Today, this holiday is called Valentine's Day. He is sometimes cited as father of Fauna, as well.

Incense Recipe

4 parts pine needles (or 1 part pitch and 3 part sandalwood)

2 part Gum Arabic

1 part Bay leaf

Enough Faunus or Pine essential oil to bind.

Oil Recipe

9 drops Pine essential oil

9 drops Bay essential oil

3 drops Patchouli essential oil

1/2 ounce Olive oil

Favonius—Male—Mediterranean

Roman god of the West Wind similar to the Greek Zephyrus. The other three are Aquilo, Auster, and Vulturnus.

Februus—Male—Mediterranean

Etruscan/Roman Underworld god for whom the month of February is named.

Felicitas—Female—Mediterranean

Roman personification and goddess of success.

Fene-Ma-So—Male—Africa
Animal association: Vulture

West African sky god who took the form of a vulture, the king of the birds, to observe happenings on Earth.

Feng-huang—Male—Central Asia
(Also known as Feng Haang)

Chinese creature guardian of the South. Similar to the phoenix, but with the head of a pheasant and the body of a peacock. He presides over the primordial attributes of divinity. The other three guardians are Ch'i-lin, Gui Xian, and Long. They are collectively known as the Ssu Ling.

Fenrir, The—Male—North Europe
(Also known as Fenris, Fenrisúlfr, and The Fenris Wolf)
Father: Loki
Mother: Angurboda
Animal association: Wolf

Scandinavian giant in the form of a wolf whom prophecy states will one day devour the world. Fearing this prophecy, the Norse gods locked the Fenrir in a cage. Even as a pup, the Fenrir was so terrifying that only their god of war was brave enough to feed it. Once it had grown into adulthood, the gods decided it had to be destroyed or rendered harmless. But they were scared to try and harm the creature, so they decided to trick it, twice. Their first trick failed. Their second is destined to fail, at which point Ragnarok, the Doom of the Gods, will be announced. One of the three children of Angurboda and Loki in which we see the number three as the number of not only good fate, but of ill fate. The other two children are Jormungand and Hel.

Fergus—Male—Central Europe
Wife: Flidais
Lover: Queen Medb (most notably)

'Virility'—The name Fergus is used widely in Irish lore; however, one Fergus stands out in respect to polyamorous (sexually open) relationships. Such was Fergus' sexual desire, that he was known widely for his adulterous relations with mortal women. Such was his wife's accepting of his practices while she was away, that she bragged that it took seven mortal women to satisfy the thirst that she alone could quench. As a very strong sexual innuendo, he is often times called 'The Great Horse.'

Feronia (1)—Female—Mediterranean
Animal association: Wolf

Roman goddess of crop fertility who was seen as patron and freer of servitude. Note: Not to be confused with Feronia (Etruscan fire goddess).

Feronia (2)—Female—Mediterranean

Etruscan Fire goddess who brought both human and plant fertility. Possibly a reference to the fire of lust that causes human fertility, or to the burning of fields to bring fertility to the soil.

Fides—Male/Female—Central Europe

'Faith'—Roman goddess (sometimes cited as god) of good faith. In the Wiccan religion, Fides is the patron of the contract set forth at any handfasting, but particularly at the third handfasting. S/he is also the patron of fidelity in a romantic relationship; however, in that aspect he should not be considered the patron of monogamous relationships alone. Instead, he is the patron of all relationships in which a promise is kept, but particularly of monogamous relationships. Patron of all oral contracts.

Fintaan—Male—Central Europe
Wife: Cesara

Irish survivor of the Great Flood. See Bith for the story.

Flidais—Female—Central Europe
Husband: Fergus
Animal association: Deer

Irish goddess who could be the patron of polyamorous couples. See Fergus for the story of her marriage.

Flora—Female—Mediterranean
Plant association: Hawthorn

Roman goddess of Spring and Spring flowers. With time she became the patron of prostitutes and young women who choose to live a sexually promiscuous lifestyle.

Fodhla—Female—Central Europe

With Eire and Banbha, she is an Irish Triple Goddess.

Forseti—Male—Northern Europe
(Also known as Vorsitzer)
Father: Baldur
Mother: Nanna

Scandinavian god of justice and the peace that justice brings to a community.

Fortuna—Female—Mediterranean
(Also known as Primigenia, Virilis, Respiciens, Muliebris, and Annonaria)

Roman personification and goddess of fortune and fertility. Historically, she was worshiped primarily by mothers and soon-to-be mothers. At some of her rituals, women who were still with their first husbands were the only ones permitted to attend.

Freya—Female—Northern Europe
(Also known as Froya)
Father: Njord
Mother: Skadi
Husband: Od
Lover: Odin
Animal associations: Cat, Falcon, Horse, Boar (sow), Bear, Hare
Plant associations: Apple, Birch, Cowslip, Daisy (especially Ox-eyed), Maidenhair, Mistletoe (European), Myrrh, Primrose, Strawberry

Scandinavian goddess of love and fertility, the most beautiful goddess in the Norse pantheon. She is patron of birth and of the desires that lead to conception. She is said for a time to have been married to Od, which has led many folk to claim she was married to Odin, but that story seems to be based on superficial associations. (Odin's wife better cited as Frigg/Frigga).

Freyr—Male—Northern Europe
(Also known as Frey, Yngvi)
Father: Njord
Mother: Skadi
Wife: Gerda
Animal associations: Boar, Horse

Norse god of rain who is both fertility god and warrior. He is called upon to bless human fertility at Wiccan handfasting. His chariot was drawn by Gullibursti and Slidrurgtanni, two boars.

Frigga—Female—Northern Europe
(Also known as Frig, Frigg)
Husband: Odin
Son: Baldur
Plant associations: Birch, Mistletoe (European)

Frigga is sometimes associated with Freya as if they were one and the same. This was probably a result of the gradual shift towards the promotion of monogamy. For the purpose of historical accuracy, it is best to identify the two separately. Frigga is patron of love, marriage, pregnancy, and childbirth, said to know the destiny of both god and human, but never telling of it. Definitely a non-monogamous goddess, she is said to have had many lovers other than her husband Odin, including Vili and Ve (both his brothers).

Fukurokuju—Male—Far East
Animal associations: Crow, Crane, Deer, Tortoise, Turtle

Japanese Shinto god of health and wisdom.

Furies, The—Female—Mediterranean
(Also known as Erinyes, Eumenides)

Animal association: Dove, Snake

Furrina—Female—Mediterranean
Husband: Neptune
   Roman Earth Mother.

Fu-Hsing—Male—Central Asia
(Also known as Fu-Xing)
Wife: Nu-Kua
Animal associations: Bat, Snake
   'Lucky Star'—Chinese god of happiness who is often depicted surrounded by children.

Gabriel—Male—Middle East/Mediterranean
(Also known as Gabri-el [Hebrew])
   'Man of God'—Semitic god of Water. He is one of the only two angels mentioned by name in the modern Christian Bible. The other is Michael. He was the angel who appeared to the Virgin Mary to foretell her conception of Christ. Gnostic archangel who is associated with the West Quarter in Wiccan, Gnostic, and Ceremonial rituals. The other Quarters are presided upon by Raphael, Michael, and Auriel.

Gad—Male/Female—Middle East
Wife: Gadda
   'Good luck' or *'Good fortune'* (masculine use of the word)—Semitic/Chaldean god of good fate and fortune. Very often, his name is mistranslated to 'God.' Sometimes appears male, other times as female with Gadda as his female counterpart.

Gadda—Female—Middle East
Husband: Gad
   'Good luck' or *'Good fortune'* (feminine use of the word)—Semitic/Chaldean goddess of fortune. See Gad.

Gadel—Male—Central Europe
   Irish god who split the Gaelic tribes into five people and five categories: warriors, poets (bards), historians, doctors, and the working class. Also created the five Gaelic dialects.

Gaia—Female—Mediterranean
(Also known as GAO, GE)
Father: Elium
Mother: Berus
Lover: Hephaestus, Uranus, Poseidon
Plant association: Apple
   'Land' or 'Earth'—Greek Earth Mother whose immaculate conception gave birth to Pontus (the Oceans) and Uranus (the Sky). With them, she forms a holy trinity of Land, Sea, and Sky (a principle generally thought to be Celtic/Druid in origin). Although she is often depicted as the Earth herself, she was historically associated more with the one-third of the Earth that is dry land.

Gama—Male—Far East
Animal associations: Deer (stag), Toad
   Japanese god of long life.

Gandharvas, The—Male—Near East
Animal association: Horse
   This is one of my absolute favorite speculations. In Hindu mythology, the Gandharvas are Air spirits who haunt the forest and mountains. They were typically associated with dry creatures, birds, and animals. They are the mates of the Apsaras (water nymphs) who were associated with fish and other damp creatures. These spirits were said to jealously protect Soma. Now, here is the interesting part. Soma is a word that not only describes the Hindu deity that the Gandharvas protect. The word is also associated with the Fly Agaric Mushroom. Moving right along, the Gandharvas are also Hindu musicians and performers who entertained the line of Indra. Like most stories of bard-type characters, the Gandharvas were rather fond of women's affections (especially young ones) but were not all that fond of formalities. Thus, they are thought of as patrons of romantic relationships prior to or without formality of a wedding or handfasting. Now then, what is that old saying about musicians having the best drugs? While I am not promoting the use of the Fly Agaric Mushroom to improve one's musical inclination (let's face it, they are also called the 'Death

Cap' mushroom), it is interesting to note that even today the use of drugs to achieve altered states of consciousness is still associated with the creative abilities of musicians and other artisans.

Ganesa—Male—Near East

(Also known as Ganessa, Ganesha)

Mother: Parvati

Wife: Buddhi, Siddhi

Animal associations: Elephant, Rat

Plant associations: Damiana, Fenugreek, Jasmine, Peanut, Sesame

Hindu god of wisdom and fortune. He is said to be the remover of obstacles and is associated with higher learning, especially of cultural matters. If you are a fan of classic literature, chances are Ganesa is your patron even if you have not noticed. He is also patron to large men in their search for gracefulness and 'Lord of Hosts.' Ganesa is married to Buddhi and Siddhi simultaneously without much conflict or jealousy. Ganesa can thus be seen as patron to marriages in the order of polyfidelity. He is sometimes described as having soft skin and breasts like a woman. As there is also a degree of lore stating that his worship has involved homoerotic rituals and anal sex, he is sometimes seen as a bisexual deity. However, his chief description would be the perfect host to the many guests invited to his worship and his home.

Incense Recipe

2 part Sandalwood (yellow/white)

1 part Jasmine flower

1 part Damiana

Enough Ganesa or Jasmine absolute to bind

Oil Recipe

12 drops Jasmine absolute

9 drops Damiana tincture

1/4 ounce sesame oil

Ganymede—Male—Mediterranean

(Also known as Granymedes)

Father: Tros

Mother: Callirhoe

Animal associations: Eagle, Peacock

Plant associations: Coconut, Olive

Greek god who served as cup bearer to Zeus. He is thus associated with the chalice of Wiccan rituals and is the patron of fathers and other men in the act of giving away the bride at Wiccan handfasting. There is clear reference to Zeus also being his lover. This union with Zeus, his title 'Cup Bearer,' and the associations made with the cup (chalice) in Wiccan ritual may well be useful to the gay Wiccan community in their development of Wiccan rituals.

Gauri—Female—Near East

Husband: Varuna

Animal association: Cow

Plant association: Rice

'Fair' (reference to her light-colored skin)—Hindu mother goddess as balance to Kali.

Gavida—Male—Central Europe

Irish god who is patron to metal workers. May be another name for Goibniu and Govannon.

Gayomart—Male—Middle East/Mediterranean

Animal association: Bull

'Dying life'—Initially the Persian first man, similar to Adam, created by Ahura Mazda. He lived for thousands of years. From his body sprang the twin children who would become the Persian Adam and Eve. Although Mashia and Mashiane are cited here as brother and sister, neither was born of mother and father. Instead, they were born as twins of the spirit of Gayomart sometime after his death. Hence, their marriage was not incestuous.

Geb—Male—Africa

(Also known as Seb, Keb)

Father: Shu

Mother: Tefnut

Wife: Nut

Animal associations: Duck, Goose

Egyptian god of the Earth whose skin was at times green as the growing plants or black as the fertile farm land surrounding the Nile. In addition to being an Earth god, he prevented evil souls from rising to Heaven. This is perhaps similar to the modern Krishna idea that earthly pleasures prevent one from ascending beyond this level of existence. In Wiccan ritual he is associated with the North/ Earth Quarter. See also Ra, Tefnut, Shu, and Nut.

Gefion—Female —— Northern Europe

(Also known as Gefjon)

Animal associations: Cattle (Ox)

'Giver'—Scandinavian fertility goddess. She is said to have used her sons (four oxen) to pull her mighty plough, driving up the Swedish earth to form the island Zealand, leaving behind huge holes that became the lakes of that part of the world. She is patron of both farmer and virgin. Girls who die before their first sexual experience are said to become the servants that she treats kindly in the afterlife. It has been speculated that she is an early Scandinavian form of Frigga/Frigg.

Genea—Female—Mediterranean

Husband: Genos

Phoenician first woman whose children are said to be Light, Fire, and Flame.

Genius—Male—Mediterranean

Roman ancestral and adopted spirits who protect individual men (women had the same, but it was called a Juno). With or without the man's recognition, every man has a Genius watching over him. Should one wish to acknowledge and thank his Genius, sacrifices are made on one's birthday. A modern interpretation of this practice can be seen in the 'Birthing Day' presents on one's birthday. This is where one gives his or her parents a present to give thanks for bringing one into this world. Should that parent be departed, then a sacrifice can be made in his name to a charity or cause that parent would have supported. As my father died of cancer, if I were to make sacrifice

unto my Genius, I would donate to the American Cancer Society in his name. My mother, being alive today, would receive a more direct present—maybe flowers or dinner.

Genos—Male—Mediterranean

Father: Protogonos

Wife: Genea

Phoenician first man whose children are said to be Light, Fire, and Flame.

Ghede—Male—Caribbean

(Also known as Guede)

Haitian Voodoo god of the dead, the division between the living and the dead, and the sexual associations made between the two. He is god of sexual orgasm, which in French means 'little death.' He stands at the entrance to the Underworld, the doorway between the living and the dead, and is thus associated with cemeteries. His female counterpart is Maman Brigidt. In understanding his nature, one should consider Ghede to be both his name and the name of the collective of his cohorts. His cohorts include Baron La Croix, Baron Piquante, Baron Cimetiere, and perhaps the best known, Baron Samedi. So well known is the name Baron Samedi to connect with Ghede, that the two are sometimes cited as being names for the same rather than one an aspect of the other. All souls must pass by the cross roads of Ghede before entering Guinee, the afterlife.

Gibil—Male—Mediterranean/Middle East

Father: Anu

Mother: Anat

Sumerian god of both Light and Fire who is called on to protect from baneful magick.

Gilgamesh—Male—Mediterranean/Middle East

Sumerian and Babylonian folk hero who shunned the affections of Ishtar. In retaliation, Ishtar brought a seven-year drought to his land. His story is a likely source on which the story of Hercules was built.

Glooskap—Male—North America

(Also known as Glooscap, Gluskap, and Nanabozho)

Creator god of the Algonquin who treated humanity as would a loving father. Unfortunately, his brother Maslum didn't much like that relationship. Maslum created all things baneful to humanity to disrupt his brother's relationship. Glooskap defeated him by using trickery and lies. Their story reminds us that sometimes good people have to use less than honorable tactics to overcome opposition.

Gnabia—Male—Australia

Australian god of ascension into manhood. He is himself the challenges that cause a boy to become a man. In today's society, he can be seen as successful completion of college, or perhaps service to the military because in his original lore, he is said to consume boys and then regurgitate only those who survived the torment, becoming men as they do. Patron of young men entering the military or college.

Gnaski—Male—North America

(Also known as Gnaska)

Animal association: Frog

Lakota spirit who drives the mind insane and the soul to paralysis. He sometimes appears as the Buffalo god to trick humanity into thinking he is friendly. For this reason, he is sometimes called 'Crazy Buffalo.' However, a direct reference to Buffalo is not made, as it is a disguise.

Goblin Spiders—Female—Far East

Animal association: Spider

Japanese personification of mischievous/evil creatures who by day take on the form of common spiders, but by night commit all forms of mischief and evil.

Goibniu—Male—Central Europe

(Also known as Govannon [Welsh])

Irish patron of brew masters, metal workers, and the creation of athame and sword. It is said that the swords and knives that he created would always strike and remain true, and his brew would sometimes grant immortality. Other times the brew brings only the feeling of immortality, which can typically be observed among the young men of campus-area taverns.

Gorgon, The—Female—Mediterranean

Father: Phorcys

Mother: Ceto

In Greek lore, the Gorgon may have at one point numbered many more, but they eventually settled on three horrific female creatures who were born as triplets from the union of Phorcys and Ceto. They are Euryale ('far roaming'), Medusa ('ruler'), and Sthenno ('forceful'). Their guardians are the Graiae. See also Medusa.

Gou—Male—Africa

Father: Lissa

West African Moon God.

Gou Mang—Male—Central Asia

(Also known as Kou Mang)

Animal association: Dragon

Holiday: Spring Equinox

Chinese messenger who arrives from the East to bring good news from the Sky God with each sunrise. He is associated with the Spring. His counterpart is Ru Shou.

Govannon—Male—Central Europe

(Also known as Gofannon)

Father: Beli

Mother: Don

Welsh metalsmith to the gods. Patron to metal workers, particularly those who make magickal tools.

Graces, The Three—Female—Mediterranean

(Also known as The Three Charities)

Greek daughters of Zeus and Euronyme who were associated with the Muses. See Aglaia, Euphrosyne, and Thalia.

Graiae, The—Female—Central Europe

(Also known as Graii, Graiae)

Father: Phorcys

Mother: Ceto

Animal association: Snake

Three old sisters of Greek lore. Each was born with gray hair and only one eye and tooth to share among the three. They were the guardians of the Gorgons (another set of three). The sisters' names are Deino ('the dread'), Enyo ('the horror'), and Pemphredo ('the alarm').

Great Spider—God—Africa

Animal association: Spider

Great spider is a term used in Africa to refer to spiders as a collective and in reference to gods and goddesses similar to Anansi. See Anansi.

Great Spirit—Male—North America/Central America/South America

(Also known as Manitou, Manito, Manitoo, Manitu)

Animal associations: Bison, Eagle (most common associations)

Generally speaking, Great Spirit is a Native American creator common to many tribes. The clearest indication of this is found in the Algonquin word *Manitou* which some translate directly to 'Great Spirit.' However, it is also important to point out that the belief that Great Spirit is a god who was shared by all Native Americans is a New Age urban legend with little basis in fact. If we lump all Native American traditions into one category, we tend to miss such information as the Chamacoco view that the Great Spirit has a wife named Eschetewuarha. Different tribes had and have specific customs and specific gods. While there is absolutely nothing wrong with adopting traditions from several sources, claiming they were all practiced by all Native Americans is rather insulting to any person following one particular tribe's traditions. No one person has the right to dictate the religion and spirituality of another. So in drawing on Native American or any cultural source, we should be careful not to claim that all others followed the ways we choose to adopt. That which today is generally called the Native American 'Great Spirit'

is a collective of views under which the modern interpretation of the Algonquin name have been placed. Some of the other names that have been variously translated into Great Spirit include Alowatsakima (Leni Lenape), Ha Wen Neyu (Iroquois), and Nagi Tanka (Dakota)

Green Lady—Female—Central Europe

(Also known as Mother Nature, Green Jill, Jill in the Green)

Husband: The Green Man

Rarely mentioned Celtic personification of the goddess of the woods and foliage. Although the Green Man image has been cited as being found in ancient architecture, many of those faces look distinctly feminine and much of the lore of the green has given yield to deities such as Mother Nature. As she is often cited as looking much as we describe Green Man, it does seem a natural conclusion that some of those green foliage images with the face of women are just that, female versions of the Green Man, or better The Green Woman.

Green Man—Male—Central Europe

(Also known as Father Nature, Green George, Green Jack, Jack in the Green)

Wife: The Green Lady

Animal associations: Goat, Elk

Plant associations: Bachelor's Buttons, Pine

Holidays: Spring Equinox, Bealtaine

Celtic personification and god of the woods and foliage who controls the rain and acts as patron over livestock of all kinds. His praise was sung far beyond the Celtic cultures. He is such a powerful concept that his images survived the Burning Times intact and can even be found on the walls and in the architecture of churches built during the persecution of Pagans by those very churches. He is seen as Father Nature.

Gronw—Male—Central Europe

Welsh god who had sex with the wife of Llew Llaw Gyffes and found out why one should not encroach on monofidelity. He met a rather nasty fate in Llew's hands.

Guaracy—Male—South America

(Also known as Guarcy)

Brazilian Sun and Creator who created all animals. One of the three Creators responsible for the world. The other two were Peruda and Jacy. In Wicca he is associated with soul and the second order of life (animal).

Gucumatz—Male—Central America

(Also known as Kucumatz)

Animal association: Snake

Mayan snake god who taught humanity the art of agriculture and negotiating with Nature.

Gui Xian—Female—Central Asia

(Also known as Kuei Hsien)

Chinese creature guardian of the North. She is described as a turtle and presides over all things that bring happiness and bliss. The other three guardians are Ch'i-lin, Gui Xian, Feng-haang, and Long. They are collectively known as the Ssu Ling.

Gula—Female—Middle East/Mediterranean

Husband: Ninurta/Enurta

Animal association: Dog

Sumerian goddess of health. Also responsible for a soul's journey to the Underworld when sickness prevails.

Gwalu—Male—Africa

Yoruba god of rain.

Gwen—Female—Central Europe

Plant association: Apple

Celtic personification and goddess of love. She appears as a beautiful sunset or an equally beautiful woman who loves all, even when that love is not returned.

Gwion—Male—Central Europe

Animal associations: Hare, Fish, Hawk

Plant association: Corn

Welsh god who splashed three drops of the contents of Cerridwen's cauldron onto his fingers. After licking it from his fingers, he received all knowledge. In a rage, Cerridwen chased him unrelentingly. In that chase, they both shape-shifted, assuming the appearance of animals—first as greyhound chasing a hare, then an otter chasing a fish, then a hawk chasing a bird, and a hen chasing a grain of grain.* She swallowed the grain, killing Gwion, but later gave birth to Taliesin from that seed.

*This story is sometimes told as a piece of barley or a piece of corn. Recently several postmodern authors have come under attack when referencing corn in European history because that which we call corn is a new world discovery. What folk have failed to mention is that the word *corn* was used in Europe to refer to a variety of grain other than what we know today as corn.

Gwydion—Male—Central Europe

Father: Beli

Mother: Don

Lover: Arianrhod (maybe sister)

Plant association: Ash

Adopted father of his sister's (Arianrhod) virgin-born son who was later named Llew Llaw Gyffes. He created a woman out of flowers (Blodeuwedd) for his adopted son. She betrayed him with infidelity and killed Llew Llaw Gyffes after plotting with her lover. Gwydion restored him and turned her into an owl.

Gwyn—Male—Central Europe

Father: Ludd

Animal association: Owl

Note: His father is sometimes cited as Llyr.

Conducted the souls of those slain in battle through the Underworld.

Ha—Male—Africa

Egyptian personification of the deserts that brought both death and protection from invaders.

Hachiman—Male—Far East

(Also known as Yawata)

Animal association: Dove

Japanese Shinto god of war who protects the island of Japan and its people from invaders.

With the decline of war, he became a god of agriculture and fishing, helping fishermen and farmers to battle against the odds they faced. Doves are his symbols, friends, and messengers.

Hadad—Male—Mediterranean/Middle East
(Also known as Baal-Hadad [Lord Thunder], Reshef [Ancient Syrian], Rimmon [Babylonian/Old Testament], Teshub [Hittite])
Father: El
Mother: Elat
Wife: Shala

'Thunder'—Syrian god of thunderstorms and the rain they bring. He has many names in the Middle East and Mediterranean area. Perhaps most notably Rimmon who appears in the Old Testament and is later identified by authors (maybe first by Milton) as a fallen angel.

Hades—Male—Mediterranean
(Also known as Clymenus, Eubuleus, Polydegmon)
Father: Cronus
Mother: Rhea
Lover: Leuce, Minth, Persephone
Plant associations: Common Aspen, Frankincense, Hibiscus, Nettle (greater), Oak, Olive, Red Poppy, White Poppy

'Unseen'—Greek god whose name is synonymous with the Underworld. He forms a sacred Triad with his brothers Zeus (land/upper world), and Poseidon (the seas and oceans)

Incense Recipe

2 parts Frankincense
1 part Hibiscus flowers
1 part Poppy flowers
Enough Hades or Frankincense essential oil to bind

Oil Recipe

12 drops Frankincense essential oil
12 drops tincture of Hibiscus
6 drops tincture of Poppy flower
1/4 ounce base oil

Hai, Mo Li—Male—Central Asia

Mo Li Hai is the Chinese Buddhism guardian of the West. His statue is often included at the west point of Buddhist temples. In the modern practice of Feng Shui, his statue is placed in the west most part of a home to protect from negative influences coming from that direction. In Wiccan ritual, he is one of the names for the Four Quarters, the other three being Hung, Shou, and Chung.

Haket—Female—Africa

Egyptian goddess who brought life to the creations of clay by her husband's hands, thus creating the first of humanity.

Hakini—Female—Near East

Hindu goddess associated with the Aja chakra (third eye). Sometimes described as an aspect of Shakti. See also Dakini, Rakini, Lakini, Kakini, and Sakini.

Halirrhothius—Male—Mediterranean
Father: Poseidon

Greek god who raped Alcippe. He met his death at the hands of her father, Ares.

Hanuman—Male—Near East
Father: Kasari
Mother: Angana
Animal association: Monkey
Plant associations: Benzoin, Mace, Sandalwood (white), Vervain

Hindu god of knowledge who takes the form of a monkey. His father is sometimes cited as Vayu.

Incense Recipe

2 parts Sandalwood (yellow/white) powder
2 parts Benzoin powder
1 part Vervain
Enough Hanuman or nutmeg essential oil to bind

Oil Recipe

9 drops Sandalwood essential oil
6 drops Benzoin essential oil
6 drops Nutmeg or tincture of Mace
1/2 ounce base oil

Haokah—Male—North America

Thunder god of the Sioux and Horned God of the hunt who seems to have his emotions backwards. He cries when he is happy and laughs when he is depressed. Perhaps a patron of the manic.

Hapi—Male—Africa

(Also known as Hep)

Father: Horus

Mother: Isis

Animal associations: Ape/Chimpanzee, Baboon

Plant association: Water Lily

Egyptian god associated with the Element Earth and the North. Associated with the Goddess Nephthys. Patron of those with illness that affects the lungs. Wiccans who have adopted an Egyptian pantheon often associate their Quarters to align with Egyptian associations made with the Four Sons of Horus. The other three are Duamutef, Imset, and Kebechsenef.

Hapikern—Male—Central America

Mayan evil antagonist to humanity who is in constant opposition and at war with Nohochacyum. Similar in concept to the Christian view of Satan in his opposition to the Christian god.

Harek—Female—Central Europe

Animal association: Hare

German Moon Goddess equivalent to Hecate.

Harpa Khrutt—Male—Africa

(Also known as Harpa-Khruti)

Plant association: Rose

A name for Horus the Child associated with the Greek Harpocrates.

Harpies—Female—Mediterranean

Animal association: Vulture

Three Greek messengers in the form of beautiful naked women who flew through the sky with wings like birds. For reasons unknown, they later became ugly and hateful, taking on monstrous appearances. I believe the Harpies were initially seen as both characters, beautiful and ugly. They were charged with keeping the peace and when enjoying the fruits of that capacity, they were beautiful. But as history has shown, war and violence are often required to keep that peace, thus they were also sometimes seen as the necessary horrible beasts. As our view of death transformed from being identified with beauty into the hideous image that is now more prevalent, so did the view of the Harpies change. They are still considered beautiful (as is the personification of Death by some), but the view of the majority has become ugly. Perhaps a reflection on the perception of increased crime and evil in our world.

Harpocrates—Male—Mediterranean

Plant association: Rose

Greek representation of Horus the Child, often depicted as a naked male infant. He is god of keeping that which is secret and that which is silent. Interestingly enough, he is prayed to by parents who wish their children to sleep quietly through the night. Sacrifice of infant formula can be made in conjunction with these prayers by donating them to shelters and food pantries.

Ha Satan—Male—Post Modern

Animal association: Coyote

Ha Satan was not, as many folk seem to believe, an ancient deity name. The use of the name to describe a deity is strictly post-modern and in particular neo-Pagan. Although Christianity did mistake the use of the word 'Satan' in their translations many hundred years earlier, I believe it is today's Neo-Pagan authors who invented and perpetuate the use of 'Ha Satan.' The best English translation of *ha* is 'the' and *satan* is 'adversary' or 'accuser.' So Ha Satan is a common noun, not a name or a proper noun. In modern English context, a court room would see the prosecution as *Ha Satan* (the satan) to the defense and the defense as *ha satan* (the satan) to the prosecutor with absolutely no association or connection to good and evil unless one took sides. In which case it just means the other party that my party sides against. See also Satan.

Hastsehogan—Male—North America
    Navajo god of the home and of home blessings.

Hathor—Female—Africa
(Also known as Hwt-Hert, Het-Heru, Het-hert)
Animal associations: Cow, Cat, Frog, Hawk, Vulture, Lion
Plant associations: Coriander, Mandrake, Myrtle, Rose, Sycamore, Vine (grape)
Holiday: Hathor's Feast November 27th
    'House of Horus' or *'House of God'*—Egyptian Sky Goddess. Her name refers to the house (sky) in which Horus takes flight. She was associated by the Greeks with Aphrodite. Her sacred instrument is the sistrum , a type of rattle that usually looks like a sling shot with tiny tambourines or bells strung between the arms.

Incense Recipe
2 parts Gum Arabic
1 part Coriander
1 part Rose
A few Raisins

Haiti—Male—Middle East
    Arabic Jinn who gave advice and warning, but who was never seen.

Hatmehyt—Female—Africa
(Also known as Hatmehyt)
Lover: Banebdjedet
Animal association: Fish
    Egyptian fish goddess who was worshiped at the banks of the Nile, especially by fishermen.

Hay-Tau—Male—Middle East/Mediterranean
Animal association: Bull
    Phoenician forest god whose tears (resin) were collected and sold to the Egyptians. Frankincense, perhaps?

Hebe—Female—Mediterranean
Husband: Hercules
Plant association: Cypress
    Greek goddess of youth and of boy's ascension into manhood. Honored at rites of passage in which boys become men. She served the nectar of the gods until she was replaced by Ganymede. Some Wiccan traditions hold that she then became cup bearer to humanity. She is associated with the chalice in Wiccan ritual.

Hecate—Female—Mediterranean
Father: Perses
Mother: Asteria
Animal associations: Dragon, Dog, Frog, Hare, Snake, Toad
Plant associations: Aconite, Belladonna, Cyclamen (especially Ivy-leaved), Cypress, Dandelion, Hemlock, Henbane, Garlic, Mandrake (European), Mint, Myrrh, Oak, Onion, Palm (date), Patchouli, Sesame, Willow, Wolf's Bane, Yew
    Greek grandmother figure. She is goddess of the crossroads. Although she is sometimes associated with the Crone stage of goddess, she is typically shown as a Triple Goddess herself in that she has three faces, one a dog, one a horse, and one a snake. Her kin familiar are two ghost dogs/hounds, which are typically shown loyally by her side. Although she has been associated with the evil stereotypical witch with of the green skin, long nose, and warts, her story is more of the champion. It was she who rescued Persephone from the Underworld, thus restoring Spring to the world. She is prayed to for easing the suffering of birth, by those who are facing Death, and by those who have realized that both birth and death are part of life. Hecate stands at an intersection of three roads that meet. One of her faces looks each way to both welcome travelers. These three crossroads are birth, life, and death, all merging at her feet.

Incense Recipe

3 parts Sandalwood

2 parts Cypress

1 part Mint

1 pinch Belladonna (optional)

Enough Sandalwood essential oil to bind

Oil Recipe

10 drops Myrrh essential oil

6 drops Cypress essential oil

4 drops Patchouli essential oil

1/2 ounce base oil

Hehaka—Male—North America

Animal association: Elk

'Elk'—A name used today to reference a Lakota and Dakota god of the hunt. However, it is unclear if that name was used initially as a god form, as the Spirit of the Elk, or simply as a name to describe the Elk. Today, the word is used more often in reference to some of the great Earthly or formerly Earthly leaders of the various tribes and the resurgence of the Native American traditions, most notably as Hehaka Sapa (Black Elk).

Heimdall—Male—Northern Europe

(Also known as Heimdallr, Gullintani)

Animal association: Ram

The guardian of Asgard who requires little sleep in his duty to prevent invasion. It is told that at Ragnarok, he will kill Loki, but he dies shortly after Loki of injuries he received in the battle.

Heket—Female—Africa

(Also known as Heqet, Heka, Hekat)

Lover: Khnum

Animal association: Frog

Plant association: Cypress

Egyptian goddess of Life and Death. She watches over both childbirth and the transition of the soul at death. She is depicted as either a frog or a beautiful woman with a frog's head. In her honor, an amulet of a frog is worn by women who hope to conceive. That amulet is then hung over a child's crib for the first year of its life that the goddess may know to watch over the child.

Hel—Female—Northern Europe

(Also known as Hell)

Father: Loki

Mother: Angurboda

Animal association: Wolf

Plant association: Elder

Norse ruler of Helheim (house of Hel/Hell), the Underworld where the souls of those who cannot rise to the Hall of their Patron/Matron will sink at the death of their body. Her lore is rather shattering to the neo-Pagan who claim Hell is a Christian invention. One of the three children of Angurboda and Loki in which we see the number three as the number of not only good fate, but also of ill fate. The other two children are Jormungand and Fenrir.

Helblindi—Male—North Europe

Father: Farbauti

Mother: Laufey

A blind Scandinavian Underworld god. Many cite him as brother to Loki. His name is sometimes cited as an alternative name for Odin. I don't agree.

Helen—Female—Mediterranean

(Also known as Helen of Troy)

Father: Zeus

Mother: Leda

Greek woman who was so lusted after that when she became of age all the eligible bachelors (and a few ineligible) sought her hand. Concerned that should one triumph over all the others their marriage and his kingdom would be harmed by the anger of those many that did not win her hand, her step-father, King Tyndareus, gathered all the suitors and told them that none would have her hand until all swore that they would with mind, body, and soul support whom ever it would be that would have her hand in marriage. He then announced that Menelaus would have her hand. After a time, she ran off with Paris (or maybe was kidnapped), the son of the King of Troy, who had earlier wanted Helen's hand. Outraged at the abduction, Menelaus called on the very men who had lusted after his wife but sworn the oath of King Tyndareus, to retrieve his wife from Paris. Their soldiers were rallied and the Trojan war began. With the fall of Troy, Helen returned to Menelaus. He did so love her that even if it was betrayal that caused her to leave, he welcomed her and treated her so well that she stayed with him ever more. After her mortal death, she even went to his side and remains there in the Greek afterworld in Elysium.

Helios—Male—Mediterranean

(Also known as Helius)

Father: Hyperion

Mother: Theia

Wife: Clymene, Perse

Plant associations: Cinnamon, Frankincense, Heliotrope, Sunflower

Greek Sun God who is most often depicted as an attractive young man with a golden halo or sun disk about his head.

Incense Recipe

2 parts Frankincense

1 part Cinnamon

A few unsalted sunflower seeds

Enough Helios or Frankincense essential oil to bind

Oil Recipe

12 drops Frankincense essential oil

6 drops Cinnamon essential oil

1/4 ounce sunflower oil

Hemera—Female—Mediterranean

Father: Erebus

Mother: Nyx

'Day'—Greek goddess of day. Being born of Darkness (Erebus) and Night (Nyx), she is one of the many foundations on which the Wiccan principle of 'Darkness before Light' is based.

Henwen—Female—Central Europe

Animal association: Boar

British fertility goddess who is depicted as a pregnant boar or sow. She brought abundance and diversity to England with her many litters. Sometimes associated with Cerridwen.

Hephaestus—Male—Mediterranean

(Also known as Hephaistos)

Wife: Aphrodite

Lover: Gaia

After Aphrodite was born, Zeus was concerned that there would be great battles over her hand. So he choose his trusted metal worker Hephaestus to take her hand. So much did Hephaestus adore Aphrodite, that he dedicated much of his greatly skilled work towards making her the finest jewelry and gifts. Adore is the important word here. You see, Hephaestus was greatly skilled, but he was nonetheless a working man. He felt he was blessed by Aphrodite because he never thought he could have a wife so beautiful. His story might have gone differently if he had wished instead for a lover that was compatible as well. One of those gifts was a girdle made from the finest woven gold. Unfortunately for his heart, the girdle made Aphrodite even more irresistible. With so many new suitors, Aphrodite quickly tired of her hard-working and skillful man and became content to run around with the 'bad boys' of the time. The message here seems to be that love is fickle. His story warns that relationships in the order of marriage will not last long if they are not based on matters other then the superficial.

Hera—Female—Mediterranean

(Also known as Bopis)

Father: Cronus

Mother: Rhea

Husband: Zeus

Animal associations: Cattle, Crow, Dove, Goose, Hawk, Peacock, Sheep (ram), Snake

Plant associations: Apple, Myrrh, Orris, Pomegranate, Willow

'Chosen one'—Greek goddess who warns us of inappropriate unions. Although she is a goddess of marriage and birth, her story is a warning to mismatched couples. Her marriage to Zeus can only be said to remain intact due to conflict theory, for most of her stories involve her jealous rage being vented on Zeus' many lovers and their many children born of Zeus. As patron of marriage, her story speaks volumes about compatibility. She tell us that folk inclined towards monogamy should be wed to those inclined to monogamy. Those not inclined to monogamy should marry those not inclined to monogamy. She is strongly associated with Juno.

Incense Recipe

2 parts Sandalwood (Yellow)

1 part Myrrh

1 part Orris root

Hercules—Male—Mediterranean

(Also known as Herakles, Heracles)

As Hercules:

Father: Jupiter

Mother: Alcmene

Step-mother: Juno

As Heracles:

Father: Zeus

Mother: Alcmene/Alcmena

Step-mother: Hera

Animal association: Deer

Here I have listed the Greek and Roman together because both names and stories overlap so well. Greek and Roman folk hero. Known to bless gay unions. His story takes the story of Hera one step further. Where her story reflects on the ill fate of a couple whose partners are not well suited, the story here is that the children of such ill-suited partnerships are the ones who commonly suffer. Told variously in his Greek and Roman tales, his step-mother tried to kill him at birth, tormented him throughout his life, and finally drove him insane. Finally reaching council (perhaps a modern interpretation of a psychologist) with an oracle, he was given several tasks, the completion of which would restore sanity.

Hermaphrodite—Male—Mediterranean

Lover: Dionysus

Greek god who united with Salmacis to become one body. From this union of male and female to form one body, we derive the modern use of the word hermaphrodite. Although many cite him as an example of a gay deity because he has the gender of both man and woman, it is hard to say that his relationship with Dionysus supports that stance. Instead, it seems to state that Hermaphrodite was bisexual.

Hermod—Male—North Europe

Father: Odin

Wife: Frigga

Scandinavian messenger of the gods who risked death to assure the safe return of his brother Baldur. He speaks volumes on the subject of brotherly love and self sacrifice.

Hermes—Male—Mediterranean

(Also known as Enagonios)

Lover: Aphrodite, Hecate, Carmenta, Persephone

Animal associations: Cock, Cattle (cow), Goose, Sheep (lamb), Hare, Lizard, Tortoise, Turtle

Plant associations: Almond, Beech, Benzoin, Gum Mastic, Hazelnut, Mace, Olive, Sandalwood (white), Vervain

Greek messenger of the gods and deity of intellect, higher learning, communication, commerce and travel. He is the patron of merchants and of the self employed. Interestingly enough, he is also patron of thieves, perhaps a reflection on the cunning necessary to keep a thief alive in a time when the profession was sometimes punishable by death. Historically and today, he is called on to bless homosexual relationships.

Incense Recipe

2 parts Sandalwood (yellow/red) powder

1 part Benzoin

1 part Gum Mastic

Enough Hermes or Sandalwood essential oil to bind

Oil Recipe

9 drops Sandalwood essential oil

6 drops Benzoin essential oil

6 drops tincture of Gum Mastic

1/2 ounce olive oil

Herne—Male—Central Europe

Animal association: Bear, Wolf, Bull, Otter, Sheep (ram), Deer (stag), Goat

Plant association: Juniper, Oak, Patchouli, Pine

Celtic Horned God of the hunt who represents the hunter, the hunted, and the connection between both. He is, in essence, the connection or mediator between Life and Death. From his lore, we see the Wiccan principle that for Life there must be Death. See also Cernunnos.

Incense Recipe

4 parts Patchouli herb

4 parts pine needles (or 1 part pitch and 3 part sandalwood)

2 parts Gum Arabic

Enough Herne oil or a mixture of patchouli and pine oil to bind

Oil Recipe

9 drops Patchouli essential oil

6 drops Pine essential oil

6 drops Juniper essential oil

1/2 ounce base oil

Hestia—Female—Mediterranean

Father: Cronus

Mother: Rhea

Greek goddess of the warmth in a home. Her altar is the hearth where family members gather to worship her with mutual love for each other. Such is her conviction to remain virgin, that she rejected the courting of both Apollo and Poseidon himself, swearing on the head of Zeus that she would now and forever more remain virgin. As you can probably guess, her Roman equivalent is Vesta.

Himavat—Male—Near East/Central Asia

(Also known as Himavan)

'*Snow top*'—Hindu personification and god of the Himalayas.

Hine Au One—Female—Polynesian Islands

(Also known as Kane [Hawaii])

Plant association: Bamboo

Polynesian first woman, molded out of clay by her father Tane. Without knowing he was her father, she welcomed him to her bed and bore him one daughter, Hina Titama. Upon discovering her lover was also her father, she fled to the Underworld in the shame of her incest.

Hino—Male—North America

Iroquois god of thunder who fought against the original inhabitants of North America. Described as giants, this could be one of the many surviving hints that European migration occurred much earlier than currently thought.

Hinokagu—Male—Far East

Father: Izanagi

Mother: Izanami-No-Kami

Japanese Fire god and patron of those seeking sudden change.

Hit—Female—Micronesia

Animal association: Octopus

Octopus goddess who is prayed to for assurance of safe passage over the ocean.

Hjordis—Female—North Europe

Husband: Sigmund

See Sigmund for her story.

Hulda—Female—Central Europe/Northern Europe

(Also known as Holda, Bertha and maybe Holle)

Animal association: Dog, Goat, Goose, Hare, Spider

Plant association: Elder, Flax, Hellebore, Rose

'The Benignant'—Initially a German goddess who began as Hulda, a beautiful young maiden. Gradually, she became a guardian of marriage. Her lore then grew into Bertha, and she is said to tend children as would a grandmother. She is also the terror of children who have been bad or who have committed evil deeds. Her lore spread to most of Europe. She is patron to everyone who has ever been bullied in school. Along the way, she became a wonderful example of the principle of Maiden, Mother, and Crone as seen in the Triple Goddess.

Hoder—Male—North Europe

Father: Odin

Scandinavian god of the night who was born blind.

Honos—Male—Mediterranean

Roman god and personification of morality and ethics, especially those in the course of conflict. Speaks to us of conducting ourselves within personal ethics and social morals, even when it seems setting those things aside might quicken victory.

Hora—Female—Mediterranean

Husband: Quirinus

Animal association: Butterfly

Roman goddess of both time and beauty. Perhaps a reflection on the fading of beauty as one gets older.

Horae—Female—Mediterranean

Father: Zeus

Mother: Themis

'The Hours'—Three Greek sisters who kept track of time and the seasons. Individually, they are Dike (natural law/justice), Irene (peace), and Eunomia (order)

Horus—Male—Africa

(Also known as Hrw, Hr)

Egyptian word, which is misunderstood to be reference to a specific deity. In essence, this word denotes any one of several different deities, most notably Horus the Elder and Horus the Younger.

Horus The Elder—Male—Africa

(Also known as Heru-ur)

Father: Geb

Mother: Nut

Animal associations: Antelope, Cat, Falcon, Goose, Hawk, Dragon, Wolf

Plant associations: Dragons Blood, Horehound (white), Nettle (greater), Oak, Pepper (black), Rose, Rue, Sunflower, Water Lily, Wormwood, Yarrow

Egyptian god.

Incense Recipe

2 parts red rose petals and buds

1 part Yarrow flowers

1 part Dragon's Blood resin

Enough Horus oil or Otto of Rose to bind

Oil Recipe

9 drops Dragon's Blood perfume oil

6 drops Otto of Rose

6 drops Yarrow essential oil

1/2 ounce Sunflower oil

Horus The Younger—Male—Africa

(Also known as Heru-sa-Aset)

Father: Osiris

Mother: Isis

Animal associations: Cat, Goose, Hawk

Plant associations: Dragon's Blood, Water Lily

The use of the word *Horus* to describe the Horus that is son of Isis. This is the most popular use of the term Horus to describe an Egyptian god form. He is often depicted suckling his mother's breast or standing as a young child between Osiris and Isis.

Hou-Chi—Male—Central Asia

(Also known as Hou Ji)

Chinese hero who taught farming and the negotiation with Nature.

Hsi Wang-Mu—Female—Central Asia

(Also known as Xi Wang-mu)

Father: Yu-huang

Husband: Mu Gong

Animal association: Tortoise

Chinese Taoist personification of the female principle of the soul (the yin). She is called the 'Royal Mother of the West.' She is goddess of immortality and presides over the western half of Paradise in the afterlife.

Hu—Male—Africa

Egyptian god who was born from a drop of Ra's blood. He is the embodiment of duty corresponding to authority. He is the patron of anyone who must follow orders once they are given and can be called on to assist in following through with matters that are necessary but perhaps not pleasant.

Hu Gadarn—Male—Central Europe

Welsh hero who taught farmers how to plow. He is most noted for his instruction of the use of rhyme and song to improve memory, which is later reflected in the Wiccan Rede as 'To cast ye spell well every time, let that spell be spake in rhyme.' Many cites state that Hu Gadarn is another name for Cernunnos/Herne.

Huitzilopochtli—Male—Central America

(Also known as Uitzilopochtli)

Mother: Coatlicue

Animal association: Hummingbird, Snake

Aztec god of storms and wars who was born in a full suit of armor. Although he was honored with human sacrifice, he was also the protector of peaceful travelers. The association with human sacrifice is centered in his mother's death. See Coatlicue.

Hunab Ku—Male—Central America

Mayan Creator god. He created three worlds, each with its own people. The first and second were destroyed by other than his hand, so he tried again and again. We now live in the third world of his creation, but our destruction is foretold. At that point he will create anew. This is, perhaps, a commentary on ages of humanity that preceded our current age. It is interesting to note that occasionally there is found anomalies that simply do not fit with our current thinking on the way humanity evolved; metal projectiles reportedly found in dinosaur skulls, near perfectly machined spheres dug from stone that dates to millions of years, and others that boggle archeologists. While I am not stating that these many anomalous finds are fact, they certainly make a person wonder, especially with lore such as this.

Hung, Mo Li—Male—Central Asia

Mo Li Hung is the Chinese Buddhism guardian of the South. His statue is often included at the south point of Buddhist temples. In the modern practice of Feng Shui, his statue is placed in the south most part of a home to protect from negative influences coming from that direction. In Wiccan ritual, he is one of the names for the Four Quarters, the other three being Shou, Chung, and Hai.

Hu Nonp—Male—North America

Animal association: Bear

Lakota Bear God who is patron of wisdom.

Hun-Tun—Male—Central Asia

Chinese god form similar to the Nameless One from the Book of Genesis. A better equation would be to Diana before separating into Light and Dark. Here the same story is told, except instead of Light and Dark or male and female, Hun-Tun predates Yin and Yang.

Huruing Wuhti—Male—North America

Hopi Creator god, of which there were two.

Hygeia—Female—Mediterranean

(Also known as Hygieia)

Father: Asklepios

Animal association: Snake

Greek goddess of health, healing, and the maintaining of that health with hygiene. So inseparable is this goddess from the concept that good personal hygiene is essential to health that the word itself, *hygiene*, is based on her name. Her symbols has survived today in the symbol of medicine. There we still see her sacred snake and the rod of her father, Asklepios.

Hymen—Male—Mediterranean

(Also known as Hymenaeus)

Father: Dionysus

Mother: Aphrodite

Plant association: Hawthorn, Juniper, Olive, Vine (grape)

Greek god who blessed marriages and the receptions that follow. Keep in mind who his parents are prior to calling on him for assistance. He is also patron of celebrating anniversaries and is most applicably called on when one wants an anniversary to rekindle a lustful spark. Patron of marriages and celebrations of marriage.

Incense Recipe

3 parts Sandalwood (yellow/white) powder

2 parts Hawthorn berries

2 parts juniper berries

1 part raisins

1 part Gum Arabic

Enough Hymen oil or red wine to bind

Oil Recipe

9 drops Juniper essential oil

1 teaspoon tincture of Hawthorn berries

1 pinch sugar (dissolve first into the tincture of Hawthorn berries)

1/2 ounce grape seed oil

1/2 ounce olive oil

Hyperion—Male—Mediterranean

Father: Uranus

Mother: Gaia

Lover: Theia

'He who goes before the sun'—Greek god whose children are Helios (the son), Selene (the moon), and Eos (the dawn). As father of the son, his name is support for the Wiccan principle that darkness comes before light.

Hypnos—Male—Mediterranean

Plant Association: Poppy (especially white)

Greek personification and god of sleep from whom we receive the word *hypnosis*. Ensures a restful sleep and sends his son Morpheus to bring the sleeper dreams. Also responsible for peaceful transition into death, for he could also send his son Thanatos. Patron of euthanasia and dreams.

Iah—See Aah

Iasion—Male—Mediterranean

(Also known as Iasius)

Greek god who is associated with fertility rites at Spring Equinox and Bealtaine. The association is probably made from records that Iasion and Demeter were involved in such fertility rites. Patron of fertility and male sexual virility.

Ibey—Male/Female—African/Caribbean/South America

In Santeria, they are called The Jimaguas/Ibey/Omo-Melli

In Voodoo, they are called The Marrasa

In Africa, they are called the Ibeji (twins)

Saint and Catholic associations (in pairs): St. Cosme and St.Damian, St. Crispin and St. Crispinian, St. Justa and St. Rufina

Holiday: Feast of Saint Cosme and Saint Damian on September 27

'The twins' (loosely)—The twins, named Taebo (male) and Kainde (female), are seen as messengers of the gods and good omens. Wood statues are given as presents to bring good luck to a home (especially at weddings). Although they are both male, the modern tradition of placing a statue of the groom and bride atop a wedding cake may come from the African tradition of giving Ibeji statues to a

couple as wedding presents. They are the playful patrons of children.

Ictinike—Male—North America

Sioux son of God who was cast from the heavens down to Earth due to his deceit and challenges to his father, the Sun God. Much like the Christian Satan, he is known for his lies and deceit.

Idris—Male—Central Europe

Welsh giant who knew the day, the morrow, and each day until end day from his careful study of the stars and heavenly bodies. He is patron of both poet and madman, for it is said that should a man spend one night in his chair that man would become the greatest of one of the two.

Igaluk—Male—Arctic North America

Animal associations: Fish and all sea creatures

Eskimo moon god. In some traditions he is seen as supreme god and All Father. In a much smaller capacity, he is sometimes linked to the Inuit god Aningan in and around Greenland. I believe this link is only made because they are both seen as moon gods and not for any attribute that they share.

Igraine—Female—Central Europe

(Also known as Igerna, Yguerne, Igrayne)

Husband: The Duke of Cornwall, Uther Pendragon

In Arthurian legend, she is the wife of the Duke of Cornwall and mother by he of Morgan la Fay. Later, she married Uther Pendragon, whose army had killed her husband, after conceiving his child, King Arthur.

Ihy—Male—Africa

Father: Horus (sometimes listed as Ra)

Mother: Hathor

Egyptian god who was particularly skilled with the sistrum, a musical instrument sacred to his mother, Hathor. Patron of musicians, especially string instruments.

Ikto—Male—North America

Sioux inventor and personification of human speech, as well as the many languages of North America.

Iktomi—Male—North America/Lakota

(Also known as Unktomi)

Animal association: Spider

Lakota spider god who brought culture to the Lakota. He is sometimes seen as a trickster who plays jokes on the young in the hopes that the tricks will bring about an understanding of the cultural principles known by their parents. Associated with the Sioux, Ikto but not interchangeable.

Ilmaqah—Male—Middle East

Early Semitic moon god.

Imhotep—Male—Africa

(Also known as Imhetep)

Father: Ptah

Mother: Nut

Egyptian man who is believed to be the first to use cut and shaped stones for the creation of buildings. His best-known example is the first pyramid (Step Pyramid). Due to the great work during his lifetime, he was deified after his death and given a spot in the lineage of the Egyptian pantheon of gods, thus becoming the son of Ptah and Nut posthumously. Patron of the skilled working class.

Imset—Male—Africa

(Also known as Amset, Mesti, Mesta)

Father: Horus

Mother: Isis

Egyptian god associated with the Element Water and the South. Associated with the goddess Isis. Patron of those with illness of the liver. Wiccans who have adopted an Egyptian pantheon often associate their Quarters to align with Egyptian associations made with the Four Sons of Horus. The other three are Duamutef, Hapi, and Kebechsenef.

342 A Wiccan Bible

In—Female—Far East

Japanese principle of the feminine portion of the soul. Similar in idea to the better-known Chinese Yin.

Inanna—Female—Mediterranean
(Also known as Inannu)
Father: Ea
Mother: Kishar
Lover: Dumuzi
Animal associations: Dog (especially hunting dogs), Lion, Snake (serpent)
Holiday: The Nativity of Inanna on January 2nd

Sweet Inanna is the most important goddess in the Sumerian pantheon. Although predominantly a goddess of love and fertility, she is also a goddess of war, especially when love and fertility are threatened. One of her dominant stories parallels the story of Persephone in many ways. In that story, she traveled to the Underworld and declared herself its ruler. That didn't sit too well with her sister Ereshkigal, who had already secured that title. Ereshkigal killed Inanna for her insolence. With the death of Inanna came the death of love and fertility, so the world suffered and begged of the god Enki that she be restored. He negotiated with Ereshkigal, who conceded that Inanna could return to the world of the living only if she made sacrifice of her beloved Dumuzi. She did. That sacrifice is repeated every year, and from that sacrifice we have Winter and Summer. During the Summer, she is in the world of the living bringing love and fertility, but her lover is in the Underworld. During the Winter, she replaces him there (self-sacrifice), and her beloved is allowed to leave.

Inari—Male—Far East
Animal associations: Fox, Spider
Plant association: Rice

Japanese god of prosperity, farming, and harvest. He was also a revered swordsmith. Wiccans associate him with the blessing of the athame, often including rice within the box that stores the athame. Patron of farmer and metal smiths (tools/weapons) and one who gives lessons and punishment to folk of evil ways.

Indra—Male—Near East
Father: Dyaus
Mother: Prithvi
Animal associations: Cattle (bull), Eagle, Hawk, Elephant (white), Horse, Dog (hunting dogs), Snake (cobra), Bee, Dragon
Plant associations: Aloe, Cedar, Olive, Orange (sweet), Saffron (Spanish)

Hindu god of war, whose wisdom was expressed in a conversation with his boyhood friend Arjuna, as recorded in the Bhagavad Gita. In the Hindu pantheon, Indra is one of the gods who favored communication with humanity. He is confidant, advisor, and guide to humanity, especially when confronting matters where one's true will comes into question. Patron of all who would seek their place in life (true will). One of the eight Hindu guardians of the principle directions. Indra is the guardian of the East. The other seven are Agni, Yama, Surya, Varuna, Vayu, Kubera, and Soma. Indra is also one of the Adityas. The Hindu month Asvini (September 23–October 22) is sacred to Indra. See Adityas.

Incense Recipe

Peel an orange and sprinkle the peel with saffron. Place the peel in a warm, moist, and dark place. Keep it damp by spraying a weak mixture of warm water (not hot) and honey on the peel each day. After a month, a mold will form on the peel. This mold is the incense or tincture base, not the peel itself. Scrape the mold, dry it, and burn as an incense powder.

Oil Recipe

12 drops Cedar Wood essential oil
9 drops Petitgrain essential oil
1/2 ounce olive oil

Inktomi—Male—North America
(Also known as Iktomi)
Animal association: Spider

Lakota spider god who established the Lakota community and culture. He is also a trickster who teaches children much needed lessons on matters of community.

Inle—Male—African/Caribbean/South America

Saint and Catholic association: Archangel Raphael

Holiday: Feast of the Archangel Raphael on October 24th

Yoruba god of fishing who, upon his migration into Santeria, became a god of healing. He is the owner with Ochun of the rivers and fish from those waters. He is patron of doctors and fishermen.

Io (1)—Female—Mediterranean

Animal association: Cow

Greek priestess who was beloved by Zeus. Of course, that meant Hera made her life miserable. In this case, Zeus turned her into a cow to escape Hera's rage. Of course, Hera didn't fall for it and hounded the poor thing even as a cow.

Io (2)—Male/Female—Polynesian Islands

(Also known as Kiho)

Supreme Creator on several of the Polynesian Islands (not all). Actually a marriage of Te Io Ora (male) and Io Wahine (female), but it is important to note that neither was seen as an individual. Te Io Ora can be seen as the Yang or masculine principle of Io, and Io Wahine can be seen as the Yin or the feminine principle of Io.

Ioskeha—Male—North America

Iroquois/Huron Creator god who taught humanity how to negotiate with Nature. He was in opposition with his brother Tawiskara, who created nothing but evil. Patron of farmers and others in negotiation with Nature.

Irene—Female—Mediterranean

(Also known as Eirene)

Animal association: Dove

Plant association: Olive

'Peace'—Greek goddess of peace and personification of wealth. Often depicted with a cornucopia, scepter, and torch. Her lore tells us that peace is achievable when all sides have wealth, warning that war is often the result of poverty and imbalance. She is one of the Horae with her sisters Dike and Eunomia.

Iris—Female—Mediterranean

Father: Thaumas

Mother: Electra

Plant associations: Iris, Orris Root, Rose, Wormwood

'Rainbow'—Greek personification of the rainbow for which the colored portion of our eyes is named. She is the winged messenger who brings messages from the gods (especially Hera) to humanity. With the modern association of the rainbow to the message brought forth by both the gay, lesbian, bisexual community and the Rainbow Coalition, we might see in her the message that communication with the gods comes in all colors and preferences.

Ishtar—Female—Middle East/Mediterranean

Father: Anu, Sinn

Mother: Anat

Lover: Marduk, Asshur

Animal associations: Lion, Snake (serpent), Dragon, Dove, Cow (calf), Scorpion, Hedgehog, Dolphin, Fish

Plant associations: Acacia, Apple, Juniper and all grains (especially Wheat)

Note: Due to the merging of the Sumerian and Babylonian pantheons, her mother and father are often cited completely differently.

Sumero-Babylonian goddess who inherited the attributes and stories of the moon goddess Nuah. One of the most noted stories that was adopted was that of her involvement in the Great Flood. Although exactly what Ishtar/Nuah complained about is not recorded, some speculate that it was issues concerning humanity's procreation or migration. In response to the complaint, the gods decided to destroy great amounts of humanity with the Great Flood. As the story comes originally from the moon goddess Nuah and as the moon controls the tides, we can see a connection in this story to Ishtar being responsible for the flood.

Isis—Female—Africa
(Also known as Aset)
Father: Seb
Mother: Nut
Animal associations: Cat, Cow, Dove, Goose, Hawk, Swallow, Peacock, Antelope, Vulture, Deer, Snake (cobra), Scorpion, Dolphin, Fish, Dog
Plant associations: Barley, Frankincense, Heather, Iris, Myrrh, Onion, Orris Root, Palm (date), Persea, Rose, Vervain, Wheat, Wormwood

Egyptian sister and wife to Osiris. She has been seen as Mother Goddess, with Horus on her lap or suckling at her breast. She has been seen as Sun Goddess, with the solar disk on her head. She has been seen as the seat of royalty, often shown with a throne on her head. Perhaps a comment on a wife's role as seat (comforter) of her husband. She is one of the popular goddess images in modern Pagan culture.

Incense Recipe
2 parts Frankincense
2 parts Sandalwood
1 part Myrrh
1 part Heather flowers
Enough Sandalwood oil to bind

Iskur—See Addad

Ison—Female—Africa
(Also known as Eka Obasi, Obasi Nsi, Ibibio, Ekoi)
Animal Association: Tortoise

West African fertility goddess. She is strongly associated with both Earth and Water.

Itokaga—Male—North America
(Also known as Okaga)
Animal association: Lark

Lakota word that literally means 'South' or the power of prayer sent to the South. Personification of South.

Itzamna—Male—Central America
(Potentially also known as Kinich-Auau)
Father: Hunab Ku
Lover: Ixchel
Animal association: Lizard, Jaguar

Mayan creator of community, moon god, and teacher of the written language. Patron of teachers and educators. He is called 'Lord of knowledge' and is said to have either invented or instructed in the Mayan calendar.

Itzpaplotl—Female—Central America
Animal association: Butterfly

Beautiful Aztec goddess associated with the door between Life and Death. Although she is portrayed as most healthy and attractive, her face reveals symbols of death. She is yet another example of the connection between sex and death or Life and Death.

Iwazaru—Male—Far East
Animal association: Monkey

'*Speak no evil*'—There is a 17th century temple in Japan which has a statue of three monkeys. The best translation of the inscription on that statue is 'See no evil, hear no evil and speak no evil' or 'Mizaru, Kikazaru, Iwazaru.' The statuary is most likely a representation of the three faces of a much earlier deity form, Vadjra.

Ix—Male—Central America
Father: Itzamna
Mother: Ixchel

One of the Bacabs, the four Mayan gods of the principle directions. Associated with the color black. In Wiccan ritual he is associated with the West Quarter. See also Cauac, Kan, and Mulac.

Ixchel—Female—Central America
Potentially equivalent to Ixalvoh
Husband: Voltan
Lover: Itzamna

Mayan moon goddess and patron of pregnant women. She invented the art of weaving and taught that art to humanity, as did her lover Itzamna teach in many of the other arts of community.

Ixtlilton—Male—Central America

Aztec god of health, medicine, and healing magic, especially for children. He is patron of children, feasting, and games. An example of the connection between revelry and games found outside of the Greek pantheon.

Izanagi—Male—Far East
Wife: Izanami

'Man who invites'—Japanese Shinto sky god, with his wife Izanami, responsible for creating the island of Japan. When his wife died, he went to the Underworld to retrieve her. She would not return, believing she was where Fate had placed her. Upon his return, he washed himself to remove anything remaining from the Underworld. In that cleansing rite, he washed his left eye. In so doing, he created the Sun Goddess Amaterasu. He washed his right eye and in so doing created the moon goddess Tsuki-Yumi. He blew his nose and in so doing created the Storm God Susanowa who, with his falling rain, became god of the oceans.

Izanami—Female—Far East
Husband: Izanagi

'Woman who invites'—Japanese creator. See Izanagi.

Jacy—Male—South America

Brazilian moon god who created all plant life. One of the three Creators responsible for the world. The other two were Peruda and Guaracy.

Jagannatha—Male—Near East

Hindu god whose name is often used to reference Krishna births and from which originated the term 'juggernaut': "Something, such as a belief or institution, that elicits blind and destructive devotion or to which people are ruthlessly sacrificed." (*The American Heritage*

Dictionary of the English Language, Fourth Edition). The word juggernaut was an offshoot of the god's name used to describe a structure (car or cart) used to transport the new bride (sacrifice?) of Jagannatha each year. So large was the structure that it had 16 wheels and took 50 men to move. As the procession traveled to the temple, devotees hurled themselves to a certain death under its wheels believing such a death would favor them in the afterlife. He is considered the patron of those who wish to be slaves and while slavery may not sound like an admirable aspiration, Wicca speaks greatly of free will and self determination. The story of Jagannatha thus speaks to us of allowing those who wish to serve to be afforded the right to do as they please. Where we might become angry with the mindless ranting of sidewalk ministries, those who honestly wish to follow blindly should be allowed to do just that. In the words of Aleister Crowley, "The slaves shall serve."

Jana—Female—Mediterranean
Husband: Janus

Roman moon goddess. She is patron of the process of change, of walking through doorways. With her husband Janus, she is the foundation for the word that is the month of January.

Janus—Male—Mediterranean
(Also known as Ianus)
Wife: Jana
Plant associations: Oak, Olive

Roman oak god who evolved from Dianus and from whose name we receive January, the month sacred to Janus. He is the guardian of transition and doorways who is often depicted with two faces, one looking forward and the other looking back.

Jehovah—Male—Middle East
(Also known as Yahweh)

'Lord' or *'God'*—The name Jehovah has come to mean either 'Lord,' 'God,' or 'Lord God' without respect to specific pantheon. However, the use of this name is a modern use

based on a mistaken translation. The original Hebrew was written *Yhvh*, because ancient Hebrew had no vowels. After generations in which it was forbidden to speak the name, vowels were added. Although no one could know what the original word sounded like, they created the word *Yehova*, which eventually found its way into English as Jehovah. See Yahweh.

Jesus—Male—Middle East

(Also known as Christ, Yeshue)

Father: Yahweh

Mother: Virgin Mary

Wife: Mary Magdalene

Animal association: Fish

Plant association: Holly

Holiday: Christmas on December 25th/Easter (date changes with the year)

An avatar/incarnation of Yahweh who was born of a willing virgin without the act of sexual intercourse with Yahweh. In this incarnation, Yahweh removed the original sin (rape) from humanity by allowing himself to take earthly form and then be violated in much the same way Mother Earth was when under his orders she was raped to create Adam. See Adam and Yahweh.

Jikoku—Male—Far East

Japanese god subordinate to Taishaku-ten who guarded the East. In Wiccan ritual, he is sometimes connected with the East Quarter. The other three were Komoku, Zocho, and Bishamon.

Jok—Male—Africa

(Also known as Jok Odudu)

Animal association: Goat (black)

'Creator'—All Father and Creator to the Alur (tribe of the Uganda/Zaire area).

Jormungand—Male/Female—Northern Europe

Norse serpent who will kill Odin in the end time. Jormungand dies too at that conflict. One of the three children of Angurboda and Loki in which we see the number three as the number of not only good fate, but of ill-fate.

The other two are Fenrir and Hel. Note that sometimes Jormungand is cited as male and other times as female.

Julunggul—Female—Australia

Animal association: Snake

Rainbow goddess of the Aboriginal Australians. She is patron of children and presides over their transition and initiation into adulthood.

Juno—Female—Mediterranean

(Also known as Juno Februa, Regina [Queen])

Father: Saturn

Husband: Jupiter (also brother)

Animal associations: Eagle, Goose, Peacock, Vulture

Plant associations: Crocus, Date (fig), Lily, Lettuce (especially wild), Mint, Pomegranate, Quince, Vervain

Roman state goddess who is associated more with national or state matters than with individual needs. To her are sacred the months of June and February. She was seen as the Queen of Rome and thus presided over litigation between Rome and other nations. She is patron and protector of women and the rights of women, but generally not the individual woman. Here is where it gets tricky. Juno is also the word used to denote a protective spirit for an individual woman. The male equivalent is Genius. These spirits are usually ancestral, but there is nothing stating that such spirits are above adoption rites. See Genius for more information.

Jupiter—Male—Mediterranean

(Also known as Dies Pater ['*Shinning Father*'], Ivppiter, Jove, Optimus Maximus ['*All Good*'])

Wife: Juno, Minerva

Animal associations: Eagle, Goat, Sheep, Woodpecker

Plant associations: Acorn, Agrimony, Almond, Aloe, American Aspen, Beech, Cassia, Carnation, Cedar, Common Aspen, Cypress, Daisy (Ox-eyed), Fig, Gorse, Hyssop, Leek, Mullein, Oak, Olive, Orange (sweet), Palm (date), Pine, Sage, Vervain, Violate

Roman Supreme God, identified with the Greek Zeus, who is known by many names in accordance with his many functions of state. Like his wife Juno, he is a state god. While oaths are often sworn to him, he is more concerned with matters of the community as a whole rather than individual needs. Some of his many names and the roles that they play:

Jupiter Caelestis—The All or Heavenly Father

Jupiter Lucetius—The god of light and sun that blesses crops

Jupiter Totans—The god of thunder (also nourishing rains)

Jupiter Fulgurator—The god of lightning (also nourishing rains)

Jupiter Victor—The god of victory

Incense Recipe

2 parts Orange peel powder

1 part Cypress

1 part Carnation flowers

1 part Gum Arabic

Add a bit of dried fig (optional)

Enough Jupiter or Cedar wood essential oil to bind

Oil Recipe

9 drops Galbanum essential oil

6 drops Cypress essential oil

6 drops Cedar Wood essential oil

1/2 ounce Almond oil

Jurupari—Male—South America

Brazilian god and patron of men's mysteries. His rituals were so guarded from women that there are more than a few accounts of women being put to death for having intruded upon them.

Justitia—Female—Mediterranean

Roman goddess of justice. She is most often recognized as the blindfolded goddess who holds scales in one hand and a sword in the other. Her statue is found in many buildings of law and justice in the modern world. Previously she was depicted with a scale in one hand

and a cornucopia or horn of plenty in the other, as if to note that only the just would receive plenty. This is in keeping with the Wiccan principle found in the Rede that instructs that one should fairly take and fairly give, not support hand-outs to those who are not deserving.

Juturna—Female—Mediterranean

Roman goddess of wells and the springs that feed them.

Juventas—Female—Mediterranean

Roman goddess of youth who is associated with the ascension into manhood. During such rites, boys would sacrifice a coin to her. Very similar to the Greek Hebe.

Kaikias—Male—Mediterranean

Greek personification of the North West Wind. See Book of Four.

Kakini—Female—Near East

Hindu goddess associated with the Ahahata chakra (heart). Sometimes described as an aspect of Shakti. See also Dakini, Rakini, Lakini, Sakini, and Hakini.

Kali—Female—Near East

(Also known as Kalika)

Husband: Shiva

Animal associations: Cow, Snake, Jackal, Raven

'Black one'—Hindu avatar/incarnation of Parvati who brings what can best be described as *dissolution*. Some are quick to point out that dissolution and Kali are Death. While it is true that the word dissolution can indeed mean death, it also indicates the fragmenting of a thing. In that we see a very different story. Kali becomes almost Zen-like. Dissolution also indicates the sensual pleasures, also attributed to Kali. Yes, she is the destroyer. But in that attribute, she is the destroyer of ignorance who frees the mind of men who seek to know god by allowing the dissolution of god such that the illusion cast upon such a force by cultural norms does not interfere with the understanding of the truth.

Kalki—Male—Near East

Animal associations: Horse, Peacock

'Time'—Hindu 10th and last avatar of Vishnu, foretold but not yet born. He will come from the sky, riding a great horse down to Earth where he will begin the great battle which will eventually kill all who are unrighteous. In the process, the world as known today will be destroyed, but Kalki will build a new world. One that is free of evil.

Kama—Male—Near East

Father: Vishnu

Mother: Lakshmi

Wife: Rati

Animal associations: Bee, Parrot

Hindu god of romantic love. He is seen as a winged messenger with bow and arrows, similar to Eros. His wife's name is Rati ('pleasure'). Together their names are united as 'Kama Rati' to describe the sexual unions of people who are deeply in love. This is one of the secret names for the Great Rite in Wiccan Ritual when the love and erotic passion of the host/priest and hostess/priestess is practiced in the form of coitus. From his name comes the title of the book *Kama Sutra*. Written in Sanskrit, the *Kama Sutra* provides rules for sensuous and sensual pleasure, love in the order of the erotic, and marriage in accordance with the Hindu laws of the time.

Kan—Male—Central America

Father: Itzamna

Mother: Ixchel

One of the Bacabs, the four Mayan gods of the principle directions. Associated with the color Yellow. In Wiccan ritual he is associated with the East Quarter. See also Cauac, Ix, and Mulac.

Kanaloa—Male—Islands

Animal association: Octopus

Plant associations: Banana, Kava Kava

Hawaiian Creator god. Although he created Above and Below, he is today associated mostly with the Underworld, leaving the others in his pantheon to dictate the lives of men. He is depicted as a giant octopus.

Kanati—Male—North America

(Also known as Kana'tu)

Wife: Sheu

'Lucky Hunter'—Cherokee god of the hunt and of tools of the hunt.

Kane—Male—Polynesian Islands

Plant association: Kava Kava

Hawaiian All Father who created all of humanity. He created the three worlds, Land, Sea, and Sky (the heavens).

Karma, Dakinis—Female—Central Asia

Dakinis Karma is the Tibetan goddess associated with the North, sternness, and impartiality. See also Vajra, Ratna, Padma, and Buddha.

Karttikeya—Male—Near East

(Also known as Skanda, Muruhan, Subramanya, Kartikeya)

Animal association: Peacock

Hindu god of war and male virility. He commands the armies of Heaven and rides a giant peacock into battle where his six heads and 12 arms make him master of the bow in combat.

Kashyapa—Male—Near East

(Also known as Kasyapa)

Lover: Aditi

With Aditi, he is the Hindu father of the Adityas (the months). See Adityas.

Kebechsenef—Male—Africa

(Also known as Qebesenuf)

Father: Horus

Mother: Isis

Animal association: Falcon

Egyptian god associated with the element Air and the West. Associated with the Goddess Selkhet. Wiccans who have adopted an Egyptian pantheon often associate their Quarters to align with Egyptian associations made with the Four Sons of Horus. The other three are Duamutef, Hapi, and Imset.

Kephra—Male—Africa

Animal associations: Dolphin, Fish, Ram, Scorpion, Turtle, Wolf

Plant associations: Cactus, Benzoin, Lotus, White Poppy

Egyptian Creator scarab beetle associated with the dawn sun. From him rises the Sky Goddess Nut.

Khenmu—Male—Africa

(Also known as Khnum, Khnemu)

Wife: Haket

Animal association: Sheep

Early Egyptian, possibly Nubian, creator of humanity. Called the 'Great Potter,' it is sometimes said that he created humanity on his potter's wheel.

Khentyamentiu—Male—Africa

Animal association: Wolf

Egyptian god form who was once the personification and representation of the spirit of all previous kings. His lore was later absorbed by Osiris.

Khons—Male—Africa

(Also known as Chons, Khonsu, Khons, Khensu)

Father: Amun

Mother: Mut

Animal associations: Baboon, Hawk

Egyptian moon god who is called the 'Master of time,' probably a reference to a lunar calendar.

Kikazaru—Male—Far East

'Hear no evil'—There is a 17th century temple in Japan which has a statue of three monkeys. The best translation of the inscription on that statue is 'See no evil, hear no evil, and speak no evil' or 'Mizaru, Kikazaru, Iwazaru.' The statuary is most likely a representation of the three faces of a much earlier deity form, Vadjra.

King Arthur—Male—Central Europe

Father: Uther Pendragon

Mother: Igraine

Wife: Weynhwyfar

Lover: Morgan le Fay

Plant association: Alder

Historic British-Celtic figure, Artorius, who was mythologized into a position in Celtic lore where he attains godlike status. Often overlooked by modern Pagans due to the fictionalization of his story, it is clear that Arthur warns of the perils one brings to the workplace when matters of interpersonal relationships fail. May also be seen as a warning about incest. Clearly we see the warning that what begins as a small indiscretion can grow to haunt us.

Kishar—Female—Middle East/Mediterranean

Father: Lakhamu

Mother: Lakhmu

Husband: Ansar

Mother of Anu and Ea.

Kitche Manitou—Male—North America

In popular reference, he is the Muskwari demon who destroyed the known world once by fire and once by flood. It is likely the destruction of the known world was by volcano. This is probably not a cite to the Great Flood that allowed migration from the Middle East into Europe, as the timing is not consistent with humanity's presence in North America.

Koevasi—Female—Melanesia

Animal association: Snake

Melanesian snake goddess associated with healing and the arts.

Kokyangwutl—Female—North America

Animal association: Spider

Hopi spider goddess who created all living things, humanity last. Upon realizing the world was filled with evil, she hid the good folk in underground caverns and then destroyed all that lived on the surface. Two more times, the surface of the world had to be destroyed while the good spirited folk hid from the destruction until finally she returned the good spirited folk to the surface, created Tuwaqachi which she filled with rich soil, and then settled those good folk there...in Arizona. Interesting enough, the state motto of Arizona is *Ditat Deus*, which means 'God Enriches.'

Komoku—Male—Far East

Japanese god who guarded the South, subordinate to Taishaku-ten. In Wiccan ritual he is sometimes connected with the South Quarter. The other three were Zocho, Bishamon, and Jikoku.

Koodjanuk—Male—Arctic North America

Eskimo god who is prayed to for health and healing.

Krishna—Male—Near East

Father: Vaseduva

Mother: Devaki

Lover: Radha

Animal associations: Bee, Elephant, Lion, Snake (cobra)

Plant associations: Acacia, Bay, Frankincense, Vine (grape)

Hindu god and twin brother of Balarama, eighth avatar of Vishnu, and boyhood friend of Arjuna. Krishna is one of the most popular of the Hindu deities in India. In the United States, he is Supreme God of the Hare Krishna.

Incense Recipe

4 part Frankincense

2 part Acacia flowers

1 part Bay leaf

A few raisins

Kuan Yin—Male—Central Asia

(Also known as Chenresi (Tibet), Guan Yin, Kuan-shi-yin)

Animal associations: Horse (white), Fish

Plant association: Lily

Recently, interest in the Chinese goddess Kuan Yin has become very popular. Interesting

enough, very few seem to have noticed that she was initially male, not female. He was initially depicted as definitively male, a god whom women who wanted children but who had failed in many attempts would seek. Gradually, he became a god of compassion. In that transition, his appearance became softer and more rounded. Yes, there have been references and depictions of the Chinese Kuan Yin as female for many years, but to print modern literature without even the mention that she was once seen as male is an insult. It is in as much as to say that compassion is not an attribute that can be held by men. Now, wouldn't one think that in the natural order of things, a woman who wants a child would do much better to turn to a male for assistance? I thus list him here as male.

Kubera—Male—Near East

(Also known as Dhanapati, Kuvera)

Hindu god of prosperity and wealth. One of the eight guardians of the principle directions. Kubera is the guardian of the North. The other seven are Indra, Agni, Yama, Surya, Varuna, Vayu, Soma.

Kul—Male/Female—North Europe

(Also known as Kul-Jungk)

Animal association: Fish

Siberian water sprite, male and female, who jealously guard fresh water ponds and lakes. They are typically the ill-fate of humans who approach on them. Perhaps an explanation of the dangers of water in cold weather.

Kul-Jungk—See Kul

Kulkulcan—Male—Central America

Animal association: Snake (serpent)

Mayan feathered serpent god whose lore was absorbed by Quetzalcoatl.

Kurkil—Male—Central Asia

Mongolian Creator god who instructed humanity in the art of building community.

Kurma—Male—Near East
Animal associations: Elephant, Tortoise
Plant associations: Banyon, Damiana, Mandrake

Hindu second avatar of Vishnu who went to the bottom of the sea to recover things lost during the Great Flood. Patron of treasure hunters in all capacities.

KuzunoHa—Female—Far East
(Also known as She-Fox of Shinoda)
Animal association: Fox

Japanese fox who so fell in love with the man who saved her life that she gave up her natural form, assumed the form of a human, and married him.

Kwannon—Female—Far East
Animal associations: Fish, Horse (white)

Japanese variant of the Chinese Kuan Yin.

Lada—Female—Central Europe/Northern Europe
Plant association: Lime tree

Slavic goddess of Beauty.

Lahar—Male—Middle East/Mediterranean
Animal association: Sheep (ram)

Sumerian god of all domestic farm animals, but particularly sheep. May have also been a Babylonian goddess with the same associations, but those cites are sketchy at best.

Lakini—Female—Near East

Hindu goddess associated with the Manipura chakra (solar plexus). Sometimes described as an aspect of Shakti. See also Dakini, Rakini, Kakini, Sakini, and Hakini.

Lakshmi—Female—Near East
(Also known as Shri, Sri)
Husband: Vishnu
Animal association: Peacock

Hindu goddess of luck, prosperity, and good fortune.

Lamashtu—See Lamia

Lamastu—See Lamia

Lamia—Male/Female—Mediterranean/Middle East
(Also known as Lamashtu, Lamastu)
Animal associations: Donkey, Snake

A Libyan Queen who fell in love with Zeus and bore him several children. In outrage, Hera killed each of her children. In grief, Lamia became a bisexual snake deity who, knowing the grief that love and sex had brought her, would never again need a man to conceive children. From her story we see explained the horrible cycle of abuse that causes an abused child to become an abusive parent. So horrific was the death of her children at the hands of Hera and her jealous rage that Lamia quickly became jealous of all who have children and is sometimes said to gobble them up at every chance.

Lares—Male/Female—Mediterranean
(Also known as Lases)
Animal association: Dog

Generally speaking, Roman term to describe ancestral spirits who remained in the home to protect it and its inhabitants. They bring blessings to the home and to any farm land connected with the home. See Lemures, their unpleasant counterparts. When used in the more specific, the Lares were guardians of specific locations or places.

Lares Compitales: protect crossroads (decision-making)
Lares Domestici: protect the home
Lares Familiares: protect the family
Lares Permarini: protect the oceans and sea travels
Lares Praestitis: protect formal community (government)
Lares Rurales: protect open land
Lares Viales: protect travelers

Lemures—Male/Female—Mediterranean
(Also known as Larvae)

Roman term to describe ancestral spirits who remained in the home and taunted its inhabitants. To appease them (or maybe drive them away), the master of the home led the 'Feast of the Lemures.' During the event, they would either be appeased with offerings of food (black beans are cited often) or driven off with loud noise. See also Lares (their friendly counterparts).

La Sirene—See Erzulie

Latona—Female—Mediterranean
   Roman name for the Greek Leto.

Laufey—Female—North Europe
Husband: Farbauti
   Scandinavian giant and mother of Loki.

Leda—Female—Mediterranean
Husband: Tyndareus
Lover: Zeus
   Leda was married to Tyndareus, King of Sparta. To him she bore Tyndareus and Clytemnestra. While still married to Tyndareus, she was seduced/tricked by Zeus into his embrace where she conceived Pollux and Helen. As part of Zeus' seduction involved taking the form of a swan and the result of that seduction was the Trojan War, we see a clear warning that deception and magick should not be involved in matters of love. Because Tyndareus and Leda were apparently monogamous, we also see a warning against disturbing monogamous relationships.

Leib-Olmai—Male—Central and Northern Europe
Animal association: Bear
   Finnish personification of Nature's strength as a bear god.

Leshi—Gods/Goddesses—Central Europe/Northern Europe
Animal association: Goat
   Russian woodland creatures, both male and female, whose antics are similar to Pan's.

Leto—Female—Mediterranean
Father: Coeus
Mother: Phoebe
Lover: Zeus
   'Hidden one'—When Leto became pregnant with Artemis and Apollo by Zeus, Hera forbade her from giving birth on land or any island. The children grew in her womb until it was incredibly painful. To circumvent Hera and finally give birth, she went to a floating island of which Hera did not say she could not. The Romans called her Latona.

Leucippe—Female—Mediterranean
Husband: Evenor
Lover: Poseidon
Animal association: Horse (white mare)
   Greek nymph who accompanied Persephone into the Underworld. Although she is married to Evenor, Poseidon fell in love with her. Together, she and Zeus had five pairs of male twins to whom Zeus gave Atlantis.

Liber Pater—Male—Mediterranean
Plant associations: Almond, Vine (grape)
   Roman god of wine and fertility. His female counterpart is the goddess Libertas. He is closely associated with Dionysus.

Libertas—Female—Mediterranean/North America
(Also known as Liberty)
Animal association: Cat
   Roman goddess who was later adopted by North America as the personification of the United States. Her male counterpart, Liber Pater, is goddess of Freedom, both personal and national.

Lilith—Female—Middle East
Husband: Adam
Animal association: Owl, Snake (serpent)
   'She of the night'—The first wife of Adam, later replaced with Eve. She and Adam were created as conjoined twins. But Lilith demanded more autonomy, so they were separated. From there, much like the story of Diana and Lucifer, she pursued Adam for reunion (sex), but Adam would have nothing of it. Some cite her banishment and transformation

into the serpent that tempted Eve, Adam's second wife. Others feel Lilith became an aspect of Eve in the way the pre-separation Diana must surely be an aspect of the Diana after separation. It is very interesting to note the meaning of her name and the association between Diana and Night/Darkness.

Lips—Male—Mediterranean
(Also known as Livos)

Greek personification of the South West Wind.

Lissa—Male—Africa
(Also known as Lisa, Leza)
Animal associations: Chameleon, Dog

Supreme God of Central Africa who instructed humanity on building community and culture. He does not listen to prayers much anymore because he has grown old and deaf.

Llew Llaw Gyffes—Male—North Europe/ Central Europe
(Also known as Lleu)
Wife: Blodeuwedd

'Bright lion with sure hand'—Welsh god who died at the hands of Gronw while fighting over his wife, who had been unfaithful to him with Gronw. Llew and Gronw died in that conflict, but Llew was magickly restored. Patron of those whose spouses have been unfaithful.

Llyr—Male—Central Europe
Wife: Iweridd
Son: Bran the Blessed by Iweridd

Welsh god of the sea and origin of Shakespeare's character King Lear.

Loa, The—Male and Female—Caribbean

Caribbean Voodoo guardians of natural forces and of humanities negotiations with those forces. The loa are either ancestral spirits (protectors of the family line) or protectors of certain locations (personified natural forces) who are governed by Damballah. They are called by drawing a 'veve' on the ground.

Lokapalas, The—Male—Near East

Hindu gods who are personification and guardians of the eight principle directions: Indra, Agni, Yama, Surya, Varuna, Vayu, Kubera, and Soma.

Loki—Male—North Europe
(Also known as Look)
Father: Farbauti
Mother: Laufey
Wife: Sign
Lover: Angurboda
Animal associations: Coyote, Horse, Jackal, Salmon, Wolf
Plant association: Benzoin

Scandinavian trickster god. He is one of the Aesir, but often finds himself at odds (and war) with them. He is also father, by Angurboda, of the three monstrous children of ill-fate; Fenrir, Hel, and Jormungand.

Long—Male—Central Asia
(Also known as Lung)
Animal association: Dragon

Chinese creature guardian of the North. He is described as a dragon. The other three guardians are Ch'i-lin, Gui Xian, and Feng-haang. They are collectively known as the Ssu Ling.

Lono—Male—Polynesian Islands
Plant association: Kava Kava

Hawaiian god of song and fertility who fell in love with the mortal Kaikilani. They were wed and lived happily ever after in monogamous bliss where each filled the other's needs and desires. Well, happily ever after until Lono mistakenly thought Kaikilani had been unfaithful, at which point Lono killed his beloved wife. Realizing his loss, he left the island promising to return when he had recovered from heartache and overcome rage. He has not yet returned. His story speaks much to those of us who suffer from anger management problems. Patron of those who battle jealousy and anger management issues.

Lucifer—Male—Mediterranean/Middle East

Roman god who is all but overlooked by modern-day Wiccans because of the Christian connection to Satan. Others overlook him due to his reportedly incestuous relationship with his sister Diana. You see, Diana and Lucifer were not brother and sister at all; to be such, one would have to be born of mother and father. They were not. Their story is that which is presented in the Book of Genesis. The name Diana is used to describe that which was both Darkness (Diana) and Lucifer (Light) prior to the separation of Light and Darkness. After separating into Diana (Darkness) and Light (Lucifer), Diana, having known what it was like to be truly alone, sought instantly to unite with Lucifer. Lucifer, not having known what it is like to be truly alone, resisted her advances. Eventually, the two did become lovers when Diana shape-shifted into a cat and tricked her way into his bed. The use of his name is one of the Inner Court secrets of many Wiccan traditions. However, in hiding the use of this story, we lose much on which Wicca has been built. After all, what would the Charge of the Goddess—a text considered sacred—be without the words of Aradia (daughter of Lucifer and Diana) found in *Aradia: Gospel of the Witches*?

Ludd—Male—Central Europe

(Also known as Nuada)

Animal associations: Dog, Fish, and all sea creatures

'Silver Hand'—Celtic river god who lost his hand in combat. His brother created a silver hand to replace it. He is sometimes seen as Sun God and protector of children, but with his invincible and indestructible magick sword, he is more often associated with war, combat, and the ability to overcome great odds by using magick.

Lugh—Male—Central Europe

See also Llew Llaw Gyffes

Father: Cain

Mother: Eithne, Tailtiu (adopted)

Lover: Dechtire

Animal associations: Raven, Deer (white stag), Dog

Plant associations: Alder, Blackberry, Gorse, Holly

Holiday: Lughnasadh (the Gaelic word for August)

Irish god who excelled at many skills. Sometimes known as 'Lugh of many arts' or 'Lugh of the long hand,' he was said to be particularly skilled with precision and attention to detail. In a modern world, Lugh can be seen as patron of such matters as computer repair or automotive maintenance. But in an older time, we was seen as man about the home, able to repair or build just about anything.

Luna—Female—Mediterranean

Plant association: Willow

'Moon'—Roman personification and Goddess of the Moon. She was later absorbed or identified with Diana and Hecate.

Lupa—Female—Mediterranean

Animal association: Wolf

Potentially the name given to the promiscuous aspect of Acca Larentia.

Lu-xing—Male—Central Asia

(Also known as Lu-Hsing)

Animal association: Deer

Chinese god of status and wealth.

Maat—Female—Africa

Animal associations: Ostrich, Lynx

Egyptian goddess of truth and divine justice in the natural order of things. It is her symbol, the feather of Maat, that a person's soul is weighed against in the afterlife to determine the eventuality of the soul.

Macha—Female—Central Europe

Father: Delbaeth

Mother: Ernmas

Animal associations: Crow, Raven

Irish goddess of war and one of the Irish Triple Goddesses of Fate. The other two are Badb and Anu. See also Morrigan.

Mafdet—Female—Africa
Animal associations: Cat, Mongoose

Very early Egyptian goddess form. She was invoked to protect against snakes and scorpions and for the healing of snake bites and scorpion stings.

Mah—Male—Middle East
Animal associations: Cattle (Cow)
Holiday: The seventh day after each new moon

Persian moon god who presides over time and the tides.

Maia—Female—Mediterranean
Father: Atlas
Mother: Aethra or Pleione
Lover: Zeus

Greek goddess whose sacred month is May. She is the eldest and most beautiful of the Pleiades.

Mait Carrefour—Male—Caribbean
(Also known as Maitre Carrefour, Kalfu)

Haitian Voodoo 'Lord of the Crossroads' and master of magick.

Maman Brigidt—Female—Caribbean

Haitian Voodoo goddess of death, resurrection, and the erotic associations made with both. Her male counterpart is Ghede.

Mama Occelo—Female—Inca
Husband: Manco Capac

Inca goddess. For her story, see Manco Capac.

Manannan Mac Lir—Male—Central Europe
Wife: Fand
Animal associations: Boar, Crane, Horse, Gull, Cow

'Manannan Son of the Sea'—Irish god of the sea who could forecast the weather.

Manco Capac—Male—South America
Wife: Mama Occelo

Inca fire and solar god who founded the first Inca city and capital Cisco and began the empire of the Inca. He and his wife taught community building to humanity while his brother, Pachacamac, created the world, humanity, and all things.

Mani—Male—Northern Europe
Father: Mundilfari
Mother: Glaur

Scandinavian personification and God of the moon. His sister is Sol, the Sun.

Mania—Female—Mediterranean
Husband: Mantus

Roman/Etruscan goddess of death and Greek personification of insanity.

Mantus—Male—Mediterranean
Wife: Mania

Roman/Etruscan god of the Underworld.

Maou—Male—Africa
Father: Lissa

West African sun god.

Maponos—Male—Central Europe
(Also known as Mabon)
Animal associations: Horse, Dog (hound)
Holiday: Autumn Equinox (AKA Mabon)

'Divine son'—Celtic god of youth and youthful endeavors. He is patron and protector of children, folk hero, and great hunter.

Marduk—Male—Mediterranean
Father: Ea
Mother: Damkina
Wife: Zarpanitu
Lover: Ishtar
Animal associations: Eagle, Dragon (snake), Lion, Antelope

Babylonian god who became Supreme God of the Babylonian pantheon. Initially he was a god of thunderstorms and the fertility that the rain brings to the Earth.

Mari—Female—Mediterranean

Animal association: Owl

'Queen'—Queen/Supreme Goddess of the Basque pantheon. She is the personification of Earth and storm, especially in the association with death by natural forces. When the old religions were replaced with Christianity, she became Santa Marina.

Marian—Female—Central Europe

Plant association: Myrrh, Myrtle

Holiday: Bealtaine

The Sea Goddess Marian is a potential origin for both the stories of the mermaid as well as Robin Hood's Maid Marian. Now, before one jumps to the conclusion that she is not a legitimate goddess form, let me point out that the difference between mythology and lore is often nothing more than the age of the story. In more contemporary culture she is Queen of the May.

Marici—Female—Near East

Animal association: Boar (sow)

Hindu goddess of dawn who travels in front of the sun. For this reason she is said to be invisible. Also seen as controlling the fate of reincarnation based on a soul's karma from past lives.

Mars—Male—Mediterranean

Wife: Bellona

Lover: Rhea Silvia

Animal associations: Vulture, Woodpecker, Horse, Wolf, Boar, Sheep

Plant associations: Aloe, Ash, Benzoin, Buttercup, Coconut, Dogwood, Dragon's Blood, Geranium, Myrrh (sweet/opoponax), Nettle (greater), Oak, Olive, Pepper (black), Rue, Vervain, Wormwood

Roman god of war. His wife, Bellona, is sometimes cited as his sister. The months February and October are sacred to him as is March, which was named after him. On the Quinquatrus, the weapons of war were cleaned in connection with his festival. Although most often called the god of war, he is often depicted named and in the embrace or partial embrace of a beautiful woman (who is not always described as his wife). He was initially associated with fertility, Spring, crops, and livestock. He most likely became a god of war as crops and live stock were threatened.

Incense Recipe
(for offensive and projective defense)

1 part Dragon's Blood resin

1 part Benzoin

1 part Vervain

1 pinch Wormwood

Enough Mars (from the second Recipe) or Opoponax oil to bind

Mars Oil Recipe
(for protection and fertility)

9 drops Opoponax (sweet myrrh) essential oil

6 drops Benzoin essential oil

3 drops Black Pepper essential oil

1/2 ounce Olive oil

Mars Oil Recipe
(for offensive and projective defense)

9 drops Dragons Blood perfume oil

6 drops Black Pepper essential oil

6 drops Benzoin essential oil

1/2 ounce Olive oil

Mary Cleopas—Female—Middle East/Mediterranean

Half-sister of the Christian mother of Jesus. Sometimes said to form a Triple Goddess with the Virgin Mary and Mary Magdalene; however, the Virgin Mary had two half-sisters. The other is Mary Salome, so the names of the Christian Triple Goddess sometimes vary.

Mary Magdalene—Female—Middle East/Mediterranean

Husband: Jesus

Sometimes said to form a Triple Goddess with the Virgin Mary and Mary Cleopas. However, as the Virgin Mary had two sisters by the name Mary, some feel citing those three is a better reference to a Christian Triple Goddess. In addition to the Virgin Mary, the other two are Mary Cleopas and Mary Salome (as opposed to Mary Magdalene). Additional lore seems to indicate that Mary Magdalene is Mary Salome. That the name change was made to protect the blood-line of Jesus.

Mary Salome—See Mary Magdalene

Mashia—Male—Middle East/Mediterranean
Father: Gayomart
Wife: Mashiane
Persian first man who, like the Christian Adam, was led away from god (Ormazd) by the evil adversary of god (Ahriman).

Mashiane—Female—Middle East/Mediterranean
Father: Gayomart
Husband: Mashia
Persian first woman.

Maslum—Male—North America
Algonquin antagonist of his brother, Glooskap. Maslum is credited with the creation of all things that are baneful to humanity.

Massim Biambe—Neutral—Africa
Creator god of the Congo who was neither male, nor female, nor hermaphrodite. Supreme God who created humanity with Phebele and Mebeli. Phebele and Mebeli gave birth to a son, thus giving humanity form (body), but it was not until Massim gave that body the breath of life (soul) and mind that humanity was truly born.

Matarisvan—Male—Near East
Hindu messenger of the gods who captured lightning and gave it to humanity in the form of fire.

Matowelia—Male—North America
God of the Mojave tribe who guided and protected tribe members in their travels. It was widely believed that to be with him after death, one's body must be cremated. Sacrificing a meal or the value of that meal to one in need just prior to traveling was said to bring his blessings on a journey.

Matsya—Male—Near East
Animal associations: Dolphin, Fish
Plant association: White Poppy
Hindu first avatar of Vishnu. Prior to the Great Flood, a mortal named Manu discovered a small fish that asked for his protection. That man granted the fish his protection and allowed no harm to come to it, even though the man was very hungry. In return, the fish warned Manu of the flood that was approaching. Eventually the fish grew to a great size, and the man recognized it as an incarnation of Vishnu. After the Great Flood, Matsya (incarnation of Vishnu) assisted Manu in reseeding the Earth.

Matuta—Female—Mediterranean
(Also known as Mater Matuta)
Roman personification of Dawn and goddess of growth. She is patron and protector of newborn babies.

Maui—Male—Polynesian Islands
Plant association: Banyan
Polynesian/Hawaiian sun god.

Mayauel—Female—Central America
Animal associations: Snake, Tortoise
Aztec goddess who, with Quetzalcoatl, brought love to humanity. Interestingly enough, she also brought all intoxicants.

Mebeli—Female—Africa
Husband: Phebele
Congo creator of the first of humanity. See Massim Biambe.

Medha—Female—Near East
Husband: Dharma
'Understanding'—Hindu goddess of empathy and compassion.

Meditrina—Female—Mediterranean

'Healer'—Roman goddess of wine and health. Perhaps an early observation of the connection between moderate alcohol use and health benefits.

Medusa—Female—Mediterranean
Animal associations: Snake, Horse (Pegasus), Moth

Ruler of the Gorgon. She is so hideous that any man who looks upon her gaze becomes stone. One story on how this happened says that Medusa was initially very beautiful—so beautiful that Poseidon welcomed her to his godly embrace. The jealous Athena would have none of it, so she turned Medusa's hair to snakes.

Megaera—Female—Mediterranean

'Jealous One'—Greek goddess of justice and vengeance. One of the three Erinyes (Furies) with Alecto and Tisiphone.

Mehilainen—Female—Northern Europe
Animal association: Bee

Finish sacred messengers manifest in the bee. May be connected to Mellonia (who taught bee-keeping), or may just be a word for bee.

Meilikki—Female—North Europe
Animal association: Bear

Finnish goddess of the green. Sometimes depicted as a female incarnation of the Green Man.

Melanion—Male—Mediterranean
Wife: Atalanta

Greek god who fell in love with Atalanta. His advances were originally rejected by Atalanta who said that he could not have her hand unless he first beat her at sport. So he and she had a foot race in which Melanion dropped three golden apples given to him by Aphrodite. Melanion won the race and her hand because Atalanta stopped to pick up the apples. In so doing he set the stage for the later observation that 'All is fair in love and war.' Patron of suitors of women playing hard to get.

Melkart—Male—Middle East/Mediterranean
Animal association: Quail

Phoenician folk hero, god, and patron of city dwellers and dwellings. Some cite as a Phoenician equivalent of Hercules.

Mellonia—Female—Mediterranean
(Also known as Mellisa)
Animal association: Bee

Perhaps an aspect of Demeter, Mellonia is a fertility goddess. She is said to have taught humanity the art of bee-keeping.

Melpomene—Female—Mediterranean

'Choir'—Greek Muse of the tragedy. See also Muses, The.

Menat—Female—Middle East
(Also known as Manat)
Father: Allah
Holiday: Dark Moon

An aspect of the Triple Goddess Allat. She is goddess of time and fate. Her holiday is the dark moon, but the whole of the waning moon cycle is also sacred to her. See also Allat.

Menthu—Male—Africa
Animal associations: Falcon, Bull

Egyptian god of war who is often depicted as having the head of a falcon or hawk.

Mercury—Male—Mediterranean
(Also known as Mercurius, Alipes)
Lover: Venus
Animal associations: Ape, Jackal, Snake, Swallow, Turtle, Tortoise
Plant associations: Almond, Beech, Broom, Cinnamon, Hazelnut, Lavender, Lemongrass, Lotus, Mulberry, Olive, Palm (date), Vervain, Willow

Roman god of communication, travel, and merchants. He is the father of Cupid by Venus; as messenger of the gods this is perhaps commentary on the relationship between love and good communication. The month of June was sacred to Mercury. At one time the worship of this Roman god was so far reaching that the Celts and Norse also joined in his praise.

Incense Recipe

2 parts Lavender flowers

1 part Lemon Grass

1 part Gum Arabic

Enough Mercury or Lavender essential oil to bind

Oil Recipe

11 drops Lavender essential oil

9 drops Lemongrass essential oil

1/2 ounce almond or olive oil

Merope—Female—Mediterranean

(Also known as Aero)

Husband: Sisyphus

Greek virgin and one of the seven Pleiades. Her hand was wildly pursued by Orion (and the other Pleiades), but she did not love them. Even when her suitors' powerful mothers became insistent that she take the hand of a god, she refused and instead chose Sisyphus, a mortal, because he had won her heart.

Meshkent—Female—Africa

(Also known as Mesenet, Meskhenet, Meskhent)

Husband: Shai

Egyptian goddess of childbirth and the personification of the birthing place. As she is responsible for shaping the child in the mother's womb and giving to that child its 'ka' (life force), she is goddess of initial fate.

Meztli—Male—Central America

Animal association: Butterfly

Aztec word for both moon and month used in the Meztlian religion and calendar. He became chief god of the Meztlian religion at its inception. A priest of the sun worshipping religion, Teotlahtolli, had instructed his son never to look directly at the sun. He ignored his father's wishes and went blind. Taking his

son to a priest of the sun, he asked him why their god would strike blind his son only for adoring the sun's brilliance. The priest told the father it happened because the child was insolent in trying to see, and thus know, the face of God. So outraged was the father that their god would blind his son for such a natural curiosity that he left the Teotlahtolli religion and formed his own, the Meztlian who worshipped a loving god—the Moon or Meztli.

Miach—Male—Central Europe

Father: Dianchecht

Irish god who, like his father, was known as a great healer. Unfortunately, he is also a rather jealous god, having occasion to destroy the superior work of others.

Michabo—Male—North America

Wife: Muskrat

Animal association: Hare

Sometimes appears as an Algonquin folk hero, similar to Mungan Ngana of Australia, who invented a system by which one can write music, make fish nets, boats, advanced tools and weapons, as well as a host of other devices that greatly improved the lives of his people. Other times he appears as the Algonquin Creator, a great hare.

Michael—Male—Middle East/Mediterranean

(Also known as Mika'il [Arabic])

Semitic God of Fire. He is also one of the only two angels mentioned by name in the modern Christian Bible. The other being Gabriel. Gnostic archangel who is associated with the South Quarter in Wiccan, Gnostic, and Ceremonial rituals. The other Quarters are presided upon by Raphael, Gabriel, and Auriel.

Mictancihautl—See Mictlantecuhtli

Mictlantecuhtli—Male—Central America

Wife: Mictlancihautl

Animal associations: Bat, Owl, Raven, Spider

God and ruler (with his wife) of the lowest level of the Aztec Underworld, Mictlan.

Mimir—Male—North Europe
Plant association: Yew

Scandinavian god of fresh water, especially streams, who grants the gift of wisdom and divination but insists a price be paid such that his gifts be honored. He is associated with the Yggdrasil, the world tree most often said to be ash, but which a growing number of folk, including myself, cite as yew. Patron of poets and those seeking wisdom. Yggdrasil is also called the Tree of Life. The story of Mimir and Odin is that Mimir was the guardian of the Yggdrasil who commonly drank from the streams (Mimir's Well). Odin asked Mimir for a drink, but Mimir wanted his eye in exchange. Upon giving him his eye, Odin drank deeply and received the same gifts of wisdom and divination. This is probably a reference to the shamanic practice of using chemically achieved altered states as reportedly the vapors (streams) that rise from the roots of the yew will induce intoxication and visions.

Min—Male—Africa
(Also known as Menu, Minu)
Animal associations: Bee, Bull (white), Lion
Plant associations: Lettuce, Wheat

Egyptian god of sexual potency. He was always depicted with an erect penis. He was also the protector of travelers, especially those who traveled across the desert. Patron of the travelers and sexual potency. As 'Menu', sometimes cited as a Lithuanian moon god.

Minerva—Female—Mediterranean
Husband: Jupiter
Animal associations: Owl, Horse, Cattle (ox), Sheep (ram), Snake
Plant associations: Dragon's Blood, Geranium, Olive, Lily (tiger), Mulberry, Thistle

Roman goddess of both education and war. Patron of commerce, entertainers, and minstrels. She was the inventor of the alphabet and of mathematics (numbers) and is thus associated with the science of the written language, although not with words themselves. She is also said to have invented either musical instruments or the method by which the sounds of those instruments can be recorded in a written form (sheet music).

Minos—Male—Mediterranean
Wife: Pasiphae
Animal associations: Cattle (bull), Elephant
Plant associations: Aloe, Myrrh, Olive

Greek king who called on Poseidon in a dispute over land and its rule, he later became the judge of the Underworld. He decides who would move on to Elysian Fields (Heaven) and who would go to Tartarus (Hell).

Incense Recipe

Yellow Sandalwood powder with enough Galbanum oil to bind

Oil Recipe

21 drops Galbanum oil
1/2 ounce Olive oil

Minth—Female—Mediterranean
Lover: Hades
Plant association: Mint

Greek nymph who slept with Hades, thus bringing on the wrath of Persephone, who flattened her into the Earth with such force that the only thing that remained was the plant that we now call mint.

Misharu—Male—Middle East/Mediterranean

Babylonian god of law who brings order to civilization.

Mithras—Male—Middle East/Mediterranean/Near East
(Also known as Mitra [Hindu])
Animal associations: Eagle, Cattle (bull), Chicken (cock), Hawk, Raven, Lion, Dog, Horse, Snake, Dragon
Plant associations: Cypress, Violet

In the Near East, he is a lesser sun god called Mitra. There his worship was not abundant. But in Persia, we see a different story. There he is god of morality, friendship, and truth. He developed into a war god who granted victory to the just when found to be in conflict with the unjust. Eventually his worship found its way to Rome where he is Mithras. Animal sacrifice was paid to him, most often in the form of a bull. Those sacrifices were thought to assure fertility to the land. This reinforces the Wiccan belief that for life there must be death. See Mitra for the attributes specific to the Near East.

Mitra—Male—Near East
(Also known as Mithras)
Father: Kashyapa
Mother: Aditi

Mitra is one of the Adityas. The Hindu month Agrahayana (November 22–December 21) is sacred to Mitra. See Adityas. See also Mithras for the evolution of this deity from Near East into Rome.

Mixcoatl—Male—Central America
Mother: Cihuatcoatl

Aztec god of hunting and war who brought the secret of fire to his people.

Mizaru—Male—Far East
Animal association: Monkey

'*See no evil*'—There is a 17th century temple in Japan which has a statue of three monkeys. The best translation of the inscription on that statue is 'See no evil, hear no evil, and speak no evil' or 'Mizaru, Kikazaru, Iwazaru.' The statuary is most likely a representation of the three faces of a much earlier deity form, Vadjra.

Mobo—Female—Central Asia/Far East

Chinese/Japanese personification of the perfect mother.

Modron—Female—Central Europe

Welsh Great Mother who may have been the historic figure 'Morgain la Fee,' who was included in the mythology of King Arthur. That is to say, Modron likely existed as a flesh and blood woman, as did King Arthur, but with the creation of lore they both became mythologized.

Moingfhion—Female—Central Europe
Holiday: Samhain

Irish Crone/grandmother goddess associated with Samhain.

Moko—Male—Polynesian Islands
Animal association: Lizard

Polynesian magician, god, and teacher of magick. He is seen as a large lizard.

Mo Li, The—Male—Central Asia

The four guardians of Chinese Buddhism. See Shou, Hung, Chung, and Hai.

Monan—Male—South America

Brazilian Creator god to the Tupis and other people along the Amazon Valley.

Montu—Male—Africa
Father: Amun Ra (adopted)
Mother: Mut (adopted)
Animal associations: Cattle (bull), Falcon, Hawk, Sheep (ram), Owl, Horse, Bear, Wolf
Plant associations: Dragon's Blood, Lily (tiger), Geranium, Pepper (black), Rue, Wormwood

Initially a minor sun god of the southmost areas of Egypt. As war became more a part of Egyptian life, he evolved into a war god of greater importance. Soon, his worship spread to much of Egypt.

Incense Recipe

4 parts Dragon's Blood
1 part Wormwood
1 pinch black pepper

Morgan le Fay—Female—Central Europe
(Also known as Morgain la Fee)
Father: The Duke of Cornwall
Mother: Igraine
Lover: King Arthur, Myrddin

Half-sister of King Arthur. In some stories, she bore to King Arthur his only son, Mordred. In other stories, Mordred was Arthur's cousin. In some stories, she is Merlin's (Myrddin) lover and plotted to destroy the reign of Arthur by causing his wife's infidelity. As the story cannot be proven to be historic, no one can be sure what the events really were. I think that as Arthur was conceived using manipulative love magick, his downfall came from the manipulative love magick used to create Mordred. Thinking that way reminds us that those who do not remember history are condemned to repeat it.

Morpheus—Male—Mediterranean

Father: Thanatos

Plant association: Broom

    'He who forms'—Greek god of dreams and their manifestation in the world of the living, who lived in the darkness of the Underworld. From his name and his attributes, we see that the Greeks saw a connection between the dream world and the manifestation of reality.

Morrigan, The—Female—Central Europe

(Also known as Morrigu)

Father: Delbaeth

Mother: Ernmas

Animal associations: Crow, Raven

Plant association: Sloe (blackthorn)

    Irish goddess of war and fate. In her role as goddess of fate, she is seen as a Triple Goddess of Fate and is the embodiment of her three daughters, Badb, Macha, and Anu.

Mu Gong—Male—Central Asia

(Also known as Mu Kung)

    Chinese Taoist personification of the male principle of the soul, the yang. He is called the 'Royal Father of the East.' He is god of immortality and presides over the east half of Paradise in the afterlife.

Mullissu—See Belitis

Mullo—Male—Central Europe

Animal association: Mule

    Celtic god of mules and those who work with or drive mules.

Muluku—Male—Africa

    Mozambican Creator god who became so frustrated with humanity's unwillingness to support themselves and each other that he created monkeys. He then took the monkeys' tails away, placed those tails on humanity, and told each to be the other, thus making monkeys of humanity and humanity of monkeys. Some might argue he missed a few. Patron of those who work with folk who act like monkeys and everyone who works retail.

Mungan Ngana—Male—Australia

    Australian Aboriginal folk hero, similar to Michabo of Africa, who taught his people how to make fish nets, boats, advanced tools and weapons, as well as a host of other devices that greatly improved the lives of his people.

Mulac—Male—Central America

Father: Itzamna

Mother: Ixchel

    One of the Bacabs, the four Mayan gods of the principle directions. Associated with the color white. In Wiccan ritual he is associated with the North Quarter. See also Cauac, Ix, and Kan.

Muses, The—Female—Mediterranean

Animal associations: Swan, Horse (Pegasus)

    Greek goddesses of inspiration. Most often cited as daughters of Zeus and Mnesyne. Their number has varied with time, most commonly cited as nine: Clio, Euterpe, Thalia, Melpomene, Terpsichore, Erato, Polyhymnia, Urania, and their leader, Calliope.

Mut—Female—Africa

Husband: Amun Ra

Animal associations: Eagle, Vulture, Cow, Cat, Lioness

Plant associations: Aspen, Cypress, Frankincense, Myrrh, Poppy (white)

    'Mother'—Egyptian Creator and Mother Goddess. She is said to make the soul strong and the body sound.

Incense Recipe

3 parts Frankincense
1 part Myrrh
1 part Poppy Flowers (white is best but red/blue will do)
1 part Cypress

Oil Recipe

8 drops Frankincense oil
6 drops Myrrh oil
6 drops Cypress oil
1/2 ounce base oil

Mylitta—Female—Middle East/Mediterranean

Babylonian moon goddess associated with love, fertility, and childbirth. Her temples were served by sacred prostitutes who sacrificed their virginity to strangers in exchange for the receipt of teachings in the ways of love.

Myrddin—Male—Central Europe

(Also known as Merlin)

Sister: Gwendydd

Lover: Morgan le Fay, Vivienne (Nimue)

Celtic and Welsh bard, magician, and speaker of prophecy who was associated with the mythic, or perhaps mythologized, Merlin of the King Arthur story.

Nabu—Male—Mediterranean

Father: Marduk

Animal association: Dragon (serpent-headed)

Sumero-Babylonian god of the written language, the alphabet, record-keeping, and wisdom. He maintains the tablets of fate and is the patron of librarians and record keepers.

Nago—Male—Africa/Caribbean

(Also known as Nago Shango)

Haitian Voodoo loa and African Yoruba god of power, especially power derived from ancestors and lineage.

Nah-Hunte—Male—Mediterranean

Babylonian Sun God of law and order. Patron of police officers and those working in the criminal justice system.

Nahmauit—Female—Africa

Husband: Thoth

Egyptian goddess who opposed and removed evil.

Nala—Male—Near East

Father: Visvakarma

Animal association: Monkey

Hindu metalsmith who built a bridge across the ocean with the help of monkeys. Patron of working animals and their masters.

Namagiri—Female—Near East

Hindu goddess of divination, inspiration, education, and teaching.

Nanan Bouclou—Male—Africa/Caribbean

African Creator (maybe bisexual) of the gods from what is now eastern Senegal. Upon his migration to the Caribbean, he became a Haitian Voodoo deity of plant life and the natural medicines made from plants.

Nanaya—See Nanna

Nanna—Female—North Europe

Husband: Baldur

Son: Forseti by Baldur

Scandinavian goddess whose story has partly led to the Wiccan tradition of the third rite of handfasting. Upon the death of her husband Baldur, Nanna committed suicide by throwing herself on the funeral pyre. Her story helps us to understand the nature of the third handfasting as an act that unites a couple even after they have left this world. Although the Wiccan rite does not involve suicide, the intent remains the same.

Nannar—Male—Middle East/Mediterranean

Sumerian moon god is called 'Lord of Destiny.'

Nanshe—Female—Mediterranean/Middle East

Father: Ea

Mother: Kishar

Babylonian goddess of fertility, water, and childbirth. She is said to give her followers the ability to interpret dreams and perhaps divine the future from dreams.

Nantosuelta—Female—Central Europe/ Northern Europe

Animal association: Raven

'Winding river'—Gallic river and water goddess who is said to bless and protect the home. As her name implies, the association to protecting the home is probably found in the observation that her people often build settlements with the entrance facing a river such that the river offered an element of protection.

Narasinha—Male—Near East

(Also known as Narasingha)

Animal association: Lion

Plant associations: Frankincense, Sunflower

Hindu fourth avatar of Vishnu. He is depicted as part man and part lion.

Na Reau—Male—Polynesian Islands

Polynesian god who created the first man and woman. He told them not to procreate, but of course they didn't listen. This could be a reflection of the Christian Adam and Eve theme. Many Christians seem to believe that the forbidden fruit that their Bible speaks of was an analogy to sex. The difference is that Na Reau forgave them. Patron of children who become parents before they are ready

Nasr—Male—Middle East

(Also known as Nesr)

Animal association: Vulture

Mentioned in the Koran (71:23) as an idol. His condemnation as a false god in the Koran is similar to the condemnation that Moses gave to similar deities. When we consider the great amount of death that has been brought about as a result of such statements, we begin to see that although religious leaders and prophets have every right to express their opinion, giving name to one Supreme God and demanding that other images and names be forsaken is the first step towards genocide.

Natigai—Male—Central Asia

Mongolian Earth god who, with his wife, were the patrons of humanity in its attempts to raise plants and animals. Patron of farmers of crop and animal.

Ndengei—Male—Polynesian Islands

Animal association: Snake (serpent)

Creator seen by the folk of Fiji.

Nebo—Male—Middle East/Mediterranean

Babylonian god of teaching and education. He and his wife Tashmit invented the written language. Also the name of the island on which the Hebrew prophet Moses died.

Nehalennia—Female—Central Europe/ Northern Europe

Animal association: Dog

Teutonic goddess of fertility and navigation at sea. She became associated with commerce in association with trade as linked to ocean navigation.

Neith—Female—Africa

Animal associations: Bee, Vulture, Snake (golden cobra), Spider

Egyptian goddess associated with the Element Fire and the protection of the god Duamutef. As her worship spread, she gradually became a war goddess.

Nekhebet—Female—Africa

Animal associations: Vulture, Snake (serpent), Lion

Protective goddess of southern Egypt.

Nemesis—Female—Mediterranean

(Also known as Rhamnusia)

Father: Erebus

Mother: Nyx

Animal association: Deer

Plant associations: Apple, Ash

Greek goddess of anger and fate. She brings great punishment to mortals who break with moral law, especially against those who do so for personal gain.

Nephthys—Female—Africa

(Also known as Neb-hut, Nebthet)

Lover: Osiris (or maybe Set)

Animal associations: Chicken (cock), Dog, Horse

Plant associations: Cypress, Lily, Myrrh, Nettle, Poppy (white)

'Friend of the Dead'—Egyptian goddess associated with the Element Earth and the protection of the god Hapi. As Nephthys she is as her name implies, friend of the dead, but she is also Neb-hut (Nebthet), which means 'Mistress of Home.' In that capacity, she is protector of children and women during childbirth. Here we see again the connection between birth and death.

Incense Recipe

2 parts Gum Arabic

1 part Sandalwood

1 parts Myrrh

1 part Cypress

1 part Poppy

Neptune—Male—Mediterranean

Wife: Furrina, Salacia

Animal associations: Dolphin, Horse, Bull, Fish, Shark, Whale

Plant associations: Ash, Bladderwrack, Lotus*, Myrrh, Olive, Water Lily, Poppy (white), Seaweed (all)

* May have been connected to Lotus due to the folk name use of the term Water Lily.

Roman god of fresh water who gradually became associated with the sea through his wife Salacia and his association with the Greek Poseidon.

Nergal—Male—Middle East/Mediterranean

Lover: Ereshkigal

Animal association: Lion

Sumero-Babylonian god of the Underworld who brings baneful things to humanity. He is responsible for sickness, blight, and war. With his lover Ereshkigal, we see a clear personification of many of the attributes Christianity have given to Satan. In that connection, we take note that Nergal is often described as the evil attribute of Shamash. This gives rise to an interesting thought: In Christian mythology, is not Satan an aspect of the Christian God?

Nereids—Female—Mediterranean

Animal associations: Dolphin, Fish, and to some degree all sea creatures

The 50 daughters of Nereus and Doris who live in the Mediterranean sea. Unlike the mermaids and mermen of lore, the Nereids are depicted fully human. Instead of having the tails of fish, they ride dolphin and other sea creatures for transportation.

Nereus—Male—Mediterranean

Father: Pontus

Mother: Gaia

Animal associations: Fish and other sea creatures

Greek 'Old Man of the Sea.' Father of the Nereids.

Nerthus—Female/Male—Northern Europe

(Also known as Hertha)

Animal association: Cow

Scandinavian deity sometimes described as a hermaphrodite, but most often cited as female. She is a goddess of prosperity and peace. Again we see the association between prosperity and war. When there is peace, there is prosperity.

Ngai—Male—Africa

'Rain'—Masai god of rain. Often cited as a Supreme sky god. He is the personification of the black rain cloud when he is in a good mood and a red rain cloud when he is in a bad mood.

Nganaoa—Male—Polynesian Islands

Animal association: Whale

Polynesian folk hero who kills three horrible sea monsters (maybe whales), then guts the beasts to find both his mother and father inside, still alive.

Nicneven—Female—Central Europe
Holiday: Samhain

Scottish goddess of Witches who is associated with Samhain.

Nidaba—Female—Middle East/Mediterranean
Animal association: Snake

Sumerian goddess of education, learning, and the written language.

Nike—Female—Mediterranean
Father: Pallas
Mother: Styx
Animal association: Lynx
Plant associations: Benzoin, Sandalwood (red), Rose

'Victory'—Greek personification and goddess of victory. Seen as the constant companion to Athena, she is said to be able to run and fly at speeds far in excess of human standards. Her name was probably chosen for the now famous shoe company for her talents at running, but years later we see that her attribute as goddess of victory may have lent itself to that company's great success.

Incense Recipe
2 parts Benzoin
1 part Sandalwood (red)
1 part Rose (red or white)

Nikkal—Female—Middle East/Mediterranean
Husband: Yerah

Phoenician moon goddess and the goddess of wild crafted harvests. She is associated with the Sumerian Ningal, an Earth goddess. With that and her husband being a moon god, one thinks that perhaps her association with the moon is more from her husband's role and her role might better be seen as Earth goddess who presides over the wild crafted harvest.

Nina—Female—Middle East/Mediterranean/Central Europe
(Also known as Eviene, Nimue, Niviene, Viviane)
Animal association: Snake

Perhaps a Babylonian Water goddess as the origin of the story of the Lady of the Lake as it found its way into European lore and eventually into the story of King Arthur. Her name is more likely an early generic term for goddess (Lady or Queen).

Ningal—Female—Mediterranean/Middle East
Husband: Nanna or Sinn (Babylonian)
Animal association: Mongoose

'Lady of the Summer' or 'Queen of Summer'—Sumerian Earth Goddess. She is associated with the Phoenician Nikkal.

Ningirsu—Male—Middle East/Mediterranean
Animal associations: Goat, Lion

'Lord of Girsu' or 'King of Girsu'—Sumero-Babylonian rain god who instructed humanity in the art of negotiating with nature. Specifically, he is god of irrigation and the knowledge of irrigation. As such, he is seen as a fertility god of crops. His name is a reference to the ancient city of Girsu.

Ninhursag—Female—Middle East/Mediterranean
Husband: Enki
Daughter: Ninsar by Enki
Animal associations: Cow (calf), Snake

'Lady of the Mountain' or 'Queen of the Mountain'—Sumerian Earth Goddess associated mostly with mountains. See Enki for her story.

Ninkurra—Female—Middle East/Mediterranean
Father: Enki
Mother: Ninsar
Daughter: Uttu by Enki
Lover: Enki

Sumerian goddess whose father, lover, and grandfather was Enki. See Enki for their story.

Ninlil—Female—Mediterranean/Middle East
(Also known as Belitis, Mullissu)
Husband: Enlil

Animal associations: Lion, Snake

'Lady of the Wind' or *'Queen of the Wind'*—Sumero-Babylonian grain goddess whose name probably comes from association with her husband, who is Lord of the Wind.

Ninsar—Female—Middle East/Mediterranean
Father: Enki
Mother: Ninhursag
Lover: Enki

Sumero-Babylonian goddess who was daughter and lover to Enki. See Enki for the story.

Ninurta—Male—Middle East/Mesopotamia
Wife: Gula
Animal associations: Eagle, Lion, Dragon (lion)

'Lord of the Earth' or *'King of the Earth'*—Sumero-Babylonian rain god who taught humanity the art of negotiating with Nature, specifically in the use of the plough to raise soil for planting. He, like his cousin Ningirsu, is chiefly concerned with humanity's ability to grow food and support itself.

Niu Wang—Male—Central Asia
Animal association: Cattle (ox)

Chinese guardian and patron of livestock, especially cattle.

Njord—Male—North Europe
Wife: Skadi
Animal associations: Fish and all sea creatures

Father of Freyr and Freya. He is lord of the sea and of the winds that push ships over it.

Noah—Male—Middle East/Mediterranean/Central Europe

'Rest'—In Christian lore, he is found in the ninth generation after Adam and Eve. This is a crucial bit of information as it helps to place the story of Adam and Eve into the historical accounts of the Great Flood which allowed migration into Europe. Although attempts to defeat such placements often cite that Noah died at the ripe old age of 950, generations are determined not by death but by birth. Even if Noah had lived to be 950 years old, he (and Adam and Eve) would have created children much earlier. For the Irish lore which likely lent itself to the modern Christian story, please see Bith.

Nodens—Male—Central Europe
(Also known as Nodons)
Animal association: Dog

Celtic river god and protector of the home. He is sometimes associated with crop fertility.

Nohochacyum—Male—Central America

Mayan Creator god who is constantly at war with Nohochacyum in the way that the Christian god is in opposition to Satan.

Nootaikok—Male—Arctic America
Animal association: Seal

Eskimo spirit who dwells on icebergs. Protector of wildlife, especially seals.

Noncomala—Male—Central America/Caribbean

Costa Rican Creator who sent a Great Flood to destroy humanity because it had become evil.

Norianahary—Male—Madagascar

Madagascan god who sent his son, Ataokoloinona, to Earth to help him decide if Earth should be populated. When his son did not return, he sent a search party hoping to find his son. When they did not return, he sent a second, a third, and more. On and on he sent folk to find his beloved son and continues to do so today. Those he sent became the progenitors of humanity.

Norns, The—Female—North Europe
(Also known as The Three Wyrds, The Weird Sisters [Shakespeare])
Animal association: Spider
Holiday: New Year's Eve

Teutonic Three Fates represented by Urd, Verdandi, and Skuld who were collectively known as Wyrd. See also Wyrd.

Notus—Male—Mediterranean
Father: Astraeus
Mother: Eos

Greek god of the South Wind associated with the South Quarter (Fire) in Wiccan ritual.

Nu-Kua—Female—Central Asia
Husband: Fu-Hsing
Animal association: Snake

Chinese Creator who made the first humans of yellow clay.

Nuah—Female—Middle East/Mediterranean

Babylonian moon goddess involved in the Great Flood. Because her tale was absorbed by Ishtar, she is often overlooked. This is unfortunate as her name show the clear connection between the Babylonian Great Flood and the one recorded in the Old Testament. The Old Testament Noah is likely a masculine version of the name Nuah, although in the Babylonian story she is the goddess whose actions began the Great Flood. See Ishtar.

Nurelli—Male—Australia

Australian god of law and order to the Wiimbaio tribe. Patron of those who work in criminal justice and politics.

Nusku—Male—Middle East/Mediterranean/ Central Asia

Sumerian god of fire and light. His sacred flame was said to destroy evil. Eventually he migrated into Western Asia. There he acquired an association with the building of civilization.

Nut—Female—Africa
(Also known as Nuit [Thelemic])
Father: Shu
Mother: Tefnut
Lover: Geb
Animal associations: Cow, Eagle, Peacock
Plant associations: Amaranth, Coconut, Olive, Sycamore
Holidays: August 24–28, December 25.

Egyptian personification and Goddess of the Sky, the Heavens, and the Stars that burn there. She is the veil between chaos and order. She is depicted as a skyclad woman painted with the burning stars of heaven who is held to the sky by her father Shu. Her husband Geb is the Earth below her. The name Nuit is an alternative spelling made popular by Aleister Crowley. In Wiccan ritual she is associated with the South/Fire quarter. See also Ra, Tefnut, Shu, and Geb.

Nyame—Male—Africa
(Also known as Nyankopon)

Ashanti god of sky, storms, and lightning. Nyame is the supreme deity of his pantheon. Provided humanity with sun, moon, rain, and the other requirements of farming after requested by Anansi. As creator of humanity, his story is loosely the story of Adam, Lilith, and Eve, except here it was the first man that became rebellious and later described as evil. So Nyame buried him and created a second man to be the husband of the first woman, whom Nyame created from a tree. They went on to become the progenitors of humanity.

Nymphs—Female—Mediterranean
Animal association: All wild animals

Greek Nature spirits most commonly represented as beautiful women clad only by the sky. The male counterparts are the Satyr.

Nyx—Female—Mediterranean
Lover: Erebus

'Night'—Chaos is sometimes cited as her father, brother or lover. See Chaos for an explanation. Nyx and Erebus are often cited as brother and sister because they share the same father. However, their birth did not involve the Great Rite. Instead, they were the son and daughter of Chaos in the way Darkness and Light were the children of the Nameless One of the Book of Genesis.

Oba—Female—Africa

Yoruba river goddess who tried to win the favor of Shango by offering him her ear to eat.

Ochun—Female—Africa/Caribbean

(Also known as Carida)

Plant associations: Adam and Eve Root, Apple (blossom), Apricot, Allspice, Almond, Anise, Basil, Catnip, Chamomile (common), Chickweed, Cinnamon, Clove, Copal, Coriander, Cumin, Calamus, Cedar, Dill, Dragon's Blood, Deerstongue, Elder, Five Finger Grass, Frangipani, Galangal, Grains of Paradise, Ginger, Ginseng (American), Hyacinth (wild), Hibiscus, Hazel, Heather, Heliotrope, Honeysuckle, Hyssop, Irish Moss, Jasmine, Lemon Grass, Lavender, Lucky Hand Root, Marjoram, Meadowsweet, Myrtle, Nettle (greater), Nutmeg, Olive, Orange (sweet), Oakmoss, Orris, Patchouli, Parsley, Peppermint, Red Clover, Roses (yellow), Rosemary, Sesame, Saffron (Mexican), St. John's Wort, Tonka, Vervain, Vanilla, Yarrow

Yoruba goddess who migrated into the Caribbean and became the Orisha of love, marriage, and motherhood. Similar to the goddess Venus. Her story illustrates how struggle and adversity are often times the price of a harmonious life. Early in her life, she owned only one dress and found it necessary to become a prostitute to feed her children. When the rest of the pantheon discovered this, they removed her children, feeling that a prostitute was not an appropriate role model. This caused her to become insane and wander about aimlessly. However, because she still had her pride she continued to wash her one dress every day to remove the soils that gathered there from her work as a prostitute. There, by the river where she always washed that dress, she was seen by the Orisha Aje-Shaluga who immediately fell in love with her. With his love, she regained not only her sanity but her children. Although this story is often rejected because it is seen as overly patriarchal, it is a wonderful example of how love triumphs adversity and support for the belief that two people are much better suited to face adversity than one.

Incense Recipe

2 parts Dragon's Blood

2 parts Copal

1 part Jasmine

1 part Lavender

Oil Recipe

8 drops Patchouli oil

4 drops Cinnamon oil

4 drops Basil oil

4 drops Cedar oil

½ ounce base oil (try a 50/50 mix of Almond and Sesame oil)

Odudua—Female—Africa/South America

(Also known as Oduduwa, Odudu)

Husband: Obatala

Brazilian Voodoo Earth Goddess who migrated from the Yoruba. She was created by Olorun on the island of Ife much as Adam and Lilith were created in Eden. But she, as some say was Lilith, was far more interested in sex and procreation, so she left Obatala in favor of many other lovers. She is sometimes described as male and her husband female in an effort to place the wander lust with the male half of the union. Patron of those who prefer polyamory.

Obask Nsi—See Ison

Obatala—Male—African/Caribbean/South America

(Also known as Orisanla)

Wife: Odudua

In Santeria, his name is Obatala

In Voodoo, his name is Batala/Blanc Dani

In Africa, his name is Obatala

Saint/Catholic associations: Our Lady of Mercy, Jesus (Crucified)

Plant associations: Almond, Angelica, Allspice, Basil, Bay, Calamus, Calendula, Carnation, Cedar, Citron, Clove, Copal, Cumin, Coriander, Dragon's Blood, Eucalyptus, Fern, Fennel, Frankincense, Garlic, Gardenia, Galangal, Geranium, Heliotrope, Horehound (white),

Honeysuckle, Heather, Hyssop, Lilac (white), Lime, Lemon Balm, Lavender, Lotus, Mallow (blue), Myrrh, Mistletoe (American), Mugwort, Mandrake (American), Orange (bitter), Orris, Peppermint, Pine, Patchouli, Pennyroyal, Peony, Rose (white), Rose Geranium, Rue, Sage (common), Sandalwood (white), Snapdragon, Thistle (greater), Thyme, Violet, Vervain, Vetivert, Valerian, Yarrow

Holiday: Feast of Our Lady of Mercy on September 24

Nigerian creator of humanity. He created the human body. His father, Olorun gives to that body the distinctly human soul (mind). His sister and wife, Odudua, gave humanity the desire to procreate. In his African aspect he is also sky god (sometimes goddess). He migrated into Santeria where he is the Orisha of purity and light. In different traditions he was associated with both the Virgin Mary (Our Lady of Mercy) and her son Jesus.

Incense Recipe

2 parts Frankincense

2 parts Copal

1 part Clove

1 part Orris Root

1 pinch Mistletoe

Oil Recipe

10 drops Sandalwood oil

4 drops Clove oil

4 drops Frankincense oil

2 drops Cedar oil

1/2 ounce almond oil as a base

Obba—Female—African/Caribbean/South America

Saint association: St. Catalina

Holiday: Feast of Saint Catalina of Palermino on November 25

Orisha of both death and birth, she owns the cemeteries with Yeggua and Oya but also presides over sexual fertility, thus providing yet another example of the connection between Life and Death in a never-ending cycle.

Obbaloke—Male—African/Caribbean/South America

Saint association: St. Santiago

Holiday: Feast of Saint Santiago on July 25

Orisha of strength, he is patron of mountain climbers, the mountain itself, and anything that stretches into the sky.

Oceanus—Male—Mediterranean

(Also known as Okeanos)

Father: Uranus

Mother: Gaia

Wife: Tethys

Animal association: Snake

Initially a Greek personification of fresh water streams and rivers. He is called on for protection when traveling across and along fresh water. He fathered thousands of river nymphs with his wife and sister Tethys. Some references state that he and his wife adopted Hera when she was an infant. As his lore expanded, he became god of the ocean.

Ochosi—Male—Africa/South America

In Santeria, his name is Ochosi Odemata

In Voodoo, his name is Agao Wedo

In Africa, his name is Ochossi

Saint associations: St. Norbert, St. Albert, St. Hubert, St. James, St. Isidro, St. Sebastian

Holiday: Feast of Saint Norbert on June 6

Plant associations: Allspice, Asafoetida, Anise, Basil, Broom, Coriander, Cumin, Clove, Deerstongue, Dragon's Blood, Five Finger Grass, Galangal, Ginger, Hyssop, Honeysuckle, Mistletoe (American), Maple, Nettle (greater), Rosemary, Sage (diviner's) Tobacco, Wormwood, Woodruff

In his African aspect, he is god of vegetation and divine justice. Migrating into Haitian Voodoo he becomes a loa of thunder. In Santeria, he is associated with many of the Catholic saints.

Incense Recipe

2 parts Dragon's Blood

1 part Coriander

1 part Clove

Enough Ochosi or Rosemary oil to bind

Oil Recipe

8 drops Basil

6 drops Coriander

3 drops Clove

3 drops Rosemary

1/2 ounce base oil

Ocypete—Female—Mediterranean

'Swift Wing'—Greek Harpy who was charged with creating peace. In that capacity, she and the others are beautiful winged maidens (sometimes virgins). But to keep that peace, she and the others were also the punisher of crime. In that capacity, they are horrid winged beasts. One of the three Harpies. The other two are Celaeno and Aello.

Oddua—Male—African/Caribbean/South America

An avatar/incarnation of Obatala who participated in the creation of the world. He created and now administers justice. As such he is the patron of those who have been unjustly accused, but treats bitterly those unjust folk who call on him for assistance.

Odin—Male—North Europe

(Also known as All Father)

Father: Bor

Mother: Bestla

Wife: Frigga

Animal associations: Crow, Eagle, Falcon, Raven, Wolf, Horse, Dog, Bear

Plant associations: Alder, Almond, Ash, Beech, Benzoin, Cedar, Elm, Mistletoe (European), Olive, Patchouli, Yew

Scandinavian god who was lovingly called All Father. Much of his great wisdom came from two visits to the Yggdrasil (Tree of Life/World Tree). On one visit, he asked Mimir for a drink of the streams that run from the Yggdrasil's roots (Mimir's Well). Mimir granted him that drink, but only at the cost of one of Odin's eyes. From that experience, Odin received great knowledge of those who had gone before. On another visit, Odin hung from the World Tree for nine days and nights. From that visit, he received knowledge of runes. While there is a great amount of debate as to if the runes were first used for magick or for language, we see clearly a connection between Odin and the written language. Although commonly thought to be a god of war, Odin is also a patron of poetry, science, and magick. Odin and Thor can be seen to have many similarities, although Odin was the god of warriors, and Thor the god more akin to the common man.

Incense Recipe

2 parts Benzoin

2 parts Cedar

1 part Patchouli

1 pinch Mistletoe

Enough Odin or Patchouli oil to bind

Oil Recipe

8 drops Benzoin oil

6 drops Cedar oil

6 drops Patchouli oil

1/2 ounce Olive oil as a base

Odomankoma—Male—Africa

Ashanti Creator god who created death to prevent over population, thus allowing himself to die for the good of all. He can thus be seen as a sacrificial god.

Oeneus—Male—Mediterranean

Wife: Althea

Plant association: Vine (grape)

Greek man who received the grapevine from Dionysus in exchange for the sexual services of his wife Althea. He became the first man to create a vineyard in Greece. I believe this story is a warning that alcohol can be detrimental to the judgment of folk involved in monogamous relationships.

Oengus Mac Og—See Aengus Mac Og

Oghma Grainaineach—Male—Central Europe
(Also known as Oghma)
Father: Dagda
Mother: Boann
Son: Delbaeth

Irish God who was said to have created/received and give to humanity the Ogham. In this capacity, his story can be seen similar to that of Odin, both being scholars, warriors, and providers of an alphabet/magical written language. Oghma is an ideal patron deity of the modern high-tech soldier.

Oggue—Male—African/Caribbean/South America

Patron of all horned animals. Perhaps originally a Horned God of the hunt. He is described often as Shango's companion.

Oggun—Male—African/Caribbean/South America
(Also known as Ogun)
In Santeria, his name is Oggun/Ogun
In Voodoo, his name is Ogu
In Africa, his name is Ogum
Saint and Catholic associations: St. Anthony, St. Peter, St. Paul, St. John the Baptist, St. James, St. George, St. Joan of Arc
Father: Aganyu
Mother: Yemaja
Holiday: Feast of Saint Peter on June 29
Plant associations: Angelica, Anise, Asafoetida, Basil, Bay, Bergamot (orange), Clove, Cypress, Cumin, Carnation, Caraway, Copal, Dragon's Blood, Eucalyptus, Galangal, Heather, Hyacinth (wild), Hyssop, Honeysuckle, Juniper, Lotus, Lime, Lilac, Mandrake (American), Mistletoe (American), Mugwort, Myrrh, Orange (bitter), Orris, Peony, Patchouli, Rosemary, Rose, Sage (diviner's), Violet, Vervain, Vetivert

Yoruba god of iron. With his associations to iron smithing, he became a god of fire and water. He migrated into Santeria where he became the Orisha who is called on to protect his followers from accidents.

Incense Recipe

1 part Dragon's Blood
1 part Copal
1 part Juniper Berries
1 part Orris Root

Oil Recipe

8 drops Clove
6 drops Cypress
6 drops Cumin

Okaga—See Itokaga

Oko—Male—African/Caribbean/South America
Father: Aganyu
Mother: Yemaja
Plant associations: Allspice, Apricot, Almond, Angelica, Anise, Asafoetida, Basil, Bergamot (orange), Bay, Calamus, Calendula, Camphor, Coriander, Cumin, Corn, Coconut, Clove, Crocus, Deerstongue, Daisy, Ginger, Ginseng, Grains of Paradise, Galangal, Geranium, Heather, Hyacinth (wild), Iris, Jasmine, Lemon, Myrtle, Magnolia, Myrrh, Nettle (greater), Peppermint, Red Poppy (seed), Rosemary, Sandalwood (white), Tobacco, Willow, Pepper (black)
Saint association: St. Isidro
Holiday: Feast of Saint Isidro on March 22 and/or May 15

African god who migrated with the slave trade and became one of the Orisha of the Santeria. Oko is Orisha of agriculture and the harvest. He is associated with fertility of the land. He is a deified ancestor.

Incense Recipe

3 part Sandalwood (white)
1 part Myrrh
1 part Jasmine

Oil Recipe

8 drops Sandalwood

6 drops Myrrh

4 drops Jasmine absolute or Lemon oil

2 drops Black Pepper oil

1/2 ounce base oil

O-Kuni-Nushi—Male—Far East

Father: Susanowo

Wife: Suseri-Hime

Japanese god of medicine and patron of healers, doctors, and especially folk who work with herbal medicine.

Old Spider—Female—Malaysia

Nauru Island creator of the moon, sun, Earth, and sky.

Old Woman—Female—North America

(Also known as Old Woman Who Never Dies)

Animal associations: Goose, Swan, Duck

Madan Crone goddess associated with fertility.

Oloddumare—Male—African/South America

(Also known as Olofi)

Supreme god of the Santeria from whom the Orisha receive their attributes and powers. In his many aspects he has been given many names:

Olorun—Owner of Heaven.

Olorun Oloddumare—The Lord who lives in Heaven.

Eledaa—The Creator

Elemi—Owner of Life

Alaaye—The Living One

Olojo Oni—The master of daily events

Olofi—God of the Earth and protector of crops.

But one name/aspect is most commonly used, that being Olofi. In his role as god on Earth, he is the aspect of Oloddumare most related to by humanity. In the blending of Yoruba and Christian traditions, he becomes associated with Jesus Christ. However, he is not prayed to directly for any one need or want, that job being delegated to the Orishas (his children).

Olocun—Male—Africa/South America

(Also known as Olokun)

Father: Aganyu

Mother: Yemaja

Plant associations: Allspice, Angelica, Anise, Apple (blossom), Almond, Bergamot (orange), Bay, Calamus, Chamomile (common), Cumin, Camphor, Coconut, Caraway, Crocus, Dragon's Blood, Elder, Jasmine, Lotus, Lavender, Lemon Grass, Lemon Verbena, Magnolia, Myrtle, Myrrh, Mandrake (American), Peppermint, Red Poppy (seed), Sandalwood (white), Spearmint, Thyme, Willow, Watermelon

Yoruba ocean god who migrated with the slave trade to become the Orisha Olocun of Santeria.

Incense Recipe

2 parts Sandalwood

2 parts Dragon's Blood

1 part Jasmine or Lemon Grass

1 part Lavender

1 part Chamomile

Oil Recipe

8 drops Sandalwood

6 drops Jasmine Absolute or Lavender oil

6 drops Lemon Grass oil

1/2 ounce base oil (almond oil is best)

Olorun—Male—Africa

Nigerian creator of Obatala and Odudua (Nigerian/Yoruba Adam and Eve). Patron of parents with wildly different children.

Olwyn—Female—Central Europe

Husband: Culhwch

Plant associations: Apple, Hawthorn

Welsh goddess of Spring and Summer.

Omacatl—Male—Central America

'Two Reeds'—Aztec god of bliss and happiness whose body and bones are symbolically eaten with great joy at his holiday. However, he was certainly a trickster god and while his blessings were many, they only came when he was given great respect. May be an aspect of Tezcatlipoca.

Omeciuatl—Female—Central America
(Also known as Omecihuatl)
Husband: Ometeuctli

Aztec Creator goddess.

Ometeuctli—Male—Central America
(Also known as Ometeoltloque, Ometecutli, Tloque Nahuaque, Citlatonac)
Wife: Omeciuatl

'Two Lords'—Aztec Creator. Like Diana and many others, he brought his mate into existence by separating her from him. Interestingly enough, he has no formal following and no cult. Instead he is seen as being found in every deity, in every rite, in all of creation. He is, in essence, the very concept of the Nameless One. His name, like Diana, only applies to the male aspect after separating his mate from himself.

Onatha—Female—North America
Plant association: Wheat

Iroquois personification of Spring, Summer, the harvest, and goddess of wheat who was kidnapped and hidden in the Underworld. Her story is incredibly similar to that of Persephone and yet they took place continents away. Both Onatha and Persephone were daughters of a chief mother goddess (Demeter in the Greek story and Eithinoha in the Iroquois story). Both were kidnapped by an Underworld being (Hades in the Greek story and a Demon in the Iroquois story). Both were rescued on the orders of a greater deity (Zeus sent Hermes in the Greek story and the Sun sent his rays in the Iroquois story).

Ooyarrauyamitok—Male—Arctic America

Eskimo god who assists hunters in finding only that which is necessary to perpetuate life. Supports the observation that for life there must be death. Patron of hunters.

Ops—Female—Mediterranean
(Also known as Opis)
Husband: Saturn

Roman fertility goddess. Her holidays also include Saturnalia, which is cited to her husband Saturn more than herself. With her inclusion at the Opalia which overlaps Saturnalia, it is clear that their marriage was just as much a part of the Saturnalia as one's family is part of the holidays during that same time of the year. Her name means 'plenty,' however she demonstrates the need to sacrifice, as she was not only associated with harvest, but also with the planting and care of a the crop. That work was sacrifice to her.

Oraea—Female—Mediterranean
Holiday: Summer Solstice

Roman Summer goddess who is celebrated at the peak of the sun.

Orestes—Male—Mediterranean
Father: Agamemnon
Mother: Clytemnestra

Greek god of revenge. After his father was killed by his father's adulterous wife and her lover Aegisthos, Orestes plotted revenge with his sister Electra. After following through with their bloody plot, he had successfully killed both Clytemnestra and her lover. As a result, he was followed and harassed by the Furies until of his own accord he sought judgment at the Aeropagus in Athens. There, he was acquitted and upon his seeking judgment, the Furies discontinued their harassment.

Orpheus—Male—Mediterranean
Father: Apollo
Mother: Calliope

The greatest Greek musician. His music is said to be able to calm raging animals and cause inanimate things to dance.

Orunjan—Male—Africa
Father: Aganyu
Mother: Yemaya

Yoruba god of the mid-day sun.

Orunla—Male—African/Caribbean/South America

In Santeria, he is known as Orúnmila/Ifa

In Voodoo, he is known as Orunla

In Africa, he is known as Orunmila

Saint and Catholic association: St. Francis of Assisi

Holiday: Feast of Saint Francis of Assisi on October 4

Plant associations: Anise, Allspice, Cinnamon, Carnation, Coconut, Calamas, Citron, Camphor, Calendula, Dittany of Crete, Dragon's Blood, Five Finger Grass, Ginger, Heliotrope, Honeysuckle, Jasmine, Lilac, Lemon Grass, Orris, Sandalwood (white), Sage (common), Wormwood

Yoruba god who became one of the Orisha of the Santeria. He is the Orisha of great prophecy and divination. Considered a divine spirit. In the mixing of Yoruba and Christian traditions, he became associated with Saint Francis of Assisi.

Incense Recipe

3 parts Sandalwood (white)

2 parts Dragon's Blood

1 part Jasmine flowers

Oil Recipe

12 drops Sandalwood oil

6 drops Jasmine absolute or Lemon Grass oil

4 drops Cinnamon oil

1/2 ounce base oil

Osain—Male—African/Caribbean/South America

Saint and Catholic associations: St. Sylvester, St. Anthony Abad, St. Ambrose, St. Joseph, St. John (San Jose), St. Benito, St. Raymond (Palo)

Holidays: Feast of Saint Sylvester on December 31, Feast of Saint Anthony Abad on January 17

African god of Nature who migrated into Santeria, without a name change, to become the patron of herbalists and doctors.

Oshun—Female—African/Caribbean/South America

Also called Carida

In Santeria, her name is Oshun/Ochun

In Voodoo, her name is Erzulie

In Africa, her name is Oshun

Plant association: Basil, Cardamom

Saint and Catholic associations: Our Lady of Charity, Our Lady of Caridad del Cobre

Mother: Yemaya

Husband: Shango

Holiday: Feast of Our Lady of La Caridad del Cobre on September 8 (Our Lady of Charity)

The connection between Oshun and Erzulie should not be considered fact. There are some who consider the connection to be just as solid as the connections made between the Greek and Roman gods. Others insist that Erzulie (aka La Siren) has no connection to Oshun. In Africa she is goddess of love, beauty, and fresh water rivers. One of two sisters who were the wives of Shango (the other is Oya). She is described as beautiful and jealous of her husband's love of her sister (his other wife), Oya. With migration into Voodoo and Santeria, she became associated primarily with beauty.

Osiris—Male —Africa

(Also known as Usire)

Wife: Isis

Lovers: Nephthys

Animal associations: Chicken (cock), Ostrich, Hawk, Goose, Heron, Vulture, Leopard, Antelope, Cattle (bull), Ram, Horse (Pegasus), Dog, Swallow, Panther

Plant associations: Acacia, Benzoin, Cedar, Clove, Dittany of Crete, Ivy (common), Orris, Palm (date), Tamarisk, Vine (grape), Willow, and all old world grains

Egyptian Earth God who is associated with not only the Underworld, but also with resurrection and fertility. In essence, he is to Isis what Geb is to Nut, who were also parents to both Osiris and Isis, indicating a cycle of rebirth.

Incense Recipe
1 part Acacia flowers
1 part Benzoin
Enough Osiris or Benzoin essential oil to bind

Oil Recipe
12 drops Benzoin essential oil
18 drops tincture of Acacia
1/4 ounce Olive oil

Otsuchi No Kami—Female—Far East
　　Japanese Earth Mother.

Ovinnik—Male—Central Europe/Northern Europe
Animal association: Cat (black)
　　Baneful spirits who set fire to homes.

Oya—Female—African/Caribbean/South America
In Santeria, her name is Oya/Olla/Yansa
In Voodoo, her name is Aida-Wedo/Brigette
In Africa, her name is Oya/Odo-Oya
Saint and Catholic associations: Our Lady of La Candeleria, Our Lady of Mount Carmel, St. Catherine, St. Theresa
Mother: Yemaja
Husband: Shango
Plant associations: Anise, Aspen (American), Cinnamon, Carnation, Calamus, Clove, Dragon's Blood, Dittany of Crete, Hibiscus, Lemon, Lime, Myrrh, Nutmeg, Oakmoss, Star Anise, Sandalwood (white), Tangerine
Holiday: Feast of Our Lady of Candlemas on February 2

　　In Africa, she is goddess of wind and lightning. Sometimes seen to also preside over water and fertility. One of two sisters who were the wives of Shango (the other is Oshun). She is described as plain-looking and jealous of her husband's love of her sister (his other wife) Oshun, as well as her beauty. In Santeria and Voodoo, she is the Orisha of the Winds and of the entrance to cemeteries.

Incense Recipe
4 parts Sandalwood (white)
2 parts Gum Arabic
1 part Dragon's Blood
1 part Clove
1 part Lemon (peel)
Enough Oya or Sandalwood oil to bind

Oil Recipe
8 drops Sandalwood
4 drops Lemon
4 drops Clove
4 drops Cinnamon
1/2 ounce base oil

Pachacamac—Male—South America
Wife: Pachamama
　　'Earth Maker'—Inca Creator but not exactly friend of humanity. He created the first man and woman, and then forgot to feed them. The man died first, so the woman complained about the god that was also an unfit father. Pachacamac caused her to become pregnant. When her first son was born, Pachacamac cut the child in half and used the body parts to create the plants of this world. He told her to dine. When her second son escaped he killed the woman, but her son came back to avenge his mother's death, driving their creator into the sea.

Pachamama—Female—South America
(Also known as Mama Pacha)
Husband: Pachacamac
　　Chincha/Inca Earth Mother. Pachamama formed her husband, Pachacamac, from herself the way Diana formed her lover Lucifer. Pachacamac then created the world, and she became a fertility goddess associated with cultivation.

Padma, Dakinis—Female—Central Asia
　　Dakinis Padma is the Tibetan goddess associated with the West, fascination, and affection. See also Vajra, Ratna, Karma, and Buddha.

Pales—Male/Female—Mediterranean
Animal associations: Cattle, Donkey, Vulture

Roman deity who was originally described as male, but who with time transformed into a female. S/he was the protector of both field and flock. Sometimes cited by the transgender community as an example of a transgender deity, due to the transition from male to female. His name comes from the Greek and Latin word *phallus,* which translates to penis.

Pan—Male—Mediterranean
Animal associations: Antelope, Eagle, Bee, Panther, Goat, Sheep (ram), Turtle, Tortoise, and in general all creatures of the wild.
Plant associations: Fennel, Fern, Fig, Myrrh, Oak, Olive, Patchouli, Pine, Reeds (all), Thistle, and meadow flowers.

'Everything' or 'All inclusive'—Greek Horned God of the woods who, in the ancient world, was almost always depicted with an erect penis. That symbolism seems to have faded, giving us the boyish and almost innocent image that we have today. Ancient lore tells a different story. There Pan remains the lustful god of the woods who chased after both men and women with whom he sought to fulfill his endless sexual desires. Of women, he preferred nymphs (especially virgins) and of the men he preferred shepherds.

Incense Recipe

4 parts Pine needles (or 1 part pitch and 3 parts Sandalwood powder)
4 parts Myrrh
Enough Pan or Myrrh essential oil to bind

Oil Recipe

9 drops Pine essential oil
6 drops Myrrh essential oil
3 drops Patchouli essential oil
1/2 ounce Olive oil

P'an Chin Lien—Female—Central Asia
Chinese spirit. Protector and patron of prostitutes.

Pandora—Female—Mediterranean
'All gifted'—Greek woman who unknowingly released baneful emotions/spirits from a box given to her by Zeus. This was Zeus' revenge on Prometheus for having stolen fire and given it to humanity. Wiccans have built on this story with the practice of the Outsider Offering, a time during ritual when baneful emotions and thoughts are symbolically removed from the circle, sometimes being placed in a mirrored box.

P'an Ku—Male/Female—Central Asia
(Also known as Pan Gu)
Animal association: Tortoise

Chinese deity born of an egg who was both the Yin and the Yang of creation. The top part of the egg grew into the Yang, forming the heavens as it did. The bottom half grew into the Yin, forming the Earth as it did. S/he kept growing for thousands of years, pushing the Yang and Yin apart until s/he split into two. His eyes became the sun and moon, his shoulders the mountains. His blood became the rain. Her womb became the oceans, filling with his blood. Her belly became the Earth. Her feet became the islands. She is always pregnant and always birthing life.

Paris—Male—Mediterranean
Greek shepherd who later became a prince. Paris sided with Aphrodite, thus starting the Trojan war, killed Achilles during that war, and then died himself. See Peleus.

Parjanya—Male—Near East
Father: Kashyapa
Mother: Aditi

Parjanya is one of the Adityas. The Hindu month Shravana (July 23–August 22) is sacred to Parjanya. See Adityas.

Papa—Female—Polynesian Islands
Husband: Rangi

New Zealand Earth Mother. With her husband Rangi, Sky God, the pair contribute greatly to the use of the Wiccan terms Father Sky and Mother Earth.

Parasurama—Male—Near East

(Also known as Parashurama)

Animal associations: Ape, Swallow

Plant associations: Benzoin, Gum Mastic, Mace, Sandalwood (white), Vervain, Marjoram, Palm (date)

Hindu sixth avatar of Vishnu. He once served Lord Shiva. During such service, Shiva gave to him an axe. Later, he went to seek advice of Lord Shiva, but Ganesha would not allow him access to his Lord. In anger, he threw his axe at Ganesha, who could surely have allowed the axe to pass without harm. Realizing the axe had been given to the young Parasurama, Ganesha allowed it to sever the tip of one of his tusks. This is why Ganesha is typically shown with one tusk that still has a point and the other with the point cut off.

Parvati—Female—Near East

Father: Himavat

Husband: Shiva

Animal association: Dove

Hindu goddess who is either one of Shiva's many lovers, or (as I believe) Shiva's wife who has many avatars/incarnations, including: Ambika, Bhairavi, Durga, Gauri, Kali, Sati, and Uma. Parvati can be seen as a Creator goddess, independent of Shiva, as her son Ganesa was created when she blessed dust with the fluids of her body. Because it was clear that in union there were none who could effectively stand against Parvati and Shiva, when she won Shiva's mind, body, and soul the Earth trembled in the quake of their love.

Pashadhari—Female—Near East

Husband: Yama

Hindu mother goddess whose symbol is the noose, associated with creation (penis and vagina) and birth (vagina and umbilical chord), much as the ankh is.

Pasiphae—Female—Mediterranean

Father: Helios

Mother: Cymene

Husband: Minos

Plant association: Ivy (common)

When her husband, King Minos, insulted Poseidon, he took his revenge by causing Pasiphae to fall deeply in love with a bull. Such was her lust for that bull that she commissioned the construction of a contraption that would allow her to mate with it. She did and later gave birth to Minotaur. Ah, now that is revenge.

Patecatl—Male—Central America

Aztec god of healing and fertility. He is also associated with intoxication and revelry, particularly fond of alcohol intoxication.

Patol—Male—Central America

Wife: Alaghom Naum

Mayan god of the Tzental tribe. Sometimes cited as the Mayan chief god.

Pax—Female—Mediterranean

(Also known as Pax Augusta)

'Peace'—Roman personification of peace. One of her holidays falls on the day the United States celebrates its independence, perhaps a hint that peace is sometimes achieved only after standing against oppression.

Peitho—Female—Mediterranean

Father: Hermes

Mother: Aphrodite

'Persuasion'—Greek personification of persuasion and seduction, especially sexual seduction.

Peleus—Male—Mediterranean

Father: Aeacus

Son: Achilles by Thetis

Wife: Thetis

Greek god who married Thetis, but did not invite Eris (Discordia). Some say the invitation list was made by Zeus, but certainly Peleus could have objected to the lack of inclusion. Eris respected the fact that she was not invited, but sent a gift of a golden apple to the feast, on which was written *kallisti*, which means 'to the prettiest one.' Athena, Hera, and Aphrodite all made claim to the apple insisting that each was 'the prettiest one.' To settle the argument, Zeus appointed Paris of Troy as arbitrator. Each tried to bribe Paris. Athena offered of victory at war. Hera offered him wealth. Aphrodite offered him the prettiest woman on Earth. Being a simple man, he decided love was more important than either victory or wealth. In that decision, Aphrodite did honor her bribe. She gave him the prettiest woman on Earth. That woman was Helen who was, unfortunately for many, married at the time to Menelaus (King of Sparta). Menelaus, not being fond of having his wife kidnapped, took his wife back and declared war on Troy. In that war, Paris sided with Troy and Achilles sided with Sparta. The result was that Achilles fell when Paris struck him in the heal with an arrow, and later Paris died himself. If you are considering a large wedding and you are not sure everyone in attendance will play nice, the moral here is to elope!

Penates—Male/Female—Mediterranean

(Also known as Di Penates)

'The Inner Ones'—Roman guardians of storage rooms and the pantry who later became the personal guardians of the home. They are praised and made sacrifice to by offering them a bit of each meal by throwing a portion of food into the fireplace.

Perse—Female—Mediterranean

(Also known as Persa, Perseis)

Lover: Helios

Greek sea nymph (one of the Oceanids) and mother of Perses and Aeetes by Helios.

Perses—Male—Mediterranean

Father: Helios

Mother: Perse

Wife: Asteria

Greek father of Hecate by his wife Asteria.

Persephone—Female—Mediterranean

(Also known as Kore)

Father: Zeus

Mother: Demeter

Lover: Hades

Animal associations: Bat, Boar, Ground Hog, Snake

Plant associations: Dittany of Crete, Ivy, Lily, Narcissus, Parsley, Pomegranate, Willow

Greek goddess of the Underworld. When she was young, all the eligible and a few ineligible men wanted her hand (as well as everything attached to it). So lustful was Hades of her that he broke open the Earth and kidnapped her, forcing her to be his queen in the Underworld. So heartbroken was her mother, Demeter, that she wandered the Earth until finally Zeus told her what had happened. So full of remorse was Demeter that she withdrew from the Earth and hid in seclusion. As she was the goddess of fertility, all growth stopped and the Earth became barren. Realizing the Earth and its inhabitants would die without Demeter, Zeus sent Hermes to recover Persephone. The story changes somewhat in its different incarnations. In one a deal was struck with Hades. In another, Persephone had eaten food from the Underworld so was trapped there and could only return to the surface for half of the year, or she would die. Whichever version one chooses, the result is the same. Persephone returns to the Underworld every Fall and then back to the Earth in the Spring. During her stay in the Underworld, her mother withdraws all fertility from the Earth, thus yielding Winter. See Minth for lore that supports the idea that Persephone had in fact fallen in love with Hades.

Perseus—Male—Mediterranean

Father: Zeus

Mother: Danae

Wife: Andromeda

Greek folk hero who rescued Andromeda from a sea monster and later married her. He is most noted for the killing of Medusa and then for the creation of Atlas Mountains when he showed Medusa's head to Atlas, thus turning Atlas into stone.

Persipnei—Female—Central Europe
Lover: Eite

Etruscan goddess similar to the Greek Persephone.

Peruda—Male—South America

Brazilian creator who was chiefly responsible for human consciousness, especially in matters of love and procreation. One of the three Creators responsible for the world. The other two were Jacy and Guaracy. In Wicca he is associated with mind and the third order of life (humanity).

Perun—Male—Central Europe
(Also known as Peroun)
Animal associations: Cock, Goat, Bear, Bull

Slavic god of storms. He was worshiped in Russia well into the second millennia despite Russia's official adoption of Christianity around the turn of the first millennium C.E.

Phaeton—Male—Mediterranean
(Also known as Phaethon)
Father: Helios
Mother: Cymene

'Shining one'—Greek god who flew his father's sun chariot too close to the Earth, creating the great deserts by setting fire to the Earth. Helios killed him to protect the Earth.

Phebele—Male—Africa
Wife: Mebeli

Congo father of the first man. See Massim-Biambe.

Phosphorus—Male—Mediterranean

One of the Greek gods who became the personification of the planet Venus (the morning star).

Picunnus—Male—Mediterranean

Roman god who, with his twin brother Pilumnus, protected the life and health of new-born babies.

Picus—Male—Mediterranean

Roman god of agriculture and prophecy.

Pidrai—Female—Middle East/Mediterranean

Canaanite Goddess of Light. One of the aspects of the Canaanite's Triple Goddess whose name means 'Maiden of Light.' See also Arai and Tallai.

Pilumnus—Male—Mediterranean

Roman god who, with his twin brother Picunnus, protected the life and health of new born babies.

Pietas—Female—Mediterranean

'Dutifulness'—Roman personification and goddess of duty to the gods, community, and family. Similar to Dharma (Hindu God) and representative of the principle presented in the Wiccan Rede as will. Her temple at the foot of the Capitoline Hill dates from the beginning of the second century before common era.

Pleione—Female—Mediterranean
Lover: Atlas

Greek mother of the Pleiades.

Pluto—Male—Mediterranean
Wife: Proserpina
Plant associations: American Aspen, Common Aspen, Cypress, Fig, Frankincense, Hibiscus, Hyssop, Mint, Nettle (greater), Oak, Olive, Peppermint, Pomegranate, Red Poppy, Saffron (Spanish), Poppy (white)

'Wealth'—Roman god of the Underworld. The etymology of his name, 'wealth,' reminds us that the Underworld is not only seen as the place of the dead, it is also the place where the riches of the Earth are found. His real name was a hidden secret, never spoken because folk were afraid it would attract his attention, and without the aspect of wealth he was not all that welcome.

Incense Recipe

1 part Hibiscus flowers
1 part Poppy flowers
1 part Frankincense
1 pinch dried Figs (optional)
Enough Pluto or Peppermint essential oil to bind

Oil Recipe

9 drops Frankincense essential oil
6 drops Peppermint essential oil
6 drops Cypress essential oil
1/2 ounce Olive oil

Pollux—Male—Mediterranean
Father: Zeus
Mother: Leda

See Leda for the story of his conception. With his twin brother Castor, he was called the Disocuri.

Polyhymnia—Female—Mediterranean

'Many songs'—Greek muse of song, dance, and mimicry. She is often shown with a finger to her lips as if in deep thought. See also Muses, The.

Pomona—Female—Mediterranean
Plant association: Apple

Roman goddess and patron of the orchard, especially apple orchards.

Pooka, The—Male—Central Europe
Animal association: Black Horse

Celtic/Pre-celtic spirit who curses all crops not harvested by Samhain. Probably the origin of Puck (Robin Goodfellow) in Shakespeare's play *A Midsummer Night's Dream*.

Porrima—Female—Mediterranean

Roman goddess of divination and prophecy. With her sisters Postvorta and Carmenta she is seen as a Triple Goddess.

Portunes—Male—Mediterranean
(Also known as Portunus, Portunis, Portuno)

Roman god of keys, entrances, and domestic animals (especially guardian animals/watchdogs). As sea trade often involved the secure storage of crops in ports, he became a god of harbors. He is honored by some with the wearing of an old fashioned key or key-like charm.

Poseidon—Male—Mediterranean
Father: Cronos
Mother: Rhea
Wife: Amphitrite
Lover: Gaia, Leucippe, Telephassa
Animal associations: Horse, Cattle (bull), Dolphin, Fish, Whale, Shark and all creatures of the sea
Plant associations: Ash, Bladderwrack, Cedar, Fig, Lotus*, Myrrh, Olive, Pine, Seaweed (all), Water Lily
* May have been connected to Lotus due to the folk name use of the term Water Lily.

Greek god and ruler of the ocean who lived there with his wife. He forms a sacred triad with his brothers Zeus (land/upper world) and Hades (Underworld).

Incense Recipe

1 part Cedar powder
1 part Myrrh (sweet myrrh is best)
A pinch of sea salt
Enough Poseidon or Myrrh essential oil to bind

Oil Recipe

9 drops Cedar wood essential oil
6 drops Myrrh essential oil
1/2 ounce olive oil

Postvorta—Female—Mediterranean

Roman goddess of history and of seeing the past for what it is rather than for how one wishes to picture it. With her sisters Carmenta and Porrima she is seen as a Triple Goddess.

Prajapati—Male—Near East
Animal association: Tortoise

Hindu god and patron of parents.

Protogonos—Male—Mediterranean

Phoenician god and father to the first of humanity. His name means 'first born,' his wife's name means 'life,' his children are the combination of the two, giving us 'first born life.'

Priapus—Male—Mediterranean/Middle East
Father: Dionysus
Mother: Aphrodite
Animal associations: Bee, Goat, Donkey
Plant associations: Myrrh, Olive, Pine, Thistle

Greek fertility god who was honored with statues carved out of wood and sporting huge penises. He protects and oversees family gardens and animal husbandry, granting fertility to both endeavors.

Incense Recipe

4 part Pine needles (or 1 part pitch and 3 part sandalwood)
4 parts Myrrh
4 parts Gum Arabic
Enough Priapus or Pine essential oil to bind

Oil Recipe

9 drops Pine essential oil
6 drops Myrrh essential oil
1/2 ounce Olive oil

Pritha—Female—Near East
Lover: Dharma

Hindu goddess. Some cite her as Dharma's close friend, others as his lover.

Prithvi—Female—Near East
Husband: Dyaus
Animal association: Cattle (cow)

Hindu Earth Mother and fertility goddess.

Priti—Female—Near East

Hindu personification of joy.

Prometheus—Male—Mediterranean
Animal association: Coyote
Plant associations: Dragon's Blood, Fennel seeds

Greek god of divination who created man of clay. Athena then breathed life into them. Because his brother had given animals everything he was allowed to give humanity, he gave us something he was not allowed to give: fire. So concerned was Zeus that humanity might become gods themselves with fire, he took fire back from humanity. In response, Prometheus stole the fire from Zeus and secreted it back to humanity. When Zeus discovered the theft, he sent Prometheus to be tortured daily, and to humanity he sent Pandora with her box of misfortune. In this story, we see why so many Wiccans hold to the use of the athame rather than the wand. It takes fire to create the athame, thus denoting the separation between humanity and other animals who use sticks as tools.

Incense Recipe

2 part powdered Fennel seed
1 part Dragon's Blood
1 part Gum Arabic
No need for an oil to bind this one

Oil Recipe

1 part Fennel Seed oil
1 part Dragon's Blood perfume oil

Proserpina—Female—Mediterranean
Animal associations: Bat, Boar

Roman goddess who equates to the Greek Persephone.

Psyche—Female—Mediterranean
Plant associations: Dittany of Crete, Ivy, Lily, Willow

'Soul'—Greek goddess who deeply loved Eros as did he love her, but she broke a promise to him which seemed a bit silly. He insisted that if they were to be lovers, it could only be at night with no light on the union. Although she thought the request was silly, she agreed. Later, she broke her promise and shed light on their lovemaking. He left her, deeply hurt by her actions. She later won him back, but not before much grief, both hers and his. Their story tells us that even when we think our lover's requests are silly, if we fail to honor them we risk hurting both ourselves and our lovers.

Ptah—Male—African
Wife: Sekhmet
Animal associations: Cattle (bull), Donkey, Hawk

Plant associations: Almond

'Creator'—Egyptian god and patron of folk who create with their hands. He is sometimes seen as an All Father of the other gods, having created them all.

Pukkeenegak—Female—Arctic North America

Eskimo goddess of conception, child birth, and the making of clothing (especially for children)

Pusha—Male—Near East

(Also known as Pushan)

Father: Kashyapa

Mother: Aditi

Hindu god of relationships in the order of all things, casual or personal, living or not living. One of the Adityas. The Hindu month Pausa (December 22–January 20) is sacred to Pusha. See Adityas.

Pyrrha—Female—Mediterranean

Husband: Deucalion

Greek goddess who survived the Great Flood. See Deucalion.

Queen Maya—Female—Far East

Mother of the Buddha.

Quetzalcoatl—Male—Central America

(Also known as Quezalcoatl)

Animal associations: Hummingbird, Dog, Lizard, Snake

Aztec and Toltec god of wind, fertility, and knowledge. He invented methods of negotiating with Nature, as well as the calendar by which his people could predict the seasons. With Mayauel, he brought love to humanity.

Quezalcoatl—See Quetzalcoatl

Quirinus—Male—Mediterranean

Wife: Hora

Roman god of community and state. Most likely an avatar/incarnation of Mars as Mars Quirinus. No longer a god of war in this incarnation, he is more of a father figure.

Ra—Male—Africa

(Also known as Re)

Animal associations: Cat, Duck, Falcon, Hawk, Lion

Plant associations: Acacia, Bay, Cinnamon, Frankincense, Heliotrope, Myrrh, Olive, Sunflower, Vine (grape)

Egyptian predecessor to Amun-Ra who was actually a fusing of two gods, Amun and Ra, due to a political merging of cultures. Ra is a sun god and Supreme God of the Heliopolis pantheon. In his aspect as Atum-Ra we see that although typically cited as male, Ra, is cited as generating the first gods from himself. Because this creation comes in a form devoid of the human attributes of procreation, he can be seen as being neither male nor female. He can also be associated with the Fifth Element in the Wiccan belief system in that even though he was neither male nor female at the point of creation, he was driven to create. In his case he is said to have created Tefnut and her mate Shu through masturbation. They in turn united in the Great Rite and formed Nut and Geb, thus giving us the four Quarters/Elements, as well as the Fifth Element (heart/spirit) that brings on the act of sex, the principle of both separation and union.

Rabefihaza—Male—Madagascar

Madagascan folk hero who taught man how to negotiate with Nature for meat and fish. He invented the snare trap. Patron of those who fish and trap for food.

Radha—Female—Near East

Holiday: September 1st

Hindu avatar/incarnation of Lakshmi as Krishna's favorite mortal lover, or maybe wife.

Rahula—Female—Far East

Father: The Buddha

Mother: Yasodhara

Son of the founder of modern Buddhism. See Buddha, The.

Rainbow Snake—Male/Female—Australia

Australian Aborigine god who was cited as male in some areas and female in other areas. S/he was seen as a life giving deity of fertility in the order of bringing rain, which fertilized the land and gave life to all creatures.

Raka (1)—Female—Near East

Hindu moon goddess associated with the full moon.

Raka (2)—Male—Polynesian Islands

Polynesian god of the wind.

Rakini—Female—Near East

Hindu goddess associated with the Swadishthana chakra (genitals). Sometimes described as an aspect of Shakti. See also Dakini, Lakini, Kakini, Sakini, and Hakini.

Raktavija—Male—Near East

Hindu demon general who led the attack against humanity that Kali put down. Kali is often depicted with Raktavija's head in her hand, so we know how that war ended.

Rama—Male—Near East
Wife: Sita

Hindu seventh avatar/incarnation of Vishnu.

Ran—Female—Scandinavian
Husband: Aegir
Animal associations: Fish and all creatures of the sea.

'The Ravisher'—Ran brought bad weather to sailors. Her daughters furthered her efforts by tempting sailors unto their death. She rules the Underworld at the bottom of the ocean. Should men die by drowning, they become an honored guest in her domain.

Rangi—Male—Polynesian Islands
(Also known as Hanui-o-Rangi)
Wife: Papa

New Zealand Sky God. With his wife Papa, Earth Goddess, the pair contribute greatly to the use of the Wiccan terms Father Sky and Mother Earth.

Raphael—Male—Middle East/Mediterranean

Semitic God of Air. Archangel who is associated with the East Quarter in Wiccan, Gnostic, and Ceremonial rituals. The other Quarters are presided upon by Michael, Gabriel, and Auriel.

Rati—Female—Near East
Father: Dyaus
Mother: Prithvi
Husband: Kama

'Pleasure'—Hindu goddess of sexual delight. See Kama.

Ratna, Dakinis—Female—Central Asia

Dakinis Ratna is the Tibetan goddess associated with the South, compassion, and all things precious. See also Vajra, Padma, Karma, and Buddha.

Ratri—Female—Near East

Hindu goddess of darkness and the night. Her sister is Ushas (Dawn).

Ravana—Male—Near East
Animal association: Donkey

Demon king who kidnapped Sita only to find the revenge of her husband, Rama, at the end of a sword.

Raven—Male—North America
Animal association: Raven

Common to Native American tribes of the Pacific North West. Similar to Coyote of other tribes. Raven, like Coyote, is a trickster god. However, although a trickster, Raven also created humanity from wood and clay. Now humanity waits to see if we too were one of his tricks. Time will tell.

Re—See Ra

Remus—See Romulus

Renenet—Female—Africa
Animal associations: Lion, Snake (serpent)

Egyptian goddess of breastfeeding who is present at birth and death—at birth to nurture and at death for judgment. She is the personification of fortune, but is usually accompanied by her sister Shai (Fate).

Rhadamanthus—Male—Mediterranean
Father: Zeus
Mother: Europa
Animal association: Elephant
Plant association: Aloe

Greek god of justice, wisdom, and education. He became one of the judges of the Underworld. Not a patron of those fairly accused of a crime or those who would defend them as he is associated with justice, not simply winning.

Rhea—Female—Mediterranean
(Also known as Dindumene)
Lover: Cronos
Animal associations: Bee, Crow, Wolf
Plant associations: Cypress, Myrrh, Oak, Pine, Poppy (white)

Greek mother of many of the gods. She gave birth to Demeter, Hades, Hera, Hestia, Poseidon and Zeus. When her husband and brother, Cronos tried to kill her children to prevent them from becoming more powerful than he, she tricked Cronos into missing Zeus. Cronos swallowed the others. When Zeus came of age, he overpowered his father, took his throne, and forced him to vomit up the other children, ushering forth the new pantheon as he did. Rhea is an Earth Mother who was worshiped with wild orgies and indulgences in wine and other intoxicants.

Rhiannon—Female—Central Europe
Animal associations: Blackbird, Horse (white), and to some extent, all birds.

Welsh fertility goddess and patron of the falsely accused. She was once punished for the murder of her son, but was later discovered to be innocent.

Robin Good Fellow—Male—Central Europe
Plant association: Bachelor's Buttons

Potentially another name for Puck. Perhaps two separate deities merged into one by Shakespeare, or maybe built on the lore of the Pooka.

Robigo—Female—Mediterranean
Husband: Robigus

Roman goddess who is called on to prevent the blight of crops by calling her attention to the weapons of war. Her name loosely means decay, and by drawing her attention to the weapons of war one brought on the rust of those weapons rather than the blighting of crops. Perhaps a commentary on the destructive nature of war on the infrastructure of a nation. Let the weapons rust and the crops will do well. She is sometimes cited as a female avatar/incarnation of Robigus, other times as his wife.

Robigus—Male—Mediterranean
Wife: Robigo

Roman god who protected grain crops from disease. Often worshiped with Flora. See Robigo, the goddess who is sometimes cited as his wife and other times cited as a female avatar/incarnation of Robigus. Their functions were shared.

Romulus—Male—Mediterranean
Father: Mars
Mother: Rhea Silvia
Mother: Acca Larentia (adopted)
Animal association: Wolf

With his brother Remus, he was the founder of Rome who was later deified. He was forced to kill his brother Remus after Remus started a horrible dispute over the naming of a new city they had hoped to found.

Roua—Male—Polynesian Islands
(Also known as Ra)
Lover: Taonoui
Son: Fati by Taonoui

Father of the stars as seen by his followers on Society Island.

Ru Shou—Male—Central Asia
(Also known as Ju-Shou)
Animal association: Dragon
Holiday: Autumn Equinox

Chinese messenger who arrives from the west to bring bad news from the sky god with each sun set. He is associated with the Fall. His counterpart is Gou Mang.

Rudra—Male—Near East
(Also known as Nilakantha)
Animal associations: Cattle (bull), Boar, and all creatures of the wild.

'Howler'—Pre-Hindu personification of untamed Nature as seen in the power of thunderstorms and wild animals. Because he was being viewed by folk who had become accustomed to city life, he was associated with death. In a way, he is the male opposite of the loving, life-giving modern view of Mother Nature. As the Hindu religion developed, he became similar to Mother Nature and became associated with the life giving attributes of wild animals who were hunted and raised as cattle. His associations with the rain and thunder became beneficial to the raising of crops and to the prosperity of humanity. Eventually he grew into what we now call Shiva, a god who retains his attributes as a wildly destructive force who is most often depicted with Shakti in the very act of creation (sex).

Rutbe—Female—Central America
Guaymian water goddess.

Sabazius—Male—Middle East/Mediterranean
Wife: Bendis
Animal associations: Ram, Scorpion, Snake, Toad

Early Hebrew sun god and maybe ultimately the origin of the term Sabbat. However, this is probably just wild speculation on my part. Eventually he was associated and maybe absorbed by both Dionysus and Bacchus.

Sadhbh—Female—Central Europe
Irish goddess of deer who was herself transformed into a deer against her will.

Sakini—Female—Near East
Hindu goddess associated with the Vishuddhi chakra (throat). Sometimes described as an aspect of Shakti. See also Dakini, Rakini, Lakini, Kakini, and Hakini.

Sakkan—Male—Middle East/Mediterranean
Father: Samas
Animal associations: Bear, Lion, Cheetah, Wolf, Jackal, Hyena, Cattle (ox/wild), Gazelle, Boar, Wild Cat, Lynx, Beaver, Mongoose, Deer, Goat, Sheep, Leopard, Bear, Bobcat, Panther

Mesopotamian patron of animals. Depicted most often as a shepherd, he presides over animal fertility.

Salacia—Female—Mediterranean
Husband: Neptune
Animal associations: Dolphin, Fish, Shark, and all sea creatures.

Roman goddess of the oceans and of salt water.

Salmacis—Female—Mediterranean
Greek nymph who joined with the god Hermaphrodite to become the first bisexual being.

Salus—Female—Mediterranean
Roman goddess of health and well-being.

Samnati—Female—Near East
Husband: Dharma
Hindu goddess of humility.

Sampsa—Male—Northern Europe/Central Europe
(Also known as Sampsa Pellervoinen)
Finnish god who goes to sleep every Fall. In so doing, he causes Winter. But when he wakes, he is reunited with his bride in Holy Matrimony, and Summer returns.

Sams—Female—Middle East
Semitic moon goddess.

Sancus—Male—Mediterranean

(Also known as Semo Sancus, Dius Fidus [divine faith])

Elder Roman god of good faith, oaths, and oral contracts. Patron and protector of those who act in good faith. But such oaths over which he presides must be made outside, in view of the sky.

Sanjna—Female—Near East

Husband: Surya

Animal associations: Horse

See Surya for her lore.

San-Ch'ing—Male—Central Asia

(Also known as San-qing)

Animal association: Frog

'Three pure ones'—The name given to the Taoist Triple God and to the heavens in which they rule. The first is Yuan-shi tian-zong who rules Yu-qing (the highest heaven). The second is Ling-bao tian-zong who rules Shang-qing (the middle heaven). The third is Tao-de tian-zong who rules Tai-qing (the lower heavens).

San-xing—Male—Central Asia

(Also known as San-hsing)

Three Chinese gods of good fate and fortune. They are Fu-xing (Luck/Health), Lu-xing (Honor/Status/Prosperity) and Shou-xing (Longevity/Wisdom). Perhaps the root of the expression early to bed and early to rise makes one *'healthy, wealthy, and wise.'*

Sarama—Female—Near East

Indra's faithful companion, a dog.

Sarasvati—Goddess—Near East

Animal associations: Peacock, Swan

Hindu goddess and protector of the river by her name.

Sati—Female—Near East

Husband: Shiva

Hindu avatar/incarnation of Parvati. When she was mistreated by her husband Shiva, she took her own life by throwing herself onto a sacrificial fire that had been lit in his praise.

Saturn—Male—Mediterranean

Wife: Ops

Son: Picus

Animal associations: Donkey, Crocodile, Goat, Vulture

Plant associations: Ash, Belladonna, Blackberry, Cypress, Fig, White Poppy, Hellebore (white), Yew

Roman god of harvest. With his wife Ops by his side, who is the goddess of plenty, he is king of the Saturnalia. This annual festival amounts to an entire week of feasting, revelry, and present giving. One of the key practices of the Saturnalia was the reversal of social roles. Masters became servants to their servants who became masters. Saturday receives its name from this god.

Satyr—Male—Mediterranean

Animal association: Goat

Greek Nature spirits of the wood and mountains. Their female counterparts are the nymphs. They are often depicted as having the upper torso, horned head, and arms of a man, but the bottom of a goat or other beast. However, they are sometimes shown in much more human-like form.

Scylla—Female—Mediterranean

Animal association: Dog

Greek sea nymph. The sea god Glaucus fell deeply in love with her, but she showed him little attention. So he went to Circe for a remedy, something to warm her heart to him. In talking to him, Circe fell deeply in love and became furious with Scylla either seeing her as competition or for the insult of not being attracted to Glaucus. Circe made a powerful potion and poured it into the pool where Scylla bathed. The moment Scylla stepped into that pool, she was changed into a hideous monster. So bitter is Scylla about the transformation, that to this day she devours and destroys any ship that passes her.

Sebek—Male—Africa

(Also known as Sobek)

Animal association: Alligator, Crocodile

Egyptian personification of the authority and power of the Pharaohs. He is depicted with the body and legs of a human but the head and upper torso of a crocodile or alligator.

Sedna—Female—Arctic North America

Animal associations: Seal, Fish, and all creatures of the sea.

Inuit Goddess of the Sea and of sea creatures.

Shaya—Female—Near East

Husband: Surya

Hindu handmaiden to Surya and sister to his wife Sanjna. See Surya.

Sheu—Female—North America

Husband: Kanati

'Corn'—Cherokee corn goddess. Often seen as a Crone goddess as well.

Seker—Male—Africa

(Also known as Sokar, Sokaris)

Animal association: Hawk

Egyptian hawk-headed god of plant fertility. He would later become associated with the Underworld.

Selene—Female—Mediterranean

Father: Hyperion

Mother: Theia

Lover: Endymion

Plant association: Willow

'Moon'—Greek goddess who fell so in love with the mortal Endymion that she begged Zeus to make him immortal, so she and her love could be together forever. Zeus granted her wish with the condition that Endymion would forever sleep. Selene accepted the condition and goes to her lover's side every night just to watch him sleep. I believe this story tells of the love our Lady has for humanity. As we sleep, Selene (the Moon) watches over us all.

Sekhmet—Female—Africa

Husband: Ptah

Animal associations: Cat, Lion, Snake (cobra)

Plant association: Pomegranate

Holiday: January 7th

Egyptian war goddess. Powerful and destructive, she was sent to Earth to put humanity in its place when it considered rising against the gods and achieving dominance over the world. She tells us that war and destruction are sometimes necessary tools against the rise of nations who wish dominance over the world.

Selkhet—Female—Africa

Animal association: Scorpion

Egyptian fertility goddess and protector of marriages. Associated with the Element Air and the protection of the god Kebechsenef.

Set—Male—Africa

(Also known as Seth, Setekh, Setesh, Seti)

Animal associations: Dog, Donkey, Antelope, Hippopotamus, Boar (black), Crocodile, Scorpion, Goose, Turtle, Snake, Wolf, and to some degree all creatures of the desert.

Plant associations: Myrrh, Patchouli, Thistle

Set begins his journey through Egyptian lore as a minor deity of wind and storms. He ruled over confusion and the destruction that came with severe weather. Gradually, he gained favor and his name became widespread. So popular was he that eventually he fell into opposition with Osiris. Their story is no doubt another reflection on the relation between prosperity and war. Set is guardian of the dessert who protected the caravans which conducted trade with other nations. He was also a protector of Egypt and god of war. Osiris, on the other hand, is in part a fertility god.

Incense Recipe

2 part Patchouli

1 part Myrrh

1 part Gum Arabic

Enough Set or Patchouli oil to bind

Oil Recipe

11 drops Patchouli essential oil

9 drops Myrrh essential oil

1/2 ounce olive oil

Shai—Female—Africa

Egyptian Goddess of Fate. She followed the soul from birth, always watching over its shoulder, until death when she appeared at the soul's judgment. Part of that judgment was if one fulfilled one's destiny and lived in accordance with one's true will. She is usually accompanied by her sister Renenet (Fortune). Sometimes Shai is seen as female and wife to Meshkent. Other times, the female version is cited as Shait and the male version as Shai. I prefer to think of her as Shai because I just can't state with a straight face that my fate is Shait.

Shait—Female version of Shai

Shaitan—Male—Middle East

An order of Jinn (genie) in the pre-Islam tradition. Although all orders of Jinn could do good or evil, this particular order seems to have been adopted by Christianity as yet another example of the manifestation of the adversary to the Christian god.

Shakti—Female—Near East

Husband: Shiva

Hindu goddess associated with the active forces. Her husband Shiva is inactive except by her influence. Although she is typically cited as an incarnation/avatar of Shiva's wife Parvati, she is more often depicted with Shiva. Interestingly enough, the most common goddesses to accompany Shiva in depiction seem to be Shakti (which whom he is shown as having sex with and thus creating) and Kali (under whom he sacrifices himself). So then, our Lord Shiva (Lord of Destruction) is most often depicted either creating or sacrificing. See also Dakini, Rakini, Lakini, Kakini, Sakini, and Hakini.

Shamash—Male—Mediterranean/Middle East (Also known as Sumerian Utu, Uta [Sumerian])

Father: Sinn

Mother: Ningal

Wife: Aya

Animal associations: Cattle (bull), Horse

Note: Due to the merging of Sumerian and Babylonian pantheons, his mother and father are often cited differently.

Sumero-Babylonian sun god of the law and law abiding. Known as 'Chemosh' in the Old Testament. Interestingly enough, he is sometimes seen as having Nergal as an aspect. Nergal is other times seen as a separate entity in opposition to Shamash. The implication is that good and evil are parts of the same whole. With the debunking of the anti-Pagan myth that Samhain was an evil Celtic god of the dead, Shamash became Samhain's replacement as the deity of choice for the nuttier of the anti-Pagan movement to claim is worshipped at Samhain. At least this time they picked a deity name that actually exists.

Shango—Male—African/Caribbean/South America

In Santeria, his name is Chango

In Voodoo, his name is Shango/John the Conqueror

In Africa, his name is Shango

Saint and Catholic associations: Saint Barbara and St. Jerome

Father: Aganyu

Mother: Yemaja

Wife: Oya, Oshun

Holiday: Feast of Saint Barbara on December 4

Plant associations: Allspice, Apricot, Apple (blossom), Angelica, Anise, Asafoetida, Basil, Balm of Gilead, Bay, Bergamot, Calendula, Chamomile (common), Caraway, Clove, Carnation, Cedar, Cypress, Cumin, Dragon's Blood, Deerstongue, Dill, Frankincense, Geranium, Ginger, Ginseng, Grains of Paradise, Galangal, Heather, Honeysuckle, Hyacinth (wild), Hyssop, Hibiscus, Juniper, Lilac, Lime, Lotus, Lavender, Mandrake (American), Mimosa, Mistletoe (American), Myrrh, Patchouli, Pennyroyal, Peppermint, Pine, Pepper (black), Rue, Sage (common), Sandalwood (white), Saffron (Mexican), Sesame, Thistle, Vanilla, Vervain, Violet

Yoruba Fire god of thunder and legendary first king of the Yoruba tribe. He was married to Oya and Oshun simultaneously. Do not confuse with the Central Asia Ch'ang-O.

Incense Recipe
4 parts Dragon's Blood
2 parts Sandalwood (white)
1 part Cedar
1 part Cumin

Oil Recipe
8 drops Sandalwood oil
4 drops Clove oil
4 drops Cypress oil
4 drops Cedar oil
1/2 ounce Sesame oil as a base

Shasti—Female—Near East
Animal association: Cat

Hindu protector and patron of children.

Sheila Na Gig—Female—Central England

Irish fertility goddess who is depicted with her legs spread and her hands opening and exposing the inner folds of her vagina. Her image is used in both pre-Christian and Christian cultures to ward off evil as if to say, here is life.

Skeiron—Male—Mediterranean

Greek personification of the North East Wind.

Shen Mu—Female—Central Asia

Chinese Mother Goddess. Patron and protector of pregnant women, children, and the act of childbirth.

Shen Nung—Male—Central Asia
Wife: Shen Tsan

Chinese emperor who taught his people how to negotiate with Nature in the order of farming.

Shen Tsan—Female—Central Asia

Chinese wife of emperor Shen Nung who became a goddess associated with silk.

Sheu—Female—North America
Husband: Kanati

Cherokee corn goddess.

Shezmu—Male—Africa

Egyptian god of wine who played many roles, the most noted being the person who ripped the souls of evil people apart in the Underworld, forcing them to endure great suffering.

Shing Mu—Female—Central Asia

Chinese Mother goddess of intelligence. Patron and protector of prostitutes.

Shitateru-Hime—Female—Far East
Husband: Ame-No-Wakahiko

Japanese mortal woman who married the god Ame-No-Wakahiko.

Shiu Mu—Female—Central Asia
Holiday: February 1st

Chinese Mother and Water goddess.

Shiva—Male—Near East
Wife: Parvati
Note: Many of the wives cited to Shiva are aspects of Parvati. See Parvati and Shakti for more information.
Animal associations: Antelope, Cattle (bull), Elephant, Jackal, Snake (serpent),Tiger
Plant associations: Dragon's Blood, Geranium

Hindu god who forms the sacred triad with Vishnu and Brahma. He retook the heavens after they were taken in combat by Jalandhara. When Jalandhara tried to abduct Shiva's wife Parvati it renewed his will to fight, causing him to rally the other gods to defeat Jalandhara. Although commonly thought of as a God of destruction, he is most often depicted either meditating or making love with wife Parvati in one of her many forms.

Incense Recipe
2 parts Dragon's Blood resin
1 part Geranium flowers or Sandalwood powder dampened with geranium essential oil
Enough Shiva or Dragon's Blood perfume oil to bind

Oil Recipe

9 drops Dragon's Blood perfume oil

6 drops Geranium essential oil

1/2 ounce base oil

Shou-Xing—Male—Central Asia

(Also known as Shou-Hsing)

Animal associations: Bat, Stag

'Star of longevity'—One of the three Chinese gods of good fortune, the San-Xing. He is the god of long life and wisdom.

Shou, Mo Li—Male—Central Asia

Animal association: Dragon

Mo Li Shou is the Chinese Buddhist guardian of the North. His statue is often included at the North point of Buddhist temples. In the modern practice of Feng Shui, his statue is placed in the North most part of a home to protect from negative influences coming from that direction. In Wiccan ritual, he is one of the names for the four Quarters, the other three being Hung, Chung, and Hai.

Shu—Male—African

Animal associations: Ostrich, Ram

Plant associations: Banyan, Damiana, Jasmine

Egyptian Air god who holds his daughter Nut above her brother and husband Geb. He was created by Ra and is often associated with the East/Air Quarter in Wiccan ritual. See also Ra, Tefnut, Seb, and Nut.

Incense Recipe

2 parts Jasmine

2 parts Gum Arabic

1 part Damiana

Enough Shu oil or Jasmine absolute to bind

Oil Recipe

12 drops Jasmine absolute

18 drops tincture of Damiana

6 drops tincture of Gum Arabic

1/2 ounce base oil

Sida—Male—Malaysia

(Also known as Sido)

Melanesian folk hero of Torres Island who taught his people both oral and written language. Later, he was viewed as a fertility god who created many useful plants and instructed humanity in the use of those plants.

Sif—Female—North Europe

Husband: Thor

Scandinavian Earth Mother described as having beautiful golden hair. As a joke, Loki once snuck into her bed chambers and lopped off her hair. So furious was Thor that he put fear of death into Loki should he not return and repair the hair. Fearing for his life and realizing he had gone way too far in his trickery, Loki replaced the hair with magickly spun gold.

Sigmund—Male—North Europe

Wife: Hjordis

Scandinavian folk hero, loyal to Odin. After Odin plunged a sword into a tree, he declared the sword would belong to the man who had the might to draw it from the tree. Sigmund was that man and later won many victories with it. His last battle was with Odin who defeated Sigmund while in disguise by breaking the sword and wounding him severely. His wife Hjordis wanted to heal his wounds, but he declared that if his lord Odin desired him dead, then he must surely die. Upon his deathbed, he still valued the sword so much that he willed it to his unborn son, Sigurd, that he might continue the family tradition in service to Odin. Sigurd became the most noted of the Germanic heroes.

Silenus—Male—Mediterranean

Greek tutor and friend to Dionysus. Always drunk but also full of knowledge and able to divine the future. He presents the most unusual form of divination one can find. If you could knock him down and tie him up, forcing him to stop drinking long enough to sleep, he would dream of your future. If, however, you failed in your attempts, then your future would be filled with bruises from where he struck you repeatedly.

Silvanus—Male—Mediterranean
Animal associations: Woodpecker, Wolf, Sheep
Plant associations: Juniper, Olive, Pine

Roman Horned God of the wild and guardian of boarders, particularly of the boarders between those areas between civilization and the wild.

Incense Recipe

4 part Pine needles (or 1 part pitch and 3 part Sandalwood)
4 parts Juniper berries
3 parts Gum Arabic
Enough Silvanus or Juniper essential oil to bind

Oil Recipe

9 drops Juniper essential oil
6 drops Pine essential oil
1/2 ounce Olive oil

Simbi—Male—Africa/Caribbean
(Also known as Sim'bi, Sim'bi d'l'eau)
Animal association: Snake

Haitian Voodoo deity of fresh water and friend to those who work magick.

Sin (1)—Male—North America
'Day'—Sky god of the Haida (North Pacific coastal area).

Sin (2)—Female—North Europe
Scandinavian goddess of truth.

Sin (3)—Male—Mediterranean/Middle East
(Also known as Sinn, Sin-Nanna, Suen)
Father: Enlil
Mother: Ninlil
Wife: Ningal
Animal associations: Cattle (bull), Dragon (lion)

Sumerian god of the moon and of measuring time. He gave wise council to the other gods who met with him at the end of each moon.

Sita—Female—Near East
Husband: Rama

Hindu goddess who was abducted and thought raped by Ravana. She escaped, killing Ravana, but did not at first reunite with Rama because it was thought that she had been raped by Ravana and was thus unclean. To demonstrate her virtue, she built a huge fire and walked into it. Rather than consuming her in its flames, the fire lifted her unharmed, proving her purity. She and Rama were thus reunited.

Skadi—Female—North Europe
Husband: Njord (first), Ull (second)

Scandinavian personification of Winter as the 'snow-shoe goddess.'

Sobek—See Sebek

Sol (1)—Male—Mediterranean
Roman god and personification of the sun.

Sol (2)—Female—North Europe
(Also known as Sunna)
Father: Mundilfari
Mother: Glaur
Husband: Glen

Scandinavian goddess and personification of the sun. Her brother is Mani, the Moon.

Soma—Male—Near East
Son: Budha by Tara
Animal association: Antelope
Plant association: Agaric Mushroom

Hindu moon god who fathered Budha by Tara after abducting and raping her. It is often mentioned that his name is shared by a plant and that the plant is associated with the drink of the gods, providing immortality and inspiration, a link between Heaven and Earth. But what most books don't mention is why the above is so funny. You see, Soma is one of the folk names of the Agaric Mushroom (*Amanita muscaria*), which is commonly sold (illegally so) in the United States as 'magic mushrooms.' One of the eight Hindu guardians of the principle directions. Soma is the guardian of the North East. The other seven are Indra, Agni, Yama, Surya, Varuna, Vayu, Kubera.

Sophia—Female—Middle East/Mediterranean
(Also known as Hakhma, Chochma)
Husband: Yahweh
Holiday: August 15th, October 5th

'*Wisdom*'—Hebrew, Greek and eventually Gnostic personification of Wisdom. Some cite her as wife of the Christian Yahweh. She is also said to be pictured in the famous painting at the Sistine Chapel in that capacity, her arm around Yahweh's shoulder.

Spider Grandmother—Female—North America
Animal association: Spider

Common to several Native American tribes as trickster or messenger.

Spider Woman/Man—Female—Japan/North America
Animal association: Spider

Both Spider Man and Spider Woman are Navaho deities who instructed the Navaho in the art of weaving. Among the Pueblo of Mexico and Arizona, Spider Woman is found in much the same capacity. In Japan, Spider Woman seems to be a female incarnation of Inari.

Sradda—Female—Near East
Husband: Dharma

Hindu goddess whose name means 'Confidence.'

Ssu Ling—Male/Female—Central Asia
(Also known as Ling)

The four creature guardians of Chinese mythology similar to the Wiccan four Quarters. They are Ch'i-lin, Feng-huang, Gui Xian, and Long.

Subhadra—Female—Near East

Hindu goddess and sister of Krishna.

Suitengu—Male—Far East

Japanese god of the sea who protects both sick children and sailors.

Summanus—Male—Mediterranean

Roman god of nighttime thunderstorms. Jupiter is the god of daytime thunderstorms.

Sun Hou Tzu—Male—Central Asia
(Also known as Sun Wu-kong, Sun Hou-zi)
Animal association: Monkey/Ape

Chinese folk hero who became an immortal after his death and venture to the Underworld, where he found his name in the Book of the Dead and ripped its page from the book. He became god of the monkeys, which might be commentary on how the other gods felt about his defiance of that which was written. One of his other names, Wu-kong, is probably the source for the name on which the story of King Kong was based. The word *wu* loosely means 'king.'

Sura—Female—Near East
Plant association: Vine

Hindu goddess of grape and wine.

Surya—Male—Near East
Wife: Sanjna, Shaya
Animal association: Horse (mare)
Plant associations: Cinnamon, Frankincense, Sandalwood (white), Sunflower

Hindu sun god whose wife, Sanjna, left him because she could not stand his brilliance. In her place, Sanjna placed Shaya, hoping her husband would not notice. Surya did notice and fell in love with Shaya, but also reconciled with his wife by sacrificing an eighth of that which he was to bring her back. His story is why I have promised my love that when I finish this book, she will be more of a focus in my life. One of the eight Hindu guardians of the principle directions. Surya is the guardian of the South West. The other seven are Indra, Agni, Yama, Varuna, Vayu, Kubera, Soma.

Incense Recipe

4 parts Frankincense
2 parts Sandalwood
1 part Cinnamon
Enough Surya or Sandalwood essential oil to bind

Oil Recipe

9 drops Frankincense essential oil

6 drops Cinnamon essential oil

1/2 ounce Sunflower oil

Susanoo—Male—Far East

Son: O-Kuni-Nushi

Animal association: Snake

Japanese moon god who was banished from Heaven by his sister, the sun goddess Amaterasu.

Sus Sistinnako—Male—North American

Animal association: Spider

Sia Creator god who made mankind by strumming a spider's web as an instrument and singing life into creation. Patron of musicians of string instruments and song.

Suwa—Female—Middle East

Arabic sun goddess. She is mentioned as an idol in the Koran. If a she had a central temple or icon, it was destroyed by Islam.

Svarog—Central Europe/Northern Europe

(Also known as Svarozic, Svarozits)

Animal association: Horse (white)

Slavic sun and Fire god. Initially seen as a supreme deity, he gradually became god of the metalsmith. He is responsible for formalizing the rites of marriage, declaring that the marriage under one culture or religion should be respected under all. In essence, he tells us that the unification of two people in such bonds transcends the structures of individual religions. Interestingly enough, after such a structure was established he gradually fell into the role of a fire demon.

Tailtiu—Female—Central Europe

Holiday: Lughnasadh

Irish patron of foster parents. She raised Lugh from infancy till the day he could bear arms. She was so loved by her foster child Lugh that he created the Tailteann games as a central part of the celebrations on Lughnasadh.

Takami-Musubi—Male—Far East

Wife: Amaterasu

Japanese Shinto Supreme Sky God and Creator who rules the world with his wife Amaterasu. With his wife, he is considered the greatest source of divine love.

Taliesin—Male—Central Europe

Plant association: Barley

Welsh son of Cerridwen who conceived him by eating a piece of grain that was really Gwion in disguise. He became a god of barley and most popular bard. Such was his fame that many historic bards have since taken his name. See Gwion for more of the story.

Tallai—Female—Middle East/Mediterranean

Canaanite goddess of rain. One of the aspects of the Canaanite's Triple Goddess whose name means 'Maiden of Rain.' See also Arsai and Pidrai.

Tammuz—Male—Middle East/Near East

(Also known as Damuzi [Sumerian])

Father: Ea

Wife: Ishtar

Animal association: Boar

Plant associations: Pomegranate, Wheat, and all old world grains.

Akkadian Green Man. Here again we see the story of Persephone reversed in both gender and climate. Each year he travels to the Underworld as the hot summer approaches. His wife Ishtar mourns his loss and all fertility leaves the Earth. Eventually Ishtar negotiates his release (by trial and tribulation) and he returns as the year cools down, fertility returned to the Earth.

Tane—Male—Polynesian Islands

Father: Rangi

Mother: Papa

Wife: Hine-Ahu-One

Plant association: Kava Kava

Animal associations: Fish, Lizard, and to a degree all reptiles

Polynesian god of light and Creator who separated the primordial egg, divided it into Earth (his own mother Papa) and Sky (His own father Rangi). Interestingly enough, this is relatively the same story found in the creation and separation of the Yin and Yang told in the story of Pan-gu (Chinese)—right down to the egg.

Tangaroa—Male—Polynesian Islands
(Also known as Ta'aroa, Tangaloa)
Animal association: Fish, Lizard

Polynesian sea god. He is sometimes cited with similar attributes as his brother Tane, but those cites are probably due to confusion in the names. Tangaroa lives in the sea and needs to breath air only once a day. When his huge body surfaces to breath, the resulting water displacement causes the waves that lap the shore.

Tantalis—Male—Mediterranean

Greek king who made his son a sacrifice to the gods. In response, Zeus restored the son to life and told Tantalis to go to Hades. There he was kept constantly hungry and constantly thirsty in the presence of the finest food and drink, chained in such a way that he could almost, but not quite, get to it. From his story we have the word *tantalize*. His story warns that those who harm children will be punished.

Taonoui—Female—Polynesian Islands
Lover: Roua
Son: Fati by Roua

Polynesian mother of the stars as viewed from Society Island.

Tara—Female—Near East
Husband: Brihaspati

Hindu star goddess who was kidnapped by Soma, raped, and released after Soma was forced to release her by Brahma but not before becoming pregnant with Budha.

Taranis—Male—Central Europe
Plant association: Holly, Oak

'Thunder'—Sky god of the Gaul. Roman records state clearly that he demanded and received human sacrifice. While this may be true, Roman records were given to disinformation about the folk they wished to defeat.

Tashmit—Female—Middle East/Mediterranean

Babylonian goddess of prayer and the written word. She and her husband Nebo invented the written language.

Ta Tanka—Male—North America
Animal association: Bison

'Great Beast'—Lakota word for Buffalo and sometimes a word used to describe the 'Great Spirit.' However, the term Nagi Tanka is used by the Dakota and most often translated to 'Great Spirit' or 'Great Mystery.' I have little doubt that word *tanka* is being translated as 'Great,' but I am not so sure the word *tanka* translates well into *spirit*. While the Buffalo were no doubt a great food source, I believe the idea that all Native Americans worshiped the 'Great Spirit' as a buffalo god is a fabrication of the New Age movement.

Tatenen—Male—Africa
(Also known as Tathen, Tanen, Tenen, Ten)
Animal association: Sheep

'Honored Earth'—Early Egyptian Earth God and Green Man image who represents the land that initially rose from the waters of the Earth. In essence, he can be seen as a Father Nature image.

Taukiyomi—Male—Far East
Japanese moon god.

Ta-Urt—Goddess—Egypt
(Also known as Taurt)
Husband: Bes
Animal association: Hippopotamus

Egyptian goddess of good fortune and childbirth. With her husband, she is the protector of women during pregnancy, birth, and for a time after birth. She is also a protector of children. Her lore illustrates the early principle that childbirth led to good fortune, after all it was one's children who provided the family work force. Her husband, Bes, is god of pleasure.

Tawhaki—Male—Polynesian Islands
(Also known as Tawhiki)

Polynesian god of beneficial thunderstorms and good health.

Tawhiri—Male—Polynesian Islands
(Also known as Tawhiri-ma-tea, Tawhiri-Matea)
Father: Rangi
Mother: Papa

Polynesian god of the winds and baneful storms.

Tawiskara—See Ioskeha

Taygete—Female—Mediterranean
Father: Atlas
Mother: Aethra or Pleione

One of the Greek Pleiades. One of the many for whom Zeus lusted. Although she called on Artemis to hide her, Zeus discovered her hiding place. From that union she conceived Lacedaemon.

Tefnut—Female—Africa
Lover: Shu

Egyptian personification and goddess of Water and moisture. Her name is associated with the Wiccan Four Quarters. She is associated with Water and the West Quarter.

Tegid—Male—Central Europe
Lover: Cerridwen
Animal association: Boar (sow)
Plant association: Apple, Vervain, Willow

Welsh father of the ugliest boy (Avagdu) and most beautiful girl (Creirwy) in the history of the world.

Tekkeitsertok—Male—Arctic North America
Animal association: Deer

Eskimo Earth God who owned all the deer. He was given prayer and sacrifice in the order of fair exchange, prior to hunting deer. Without that exchange, the taking of deer was considered theft.

Tellumo—Male—Mediterranean
(Also known as Telluno)

Roman god of fertility. His female counterpart is Tellus Mater.

Tellus Mater—Female—Mediterranean
Animal association: Boar

'Earth Mother'—Roman Earth Mother and goddess of fertility. She is patron and protector of children and marriages. Her male counterpart is Telluno. The Sementivae honored her and Ceres.

Tempestes—Female—Mediterranean
Roman goddess of storms.

Temu—Male—Africa
(Also known as Atum, Tum)
Animal association: Snake (serpent)

Early Egyptian creator and sun god. He evolved into a lesser role in the Egyptian pantheon, becoming associated with the setting sun rather than its entire cycle. Eventually he evolved into Atum-Ra. See Ra.

Tenazuchi-no-Kami—Female—Far East
Husband: Ashi-Nadzuchi

Japanese Earth Mother and goddess of fertility.

Terminus—Male—Mediterranean
Animal association: Sheep

Roman god of property, especially land. He defines boundaries and property lines.

Terpsichore—Female—Mediterranean
Greek muse of poetry and dance. See also Muses, The.

Tethys—Female—Mediterranean
Husband: Oceanus

Greek personification and goddess of the ocean's fertility. With her husband, Oceanus, she gave birth to the many fresh water bodies of water found on the Earth.

Tezcatlipoca—Male—Central America
(Also known as God of the Smoking Mirror)

Animal associations: Hummingbird, Jaguar, Panther

'Smoke Mirror' or *'Smoking Mirror'*—Aztec Sun God who is fond of music and ruled the dances of summer. At each of his festivals, a prisoner was made sacrifice to him, but only after that prisoner was treated as a king during his long festival, in which he received four wives who performed his every wish. That practice is immensely similar to European practices. His magick mirror resembles the scrying mirrors of today, except that smoke rises from it, and he uses it to reflect rays of sunlight to strike his enemy dead. He is patron to magicians and sorcerers.

Thalia—Female—Mediterranean

Father: Zeus

Mother: Euronyme

'Brings flowers'—One of the Three Graces found in Greek lore. Her parents are sometimes cited as Dionysus and Aphrodite. See also Euphrosyne and Aglaia. She is also the Muse of comedy. See also Muses, The.

Thanatos—Male—Mediterranean

Father: Hypnos

Greek god of death who lives in the Underworld.

Thaumas—Male—Mediterranean

Father: Pontus

Mother: Gaia

Wife: Electra

'Wonder'—Greek personification of the rainbow and messenger of the gods.

Theia—Female—Mediterranean

(Also known as Thea)

Lover: Hyperion

Greek goddess and mother to Helios (Sun), Selene (Moon), and Eos (Dawn).

Thetis—Female—Mediterranean

Animal association: Dolphin

Became the mother of Achilles after joining in the Great Rite with Peleus. Thetis

reminds us that although we might do everything we can to protect our children, there will always remain a vulnerability.

Thor—Male—North Europe

(Also known as Donar)

Animal associations: Goat, Robin, Bear

Plant associations: Ash, Mountain Ash (Rowan), Birch, Common Daisy, Gorse, Hazelnut, Holly, Houseleek, Nettle (greater), Oak, Ox-eyed Daisy, Thistle, Vervain

Scandinavian god of the common man. He had many similarities to Odin except that Odin was more the god of the warrior class. Thor is the red-haired champion of the working class, requiring no sacrifice for his protection and guidance. His symbol is the hammer, which is most likely a phallic symbol.

Thoth—Male—Africa

(Also known as Djeheuty, Tehuti, Tahuti, Zehuti)

Wife: Nahmauit

Animal association: Ape, Jackal, Snake

Plant association: Almond, Beech, Benzoin, Birch, Gum Arabic, Vervain

Egyptian god of wisdom who is often seen as the scribe of his pantheon. He is said to have created the written language. He is patron of record-keepers and the divine mediator of the Egyptian pantheon.

Incense Recipe

2 parts Benzoin

1 part Vervain

Enough Thoth or Benzoin essential oil to bind

Oil Recipe

12 drops Benzoin essential oil

18 drops tincture of Vervain

6 drops tincture of Gum Arabic

1/2 ounce Almond oil

Three Marys, The—Female—Middle East/ Mediterranean

Christian Triple Goddess seen as either Mary Magdalene, the Virgin Mary, and Mary

Cleopas or as the latter two with the former Mary Magdalene replaced by Mary Salome. As Mary Salome and Mary Cleopas were the sisters of the Virgin Mary, it does seem a better fit. Interestingly enough there is some lore stating that Mary Magdalene is an alternative name for Mary Salome that was created to protect the bloodline of Jesus. But don't tell anyone, it is supposed to be a secret.

Three Mothers, The—Female—Middle East/Mediterranean

Hebrew Triple Goddess associated with Air, Water, and Fire. Sometimes cited as having the names of the three mother letters in the Hebrew alphabet: Aleph, Mem, and Shin. Perhaps a precursor to the Three Marys of Christian lore.

Thunder Beings—Male—North America

(Also known as Thunder Birds, Wakinyan)

Animal associations: Eagle, Hawk, Moth, Woodpecker

Lakota and other Native American personification of thunder, lightning, and rain. Most often viewed as beneficial as they were responsible for providing the rain that nourished their crops. Sometimes seen as destructive in the way that most things in Nature are mostly beneficial but sometimes baneful.

Thunder Birds—See Thunder Beings

Tiamat—Female—Middle East/Mediterranean

Lover: Apsu

Animal associations: Cattle (bull), Dragon (snake), Snake (serpent and horned), Ostrich, and to some degree all birds

'Ocean'—Babylonian personification of the ocean as a huge dragon. Her lover is Apsu, who she separated from herself in a story similar to that of Diana and Lucifer. However, in the story of Tiamat, she is the personification of salt water who separates fresh water from herself. Here we see the Wiccan concept of salting unsalted water as a symbol of creation.

Tian-wang—Male—Far East/Central Asia

(Also known as T'ien-wang)

Four Kings who guarded the Four Quarters in both Chinese and Japanese lore. Their images are still found in the temples of that area. Each is shown fully armored with a different skin color and holding different items in accordance with the direction they preside over. The King of the East has white skin. He is often shown with a lute which he uses to play music that brings tranquility and peace. The King of the South has blue skin. He is often shown holding a sword which he uses to fight back ignorance and darkness. The King of the West has red skin. He is often shown holding a snake. The King of the North has green skin. He is often shown holding a mongoose that spits jewels from his mouth in one hand and a parasol in the other.

Tiberinus—Male—Mediterranean

(Also known as Tiberis)

Animal association: Fish (especially fresh water)

Roman god of the River Tiber and patron of those who fish. Although his following was noted as being widespread among fishermen, little remains of his great lore.

Tiki (1)—Male—Polynesian Islands

Polynesian god and creator of land by causing it to rise from the ocean. He is a fertility god who is prayed to for conception. In his name, a charm of a phallus is worn around the neck of a woman who wishes to conceive. That charm was also called a *tiki* in his honor and praise. Although his name has become almost synonymous with wood deity images of the area, statuary of the phallus or of a male form with a large phallus are more appropriately attributed to Tiki.

Tiki (2)—Male—Polynesian Islands

The name of the first man created by either Tane or Ta Matauenga/Tu Matauenga.

Ti Mu—Female—Central Asia

Chinese Earth Mother.

Tisiphone—Female—Mediterranean

'Avenger of Murder'—Greek goddess of justice and vengeance. One of the three Erinyes. The other two are Alecto and Megaera.

Tlazolteotl—Female—Central America

(Also known as Tlazolteotl Ixcuiname)

Animal association: Snake (red)

Aztec Earth Mother and goddess of sex. She is a protector of children and of the mother at childbirth. She is also said to offer redemption at death. In that capacity she is called 'Eater of Filth' because she is said to consume the confessed sins of a lifetime.

Toma—Female—Central Asia

Tibetan goddess associated with mind (human intellect).

Tonacatecuhtli—Male—Central America

Wife: Tonacacihuatl

'One at the center'—Aztec provider of bountiful harvests. The meaning behind his name notes that he is at the center of creation. When things are in balance, the Wheel spins properly around him and the harvest is plenty. When it is out of balance, the Wheel does not spin properly and there is a poor harvest. The Wheel in reference can be seen as the Wiccan Wheel of the Year. When Winter lasts too long, or when there is a late frost, plants die. Thus the Wheel is out of balance, and the harvest is poor.

Tonacacihuatl—Female—Central America

Husband: Tonacatecuhtli

Female aspect/wife of Tonacatecuhtli.

Toruguenket—Male—South America

Brazilian moon god and personification of evil. In opposition to Torushompek, much the way the Christian Satan is in opposition to the Christian God.

Torushompek—Male—South America

Brazilian sun god and personification of good. In opposition to Toruguenket much the way the Christian God is in opposition to the Christian Satan.

Tros—Male—Mediterranean

(Also known as Troy)

Lover: Callirhoe

Greek culture hero for whom the city of Troy was named. He is the father of Ganymede by Callirhoe.

Tsai Shen—Male—Central Asia

Animal associations: Carp, Chicken (cock), Tiger

Chinese god of wealth and prosperity.

Tsukiyomi—Male—Far East

Father: Izanagi

Mother: Izanami

Japanese moon god and keeper of time.

Tsul Kalu—Male—North America

Cherokee god of hunting. Patron of hunters.

Tvashta—Male—Near East

(Also known as Tvashtar)

Father: Kashyapa

Mother: Aditi

Hindu craftsman responsible for crafting the thunderbolt of Indra and the moon cup which was used to serve ambrosia. He is one of the Adityas. The Hindu month Phalguna (February 20–March 21) is sacred to Tvashta. See Adityas.

Twen-Ch'ang—Male—Central Asia

Animal association: Crane

Chinese god of poetry and literature. Sometimes cited as female.

Tyndareus—Male—Mediterranean

Wife: Leda

King of Sparta. See Leda for a full account of their children.

Typhon—Male—Mediterranean
Wife: Echidna
Animal associations: Donkey, Scorpion, Snake
Plant association: Cactus

Greek storm god. Born or created of Hera. He and his wife were so horrific that they even frightened the gods. It wasn't until Zeus stood up to the two that the Earth found relief. With his example, the other gods and goddesses found the courage to join and finally defeated Typhon and his wife, but not until much of the Earth and Heaven was destroyed in the battle.

Tyr—Male—North Europe

Scandinavian god of law (especially common law) who became a god of war, demonstrating the principle requirement of war to enforce law. In the Scandinavian pantheon, he is one of the gods who favors the common man. Patron of athletes and law enforcement.

Ueueteotl—Male—Central America

Aztec god of fire in order of both creative/useful and the destructive. A reminder that of the many forces in the universe which man believes he has mastered, fire will remain useful but forever unmastered.

Uga-Jin—Male—Far East
Animal association: Snake

Japanese serpent and Water god who brings fertility to the Earth. Like other serpent gods associated with water, he is seen in the rainbow.

Ukupanipo—Male—Polynesian Islands
Animal association: Fish, Shark

Hawaiian shark god who determines the abundance of ocean harvests by driving fish either into the waiting nets of fishermen or away into the deep ocean.

Uller—Male—North Europe
Father: Thor (adopted)
Mother: Sif

Scandinavian sky god of hunting and skill at archery. Patron of hunters, especially bow hunters.

Uma—Female—Near East
Husband: Shiva

Hindu avatar/incarnation of Parvati. She is the personification of Light and the beauty that comes with an inner light and divine wisdom.

Umi Bozu—Male—Far East
Animal association: Octopus

Japanese sea monster who is said to be the sometimes baneful spirit of a monk who died at sea.

Ungud—Male/Female—Australia
Animal association: Snake

Aboriginal Australian hermaphrodite snake god. Although cited most often as a hermaphrodite, s/he sometimes takes on distinctly male form and other times s/he is distinctly female. In her female form, she is the Earth. In her male form, he is the rainbow that is still seen after the rain falls to the Earth.

Uni—Female—Mediterranean/Central Europe
Animal association: Peacock

Etruscan supreme goddess who is associated with both Hera and Juno.

Unktomi—See Iktomi

Unkulukulu—Male—Africa
Animal associations: Chameleon, Lizard

Bantu Creator and educator of humanity.

Upulero—Male—Far East/Malaysia
Animal association: Chicken

Indonesian Sun God. Should a couple wish to conceive a child, the potential father calls on Upulero for his blessings and help in the matter, but only via sacrifice. Traditionally, that sacrifice took the form of a chicken. If you happen to live on a farm where the killing of chickens for food is routine, by all means do so, and then serve that animal's flesh to someone in need as you and your family go without food for a day. If, however, you are not one of those who routinely kills animals for food, purchase an amount of non perishable food equal to that which would feed you family for a day, deliver that food to a shelter or pantry and then go hungry, with your wife, for the day in which the potential father calls on Upulero. Patron of couples who want to become parents.

Ura—See Uronica

Uranus—Male—Mediterranean
(Also known as Ouranos)
Father: Elium
Mother: Berus
Lover: Gaia
Animal association: Jay
Plant association: Ash

Greek sky god. Gaia formed him out of herself in much the same way Diana formed Lucifer, then set him about the sky and caused him to become her lover.

Urcaguary—Male—South American
Animal association: Snake (serpent with deer's head)

Inca god of the richness of the Earth and of the treasures found beneath soil.

Uroica—Female—Central Europe
(Also known as Ura)
Plant association: Heather

A Brenton goddess of Summer, heather, and heather wine. She is associated with the Feast of Brewing on September 28th, with the creation of heather wine and other alcoholic beverages for that feast.

Ushas—Female—Near East
Father: Dyaus
Mother: Prithvi

Ushas is the Hindu goddess of dawn. Most often cited as sister to Agni, she is sometimes cited as his wife. Her sister is Ratri (night).

Uta—See Shamash

Uther Pendragon—Male—Central Europe
Wife: Igraine

British king during the Saxon invasions of Britain, who asked Myrddin (Merlin) for assistance in his quest for the hand of Igraine. Myrddin granted him that request and transformed Uther into the image of Igraine's husband, the Duke of Cornwall. During the night in which Uther, disguised as the Duke, and Igraine became initiated to each other, Arthur was conceived (later to become king). At the moment of Arthur's conception, the real Duke of Cornwall was killed in battle against Uther's troops. The story of the Duke of Cornwall and Arthur can be seen as founded in the roots of the ancient lore similar to the Oak and Holly King often used in Wiccan rituals to mark the Winter Solstice.

Utnapishtim—Male—Middle East/Mediterranean
(Also known as Ut-napishtim, Uta-Napishtim)

'He who saw life'—Sumero-Babylonian elder who was warned by Ea that the gods were concerned about humanity's proliferation and had planned a Great Flood. To escape that flood, Utnapishtim built a great ship. After seven days of flood, he sent out a dove but that dove returned. He then sent swallow and it too returned. Finally he sent a raven which did not return, thus indicating there must have been land somewhere for the raven to have landed on. After finding dry land, he made sacrifice for his deliverance. So humbled were the gods in this mortal's act of sacrifice even after witnessing the utter destruction of his world, that they felt great remorse for having killed so many with the flood, and they granted Utnapishtim immortality and promised never again to cause such an event. See Ishtar for more information.

Urania—Female—Mediterranean
Greek Muse of astronomy. See also Muses, The.

Utta—Female—Middle East/Mediterranean
Father: Enki
Mother: Ninkurra
Lover: Enki

Sumerian goddess whose lover, father, and great grandfather is Enki. See Enki for the story.

Uttu—Female—Middle East/Mediterranean

Sumerian goddess of vegetation and the use of vegetation by humanity. Also a name for the god Shamash.

Vach—Female—Near East

(Also known as Vac)

'Speech'—Hindu goddess of speech and of the process of experiencing the mysteries that normal speech cannot express. She is thus associated with the initiatory path of mystery religions such as Wicca.

Vadjra—Male—Far East

Japanese god of three faces. Those faces are the likely source for the statuary of three monkeys found in a 17th century Japanese temple. The best translation of the inscription on that statue is 'See no evil, hear no evil, and speak no evil' or 'Mizaru, Kikazaru, Iwazaru.' The statuary is most likely a representation of the three faces of a much earlier deity form, Vadjra. The fun part of this translation is that the Japanese word for monkey is 'saru,' which is similar in sound to the ending of each of the three faces of Vadjra. It is likely that any association between monkeys and Vadjra is made only through the pun intended on the names of his three faces whose names are actually verbs with an ending that only sounds similar to monkey. In a modern context, this supports the Wiccan principle that like attracts like and the warning in the Wiccan Rede about spending time with fools. It is the commentary that upon seeing, hearing, or speaking evil, one risks becoming evil. Now that is not a steadfast rule, but an observation. Certainly statistics show that abused children tend to grow up to be abusive parents, but it is not always the case.

Vajra, Dakinis—Female—Central Asia

Dakinis Vajra is the Tibetan goddess associated with East, peace, love, and the divine. See also Ratna, Padma, Karma, and Buddha.

Vali (1)—Male—Northern Europe

Father: Odin

Mother: Rind

Little is known about Vali other than he was born for the purpose of avenging Baldur's death. He is sometimes cited as an excellent archer, but I am unclear if this is a modern creation to connect him with the Roman Vali (son of Juno), or if perhaps the Vali of Northern Europe and Mediterranean have a connection other than the name.

Vali (2)—Male—Mediterranean

Mother: Juno

Vali is cited as an excellent archer and son of the goddess of love Juno Februa, making it a no-brainer that St. Valentine's Day is probably built on his story.

Valkyries—Female—Northern Europe

(Also known as Walkyries)

Animal associations: Horse, Eagle, Raven, Wolf, Swan

Plant association: Aspen

'Choosers of the slain'—The Valkyries are not only Odin's messengers, they are the beings sent forth to select combatants for the final battle of Ragnarok. These beautiful young women comb the battlefields of man to witness how warriors fight and just as importantly, how they die. If they fight with the fierceness necessary for the final battle of the gods, the Valkyries take note. If they die without fear and having confidence that their cause was just, then they raise the slain warrior (called the Einherjar) and bring him to Valhalla where they train every day for the end days. Interestingly enough, that training involves being wounded and killed each day, then healed at night so they can participate in combat training the next day. Where other cultures consider such an afterlife to be unpleasant, the Norse folk considered it to be one of the highest honors a man could receive. Yet another example of cultural different views of the ever present lore of an afterlife.

Varaha—Male—Near East

Animal association: Boar

Plant associations: Nettle (greater and lesser), Oak

Hindu third avatar of Vishnu. When Hiranyaksha dragged the Earth beneath the ocean, Vishnu incarnated into this third avatar (a boar) to combat Hiranyaksha. After a thousand-year battle, Varaha was successful and restored the Earth to the surface.

Varahini—Female—Near East

Husband: Vishnu

Hindu Earth goddess and avatar/incarnation of Lakshmi.

Vamana—Male—Near East

Hindu fifth avatar of Vishnu who appeared in the form of a dwarf such that he could trick Bali (a demon) to give up the Earth. First he convinced Bali to give him a tiny plot of land only three paces in size. Bali agreed, and Vamana returned to the size of Vishnu. He then counted the first place as Earth, the second as Heaven, and the third he said Bali could keep. There Bali remains today, in the Underworld.

Varuna—Male—Near East

Father: Dyaus

Mother: Prithvi

Wife: Varuni

Animal associations: Cattle (cow), Horse (white), Snake

Hindu god of sky and Water who is the charge of law and order. He is the personification of the Moon and a god with a heart, dispensing justice only with mercy. One of the eight Hindu guardians of the principle directions. Varuna is the guardian of the West. The other seven are Indra, Agni, Yama, Surya, Vayu, Kubera, Soma. Varuna is also one of the Adityas. The Hindu month Bhardra (August 23–September 22) is sacred to Varuna. See Adityas.

Varuni—Female—Near East

Husband: Varuna

Animal association: Crow

Hindu goddess of liquor and intoxicating beverages and brews of all order.

Vaya—Male—Near East

Animal association: Deer

One of the eight Hindu guardians of the principle directions. Vayu is the guardian of the North West. The other seven are Indra, Agni, Yama, Surya, Varuna, Kubera, Soma.

Vediovis—Male—Mediterranean

(Also known as Vediovis)

Animal association: Goat

Elder Roman god of health and healing. He is often depicted with his trusted goat.

Vellamo—Female—Central Europe/North Europe

Husband: Ahto

Finnish goddess of the sea who, with the help of her husband Ahto, controls matters of underwater fertility.

Venus—Female—Mediterranean

Lover: Mercury

Animal associations: Heron, Cattle (bull), Dove, Lion, Lynx, Snake, Sparrow, Swallow, Swan, Turtle, Tortoise

Plant associations: Adam and Eve root, Anemone, Angelica, Apple, Apricot, Aster, Benzoin, Carnation, Cedar, Cinnamon, Clover (red), Daisy, Elder, Frankincense, Heather, Lily, Lime Tree, Mallow (blue, dwarf, musk), Maidenhair, Marjoram, Mistletoe (European), Myrtle, Orchid, Pine, Poppy, Quince, Rose, Sandalwood (red, white), Sunflower, Vervain, Violet

Roman goddess of Spring and Springtime love. She is the mother of Cupid by either Mercury (most often cited) or Mars. As deity, she started off as a goddess of vegetation fertility. Gradually she became goddess of the vine (grape) and the fermentation thereof until she eventually arrived as goddess of love. Isn't that how it always happens? A little salad, a little wine, and all of a sudden there you are.

Incense Recipe
2 parts Sandalwood (white)
1 part Frankincense
1 part Benzoin
1 part Cinnamon
1 part Clove

Vertumnus—Male—Mediterranean

Roman god of gardens, orchards, and vineyards. One of the shape-shifters of Roman lore, probably acquiring that attribute from the change in appearance of plants as they grow and ripen.

Vesta—Female—Mediterranean

Animal associations: Donkey, Goat

Plant associations: Adam and Eve Root, Dog Bane, Lucky Hand Root, Oak, Thistle

Roman goddess of fire and flame. December is her sacred month. In the home, she was goddess to the hearth and to the preparation of family meals. At ritual, she is the ritual fire itself. From her service, we receive the term 'Vestal Virgins,' children chosen for service to Vesta who took a strict oath of celibacy for their 30 years of service. Roman records show that during the thousand or so years in which the Vestal Virgins served, only 20 broke their oath of celibacy. Unfortunately for them, the Roman records noting this are the accounts of their death as punishment for such actions.

Vica Pota—Female—Mediterranean

Roman goddess of victory. One of the older deity forms.

Victoria—Female—Mediterranean

Roman winged goddess and personification of Victory.

Vinar, The—Male/Female—North Europe

Scandinavian tribe of gods and goddesses of Nature and fertility who live in Vanaheimr. They were at one time the sworn enemies of the Aesir, but the two tribes were eventually united. The story of the conflict between the Vinar and the Aesir is told here in the Book of Exodus.

Virgin Mary—Female—Middle East/Mediterranean

(Also known as Bibi Miriam)

Plant associations: Hawthorn, Mountain Ash (Rowan)

Mother of Jesus in Christian lore. She is said to form a Triple Goddess with either Mary Magdalene and Mary Cleopas or with Mary Cleopas and Mary Salome (as opposed to Magdalene). Her worship migrated into Hindu lore where she is called Bibi Miriam and into both Voodoo and Santeria. During the last decade of the 20th century, the Pope and Vatican reaffirmed her divinity. Essentially, this was the confirmation that Catholicism sees divinity in part as female.

Vishnu—Male—Near East

Wife: Varahini

Animal associations: Ape, Eagle, Boar, Bee, Dolphin, Elephant, Fish, Horse, Lion, Peacock, Swallow, Turtle, Tortoise

Plant associations: Acacia, Amaranth, Banyon, Basil, Bay, Benzoin, Bodhi, Damiana, Frankincense, Ginseng, Gum Mastic, Jasmine, Mace, Mandrake, Marjoram, Nettle (greater and lesser), Oak, Palm (date), Sandalwood, Sunflower, Vervain, Vine (grape), White Poppy

Hindu sun god who forms the sacred triad with Brahma and Shiva. Vishnu has thus far had nine known avatars/incarnations: Matsya, Kurma, Varaha, Narasinha, Vamana, Parashurama, Chandra, Krishna, and Buddha. The foretold 10th avatar/incarnation is said to be Kalki who will come to be known only once the world has been greatly improved. Vishnu is one of the Adityas. The Hindu month Chaitra (March 22–April 20) is sacred to Vishnu. See Adityas.

Incense Recipe

6 parts Sandalwood (yellow)

3 parts Gum Arabic

3 parts Benzoin

3 parts Frankincense

1 part Jasmine flowers

1 part Bay

1 pinch Mandrake (optional)

Incense extra step: This recipe is wonderful as presented. But if you want to make the absolutely most heavenly incense you have ever burned, grind the above ingredients into a fine powder. It will be very sticky due to the large amounts of resin. Add this to a simmering pot of water along with a few dates or two and a few raisins. Simmer over low heat for an evening, adding water as necessary to keep it from boiling away. Then allow to cool and pour into a glass container. Set the mixture aside uncovered and allow it to evaporate until only dry solids remain. Depending on how much you are making and how much water you use, the drying process can take some time, but the results are worth it. Once it has dried, remove the solids and scrape the bowl of all the resins, grind into what will be a resin laden powder, allow to mellow for a couple of days, then burn over charcoal.

Oil Recipe

8 drops Sandalwood oil

3 drops Frankincense oil

3 drops Bay oil

3 drops Benzoin oil

3 drops Jasmine Absolute

1/2 ounce Sunflower (best) or Palm oil

Visvakarma—Male—Near East

Animal association: Horse

Hindu craftsman of the gods. Created the disc of Vishnu, the lance of Karttikeya, the trident of Shiva, and other magickal tools and weapons. Built the cities Lanka and Amaravati.

Vivasvana—Male—Near East

Father: Kashyapa

Mother: Aditi

Vivasvana is one of the Adityas. The Hindu month Jyaistha (May 22–June 21) is sacred to Vivasvana. See Adityas.

Vivienne—Female—Central Europe

(Also known as Nimue)

Father: Dylan

Mother: Lady of the Lake

Lover: Myrddin (Merlin)

Her father is sometimes cited as Dynes, stemming from some of the mixed legends of King Arthur and the folk who filled his story.

Voles—Male—Central/Northern Europe

(Also known as Veles)

Animal associations: Cattle, Horse, and to some degree all horned animals.

Slavic god and patron of cattle, horses, and horned animals. In the trade and production of those animals, he became a god of commerce and trade. Associated with fair exchange of value, he was said to bring prosperity only when both participants of a deal were honest. To demonstrate that honesty, deals were often sworn on his name.

Volcanus—Male—Mediterranean

(Also known as Vulcan)

Animal associations: Elephant, Lion

Plant associations: Aloe, Frankincense, Hibiscus, Nettle (greater), Red Poppy

Roman god of working metal and the fire that makes such works possible. The month of September is sacred to Volcanus.

Vulturnus—Male—Mediterranean

Roman personification and god of the East Wind. The other three are Aquilo, Auster, and Favonius.

Wekwek—Male—North America

Tuleyone falcon who stole fire from the sun and then set Earth on fire. This story is repeated in many tribes as an explanation of the western deserts of North America. The really fun part is when we see a very similar story in the Mediterranean. See Phaeton.

Wip—See Anubis

Xipe—Male—Central America

Aztec god of the first flowers of the year and to some degree all of the springtime foliage.

Yerah—Male—Middle East/Mediterranean
(Also known as Jarih)
Wife: Nikkal

Phoenician moon god.

Wadjet—Female—Africa
(Also known as Buto, Edjo, Udjo, Wadjit)
Animal association: Snake

Snake goddess and protector of the Egyptian king.

Wakinyan—See Thunder Being

Wepwawet—Male—Africa
(Also known as Upuaut, Wep-wawet, Ophois)
Animal association: Wolf, Jackal

'Opener of ways'—Egyptian god of death and war. He has been depicted variously as having the body of a man but the head of either a jackal or a wolf. His name comes from his leading the way of soldiers into both combat and the afterlife.

Wishpoosh—Male—North America
Animal association: Beaver

A giant beaver who sinks canoes and causes men to drown.

Wyrd—Female—North Europe

Teutonic personification of Fate (for lack of a better word) as a Triple Goddess. Her three aspects included Urd (Past), Verdani (Present), and Skuld (future). See also the Book of Three, Part I for a better explanation.

Xochiquetzal—Female—South America
Husband: Coxcoxtli
Animal association: Butterfly

'Flower feather'—Aztec moon goddess of flowers, love, and marriage. She was patron to all forms of the arts, especially of singing, dancing, and the creation of fabric.

Xolotl—Male—Central America
Animal association: Dog

Aztec god of lightning who guides departed souls to the Underworld (a place of rest). The only ones to escape this fate at death were women who died while giving birth and brave men who fell in battle. These folk receive a reward that is unspecified. Again, a clear connection to birth and death.

Yahweh—Male—Middle East
Also mistakenly known as Jehovah (see Jehovah)
Wife: Aholibah, Ashera, Sophia
Plant association: Willow

Christian All Father who, with his wife Aholibah, was the parent of humanity. He had a falling out with his wife, left her, and then formed his own line of humanity, beginning with the creation of Adam and Lilith. Lilith was entirely too similar to his wife Aholibah, so he replaced her with Eve. Although Hebrew scripture leads us to see Aholibah as wife to Yahweh, there is also reference to the two wives of Yahweh from his Egyptian following in the 5th century B.C.E. As a bigamist, Yahweh's wives are listed as Anatha Baetyl and Ashima Baetyl. Then there is the Canaanite reference to Ashera as wife and sister to Yahweh. So then the history of Yahweh is very similar to the history of many of the other gods. Additionally, the Goddess of Wisdom, Sophia, is depicted with Yahweh at the Sistine Chapel. Where Yahweh is reaching his hand out to touch humanity (Adam), Sophia's arm is draped over Yahweh's shoulder.

Yama—Male—Near East
(Also known as Yamantaka)
Wife: Pashadhari

Animal associations: Dove, Owl, Pigeon, Dog (watchdogs), Cattle (bull)

'The restrainer'—One of the eight Hindu guardians of the principle directions and the god of judgment at death. He decides who will and will not be reborn. Yama is the guardian of the South. The other seven are Indra, Agni, Surya, Varuna, Vayu, Kubera, Soma.

Yarhibol—Male—Middle East/Mediterranean

'Calf of the Lord'—Ancient Syrian (Pre Islam) moon god who forms a sacred triad with Bel and Aglibol.

Yasodhara—Female—Far East

Wife of the Buddha who was born spontaneously as the Buddha thought her into existence.

Yeggua—Female—African/Caribbean/South America

Saint association: Our Lady of the Forsaken

Holiday: Feast of Our Lady of the Forsaken on October 30th

Orisha who lives among the tombstones of the graveyard. She is in charge of insuring that souls find Oya.

Yemaya—Female—African/Caribbean/South America

(Also known as Yemaja)

In Santeria, her name is Yemaya

In Voodoo, her name is Agwe/La Balianne

In Africa, her name is Yemonja/Yeyeomo eja

Saint and Catholic associations: The Virgin Mary, Our Lady of Regla (Cuba)

Husband: Aganyu

Holiday: Feast of Our Lady of Regla on September 7th, December 31st (New Year's Eve)

Plant associations: Allspice, Angelica, Almond, Asafoetida, Balm of Gilead, Basil, Calamus, Coconut, Camphor, Cumin, Carnation, Citron, Daffodil, Eucalyptus, Gardenia, Grains of Paradise, Jasmine, Lemon, Lotus, Myrrh, Mugwort, Magnolia, Meadowsweet, Pennyroyal, Peony, Pine, Red Poppy (seed), Sandalwood (white), Valerian, Vetivert, Vine (grape), Watermelon

In Africa she is goddess of the ocean, and to a lesser degree, of fresh water ponds. She migrated into Voodoo and Santeria where she retains her association with the ocean and also becomes associated with the Virgin Mary.

Incense Recipe

4 parts Sandalwood (white)

3 parts Gum Arabic

1 part Myrrh

1 part Lemon peel

1 part Jasmine flowers

Oil Recipe

8 drops Sandalwood oil

6 drops Jasmine absolute

2 drops Lemon oil

1 drop Citron (optional)

1/2 ounce Almond oil as a base

Yhi—Female—Australia

Lover: Baiame

Son: Bahloo

Australian Aborigine sun goddess and All Mother who, with Bahloo, created all the animals of the Earth, including humanity. Although their relationship is occasionally recorded as incestuous, Yhi did not necessarily give birth to Bahloo. She created him as did she create Baiame, in much the way Diana created her lover Lucifer. With mixed lore, it is difficult to say which should be called son and which lover.

Yo—Male—Far East

Japanese principle of the masculine portion of the soul. Similar in ideology to the better known Chinese Yang. The Japanese Ying being In.

Yu—Male/Female—Central Asia

Animal association: Snake

Chinese hermaphrodite god who caused the world to be livable by slithering upon it. In so doing, she created the mountain passes and the valleys that hold rain long after the storm has stopped. S/he is also said to be the reason the Great Flood receded. Realizing it had caused the world to become unlivable, she guided the flood waters into the abyss.

Zephyrus—Male—Mediterranean
Father: Astraeus
Mother: Eos

Greek god of the West Wind associated with the West Quarter (Water) in Wiccan ritual.

Zeus—Male—Mediterranean
Father: Cronus
Mother: Rhea
Wife: Metis, Hera
Animal associations: Bee, Dove, Eagle, Goat, Swan, Woodpecker, Wolf, Cattle (bull), Sheep, Ram
Plant associations: Almond, Aloe, American Aspen, Apple, Common Aspen, Damiana, Fig, Hyssop, Jasmine, Myrrh (sweet), Oak, Olive, Parsley, Pine, Saffron (Spanish), Sage, Wheat

Listing the lovers of Zeus would be a book of its own. Certainly, he is a god of male virility especially when that virility is called upon to satisfy a younger lover. However, he is also a god who was not above forcing his desires on those he lusted after. Perhaps in his story we see the principle that power corrupts. With few that could stand up to him, he did seem to get his way a great number of times when he clearly should not have. Sometimes called the Father of the Gods, his lust for both goddesses and mortal women infuriated his wife Hera. Sometimes cited as his wife, other times as his consort, it is clear that Zeus felt they had an open relationship, while she felt Zeus was all hers. His list of lovers includes Aegina, Alcmena, Callisto, Calypso, Demeter, Electra, Leda, Leto, Maia, Semele, and many others. He is also cited as having a homosexual lover in Ganymede. As god chiefly responsible for land and mountains, he forms a sacred triad with his brothers Hades (Underworld) and Poseidon (the seas and oceans).

Incense Recipe
2 part Gum Arabic
1 part Jasmine flowers
1 part Hyssop
1 pinch Saffron (Spanish)
Enough Zeus or Galbanum essential oil to bind

Oil Recipe
9 drops Galbanum essential oil
6 drops Jasmine absolute
1/2 ounce base oil

Zocho—Male—Far East
Japanese god subordinate to Taishaku-ten who guarded the West. In Wiccan ritual he is sometimes connected with the West Quarter. The other three were Bishamon, Jikoku, and Komoku.

Chapter Commentary

Again, I have to remind you that this chapter is an overview of the many faces I see in our beloved Lord and Lady. There is a wealth of material available for your study. For that purpose, I strongly encourage you to visit the bibliography given at the end of this book. However, in so doing, remember that what is important is not how the ancients felt about these archetypes. Nor is what scholarly interpretation of what the ancients felt about these archetypes. What is important is what they say to you. Think of this process similar to the reading of Tarot. Yes, it is important that you read books that point out the symbolism on each card because the archetypes they represent are not nearly as clear as one might think. However, in understanding what those archetypes are and how to identify them, what is important in a Tarot reading is how the cards strike your mind and soul. It is these subtleties by which the reading of the Tarot reveals seemingly hidden information, and these subtleties will allow you to discover that same information within the many books that discuss our Lord and Lady.

Chapter Dedication

This chapter is dedicated to that school teacher mentioned in the Book of Holidays who had a mind so closed as to tell me the stories of the elder religions were not part of a valid religion. Not only were they a deeply integral part of the ancient religions, they are today a part of the fastest growing religion in the world.

A Final Word

Gay, Straight, Black, White
Same Struggle, Same Fight
Christian, Muslim, Pagan, Jew
There is just one world for me and you

During the writing of this book, I have lost two of my dearest friends. As I close this book, my brother's fiancée is in the hospital on bed rest. She is his first real love, and he is so worried about her. In the larger community, parents and families are now mourning the loss of the brave men and women in humanity's latest temper tantrum. Watching the war in Iraq in all of its video-phone realism, I thought maybe the message of Wicca had come a bit too late. Maybe humanity couldn't come together and resolve its differences. Then I read something so profound that I could not let this book go to print without it.

Where I am From

By Sharon Kay Carpenter

"I am from the defiant, free wheeling four-year-old riding her tricycle across a forbidden street, much to the dismay of Grandma Belle, and from the regretful, tear stained child with a stinging bottom.

I am from the boyish girl with a passion for climbing trees ever higher, to shout at the world, leaving my carved mark for anyone as brave as I to see, and from the safety of the earth where I returned.

I am from the mother cat and her three kittens hidden from the landlord in a closet, with my co-conspirator, Mom, helping block the view of our little guests, and ever increasing my love for her.

I am from Garfield Elementary School, ever drawing me back because I never wanted to leave, from McKinley Junior High School where children quickly learned social and class differences from the cruel remarks of older students and adults, and from Portsmouth High School where I couldn't stay because financial necessity beckoned and Mom was no longer able to provide for the many needs in our lives.

I am from the 60s, from the era of the Beatles, from bell-bottoms, from drive in theaters, and from the King of Rock and Roll, Elvis.

I am from the country that heaped shame on soldiers returning from Viet Nam, from the spiritual country that prayed for every soldier through each war, and from the country that shed tears for a multitude not returning.

I am from the starry-eyed bride who married the love of her life, from a young mother of three, from the changed roles of my mother and me as I protected a child like adult from the suddenly overwhelming issues of aging, and from my new title, Grandma.

I am from memories of my past tricycle ride as my four-year-old grandson rides away on his new bike, from my continued love of animals, from my aches and pains of increasing age, and from climbing that tall tree as my granddaughter reaches up to me with her tiny hands."

So who is Sharon Kay Carpenter? She is a 56-year-old widowed grandmother who has worked all of her life. She raised her children to be 'Good Christians' and you know what? She succeeded, despite the fact that two of her children are Pagan (we might work on the third). She is a survivor of not only the death of a man she loved dearly, but of that which took my own father's life, cancer. And after all that, she went back to college, where she wrote the essay presented here. One of her daughters, Aimee, tells me that their home was once filled with every order of animal, the wild ones spending just enough time to recover from injury or illness.

When Aimee was a teen, her mother accidentally hit a possum while driving to work. Without hesitation, she turned around to try and save the critter. She was beyond saving, but she had a pouch full of baby possums who desperately needed their mother. Sharon became that mother and bottle fed the children until they were weaned, always sure to withhold her abundant affection such that when they could leave her care they would have the best chances back in the care of Mother Nature.

Squirrels, possums, rabbits, a hawk, and a big fat raccoon that ate cat food on the front porch always had a home when it was needed. Not for her own amusement, but because she had no choice. Caring for critters is written in her soul. That is what I mean when I say a Wiccan soul. Oh, I don't care if she is Wiccan, Christian, Muslim, Jewish, or any other religion because no matter what church a person attends, what is really important are the things we do between religious services.

I care because she passed part of her soul on to her children, and I have fallen head over heels in love with one of them. Sorry, Bubba, it isn't you. I care because I want to spend the rest of my life with one of her daughters (despite the fact that she once thought all cats were girls and all dogs were boys) and because I cannot imagine having a more Wiccan mother-in-law, despite the fact that she is not Wiccan.

Mrs. Carpenter, I care because I very much want your blessing when I ask your daughter Aimee to be my wife. If after reading this, you can find it in your heart to give us your blessings, then upon Aimee's consent; I will be honored to be your son-in-law.

Blessed be and live free,

A.J. Drew

I try to be as interactive as an author can be. If you would like to discuss this or any of my books, please visit *www.PaganNation.com* and become involved in our effort to form a responsible and responsive Pagan Community.

Endnotes

Liber ab Genesis

1. A prayer was recorded by Ahmed ibn Fadlan in 922 C.E.and attributed to the "Norsemen" of south east Russia (near the Volga River) of the time. I cite Albert Stanburrough Cook's "Ibn Fadlan's Account of Scandinavian Merchants on the Volga in 922," *Journal of English and Germanic Philosophy,* vol. 22 (1923), pages 54-63.

2. I have not been able to confirm or deny this, but I believe the quote "Our creator as evidenced by our creativity" was originally the motto of the creator of the Dazzle Screen saver. Unfortunately, I think that was back in the days of DOS X when a 286 was hot property. I am afraid I cannot confirm its origin.

Liber ab Tres 1

1. *The American Heritage Dictionary of the English Language*, Fourth Edition. Houghton Mifflin Company, 2000.

2. From the story of the great flood as presented by the Gilgamesh Epic which appears in countless books. I cite here the version I copied as a teenager, but do not know the exact origin of these exact words.

3. A variation on the Serenity Prayer, originally written by Reinhold Nieburhr.

Liber ab Exodus

General:

The story of Ash and Elm and indeed all of Genesis should be considered a construct to explain evolution and the accumulation of humanity's basic knowledge of his or her world. At position one (1) on the map that accompanies this chapter, humanity probably numbered about 10,000 and not two as is implied in The Book of Genesis. The principles set forth in this chapter are based on the modern science and study of mitochondrial DNA. This is a relatively new science. I first became aware of this science and the new Out of Africa theory by watching a show on the Discovery Channel. See bibliography for specifics.

Specific:

1. As cited by the Associated Press, November 9, 2002.
2. From the story of the Great Flood as presented by the Gilgamesh Epic that appears in countless books. I cite here the version I copied as a teenager, but I do not know the exact origin of these exact words.

Liber ab Quattuor

1. Generally attributed to Aleister Crowley. This quote has appeared in several of his works.

Liber ab Tres11

1. *The American Heritage Dictionary of the English Language*, Fourth Edition. Houghton Mifflin Company, 2000.

Liber ab Planta

1. Presented here is a greatly condensed version of the manuscript originally written as Liber ab Planta. It was originally written as both a spiritual and encyclopedic look at the first order of plants in much the same way Liber ab Clementia appears. Unfortunately, due to space considerations the publisher could not include it in its entirety. As a result, the complete Liber ab Planta is now an ongoing and expanding work, which might at a later date find its way into publication.
2. A quote from notes that I took at a presentation by Tatia Kingslady. She spoke at a good pace, so I might have missed a word or two as I was recording what she said with a pen and paper.
3. *http://news.bbc.co.uk/1/hi/sci/tech/411639.stm*—published Thursday, August 5, 1999.

Liber ab Sol

1. Although the Wiccan Rede's author is often cited as Lady Gwen Thompson, she did not claim to have written it. She simply submitted it for publication under the title Rede of the Wiccae, stating that it was given to her by her grandmother, Adriana Porter. Looking back on those early days of the movement, we see there was a great deal of material provided by grandmothers and never credited to the original author.
2. Cited from "The Origins of Imbolg" by Tatia Kingslady. Published by Poison Pen as part of the Imbolg 1974 installment of *The Wheel*.

Liber ab Familia

1. Presented here is a condensed version of Liber ab Familia. The original manuscript included an expanded and encyclopedic look at our critter friends. Unfortunately, the editor felt it was far too long to be presented here. It is now an ongoing work, which I hope to one day offer for publication.
2. From *The American Heritage Dictionary of the English Language*, Fourth Edition, Houghton Mifflin Company, 2000.
3. Some cite the Neolithic Revolution as taking place 10,000 B.C.E., but the majority of cites place it at between 6,500 and 7,000 B.C.E., or 8,500 to 9,000 years ago. As the revolution was a process and not a single event, it is hard to pinpoint an exact date.

Liber ab Mentis

1. *The American Heritage Dictionary of the English Language*, Fourth Edition, Houghton Mifflin Company, 2000.

Liber ab Mortuus

1. The first line from the first letter written by Damien Echols to A.J. Drew.

Bibliography

Adkins, Lesley & Roy. *Handbook to Life in Ancient Greece*. New York: Oxford University Press, 1997.

Andrews, Ted. *Animal-Speak*. St. Paul, Minn.: Llewellyn Publications, 1993.

Angell, Madeline. *America's Best Loved Wild Animals*. New York: Bobbs-Merrill, 1975.

Arnott, Kathleen. *African Myths and Legends*. New York: Oxford University Press, 1989.

Baierlein, Ralph. *Thermal Physics*. Cambridge: Cambridge University Press, 1999.

Bandinelli, R.B. *Rome: The Center of Power 500 B.C. to A.D. 200*. New York: George Braziller, 1970.

Barthell, E.E. *Gods and Goddesses of Ancient Greece*. Coral Gables, Fla.: University of Miami Press, 1971.

Bickerman, E.J. *Chronology of the Ancient World*. Ithaca, N.Y.: Cornell University Press, 1982.

Bickerman, E.J. *Chronology of the Ancient World*. Southhampton, N.Y.: Camelot Press, 1980.

Blamires, Steve. *Celtic Tree Mysteries*. St. Paul, Minn.: Llewellyn Publications, 2002.

Blanchard-Lemee, M. *Mosaics of Romans Africa*. New York: George Braziller, 1996.

Bocking, Brian. *A Popular Dictionary of Shinto*. United Kingdom: Curzon Press, 1996.

Bonnefoy, Yves. *American, African, and Old European Mythologies*. Chicago: University of Chicago Press, 1993.

Bullock, M. *Daily Life in Ancient Egypt*. New York: McGraw Hill, 1964.

Burkert, Walter. *Greek Religion*. Cambridge: Harvard University Press, 1985.

Caesar, Julius. The Cival War. The Cival War. Rome, 46 B.C.E.*

Caesar, Julius. The Conquest of Gaul. Rome, 50 B.C.E.*

Chase, Pamela. *Trees for Healing*. New Castle, 1991.

Cicero. Political Speeches. Rome, 44 C.E.*

Cicero. The Nature of the Gods. Rome, 45 C.E.*

Cook, B.F. *Greek and Roman Art in the British Museum*. London: British Museum Publications, 1976.

Cooper, J.J., ed. *Brewer's Book of Myth and Legend*. Oxford: Helicon Publishing, 1993.

Cotterell, Arthur. *Dictionary of World Mythology*. Oxford: Oxford University Press, 1979.

Crowley, Aleister. *777*. New York: Weiser, 1973.

Cunningham, Scott. *The Complete Book of Incense, Oils, and Brews*. St Paul, Minn.: Llewellyn Publications, 1989.

———. *Cunningham's Encyclopedia of Magical Herbs*. St. Paul, Minn.: Llewellyn Publications, 1985.

———. *Magical Aromatherapy*. St. Paul, Minn.: Llewellyn Publications, 2002.

Dallapiccola, Anna. *Dictionary of Hindu Lore and Legend*. London: Thames & Hudson, 2002.

Danielou, Alain. *The Myths and Gods of India*. Rochester, Vt.: Inner Traditions, 1991

Davidson, Hilda. *Scandinavian Mythology*. New York: Peter Bedrick Books, 1986.

———. *The Road to Hel*. Westport, Conn.: Greenwood Publishing Group, 1968.

———. *Myths and Symbols in Pagan Europe: Early Scandinavian and Celtic Religions*. Syracuse, N.Y.: Syracuse University Press, 1989.

———. *The Viking Road to Byzantium*. Lanham, Md.: Rowman & Littlefield, 1976.

———. The Battle God of the Vikings: The First G. N. Garmonsway Memorial Lecture Delivered 29 October 1971 in the University of York. University of York, Centre for Medieval Studies, 1972.

———. *The Lost Beliefs of Northern Europe*. London; New York: Routledge, 1993.

Davis, F. Hadland. *Myths and Legends of Japan*. New York: Dover, 1992.

Deiss, J.J. *Herculaneum*. New York: Harper and Row, 1985.

Del Chiaro, M.A. *Roman Art in West Coast Collections*. New York: St. Martin's Press, 1973.

Dimmitt, Cornelia, ed. *Classic Hindu Mythology*. Philadelphia: Temple University Press, 1978.

Dimont, Max I. *Jews, God and History.* New York: New American Library, Times Mirror, 1962.

Discovery Communications, Inc. *The Real Eve*. Discovery Communications, 2002. Compact disc.

Dorig, J. *Onatas of Aegina*. Leiden, Netherlands: E.J. Brill, 1977.

Ellis, Peter. *Celtic Myths and Legends*. New York: Carroll & Graf, 2002.

———. *A Brief History of the Druids*. New York: Carroll & Graf, 2002

Euripides. The Heracleidae. Athens, 425 B.C.E.*

Fagles, Robert, trans. *The Odyssey*. New York: Penguin Group, 1999.

Farrar, Janet and Stewart. *The Witches' God*. Washington: Phoenix, 1989.

———. *The Witches' Goddess*. Washington: Phoenix, 1987.

Fast, Howard. *The Jews, Story of a People.* New York: Bantam, Doubleday, Dell Publishing, 1992.

Ferguson, J. *The Religions of the Roman Empire*. Ithaca, N.Y.: Cornell University Press, 1970.

Finnegan, Ruth. *Oral Literature in Africa*. Oxford: Oxford University Press, 1976.

Forman, W. *The Romans: Their Gods and their Beliefs*. London: Orbis Publishing, 1984.

Fowler, W.W. *The Religious Experience of the Roman People*. London: MacMillan, 1911.

Frazer, James. *The Golden Bough.* New York: Collier Books, 1922.

Gardner, J.F. *Roman Myths*. London: British Museum Press, 1993.

Gibbon, E. *The Decline and Fall of the Roman Empire*. New York: Knopf Publishing, 1993.

Gikatilla, Rabbi Joseph. *Gates of Light (Sha'are Orah)*. San Francisco: Harper Collins Publishers, 1994.

Glare, P.E.,, ed. *Oxford Latin Dictionary*. Oxford: Oxford University Press, 1983.

Glassman, Sallie. *Vodou Visions: An Encounter with Divine Mystery*. New York: Random House;Villard Books, 2000

Gonzalez-Wippler, M. *Powers of the Orishas*. New York: Original Publications, 1992.

Graves, Robert. *The Greek Myths*. New York: George Brazillier, Inc., 1955.

———. *The White Goddess*. New York: Farrar, Straus and Giroux, 1948.

Guerber, H.A. *Myths of the Norsemen*. New York: Dover, 1992.

Holme, B. *Bullfinch's Mythology*. New York: Viking Press, 1979.

Hope, Murry. Practical Egyptian Magic. New York: St. Martin's Press, 1984.

Hopman, Ellen Evert. *Tree Medicine Tree Magic*. Washington: Phoenix, 1991.

Hurbon, Laennec. *Voodoo: Search for the Spirit*. New York: Harry N Abrams, 1995

Ions, Veronica. *Indian Mythology*. New York: Peter Bedrick Books, 1983.

Johnson, Sylvia. *The Wildlife Atlas*. Minneapolis: Lerner Publishing, 1977.

Jung, Carl. *Man and His Symbols*. New York: Anchor Press, 1964.

Karade, Baba Ifa. *Handbook of Yoruba Religious Concepts*. New York: Weiser, 1994.

———. *Ojise: Messenger of the Yoruba Tradition*. New York: Weiser, 1996.

———. *Imoye: A Definition of the Ifa Tradition*. New York: Athelia Henrietta Press, 1999.

Knappert, Jan. *Pacific Mythology*. London: Harper Collins 1992.

———. *The Encyclopedia of Middle Eastern Mythology & Religion*. Shaftesbury: Element Books, 1993.

Kovacs, Maureen. *The Epic of Gilgamesh*. Stanford University Press, 1989.

Leach, Maria, ed. *Funk & Wagnalls Standard Dictionary of Folklore, Mythology, and legend*. New York: Harper Collins, 1984.

Leland, Charles G. *Aradia: Gospel of the Witches*. New York: Buckland Museum, 1968.

Littleton, C. Scott . *Shinto: Origins, Rituals, Festivals, Spirits, Sacred Places*. Oxford: Oxford University Press, 2002.

Lyttleton, M. *The Romans: Their Gods and their Beliefs*. London: Orbis Publishing, 1984.

McElheny, Victor. *Watson and DNA: Making a Scientific Revolution*. Perseus Publishing, 2003.

McLaughlin, Marie. *Myths and Legends of the Sioux*. Lincoln, Nebr.: University of Nebraska Press, 1990.

Michels, A.K. *The Calendar of the Roman Republic*. New Jersey: Princeton University Press, 1967.

Mikalson, J.D. The Sacred and Civil Calendar of the Athenian Year. Princeton University Press, 1975.

Miller, Richard. *The Magical and Ritual Use of Aphrodisiacs*. Rochester, Vt: Destiny Books, 1993.

————. *The Magical and Ritual Use of Herbs*. Vermont, Destiny Books, 1993.

————. *The Magical and Ritual Use of Perfumes*. Vermont, Destiny Books, 1993.

Montenegro, Carlos. Magical Herbal Baths of Santeria. New York: Original Publications, 1996.

Muryn, Mary. *Water Magic*. New York: Fireside, 1995.

Nicholson, Irene. *Mexican and Central American Mythology*. New York: Peter Bedrick Books, 1982.

O'Hara, Gwydion. *The Magick of Aromatherapy*. St. Paul, Minn.: Llewellyn Publications, 1998.

Palmer, Jessica Dawn. *Animal Wisdom*. London: Thorsons, 2001.

Pantel, Pauline. *Religion in the Ancient Greek City*. Cambridge: Cambridge University Press, 1992.

Parke, HW. *Festivals of the Athenians*. Ithaca, N.Y.: Cornell University Press, 1994.

Patai, Raphael. *On Jewish Folklore.* Detroit: Wayne State University Press, 1983.

Pliny the Elder. *Natural History*, 10 vols. Harvard University Press, 1992.

Poinsias, Mac Cana. *Celtic Mythology*. New York: Peter Bedrick, 1983.

Reed, Ellen Cannon. *The Heart of Wicca*. York Beach, Maine: Samuel Weiser, 2000.

Richter, G. *Engraved Gems of the Romans*. New York: Phaidon Press, 1971.

Salzman, M.R. *On Roman Time: The Codex-Calendar of 354 and the Rhythms of Urban Life in Late Antiquity*. Berkeley: University of California Press, 1990.

Sameh, W. *Daily Life in Ancient Egypt*. New York: McGraw Hill, 1964.

Saxo, Grammaticus. *The History of the Danes Books I-IX*. Cambridge: DS Brewer, 1998.

Scholem, Gershom. Major Trends in Jewish Mysticism. New York: Schocken Books, 1972.

Seneca. Hercules. Rome, 50 c.e. *

Shafer, B. *Religion in Ancient Egypt*. Ithaca, N.Y.: Cornell University Press, 1991.

Smith, Steven. *Wylundt's Book of Incense*. Maine, Samuel Weiser, 1989.

Speak, Graham, ed. *Encyclopedia of Greece and Hellenic Traditions*. Independence, Ky: Fitzroy Dearborn Publications, 2000.

Spence, Lewis. *Myths of the North American Indians*. New York: Dover, 1992.

Spretnak, Charlene. *Lost Goddesses of Early Greece*. Boston: Beacon Press, 1992.

Strouhal, E. *Life of the Ancient Egyptians*. London: Opus Publishing, 1992.

Sympson, Jacquelyn. *European Mythology*. New York: Peter Bedrick, 1987.

Tacitus, C. *The Annals of Imperial Rome*. Rome, 120 c.e.*

Tacitus, C. *The Agricola*. Rome, 98 C.E.*

Tarostar. *The Witch's Formulary and Spellbook*. New York: Original Publications, 1996.

Taube, Karl. *Aztec and Maya Myths*. Austin: University of Texas Press, 1994.

———. *The Gods and Symbols of Ancient Mexico and the Maya*. London: Thames & Hudson, 1993.

———. *The Major Gods of Ancient Yucatan*. Washington, D.C.: Dumbarton Oaks Publishing Service, 1992.

Thorsson, Edred. *Witchdom of the True*. Smithville, Tex.: Runa Raven Press, 1999.

Waters, Mary. *Black Identities*. Harvard University Press, 2001

Weinstein, Marion. Positive Magic. Franklin Lakes, N.J.: New Page Books, 2002.

Wolkstein, D. *Inanna Queen of Heaven and Earth*. New York: Harper & Row, 1983.

York, M. *The Roman Festival Calendar of Numa Popillius*. New York: Peter Lang, 1986.

Zaidman, Louis. *Religion in the Ancient Greek City*. Cambridge Press, 1992.

Zerubavel, E. *The Seven Day Circle*. New York: The Free Press, 1985.

* A collection of photocopies of unknown English translations routinely reproduced at the Ohio State University with no cite to origin, translator, publisher, or date.

Index

A

B

C

Y